Biographical Dictionary
of American Educators

Biographical Dictionary of American Educators

edited by JOHN F. OHLES

Volume 2

GREENWOOD PRESS

WESTPORT, CONNECTICUT
LONDON, ENGLAND

Library of Congress Cataloging in Publication Data

Main entry under title:

Biographical dictionary of American educators.

Includes index.
1. Educators—United States—Biography. I. Ohles, John F.
LA2311.B54   370'.973 [B]   77-84750
ISBN 0-8371-9893-3

Library of Congress Catalog Card Number: 77-84750
ISBN: 0-8371-9893-3 (set)
      0-8371-9895-X (vol. 2)

First published in 1978

Greenwood Press, Inc.
51 Riverside Avenue, Westport, Connecticut 06880

Printed in the United States of America

10 9 8 7 6 5 4 3 2 1

____CONTENTS _____

Contributors   ix

Preface   xlvii

Introduction   xlix

Abbreviations   li

BIOGRAPHIES   3

    APPENDIX A.   Place of Birth   1461

    APPENDIX B.   State of Major Service   1500

    APPENDIX C.   Field of Work   1521

    APPENDIX D.   Chronology of Birth Years   1546

    APPENDIX E.   Important Dates in American Education   1569

Index   *1573*

Biographical Dictionary
of American Educators

G

GAGE, Lucy. B. October 17, 1876, Portsmouth, Ohio, to William and Caroline (Angele) Gage. M. no. D. October 30, 1945, Nashville, Tennessee.

Lucy Gage received her elementary school education in the schools of Portsmouth, Ohio. She received her high school education in Superior, Wisconsin, and then assisted in a kindergarten in the mill district of Superior. Gage studied under Anna E. Bryan *(q.v.)* at the normal department of the Chicago Free Kindergarten Association and was graduated in 1896. She studied at Teachers College, Columbia University, in 1907, 1915, and 1921–1922 and received the bachelor's degree.

Following graduation from the Chicago school, she taught in the kindergartens of Chicago (1895–1900). She moved to Oklahoma and taught in a three-room school at Fort Cobb (1901–02). She went to Oklahoma City and organized a kindergarten. She helped prepare a bill for the Oklahoma legislature that would require normal schools to establish kindergarten training programs; the bill was passed in 1903. Epworth University (later, Oklahoma City University) in Oklahoma City started a kindergarten training program, and Gage taught some courses, while also directing her own kindergarten and supervising others.

In 1907 Gage became head of early elementary education in the State Normal School (later, Western Michigan University) at Kalamazoo, Michigan, where she developed the program in kindergarten education. She joined the faculty of George Peabody College for Teachers in Nashville, Tennessee, in 1920, remaining to her death in 1945. Nursery school education was added to early childhood education. Gage believed in the continuity of education from nursery school through the elementary grades.

She wrote articles for professional journals and spoke before many groups throughout the United States. She was a member of a number of local and national organizations. In the National Council of Primary Education, Gage served as vice-chairman (1923–25), chairman (1925–27), and on the board of directors (1929–31). The council merged with the International Kindergarten Union in 1931. Gage wrote, along with Ella Dobbs *(q.v.)* and Julia Hahn, *History of the National Council of Primary Education* (1932).

REFERENCES: *LE* (II); Agnes Snyder, *Dauntless Women in Childhood*

Education, 1856–1931 (Washington, D.C.: Association for Childhood Education International, 1972).   *Betty S. Harper*

GALE, George Washington. B. December 3, 1789, Stamford, New York, to Josiah and Rachel (Mead) Gale. M. 1820 to Harriet Selden. M. 1841 to Esther (Williams) Coon. M. 1844 to Lucy Merriam. Ch. ten. D. September 13, 1861, Galesburg, Illinois.

George Washington Gale was instrumental in getting the manual labor education movement under way. He attended Troy Latin School and the Academy at Middlebury, Vermont, where he studied under John Frost for several months. In 1814 Gale was graduated from Union College in Schenectady, New York. He attended Princeton (New Jersey) Theological Seminary, but ill health forced him to discontinue his studies. The Hudson presbytery at Fishkill, New York, licensed him to preach, and Gale became an itinerant missionary to communities along the southern shore of Lake Ontario. His health improved, and he resumed his studies at Princeton. After his ordination, he became the Presbyterian minister at Adams, New York.

In 1824 recurring health problems forced him to resign his pastorate. He traveled in Virginia for a year and returned to settle on a farm near Western, New York, where he established a course of studies for seven young men who wanted to enter the ministry. Gale set up a program for trading instruction, books, and room and board for work on the farm. Gale had found a way for poor young men to prepare for the ministry. He persuaded the Hudson presbytery to establish the Oneida (New York) Institute in 1827, based on his principles. The institute allowed young men who wanted to enter the ministry to work their way through school. By the third year, five hundred applicants had to be turned away. Gale headed the institute from 1827 to 1834.

While at Oneida, Gale planned to found a new manual labor school in the West. A prospectus for the new colony that was distributed in 1834 proposed a college based on a manual labor plan with a course of liberal studies. Gale proposed to buy a township on the frontier from the federal government. Gale's colony moved to Illinois in 1836 and founded the town of Galesburg. The Illinois legislature granted a charter for the Knox Manual Labor College (later, Knox College) in 1837. Gale and two former Oneida teachers constituted the faculty; women were admitted to a new women's department in 1849.

Gale was a trustee of the college (1837–61) and taught languages (1837–42) and moral philosophy and belles lettres (1843–57). By 1857 Knox was involved in a denominational struggle between Congregationalists and Presbyterians over control of the school. In June the board of trustees asked Gale to resign his teaching post; he did but continued to serve on the board of trustees until his death.

Gale was called the "greatest champion of abolitionism in Illinois" by the *Peoria Register and Northwestern Gazeteer*. He represented Illinois at the annual meeting of the American Anti-Slavery Society in 1839 and persuaded the Knox presbytery to excommunicate slaveholders.

REFERENCES: *AC; DAB; NCAB* (24:26); *WWW* (H); Earnest Elmo Calkins, *They Broke the Prairie* (New York: Charles Scribner's Sons, 1937); Charles P. Coates, "From George Gale to Arthur Morgan," *Educational Review* 72 (June 1926): 53-55; Herman R. Muelder, *Fighters for Freedom: The History of Anti-slavery Activities of Men and Women Associated with Knox College* (New York: Columbia University Press, 1959); Martha F. Webster, *Seventy-five Significant Years: The Story of Knox College, 1837-1912* (Galesburg, Ill.: Wagoner Printing Co., 1912).   *Erika Hugo*

GALLAUDET, Edward Miner. B. February 5, 1837, Hartford, Connecticut, to Thomas Hopkins *(q.v.)* and Sophia (Fowler) Gallaudet. M. July 1858 to Jane M. Fessenden. M. December 22, 1868, to Susan Denison. Ch. six. D. September 26, 1917, Hartford, Connecticut.

Edward Miner Gallaudet, youngest son of Thomas Hopkins Gallaudet *(q.v.)*, attended Trinity College in Hartford, Connecticut, from which he received the B.S. degree (1856).

Gallaudet taught at his father's school for the deaf while he was a student and after his graduation from Trinity College (1856–57). A group establishing a school for deaf children in Washington, D.C., asked him to serve as principal. In 1857 Gallaudet organized the Columbia Institution for the Deaf, Dumb, and Blind and served as principal. Congress granted the institution the right to grant degrees in 1864, and Gallaudet served as first president (1864–1911). Named after Gallaudet's father, Gallaudet College was the only institution of its kind in the world.

Gallaudet established a basic college program and obtained financial support from Congress. Gallaudet was a leader in promoting the combined system of educating the deaf in which speech and lip reading were taught, as well as sign language. In 1886 he appeared before the British Royal Commission on the education of the deaf to promote his ideas.

Gallaudet was a frequent contributor of articles on the education of the deaf and was the author of *Popular Manual of International Law* (1879) and *Life of Thomas Hopkins Gallaudet* (1888).

He was active in civic and professional organizations. He was first president of the Convention of American Instructors of the Deaf (1895–1917). He was a director of American School for the Deaf and a trustee of George Washington and Howard universities. He was made chevalier of the Legion of Honor by France (1912) and received honorary degrees from American universities.

REFERENCES: *AC; DAB; NCAB* (18:128) *NYT,* September, 27, 1917, p. 13; *TC; WWW* (I).   *Thomas Meighan*

GALLAUDET, Thomas Hopkins. B. December 10, 1787, Philadelphia, Pennsylvania, to Peter Wallace and Jane (Hopkins) Gallaudet. M. August 29, 1821, to Sophia Fowler. Ch. two, Thomas Gallaudet, clergyman for the deaf, and Edward Miner Gallaudet *(q.v.),* founder of a school for the deaf in Washington, D.C. (later, Gallaudet College). D. September 10, 1851, Hartford, Connecticut.

Thomas Gallaudet was graduated from Yale College in 1805. He worked in a law office for one year and then continued studies in literature and the ministry. He was graduated from Andover (Massachusetts) Theological Seminary in 1814, but ill health prevented him from accepting a ministerial position.

He met Alice Cogswell, a deaf child, and attempted to teach her to speak. He became interested in studying educational techniques for the deaf. The girl's father, Dr. Mason Cogswell, and some friends raised money to send Gallaudet to Europe to study. He studied in England and at the Institut royal des sourds-muets in Paris, France, under Abbé Roch A. C. Sicard.

Gallaudet returned to the United States in 1816 with Laurent Clerc *(q.v.),* a brilliant deaf teacher from the Institut royal des sourds-muets. They solicited money for the first free school for the deaf in America, established in Hartford, Connecticut, in 1817. Gallaudet was principal of the school (1817–30). He served as chaplain for the Connecticut Retreat for the Insane (1833–51).

Gallaudet made significant contributions to the education of the deaf and was active in supporting the establishment of normal schools in Connecticut, advancement of education for the Negro, establishment of manual training in schools, and improvement in higher education for women.

Gallaudet wrote articles on the education of the deaf in the *American Annals of the Deaf* and contributed to *Discourses on Various Points of Christian Faith and Practise* (1818). He also wrote *The Child's Picture Defining and Reading Book* (1830), *The Child's Book on the Soul* (1830), *The Child's Book on Repentance* (1834), *The Class Book of Natural Theology* (1835), *Scripture Biography for the Young* (1838), *The Practical Spelling-Book* (1840), and *The School and Family Dictionary* (with Horace Hooker, 1841).

Gallaudet College in Washington, D.C., was named in his honor. A bronze monument by Daniel French was erected by grateful deaf people on the college grounds as a tribute to Gallaudet's contribution to deaf education in America.

REFERENCES: *AC; DAB; EB; NCAB* (9:138); *TC; WWW* (H); Edward Miner Gallaudet, *The Life of Thomas Hopkins Gallaudet* (New York: Hold, 1910). *Raymond Quist*

GALLOWAY, Samuel. B. March 20, 1811, Gettysburg, Pennsylvania, to James and Sarah (Buchanan) Galloway. M. 1843 to Joan Wallin. Ch. one.

D. April 5, 1872, Columbus, Ohio.

After the death of his father, Samuel Galloway's family moved from Columbus to Greenfield, Ohio, in 1819. Following his graduation from Miami University (Ohio) in 1833, he taught in a classical school in Hamilton, Ohio (1834–35). He spent a year as a student at the Princeton Theological Seminary (1835–36) and taught classical languages at Miami University (1837–38) and at Hanover (Indiana) College (1838–40).

Galloway returned to Ohio and the study of law in 1841 and was admitted to the Ohio bar in 1843. He was elected by the legislature to be secretary of state (1844–50) and ex officio superintendent of schools. He was a strong supporter of education; his reports to the legislature drew public attention to the problems of the common schools. He was responsible for reforms in education, including raising teaching standards, organizing teachers' institutes, and appointing district and county superintendents to supervise the schools.

Galloway was a supporter of temperance reform and abolition. He served one term in the United States House of Representatives (1854–56) but was defeated in two successive elections because of his anti-slavery views. Returning to private law practice, Galloway took an active part in the Presbyterian church and participated in the Republican party in Ohio.

Galloway declined offers of governmental positions under the administration of President Abraham Lincoln, but did accept a federal appointment as judge advocate of Camp Chase, Ohio. He was appointed to investigate conditions in the South during Reconstruction.

Galloway was the first president of the State Teachers' Association of Ohio (1847).

REFERENCES: *AC; DAB; NCAB* (23:198); *WWW* (H); *NYT*, April 6, 1872, p. 1; William Alexander Taylor, *Centennial History of Columbus and Franklin County, Ohio* (Chicago: The S. J. Clarke Publishing Co., 1909), vol. 1.   *Robert H. Truman*

GAMMAGE, Grady. B. August 5, 1892, Prescott, Arkansas, to Thomas Mancion and Elizabeth (Greer) Gammage. M. August 21, 1913, to Dixie Dees. M. November 19, 1949, to Kathryn R. Klink. Ch. one. D. December 22, 1959, Tempe, Arizona.

Grady Gammage attended the University of Arizona, where he received the A.B. (1916) and A.M. (1922) degrees; he received the Ed.D. degree (1940) from New York University.

Gammage was a deputy clerk of the circuit court of Nevada County, Arkansas (1909–10), a public school teacher in Arkansas (1909–12), principal of the Winslow, Arizona, high school (1920–22), and superintendent of the Winslow public schools (1922–25). He was director of the training school at the Northern Arizona State Teachers College (later, Northern

Arizona University) at Flagstaff, during 1925 and 1926 and president of the college (1926–33). He was president of Arizona State Teachers College (later, Arizona State University) at Tempe (1933–59). Successful at both institutions, Gammage governed over a profound period of growth at Arizona State from a student body of 875 in 1933 to over 10,000 in 1959. He expanded the curriculum to include agriculture, science, and business, and the institution was organized into colleges of education, liberal arts, business administration, applied arts and sciences, and graduate studies.

Gammage was the author of *Rural Education in Arizona* (1922) and *A Survey of the Arizona State Teachers College* (1940).

He was active in state and national professional organizations, including the American Association of Teachers Colleges (president, 1945–46), and was a member of the Arizona State Board of Education and the Arizona Board of Vocational Education. He received awards from Denmark and China and was the recipient of honorary degrees from the University of Arizona and the Southwest Christian Seminary.

REFERENCES: *LE* (III); *NCAB* (47:91); *WWAE* (XVI); *WWW* (III).

John F. Ohles

GAMORAN, Emmanuel. B. November 23, 1895, Beltz, Russia, to Abraham Dov and Fanny Leah (Simchovitz) Gamoran. M. December 17, 1922, to Mamie Goldsmith. Ch. three. D. November 14, 1962, New York, New York.

Emmanuel Gamoran was brought to the United States in 1907 and was educated in New York City public schools and at Rabbi Jacob Joseph School in New York City (1907–10). He received a teacher's certificate from Teachers Institute of the Jewish Theological Seminary of America in New York City (1913). He attended City College of New York, where he received the B.A. degree (1917), and Teachers College of Columbia University, where he was awarded the M.A. (1919) and Ph.D. (1924) degrees.

A teacher in Jewish schools (1914–17), he served as educational director of the Circle of Jewish Children of America of the Bureau of Jewish Education of New York City (1917–20) and director of extension schools (1920–21). He was principal of the Washington Heights Hebrew School in New York City (1921–23) and a member of the faculty of the extension department of the Teachers Institute of Jewish Theological Seminary of America (1921–23). He was educational director (1923–58) and adviser (1958–62) to the Union of American Congregations and Commission on Jewish Education. He revolutionized the curriculum and methods of instruction in Jewish education in the United States and influenced Judaism in the rest of the world.

The author of textbooks on Jewish history and literature, Gamoran wrote *Changing Conceptions in Jewish Education* (1924), *Teacher-*

Training for Jewish Schools (1924), *Methods of Teaching the Jewish Subjects* (1932), *Gilenu–The Play Way to Hebrew* (with A. H. Friedland, volume 1, 1933, and volume 2, 1934), *Gilenu Primer* (volume 3, 1935), *Torah-Li* (volume 1, 1939), and *Talks to Jewish Teachers* (with M. G. Gamoran, 1966, published posthumously). He was a contributing editor to *National Jewish Monthly*.

Gamoran was a member of many organizations, including the Religious Education Association (vice-president), the Hebrew Federation of America (executive committee, 1958), and the National Council for Jewish Education (president, 1927–28), and he was a director of the Bureau of Jewish Education of Cincinnati and a member of the executive boards of the Hebrew Federation of America and the Jewish Academy of Arts and Sciences. He was a delegate for the Union of American Hebrew Congregations to the First International Conference on Jewish Education in Jerusalem, Palestine. He was awarded citations by the Jewish Theological Seminary of America for distinguished service to Jewish education (1945), and the Union of American Hebrew Congregations (1953) and received an award of the educators' council of the Federation of Jewish Philanthropies (1958). He received honorary degrees from the Jewish Theological Seminary of America (1913) and Hebrew Union College (1956).

REFERENCES: *LE* (III); *NYT,* November 16, 1962, p. 31; *WWW* (IV); *Jewish Education* 34 (1964): 67–68; "Dr. Emmanuel Gamoran: Tribute," *Religious Education* 58 (January 1963): 71.   *John F. Ohles*

GANTVOORT, Arnold Johann. B. December 6, 1857, Amsterdam, Holland, to Martienus Johannes and Jansje (Voogt) Gantvoort. M. August 29, 1881, to Netti Mar Looker. Ch. seven. D. May 18, 1937, Los Angeles, California.

Arnold Johann Gantvoort was noted for his work in music, music education, and higher education. He was educated in the Netherlands in private schools and a gymnasium. He studied music under Joseph Coenen and others.

He traveled to the United States for the International Centennial Exposition in Philadelphia (1876). He stayed in America and settled in the Cincinnati, Ohio, area. He engaged in giving private music lessons and teaching music in schools at Bowling Green, Kentucky, and Oxford and Piqua, Ohio (1878–94).

Gantvoort became head of the department preparing public-school music teachers at the Cincinnati College of Music (1894–1901). He became the general manager of the college in 1901 and remained there until 1921. At the college, Gantvoort taught courses in solfeggio and harmony, in which he developed a wide reputation. He served as the director of music education in the public schools of Norwood, Ohio, a neighboring community.

Following his many years in Ohio, Gantvoort was appointed to the music faculty of the University of California at Los Angeles where he was lecturer (1924–32). He was dean of the Zoellner Conservatory in Los Angeles for many years.

Gantvoort arranged numerous songs for choral groups. He authored several books, including *Gantvoort's Shorter Music Course* (1894), *The High School Ideal* (1895), *Gantvoort's Music Reader* (1897), *The Model Music Course* (with J. A. Broekhoven, 1907), *Progressive Harmony* (1910), and *Familiar Talks on the History of Music* (1913).

He served as president of Music Teachers National Association. He chaired a committee of the National Education Association established to revise national songs. Gantvoort presided over the International Music Congress that met in Rome in 1911. He was one of two representatives from the United States.

REFERENCES: *NCAB* (40:77); *WWW* (I); Nicholas Slonimsky, *Baker's Biographical Dictionary of Musicians*, 5th ed. (New York: G. Schirmer, 1958).   *Dana T. Elmore*

GARDNER, Helen. B. March 17, 1878, Manchester, New Hampshire, to Charles Frederick and Martha Washington (Cunningham) Gardner. M. no. D. June 4, 1946, Chicago, Illinois.

Helen Gardner's father moved to the Chicago South Side Hyde Park area about 1891 to open a tailor shop. Gardner attended Hyde Park High School and was graduated from the University of Chicago with the B.A. (1901) and M.A. (1918) degrees.

She taught at Brooks Classical School in Chicago (1901–05), where her sister was the principal, and she was assistant principal from 1905 to 1910.

About 1919 Gardner took the position of head of the photograph and lantern-slide department at the Ryerson Library of the Art Institute of Chicago, and in 1920 she inaugurated an art history course at the Art Institute School. She taught at that school for twenty-three years and was professor and chairman of the history of art department (1933–43).

Gardner was the author of *Art Through the Ages* (1926), a significant contribution to art education. The book included design analysis and historical development of various periods of art. She also wrote *Understanding the Arts* (1932).

REFERENCES: *DAB* (supp. 4); *NAW; WWW* (II); *NYT*, June 7, 1946, p. 19.   *Darlene E. Fisher*

GARLAND, Landon Cabell. B. January 21, 1810, Nelson County, Virginia, to Spotswood and Lucinda (Rose) Garland. M. December 1835 to Louisa Frances Garland. Ch. none. D. February 12, 1895, Nashville, Tennessee.

At the age of sixteen, Landon Cabell Garland entered Hampden-Sydney (Virginia) College and was graduated in 1829.

He was appointed teacher of natural science at Washington (later, Washington and Lee) College in Lexington, Virginia. During his early teaching years he developed a laboratory method of instruction for his classes. When Randolph-Macon College opened in Ashland, Virginia in 1832 Garland joined the faculty as a teacher of mathematics (1832–36) and served as president (1836–46). Following his resignation in 1846 he received several offers of college presidencies.

In 1847 Garland joined the faculty at the University of Alabama. He was president of the university from 1855 to 1865, when federal troops demolished the university buildings. He immediately undertook to raise funds to restore the university buildings. From 1867 to 1875 Garland taught physics and astronomy at the University of Mississippi.

Encouraged by Bishop Holland McTyeire, Garland wrote a series of articles for the *Christian Advocate* favoring a trained ministry and advocating establishment of a theological seminary for the Methodist Episcopal Church, South. Despite opposition, Garland's dream was realized with the establishment of Vanderbilt University in Nashville, Tennessee (1875), as a Methodist college and seminary. Garland became the first chancellor of the university while Bishop McTyeire became president of the board of trustees. In 1893 Garland resigned the presidency and returned to the classroom; he died two years later.

In addition to his articles in the *Christian Advocate,* Garland was the author of a mathematics textbook, *Trigonometry, Plane and Spherical* (1841).

REFERENCES: *AC; DAB; NCAB* (8:226); *TC; WWW* (H).

Harold D. Lehman

GARRETT, Emma. B. c. 1846, Philadelphia, Pennsylvania, to Henry and Caroline Ruch (Cole) Garrett. M. no. D. July 18, 1893, Chicago, Illinois.

Emma Garrett was graduated from the Boston University School of Oratory. She founded the Pennsylvania Institution for the Deaf and Dumb in 1878, where she favored use of the oral lip-reading system for communication rather than the manual alphabet. She headed the newly established oral branch of the Pennsylvania Institution (1881) and began a summer school to train teachers in the lip-reading techniques of communication for the deaf. She addressed the convention of American Instructors of the Deaf and Dumb in 1882 and urged them to make wider use of the vocal method of teaching deaf children. She became principal of a Scranton, Pennsylvania, day school for the deaf (1884) and raised funds for a new building.

After a visit to European schools for the deaf in 1890, Garrett sought to establish an institution for preschool deaf children. The Pennsylvania legislature appropriated money, and a site was donated for the building in Philadelphia. Emma Garrett and her sister Mary opened their Home for the

Training in Speech of Deaf Children Before They Are of School Age in 1892. The state of Pennsylvania assumed financial responsibility for the institution in 1893, and it became the Bala Home. Children were admitted from the age of two and remained for limited periods or until the age of eight. The child was surrounded with functional speech and associated with hearing and speaking people. This method attracted attention, and the two sisters presented demonstration classes at the World's Columbian Exposition in Chicago (1893).

Emma Garrett had a nervous breakdown and died by leaping from a Chicago hotel window in 1893.

REFERENCES: *NAW;* Edward A. Fay, ed., *History of American Schools for the Deaf, 1817–1893* (Washington, D.C.: The Volta Bureau, 1893); Mary S. Garrett, "Emma Garrett's Methods," *The American Association to Promote the Teaching of Speech to the Deaf Infants: Proceedings, 1894; NYT*, July 19, 1893, p. 5.   *Thomas Meighan*

GARRETT, William Robertson. B. April 12, 1839, Williamsburg, Virginia, to Robert Major and Susan Comfort (Winder) Garrett. M. November 12, 1868, to Julia Flournoy Batte. Ch. eight. D. February 12, 1904, Nashville, Tennessee.

William Robertson Garrett was graduated at the age of fifteen from Williamsburg (Virginia) Military Academy and entered the College of William and Mary. He was graduated with the A.M. degree (1858) and studied law at the University of Virginia (1858–59).

Garrett practiced law at Williamsburg until the Civil War, when he served as a private and then a captain in the Confederate army. After the war he returned to Williamsburg and accepted a position as master of the grammar school at the College of William and Mary. In 1868 he moved to Pulaski, Tennessee, where he served as president of Giles College and principal of Cornersville Academy (1868–73). Garrett was superintendent of schools for Giles County (1873–75) and was a leader in the organization of the first public schools in the county (1873). He was associate principal and professor of mathematics at Montgomery Bell Academy in Nashville, Tennessee (1875–91).

Garrett was appointed state superintendent of public instruction (1891–93). After his service as state superintendent, he was principal of Garrett Military Academy (1893–95). In 1895 he was appointed professor of American history and in 1899 became dean of George Peabody College for Teachers; he held both positions until his death in 1904.

Garrett organized the Watkins Night School for the benefit of laboring men financed by a gift of $200,000 to the state. He raised a volunteer regiment of cavalry in 1898 and offered their services to fight in the Spanish-American War, but his offer was declined by the government.

Garrett wrote numerous articles and books, including *Complimentary Squares* (1883), *History of South Carolina Cession and the Northern Boundary of Tennessee* (1884), *Public School Laws of Tennessee* (1892), *Geography of Tennessee* (1896), *History of Tennessee* (with Albert V. Goodpasture, 1900), and *The Civil War from a Southern Standpoint* (finished after his death by Robert A. Halley, 1905). He edited *The Southwestern Journal of Education* (1886–91) and *The American Historical Magazine* (1896–1902).

A prominent figure in the National Educational Association, he was state director for Tennessee, vice-president, and president (1891). He was awarded an honorary degree by the University of Nashville (1891).

REFERENCES: *DAB; NCAB* (12:560); *TC; WWW* (I); Albert V. Goodpasture, "William Robertson Garrett," *The American Historical Magazine* 9 (April 1904).   *Jerry C. McGee*

GATES, Arthur Irving. B. September 22, 1890, Red Wing, Minnesota, to William P. and Lenore (Gaylord) Gates. M. August 14, 1920, to Georgina Strickland. Ch. two. D. August 24, 1972, Montrose, New York.

Arthur Irving Gates received the B.L. (1914) and M.A. (1915) degrees from the University of California at Berkeley. He accepted a teaching assistantship in experimental psychology at Columbia University, where he was awarded the Ph.D. degree (1917) in psychology.

Gates remained at Columbia as a member of the faculty (1917–56). While at Columbia, he was director of the Institute for Educational Research, Section D (1921–30), head of the department of educational research in the advanced school of education (1933–37), executive officer of the department of psychology and research methods (1933–56), and director of the division of the foundations of education (1948–56). After retirement in 1956, he was supervisor of research in the Institute of the Language Arts. Gates was able to translate theory into practice and to make his findings applicable to classroom situations. He was one of the first to supply a factual foundation for reading instruction.

An authority in the areas of reading and psychology, his bibliography includes approximately three hundred books, articles, and addresses. Among his books were *Psychology for Students of Education* (1923), *The Improvement of Reading* (1927), *New Methods in Primary Reading* (1928), *Elementary Principles of Education* (with E. L. Thorndike, *q.v.*, 1929), *Interest and Ability in Reading* (1930), *Reading for Public School Administrators* (1931), *Improvement of Reading* (1936), *Spelling Difficulties* (1937), *Educational Psychology* (with others, 1942), and *Teaching Reading to Slow Learning Pupils* (1943).

Gates received medals and citations from many organizations, including the International Reading Association (1961), the American Educational

Research Association (1964), Phi Delta Kappa (1964), the American Psychological Association (1967), Teachers College, Columbia University (1968), and the World Congress on Language Arts (1968). He served as president of the American Association for Educational Research (1942), and the education section of the Council of the American Psychological Association (1948–49). He was a fellow of the American Association for the Advancement of Science.

REFERENCES: *CA* (37–40); *LE* (III); *NYT,* August 25, 1972, p. 36; *WWAE* (XVI); *WWW* (V); Robert J. Havighurst *(q.v.),* ed., *Leaders in American Education* (Chicago: University of Chicago Press, 1971).

H. Thompson Fillmer

GATES, Noah Putnam. B. November 18, 1832, near Princeton, Kentucky, to Nathan and Caroline Wilson (Davidson) Gates. M. July 4, 1860, to Lucy Jane Lawrence. Ch. eleven. D. April 18, 1909, Little Rock, Arkansas.

Noah Putnam Gates was educated at Chapel Hill (Missouri) College, Princeton (Kentucky) College, and the Illinois Normal School. He prepared for the ministry but decided to become a teacher. He taught in western Kentucky and moved to Illinois, where he taught for nine years.

In 1869 Gates went to Little Rock, Arkansas, where he organized the public school system and became its first superintendent, serving to 1871. He moved to Fayetteville, Arkansas, to organize the new Arkansas Industrial University (later, University of Arkansas) and served as its first president (1871–73). The first state university in Arkansas, the institution was founded in response to the Morrill Act for the establishment of agricultural colleges. The university was located on the site of a 160-acre farm at Fayetteville.

Seeking to serve education and improve public school teaching, Gates remained as president of the university only until a suitable replacement could be found, and he became director of the normal school department until 1884. With the three teachers who made up the original faculty, Gates organized the university and worked with the board of trustees to promote it. He was instrumental in getting a railroad to construct its line through Fayetteville.

Resigning from the university in 1884, Gates became superintendent of schools at Fort Smith, Arkansas, where he reorganized the school system. He returned to Fayetteville in 1889, where he served as superintendent of schools until his retirement in 1902.

Gates was president of the Arkansas Education Association (1873 and 1880) and was active in the National Educational Association. He was awarded an honorary M.A. degree by Arkansas Industrial University in 1880.

REFERENCES: *NCAB* (26:240); Harrison Hale, *University of Arkansas,*

1871–1948 (Fayetteville: University of Arkansas Alumni Association, 1948); Robert A. Leflar, *The First 100 Years* (Fayetteville: University of Arkansas Foundation, 1972); John Hugh Reynolds and David Yancey Thomas, *History of the University of Arkansas* (Fayetteville: University of Arkansas, 1910); T. M. Stinnett and Clara B. Kennen, *All This and Tomorrow Too* (Little Rock: Arkansas Education Association, 1969).

Robert Wyly

GAULT, Franklin Benjamin. B. May 2, 1851, Wooster, Ohio, to Joseph and Caroline (Zinn) Gault. M. May 18, 1875, to Martha Ellen Secrest. M. June 29, 1886, to Jennie F. Perrett. Ch. one. D. March 16, 1918, Sumner, Washington.

Franklin Benjamin Gault was educated in the public schools of Jones County, Iowa, and the Monticello (Iowa) high school. He received the B.Sc. (1877) and M.Sc. (1880) degrees from Cornell College in Mount Vernon, Iowa. He studied at the University (later, College) of Wooster (Ohio) and was awarded the Ph.D. degree in 1901.

Gault served as superintendent of schools in Iowa at Tama (1877–81) and Mason City (1881–83). He was also superintendent at Pueblo, Colorado (1883–88), and Tacoma, Washington (1888–92), where he organized the public school systems.

On the admission of the state of Idaho to the Union in 1890, a state university was authorized in the constitution. In 1892 Gault accepted the position as first president of the University of Idaho and saw the institution through the formative years to 1898. In 1898 he took over Whitworth College in Sumner, Washington, reorganized the college, and relocated it in Tacoma, Washington (it was moved to Spokane, Washington, in 1914). He served as president of Whitworth to 1906, when he accepted the presidency of the University of South Dakota at Vermillion. He served as president until he retired in 1913 to Sumner, Washington.

Gault participated in formulating educational policies of the Presbyterian church. He was a member of professional organizations, serving as president of the Idaho State Teachers Association (1893) and the first director of the National Educational Association for the states of Washington and Idaho. He was a member of the Washington State Board of Education (1891–92) and chairman of the Idaho Free Text Book Commission (1893). He received an honorary degree from Cornell College in 1897.

REFERENCES: *NCAB* (18:200); *TC; WWW* (I).   *John F. Ohles*

GAYLEY, Charles Mills. B. February 22, 1858, Shanghai, China, to Samuel Rankin and Sarah Sophia (Mills) Gayley. M. December 17, 1891, to Sallie Pickett. Ch. two. D. July 26, 1932, Berkeley, California.

Charles Mills Gayley was a student at Blackheath, England (1867–74), and at the Royal Academical Institution, Belfast, Ireland (1875). He emigrated to the United States and was graduated from the University of Michigan with the B.A. degree (1878). He studied on the graduate level at Giessen and Halle, Germany (1886–87).

After a two-year period as principal of Muskegon (Michigan) High School (1878–80) he joined the staff at the University of Michigan as an instructor in Latin and later taught English to 1889. He became professor of English language and literature and head of the English department at the University of California (1889–1923), serving as dean of the faculty (1918–20), coadministrator of the presidency (1919), and research lecturer (1921). He was director of the American University Union in London, England (1924–25).

He was the author of many books, including *A Guide to Literature of Aesthetics* (with F. N. Scott, 1890), *Classic Myths in English Literature* (1893), *English in Secondary Schools* (1894), *Methods and Materials of Literary Criticism* (with F. N. Scott, 1899), *Representative English Comedies* (four volumes, 1903–14), *The Poetry of the People* (with M. C. Flaherty, 1903), *The Principles and Progress of English Poetry* (with C. C. Young, 1904), and *Lyric Epic* (with B. P. Kurtz, 1919). The *Gayley Anniversary Papers* were published in 1922.

He was a member of many organizations and societies, including the American Philological Association (president of the Pacific Coast division, 1902–03) and honorary president of the California branch of the English-Speaking Union. He was awarded the French Legion of Honor (1921) and received honorary degrees from four American colleges and universities and the University of Glasgow, Scotland.

REFERENCES: *NCAB* (A:227, 23:128); *TC; WWW* (I).   *LeRoy Barney*

GEHRKENS, Karl Wilson. B. April 19, 1882, Kelleys Island, Ohio, to Henry F. and Elizabeth (Ricker) Gehrkens. M. August 16, 1905, to Ruth Grey Bedford. Ch. two. D. February 28, 1975, Bellaire, Michigan.

Karl Wilson Gehrkens was graduated from Oberlin (Ohio) College with the B.A. (1905) and M.A. (1912) degrees and studied at Columbia University.

Gehrkens taught algebra and German at Oberlin High School (1905–07) and was professor of school music and head of the department of school music at Oberlin College Conservatory of Music (1907–42). A major music educator, he developed a plan for the preparation of music supervisors that was adopted by many colleges and universities.

Gehrkens was the author of *Music Notation and Terminology* (1914), *Essentials in Conducting* (1919), *An Introduction to School Music Teaching* (1919), *Fundamentals of Music* (1924), *Handbook of Musical Terms* (1927), *Twenty Lessons in Conducting* (1930), *Music in the Elementary Schools* (1934), *Music in the Junior High School* (1936), and *The Teaching and Administration of High School Music* (with P. W. Dykema, *q.v.*,

1941). He was coeditor of the Universal School Music Series (1923–36) and *School Music* (1925–34). He was editor of musical terms for *Webster's New International Dictionary* (2d ed.) and department editor of *The Etude* from 1934.

Active in professional associations, Gehrkens was president of the Music Supervisors' National Conference (later, Music Educators National Conference) (1923) and Music Teachers' National Association in 1934. He received honorary degrees from Illinois Wesleyan and Capital universities.

REFERENCES: *LE* (III); *WW* (XXVII); *WWAE* (XIII); Nicholas Slonimsky, ed., *Baker's Biographical Dictionary of Musicians,* 5th ed. (New York: G. Schirmer, 1958); Nicholas Slonimsky, ed., *The International Cyclopedia of Music and Musicians,* 5th ed. (New York: Dodd, Mead, 1949).   *John F. Ohles*

GESELL, Arnold Lucius. B. June 21, 1880, Alma, Wisconsin, to Gerhard and Christine (Giesen) Gesell. M. February 18, 1909, to Beatrice Chandler. Ch. two, including Gerhard Alden Gesell, lawyer and jurist. D. May 29, 1961, New Haven, Connecticut.

Arnold Gesell was a student at the State Normal School (later, University of Wisconsin—Stevens Point) at Stevens Point, Wisconsin, and received the B.Ph. degree (1903) from the University of Wisconsin, the Ph.D. degree (1906) from Clark University in Worcester, Massachusetts, and the M.D. degree (1915) from Yale University.

He taught psychology at the Los Angeles State Normal School (1908–10). In 1911 he was appointed first director of the Yale Clinic for Child Development, serving to his retirement in 1948. Under Gesell's leadership, the clinic conducted research that led to an objective description of characteristics and norms for the mental and physical growth of both normal and exceptional children. Gesell was concerned about the origins and development of individual differences in children. In 1925 he established an extensive film library on the behavior of over 12,000 children under the age of ten filmed in natural settings. Gesell used the films in establishing developmental norms and concepts of child training. He believed all development was related to biological change and was known as a maturational theorist.

Gesell served as professor of child hygiene at Yale Medical School (1915–48) and was an attending pediatrician at New Haven Hospital (1928–48). He was a child psychologist for the Connecticut State Board of Education (1915–19). He was a research associate in child vision research at the Yale School of Medicine (1948–50) and lectured at the New School for Social Research in New York City from 1950. He was a consultant to the Gesell Institute of Child Development (1950–58).

Gesell was a major writer in the field of child development. Among his many books were *The Normal Child and Primary Education* (with Beatrice Gesell, 1912), *Manual on Defective Children* (1918), *School Provisions for Exceptional Children* (1919), *Exceptional Children and Public School Policy* (1921), *Handicapped Children in School and Court* (1921), *The Preschool Child* (1923), *The Retarded Child* (1925), *The Mental Growth of the Preschool Child* (1925), *Learning and Growth in Identical Infant Twins* (with Helen Thompson, 1929), *An Atlas of Infant Behavior* (two volumes, with others, 1934), *Biographies of Child Development* (with others, 1938), *The First Five Years* (with others, 1940), *The Child from Five to Ten* (with F. Ilg, 1946), *Studies in Child Development* (1948), and *The Years from Ten to Sixteen* (with F. Ilg and L. B. Ames, 1956). He produced films on child development and established the photographic library of Yale Films of Child Development (1925).

Active in professional organizations, Gesell was a fellow of the American Association for the Advancement of Science, the American Orthopsychiatric Association, and the American Academy of Pediatrics. He was a member of the American Academy for Cerebral Palsy (president, 1952–53), the Connecticut Commission on Child Welfare (1919–21), and the National Academy of Sciences. He was a member of White House conferences on child health and protection and children in a democracy. Gesell received honorary degrees from Clark University and the University of Wisconsin and was named laureate of Kappa Delta Pi (1958).

REFERENCES: *CB* (November 1940); *DSB; LE* (III); *NCAB* (49:119); *WWAE* (XIII); *WWW* (IV); *NYT*, May 30, 1961, p. 17.

John R. Silvestro

GIBBS, Jonathan C. B. c. 1827, Philadelphia, Pennsylvania, to Jonathan C. and Maria Gibbs. M. to n.a. ch. one, Thomas Van Rensselaer Gibbs, Florida legislator. D. August 14, 1874, Tallahassee, Florida.

Jonathan C. Gibbs was a well-educated articulate Negro clergyman who rose to prominence in Florida following the Civil War. A graduate of Dartmouth College (1852) and Princeton Theological Seminary, he held Presbyterian pastorates in New York and Pennsylvania before opening a mission and school for freedmen in North Carolina and later in Florida.

Because he defied the stereotype of illiterate and arrogant blacks who ostensibly made a mockery of civil government in the South during Reconstruction, Gibbs was well respected by both black and white members of the dominant Republican party. He was elected a member of Florida's Constitutional Convention of 1868 and served as secretary of state (1868–73) and state superintendent of public instruction (1873–74). He was Florida's first and only Negro cabinet member.

In his brief tenure as superintendent, Gibbs devoted his energies to upgrading education for both races. He had some success in securing adoption of uniform textbooks; under his direction the state published its first course of studies for elementary and secondary schools. Gibbs was often discouraged by the scarcity of funds for education, the lack of trained teachers, and the hostility of many toward providing public schools for Negroes. In August 1873 Gibbs addressed the National Educational Association meeting in Elmira, New York, on the problems and progress of education in Florida since the Civil War.

A promising career was cut short when Gibbs died on August 14, 1874. He was honored by having a junior college, high schools, and a hall on the Florida Agricultural and Mechanical University campus in Tallahassee named for him.

REFERENCES: William Watson Davis, "The Civil War and Reconstruction in Florida" (Ph.D. diss., Columbia University, 1913); Leedell W. Neyland and John W. Riley, *The History of Florida Agricultural and Mechanical University* (Gainesville: University Presses of Florida, 1963); Joe M. Richardson, *The Negro in the Reconstruction of Florida, 1865–1877* (Tallahassee: Florida State University, 1965); Jerrell H. Shofner, *Nor Is It over Yet–Florida in the Era of Reconstruction, 1863–1877* (Gainesville: University Presses of Florida, 1974).   *Harry A. Kersey, Jr.*

GIBSON, William. B. March 14, 1788, Baltimore, Maryland, to John Gibson and his wife (n.a.). M. 1810 to Sarah Hollingsworth. M. to n.a. Ch. eight, including Charles Bell Gibson, prominent medical educator. D. March 2, 1868, Savannah, Georgia.

William Gibson attended St. John's College in Annapolis, Maryland, and was graduated from the College of New Jersey (later, Princeton University) in 1806. He began the study of medicine with John Owen of Baltimore, Maryland, and later attended lectures at the University of Pennsylvania. He received his degree in medicine from the University of Edinburgh (Scotland) in 1809, where he had studied with John Bell, who took him as a private pupil, and attracted the attention of Sir Astley Cooper, the great surgeon of Guy's Hospital. Gibson was greatly influenced by his early association with these two men and their colleagues.

Gibson returned to America in 1810 and set up a medical practice in Baltimore. He organized a medical department at the University of Maryland and became professor of surgery (1811). He stayed at Maryland until 1819 when he accepted a position teaching surgery at the University of Pennsylvania, succeeding Philip S. Physick *(q.v.)*. He held this post until his retirement in 1855.

He was the first in America to tie the iliac artery (1812) and legate the subclavian artery (1828). He became famous in America and Europe for performing a caesarian section twice upon the same woman; both mother and child were saved both times.

Gibson wrote *The Institutes and Practice of Surgery* (1824), which was a long-used text in the United States and Europe. He also wrote *Rambles in Europe* (1839), which contained sketches of eminent surgeons, and *Lectures on Eminent Belgian Surgeons and Physicians* (1841).

REFERENCES: *AC; DAB; NCAB* (2:441); *TC; WWW* (H).

C. Roy Rylander

GIDDINGS, Franklin Henry. B. March 23, 1855, Sherman, Connecticut, to Edward J. and Rebecca Jane (Fuller) Giddings. M. November 8, 1876, to Elizabeth Patience Hawes. Ch. three. D. June 11, 1931, Scarsdale, New York.

Franklin Giddings was uninspired by elementary schooling, but entered Union College (Schenectady, New York) in 1873 with the intention of becoming a civil engineer. Because of ill health, he gave up formal education to enter the teaching profession. After two years of teaching, he began a career in journalism. He was involved in newspaper work and conducted an investigation of cooperation and profit sharing in the United States for the Massachusetts Bureau of Statistics of Labor. Union College granted him the A.B. degree in 1888 and a year later conferred on him the A.M. degree.

In 1888 he succeeded Woodrow Wilson *(q.v.)* in teaching at Bryn Mawr (Pennsylvania) College. In 1894 Columbia University selected him as the first professor of sociology in any American college. He remained with Columbia for the rest of his life, retiring from teaching in 1928, but continued productive work as professor emeritus in residence.

He was the author of *The Modern Distributive Process* (1888), a volume in economics, and *The Theory of Sociology* (1894). His first volume to be widely acclaimed was *The Principles of Sociology* (1896). It was translated into seven foreign languages. He also wrote *The Theory of Socialization* (1897), *The Elements of Sociology* (1898), *The Western Hemisphere in the World of Tomorrow* (1915), *The Responsible State* (1918), *Studies in the Theory of Human Society* (1922), *The Scientific Study of Human Society* (1924), and *The Mighty Medicine–Superstition and Its Antidote* (1929).

Giddings was president of the American Sociological Society (1910–11) and the Institut international de sociologie (1913). He was a member of the board of education of New York City from 1915 to 1917 and of the board of trustees of Union College, being made honorary chancellor in 1926.

REFERENCES: *DAB* (supp. 1); *NCAB* (39:78); *TC; WWW* (I); *NYT,* June 12, 1931, p. 21.

Paul J. Schafer

GIDEONSE, Harry David. B. May 17, 1901, Rotterdam, the Netherlands, to Martin Cornelius and Johanna Jacoba Helena Magdalena (de Lange) Gideonse. M. June 15, 1926, to Edmee Koch. Ch. two.

Harry D. Gideonse emigrated to the United States from the Netherlands at the age of three. He attended public school in Rochester, New York, and the Hague, the Netherlands. He was graduated from Columbia University with the B.S. (1923) and M.A. (1924) degrees. He studied at the University of Geneva, Switzerland, where he received the Diplome des hautes études Internationales (1928).

Gideonse was a research chemist for the Eastman Kodak Company (1919–21) and a lecturer in economy at Barnard and Columbia colleges of Columbia University (1924–26) and director of international students' work at Geneva, Switzerland (1926–28). He was assistant professor of economics at Rutgers University in New Brunswick, New Jersey (1928–30), and joined the faculty of the University of Chicago in 1930, where he stayed to 1938. At Chicago he served as chairman of the social science unit and integrated social science courses. He was one of the originators of the University of Chicago Round Table broadcasts. He was professor of economics and chairman of the economics and social science department at Hunter College of Columbia University (1938–39). In 1939 he assumed the presidency of Brooklyn College of the City of New York, where he remained to his retirement in 1966. During his tenure, enrollment doubled and the physical plant was enlarged. He served as chancellor of the New School for Social Research at New York City from 1966.

Gideonse was the author of *Transfert des Réparations et Plan Dawes* (1928), *The International Bank* (1930), *The Higher Learning in a Democracy* (1937), *The Economic Foreign Policy of the United States* (1953), and *Against the Running Tide* (1967). He was the editor of the Public Policy pamphlets of the University of Chicago (1932–42).

Gideonse was a member of many organizations, including the Chicago Council on Foreign Relations (executive committee, 1936), the Economist's National Committee on Monetary Policy (executive vice-president, 1937–46), the Woodrow Wilson Foundation (member of the board of directors from 1946 and vice-president), Freedom House (board of directors since 1942), and the Commission of Inquiry into Forced Labor (chairman, 1948–50). He was decorated by the governments of Denmark, the Netherlands, and France and was the recipient of many honorary degrees from colleges and universities.

REFERENCES: *CB* (May 1940); *LE* (III); *NCAB* (I:289); *WW* (XXXVI); *WWAE* (XVI).   *John F. Ohles*

GILBERT, Eliphalet Wheeler. B. December 19, 1793, New Lebanon, Connecticut, to Elisha and Ellen (Venderpoel) Gilbert. M. October 21, 1819, to Lydia Hale Monroe. M. to Mary Ann Singer. Ch. six. D. July 31, 1853, Philadelphia, Pennsylvania.

Eliphalet Wheeler Gilbert received his early education from his grandfather, Elisha Gilbert, and was graduated from Union College in Schenectady, New York, in 1813. He studied at the Princeton (New Jersey) Theological Seminary (1814–16), was licensed to preach in 1817, and was ordained by the presbytery of New Castle, Delaware, in 1818.

Gilbert was pastor of the Second Presbyterian Church in Wilmington, Delaware (1818–29). In 1829 the congregation split over the issue of constructing a new church, and Gilbert and part of the congregation established the Hanover Street Church in the new building (1829–34).

Appointed in 1833 to the board of trustees of a new college, which was to be part of the Newark (Delaware) Academy, Gilbert became president of the board and president of Newark College in 1834. He resigned in 1835 to protest the financing of the college through a lottery. He returned to the Hanover Street Church (1835–41), but reassumed the presidency of the college in 1841 with agreement to discontinue the lottery. In 1843 the legislature changed the name to Delaware College, and the school became the University of Delaware in 1921. Gilbert served as president until 1847, when he assumed charge of the Western Presbyterian Church in Philadelphia, Pennsylvania, where he served until his death in 1853.

Gilbert was a major figure in the New School group during the controversy in the Presbyterian church during the 1830s. He served as coeditor of the *Presbyterian Quarterly Review* and was active in church affairs as a trustee of the Princeton Theological Seminary and a member of the American Board of Commissioners for Foreign Missions. He received an honorary degree from the University of Vermont (1841).

REFERENCES: *DAB; NCAB* (24:213); *WWW* (H).   *John F. Ohles*

GILDERSLEEVE, Basil Lanneau. B. October 23, 1831, Charleston, South Carolina, to Benjamin and Emma Louisa (Lanneau) Gildersleeve. M. September 18, 1866, to Eliza Fisher Colston. Ch. two. D. January 9, 1924, Baltimore, Maryland.

Basil Lanneau Gildersleeve, accaimed as the greatest American classical scholar, had read through the entire Bible by the age of five and learned Latin well enough to have read Caesar, Sallust, Cicero, Virgil, and Horace by his sixth birthday. His early education was obtained under the tutelage of his father and at the age of sixteen he entered Jefferson College in Canonsburg, Pennsylvania. He enrolled at the College of New Jersey (later, Princeton University), graduating at the age of seventeen with the A.B. degree (1849) and in 1852 with the M.A. degree. He was considered precocious in Latin and Greek, and superior in French, German, Italian, and Spanish. He studied the classics in three German universities, Berlin, Bonn, and Göttingen, and received the Ph.D. degree (1853) from the University of Göttingen at the age of twenty-two. He studied at home from 1853 to 1856.

Gildersleeve taught in a school in Richmond, Virginia, in 1850. He was named professor of Greek and Hebrew at the University of Virginia in 1856 and taught Latin from 1861 to 1866. When the Civil War began, he served during summers in the Confederate army (1861–63), joined a general staff in 1864, and was wounded in action. He returned to the University of Virginia and served until 1876.

When Johns Hopkins University opened in 1876, Gildersleeve was offered the first chair in the classics as a professor of Greek. He served at Johns Hopkins from 1876 to his retirement in 1915.

Gildersleeve was the author of *Latin Grammar* (1867), *Latin Primer* (1871), *Latin Reader* (1871), *Essays and Studies* (1890), *Greek Syntax* (with C. W. E. Miller, 1900 and 1911), *Hellas and Hispera* (1909), and *The Creed of the Old South* (1915). He was editor of *Persius* (1875), *Justin Martyr* (1877), and *Odes of Pindar* (1885). He was founder and editor of the *American Journal of Philology* (1880–1920).

He was named a fellow in the British Academy and American Academy of Arts and Sciences. He was a member of the American Academy of Arts and Letters and the American Philological Association (president, 1878 and 1909). He was an honorary corresponding member of foreign learned associations and was awarded nine honorary degrees from American and English colleges and universities.

REFERENCES: *AC; DAB; EB; NCAB* (10:469); *TC; WWW* (I); *NYT,* January 10, 1924, p. 21.   *Franklin Ross Jones*

GILDERSLEEVE, Virginia Crocheron. B. October 3, 1877, New York, New York, to Henry Alger and Virginia (Crocheron) Gildersleeve. M. no. D. July 7, 1965, Centerville, Massachusetts.

Virginia Crocheron Gildersleeve's father was justice of the supreme court of New York (1894–1909). Gildersleeve was graduated with the A.B. degree (1899) from Barnard College of Columbia University. She joined the Barnard faculty as an English instructor in 1900 and left in 1905 to pursue doctoral studies at Columbia, where she received the Ph.D. degree (1908).

Gildersleeve returned to Barnard as an instructor and became dean in 1911, where she remained to her retirement in 1947. Regarded as one of the country's foremost educators, she was practical in her beliefs about college-educated women in the modern world and was a champion of women's rights and supranationalism. She disapproved of coeducational schooling, allowed smoking, and introduced courses in sex hygiene.

Gildersleeve's autobiography, *Many a Good Crusade,* was published in 1954. She also wrote *Government Regulation of Elizabethean Drama* (1908) and *A Hoard for Winter* (1962), a collection of essays, articles, and broadcasts.

Active in educational organizations, Gildersleeve was chairman of the

American Council on Education and president of the International Federation of University Women and of Reid Hall, the resident center for American college students in Paris, France. She was a trustee of the American College for Girls of Istanbul, Turkey, Spence School, the Masters School, and the Institute of International Education. She was first chairman on international relations of the American Association of University Women.

Gildersleeve was appointed by President Franklin D. Roosevelt as the only woman delegate to the United Nations Conference on International Organization in San Francisco, California (1945), was chairman of the executive committee for American Middle East Relief, and was a member of the American Educational Mission to Japan (1946). She was decorated by the governments of France (Legion of Honor) and the Dominican Republic and received many awards for distinguished service and seven honorary degrees.

REFERENCES: *CB* (August 1941); *LE* (III); *NCAB* (G:104); *WWAE* (XIV); *WWW* (IV); Alice Fleming, *Great Women Teachers* (Philadelphia: J. B. Lippincott Co., 1965); *NYT,* July 9, 1965, p. 1; *Newsweek,* October 25, 1954, p. 86.   *Linda C. Gardner*

GILLESPIE, Eliza Maria (Mother Angela). B. February 21, 1824, Brownsville, Pennsylvania, to John and Mary (Miers) Gillespie. M. no. D. March 4, 1887, Notre Dame, Indiana.

A pioneer in equal education for Catholic women, Eliza Gillespie was raised in Lancaster, Ohio. She was educated at Georgetown Visitation School in Washington, D.C., graduating in 1842. She taught in a non-Catholic school in St. Mary's, Maryland, where she introduced religion courses for Catholic students despite initial objections of school officials. She organized a Sunday school for blacks and worked as a nurse among the poor. She decided upon a career as a religious but did not join the Congregation of the Holy Cross until after she had met Father Edward Sorin *(q.v.)*, founder of the University of Notre Dame. She entered the order in 1853 and went to France to spend two years in the novitiate.

She returned to the United States and took charge of the educational program of St. Mary's College at South Bend, Indiana. She believed that the educational preparation of young women should be as complete as that for men. She strengthened the traditionally feminine subjects, such as art and music, and introduced enriched offerings in science, higher mathematics, foreign languages, philosophy, and theology.

She was active in providing nurses during the Civil War. In 1869 she was named provincial superior of her order. She was the founder of St. Catherine's Institute in Baltimore, Maryland, a teacher-training institution. By 1887 she had established forty-five foundations for her order throughout the country.

Mother Angela was noted as the publisher of the Metropolitan Readers, which later became the Excelsior Series. After 1866 she was an editor of *Ave Maria*. She worked with Sorin to promote higher education for Catholics in the Midwest. She remained as superior of her province until her death near South Bend in 1887.

REFERENCES: *DAB; NAW; WC; WWW* (H); *New Catholic Encyclopedia* (New York: McGraw-Hill, 1967).   *James M. Vosper*

GILLETTE, John Morris. B. August 9, 1866, near Marysville, Missouri, to William Wilgus and Jane (Radford) Gillette. M. September 4, 1901, to Margaret Carolyn Morgan. Ch. one. D. September 24, 1949, Grand Forks, North Dakota.

John Morris Gillette was graduated with the A.B. degree (1892) from Park College in Parkville, Missouri. He was graduated from Princeton Theological Seminary (1895), received the A.M. degree (1895) at Princeton University and received Ph.D. degrees from the Chicago Theological Seminary (1898) and the University of Chicago (1901). He also studied at the San Francisco (California) Theological Seminary, Union Theological Seminary in New York City, Columbia University, and Auburn (New York) Theological Seminary.

Gillette was an ordained Presbyterian minister and served pastorates in Kansas at Perry, Bethel, and Dodge City. He was a lecturer and librarian at the Bible Normal College in Springfield, Massachusetts (1898–99). He was president of Chadron (Nebraska) Academy (1899–1900) and the Academy for Young Women at Jacksonville, Illinois (1901–03). He was professor of history and social sciences at the State Normal School (later, Valley City State College) in Valley City, North Dakota (1903–07). He was professor of sociology and head of the department of sociology and anthropology at the University of North Dakota (1907–49), where he was called the Father of Rural Sociology.

Gillette authored *Cultural Influences in a Typical Manufacturing Group—South Chicago* (1901), *Vocational Education* (1910), *Constructive Rural Sociology* (1913), *The Family and Society* (1914), *Rural Communities* (1915), *Sociology* (1916), *Rural Sociology* (1922), *Current Social Problems* (with James M. Reinhardt, 1933), *Mounds and Mound-builders of the United States* (1944), and *North Dakota Weather and the Rural Economy* (1945). He also wrote nearly a hundred papers and monographs.

He was a member of professional associations, including the American Sociological Society (president, 1928) and the North Dakota Historical Society (director). He was a state supervisor of rural research for the Federal Emergency Relief Administration, chairman of the advisory committee on personnel of the North Dakota Workmen's Compensation and

Unemployment Insurance Division (1937–40), a member of the advisory board of the National Child Labor Committee (1918–22), and chairman of the North Dakota State Child Labor Commission (1913–20). He was the recipient of honorary degrees.

REFERENCES: *LE* (II); *NCAB* (37:269); *WWW* (III).

Lawrence S. Master

GILMAN, Arthur. B. June 22, 1837, Alton, Illinois, to Winthrop Sargent and Abbia Swift (Lippincott) Gilman. M. April 12, 1860, to Amy Cooke Ball. M. July 11, 1876, to Stella Haughton Scott. Ch. seven. D. December 28, 1909, Atlantic City, New Jersey.

Arthur Gilman received his early education in private schools in St. Louis, Missouri, and Lee, Massachusetts. In 1849 his family moved to New York City, and he attended Chrestomathic Institute at Rye, New York. He attended Mr. Leggett's School in New York City in 1851.

Gilman began a successful career in his father's banking firm in 1857, but his health failed, and in 1862 he moved to Berkshire County, Massachusetts, near Lenox. He engaged in agriculture, philanthropy, and education, serving twice on the local school committee and as a visitor to the public schools. In 1865 he toured Europe, visiting England to prepare a family genealogy. On his return from Europe, he moved to Cambridge, Massachusetts. He was an editor of the American Tract Society in Boston in 1871 and served for many years as a literary adviser to the Riverside Press.

In 1877 Gilman and his wife devised a plan for the education of women by the Harvard College faculty. The plan took form as the Society for the Collegiate Instruction of Women, or more familiarly, the Harvard Annex, with Gilman as the first executive officer.

In 1886 he bought an estate next to the Harvard Annex and founded the Cambridge School where modern educational methods were used to prepare girls for college and give them a literary education. When the Harvard Annex became Radcliffe College in 1893, he was named regent.

Gilman was the author of *First Steps in English Literature* (1870), *Story of the Saracens* (1883), *Story of Rome* (1885), *Short Stories from the Dictionary* (1886), *Discovery and Exploration of America* (1887), *The Colonization of America* (1887), *The Making of the American Nation* (1887), and *The Story of Boston* (1889).

REFERENCES: *AC; DAB; NCAB* (6:162); *WWW* (I); *NYT,* December 29, 1909, p. 9.   *Joseph P. Cangemi*

Thomas E. Kesler

GILMAN, Daniel Coit. B. July 6, 1831, Norwich, Connecticut, to William Charles and Eliza (Coit) Gilman. M. December 4, 1861, to Mary Ketcham.

M. June 13, 1877, to Elizabeth Dwight Woolsey. Ch. two. D. October 13, 1908, Norwich, Connecticut.

Daniel Coit Gilman attended Norwich (Connecticut) Academy and was graduated from Yale College in 1852, receiving the A.M. degree in 1855. He studied at Harvard University for a few months. Gilman left for Europe in late 1853 with Yale classmate Andrew D. White *(q.v.)*. They remained for two years as attachés of the American legation at St. Petersburg, Russia.

On his return to the United States, Gilman accepted a position at Yale College, where he helped plan the new Sheffield Scientific School, which he served as librarian, secretary, and professor of physical and political geography. In 1872 Gilman accepted the presidency of the University of California where he succeeded in laying the groundwork for a modern university. In 1875 he accepted the presidency of Johns Hopkins University, which was to be founded in Baltimore, Maryland, by the beneficence of Quaker merchant Johns Hopkins.

Gilman served as president of Johns Hopkins University for over a quarter century (1875–1901). Under Gilman, Johns Hopkins became an important research university as a unique institution that was not German, English, or American. In 1902, on the occasion of Gilman's retirement as president of Johns Hopkins, Woodrow Wilson *(q.v.)* noted that Gilman was "the first to create and organize in America a university in which the discovery and dissemination of new truth were conceded a rank superior to mere instruction; and in which the efficiency and value of research as an educational instrument were exemplified in the training of many investigators." Gilman served as first president (1902–04) of the Carnegie Institution, which had been endowed by Andrew Carnegie.

Gilman was the author of *Life of James Monroe* (1883), *University Problems* (1888), *The Life of James Dwight Dana* (1899), *Science and Letters in Yale* (1901), and *The Launching of a University* (1906). He was editor-in-chief of the *New International Encyclopedia*.

Gilman held a number of important offices, including president of the American Social Science Association (1879). He was one of the original trustees of the John F. Slater Fund in 1882 and served as president (1893–1908). He became a trustee of the Peabody Education Fund (1893) and the Russell Sage Foundation (1907) and was a member of the General Education Board (1903). He was president of the National Civil Service Reform League (1901–07). He was a member of the United States commission that determined the boundary between Venezuela and British Guiana (1896–97). Gilman was awarded honorary degrees by nine American colleges and universities and the University of Toronto, Canada.

REFERENCES: *AC; DAB; EB; NCAB* (5:170); *TC; WWW* (I); F. Cordasco, *Daniel Coit Gilman and the Protean Ph.D.* (Leiden, the Netherlands: E. J. Brill, 1960); Fabian Franklin, *Daniel Coit Gilman* (New York:

Dodd, Mead & Co., 1910); *NYT,* October 14, 1908, p. 9; Abraham Flexner (*q.v.*), *Daniel Coit Gilman* (New York: Harcourt, Brace, 1946).

Francesco Cordasco

GIVENS, Willard Earl. B. December 10, 1886, Anderson, Indiana, to John Luther and Amanda Elizabeth (Hershberger) Givens. M. December 10, 1917, to Neva Lillian Galbreath. Ch. two. D. May 20, 1971, Detroit, Michigan.

Willard Earl Givens was a student at Butler College (later, University) in Indianapolis, Indiana (1908–09), and attended Indiana University, where he received the A.B. degree (1913). He received the M.A. degree (1915) from Columbia University, a diploma from Union Theological Seminary in New York City in 1916, and studied at Columbia University (1915–17) and the University of California (1925–33).

Givens taught in a one-room rural school in Madison County, Indiana (1906–09), and at Noblesville (Indiana) High School (1911–13), and was a high school principal in Honolulu, Hawaii (1919–21), Oakland, California (1921–22), and at the Kamehameha Boys School in Honolulu (1922–23). He was superintendent of public instruction in the Territory of Hawaii (1923–25) and served in California as assistant superintendent of schools in Oakland (1925–27) and superintendent of schools in San Diego (1927–28) and Oakland (1928–35).

He was executive secretary of the National Education Association (NEA) from 1935 until his retirement in 1952. Experience as president of the California State Teachers Association (1932–35) and as state director of the National Education Association in both Hawaii and California prepared Givens for his job as executive secretary of the NEA. Givens expanded the NEA membership, budget, research, number of local associations, leadership among classroom teachers, the association journal, and services to members of the teaching profession. He served in many national and international posts, including consultant for the United States to the Philippines (1953), chairman of the United States National Commission for the United Nations Educational, Scientific, and Cultural Organization (UNESCO) (1956), and educational adviser to the United States delegation to the World UNESCO Conference in New Delhi, India (1956).

REFERENCES: *CB* (September 1948); *LE* (III); *WWAE* (XXII); *WWW* (V); "Willard E. Givens," *NEA Journal* 41 (March 1952): 269–70.

Stratton F. Caldwell

GLASS, Hiram Bentley. B. January 17, 1906, Laichowfu (later, Yehsien), Shantung, China, to Wiley B. and Eunice (Taylor) Glass. M. August 10, 1934, to Suzanne G. Smith. Ch. two.

H. Bentley Glass, son of Baptist missionaries, received his elementary and secondary education in China. At the age of seventeen, he left China to attend Decatur (Texas) Baptist College. He transferred to Baylor University in Waco, Texas, where he was awarded the B.A. degree (1926). For the next two years, he taught high school biology and physics at Timpson, Texas, and then resumed studies at Baylor to complete the M.S. degree (1929). He earned the Ph.D. degree in biology from the University of Texas in Austin (1932).

Glass was awarded a National Research Council postdoctoral fellowship to study genetics at the University of Oslo (Norway) and in 1933 resumed these studies at the Kaiser Wilhelm Institüt (Berlin). However, because of increasing Nazi control over the academic community, he returned to the United States (1933) to complete these studies at the University of Missouri in Columbia.

He taught zoology at Stephens College in Columbia, Missouri (1934–38), and biology at Goucher College in Towson, Maryland (1938–47). He joined the Johns Hopkins University faculty as associate professor of biology in 1948 and was appointed professor in 1952. In 1965 he was appointed chief executive officer of the State University of New York at Stony Brook.

While at Johns Hopkins, he became known for his genetic drift theory, a model that explains the spread of genetic characteristics from one population to another. He suggested ways in which to estimate the amount of exchange between gene pools of neighboring populations, enabling population geneticists to quantize genetic traits in human populations. As a member of the Baltimore School Board (1954–58), Glass convinced the board that the differences in intelligence between races were the result of differences in opportunities.

Glass led the fight against a nationwide threat to academic freedom. As president and spokesman of the American Association of University Professors (1958), he initiated action toward the repeal of the loyalty-oath clause of the National Defense Act. He was among the first scientists (1963) to advocate a ban on atomic testing.

Among Glass's most important contributions was his chairmanship of the Biological Sciences Curriculum Study and the development of instructional materials and techniques for the secondary schools. Glass was the author of *Genes and the Man* (1943), *Science and Liberal Education* (1959), and *Science and Ethical Values* (1965). He was editor of *McCollum-Pratt Symposia* (with W. D. McElroy), *Survey of Biological Process* (volumes 3 and 4), *Forerunners of Darwin* (1959), and *Quarterly Review of Biology* and a member of the editorial boards of *Human Biology* and *Isis*.

Six times a member of the International Genetics Congress, Glass was a member of the advisory committee on biology and medicine to the Atomic Energy Commission (1956–63, chairman, 1962–63) and the American

Philosophical Society (council member, 1966–69), and he was president of the Maryland branch of the American Civil Liberties Union (1955–65), the Fund for Overseas Research Grants and Education (from 1966), the American Institute for Biological Sciences (1954–56), the American Society of Naturalists (1965), the American Society of Human Genetics (1967), Phi Beta Kappa (1967), and the American Association of University Professors (1958–60). He was a trustee of *Biological Abstracts* (1954–60), Cold Spring Harbor Laboratory for Quantitative Biology (from 1965), and the Eastern Regional Institute of Education (1966–69). He was the recipient of honorary degrees from several American colleges and universities.

REFERENCES: *CB* (April 1966); *WW* (XXXVIII); *New Republic* 142 (June 27, 1960): 16; *NYT*, April 9, 1965, p. 8; Edwin Diamond, "Biologist in Society's Laboratory," *Saturday Review* 40 (November 2, 1957): 47.   *Isadore L. Sonnier*

GLENN, Gustavus Richard. B. December 5, 1848, Jackson County, Georgia, to James Russell and Anne (Williams) Glenn. M. July 22, 1875, to Nellie Verstille. Ch. eleven. D. January 23, 1939, Decatur, Georgia.

Gustavus R. Glenn attended the common schools of Georgia and entered the University of Georgia at Athens. He was graduated with the A.B. (1871) and A.M. (1872) degrees.

Glenn was the principal of a select school for boys in Columbus, Georgia, and in 1875 founded and was president of the Columbus (Georgia) Female College until the college was destroyed by fire in 1884. From 1884 to 1894 he occupied the chair of natural science at Wesleyan College in Macon, Georgia.

Glenn became state school commissioner in 1895 under Governor William Y. Atkinson and served for eight years. He was president of North Georgia Agricultural College (later, North Georgia College) at Dahlonega from 1904 until his resignation in 1922.

Glenn was active in professional organizations and was president of the Southern Educational Association (1900) and the department of superintendence of the National Educational Association (1901). He was general agent of the Peabody Fund from 1903 until the office was discontinued in 1905. He received an honorary degree from the Peabody Normal School (later, George Peabody College for Teachers) in 1899.

REFERENCES: *NCAB* (13:96); *WWW* (III); Dorothy Orr, *A History of Education in Georgia* (Chapel Hill: University of North Carolina Press, 1950), pp. 393–94.   *Edward B. Goellner*

GODDARD, Henry Herbert. B. August 14, 1866, Vassalboro, Maine, to Henry C. and Sarah (Winslow) Goddard. M. August 7, 1889, to Emma

Florence Robbins. Ch. none. D. June 20, 1957, Santa Barbara, California.

Henry Goddard received his preliminary education in Providence, Rhode Island, and the A.B. (1887) and A.M. (1889) degrees from Haverford (Pennsylvania) College. He was a fellow in psychology at Clark University in Worcester, Massachusetts (1896–99), where he received the Ph.D. degree (1899). He studied in German universities.

Goddard began his professional career as principal of Damascus (Ohio) Academy (1889–91), assistant principal and principal of the Oak Grove Seminary in Vassalboro, Maine (1891–96), and professor of psychology at Pennsylvania State Normal School in West Chester (later, West Chester State College) from 1899 to 1906. In 1906 he became psychologist and director of the new research laboratory at the Training School in Vineland, New Jersey. He founded the first laboratory for the psychological study of mental deficiency. Goddard studied the causation, amelioration, and prevention of mental deficiency. He originated the word *moron*. In 1918 he became director of the State Bureau of Juvenile Research in Columbus, Ohio, and in 1922 was professor of clinical and abnormal psychology at Ohio State University, a position he held until he retired in 1938.

Goddard was the author of *The Kallikak Family* (1912), *Feeblemindedness* (1914), *The Criminal Imbecile* (1915), *School Training of Defective Children* (1915), *Psychology of the Normal and Subnormal* (1919), *Human Efficiency and Levels of Intelligence* (1920), *Juvenile Delinquency* (1921), *Two Souls in One Body?* (1927), *The School Training of Gifted Children* (1927), and *How to Raise Children in the Atomic Age* (1948). He published a translation and revision of the Binet-Simon intelligence scale in 1910.

Goddard held memberships in the American Association for the Study of the Feebleminded (later, American Association on Mental Deficiency), serving as president (1914–15), the American Psychological Association, and the American Association for the Advancement of Science. He was the recipient of three honorary degrees.

REFERENCES: *LE* (III); *NCAB* (15:236); *WWW* (IV); *American Men of Science,* 5th ed. (New York: Science Press, 1933); *NYT,* June 22, 1957, p. 15.   *Bruce D. Mattson*

GOETSCHIUS, Percy. B. August 30, 1853, Paterson, New Jersey, to John Henry and Mary Ann (Berry) Goetschius. M. July 29, 1889, to n.a. M. July 14, 1899, to Maria C. Stephany. Ch. two. D. October 29, 1943, Manchester, New Hampshire.

Percy Goetschius received his early education in a private school at Paterson, New Jersey. In 1873 he went to Germany to study music with Siegmund Lebert and Dionys Pruckner in piano, Immanuel Faiszt in composition, and Karl Doppler in instrumentation in the Conservatory of Music at Stuttgart. He was graduated from the conservatory in 1878.

Before his graduation he was an instructor of English classes in harmony, counterpoint, composition, and musical history at the conservatory. In 1885 he was honored by the king of Württemberg with the title "royal professor of music" and in 1886 he became musical editor of the (Stuttgart) *Schwäbischer Merkur* and *Neues Tagblatt;* he was also a correspondent for other German musical publications.

Goetschius taught at Stuttgart until 1890 when he returned to America to teach musical theory, history and advanced piano-forte at Syracuse (New York) University. He became professor of harmony, counterpoint, composition, and musical history at the New England Conservatory of Music in Boston, Massachusetts (1892–96). He engaged in private teaching and was a church organist and choir director of the First Parish Church, Brookline, Massachusetts. In 1905 he became head of the department of theory and composition at the new Institute of Musical Art in New York City, remaining there until his retirement in 1925.

Goetschius developed an international reputation through his books, including *The Material Used in Musical Composition* (1889), *The Theory and Practice of Tone Relations* (1892), *Models of the Principal Musical-Forms* (1894), *Syllabus of Musical History* (1895), *The Homophonic Forms of Musical Composition* (1898), *Exercises in Melody Writing* (1900), *Applied Counterpoint* (1902), *Lessons in Music Form* (1904), *Twelve Lessons in Harmony* (1904), *Elementary Counterpoint* (1909), *The Essentials of Music History* (with Thomas Tapper, *q.v.*, 1913), *The Larger Forms of Musical Composition* (1915), *Masters of the Symphony* (1929), and *The Structure of Music* (1933). He also wrote many musical compositions, including a symphony, two overtures, an orchestral suite, and numerous smaller works.

REFERENCES: *DAB* (supp. 3); *NCAB* (14:258); *WWW* (IV); *NYT,* November 19, 1943, p. 19; Nicholas Slonimsky, ed., *The International Encyclopedia of Music and Musicians,* 8th ed. (New York: Dodd, Mead & Co., 1953), pp. 680–81; A Shepard, "Papa Goetschius in Retrospect," *Musical Quarterly* 30 (July 1944): 307–18.   *Norman J. Bauer*

GOFF, Milton Browning. B. December 17, 1831, Pittsburgh, Pennsylvania, to Philo and Prudence (Brown) Goff. M. November 20, 1856, to Emily Virginia Locke. Ch. four. D. November 8, 1890, Pittsburgh, Pennsylvania.

Milton Browning Goff was educated in the public schools of Sewickley, Pennsylvania, and at Dr. J. S. Travelli's Academy. He studied at Allegheny College in Meadville, Pennsylvania, receiving the A.B. (1854) and A.M. (1858) degrees.

As a youth, he was a typesetter for the *Pittsburgh* (Pennsylvania) *Gazette.* After graduation from college he was professor of mathematics and natural sciences at Madison College in Uniontown, Pennsylvania (1854–

56). He was principal of Northern Illinois University in Henry (1858–61) and the Sharpsburgh Academy and Third Ward School in Allegheny, Pennsylvania (1861–65). He was professor of mathematics at Western University of Pennsylvania (later, University of Pittsburgh) from 1867 to 1882 and professor of mathematics and astronomy at Allegheny College from 1882 to 1884. He returned to the Western University of Pennsylvania in 1884 as chancellor, serving to his death in 1890. Under Goff, the university erected new buildings and opened a school of engineering with courses in civil, electrical, and mechanical engineering.

Goff was a contributor to the *United States Nautical Almanac* and wrote articles on astronomy and other scientific subjects. He was the author of *The Complete Arithmetic* (1876), *First Book in Arithmetic* (1876), *A Book of Arithmetic Problems* (1877), *Elementary Arithmetic* (1888), *Goff's Practical Arithmetic for Graded and Common Schools* (1889), and *Key to Practical Arithmetic* (1891). He received an honorary degree from Allegheny College.

REFERENCES: *NCAB* (21:100); *TC; NYT,* November 9, 1890, p. 5; Agnes Lynch Starrett, *Through One Hundred and Fifty Years* (Pittsburgh: University of Pittsburgh Press, 1937).   *Steven A. Thiel*

GOLDBECK, Robert. B. April 19, 1839, Potsdam, Prussia, to n.a. M. (first and second wives, n.a.). M. June 22, 1880, to Elise F. Haenschen. Ch. none. D. May 16, 1908, St. Louis, Missouri.

There are no records to indicate who the parents of Robert Goldbeck were; yet, early in life he was associated with celebrated personalities. Goldbeck was born in Potsdam, Prussia (later, Germany), and at the age of fourteen appeared in concert before the king of Prussia. The boy's talents were recognized and developed at an early age by his maternal uncle, composer Louis Kohler. Goldbeck continued his study of piano at Brunswick for four years and in Paris for three years and made his debut in London.

In 1861 Goldbeck traveled to New York, where he spent six years composing and teaching, and in 1867 he went to Boston and aided Eben Tourjée *(q.v.)* in founding the New England Conservatory. Goldbeck went to Chicago in 1868 where he founded the Goldbeck Conservatory of Music. He left Chicago in 1873 to become director of the St. Louis (Missouri) Harmonic Society and codirector and teacher in the Beethoven Conservatory. Goldbeck established his own school, the St. Louis College of Music, in 1880. He went to New York City in 1880 and in 1886 returned to Germany to take charge of the Conservatory at Königsberg, which Louis Kohler had willed to him. In 1891 Goldbeck returned to St. Louis, where he remained to his death in 1908.

Goldbeck was the author of *Musical Questions and Answers* (1860),

Love Songs (1866), *The Art and Science of Music* (1881), *Music Science Primer* (1881), *Harmony Primer* (1886), and the *Encyclopedia of Music Education* (three volumes, 1903). He produced piano methods courses, including graduating courses for piano, general piano techniques, and primary piano methods and vocal music courses, such as graduating courses in voice. He was founder and editor of professional journals, including *Goldbeck's Monthly Journal of Music* (1873), and *Goldbeck's Musical Instructor* (1882, later, *Goldbeck's Musical Art*) and *Musical World*. These journals contained valuable pedagogical material, especially techniques for piano, voice, and harmony. He also published an eight-page biweekly paper, *Goldbeck's Art Critic: or Musical and General Observer* (1884). He composed many and varied musical pieces.

REFERENCES: *DAB; NCAB* (23:251); *WWW* (I); Ernst C. Krohn, *Missouri Music* (New York: Da Capo Press, 1971).   *James R. Layton*
Mary Paula Phillips

GOLDSTEIN, Max Aaron. B. April 19, 1870, St. Louis, Missouri, to William and Hulda (Loewenthal) Goldstein. M. June 4, 1895, to Leonore Weiner. Ch. one. D. July 27, 1941, Frankfort, Michigan.

Max Aaron Goldstein attended local public schools in St. Louis, Missouri, and received the M.D. degree (1892) from the Missouri Medical College (later, Washington University School of Medicine). He was an intern at the St. Louis City Hospital for a year and studied in Berlin, Germany, Vienna, Austria, and London, England (1893).

Returning to St. Louis, he practiced medicine, specializing in otolaryngology. He had become interested in treatment of the deaf while in Europe. He established a class of deaf girls at St. Joseph School for the Deaf in St. Louis. In two years he demonstrated that his pupils had developed an ability to distinguish sounds and changes in pitch and to engage in some conversation.

In 1914 Goldstein established the Central Institute for the Deaf in St. Louis, where he instituted the acoustic method of instruction. He established the first training school for teachers of the deaf, providing a two-year course of study. He provided a nursery school for deaf children and engaged in research in the compensation for deafness through the use of other senses.

Goldstein also served in St. Louis as professor of ontology at Beaumont Hospital Medical College (1895–1900), professor of otolaryngology at St. Louis University (1900–12), director of the department of ontology and laryngology at the Jewish Hospital of St. Louis, and professor of research otology and speech pathology at Washington University (1931–39).

Goldstein was the author of *One Hundred Years of Medicine in Missouri* (1900), *Problems of the Deaf* (1933), and *The Acoustic Method for Train-*

ing of the Deaf and Hard of Hearing Child (1939). He was founder and editor of *The Laryngoscope* (1896) and *Oralism and Auralism* (1922).

He served in the United States Army in World War I as head of the department of head surgery at Camp Dodge, Iowa, and was a member of the committee on reconstruction for deaf and defective-speech soldiers. He received an honorary degree from George Washington University in 1937.

REFERENCES: *DAB* (supp. 3); *NCAB* (37:278); *WWW* (I).

John W. Schifani

GOOD, Carter Victor. B. September 16, 1897, Dayton, Virginia, to Jacob S. H. and Anna Victoria (Early) Good. M. September 6, 1920, to Irene Cooper. Ch. one.

Carter V. Good was a student at Shenandoah College at Dayton, Virginia (1914–15), and received the A.B. (1918) degree from Bridgewater (Virginia) College and the A.M. degree (1923) from the University of Virginia. He studied as a fellow and scholar at the University of Chicago, where he received the Ph.D. degree (1925).

Good was assistant principal of the high school at Shenandoah, Virginia (1919–20), and high school principal in Virginia high schools at New Hope (1920–21) and Marshall (1921–22) and superintendent of Burnsville, West Virginia, schools (1922–23). He was professor of education at Miami University in Oxford, Ohio (1925–30). He joined the University of Cincinnati, Ohio, as professor of education (1930–68), director of graduate study in the teachers' college (1944–59), acting dean (1944–47), and dean (1947–59). He was dean and director of graduate studies in the college of education and home economics at the University of Cincinnati (1959–68) and dean of institutional research (1966–68).

Good was the author of several books, including *The Supplementary Reading Assignment* (1927), *How to Do Research in Education* (1928), *Teaching in College and University* (1929), *The Methodology of Educational Research* (with A. S. Barr, *q.v.* and Douglas Scates, *q.v.*, 1936), *Methods of Research* (with Douglas Scates, 1954), *Introduction to Educational Research* (1959), and *Essentials of Educational Research* (1966). He was editor of *Dictionary of Education* (1945) and *Guide to Colleges, Universities and Professional Schools* (1945). He was a member of the editorial board of the *Journal of Educational Research* (1930–46), *Journal of Experimental Education,* and the *Encyclopedia of Educational Research.*

Good served in the United States Navy (1918–19). He was a member of educational associations, including a fellow of the American Association for the Advancement of Science (vice-president, 1955) and the American Psychological Association and a member of the American Educational

Research Association (president, 1940–41), the National Society of College Teachers of Education (president, 1947–48), and Phi Delta Kappa (national historian, 1946–48). He received an honorary degree from Bridgewater College (1950).

REFERENCES: *CA* (5–8); *LE* (V); *WW* (XXXI); *WWAE* (XVI).

John F. Ohles

GOOD, Harry Gehman. B. July 14, 1880, Lancaster, Pennsylvania, to Joseph B. and Anna (Gehman) Good. M. June 23, 1910, to Maud Alice Wayre. Ch. three. D. April 11, 1971, Columbus, Ohio.

H. G. Good received the A.B. degree (1909) from the University of Indiana and the Ph.D. degree (1915) from the University of Pennsylvania.

Good was an elementary school teacher in Pennsylvania (1898–1906) and high school mathematics teacher at Camden, New Jersey, and West Chester and Philadelphia, Pennsylvania. He was professor of education at Bluffton (Ohio) College (1910–15). He was associate professor of psychology and education at Colgate University in Hamilton, New York (1919–22), and professor of education at Ohio University in Athens (1922–26). Good joined the faculty of Ohio State University as professor of the history of education (1926–33) and professor of education (1933) to his retirement in 1950.

The author of over one hundred articles and books, Good wrote *Benjamin Rush and His Services to American Education* (1918), *A History of Western Education* (1947), *A History of American Education* (1956) and *The Rise of the College of Education of the Ohio State University* (1960). *A History of Western Education* was regarded as the most scholarly and comprehensive American book in its field.

REFERENCES: *CA* (1–4); *LE* (III); James D. Teller, "Harry Gehman Good, Educational Scholar, 1880–1971," *School and Society* 100 (February 1972): 99; *Ohio State University Monthly* 18 (October 1926):17.

John F. Ohles

GOODALE, George Lincoln. B. August 3, 1839, Saco, Maine, to Stephen Lincoln and Prudence Aiken (Nourse) Goodale. M. December 1866 to Henrietta Juel Hobson. Ch. five. D. April 12, 1923, Cambridge, Massachusetts.

George Lincoln Goodale was graduated from Amherst (Massachusetts) College with the A.B. (1860) and A.M. (1866) degrees and received the M.D. degree from Harvard University and Bowdoin College in Brunswick, Maine, in 1863.

Goodale practiced medicine in Portland, Maine (1863–66), and was an instructor in anatomy, materia medica, and surgery in the Portland School for Medical Instruction. He traveled for health reasons to California via

Panama and on his return served as professor of natural history at Bowdoin College (1868–72). He moved to Harvard in 1872, where he succeeded Asa Gray *(q.v.)* as Fisher Professor of Botany in 1888. He was director of the Harvard Botanical Museum (1879–1909) and a member of the faculty of comparative zoology from 1881. He retired from Harvard in 1909. Goodale was credited with pioneering in the use of lantern slides to illustrate his lectures.

Goodale was first to write a physiological botany, volume two of Asa Gray's *The Botanical Text-Book* (1885). He was a founder with C. F. Brackett of the *Bowdoin Scientific Review* (1870–72) and was an associate editor of the *American Journal of Science* from 1888.

A member of many scholarly and scientific societies, Goodale was a fellow of the American Academy of Arts and Sciences and the American Association for the Advancement of Science (vice-president of the section on biology, 1888; association president, 1890). He was president of the Society of American Naturalists. Goodale received two honorary degrees from both Amherst and Bowdoin colleges and an honorary degree from Princeton University.

REFERENCES: *DAB; NCAB* (6:427); *NYT*, April 13, 1923, p. 17; *TC; WWW* (I).   *John F. Ohles*

GOODE, John Paul. B. November 21, 1862, Stewartville, Minnesota, to Abraham John and Hulda Jane (Van Valkenburgh) Goode. M. September 12, 1901, to Ida Katherine Hancock. Ch. one. D. August 5, 1932, Little Point Sable, Michigan.

J. Paul Goode received the B.S. degree (1889) from the University of Minnesota, was a graduate student at Harvard University (1894), and a fellow in geology at the University of Chicago (1895–99). He was awarded the Ph.D. degree (1901) from the University of Pennsylvania.

Goode was a teacher of general science at the State Normal School (later, Moorhead State College) at Moorhead, Minnesota (1889–98), professor of physics, physical sciences, and geography at the Charleston (Illinois) State Normal School (later, Eastern Illinois University) from 1898 to 1901, assistant professor of geography at the University of Pennsylvania, and director of the Geographical Society of Philadelphia (1901–03). He spent the rest of his professoriate at the University of Chicago (1903–28).

Goode toured and traveled widely in the United States, Europe, and parts of the Far East. His lectures, mostly on geography and economic subjects, were illustrated by thousands of hand-painted slides. He was credited with inventing the interrupted homolographic map projection (1916), the homolosine projection (1923), and the polar equal-area projection (1928). He also devised the sunboard, an instrument for working with sun shadows, patented in 1904.

Goode was noted for his maps, including a series of base maps (1908) and a series of physical and political and wall maps. In 1912 he issued a popular series of eighteen maps for schools use that dealt with human geography, a term he coined. In the 1920s he published two hundred hand-colored map slides and developed geographic globes and base maps.

Goode's publications include *The Goode School Atlas* (1923), *The Development of Commercial Ports* (a report for the Chicago Harbor Commission about Western Europe, 1908), *Chicago, City of Destiny* (1923), and *The Geographic Background of Chicago* (1926). He also wrote many articles for professional journals. Goode received the Helen Culver Gold Medal of the Geographic Society of Chicago in 1923. He was a consultant to Rand McNally & Co., publishers. He was a fellow of the American Association for the Advancement of Science and a member of the American Association of Geographers (president, 1926–27), the Geographic Society of Chicago (president), and the Illinois Academy of Science.

A man of broad interests, Goode was skilled in photography, versed in music, and interested in art and nature. His work advanced geography from a grade-school subject to a university-level course of study.

REFERENCES: *DAB* (supp. 1); *LE* (I); *NCAB* (23:386); *WWW* (I).

Albert Nissman

GOODELL, Henry Hill. B. May 20, 1839, Constantinople, Turkey, to William and Abigail Perkins (Davis) Goodell. M. December 10, 1873, to Helen Eloise Stanton. Ch. two. D. April 23, 1905, at sea.

Henry Hill Goodell was sent from his parents' mission in Constantinople (later, Istanbul) Turkey, to the United States at the age of seventeen for his formal education. He attended Williston Seminary in Easthampton, Massachusetts, and was graduated from Amherst (Massachusetts) College in 1862; he received the A.M. degree from Amherst in 1865.

Goodell served in the Union army during the Civil War. In 1867 he became professor of modern languages and English literature at the new Massachusetts Agricultural College in Amherst, which had been founded under the provisions of the 1862 Morrill Land Grant Act. From 1887 until his death in 1905 he was president of the college. He was one of the four original teachers who taught a handful of students in four antiquated buildings and helped lay the groundwork for what became the Massachusetts State College in 1931 and the University of Massachusetts in 1947. During his tenure as teacher and administrator, he helped organize the college library and served as librarian. He directed the Hatch Agricultural Experimental Station (1886–1905). In 1896 the college admitted women as students.

Goodell served as chairman of the Association of Agricultural Colleges and Experimental Stations.

REFERENCES: *DAB; NCAB* (8:116); *WWW* (I); Calvin Stebbins, *Henry*

Hill Goodell: The Story of His Life (Cambridge, Mass.: Riverside Press, 1911); *NYT,* April 25, 1905, p. 11.   *Richard S. Offenberg*

GOODNOW, Isaac Tichenor. B. January 17, 1814, Whitingham, Vermont, to William and Sybil (Arms) Goodnow. M. August 28, 1838, to Ellen Denison. Ch. none. D. March 20, 1894, Manhattan, Kansas.

Isaac T. Goodnow attended the local schools of Whitingham, Vermont, until he was fourteen years old, when he became a merchant's clerk. Resolving to complete his education, he walked eighty miles to enter Wesleyan Academy in Wilbraham, Massachusetts, in 1834. He remained at Wilbraham for fourteen years as a student and instructor in English literature until 1838 and then as professor of natural sciences to 1848.

He accepted an appointment as professor of natural sciences at Providence Conference Seminary in East Greenwich, Vermont. In December 1854 he attended a lecture by Eli Thayer, an ardent abolitionist and founder of the New England Emigrant Aid Company. Goodnow and the Reverend Joseph Denison, his wife's brother, decided to emigrate to Kansas, convinced that slavery or freedom in the nation would be settled on the prairies of Kansas. Goodnow resigned his professorship and spent almost three months collecting and organizing a company of two hundred emigrants. In March 1855, at the age of forty-one, Goodnow left for Kansas to begin a new life.

An active participant in Kansas politics, Goodnow served as a delegate to the first free state convention at Lawrence, contributed to the drafting of the Leavenworth constitution, and was elected to the first Kansas legislature.

Goodnow was an influential figure in the early history of Kansas education. He was a cofounder of Bluemont Central College (merged with Kansas State Agricultural College and, later, Kansas State University). He served as state superintendent of public instruction and ex officio regent of the agricultural college (1863–67). In 1867 Goodnow was appointed agent to dispose of ninety thousand acres of land belonging to the college, a post he held until he became land commissioner of the Missouri Kansas and Texas Railway.

REFERENCES: *DAB; NCAB* (23:283); *TC; WWW* (H); Hugh D. Fisher, "Memoir of Professor Isaac T. Goodnow," *Transactions of the Kansas Historical Society* 5 (1889–96): 141-42; Isaac T. Goodnow, "Personal Reminiscences and Kansas Emigration, 1855," *Transactions of the Kansas Historical Society* 4 (1886–88): 244–53; J. T. Willard, "Bluemont Central College, the Forerunner of Kansas State College," *Kansas Historical Quarterly* 13 (May 1945): 323-57.   *N. Ray Hiner*

GOODRICH, Annie Warburton. B. February 6, 1866, New Brunswick, New Jersey, to Samuel Griswold and Annie Williams (Butler) Goodrich. M. no. D. December 31, 1954, Cobalt, Connecticut.

Annie Warburton Goodrich was educated in private schools in Connecticut, England, and France. She was graduated as a registered nurse from New York Hospital in 1892.

Goodrich was a superintendent of nurses at New York Post Graduate Medical School and Hospital (1893–1900) and St. Luke's Hospital in New York City (1902–07) and was general superintendent of the training school for nurses at Bellevue and Allied Hospitals in New York City (1907–10). She became state inspector of nurses' training schools for the New York State Education Department (1910–14). She was a part-time lecturer at Teachers College, Columbia University (1904–13), and was appointed assistant professor of nursing, department of nursing and health at Columbia (1914–23). She was director of nurses at the Henry Street Visiting Nurse Service (1917–23). In 1918 she organized and served to 1919 as the first dean of the United States Army School of Nursing in Washington, D.C., which was designed to meet the special needs for nurses during World War I.

A school of nursing was organized at Yale University and Goodrich became the first dean in 1923. The school was founded on the principle of preventive nursing and was granted $1 million by the Rockefeller Foundation in 1929. Under Goodrich, the school exercised leadership in promoting and expanding nursing education.

While at Yale she lectured at other nursing schools and began an extended tour in 1935 financed by the Rockefeller Foundation to nursing schools in England, Belgium, Scandinavia, Lithuania, Estonia, Czechoslovakia, Poland, Latvia, and China. Goodrich was the author of *Social and Ethical Significance in Nursing* (1932).

Goodrich was a member of the advisory committee of Western Reserve University's school of nursing and the board of control of the school of nursing at Skidmore College. She was president of the International Council of Nurses (1912–15), the American Nurses Association (1915–18), and the Association of Collegiate Schools of Nursing (1933), and was a member of the National League of Nursing Education, the Florence Nightingale International Foundation, and other associations.

She received the United States Distinguished Service Medal (1923). The government of France awarded her the Medaille d'honneur d'hygiene publique (1928) for her work in nursing during World War I and a silver medal for public service (1933). She received honorary degrees from Mount Holyoke College and Yale University, and the Yale Medal (1953) for outstanding service.

REFERENCES: *NCAB* (42:326); *WWAE* (XI); *WWW* (III); *NYT,* January 1, 1955, p. 13.   *Joan Duff Kise*

GOODRICH, Chauncey Allen. B. October 23, 1790, New Haven, Connecticut, to Elizur and Anne Willard (Allen) Goodrich. M. October 1, 1816, to Julia Frances (Frances Juliana) Webster. Ch. four. D. February 25, 1860, New Haven, Connecticut.

A member of a family of scholars and clergymen, Chauncey Allen Goodrich was graduated from Yale College in 1810. He became rector of Hopkins Grammar School in New Haven, Connecticut, and a tutor at Yale (1812–14) and studied theology under Yale's president, Timothy Dwight *(q.v.)*. Licensed to preach in 1814, he was ordained and installed by the Middletown (Connecticut) Congregational Church in 1816. He was married to the daughter of Noah Webster *(q.v.)*.

Goodrich resigned the ministry in 1817 to become the first professor of rhetoric at Yale. He was one of the founders of a theological department at Yale in 1822. He bought the *Christian Spectator* in 1828 and edited it as the *Quarterly Christian Spectator* until 1836, using it as a sounding board for the New Haven theology. In 1838 he gave $5,000 to Yale to establish a professorship in preaching and pastoral work, and when the position was refused by the first appointee, Goodrich was named to it. He served in that post until his death. Through his pastoral work at the college, conducting weekly meetings for students and serving as a counselor on spiritual matters, Goodrich exerted an influence on the religious character of the school. He supported temperance and missionary causes.

Goodrich's first book was *Elements of Greek Grammar* (1814), written with the encouragement of Timothy Dwight. He also wrote *Lessons in Greek Parsing* (1829) and *Lessons in Latin Parsing* (1822), and two anonymous pamphlets, *Can I Conscientiously Vote for Henry Clay?* (1844) and *What Does Dr. Bushnell Mean?* (1849). He contributed a chapter to Robert Baird's *Religion in the United States of America* (1844) and wrote *Selected British Eloquence* (1852). He edited an abridgement of Noah Webster's *Dictionary* in 1829 and the first one-volume edition, a thorough revision of the *Dictionary,* in 1847. Goodrich added synonyms, a treatise on principles of pronunciation, and a memoir of Noah Webster to the dictionary.

REFERENCES: *AC; DAB; NCAB* (4:511); *TC; WWW* (H); *NYT,* February 28, 1860, p. 5.   *M. Jane Dowd*

GOODRICH, Samuel Griswold. B. August 19, 1793, Ridgefield, Connecticut, to Samuel and Elizabeth (Ely) Goodrich. M. 1818 to Adeline Bradley. M. 1826 to Mary Boott. Ch. six. D. May 9, 1860, New York, New York.

One of eight surviving children in the family of the Reverend Samuel Goodrich, Samuel Griswold Goodrich was limited in his educational opportunities and was employed by his oldest sister's husband as a store clerk apprentice at the age of fifteen. With six weeks out for service in the War of

1812, he served out his apprenticeship and established in 1814 a short-lived pocket book factory in Hartford, Connecticut. Unable to attend college, he studied French under Count Value.

In 1816 he joined in a book publishing partnership with George Sheldon, which terminated on Sheldon's death. By 1818 he had published on his own a small tract and began his publishing business, moving his office from Hartford to Boston in 1826. The following year Goodrich published the first Peter Parley book, *Peter Parley's Tales of America*. Goodrich wrote some and contracted others to write the Peter Parley books and, by Goodrich's own count, he was the author and editor of about one hundred and seventy volumes with a sale of over seven million. In addition to the Peter Parley books, this total included books and textbooks in many fields.

Goodrich published *The Token* from 1826 to 1841, one of the annual literary publications that were popular commercial enterprises in the second quarter of the nineteenth century. In 1833 and 1834 Goodrich published *Parley's Magazine* and an illustrated magazine starting as *Robert Merry's Museum* in 1841 and continuing with various name changes to 1854.

In addition to the educational uses of his publications, Goodrich also encouraged American authors and artists by commissioning from them literary selections, books, and engravings. The most notable author Goodrich employed was Nathaniel Hawthorne.

Goodrich served in the Massachusetts legislature and as United States consul in Paris from 1851 to 1853. Remaining in France until 1855, he settled in Southbury, Connecticut, about 1858.

REFERENCES: *AC; DAB; EB; NCAB* (5:355); *WWW* (H); Daniel Roselle, *Samuel Griswold Goodrich, Creator of Peter Parley* (Albany: State University of New York Press, 1968); Samuel G. Goodrich, *Recollections of a Lifetime* (New York: Miller, Orton, 1857); *NYT,* May 11, 1860, p. 4.

John F. Ohles

GOODWIN, William Watson. B. May 9, 1831, Concord, Massachusetts, to Hersey Bradford and Lucretia (Watson) Goodwin. M. to Emily Jenks. M. 1882 to Ellen Chandler. Ch. two. D. June 15, 1912, Cambridge, Massachusetts.

William Watson Goodwin received the A.B. degree (1851) from Harvard University and studied in Germany at the universities of Göttingen, Berlin, and Bonn. He received the Ph.D. degree (1855) from the University of Göttingen.

After his formal education, he visited Italy and Greece, the first of eight trips to Europe, and returned to Cambridge in 1856 to begin his long career as a teacher and officer of Harvard University. In 1860 he was appointed Eliot Professor of Greek Literature, serving to 1901. He was the first director of the American School of Classical Studies at Athens, Greece (1882–83). Goodwin was among the first to admit women to his courses.

His writings include *Syntax of the Moods and Times of the Greek Verb* (1860), *Translation of Plutarch's Morals by Several Hands* (five volumes, 1870), *Elementary Greek Grammar* (1870), *Greek Reader* (1871), *Greek Grammar* (1879), *The First Four Books of Xenophon's Anabasis* (with J. W. White, 1880), *School Greek Grammar* (1882), and *The Battle of Salamis—Papers of the American School of Classical Studies* (1879). He edited Isocrates' *Panegyricus* (1864) and Demosthenes' *DeCorona* (1901).

Active in professional organizations, Goodwin was president of the American Philological Association (1872 and 1885) and the Phi Beta Kappa Society of Cambridge (1892–94). He was a member of the Imperial Archaeological Institute of Germany, the American Academy of Arts and Sciences of Boston, and the Massachusetts Historical Society. An overseer of Harvard University (1903–09), he was an incorporator of the Society for the Collegiate Instruction of Women (later, Radcliffe College) and served on its governing boards until his death.

He was decorated by the king of Greece (1883) and was the recipient of honorary degrees from nine American and foreign colleges and universities.

REFERENCES: *AC; DAB; EB; NCAB* (6:428); *TC; WWW* (I); *Boston Transcript,* June 17, 1912; *NYT,* June 17, 1912, p. 9. *Lawrence S. Master*

GORDY, John Pancoast. B. December 21, 1851, near Salisbury, Maryland, to Elijah Melson and Martha Ellen (Sheppard) Gordy. M. March 27, 1884, to Eugenie Day. Ch. one. D. December 31, 1908, New York, New York.

John Gordy began teaching at the age of seventeen and was principal of a small academy in Farmington, Delaware, by the age of twenty-two. He attended Wesleyan University in Middletown, Connecticut, graduating in 1878 with special honors. He received the Ph.D. degree from the University of Leipzig, Germany (1884).

He was professor of philosophy and pedagogy at Ohio University at Athens (1886–96) and at Ohio State University in Columbus (1896–1900) and professor of the history of education and of American history at New York University (1901–08). Gordy believed that education should be training for the art of living and used that principle as a guide in judging the worth of school subjects. He was concerned with taste in reading and the ability to assimilate what was read. Manual training had a value of its own and should develop a respect for labor.

Among Gordy's books were *Lessons in Psychology* (1890), *Rise and Growth of the Normal School Idea in the United States* (1891), *History of Political Parties in the United States* (two volumes 1895), and *A Broader Elementary Education* (1903). He also translated Kuno Fischer's *Des-*

cartes (1887) and *History of Modern Philosophy* (1887).

Gordy and his wife committed suicide in 1908 after their daughter's death. He was a brother of Wilbur Fisk Gordy *(q.v.).*

REFERENCES: *DAB; WWW* (I); *NYT,* January 1, 1909, p. 1; "Gordy as a Historian," *Munsey* 28 (December 1902): 442–43.   *Ned V. Schimizzi*

GORDY, Wilbur Fisk. B. June 14, 1854, Salisbury, Maryland, to Elijah Melson and Martha Ellen (Sheppard) Gordy. M. July 9, 1889, to Isabel Drummond Hunter. Ch. none. D. December 23, 1929, Hartford, Connecticut.

Wilbur Fisk Gordy received the A.B. degree (1880) from Wesleyan University in Middletown, Connecticut. He was a vice-principal and classics teacher at the Middletown high school (1880–81), superintendent of schools at Ansonia, Connecticut (1881–84), and supervising principal at Hartford, Connecticut (1884–1904). He was superintendent of schools at Springfield, Massachusetts (1904–11), where he instituted educational innovations, including a vocational school, technical high school, and high school of commerce. From 1911, when he moved to Hartford, Connecticut, he engaged in writing history textbooks.

Gordy was the author of *A Pathfinder in American History* (with W. I. Twitchell, 1892), *A School History of the United States* (1898), *American Leaders and Heroes* (1901), *Language Lessons* (with W. E. Mead, 1903), *Grammar Lessons* (with W. E. Mead, 1904), *Stories of American Explorers* (1906), *Colonial Days* (1908), *Elementary History of the United States* (1909), *American Beginnings in Europe* (1912), *Stories of Early American History* (1913), *Stories of Later American History* (1915), *Abraham Lincoln* (1917), *Causes and Meaning of the Great War* (1919), *History of the United States* (1922), and *Leaders in Making America* (1923).

A member of many professional and civic organizations, Gordy was president of the Connecticut State Teachers' Association (1891), the New England History Teachers' Association, the Hartford board of education (1915–28), the Hartford public library board of directors (1915–29), the Connecticut Council of Education (1894), and the Connecticut Peace Society. He was a director of the American Peace Society and Connecticut Humane Society. He was awarded two honorary degrees by Wesleyan University and an honorary degree by Marietta College. He was a brother of John Pancoast Gordy *(q.v.).*

REFERENCES: *NCAB* (B:480, 21:85); *TC; WWW* (I).   *John F. Ohles*

GOUCHER, John Franklin. B. June 7, 1845, Waynesburg, Pennsylvania, to John and Eleanor (Townsend) Goucher. M. December 24, 1877, to Mary Cecelia Fisher. Ch. three. D. July 19, 1922, Pikesville, Maryland.

Raised in Pittsburgh, Pennsylvania, John Franklin Goucher attended

Dickinson College in Carlisle, Pennsylvania, where he earned the A.B. (1868) and A.M. (1872) degrees.

Goucher entered the Methodist Episcopal ministry in the Baltimore Conference in 1869. He served various churches in Baltimore and was involved in the founding of eight congregations and building fifteen new churches. He married a wealthy woman and engaged in many philanthropic endeavors, particularly in the field of education. He established, organized, and helped finance a number of mission schools in Europe and the Far East. He financed a system of about 120 primary and secondary vernacular schools in India. He planned and organized the Anglo-Japanese College in Tokyo, Japan, in 1882 and founded West China and Korean Missions of the Methodist Episcopal church. He gave funds to the Martin Mission Institute at Frankfort on the Main, Germany, which aided in relieving its financial problems and was the chief benefactor of Princess Anne Training School for blacks located on the Eastern Shore of Maryland. He founded Pai Chai School in Seoul, the first Christian school in Korea.

Goucher was one of the original incorporators and the largest individual donor for the establishment of a college dedicated to the education of women. Founded in 1885 as the Woman's College of Baltimore, its name was changed to Goucher College in 1910. Goucher was elected second president of the college in 1890, a position he held until 1908. During his tenure, the college experienced a growth in building, the development of a rigorous academic curriculum, and an increase in the number of students, and was among the fourteen institutions listed as first class in the 1898 *Report* of the United States Commissioner of Education.

Goucher was the author of *Young People and Missions* (1903), *Adjustment for Sovereignty* (1906), *Christianity and the U.S.* (1908), and *Growth of the Missionary Concept* (1911). He was a member of the board of trustees of Centenary Biblical Institute (later, Morgan State College) in Baltimore (1879–1922) and served as chairman of the board (1883–1922). He was a member of the board of missions of the Methodist Episcopal church (chairman of the committee on education, 1884–1922). He helped organize (1902) and was a member of the executive committee (1902–09) of the Young People's Missionary movement. He was president of the Maryland Bible Society (1909), of the board of governors of the West China Union University in Chentu, and of the Maryland Methodist Historical Society. He was a trustee of Fukien Christian University in Foochow, China, Chosen Christian College in Seoul, Korea, and Union Methodist Episcopal Theological Seminary in Seoul. He was decorated by the governments of Japan and China and received two honorary degrees from Dickinson College.

REFERENCES: *DAB; NCAB* (24:174); *NYT,* July 20, 1922, p. 17; *WWW* (I); Anna Heubeck Knipp and Thaddeus P. Thomas, *The History of Goucher College* (Baltimore, Md.: Goucher College, 1938). *Eli Velder*

GOULD, Benjamin Apthorp. B. June 15, 1787, Lancaster, Massachusetts, to Benjamin and Griselda Apthorp (Flagg) Gould. M. December 2, 1823, to Lucretia Dana Goddard. Ch. four, including Benjamin Apthorp Gould, astronomer. D. October 24, 1859, Boston, Massachusetts.

Benjamin Apthorp Gould attended Dummer Academy in Newburyport, Massachusetts, and was graduated with the A.B. (1814) and A.M. (1817) degrees from Harvard University, where he distinguished himself, especially in the classics.

In 1814 Gould was appointed headmaster of the Boston Public Latin School on the recommendation of John T. Kirkland *(q.v.),* president of Harvard. Gould continued as headmaster until he was forced to retire in 1828 because of ill health. The Latin School had experienced a period of decline when Gould took over; under his administration, the school was reorganized and became famous for the quality of its instructional program.

Following his retirement, Gould traveled throughout Europe (1829–30) and returned to Boston where he became a prosperous ship owner, merchant, and trader in the China and India areas.

Gould was the first American to prepare annotated editions of the classics: *Ovid* (1827), *Horace* (1828), and *Virgil* (1829). He revised Alexander Adams's *Latin Grammar* (1825) and edited *The Prize Book of the Publick Latin School in Boston* (1820–24).

A prominent Bostonian, Gould was the first president of the Latin School Association, a trustee of Governor Dummer Academy, a member of the Boston School Committee, and a member of the Boston Common Council (1834–37).

REFERENCES: *AC; DAB; NCAB* (3:519); *TC;* Pauline Holmes, *A Tercentenary History of the Boston Latin School, 1635–1935* (Cambridge: Harvard University Press, 1935). *Patrick J. Foley*

GOULD, James. B. December 5, 1770, Branford, Connecticut, to William and Mary (Foote) Gould. M. October 21, 1798, to Sally McCurdy Tracy. Ch. nine. D. May 11, 1838, Litchfield, Connecticut.

James Gould was the first American lawyer to devote his talents entirely to teaching law. After a common school education, he entered Yale College in 1787 and was graduated in 1791, with highest honors. He taught for a brief time at Wethersfield, Connecticut, and Baltimore, Maryland, before entering a law office in New Haven, Connecticut, early in 1793. He accepted a position as tutor at Yale. In 1795 he resumed his legal studies at Tapping Reeve's *(q.v.)* law school in Litchfield, Connecticut, the first law school in America. He was graduated in 1798.

Reeve invited Gould to teach at the school, and, when Reeve withdrew in 1820, Gould assumed sole charge, Gould was a judge of the Superior Court and Court of Errors (1816–19). His *A Treatise on the Principles of Pleading in Civil Actions* (1832), which was an expansion of one of his series of lectures, was widely used as a textbook, even into the twentieth century. Gould's influence was great; many of America's best lawyers had either studied under him or gained their legal training through the use of his books.

Litchfield declined in influence after the founding of the law schools at Harvard in 1817 and Yale in 1824 and was closed in 1833. Gould received an honorary degree from Yale College.

REFERENCES: *AC; DAB; NCAB* (19:23); *WWW* (H); Dwight C. Kilbourn, *The Bench and Bar of Litchfield County, Connecticut, 1709–1909* (Litchfield, Conn.: Published privately, 1909), pp. 59-60; William Draper Lewis, ed., *Great American Lawyers* (Philadelphia: The John C. Winston Co., 1907), 2:455-87.   *Robert H. Truman*

GOVE, Aaron Estellus. B. September 26, 1839, Hampton Falls, New Hampshire, to Jeremiah and Mary (Morrill) Gove. M. February 13, 1865, to Caroline C. Spofford, Ch. four. D. August 1, 1919, Denver, Colorado.

Aaron Estellus Gove began his schooling at three years of age in Hampton Falls, New Hampshire. At the age of eight, he was taken to Boston, where he continued his public education. The family moved to Illinois, and he began to teach in 1854 and studied at the Illinois State Normal School (later, State University).

In 1861 Gove entered the United States Army and served in the Civil War, including fighting in the battle of Vicksburg. After the war, he took charge of schools at New Rutland and Normal, Illinois, where he taught until 1874.

In 1874 he moved to Denver, Colorado, as superintendent of schools. He played an important role in developing the school system in Denver, a former transient mining town. For thirty years, he guided the schools from a two-schoolhouse, eighteen-classroom district into a sprawling district with quality school buildings. Gove participated in the design of many of the school buildings, and Denver became noted for the quality and safety of its schools. In 1904 he resigned as superintendent to go into the sugar refining industry.

Gove was founder and editor of the *Illinois Schoolmaster* and also of the *Colorado School Journal.* He was active in the National Educational Association (president, 1888) and was a founder of the National Council of Education. He was credited with writing the educational article for the Colorado constitution in 1876. He was awarded honorary degrees by Dartmouth College and the University of Colorado.

REFERENCES: *DAB; NCAB* (12:531); *WWW* (I); *History of Colorado* (Denver: Linderman Co., 1927); vol. 5; *Portrait and Biographical Record of Denver and Vicinity, Colorado* (Chicago: Chapman Publishing Co., 1898), pp. 619-20.   *Stanley A. Leftwich*

GOWAN, Mary Olivia. B. March 15, 1888, Stillwater, Minnesota, to William and Margaret (Lawler) Gowan. M. no. D. April 2, 1977, Duluth, Minnesota.

As a young girl, Mary Gowan showed great interest in the care of the sick. In 1909 she entered the first class of Saint Mary's School of Nurses in Duluth, Minnesota, and, one month after her graduation in 1912, entered the novitiate of the Sisters of Saint Benedict in Duluth. During her novitiate she began teaching at the Training School for Nurses in Saint Mary's.

After making her final vows in 1916, she became assistant superintendent of Saint Mary's Hospital and, a year later, superintendent. Under her leadership the hospital undertook a reorganization to meet the standards of the American College of Surgeons and appeared on its first list of approved hospitals.

After years of part-time study, she earned the bachelor's degree from the College of Saint Scholastica in Duluth in 1925. Shortly after her graduation she was selected, along with four other sisters, to establish Saint Gertrude's School for retarded children in Washington, D.C. During the summers of the years she spent there, she took work at Teachers College, Columbia University, and completed the master's degree (1932). The Catholic University of America began a program in nursing education for Catholic congregations of nursing sisters, and Gowan joined the faculty of the division of nursing education under the department of psychology. In 1932 she became the first dean of the school of nursing education.

Gowan served as consultant to the training committee in psychiatric nursing of the United States Public Health Service, on hospitals and nursing to the Sisters of Saint Benedict and as honorary civilian consultant to the Bureau of Medicine and Surgery, United States Navy. She served on the advisory council of nursing services of the Veterans Administration. She became an honorary fellow of the American Hospital Association and a member of the National League for Nursing, the Graduate Nurses Association, and the National Catholic Education Association. Gowan authored *Institutions and Workshops* (n.d.), was an editor of *Studies in Nursing Education,* and contributed articles to professional journals. She made a survey of the Catholic schools of nursing in Brazil and attended the International Council of Nurses in Rome, Italy (1957).

REFERENCES: *WW* (XXX); *WWAE* (XV); Edna Yost,*American Women of Nursing* (Philadelphia: J. B. Lippincott, 1947), pp. 77-95.

Anne E. Scheerer

GRACE, Alonzo Gaskell. B. August 14, 1896, Morris, Minnesota, to Richard H. and Sarah Elizabeth (Murphy) Grace. M. June 18, 1921, to Jeannette Meland. Ch. three. D. October 19, 1971, Willimantic, Connecticut.

Alonzo G. Grace attended a one-teacher Minnesota rural school and then a small village high school. He attended the University of Minnesota majoring in sociology and anthropology, and received the B.A. (1917) and A.M. (1921) degrees. He enlisted in the United States Army and served in France (1917–19). While in the Army of Occupation, he was granted a diploma from the American Musicians School in Chaumont, France. He received the Ph.D. degree (1932) from Western Reserve University (later, Case Western Reserve University) in Cleveland, Ohio.

Grace served as an instructor at the University of Minnesota before teaching in rural schools and at the Northern State Teachers College (later, Northern State College) in Aberdeen, South Dakota, In 1925 he went to Cleveland where he was director of adult education. In 1930 he joined the faculty of the University of Rochester (New York) until he became commissioner of education in Connecticut (1938–48).

Grace believed that the local community and local boards of education were responsible for establishing and maintaining public schools. He placed great emphasis on the movement to improve and strengthen local initiative and responsibility and introduced legislation leading to the first state aid to towns for education in Connecticut. He believed that the state department of education should provide leadership, service, and planning but that desirable educational growth was from the bottom up rather than domination from the top. He saw the need for democratizing and humanizing the administrative processes in education.

Grace was director of education and cultural relations with the Office of Military Government in Germany where he supervised the rebuilding of the German school system (1948–50). He resigned, protesting the inadequacy of the program implemented by the high commission that had replaced the military command in Germany. Returning to the United States, he was professor of education and chairman of the department of education at the University of Chicago (1950), professor of education and director of the division of advanced studies (1951–60) and associate dean (1952–60) of the school of education at New York University, and dean of the college of education at the University of Illinois (1960–64).

Grace was the author of *Immigration and Community Americanization* (1921) coauthor of *State Aid and School Costs* (with G. A. Moe, 1938), and editor of *Leadership in American Education* (1950).

He was a member of the National Advisory Committee on Education and a director of the Rochester School for the Deaf, the Connecticut Teachers' Retirement Board (1938–48), and the Connecticut Public Library Committee (1938–48). He was president of the Harvard Teachers Association (1946–48) and a committee member of the American Council on Education (1940–44). He was the recipient of the Order of Merit from the Federal Republic of Germany (1971) and honorary degrees from Boston University and Springfield College.

REFERENCES: *CB* (January 1950 and December 1971); *LE* (III); *WWAE* (XIV); *WWW* (V); Hartford *Courant,* October 21, 1971; *NYT,* October 23, 1971, p. 36.   *Arthur E. Soderlind*

GRAHAM, Edward Kidder. B. October 11, 1876, Charlotte, North Carolina, to Archibald and Eliza Owen (Barry) Graham. M. June 25, 1908, to Susan Williams Moses. Ch. one. D. October 26, 1918, Chapel Hill, North Carolina.

Edward Kidder Graham received his early education in the public schools of Charlotte, North Carolina. He entered the University of North Carolina and received the Ph.B. degree in 1898. He received the M.A. degree (1902) from Columbia University and continued his graduate study there (1903–04).

Following his graduation from the University of North Carolina, he returned to Charlotte and taught for one year at Baird's School for Boys. In 1899 he returned to the University of North Carolina as librarian and during the first year became an instructor in English to 1903, when he took a leave of absence to engage in graduate study. He returned to North Carolina and in 1908 became head of the department of English and dean of the college of liberal arts. In 1913 he served as acting president and was elected president in 1914.

Graham extended the services of the university to the citizens of the state through the extension division. The university experienced a significant growth in students during his term as president and changed from an elitist to a democratic institution. Graham was director of the South Atlantic Division of the Students' Army Training Corps. He was a member of professional and learned associations and received honorary degrees from four American colleges and universities.

REFERENCES: *DAB; NCAB* (19:147); *WWW* (I); Archibald Henderson, "Edward Kidder Graham," *Sewanee Review* 27 (1919): 101-06; Louis R. Wilson *(q.v.), The University of North Carolina: 1900–1930* (Chapel Hill: University of North Carolina Press, 1957).   *Linda C. Gardner*

GRAHAM, Frank Porter. B. October 14, 1886, Fayetteville, North Carolina, to Alexander and Katherine Bryan (Sloan) Graham. M. July 21, 1932, to Marian Drane. Ch. none. D. February 16, 1972, Raleigh, North Carolina.

Frank Porter Graham was the son of the founder and long-time superintendent of public schools in and around Fayetteville, North Carolina. He was educated in the local public schools and received the B.A. degree (1909) from the University of North Carolina. He studied law at North Carolina and studied at Columbia University, where he was awarded the

M.A. degree (1916). He continued his graduate studies at the University of Chicago, Brookings Institution, and the London (England) School of Economics.

Graham taught English in Raleigh, North Carolina. He received an appointment to the faculty of the University of North Carolina (1914–27) and served as dean of students (1919–20). Graham was president of the University of North Carolina (1930–49) where he was known for consolidation of the University of North Carolina system, active involvement with students, and dedication to freedom and civil liberties.

From 1949 to 1951 Graham was an appointed United States senator from North Carolina and was defeated in the 1950 election. In 1951 he was appointed defense manpower administrator in the United States Department of Labor and was United Nations mediator for India and Pakistan. In the latter capacity until 1967, he became an internationally recognized negotiator and arbitrator.

Graham was active in national public service as chairman of President Franklin D. Roosevelt's advisory committee for the Social Security Act, vice-chairman of the National Consumer's Advisory Board, and a member of the President's Commission on Education. He served on the National Defense Mediation Board, the War Labor Board, and the Maritime War Emergency Board. Graham was a member of President Harry S Truman's Commission on Civil Rights.

Graham served in the United States Marine Corps in World War I and was active in professional associations, including the National Association of State Universities (president), and he was on the board of directors of the Carnegie Foundation for the Advancement of Teaching and the North Carolina Historical and Literary Society. He was the recipient of thirteen honorary degrees from American colleges and universities.

REFERENCES: *CB* (May 1941 and July 1951); *LE* (III); *NCAB* (D:409); *NYT*, February 17, 1972, p. 40; *WWAE* (VIII); *WWW* (V).

J. K. Ward.

GRANDGENT, Charles Hall. B. November 14, 1862, Dorchester, Massachusetts, to Louis Hall and Lucy Lucretia (Burgess) Grandgent. M. 1886 to Ethel Wright Cushing. Ch. five. D. September 11, 1939, Cambridge, Massachusetts.

Charles Hall Grandgent was graduated from the Dudley School in Roxbury, Massachusetts (1875), and the Roxbury Latin School (1879). He received the A.B. degree (1883) from Harvard University. During the next three years he studied in Europe at the University of Leipzig, Germany, and the Collège de France and the Ecole des chartes in Paris, France.

In the fall of 1886, Grandgent began teaching as a tutor of modern languages at Harvard University. He was director of modern language instruction in the Boston public schools (1889–96) and was appointed professor of Romance languages at Harvard (1896–1932).

He was the author of *Italian Grammar* (1887), *Italian Composition* (1891), *German and English Sounds* (1892), *Short French Grammar* (1894), *Selections for French Composition* (1895), *Essentials of French Grammar* (1900), *Outline of the Phonology and Morphology of Old Provencal* (1905), an edition of *Dante* (1917), *The Ladus of Dante's Lyrics* (1917), *The Power of Dante* (1918), *The Discourses of Dante* (1924), and various monographs on phonetics, pedagogy, and literature.

Grandgent was a member of the Société de linguistique de Paris and the Modern Language Association of America (secretary, 1902–11, and president, 1912). He was one of the founders of the American Dialect Society, which he served as treasurer (1889–93), vice-president (1894–95), and president (1896). He was a corresponding member of several foreign learned societies. He was a fellow of the American Academy of Arts and Sciences, president of the Boston Author's Club (1927–30) and of the Italian War Relief Fund of America (1917–20), and was decorated by the governments of Italy and France and received four honorary degrees.

REFERENCES: *DAB* (supp. 2); *EB; LE* (I); *NCAB* (13:539); *WWW* (IV); *NYT,* September 12, 1939, p. 25.   *Marilyn Meiss*

GRANT, Zilpah Polly. See BANISTER, Zilpah Polly Grant.

GRATZ, Rebecca. B. March 4, 1781, Philadelphia, Pennsylvania, to Michael and Miriam (Simon) Gratz. M. no. D. August 29, 1869, Philadelphia, Pennsylvania.

Rebecca Gratz grew up in the home of a prosperous merchant. Interested in charitable and social service, she was elected the first secretary of the Female Association for the Relief of Women and Children in Reduced Circumstances in 1801. She helped establish the nonsectarian Philadelphia Orphan Society in 1815 and served as secretary (1815–59). She was the founder of the Female Hebrew Benevolent Society (1819) and originator and one of the founders of the Jewish Foster Home (1855). She also was a leader in establishing the Fuel Society and the Sewing Society.

Her most significant contribution was in the field of religious education. Determined to provide a better religious training for Jewish youngsters, she started a school in her home, assisted by a rabbinical scholar. She made a study of the Christian Sunday school movement and organized the Hebrew Sunday School Society in 1838; she served as its president to 1864. This society has served as a model for similar institutions in the United States.

Gratz brought up the nine children of her sister who had died in 1823.

REFERENCES: *DAB; NAW; NCAB* (10:130); *WWW* (H); Bertram W. Korn, *American Jewry and the Civil War* (Philadelphia: Jewish Publication Society of America, 1951); Joseph R. Rosenbloom, *A Biographical Dictio-*

nary of Early American Jews (Lexington: University of Kentucky Press, 1960).   *David E. Kapel*

GRAVES, Frank Pierrepont. B. July 23, 1869, Brooklyn, New York, to Horace and Annie (Hall) Graves. M. December 18, 1895, to Helen Hope Wadsworth. M. May 22, 1944, to Jessie Chase Malcolm. Ch. none. D. September 13, 1956, Albany, New York.

Frank Graves attended public schools in Brooklyn, New York, and completed a course at Brooklyn Polytechnic Institute Preparatory School (1886). He earned the A.B. (1890), A.M. (1891), and Ph.D. (1912) degrees from Columbia University and the Ph.D. degree (1892) from Boston University.

In 1891 Graves became assistant professor of Greek at Tufts College (later, University) in Medford, Massachusetts, and in 1893 professor of classical philology. He was named president of the University of Wyoming (1896–98) and president of the University of Washington (1898–1903).

Returning eastward, Graves was professor of education and dean of the school of education at the University of Missouri (1904–07), professor of education and dean of the summer school at Ohio State University (1907–13), and professor of education and first dean of the school of education at the University of Pennsylvania (1913–21).

In 1921 the New York State Board of Regents appointed Graves commissioner of education and president of the University of the State of New York. He held the state's highest education office for nineteen years. During his term, the basic program of school support was adopted, centralization of rural schools was begun, and the program of education was improved.

After retirement, Graves set out upon his third career, passing the New York State bar examination in 1943. He became an attorney for the New York State Teachers' Association.

Graves contributed many articles on education to professional journals and also wrote *Burial Customs of the Ancient Greeks* (1891), *A First Book in Greek* (with E. S. Hawes, 1895), *The State University Ideal* (1897), *A History of Education before the Middle Ages* (1909), *A History of Education during the Middle Ages and the Transition to Modern Times* (1910), *Great Educators of Three Centuries* (1911), *Peter Ramus and the Educational Reformation of the Sixteenth Century* (1912), *A History of Education in Modern Times* (1913), *A Student's History of Education* (1915), and *Administration of American Education* (1932). He was editor of *Educational Review* (1920–24)

Graves was active in educational associations and served as trustee of Teachers College of Columbia University, Russell Sage College, and Albany Law School. He was a fellow of the American Association for the

Advancement of Science and a member of the board of visitors of the United States Naval Academy and the National Advisory Committee on Education, the American Philosophical Society (councillor, 1933–36), College Teachers of Education (president, 1920), and Phi Beta Kappa (national president, 1937–40). He received awards from Belgium and France (the Legion of Honor), the Butler Medal for educational administration, the American Educational Award, and over thirty honorary degrees from American colleges and universities.

REFERENCES: *LE* (III); *NCAB* (A:277); *WWAE* (VIII); *WWW* (III); *NYT*, September 14, 1956, p. 23.   *Paul J. Schafer*

GRAY, Asa. B. November 18, 1810, Sauquoit, New York, to Moses and Roxanna (Howard) Gray. M. May 4, 1848, to Jane Lathrop Loring. Ch. none. D. January 30, 1888, Cambridge, Massachusetts.

Asa Gray was educated in the public schools of Sauquoit, New York. In 1825 at the age of sixteen, he entered Fairfield (New York) Academy and attended lectures at Fairfield's College of Physicians and Surgeons (1826). Gray was interested in collecting and studying local flora. His collecting continued during his medical apprenticeship in Bridgewater, New York. He practiced medicine in Bridgewater for a short time after receiving the M.D. degree in 1831 at the age of twenty.

His studies of local plants placed him in contact with the leading botanist in the United States, John Torrey of New York. Gray spent five years in collaboration with Torrey while teaching part time and working in libraries (1832–37). Torrey accepted Gray as a full assistant writing *Flora of North America;* the first volume (1838–40) received wide acclaim as a contribution to the knowledge of vegetation of the globe. The second volume was completed in 1843.

Gray accepted a professorship at the newly organized University of Michigan (1839) and spent a year in Europe to buy books and materials. He met leading botanists and studied specimens of American plants in English and Continental herbaria. The University of Michigan position did not materialize because of financial difficulties within the institution, and Gray became Fisher Professor of Natural History at Harvard University in 1842. He confined his activities to botany and the botanic garden and was the only fully supported botanist in the United States at the time.

As the West was being opened (1845–70) volumes of flora were sent to Gray and Torrey by survey and expedition parties. These specimens comprised a fair representation of the flora of the western half of the continent. After his marriage in 1848, he made a half-dozen trips to Europe and some across North America with his wife. He spent most of his time in routine work in his herbarium (200,000 species) and the botanical library (2,200 volumes), which he gave to Harvard in 1844 in return for a fireproof building.

In 1836 Gray's first botanical textbook appeared as *Elements of Botany,* followed by a number of other textbooks, which served to popularize botany in the United States, including *Botanical Text-Book for Colleges, Schools, and Private Students* (1842), *Manual of Botany* (1848), *First Lessons in Botany* (1857), *How Plants Grow* (1858), *Field, Forest and Garden Botany* (1869), and *How Plants Behave* (1872). He wrote *Statistics of the Flora of the Northern United States* (1856–57) and completed in 1878 after forty years of preparation *Synoptical Flora,* the third volume of Torrey and Gray's *Flora.* In 1880 he wrote *Natural Science and Religion.*

In 1872 he was elected president of the American Association for the Advancement of Science. He was one of the original members of the National Academy of Sciences (president, 1863–73) and was appointed a regent of the Smithsonian Institution (1874–88). He was elected to the New York University Hall of Fame in 1900. He was a regular and honorary member of many American and foreign learned and scientific societies and received honorary degrees from American and foreign institutions.

REFERENCES: *AC; DAB; DSB; EB; NCAB* (3:407) *NYT,* January 31, 1888, p. 5; *TC; WWW* (H); B. L. Robinson, "Asa Gray," *Science* 62 (July 17, 1925): 45-46.   *Isadore L. Sonnier*

GRAY, William Scott. B. June 5, 1885, Coatsburg, Illinois, to William Scott and Anna Letitia (Gilliland) Gray. M. September 14, 1921, to Beatrice Warner Jardine. Ch. two. D. September 8, 1960, Billings, Montana.

William S. Gray was best known as the "father" of Dick and Jane books. He was graduated from Illinois State Normal University (later, State University) (1910) and earned the S.B. (1913) and Ph.D. (1916) degrees from the University of Chicago and the M.A. degree (1914) from Columbia University.

He was a teacher in rural schools of Illinois (1904–05), principal of elementary schools in Fowler, Illinois (1905–08), and director of the training school at Illinois State Normal University (1910–12) before he joined the faculty of the University of Chicago in 1914. He was an active member of the University of Chicago faculty until 1950 and served as dean of the college of education (1917–31). He introduced a course in the teaching of reading at Chicago. He first conceived and initiated annual reviews of the literature of reading research. He was a leading exponent of the eclectic method of reading instruction.

Gray engaged in research in reading instruction and authored about five hundred books, articles, and research reports. He organized and directed the first annual reading conference at the University of Chicago and edited the proceedings of those conferences from 1938 to 1952. A few of his works include *Reading Interests and Habits of Adults* (with Ruth Monroe, 1929), *What Makes a Book Readable* (with Bernice E. Leary, 1935), *On Their*

Own in Reading (1948), *The Teaching of Reading and Writing* (1956 report of a worldwide study for UNESCO), *Keeping Reading Abreast of the Times* (1950), *Classroom Techniques in Improving Reading* (1949), *Reading in High School and College* (1948), and *Promoting Personal and Social Development Through Reading* (1947). He edited *The Training of College Teachers* (1930), *The Academic and Professional Preparation of Secondary-School Teachers* (1935), and *Basic Instruction in Reading in Elementary and High Schools* (1948). He was coauthor of the Basic Readers Series of Scott-Foresman (with others) and the Elson-Gray Basic Readers (with William H. Elson, *q.v.*, and Laura E. Runkel). He was chairman of the yearbook committee of the National Society for the Study of Education in 1925, 1937, and 1948.

He was a founder of the International Reading Association (president, 1956) and a member of many other organizations, including the American Educational Research Association (president, 1932–33).

REFERENCES: *LE* (III); *NCAB* (48:106); *WWAE* (XVI); *WWW* (IV); *NYT* September 9, 1960, p. 29; *Elementary English* 38 (March 1961): 187–89.   *Donavon Lumpkin*

GREEN, Jacob. B. July 26, 1790, Philadelphia, Pennsylvania, to Ashbel and Elizabeth (Stockton) Green. M. no. D. February 1, 1841, Philadelphia, Pennsylvania.

Jacob Green belonged to the early group of educators who pioneered chemical education in the United States. Like other members of this group, he had wide-ranging interests. As a boy he developed an interest in botany and made an extensive collection of plants. Shortly after graduating from the University of Pennsylvania in 1807, he demonstrated his interest in physics by coauthoring with Ebenezer Hazard *An Epitome of Electricity and Magnetism.* He considered going into the ministry and medicine but chose law and was admitted to the bar. He practiced law and continued his interest in and contributions to science.

Green was appointed professor of chemistry, experimental philosophy, and natural history at the College of New Jersey (later, Princeton University) in 1818. He resigned this position in 1822 and three years later accepted the post of professor of chemistry at the newly formed Jefferson Medical College in Philadelphia, a position he retained until his death.

Green wrote many articles for scientific journals in the fields of chemistry, physics, botany, astronomy, paleontology, and ethnology. He wrote textbooks, including *Textbook of Chemical Philosophy on the Basis of Turner's Elements* (1829), *Syllabus of a Course in Chemistry* (1835), and *Chemical Diagrams* (1837). Other books include *Catalogue of the Plants Indigenous to the State of New York* (1814), *Astronomical Recreations* (1824), *Diseases of the Skin* (1841), and *Monograph of the Trilobites of*

North America (1832), his most significant biological contribution.

Green received four honorary degrees, including an honorary M.D. degree from Yale College in 1827.

REFERENCES: *AC; DAB; DSB; NCAB* (13:552); *TC; WWW* (H).

B. Richard Siebring

GREEN, Lewis Warner. B. January 28, 1806, Boyle County, Kentucky, to Willis and Sarah (Reed) Green. M. February 1827 to Eliza J. Montgomery. M. April 1834 to Mary (Fry) Lawrence. Ch. two. D. May 26, 1863, Danville, Kentucky.

A clergyman who gained prominence as an educator and college president, Lewis Warner Green attended a classical school at Buck Pond, Kentucky. He studied for three years at Transylvania University in Lexington, Kentucky, before transferring to Centre College in Danville, Kentucky, from which he was graduated in 1824, one of two members of the first graduating class. He studied theology at Yale College and Princeton (New Jersey) Theological Seminary and was ordained by the Transylvania presbytery (1838). He also studied in Germany at Berlin, Halle, and Bonn (1834–36).

In 1832 Green was appointed professor of belles lettres and political economy at Centre College. Upon his return from Europe in 1836, he was professor of Oriental and biblical literature at the seminary connected with Hanover (Indiana) College to 1839, when he was elected vice-president of Centre College and colleague-pastor of the Danville Presbyterian Church (1839–40). He was professor of Oriental literature and biblical criticism at Western Theological Seminary in Allegheny (later, Pittsburgh), Pennsylvania (1840–47). After serving a year as pastor of the Second Presbyterian Church in Baltimore, Maryland, Green accepted election as president of Hampden-Sydney (Virginia) College (1848–56). Green successfully increased the endowment and enrollment of the college. The curriculum was extended, and the standards of scholarship were raised.

In 1856 Green was appointed president of the reorganized Transylvania University, a post he held until 1857, when state support was withdrawn from the institution. He became president of Centre College in 1858 and remained there until his death in 1863.

A collection of twenty-nine sermons by Green was edited by L. J. Halsen and published in 1871 as *Memoir of the Life and Character of Rev. Lewis Warner Green, D. D.*

REFERENCES: *AC; DAB; NCAB* (2:25, 4:515); *WWW* (H); Alfred J. Morrison ed., *The College of Hampden-Sydney: Calendar of Board of Minutes, 1776–1876* (Richmond, Va.: Hermitage Press, 1912).

Jennings L. Wagoner
Harold D. Lehman

GREEN, Samuel Bowdlear. B. September 15, 1859, Chelsea, Massachusetts, to Thomas and Anna (Marden) Green. M. September 15, 1887, to Alice C. Hazelton. Ch. none. D. July 11, 1910, Lake Itasca, Minnesota.

Samuel B. Green spent summers on a New Hampshire farm, where he developed an interest in scientific agriculture. He attended the Massachusetts Agricultural College (later, University of Massachusetts) in Amherst, where he received the B.S. degree (1879). In 1900 he spent a year studying agriculture and horticulture in Germany, Denmark, Holland, Belgium, France, and England.

By the age of twenty, Green was superintendent of the Vine Hill Farm at West Hartford, Connecticut. He worked in various agricultural vocations, managed the horticultural department at the Houghton Farm Experiment Station at Cornwall, New York, and worked in nurseries at Brighton and Newton, Massachusetts. He was superintendent of the horticultural department of the Massachusetts Agricultural College (1886–88). In 1888 he moved to the University of Minnesota, where he was horticulturist at the Minnesota Agricultural Experiment Station and professor of horticulture (1888–98) and professor of horticulture and forestry (1898–1910). He was first dean of the department of forestry but died a few months later.

Green was the author of a number of books, including *Amateur Fruit Growing* (1894), *Vegetable Gardening* (1896), *Forestry in Minnesota* (1898), *Principles of American Forestry* (1898), *Farm Wind-Breaks and Shelter Belts* (1906), and *Popular Fruit Growing* (1909). He also wrote university bulletins on agriculture and forestry and was associate editor of *Farm and Fireside* (1888–1910).

Green was active in agricultural and forestry organizations, including the Minnesota Horticultural Society (board member, 1892–1910, and president, 1907–10) and the Forestry Association of Minnesota (executive committee). He was president of the board of Minnesota Farmers' Institutes.

REFERENCES: *DAB; WWW* (I); *Minnesota Farm Review* 15 (August 1910): 170. *John F. Ohles*

GREENE, Samuel Stillman. B. May 3, 1810, Belchertown, Massachusetts, to Ebenezer and Sybil (Hitchcock) Greene. M. August 29, 1839, to Edna Amelia Bartlett. M. August 10, 1854, to Mary Adeline Bailey. Ch. four. D. January 24, 1883, Providence, Rhode Island.

Samuel Greene attended the district school taught by his father, a farmer and part-time schoolteacher. At the age of eighteen he attended a private school in which the teacher was his brother, the Reverend John Greene. He taught in the district school for three years earning money to attend college. Greene was graduated from Brown University in Providence, Rhode Island, in 1837 as the valedictorian of his class.

Upon graduation, Greene was employed as an assistant principal and later principal of the Baptist Academy in Worcester, Massachusetts. After three years he was made superintendent of schools in Springfield, Massachusetts, the first such position in Massachusetts. From 1842 to 1844 Greene taught in the English High School of Boston. He served as principal of the Phillips Grammar School of Boston from 1844 until 1849, when he accepted a position as agent of the Massachusetts Board of Education, a pioneering effort and said to be the first post of its kind in the nation. In this post, Greene was associated with Horace Mann *(q.v.)* who served as secretary of the board of education for the state of Massachusetts. In 1851 Greene was named superintendent of schools of Providence, Rhode Island, and also was appointed professor of didactics at Brown University.

In 1852 he and others opened a private normal school; the following year the school was given city support, and in 1854 it was taken over by the state as the Rhode Island Normal School (later, Rhode Island College). In 1855 Greene was appointed professor of mathematics and civil engineering and continued until 1864, when he transferred to the chair of natural philosophy and astronomy, assuming in 1875 the chair of mathematics and astronomy.

Greene was the author of *A Treatise of Structure of the English Language* and *First Lessons in Grammar,* both in 1848, followed by *The Elements of English Grammar* (1853), *Introduction to the Study of English Grammar* (1856), *A Grammar of the English Language* (1867), *An Introduction to the Study of English Grammar* (1868), and *An Analysis of English Language* (1874). These works represented attempts by Greene to improve the teaching of English grammar.

Greene served as president of the Rhode Island Institute of Instruction (1856–60), president of the National Teachers Association (1864–65), and president of the American Institute of Instruction (1869–70). He continued active in teaching and lecturing to his death.

REFERENCES: *AC; DAB; NCAB* (8:349); *TC; WWW* (H); *NYT,* January 25, 1883, p. 5.   *Franklin Ross Jones*

GREENLAW, Edwin Almiron. B. April 6, 1874, Flora, Illinois, to Thomas Bretwer and Emma Julia (Leverich) Greenlaw. M. September 1, 1898, to Mary Elizabeth Durland. Ch. three. D. September 10, 1931, Chapel Hill, North Carolina.

Edwin Almiron Greenlaw's father was a superintendent of schools and founder and proprietor of Orchard City College in Flora, Illinois. Educated primarily at home, Greenlaw was graduated from high school in 1890 after one year of study. He studied at Northwestern University in Evanston Illinois, earning the B.A. (1897) and A.M. (1898) degrees. He attended the University of Chicago and spent a year of study at Illinois College in Jacksonville, Illinois, before going on to Harvard University where he was awarded the A.M. (1903) and Ph.D. (1904) degrees.

Greenlaw was an English instructor at Northwestern University (1904–05) and head of the English department at Adelphi College (later, University in Garden City) in Brooklyn, New York (1905–13), where he concentrated his scholarship on Spenser and the Elizabethan allegory in the *Faerie Queen*. In 1913 he went to the University of North Carolina as head of the English department where his innovations in instruction attracted much attention. From 1920 to 1925 Greenlaw was dean of the graduate school. He established a board to raise requirements for both teachers and students, initiated a job placement bureau, and founded the *Bulletin of Research in Progress*. He was William Osler Professor of English Literature at Johns Hopkins University (1925–31).

Editor-in-chief of *Modern Language Notes* (1926–28) and *Studies in Philology* (1915–25), Greenlaw initiated the Johns Hopkins Monographs of Literary History. In 1931 he published *The Province of Literary History* in two volumes and in 1932, with Rockefeller Foundation Aid, established the Spenser Research Unit to publish a variorum edition of the works of Spenser. The six-volume work was completed in 1932 after his death. Greenlaw's other books include *A Syllabus of English Literature* (1912), *Outline of the Literature of the English Renaissance* (1916), and *Builders of Democracy* (1918). He also edited *Selections from Chaucer* (1907), *Irving's Knickerbocker History of New York* (1909), *Familiar Letters* (1915), *National Ideas in English and American Literature* (1918), *The Great Tradition* (with J. H. Hanford, 1918), and a four-volume *Literature and Life* (1922–24).

Greenlaw was a member of the college and university curriculum commission of the National Council of Teachers of English, the American Field Service advisory committee to award fellowships for studies in Europe, the executive committee of the British and American Association of Teachers of English, the American Council of Learned Societies Commission on Research, and the board of advisers for Guggenheim Fellowship awards. For five years he was chairman of the general research committee of the Modern Language Association. He was awarded honorary degrees by the University of North Carolina and Northwestern University.

REFERENCES: *DAB* (supp. 1); *NCAB;* (22:5); *WWW* (I).

William W. West

GREENLEAF, Benjamin. B. September 25, 1786, Haverhill, Massachusetts, to Caleb and Susanna (Emerson) Greenleaf. M. November 20, 1821, to Lucretia Kimball. Ch. nine. D. October 29, 1864, Bradford, Massachusetts.

Benjamin Greenleaf was self-educated. A voracious reader, he did most of his reading by firelight. At the age of nineteen, he was tutored for two years in preparation for college. Greenleaf studied for two years at the academy in Atkinson, New Hampshire, and taught for three years in New

Hampshire and Massachusetts. In 1810 he entered Dartmouth College in Hanover, New Hampshire, and was graduated in 1813. His primary interests were mathematics and astronomy.

After leaving Dartmouth, Greenleaf was principal of a grammar school in Haverhill, Massachusetts (1813). In 1814 he took charge of the Bradford (Massachusetts) Academy and was preceptor until 1836. He served in the state legislature (1837–39) where he advocated normal schools for teachers. He founded Bradford Teachers Seminary, a coeducational school, in 1839 and was in charge until it closed in 1848.

Greenleaf was an advocate of the formation of normal schools for the preparation of teachers. He began to write arithmetic and mathematics textbooks, which were first published in 1835. The most famous of his books was *National Arithmetic* (1835), which sold over a million copies. Among his other books were *A Concise System of Grammatical Punctuation* (1822), *Rules of Syntax* (1825), *A Practical Treatise on Algebra* (1852), *New Primary Arithmetic* (1861), *Elements of Geometry and Trigonometry* (1862), *New Elementary Algebra* (1862), and *Elements of Plane and Spherical Trigonometry* (1863). He also produced *The California Almanac* (1849) and *Cherokee Almanac* (n.d.). In his later years he made calculations for almanacs.

REFERENCES: *AC; DAB; NCAB* (8:141); *NYT,* November 10, 1864, p. 3; *TC; WWW* (H); John A. Nietz, *Old Textbooks* (Pittsburgh, Pa.: University of Pittsburgh Press, 1961).   *Robert McGinty*

GREENLEAF, Simon. B. December 5, 1783, Newburyport, Massachusetts, to Moses and Lydia (Parsons) Greenleaf. M. September 18, 1806, to Hannah Kingman. Ch. fifteen. D. October 6, 1853, Cambridge, Massachusetts.

When his parents moved to New Gloucester, Maine, Simon Greenleaf, at the age of seven, remained with his grandfather in Newburyport, Massachusetts, and was educated at the local Latin school. When he was sixteen he rejoined his parents, began studying law, and was admitted to the bar of Cumberland County, Maine, in 1806.

He practiced law briefly in Standish, Maine, before settling in Gray (1806–18). During this period he devoted much of his energies to a profound study of the basic source material of the common law and eventually became the foremost American authority on the subject. In 1818 he moved to Portland; in 1820, following the admission of Maine to the Union, Greenleaf was appointed reporter to the state supreme court (1820–32). He represented Portland in the initial term of the Maine legislature and was instrumental in forming the state's first legislation. In 1833 Greenleaf accepted the offer of Joseph Story *(q.v.)* to be Royall Professor of Law at Harvard University. Upon Story's death Greenleaf succeeded him as Dane Professor of Law (1846–48).

Greenleaf was the author of *Report of Cases Argued and Determined by the Supreme Judicial Court of the State of Maine* (nine volumes, 1821–35). In 1842 he published *A Treatise on the Law of Evidence,* which was regarded as the finest work on the subject; the second and third volumes were added in 1846 and 1853. His other major work was *Cruise's Digest of the Law of Real Property, Revised and Abridged for the Use of American Students* (seven volumes, 1849–50). He also wrote *A Brief Inquiry into the Origin and Principles of Free Masonry* (1820) and *An Examination of the Testimony of the Four Evangelists by the Rules of Evidence Administered in Courts of Justice with an Account of the Trial of Jesus* (1846), and was a frequent contributor of articles to periodicals.

Greenleaf was president for many years of the Massachusetts Bible Society and held memberships in the Massachusetts Historical Society and the American Philosophical Society. He was the recipient of several honorary degrees.

REFERENCES: *AC; DAB; NCAB* (7:360); *TC; WWW* (H); William Willis, *A History of the Law, the Courts, and the Lawyers of Maine* (Portland: Bailey and Noyes, 1863), pp. 520–36.   *Robert H. Truman*

GREENWOOD, Isaac. B. May 11, 1702, Boston, Massachusetts, to Samuel and Elizabeth (Bronson) Greenwood. M. July 31, 1729, to Sarah Clark. Ch. five. D. October 22, 1745, Charlestown, Massachusetts.

Isaac Greenwood was graduated from Harvard College in 1721. He continued his theological studies in London, England, began preaching, and became a follower of Theophilus Desaguliers, lecturer on experimental philosophy.

Greenwood returned to Boston where Thomas Hollis, a benefactor of Harvard College, proposed establishing a chair in mathematics with Greenwood as the professor. Greenwood assumed the post in 1728. He resigned in 1738 and spent his final years as a private tutor.

Greenwood was the author of *Experimental Course in Mechanical Philosophy* (1726), *A New Method for Composing a Natural History of Meteors* (1728), *A Brief Account of Some of the Effects and Properties of Damps* (1729), and *Vulgar and Decimal: With the Application Thereof to a Variety of Cases in Trade and Commerce* (1729), the first mathematics textbook written in English by a native American. Following his writing career, Greenwood launched a lecture series in Boston on the topic of astronomy.

Although Greenwood lived a relatively short life, his contributions were important to American education in the field of mathematics.

REFERENCES: *AC; DAB; DSB; TC; WWW* (H).   *John R. O'Donnell*

GREENWOOD, James Mickleborough. B. November 15, 1836, Sangamon County, Illinois, to Edmund and Jeanette (Foster) Greenwood. M. November 1, 1859, to Amanda A. McDaniel. Ch. three. D. August 1, 1914, Kansas City, Missouri.

James Mickleborough Greenwood attended the schools near Springfield, Illinois, but, when the family moved to Missouri in 1852, had little opportunity for formal schooling. He studied mathematics, Latin, and philosophy independently while working on the farm. In 1856 he attended school at Kirksville, Missouri. After one year at Kirksville, he entered the Canton Seminary (1857) in Missouri where he completed all course offerings of the institution, except Greek.

Between 1859 and 1866, Greenwood taught during the winters and farmed in the summers. That work was interrupted when he served as a soldier in the Union army (1862–64). He was a professor of mathematics, astronomy, and philosophy and logic at the Kirksville State Normal School (later, Northeast Missouri State University) from 1867 to 1874.

Greenwood's impact on education beyond the local level began in 1874 when he became superintendent of the Kansas City schools. He organized the Greenwood Club for the purpose of stimulating the mental growth of teachers. Greenwood developed a system of closely connected course work that would lead to high school graduation. The system was based on a philosophy that pursuing a high school education should not be unduly difficult for students and should be attractive to them. He added courses in physical education (1885), shorthand and typing (1886), manual training (1893), and home economics (1897) and established a kindergarten (1895). As early as 1886, the teachers in the Kansas City schools were keeping physical growth records on students.

Among his major published works were *Principles of Education Practically Applied* (1887), *A Complete Manual on Teaching Arithmetic, Algebra, and Geometry* (1890), *A History of American Arithmetics and a Biographical Sketch of the Authors* (with Artemus Martin, 1890), and *Dodge's Geography of Missouri* (with C. F. Marbut, 1906).

Greenwood was very active in teacher organizations and their development. In 1861 he helped develop the first teachers' institute at Northeast Missouri Normal School in Kirksville. Greenwood served two terms as president of the Missouri State Teachers Association and was president of the National Educational Association (1898). The University of Missouri conferred honorary degrees on Greenwood, an A.M. (1874) and LL.D. (1899).

REFERENCES: *AC; NCAB* (13:62); *WWW* (IV); *Encyclopedia of History of Missouri* (New York: Southern History Co., 1901), 3: 117–20, 121–22; Alice Lanterman and Virginia Sheoff, *Your City and You, The Story of Kansas City* (Kansas City, Mo.: Board of Education, 1947), pp. 33–34;

Carrie Westlake Whitney, *Kansas City, Missouri: Its History and Its People, 1808–1908* (Chicago: S. J. Clarke Publishing Co., 1908), 1:310, 2:238–43.   *James R. Layton*
Mary Paula Phillips

GREGG, John Robert. B. June 17, 1867, Rockcorry, County Monaghan, Ireland, to George and Margaret (Courtney Johnston) Gregg. M. July 3, 1899, to Maida Wasson. M. October 23, 1930, to Janet Fraser. Ch. two. D. February 23, 1948, New York, New York.

At the age of ten, John Robert Gregg developed an intense interest in shorthand after watching a friend record a church sermon. He moved with his family from Ireland to Scotland and had mastered at least six shorthand systems and began developing his own method when he was only fifteen years old. He sought to construct outlines that conformed to the natural motion of longhand.

Gregg arrived in Liverpool, England, in 1888, published five hundred copies of his system as Light-Line Phonography, and opened the Light-Line Phonography Institute. He moved to Boston in 1893 to protect his American copyright and moved to Chicago in 1895 where he organized and served as president of the successful Gregg School.

Gregg wrote many shorthand texts, including *Progressive Exercises in Gregg Shorthand* (1890), *Gregg Shorthand Dictionary* (1901), *Gregg Phrase Book* (1901), *Gregg Speed Practice* (1907), *Gregg Reporter* (1909), *Gregg Speed Studies* (1917), *Reporting Shortcuts* (1921), and *Basic Principles of Gregg Shorthand* (1923). He established the Gregg Publishing Company and entered the field of commercial textbook publishing, writing and publishing *Secretarial Studies* (1922), *The Q's and A's of Shorthand Theory* (1924), *Gregg Speed Building* (1932), *Applied Secretarial Practice* (1941), and *The Private Secretary* (1943). Gregg published periodicals, including *The Gregg Writer* and *American Shorthand Teacher* (later, *Business Education World*). The business continued as the Gregg Publishing Division of McGraw-Hill Publishing Company.

Gregg received several honorary degrees and medals. He was awarded the King George Medal by the United Kingdom in 1947 for services to the cause of freedom and an award in 1938 by the New York Academy of Public Education for distinguished service to public education. He was active in professional associations as a fellow of the National Academy of Design, charter member of the National Shorthand Reporters' Association, honorary life member of the National Commercial Teachers Federation and the New York State Shorthand Reporters' Association, and vice-president (1931) of the International Shorthand Congress in Paris, France. He was a delegate to the International Congress on Commercial Education in Amsterdam, the Netherlands (1929), and London, England (1932).

Following Gregg's death in 1948, his Chicago school was sold to McGraw-Hill Publishing Company and turned over to Northwestern University in 1952 to operate under his name. At the time of his death, Gregg's system was being used by millions of stenographers and had been adapted to Spanish, French, German, Portuguese, Italian, Polish, and Esperanto.

REFERENCES: *DAB* (supp. 4); *LE* (II); *NCAB* (C:273); *NYT,* February 24, 1948, p. 25; *WWW* (II); "Death of John R. Gregg," *American School Board Journal* 116 (April 1948): 75; "John R. Gregg: 80," *Business Education World* 28 (September 1947): 23; "John R. Gregg: Inventor, Educator, Benefactor of Mankind," *Business Education World* 28 (October 1947): 74–78 and (November 1947): 13; Louis A. Leslie, *The Story of Gregg Shorthand* (New York: McGraw-Hill, 1964); F. Addington Symonds, *John Robert Gregg: The Man and His Work* (New York: McGraw-Hill, 1963).

J. Lee Dye

GREGORY, John Milton. B. July 6, 1822, Sand Lake, New York, to Joseph G. and Rachel (Bullock) Gregory. M. September 6, 1848, to Julia Gregory. M. 1879 to Louisa Allen. Ch. six. D. October 19, 1898, Washington, D.C.

John Milton Gregory received his education in local public schools and the Dutchess County Academy at Poughkeepsie, New York. He was graduated from Union College in Schenectady, New York, with the A.B. degree (1846). After teaching and studying law for two years, he was ordained to the Baptist ministry in 1847 and served in pastorates in Hoosick Falls, New York, and Akron, Ohio. In 1852 he took charge of a private high school in Detroit, Michigan, and served as superintendent of public instruction in Michigan from 1859 to 1864. He was president of Kalamazoo (Michigan) College (1864–67), with notable success.

Gregory became the first regent (president) of the Illinois Industrial University (later, University of Illinois) in 1867. Opened on March 2, 1868, the university grew into a major institution. Women were admitted as students in 1871. The university was organized into four colleges and three schools. Gregory resigned as regent in 1880 and devoted several years to travel, writing, and public service.

Gregory was the author of *A Handbook of History and Chronology* (1867), *A New Political Economy* (1883), *The Seven Laws of Teaching* (1886), and numerous published articles and addresses on educational and religious subjects. He was a founder (1854) and editor (1855–70) of the *Michigan Journal of Education.*

He was president of the state board of health (1881) and superintendent of the educational work of the American Baptist Home Mission Society. He was a member of the first United States Civil Service Commission (1883–85). He was president of the National Teachers' Association (later, National Education Association) in 1868. He received an honorary degree from Madison University in 1866.

REFERENCES: *AC; DAB; NCAB* (12:497); *WWW* (H); Harry A. Kersey, *John Milton Gregory and the University of Illinois* (Urbana: University of Illinois Press, 1968).   *Paul L. Ward*

GREGORY, Samuel. B. April 19, 1813, Guilford, Vermont, to n.a. M. no. D. March 23, 1872, Boston, Massachusetts.

Samuel Gregory received the A.B. (1840) and A.M. (1845) degrees from Yale College and began teaching English evenings in manufacturing towns. He became interested in anatomy and physiology and read widely on his own. Traveling throughout New England he gave free lectures on sanitation and other subjects.

Gregory gave public lectures urging the establishment of an institution to train women in the field of medicine. In 1848 he opened the Boston Female Medical School, the first American institution to train women physicians. Gregory was president and secretary and served for a time as professor of chemistry. The Female Medical Education Society was founded in 1848 to keep the college functioning and to build a hospital; Gregory also served as secretary of the society. The college was chartered by the state in 1856 as the New England Female Medical College, was granted the right to confer the doctor of medicine degree, and a board of trustees was established. In 1870 a permanent building was erected on land donated by the city of Boston. Gregory continued with the college to his death in 1872. After Gregory's death the college merged (1874) with the Boston University Medical School as one of the first coeducational medical schools in the world.

Gregory was the author of a number of pamphlets about medicine and women physicians. He was awarded an honorary M.D. degree by Yale College in 1853.

REFERENCES: *AC; DAB; WWW* (H); *Boston Transcript,* March 24, 1872, p. 4.   *Barbara Ruth Peltzman*

GRIFFIS, William Elliot. B. September 17, 1843, Philadelphia, Pennsylvania, to John Limeburner and Anna Maria (Hess) Griffis. M. June 17, 1879, to Katherine L. Stanton. M. June 28, 1900, to Sarah F. King. Ch. two. D. February 5, 1928, Winter Park, Florida.

William Elliot Griffis served with the Union army in the Civil War. After the war, he attended Rutgers College (later, University) in New Brunswick, New Jersey, where he was graduated with the A.M. degree (1869). He studied at Union Theological Seminary in New York City and was graduated in 1877.

In 1870 Griffis made the first of two trips to Japan at the invitation of the emperor. He organized a school system in Echizen province modeled on American schools. He established the first chemical laboratory in Japan at Fukui and taught chemistry and physics (1872–74) at what later became the

Imperial University of Japan. He has been credited with advancing the development of modern manufacturing in Japan, starting with the silk industry in Fukui. He left Japan in 1874 but remained in contact with the Japanese empire all his life, returning for a six-month visit as guest of the emperor in 1927.

After his return to the United States Griffis was minister at the First Reformed Church in Schenectady, New York (1877–86), Shawmut Congregational Church in Boston, Massachusetts (1886–93), and First Congregational Church in Ithaca, New York (1893–1903). He retired in 1903 to devote his time to writing, lecturing, and travel, especially to the Netherlands, where he reported major events for American periodicals.

Griffis was best known in the United States as an interpreter of Japanese civilization. He wrote nearly fifty books and many journal articles. Among his books were *History of Japan from 660 B.C. to 1872 A.D.* (1874), *Studies in Japan* (1874), *The Influence of the Netherlands in the Making of the English Commonwealth and the American Republic* (1892), *Romance of Discovery* (1897), *The Pathfinders of the Revolution* (1900), *A Maker of the New Orient* (1902), *Young Peoples History of Holland* (1903), *The Japanese Nation in Evolution* (1907), *The Mikado–Institution and Person* (1915), *The American Flag of Stripes and Stars* (1926), and six volumes on the fairy tales of Europe and the Orient (1918–23).

Griffis was a member of many American and foreign organizations. He received honorary degrees from Union and Rutgers colleges and was decorated twice by the emperor of Japan.

REFERENCES: *DAB; NCAB* (21:118); *WWW* (I); *NYT,* February 6, 1928, p. 19.   *Daniel J. Booth*

GRIFFITH, Emily. B. February 10, 1880, Cincinnati, Ohio, to Andrew and Martha (Craig) Griffith. M. no. D. June 19, 1947, Pinecliffe, Colorado.

Emily Griffith moved to Arnold and Broken Bow, Nebraska, where she began to teach at the age of fourteen. The family was resettled in Denver, Colorado, where she taught as a substitute teacher and then as a regularly appointed teacher. She attended the Denver Normal School.

Griffith was appointed deputy superintendent of schools for the state of Colorado (1904–08 and 1910–12). She was an eighth-grade teacher in Denver, Colorado (1908–10 and 1912–16). She taught night adult classes and conceived the idea of classes for adults in a special school. She persuaded the school board to provide quarters in an old school building and opened the Public Opportunity School in 1916. The school featured a wide variety of courses for students of all ages. She continued at the school to her retirement in 1933, when the school enrolled over eight thousand students.

The Denver school was featured in 1932, when the American Association for Adult Education published *What Is This Opportunity School?* by Fletcher H. Swift and John W. Studebaker *(q.v.)*. Griffith lived in a cabin at Pinecliffe, Colorado, after retirement, where she was found shot to death in 1947.

Griffith was president of the Colorado Education Association and was the recipient of honorary degrees from Colorado State College, University of Colorado, and Colorado Women's College. In 1934 the school was named the Emily Griffith Opportunity School.

REFERENCES: *NAW;* M. A. Babich, "Programs for Adults, Emily Griffith Opportunity School, Denver," *Journal of Home Economics* 40 (November 1948): 513; "Murder in Pinecliffe," *Time* 49 (June 30, 1947): 18; "You Can Do It; Denver's Opportunity School," *Time* 48 (July 8, 1946): 70. *John F. Ohles*

GRIMKÉ, Charlotte L. Forten. B. August 17, 1837, Philadelphia, Pennsylvania, to Robert Bridges and Mary (Wood) Forten. M. December 19, 1878, to Francis James Grimké. Ch. one. D. July 23, 1914, Washington, D.C.

Charlotte L. Forten Grimké was a member of a well-known anti-slavery black family in Philadelphia, Pennsylvania. She was educated by tutoring at home rather than attend the segregated local public schools. She grew up influenced by her father, grandfather James Forten, a prominent sailmaker and reported to be the most successful black businessman of the time, and abolitionist William Lloyd Garrison. She attended the Higginson Grammar School in Salem, Massachusetts, where she was graduated with distinction in 1855. She stayed in Salem where she completed a course of study at the State Normal School (later, Salem State College) in 1856. In Salem she lived at the home of a family friend and black abolitionist, Charles L. Remond.

In 1856 she became the first black teacher in Salem at the Epes Grammar School. Poor health forced her resignation in 1858. She returned to the Salem school (1860–61). In 1862 she moved to St. Helena, one of the coastal islands between Charleston, South Carolina, and Savannah, Georgia, occupied by Union troops in 1861. She taught freedmen in schools managed in turn by the United States Treasury Department and War Department; teachers were recruited by the Philadelphia Port Relief Association. She left the South in 1863 and returned to Philadelphia. She assisted in the administration of Sumner High School in Washington, D.C. (1870–71) and was appointed as a clerk in the United States Treasury Department in 1873. In 1878 she was married to Francis James Grimké, pastor of the Fifteenth Street Presbyterian Church in Washington, D.C.

Grimké was the author of *Life on the Sea Island* (1864), published with the encouragement of John Greenleaf Whittier. She translated Emile Erckmann-Chatrian's *Madame Thérèse or the Volunteers of '92* (1869).

REFERENCES: *NAW; Afro-American Encyclopedia* (North Miami, Fla.: Educational Book Publishers, 1974), 4: 1098–99; Ray A. Billington, ed., *The Journal of Charlotte L. Forten* (New York: Dryden Press, 1953); *Two Black Teachers During the Civil War* (New York: Arno Press and the New York Times, 1969).   *Octavia B. Knight*

GRISCOM, John. B. September 17, 1774, Hancock's Bridge, New Jersey, to William and Rachel (Denn) Griscom. M. 1800 to Abigail Hoskins. M. December 13, 1843, to Rachel Denn. Ch. two. D. February 26, 1852, Burlington, New Jersey.

John Griscom attended country schools near his home in New Jersey, studied at the Friends Academy in Philadelphia, and was placed in charge of the Friends' monthly meeting school at Burlington, New Jersey, for thirteen years. Said to be the first to teach chemistry in the United States, he delivered a series of public lectures on chemistry at his school in 1806.

Griscom moved to New York City in 1807 where he established a successful school that was reorganized in 1825 as the New York High School for Boys. He engaged in the monitorial system of instruction, provided excellent equipment for the study of science, and emphasized instruction in gymnastics. Griscom also taught chemistry and natural history at the medical department of Queens College (later, Rutgers University) in New Brunswick, New Jersey, and lectured in chemistry at Columbia College.

The New York school was sold in 1831, and Griscom took charge of a Friends' boarding school in Providence, Rhode Island (1832–34). He lived in Haverford, Pennsylvania (1834–40), and was superintendent of schools in Burlington, New Jersey, from 1840 to his death in 1852. He participated in the reorganization of the common school system of New Jersey.

Griscom translated foreign articles for publication in American journals. In this way he publicized certain chemical discoveries, including the value of iodine in the treatment of goiter. He wrote *Education of Young Men* (1815), *Geographical Questions* (1816), *A Year in Europe* (two volumes, 1823), *Discourse on Character and Education* (1823), and *Monitorial Instruction* (1825).

He was one of the founders of the New York Society for the Prevention of Pauperism and Crime (1817) and the Society for the Reformation of Juvenile Delinquents. He was also a principal founder of the House of Refuge, the first reformatory in the United States.

REFERENCES: *AC; DAB; NCAB* (10:510); *TC; WWW* (H).
                                            Michael R. Cioffi

GRISWOLD, Alfred Whitney. B. October 27, 1906, Morristown, New Jersey, to Harold Ely and Elsie Montgomery (Whitney) Griswold. M. June

10, 1930, to Mary Morgan Brooks. Ch. four. D. April 19, 1963, New Haven Connecticut.

A. Whitney Griswold attended the Peck School in Morristown, New Jersey, and was graduated from the Hotchkiss School in Lakeville, Connecticut. He earned the B.A. (1929) and Ph.D. (1933) degrees from Yale University. Griswold was an instructor of English at Yale for one year (1929–30). A summer of study in Germany (1930) influenced him to change his graduate studies from English to history. He joined the Yale history department as an instructor in 1933 and advanced in rank, becoming a full professor in history in 1947 and a fellow of Yale's Timothy Dwight College. He was the director of the United States Foreign Areas and Language Curriculum of the Army Specialized Training Program (1942–45) and director of the United States Civil Affairs Training School (1943–45) at Yale.

When Yale's President Charles Seymour announced his intention to retire, Griswold was selected as his successor. Upon becoming president of Yale in 1950, Griswold found the university in difficult economic conditions. He reduced the debt, began to build the endowment funds, and gained the respect of the alumni. He worked toward slowly changing the curriculum, deemphasizing extracurricular activities, and emphasizing the liberal arts. He served as president of Yale to his death in 1963.

Griswold was a frequent contributor to a number of scholarly magazines and published several books, including *The Far Eastern Policy of the United States* (1938), *Farming and Democracy* (1948), *Essays on Education* (1954), *In the University Tradition* (1957), and *Liberal Education and the Democratic Ideal* (1959).

Griswold was a founder (1934) of the Yale Political Forum, a student forum on public affairs. He was a Guggenheim Fellow (1942 and 1945). He was an alumni trustee of Hotchkiss School (1943–47) and trustee from 1948 and a member of the board of trustees of the Carnegie Foundation for the Advancement of Teaching. He was decorated Officer of the Legion of Honor by France and Commander's Cross by Germany and was awarded honorary degrees by a number of American colleges and universities.

REFERENCES: *CB* (April 1950); *NCAB* (H:167); *NYT*, April 20, 1963, p. 1; *WWW* (IV).   *Earl W. Thomas*

GROPIUS, Walter Adolf Georg. B. May 18, 1883, Berlin, Germany, to Walter Adolf and Manon (Schwarnweber) Gropius. M. 1916 to Alma Schindler Mahler. M. October 16, 1923, to Ise Frank. Ch. two. D. July 5, 1969, Boston, Massachusetts.

Walter Gropius attended the Leibnitz Gymnasium in Berlin-Charlottenburg and was graduated (1903) from the Kaiserin Augusta Gymnasium in Berlin-Steglitz. He studied at the Technische Hochschule in

Munich (1903–04) and the Berlin Technische Hochschule (1905–07).

Gropius worked in an architect's office in Munich (1903–04) and with Peter Behrens in Berlin (1907–10) and conducted his own practice (1910–14). He served in the German army (1914–18) and was director of the Grand Ducal Saxon schools of Art and Arts and Crafts and the Grand Ducal Saxon Academy of Art in Weimar in 1918. He merged the two schools into the Staatliches Bauhaus (1919–25) and moved to Dessau in 1925, where he remained as director to 1928. Under Gropius the Bauhaus School revolutionized the teaching of architecture. He returned to private practice in 1928 and fled from Nazi Germany in 1934 to England, where he remained to 1937.

Gropius visited the United States in 1928 and returned in 1937 as senior professor of architecture at Harvard University and chairman of the department of architecture of the Harvard Graduate School of Design in 1938, serving to his retirement in 1952. Gropius designed many notable buildings in his career, reformed the architectural education program at Harvard, and influenced architectural programs across the country.

Gropius was the author of *Staatliches Bauhaus, Weimar, 1919–23* (1923), *Bauhausbauten in Dessau* (1930), *The New Architecture and the Bauhaus* (1935), *The Bauhaus, 1919–28* (1939), and *Rebuilding Our Communities* (1946) and editor with others of *The Architects Collaborative, 1945–65* (1966). He was active in professional associations in Europe and in the United States, was given honorary membership in Phi Beta Kappa (1942), and was named a fellow of the American Academy of Arts and Sciences (1944). He received honors, including the Howard Myers Memorial Award (1951) from the Architectural League of New York. He received honorary degrees from the Technische Hochschule of Hanover, Germany, Harvard University, and Western Reserve University.

REFERENCES: *CB* (November 1941, March 1952, and September 1969); *EB; LE* (II); *NYT,* July 6, 1969, p. 1; *WWW* (V).   *John F. Ohles*

GROSS, Samuel David. B. July 8, 1805, near Easton, Pennsylvania, to Philip and Johanna Juliana (Brown) Gross. M. 1828 to Louisa Weissell. Ch. eight, including Samuel Weissell Gross, medical educator, and Albert Haller Gross, lawyer. D. May 6, 1884, Philadelphia, Pennsylvania.

Samuel David Gross, a medical pioneer, teacher, and author, received his early education in a country school near Easton, Pennsylvania, and attended schools in Wilkes-Barre, Pennsylvania, and Lawrence, New Jersey. He studied medicine at Jefferson Medical College in Philadelphia, Pennsylvania, graduating in 1828.

He worked with George McClellan, a noted surgeon and founder of Jefferson Medical College. He practiced in Philadelphia after receiving his medical degree and translated to English medical books written in French and German. He left Philadelphia and returned to Easton to practice medicine (1829-34) and teach chemistry at Lafayette College (1832-34).

In 1833 he was appointed demonstrator of anatomy at the Medical College of Ohio in Cincinnati Medical College in 1835. Gross was professor of surgery at the University of Louisville, Kentucky (1840-50), where he became the most famous surgeon in the South. He left there in 1850 to teach at the University of the City of New York (later, New York University) but returned to Louisville in 1851. Gross returned to Philadelphia as professor of surgery at Jefferson Medical College (1856-82). As a surgeon, he was noted for operating for stone in the bladder.

Gross was an important writer in medicine; his most outstanding works were *Elements of Pathological Anatomy* (1839), the first systematic treatment of the subject, and *A System of Surgery, Pathological, Diagnostic, Therapeutic and Operative* (1859), called one of the greatest surgical textbooks. He also wrote *Diseases and Injuries of the Bones and Joints* (1830), *Wounds of the Intestines* (1843), *Report on Kentucky Surgery* (1851), *Diseases, Injuries and Malfunctions of the Urinary Organs* (1851), *Foreign Bodies in the Air Passage* (1854), *Manual of Military Surgery* (1861), *John Hunter and His Pupils* (1861), *History of Medical Literature* (1875), and *Century of American Medicine* (with others, 1876). He edited *American Medical Biography* (1861) and with T. G. Richardson was founder and editor of *Louisville Medical Review* (1856) and editor of *North American Medico-Chirurigical Review*.

He was one of the founders of the American Medical Association (president, 1867), the Philadelphia Pathological Society (first president), the Philadelphia Academy of Surgery, and the American Surgical Society. He was a member of many other American and foreign associations. He presided over the International Medical Congress in Philadelphia in 1876. He established the Samuel D. Gross Prize, the Academy of Surgery prize for original writing. He received honorary degrees from the English universities of Oxford and Cambridge and the University of Edinburgh, Scotland.

REFERENCES: *AC; DAB; NCAB* (8:216); *TC; WWW* (H).

Richard M. Coger

GROSSMANN, Louis. B. February 24, 1863, Vienna, Austria, to Ignatz and Nettie (Rosenbaum) Grossmann. M. no. D. September 21, 1926, Detroit, Michigan.

When he was ten years old, Louis Grossmann accompanied his father from Austria to the United States. He went to Cincinnati in 1876, where he attended the Hebrew Union College and also studied at Hughes High School. He completed his secular education at the University of Cincinnati with the B.A. degree (1884) and was graduated from the Hebrew Union College, becoming a rabbi in 1884.

Grossmann officiated as rabbi of Temple Beth El in Detroit, Michigan (1884–98), and served as associate of Congregation B'nai Yeshuran of Cincinnati, Ohio (1898–1922). At the same time he became assistant to Isaac M. Wise *(q.v.)*, founder of the Hebrew Union College, and was appointed professor of ethics and Jewish pedagogy at the college (1898–1922). Grossmann contributed to the growth of modern Jewish religious education and was a pioneer in relating modern scientific methods, especially psychological, to Jewish religious training.

He published two books on education, *Principles of Religious Instruction in Jewish Schools* (1913) and *The Aims of Teaching in Jewish Schools* (1919). He was also the author of *Some Chapters on Judaism and the Science of Religion* (1889), *Maimonides* (1890), *The Real Life* (1914), and *Glimpses into Life* (1922). He edited *Selected Writings of Isaac M. Wise* (1920) and *The Poems of B. Bettmann* (1904). He wrote two children's services for the holy days and Sabbath and arranged musical settings for children's services. During World War I he served as president of the Central Conference of American Rabbis and was also president of the Jewish Religious Educational Association of Ohio and the Rabbinical Association of Ohio. He was founder and president of the Western Association of Jewish Ministers (1924). He was a member of the international committee that organized the First Universal Congress of Races in London, England (1911). He received an honorary degree from Hebrew Union College in 1922.

REFERENCES: *DAB; NCAB* (23:302); *WWW* (I).   *Iris Hiller Berwitt*

GROVES, James Henry. B. May 17, 1837, Red Lion, New Castle County, Delaware, to Richard and Anne Benson (Henderson) Groves. M. October 15, 1874, to Emma F. Flowers. Ch. two. D. June 19, 1923, Wilmington, Delaware.

James Henry Groves was a teacher, principal, and Delaware's first state superintendent of free schools. He attended the public schools of New Castle County until he was fifteen years old and then spent one year at the Conference Academy in Charlotteville, New York. He entered Dickinson College in Carlisle, Pennsylvania, in 1859 and seven months later entered Wesleyan University in Middletown, Connecticut.

Groves began a long educational career in the fall of 1862 in a public school near Kirkwood, Delaware. He taught there for five years, and for seven months in 1867 he taught at a Friends' school in Bucks County, Pennsylvania. He was principal of the Odessa Grammar School for two years, principal of a private school in Odessa for two years, headmaster of the Bucks County Friends' School for three years, and principal of Smyrna Seminary for one year.

In 1875, on passage of the public school law providing for the establishment of a state superintendent of the free schools of Delaware, Governor John P. Cochran appointed Groves as state superintendent. He held that post until 1883, organizing Delaware's educational system and establishing it on a sound basis. His development of teachers' institutes resulted in a decided improvement in the efficiency and competency of the teachers' school accommodations.

REFERENCES: Henry C. Conrad, *History of the State of Delaware* (Wilmington, Del.: By the author, 1908), 3: 802; H. Clay Reed, *Delaware: A History of the First State* (New York: Lewis Historical Publishing Corp., 1947), 3: 74. *C. Roy Rylander*

GRUENBERG, Benjamin Charles. B. August 15, 1875, Bessarabia, Russia, to John Benedict and Charlotte (Mayberg) Gruenberg. M. June 30, 1903, to Sidonie Matzner (later, Matsner)*(q.v.)*. Ch. four. D. July 1, 1965, New York, New York.

Benjamin Charles Gruenberg was a leader in American science education. Born in the area of Eastern Europe bordered by the Dniester and Prut rivers, Gruenberg was brought to Minnesota as a young child. He received the B.S. degree (1896) from the University of Minnesota. He earned the A.M. (1908) and Ph.D. (1911) degrees from Columbia University.

He was a polarscopist for the United States Laboratory in New York City (1898–1902). He was employed by the New York public schools as a teacher of biology at De Witt Clinton High School (1902–10) and head of the biology department at Commercial High School (1910–14) and Julia Richman High School (1914–22). He was on a leave of absence (1920–22) to inaugurate sex education programs for the United States Bureau of Education and the United States Public Health Service. He was active in the development of the Rand School for Social Science (1907–20).

After leaving the public schools, Gruenberg served as a consultant to state and federal agencies and was education director for Urban Motion Picture Industries in an attempt to develop science films for classroom use (1922–23).

Perhaps best known for his textbooks, Gruenberg anticipated the trend of teaching high school biology and actually preceded the thinking of the Seven Cardinal Principles of the Commission on the Reorganization of Secondary Education (1918). His *Elementary Biology* text (1919) was judged to be the best of twelve existing texts in meeting these goals in 1924. *Elementary Biology* was the first high school biology text in the United States, and in his other works Gruenberg continued to advance the anthropocentric concept of man as the center of a complex and interacting chain. He also wrote *Student Manual of Exercises in Elementary Biology* (with F. M. Wheat, 1920), *Parents and Sex Education* (1923), *Biology and Human Life* (1925), *Experiments and Projects in Biology* (with N. E.

Robinson, 1925), *Outlines of Child Study: A Manual for Parents and Teachers* (1927), *Parents and Sex Education* (1928), *Story of Evolution, Facts and Theories on the Development of Life* (1929), *Instructional Tests in General Science* (1932), *Science and the Public Mind* (1935), *Science in Our Lives* (with S. P. Unzicker, 1938), *Activities in General Science* (1939), *Biology and Man* (with N. E. Bingham, 1944), and *How Can We Teach About Sex?* (1946). He coauthored many articles, book chapters, and books with his wife Sidonie M. Gruenberg, including *Parents, Children and Money* (1933), *Children for the Childless* (1954), and *The Wonderful Story of You* (1960). He was a cofounder of the *American Teacher* magazine and served as editor (1912–16).

Gruenberg was a fellow of the American Association for the Advancement of Science and the American Public Health Association and a member of many professional and learned associations. He organized the American Association for Medical Progress (1925–29).

REFERENCES: *CA* (13–16); *LE* (III); *WWAE* (XIII); *WWW* (IV); *NYT*, July 2, 1965, p. 29; *Science Education* 50 (February 1966): 83–89.

Jo Ann Kaufman

GRUENBERG, Sidonie Matsner. B. June 10, 1881, Vienna, Austria, to Idore and Augusta Olivia (Bassaches) Matsner (originally Matzner). M. June 30, 1903, to Benjamin C. Gruenberg *(q.v.)*. Ch. four. D. March 11, 1974, New York, New York.

Sidonie Matsner Gruenberg came to the United States with her parents at the age of fourteen. She was educated at the Höhere Töchterschule in Hamburg, Germany (1894), the Ethical Culture School in New York City (1897 and 1905–06), and Teachers College of Columbia University (1906–10).

Gruenberg joined the Child Study Association of America in 1906, became its director (1923–50), and served as special consultant to it after 1950. She was a lecturer in parent education at Teachers College, Columbia University (1928–36, 1941), New York University (1936–37), the New York School of Social Work (1936–37), and the University of Colorado (1940–42).

Gruenberg was the author and coauthor of many books, including *Your Child Today and Tomorrow* (1913), *Sons and Daughters* (1916), *Parents, Children and Money* (with Benjamin C. Gruenberg, 1933), *The Family in a World at War* (1942), *Your Child and You* (1950), *The Many Lives of Modern Woman* (with her daughter Hilda Sidney Krech, 1952), *The Wonderful Story of How You Were Born* (1952), and *Guiding Your Child from Five to Twelve* (1958). She was editor of many titles under the Child Study Association of America, including *Our Children* (with Dorothy Canfield Fisher, 1936), and was editor of *The Encyclopedia of Child Care and Guidance* (1954). She was a member of the editorial board of the Junior Literary Guild and *Parents Magazine* (1926–43) and was an editorial consultant to Fawcett Publications (1943–45), *Woman's Day* (1947–49), and Doubleday and Company.

Gruenberg was a member of the executive boards of many organizations, and she served as chairman of the National Council for Parent Education (1947–51), the parent education committee of the National Advisory Council on Radio in Education, and a subcommittee of the White House Conference on Child Health and Protection (1930); she was a member of the White House Conference (1940) and the Mid-century White House Conference (1950) and director of the Public Affairs Commission (1947) and Social Legislation Information Service (1947–61).

REFERENCES: *CA* (13–16); *CB* (May 1940); *LE* (III); *NYT,* March 13, 1974, p. 44; *WWAE* (XIII); *WW* (XXXVI); *WWW* (VI).

Ronald E. Ohl

GRUHN, William Theodore. B. November 11, 1904, Bridgeport, Connecticut, to Carl S. and Louisa (Vahlsing) Gruhn. M. July 14, 1928, to Myrtis Clark. Ch. one.

William Theodore Gruhn received the B.A. degree (1926) from Northern State College in Aberdeen, South Dakota, the M.A. degree (1933) from the University of Minnesota, and the Ph.D. degree (1940) from the University of North Carolina.

Gruhn initiated his career in education in Aberdeen at Roosevelt Junior High School where he was a teacher of social studies (1926–30) and as principal at Simmons Junior High School (1930–37). He was a graduate assistant at the University of Minnesota (1937–38) and a teaching fellow and instructor at the University of North Carolina (1938–40). He taught secondary education at the University of Connecticut at Storrs (1940–48) and was acting dean of the school of education (1948–49) and director of teacher education (1949–58). He was active as a lecturer, workshop director, and seminar leader.

In 1947 Gruhn teamed with Harl Douglass *(q.v.)* to write *The Modern Junior High School,* which was a significant contribution to the literature about the junior high school. Gruhn also wrote *Principles and Practices of Secondary Education* (1951), *Student Teaching in the Secondary School* (1954), and *Student Teaching in the Elementary School* (with Margaret Lindsey, 1957).

He received citations from the Connecticut Association of Secondary Schools and the Massachusetts Association of Secondary School Principals. He was made chairman of the committee on junior high school education of the National Association of Secondary School Principals (1955–62). He was a member of several professional associations.

REFERENCES: *LE* (IV); *WWAE* (XXIII). *M. Dale Baughman*

GUERIN, Anne-Thérèse. B. October 2, 1798, Etables, Cotes-du-Nord, France, to Laurent and Isabelle (LeFevre) Guerin. M. no. D. May 14, 1856, St. Mary-of-the-Woods, Indiana.

Anne-Thérèse (Mother Theodore) Guérin spent most of her life in France, but became noted in American educational circles after she emigrated to the United States in 1840.

In her early years she was educated in a local private school and later by a tutor. At the age of twenty-four, she entered the congregation of the Sisters of Providence at Ruillé-sur-Loir. In 1825 she took her vows and was appointed superior of a school at Rennes. In 1835 she went to Soulaines where she studied medicine and pharmacy and gained a reputation as an excellent teacher of mathematics. In 1840 she and other nuns answered the call of the bishop of Vincennes, Indiana. Guérin established a girls' academy, the first in Indiana, which received a charter in 1846. She built a motherhouse for her order and initiated the establishment of ten more schools.

She corresponded with national and local political and religious leaders and kept careful diaries and journals of her travels.

REFERENCES: *DAB; NCAB* (23:388); *WWW* (H), *New Catholic Encyclopedia* (New York: McGraw-Hill, 1967).   *James M. Vosper*

GUILFORD, Nathan. B. July 19, 1786, Spencer, Massachusetts, to Jonas and Lydia (Hobbs) Guilford. M. August 19, 1819, to Eliza Wheeler Farnsworth. Ch. none. D. December 18, 1854, Cincinnati, Ohio.

Nathan Guilford was graduated from Leicester (Massachusetts) Academy and Yale College (1812). He studied law and practiced in Worcester, Massachusetts.

Guilford later practiced law and taught in Lexington, Kentucky (1814–16). He formed a law firm with Amos Kendall in Alexandria, Kentucky, and Georgetown, Kentucky (1816), and moved to Cincinnati, Ohio, in 1816, practicing law there.

Guilford joined with Samuel Lewis and others in advocating free education. In 1822 he published a letter urging a general county tax. The letter was later published by the Ohio General Assembly, but no legislation resulted. Guilford ran for the state senate to secure enactment of a law that would provide an adequate system of education. A bill he wrote authorizing assessment of taxes for support of the schools was enacted in 1825. He returned to Cincinnati, where he proposed that the tax permitted by the legislature be levied to support local schools. In the ensuing struggle, he successfully ran as a candidate for the city council and persisted until the tax measure was enacted.

Guilford edited an educational almanac under the pseudonym Solomon Thrifty (1818–25). In addition to the usual information found in almanacs,

Solomon Thrifty's Almanac contained a statement on each page emphasizing the value of education and the need for public schools in Ohio. He gradually withdrew from the practice of law and devoted more time as a publisher. He published *The Western Spelling Book* (1831) and *The Juvenile Arithmetic* (1836).

A special act of the Ohio legislature in 1850 authorized the popular election of a superintendent of common schools for the city of Cincinnati. Nathan Guilford was elected and held the position for two years. He was city magistrate of Cincinnati in 1854. In 1914 the new Guilford Elementary School was named in his honor.

REFERENCES: *DAB; NCAB* (12:385); *WWW* (H); James J. Burns, *Educational History of Ohio* (Columbus: Historical Publishing Company, 1905). *Jerrold D. Hopfengardner*

GULICK, Luther Halsey. B. December 4, 1865, Honolulu, Hawaii, to Luther Halsey and Louisa (Lewis) Gulick. M. August 30, 1887, to Charlotte Emily Vetter. Ch. six. D. August 13, 1918, Sebago, Maine.

Luther Halsey Gulick, son of missionaries, studied at the preparatory department of Oberlin (Ohio) College (1880–82) and in the college (1883–86). Plagued by ill health, Gulick became concerned with physical development. He studied at the Sargent Normal School of Physical Training (later, part of Boston University) but left after six months to become gymnasium superintendent at the Young Men's Christian Association (YMCA) in Jackson, Michigan. He studied at the New York University Medical School (1886–89) and earned the M.D. degree (1889). He supported himself teaching at a girls' school in Harlem and acting as medical examiner at the Twenty-third Street YMCA.

In 1887 Gulick and Robert J. Roberts *(q.v.)* conducted the first summer school of special training for gymnasium instructors at the School of Christian Workers (later, International Young Men's Christian Association College and Springfield College) at Springfield, Massachusetts. Gulick remained director until 1903. He devised the YMCA triangle emblem denoting the physical, social, and spiritual goals of the organization. He also served as secretary for the physical training department of the YMCA International Committee.

Gulick was principal of Pratt High School in Brooklyn, New York (1900–03). He served as director of physical education for the schools of New York City (1903–08) where he reorganized and coordinated physical education activities and instruction in hygiene, wrote the Gulick Hygiene Series, and organized the Public School Athletic League. He also lectured at the New York University School of Pedagogy (1905–09). In 1907 Gulick organized the child hygiene department of the Russell Sage Foundation; he served as its director until 1913 when his health began to decline. Gulick was credited with assisting in the founding of the Boy Scouts of America, establishing the Camp Fire Girls with Charlotte Gulick, and developing the game of basketball with James Naismith.

Gulick served the National War Council in 1917 by conducting a survey in France of the work of the YMCA with the American Expeditionary Force. *The Dynamic of Manhood* (1917), considered his best book, was the outgrowth of his two months in France. He also wrote *Physical Measurements and How They Are Used* (1899), *The Efficient Life* (1907), *Mind and Work* (1908), *The Healthful Art of Dancing* (1910), and many monographs. He was editor of *Physical Education* (1891–96), *Association Outlook* (1897–1900), and *Physical Education Review* (1901–03).

Gulick was active in professional associations, serving as president of the American Physical Education Association (1903–07), the Public School Physical Training Society (1905–08), and the Playground Association of America (1906–09). He was a member of the American Association for the Advancement of Physical Education (secretary, 1892–93), and the School Hygiene Association of America (organizing secretary) and a fellow of the American Medical Association and other medical societies. He was a member of Olympic Games committees (1906 and 1908), chairman of the physical training lecture committee of the St. Louis Exposition (1904), and United States delegate to the Second International Congress on School Hygiene in London, England (1907). The American Alliance for Health, Physical Education and Recreation established the Gulick Award in his honor.

REFERENCES: *DAB; NCAB* (26:371); *WWW* (I); *NYT,* August 14, 1918, p. 9; Ethel J. Dorgan, *Luther Halsey Gulick* (New York: Teachers College, Columbia University, 1934).   *Kathryn D. Lizzul*

GULLIVER, Julia Henrietta. B. July 30, 1856, Norwich, Connecticut, to John Putnam and Frances Woodbury (Curtis) Gulliver. M. no. D. July 25, 1940, Eustis, Florida.

Julia Henrietta Gulliver was the daughter of John Putnam Gulliver, president of Knox College in Galesburg, Illinois. After graduating from high school in Binghamton, New York, she entered the first class of the newly founded Smith College, graduating with the A.B. degree in 1879. In 1888 she received the second Ph.D. degree awarded by Smith. She traveled to Leipzig, Germany, where she received special permission as a woman to study with Wilhelm Wundt. She translated part of his *Ethics* into English.

In 1890 Gulliver became head of the department of philosophy and biblical literature at Rockford (Illinois) Seminary. After European studies she returned to Rockford where the seminary became a college; in 1902 she was appointed president of Rockford College.

Rockford College was in a precarious condition when Gulliver assumed the presidency, but she was able to recruit new faculty, eliminate the preparatory department, build a new hall, double endowment funds, and gain national accreditation. She added courses in home economics and secretarial studies to the college curriculum. She banned sororities as undemocratic in 1909. Gulliver retired from Rockford in 1919.

Gulliver expressed her beliefs in the role of women in the larger community as well as in the home in *Studies in Democracy* (1917). She was decorated officer d'académie by the French government in 1909 and received an honorary degree from Smith College in 1910.

REFERENCES: *LE* (I); *NAW; WWW* (I); *NYT*, July 28, 1940, p. 27.

Darlene E. Fisher

GUMMERE, John. B. 1784, Willow Grove, Pennsylvania, to Samuel and Rachel (James) Gummere. M. 1808 to Elizabeth Buzby. Ch. eleven, including Samuel James Gummere, president of Haverford College. D. May 31, 1845, Burlington, New Jersey.

John Gummere taught himself mathematics and astronomy. He attended the Friends' Boarding School in Westtown, Pennsylvania, where he was instructed by Enoch Lewis *(q.v.)*.

At the age of nineteen, Gummere taught school in Horsham, Pennsylvania. He taught in Rancocas, New Jersey (1805–11), and returned to teach in the Westtown boarding school (1811–14) that later was the Haverford School (1833) and Haverford College (1856). Gummere established a highly successful boarding school in Burlington, New Jersey (1814–33), which attracted students from across the country and from as far as the West Indies. Gummere was one of the first to introduce laboratory work in chemistry teaching in his school.

In 1833 Gummere closed his school to become a mathematics teacher at the newly established Haverford (Pennsylvania) School; he also served for a time as principal of the school. A difference of opinion over the management of the Haverford School in 1843 led to Gummere's resignation, and he reopened a school in Burlington, New Jersey, with his son Samuel.

Gummere was elected to the American Philosophical Society in 1814. He was the author of *A Treatise on Surveying* (1814), *Elementary Treatise on Astronomy* (1822), and several articles for the American Philosophical Society journal *Transactions*. He received honorary degrees from the College of New Jersey (later, Princeton University) and the University of Pennsylvania.

REFERENCES: *AC; DAB; NCAB* (23:409); *TC; WWW* (H).

Barbara Ruth Peltzman

GUNN, Frederick William. B. October 4, 1816, Washington, Connecticut, to John and Mary (Ford) Gunn. M. April 16, 1848, to Abigail I. Brinsmade. Ch. none. D. August 16, 1881, Washington, Connecticut.

Frederick William Gunn was raised by his oldest brother John after both his mother and father died when he was ten years old. Gunn was graduated from Yale College in 1837 where he was known for feats of physical strength rather than for his scholarly activities and acquired a reputation as a nonconformist.

Intending to study medicine, Gunn began teaching at New Preston, Connecticut, to earn money for his studies (1838–39). In 1839 he opened an academy at Washington, Connecticut. His nonconformist ideas brought him in conflict with the local citizenry when he advocated in a town dependent on rum trade abstinence from alcoholic beverages and became active in the abolitionist movement. Students were withdrawn from his academy, and he returned to teaching in New Preston in 1845. He operated an academy in Towanda, Pennsylvania (1847–48).

Gunn returned to Washington, Connecticut, to resume teaching at the academy; later it came to be called the Gunnery. The school became widely known for its unique methods and the general character of the institution. The Gunns adopted a parental attitude toward the boys, and self-government was encouraged. There was no marking system in the school, and intellectual training was secondary to moral and physical development.

Gunn conducted a summer encampment at Lake Waramaug for a number of years with some of his Gunnery students in attendance. A monument was erected to Gunn by his former pupils in Washington, Connecticut.

REFERENCES: *DAB; NCAB* (13:349); *TC; WWW* (H); *New Haven Journal-Courier,* August 18, 1881; *New York Daily Tribune,* August 17, 1881.   *Robert V. Shuff*

GUTHE, Karl Eugen. B. March 5, 1866, Hanover, Germany, to Otto and Anna (Hanstein) Guthe. M. August 18, 1892, to Clara Belle Ware. Ch. three. D. September 10, 1915, Ashland, Oregon.

Karl Eugen Guthe received his early education at the gymnasium and technical high school in his home town, Hanover, Germany. He later attended and was graduated from the University of Marburg, Germany (1889), with a teaching certificate in physics, chemistry, geography, and the natural sciences. For the next two years, he taught and studied at the University of Strassburg. In 1892 he returned to Marburg for a brief residency to complete and submit his dissertation on the mechanical telephone. Guthe was awarded the Ph.D. degree from the University of Marburg in 1892 and that summer emigrated to Grand Rapids, Michigan.

He was a research assistant in the physics department at the University of Michigan and was given a regular appointment in the department in 1893, continuing to 1903. On a sabbatical leave, he studied under Professor Max Planck at the University of Berlin (1900–01) and returned to the University of Michigan as an assistant professor of physics.

Guthe served in the United States Bureau of Standards in Washington, D.C. (1903–05). He was professor and chairman in physics at the University of Iowa (1905–09). He returned to the University of Michigan as professor of physics in 1909 where he was instrumental in the organization of the graduate school and was appointed its first dean in 1912. Guthe was an able administrator and was a recognized authority in the field of electricity.

Guthe was the author of *Manual of Physical Measurement* (with John O. Reed, 1902), *Laboratory Exercise with Primary and Storage Cells* (1903), *Textbook of Physics* (with others, 1908), *College Physics* (with J. O. Reed, 1911), and *Definitions in Physics* (1913). He contributed many papers on scientific subjects, particularly electricity, to scholarly and technical journals.

Guthe was a member of the jury of awards in electricity at the St. Louis (Missouri) Exposition (1904). He was a fellow of the American Association for the Advancement of Science (vice-president, 1908) and a member of other scientific and professional associations.

REFERENCES: *DAB; NCAB* (22:348); *WWW* (I); *NYT,* September 12, 1915, p. 17. *Isadore L. Sonnier*

GUYOT, Arnold Henry. B. September 28, 1807, Boudevilliers, Switzerland, to David Pierre and Constance (Favarger) Guyot. M. July 2, 1867, to Sarah Doremus Haines. Ch. none. D. February 8, 1884, Princeton, New Jersey.

Arnold Guyot, Swiss-born geographer and geologist, was an eminent scientist and educator. He was first interested in the ministry; while never abandoning religion, he became interested in science after his entrance into the University of Neuchâtel, Switzerland (1821). He studied sciences in Germany at Karlsruhe, Stuttgart, and Berlin and attended lectures by the greatest scientists of the period including the physical geographer Carl Ritter. Guyot earned a doctorate from the University of Berlin (1835) and in 1839 became a colleague of Louis Agassiz *(q.v.)* at the College of Neuchâtel, where his attention turned to the study of glaciers and glacial action.

Political turmoil swept Europe in 1848 and Agassiz, then at Harvard University in Cambridge, Massachusetts, convinced Guyot that his professional and scientific interests would be best served by going to the United States. Guyot delivered the Lowell Institute lectures in Boston on the "new geography" in 1849, and the subsequent publication of these lectures served to popularize geographic education, as well as Guyot's views.

Guyot lectured on the new geography for six years for the Massachusetts Board of Education, and his influence on public education became widespread. He believed that the starting point for geographic education should be nature and not books, and he urged teachers to take their pupils outside to observe landforms as a prerequisite for broader geographic study.

Guyot became professor of physical geography and geology at the College of New Jersey (later, Princeton University) in 1854, and his work in meteorology, topology, and geology continued until his retirement in 1880. He also lectured on physical geography at the State Normal School (later, Trenton State College) in Trenton, New Jersey (1861–66), and he was Lecturer Extraordinary at the Princeton (New Jersey) Theological Seminary. He founded the geological museum at Princeton University, which bears his name.

Guyot was the author of *The Earth and Man* (1849), *A Collection of Meteorological Tables* (1852), *Geographical Teaching* (1866), *Primary; or Introduction to the Study of Geography* (1866), *The Earth and Its Inhabitants* (1866), *Elementary Geography for Primary Classes* (1868), *Physical Geography* (1873), *Guyots New Intermediate Geography* (1875), with supplements on individual states, *The Geographical Primer* (1882), and *Creation; or, The Biblical Cosmogony in the Light of Modern Science* (1887). He was editor with F. A. P. Barnard *(q.v.)* of *Johnson's Cyclopaedia.*

Guyot was a member of many American and foreign scientific societies and was one of the original members of the National Academy of Sciences. He was awarded medals at the Paris Exposition of 1878 and the Vienna Exposition of 1873. He received an honorary degree from Union College in 1873.

REFERENCES: *AC; DAB; DSB; EB; NCAB* (4:448); *TC; WWW* (H); James D. Dana, "Memoir of Arnold Guyot, 1807–1884," *National Academy of Science, Biographical Memoirs, II* (Washington, D.C.: National Academy of Science, 1886), pp. 309–47; Preston E. James, *All Possible Worlds: A History of Geographic Ideas* (New York: Odyssey Press, 1972); *NYT,* February 9, 1884, p. 5; *Science* 55 (February 22, 1884): 218–20.

Stuart B. Palonsky

H

HADDOCK, Charles Brickett. B. June 20, 1796, Salisbury, New Hampshire, to William and Abigail Eastman (Webster) Haddock. M. August 19, 1819, to Susan Sanders. M. July 21, 1841, to Caroline (Kimball) Young. Ch. nine. D. January 15, 1861, West Lebanon, New Hampshire.

Charles Brickett Haddock was graduated from Dartmouth College in 1816 and from Andover (Massachusetts) Theological Seminary in 1818. He was ordained a Congregational minister.

He was made professor of rhetoric at Dartmouth in 1819 and later became professor of intellectual philosophy and political economy. He resigned in 1850 when he was appointed minister to Portugal by President Millard Fillmore. He returned in 1854 and retired to West Lebanon, New Hampshire, where he remained until his death in 1861.

Haddock was interested in public affairs and served as a member of the New Hampshire state legislature (1845–48). He was the first New Hampshire commissioner of public schools (1846–47). His initial survey of the New Hampshire school system, *Report of the Commissioner of Common Schools* (1847), was a notable document. He was active in developing teachers' institutes for normal training. He supported building railways in New Hampshire. His occasional addresses, magazine articles, and speeches were published in 1846 as *Addresses and Miscellaneous Writings*.

Haddock served for many years as secretary of the New Hampshire Education Society. He was awarded an honorary degree by Bowdoin College.

REFERENCES: *AC; DAB; NCAB* (9:96); *WWW* (H). *Connie S. Menges*

HADLEY, Arthur Twining. B. April 23, 1856, New Haven, Connecticut, to James (*q.v.*) and Anne Loring (Twining) Hadley. M. June 30, 1891, to Helen Harrison Morris. Ch. three. D. March 5, 1930, Kobe, Japan.

Arthur Twining Hadley, president of Yale University and international authority on the operation and financing of railroads, attended the Hopkins Grammar School in New Haven, Connecticut, in preparation for entering Yale College, where he was graduated with the A.B. degree (1876) as a twenty-year-old class valedictorian. He studied history and political science at Yale (1876–77) and the University of Berlin (1878–79).

Hadley returned to Yale as a tutor in German, Greek, logic, and Roman law in 1879 and established a reputation as one of the most brilliant and popular professors at the institution. In 1883 he was an instructor and three years later a graduate professor in political economy. He served as dean of the graduate department (1892–95) and became the thirteenth president of Yale in 1899, the first layperson since the founding of Yale in 1701.

During his twenty-two years as the chief administrator, Yale University became an institution of national and international prominence. Under Hadley, it became a mature university with a coordinated organization of the various schools and colleges. The size of the staff, student enrollment, and physical plant were increased. The school of forestry was established in 1900, and the Yale University Press and *Yale Review* were founded.

Upon retirement in 1921, Hadley lectured at many universities and to many learned societies, including Harvard, Oxford, and Cambridge universities, Lowell Institute, and the New York School of Philanthropy. In fulfillment of a lifelong dream he sailed in December of 1929 on a trip around the world that ended in Kobe, Japan, on March 5, 1930, where he contracted pneumonia and died aboard ship.

Hadley was the author of *Railroad Transportation* (1885), *Economics* (1896), *The Education of the American Citizen* (1901), *Standards of Public Morality* (1907), *The Moral Basis of Democracy* (1919), and *The Conflict Between Liberty and Equality* (1925).

Hadley was appointed chairman of the Railroad Security Commission (1910) and served as trustee of the Carnegie Foundation for the Advancement of Teaching (1905–21) and chairman of the board (1917–20). He was a member of the American Economic Association (president, 1898–1900), the National Institute of Arts and Letters (president, 1925–27), the British Association for the Advancement of Science, and other professional associations. He was awarded many honorary degrees, including one from the University of Berlin.

REFERENCES: *DAB; EB; NCAB* (32:9); *WWW* (I); *NYT,* March 6, 1930, p. 1.   *Franklin Ross Jones*

HADLEY, Hiram. B. March 17, 1833, Wilmington, Ohio, to John and Lydia (Harvey) Hadley. M. April 30, 1856, to Hannah Fulghum. M. May 20, 1880, to Katherine E. Coffin. Ch. four. D. December 3, 1922, Kansas City, Missouri.

Referred to as the Father of Education in New Mexico, Hiram Hadley went to Las Cruces, New Mexico, in 1887 after fifty-four years in the Midwest. He received his education at the Friends' boarding school (later, Earlham College) in Richmond, Indiana, and at Haverford College in Pennsylvania.

While a student he began teaching, first at a Friends' schoolhouse at Grassy Run, Ohio (1850), then at Carthage, Indiana (1854–56), and then at Friends' Academy in Richmond, Indiana (1856–63). In 1861 he was appointed county examiner of schools in Wayne County, Indiana. In 1865 he established Hadley's Normal Academy in Richmond, Indiana.

In 1869 he became associated with Scribner, Armstrong and Company, publishers, as a traveling representative. He and his brother Seth S. Hadley then formed the bookselling firm of Hadley Bros. In 1876 the firm was closed because of a fire, and Hadley established another academy, Hadley's Classical Academy at Indianapolis in 1880; he left the academy in 1883. He was principal of the Friends' Academy at Bloomingdale, Indiana, in 1885. In 1887 he resigned his post and went to Las Cruces, New Mexico.

In 1888 Hadley was appointed president of Las Cruces College, an institution he had helped to found. He was instrumental in establishing the New Mexico College of Agriculture and Mechanic Arts (later, New Mexico State University), and in 1889 the two colleges were merged with Hadley as president of New Mexico College of Agriculture and Mechanic Arts (1889–94). In 1894 Hadley went to the University of New Mexico at Albuquerque as vice-president, a position he held for three years. Upon retiring from that position he returned to the college at Las Cruces as professor of history and philosophy.

In 1905 Governor Miguel A. Otero appointed Hadley, then seventy-two, to the position of superintendent of public instruction of the Territory of New Mexico. His work as superintendent was hailed as outstanding. Upon retirement from this position, he served on the state board of regents (1907–13).

He was active in the New Mexico Education Association, (president, 1890 and 1891). He formed the Anti-Tobacco League and represented New Mexico at several national peace congresses. Hadley wrote *Lessons in Language* (1871) and *English Grammar* (with Mary V. Lee, 1873).

REFERENCES: *NCAB* (21:207); *WWW* (I); Anna R. Hadley Bowman, Caroline H. Allen, and Frank Allen, *Hiram Hadley, March 17, 1833–December 3, 1922* (Boston: The authors, 1924). *Nelson L. Haggerson*

HADLEY, James. B. March 30, 1821, Fairfield, New York, to James and Marcia (Hamilton) Hadley. M. August 31, 1851, to Anne Loring Twining. Ch. one, Arthur Twining Hadley *(q.v.)*, president of Yale University. D. November 14, 1872, New Haven, Connecticut.

James Hadley received his early education and training for college at the Fairfield (New York) Academy which was run by the Reverend Dr. David Chassel. His father, a professor of chemistry at the College of Physicians and Surgeons of the western district of New York, developed his scientific interest. Young Hadley occasionally conducted recitations of his own class; at sixteen, Chassel made him his assistant in hearing the recitation of other classes. At the age of nineteen, he entered Yale College at the junior year level and was graduated as salutatorian in 1842.

He spent a year as a resident graduate student and was tutor of mathematics at Middlebury (Vermont) College (1844–45). He was a tutor of classical history at Yale (1845) and became professor of Greek (1851), holding that chair until his death in 1872, with interruptions caused by periods of illness.

Hadley had a gift for languages; his philological studies made him known throughout the world. He was a scholar in Latin, Greek, Hebrew, and the principal modern languages, including Swedish, and also in Arabic, Armenian, several Celtic tongues, Sanskrit, and the different forms of Gothic. He also was an expert in mathematics, chronology, and history and was interested in Roman law, on which he lectured, and political science and English literature.

Hadley was the author of *A Greek Grammar for Schools and Colleges* (1860), *A Brief History of the English Language* (1864), *Elements of the Greek Language* (1869), and *Introduction to Roman Law* (1873). *Essays Philological and Critical, Selected Papers of James Hadley* was published posthumously in 1873.

He was an active member of the American Philological Association and the National Academy of Sciences. He served on the American Committee for the Revision of the New Testament and was president of the American Oriental Society (1870–72).

REFERENCES: *AC; DAB; NCAB* (1:175); *WWW* (H).

Joseph P. Cangemi
Thomas E. Kesler

HAGAR, Daniel Barnard. B. April 22, 1820, Newton Lower Falls, Massachusetts, to Isaac and Eunice (Steadman) Hagar. M. August 25, 1848, to Mary Bradford McKim. Ch. seven. D. August 4, 1896, Sharon, Massachusetts.

Daniel B. Hagar, one of the pioneers in the development of the American normal school, attended the village district school in Newton Lower Falls, Massachusetts, and Seth Davis Academy in nearby West Newton. In 1829 his father died, and nine-year-old Hagar had to help support the family. He worked in a local papermill for several years and then in a Boston dry-goods store.

Hagar entered Union College in Schenectady, New York, where he supported himself by teaching in academies in Schuylerville and Kingston, New York. He was graduated in 1843 with highest honors and for a time pursued theological studies. He accepted the principalship of the Canajoharie (New York) Academy for five years and then served for a year as principal of the Norwich (New York) Academy before moving to Boston as headmaster of the Eliot High School in Jamaica Plain, where he served for the next sixteen years. Hagar established a reputation as one of the most eminent educators in New England. He was an early member of the American Institute of Instruction where he read an influential paper, "School Supervision."

In 1865 he accepted an offer to become the third principal of the Salem (Massachusetts) State Normal School (later, Salem State College) and served there to 1896. His years at Salem were marked by the introduction of chemistry, physics, and manual training, greater attention to music and art, and an enlarged gymnastics program. He established a liaison with a nearby primary school so that Salem seniors could give lessons at the school under near-normal teaching conditions.

Hagar was an editor of *The Massachusetts Teacher* (1852–56 and 1865–70) and the author of *Primary Lessons in Numbers* (1871), *Elementary Arithmetic* (1877), *Common School Arithmetic* (1877), and *Elementary Algebra* (1874).

Hagar served as president of various local teachers' associations in New York and Massachusetts and of the Massachusetts State Teachers' Association (1856–58). He was a founding member of the National Teachers' Association (later, National Education Association) in 1857 and its president (1871). He was president of the American Institute of Instruction (1860–61), the American Normal Association (1858), and the National Council of Education (1885–86).

He was president of Salem Young Men's Christian Association, vice-president of Essex Institute, and a member of the Salem school board (1866-75). He received an honorary degree from Union College (1871).

REFERENCES: *NCAB* (13:578); *Salem* (Massachusetts) *Evening News,* August 5, 1896; *Salem State College 100th Anniversary Booklet* (Salem, Mass.: Salem State College Library Archives, 1954).

Stephen J. Clarke

HAILMANN, William Nicholas. B. October 20, 1836, Glarus, Switzerland, to William Alexander and Babette Hailmann. M. December 24, 1857, to Eudora Lucas. M. December 25, 1907, to Helena Kuhn. Ch. one. D. May 13, 1920, Pasadena, California.

At the age of thirteen, William Nicholas Hailmann entered the polytechnic division of the Cantonal College at Zurich, Switzerland. Three years later (1852) he emigrated to Louisville, Kentucky, where he taught modern languages at Henry College. He studied at the Medical College in Louisville (1855–56).

Hailmann taught modern languages and natural sciences in high schools in Louisville (1856–65). Shocked at the use of rote memory and formalism, he saw the need for a progressive primary education and revisited Zurich in 1860 to study kindergartens and primary education. Hailmann directed the German-American Academy in Louisville (1865–73), the German-

American Academy in Milwaukee, Wisconsin (1873–78), and the German-American Seminary in Detroit, Michigan (1878–83). He was superintendent of schools in LaPorte, Indiana (1883–94). He established kindergartens, conducted training schools in kindergarten methods (often with his wife), and promoted manual training and the study of art.

From 1894 to 1898 Hailmann was the federal supervisor of Indian schools in Washington, D.C.; he established kindergartens for Indian children and training schools for kindergarten teachers. He was supervisor of schools in Dayton, Ohio (1898–1903), head of the department of psychology at the Chicago Normal School (later, Chicago State University) from 1904 to 1908, and professor of the history of education at the Cleveland (Ohio) Normal Training School (1909–14). In 1914 he moved to California where he served until his death in 1920 as a professor at Broadoaks Kindergarten Normal School in Pasadena.

Hailmann was a leading exponent of the doctrine of Froebel, and in 1887 translated, with a commentary, *Froebel's Education of Man*. His *Application of Psychology to the Work of Teaching* (1884) was awarded the Bicknell Prize by the American Institute of Instruction. His other writings include *Outlines of a System of Objective Teaching* (1867), *History of Pedagogy* (1870), *Kindergarten Culture in the Family and Kindergarten* (1872), *Twelve Lectures on the History of Pedagogy* (1874), *Lectures to a Mother (1876)*, *Early Education* (1878), *Four Lectures on Early Child Culture* (1880), *Primary Methods* (1887), *Laws of Childhood and Other Papers* (1889), *Constructive Form-Work* (1901), *The English Language* (with Frederick Manley, 1902), *The Laurel Primer* (1903), and *Education of the Indian* (1904). He was editor of *Erziehungsblätter* (1870–73) and *Kindergarten Messenger and New Education* (1876–83). He contributed to publications of the United States Bureau of Education and wrote widely in newspapers about education.

Hailmann was active in professional associations, including serving as the first chairman of the kindergarten section of the National Educational Association, organized in 1885. In California, he organized the Kindergarten-Primary Council of the West. The William N. Hailmann Memorial Library of the University of Southern California was dedicated in his honor. He received honorary degrees from the University of Louisville and Ohio University.

REFERENCES: *DAB; WWW (IV); Barbara Greenwood, "William Nicholas Hailmann, 1836–1920,"* in the International Kindergarten Union, Committee of Nineteen, *Pioneers of the Kindergarten in America* (New York: The Century Co., 1924).   *Robert R. Sherman*

HALDEMAN, Samuel Stehman. B. August 12, 1821, Locust Grove, Pennsylvania, to Henry and Frances (Stehman) Haldeman. M. 1835 to Mary A. Hough (or Hugh). Ch. six. D. September 10, 1880, Chickies, Pennsylvania.

Samuel Stehman Haldeman completed classical school training in Harrisburg, Pennsylvania. He entered Dickinson College in Carlisle, Pennsylvania, but returned home after two years of study and engaged in the study of nature. His father decided that he needed a practical type of employment and made him manager of a sawmill (1831–36), and he was in the iron smelting business with his brother from 1842.

Haldeman was asked by H. D. Rogers, a former Dickinson College professor, to assist in conducting geological field studies in New Jersey (1836). He next conducted surveys in Pennsylvania (1837–42). Continuing in partnership in the family iron business, he also lectured at the Franklin Institute in Philadelphia (1842–43), was professor of natural history at the University of Pennsylvania (1851–55), and lectured on geology and chemistry at the State Agricultural College of Pennsylvania (later, Pennsylvania State University) from 1855 to 1869. He also taught at Delaware College (later, the University of Delaware) in Newark (1853–58).

In 1869 Haldeman became the first professor of comparative philology at the University of Pennsylvania, serving to his death in 1880. Haldeman made significant contributions in several areas, including discovery of a new sound emitted by certain Lepidoptera, a result of an acute sense of hearing. He also identified the oldest organic remains found in Pennsylvania and conducted extensive research on American Indian dialects.

He was the author of a prize-winning essay, *Analytical Orthography* (1860), and *Elements of Latin Pronunciation* (1851), *Tours of a Chess Knight* (1864), *Affixes in Their Origin and Application* (1865), *Pennsylvania Dutch* (1872), *Outlines of Etymology* (1877), and *Word-Building* (1881). He edited the *Pennsylvania Farmers Journal* (1851–52).

Haldeman was a member of many scientific societies and was founder and president of the American Philological Society and one of the early members of the National Academy of Sciences. He received an honorary degree from the University of Pennsylvania in 1876.

REFERENCES: *AC; DAB; NCAB* (9:246); *TC; WWW* (H); *NYT,* September 12, 1880, p. 2.   *Gorman L. Miller*

HALE, Benjamin. B. November 23, 1797, Newburyport, Massachusetts, to Thomas and Alice (Little) Hale. M. April 9, 1823, to Mary Caroline King. Ch. two. D. July 15, 1863, Newburyport, Massachusetts.

Benjamin Hale was graduated with high honors from Bowdoin College in Brunswick, Maine, in 1818, taught a year at Saco (Maine) Academy, studied theology at the Andover (Massachusetts) Theological Seminary, became a tutor at Bowdoin in 1820, and received a license to preach in the Congregational church in 1822.

The Gardiner (Maine) Lyceum opened in 1823 with twenty students and Hale as principal. He developed the lyceum after Philipp von Fellenberg's manual-labor school in Switzerland. Based on Pestalozzian principles, the lyceum emphasized practical subjects, such as navigation, carpentry, and agriculture. Hale established short courses in different branches of husbandry and experimented with student government.

The lyceum declined, and Hale accepted the chair of chemistry and mineralogy at Dartmouth College in Hanover, New Hampshire, in 1827 and helped build an important collection of minerals. In 1835 his position was suddenly abolished by the college trustees. In 1828 he was ordained a priest of the Episcopal church.

Hale was the third president of the almost bankrupt Geneva (later, Hobart) College, a small Episcopalian institution at Geneva, New York (1836–58). He was an educational liberal, supporting the English course in which students could substitute modern languages for the classics. Hale served as a trustee of Geneva College during his presidency and to 1860. At the time of his resignation he was commended for his success in solving the college's financial problems.

Hale was the author of *Introduction to the Mechanical Principles of Carpentry* (1827), *Scriptural Illustrations of the Daily Morning and Evening Service* (1835), *Litany of the Protestant Episcopal Church* (1835), *Liberty and Law* (1838), *Education and Its Relation to Free Government* (1838), *Historical Notes of Geneva College* (1849), and *The Sources and Means of Education: a Lecture* (1846). He received honorary degrees from Dartmouth and Columbia colleges.

REFERENCES: *AC; DAB; NCAB* (13:39); *WWW* (H). *Norman J. Bauer*

HALE, Florence Maria. B. October 26, 1880, Athol, Massachusetts, to Henry and Anna (Perry) Hale. M. no. D. December 2, 1959, Stamford, Connecticut.

Florence M. Hale was graduated from the Athol (Massachusetts) High School (1898) and the Massachusetts State Normal School (later, Fitchburg State College) at Fitchburg (1903) and studied at the graduate level at Harvard and Columbia universities.

Hale was an elementary (1902–04) and high school English (1904–05) teacher in the Leominster, Massachusetts, schools. She served as director of teacher training for the Aroostock (Maine) State Normal School (later, University of Maine at Presque Isle) from 1905 to 1916 and was director of rural education for the state of Maine (1916–32). She was editor of *Grade Teacher* (1927–52).

Hale was the author of a number of monographs, including *How to Use the Contents of an Educational Magazine* (1930), and editor of *Classroom Posters and Decorations* (1933), *Autumn Plays and Programs* (1934), *Spring Plays and Programs* (1934), *Modern Objective Tests* (1934), and *Democracy and Patriotism* (1941).

Active in professional organizations, Hale was a member of the National

Education Association (vice-president, 1927, president, 1931–32, life director, lecturer, and radio broadcaster), the National Council of Administrative Women in Education (director), the Good Teeth Council for Children (board member), the National Motion Picture Council of America (charter member), and the board of trustees of Westbrook Junior College in Portland, Maine. She was chairman of the committee on rural education for the White House Conference on Education (1930). She was a consultant on education to the National Broadcasting Company. She received an honorary degree from Colby College (1932).

REFERENCES: *LE* (III); *NYT,* December 5, 1959, p. 23; *WWW* (III); *Grade Teacher* 77 (February 1960): 5; *The Athol Transcript,* July 8, 1931, p. 1. *John F. Ohles*

HALE, Horace Morrison. B. March 6, 1833, Hollis, New Hampshire, to John and Jane (Morrison) Hale. M. August 4, 1859, to Martha Eliza Huntington. Ch. one. D. October 24, 1901, Denver, Colorado.

Horace Morrison Hale's father died in 1852, and the family became separated. Hale taught in a country school to earn money to attend Genesee Wesleyan Seminary in Lima, New York, in 1853 and was graduated from Union College in Schenectady, New York, with the A.B. degree (1856).

Hale taught in schools at West Bloomfield, New York (1856–57), and at Nashville, Tennessee (1857–61). He moved to Detroit, Michigan, where he taught English in a German school. While in Detroit, he read law and was admitted to the bar in 1863. Moving to Colorado in 1863, Hale was principal of the Central City, Colorado, high school (1868–73 and 1877–87). He was territorial superintendent of public instruction (1873–76) and served as president of the University of Colorado (1887–92).

Hale was mayor of Central City, Colorado (1882–83), and regent of the University of Colorado (1878–84). He was president of the Charity Organization of Denver (1895–1901) and was awarded an honorary degree by Iowa Wesleyan University. The Hale Scientific Building at the University of Colorado was named in his honor.

REFERENCES: *NCAB* (6:492); *TC; Education in Colorado, 1861–1885* (Denver: News Print Co., 1885). *John F. Ohles*

HALE, William Gardner. B. February 9, 1849, Savannah, Georgia, to William Bradford and Elizabeth Scott (Jewett) Hale. M. June 13, 1883, to Harriet Knowles Swinburne. Ch. four, including Gardner Hale, artist. D. June 24, 1928, Stamford, Connecticut.

William Gardner Hale was graduated from Phillips Academy in Exeter, New Hampshire, and attended Harvard University, from which he was graduated with the A.B. degree (1870). After graduation he was a fellow

(1870–71) and tutor (1871–76 and 1877–80). He studied in Germany at Leipzig and Göttingen (1876–77), but his health failed and he returned to the United States.

In 1880 Hale became professor of Latin at Cornell University in Ithaca, New York. He was appointed head of the department of Latin at the new University of Chicago in 1892 and remained there until his retirement in 1919. He then moved to Stamford, Connecticut. He was the first director of the American School of Classical Studies established in Rome, Italy, in 1895.

Hale used a dialogue form of instruction and wrote *The Art of Reading Latin: How to Teach It* (1887). He also was the author of *The Sequence of Tenses in Latin* (1887–88), *A Latin Grammar* (with Carl D. Buck, 1903), and *First Latin Book* (1907). He was editor of *American Journal of Archaeology* (1897–99), associate editor of *Classical Review* (1895–1907), *Classical Quarterly,* and joint editor of Cornell University Studies in Classical Philology (1887–92).

Browsing in the Vatican Library, Hale discovered a manuscript by Catullus that had been assumed lost because it did not appear in the master catalog. He named his discovery *R* and compared it in importance with the Mss. *O* (Oxford) and *G* (Paris), other fragments of the original manuscript. He decided he wanted to trace the history of the entire Catullus manuscript but died before the task was completed. Hale received honorary degrees from American and Scottish universities.

REFERENCES: *DAB; NCAB* (23:80); *TC; WWW* (I); *NYT,* June 24, 1928, p. 26.   *LeRoy Barney*

HALEY, Margaret Angela. B. November 15, 1861, Joliet, Illinois, to Michael and Elizabeth (Tiernan) Haley. M. no. D. January 5, 1939, Chicago, Illinois.

Margaret Haley was graduated from St. Angela's Convent high school in Morris, Illinois, and attended a summer institute at the State Normal School in Bloomington, Illinois. She began her teaching career at the age of sixteen in a country school in Dresden Heights, Illinois, and taught in Joliet, Lake Township, and at the Hendricks Elementary School in Chicago.

Haley resigned her position in 1901 to become the full-time business representative of the Chicago Federation of Teachers, a group of women elementary teachers who had united in 1897 to protest low salaries and an inadequate pension plan. She continued in that position until her death in 1939.

In 1900 Haley spearheaded a tax case involving the failure of the Illinois State Board of Equalization to tax five Chicago utility companies fully. After protracted litigation, the teachers were compensated in salary increases from the new funds that their action had won for the Chicago school board. Haley and the federation gained power in Chicago and Illinois politics.

Haley prevented the board of education from selling school-fund lands without the consent of the city council, lobbied for the 1928 and 1929 tax reassessment programs in Chicago, and traveled to Washington, D.C., in 1933 and helped secure a loan from the Reconstruction Finance Corporation so that Chicago could pay its teachers.

Haley was a champion of the classroom teacher. She prevented a move toward automatic presidential power at the 1903 National Educational Association (NEA) convention. The election of Ella Flagg Young (*q.v.*) to the NEA presidency in 1910 was a personal triumph for Haley. However, she became disillusioned with the organization and in 1918 withdrew her membership because classroom teachers were still largely excluded from its hierarchy. Instead, she encouraged the teachers' federation to associate with the League of Teacher Associations, which met annually at the same time as the NEA. Haley strove to make teachers a major political force.

Haley was active in the feminist movement, the Public Ownership League, and the Women's Trade Union-League. She affiliated the teachers' federation with the Chicago Federation of Labor in 1902. Although this association ended in 1917, she continued to support labor political candidates and causes and helped organize the American Federation of Teachers in 1916.

REFERENCES: *NAW; NYT,* January 8, 1939, p. 43; George S. Counts (*q.v.*), *School and Society in Chicago* (New York: Harcourt, Brace and Co., 1928); George Creel, "Why Chicago's Teachers Unionized," *Harper's Weekly* (June 19, 1915): 598–99.   *Robert H. Truman*

HALL, Granville Stanley. B. February 1, 1844, Ashfield, Massachusetts, to Granville Bascom and Abigail (Beals) Hall. M. September 1879 to Cornelia Fisher. M. July 1899 to Florence E. Smith. Ch. two. D. April 24, 1924, Worcester, Massachusetts.

G. Stanley Hall, psychologist, philosopher, educator, and college president, was graduated with the B.A. (1867) and M.A. (1870) degrees from Williams College in Williamstown, Massachusetts, and received the Ph.D. degree (1878) from Harvard University. He studied at Union Theological Seminary in New York City (1867–68). With support from Henry W. Sage, Hall studied theology and philosophy in Germany and reported the Franco-Prussian War for American newspapers and periodicals (1868–71).

Hall taught literature and philosophy at Antioch College in Yellow Springs, Ohio (1872–76), and English at Harvard (1876–77). Wilhelm Max Wundt's book, *Grundzuge der Physiologischen Psychologie,* aroused his interest in psychology. He returned to Germany in 1878 to study physics with Hermann Helmholtz, physiology with Karl Ludwig, and experimental psychology with Wundt. He returned to Massachusetts as a lecturer in psychology at Harvard and Williams College (1880–81).

Hall joined the faculty at Johns Hopkins University in Baltimore, Maryland (1881–88). In 1882 he was given a special lectureship and was granted a thousand dollars to establish a psychological laboratory at Johns Hopkins. He continued his research in experimental psychology and attracted eminent scholars as students, including James McKeen Cattell *(q.v.)* and John Dewey *(q.v.)*.

By 1888 Hall had gained a reputation as an educational writer and critic and was chosen the first head of Clark University in Worcester, Massachusetts. On the opening of the university in 1889, he became president and professor of psychology, positions he maintained until he retired in 1919.

Some of Hall's most important writings were *Aspects of German Culture* (1881), *The Contents of Children's Minds* (1883), *Hints Toward a Select and Descriptive Bibliography of Education* (with John Mansfield, 1886), *Adolescence: Its Psychology and Its Relation to Physiology, Anthropology, Sociology, Sex, Crime, Religion, and Education* (two volumes, 1904), in which he coined three hundred new words, *Youth—Its Education, Regimen, and Hygiene* (1907), *Educational Problems* (two volumes, 1911), *Founders of Modern Psychology* (1912), *Jesus Christ, in the Light of Psychology* (1917), *Morale* (1920), *Recreations of a Psychologist* (1920), *Senescence* (1922), and *Life and Confessions of a Psychologist* (1923). To provide an outlet for writings in the area of child study he founded *The Pedagogical Seminary* (editor, 1891–1924). He also founded *American Journal of Psychology* (editor, 1887–1921), *American Journal of Religious Psychology and Education* (editor, 1904–15), and *Journal of Applied Psychology* (editor, 1917–24).

Hall was a founder of the Child Study Association of America in 1888 and was the first president of the American Psychological Association (1881). He presided over a congress of experimental psychology held during the World's Columbian Exposition in Chicago, Illinois, in 1893. He was a fellow of the American Association for the Advancement of Science and was a member of other professional and learned groups. He was the recipient of three honorary degrees.

REFERENCES: *DAB; EB; NCAB* (39:469); *TC; WWW* (I); *NYT,* April 25, 1924, p. 17; Lorine Pruette, *G. Stanley Hall: A Biography of a Mind* (New York: D. Appleton and Co., 1926); Dorothy Ross, *G. Stanley Hall: The Psychologist as Prophet* (Chicago: University of Chicago Press, 1972).   *Harold G. MacDermot*

HALL, Samuel Read. B. October 27, 1795, Croyden, New Hampshire, to Samuel Read and Elizabeth (Hall) Hall. M. June 17, 1823, to Mary Dascomb. M. June 6, 1837, to Mary Holt. Ch. ten. D. June 24, 1877, near Burlington, Vermont.

Samuel Read Hall received his only formal education pursuing a course of classical study at Kimball Union Academy in Meriden, New Hampshire. He suffered poor health as a child and experienced family financial misfortunes.

In 1814, at the age of nineteen, Hall began to teach school in Rumford, Maine. He has been credited with the first use of blackboards for instructional purposes. About 1822 he was principal of an academy in Fitchburg, Massachusetts, and was licensed as a Congregational minister. He engaged in missionary work and established a training school for teachers at what became Concord (Vermont) Academy in 1823. This school is credited with being the first normal school in the United States.

For the next forty-five years, Hall continued his career as minister, teacher, writer, and lecturer. He was principal of Phillips Academy at Andover, Massachusetts (1830–37), and Holmes (Plymouth, New Hampshire) Academy (1837–40). He served a church in Craftsbury, Vermont (1840–58), and was principal of the Craftsbury Academy (1840–46), where he instituted a teacher seminary. He served churches in Vermont at Browington (1858–67) and Granby (1872–75).

Hall lectured widely and wrote in areas of geography, history, and education. His principal written works include *The Child's Assistant* (1827), *Lectures on School-Keeping* (1828), *Lectures to Female Teachers on School-Keeping* (1832), *The Grammatical Assistant* (1833), *A School History of the United States* (1833), *The Arithmetical Manual* (1832), *The Geography and History of Vermont* (1864), and *The Alphabet of Geology* (1868).

Hall was awarded honorary degrees by Dartmouth College (1838) and the University of Vermont (1865). He was one of the organizers of the American Institute of Instruction (1830), an early educational association.

REFERENCES: *AC; DAB; NCAB* (3:504); *TC; WWW* (H). *J. K. Ward*

HALL, Willard. B. December 24, 1780, Westford, Massachusetts, to Willis and Mehetable (Poole) Hall. M. 1806 to Junia Killen. M. 1829 to Harriet Hilliard. Ch. one. D. May 10, 1875, Wilmington, Delaware.

Willard Hall was a lawyer, congressman, jurist, and an advocate of public education in the state of Delaware. In 1792 he entered the academy at Westford, Massachusetts, which had been established mainly through his grandfather's efforts. He was graduated from Harvard University in 1799. In March 1800 he became a law student in the office of Samuel Dana of Groton, Massachusetts, and in March 1803 was admitted to the bar in Hillsboro, New Hampshire.

Because of the large number of lawyers in New England, he moved to

Delaware in April 1803 and was admitted to the Delaware bar. Hall served as secretary of state for Delaware (1812–14)and was elected to Congress on the Republican ticket, serving two terms (1817–21). On May 6, 1823, he was appointed a United States district judge by President James Monroe, a post he held until he retired on December 6, 1871. At the request of the state legislature in 1824, Hall revised the laws of Delaware. In 1831 he was elected a delegate to the constitutional convention on the ticket of both parties.

Hall was the founder and guardian of public school instruction in Delaware. He advocated the establishment of public schools when he was secretary of state in 1822; in 1829, at the request of the state legislature, he authored a bill providing for a school system for the state. The school law of 1829 recognized the principle of general free education and authorized the counties to establish and maintain free schools. The counties were divided into school districts with taxing power for educational purposes.

In 1852, the board of education in Wilmington established a separate school system for the city. Hall presided over this board from its organization in 1852 until he announced his retirement on March 28, 1870, closing a record of forty-eight years of service to the educational interests of the state. Hall took an active part in the establishment and management of the Delaware Society for the Education of the Colored People.

REFERENCES: *AC; DAB; NCAB* (11:500); *TC; WWW* (H); *NYT,* May 12, 1875, p. 6; J. Thomas Scharf, *History of Delaware* (Philadelphia: L. J. Richards and Co., 1888), pp. 555–60.   *C. Roy Rylander*

HALLECK, Reuben Post. B. February 8, 1859, Rocky Point, Long Island, New York, to Luther and Fannie (Tuthill) Halleck. M. October 29, 1896, to Annie Ainslie. Ch. none. D. December 24, 1936, Louisville, Kentucky.

Reuben Post Halleck attended General Russell's Military School in New Haven, Connecticut, and was graduated from Yale University with the B.A. (1881) and A.M. (1896) degrees. He was principal of Cherry Valley (New York) Academy (1881–83) and instructor (1883–86) and principal (1896–1912) at Louisville (Kentucky) Male High School. Halleck established a reputation as an outstanding leader in secondary education.

In 1861 the Kentucky General Assembly had chartered Male High School, granting it "all the rights and privileges of a university." Until 1912 graduates of Male received the B.A. degree and outstanding students were sometimes awarded the M.A. degree. Halleck sought to elevate the high standards at Male and also stressed physical development and sports, which previously had no supervision or regulation of games or players. Halleck resigned as principal of Male High School in 1915 to devote more time to writing textbooks.

Halleck wrote many books, including *Psychology and Psychic Culture*

(1895), *The Education of the Central Nervous System* (1896), *History of American Literature* (1911), *New English Literature* (1913), and *Readings from Literature* (with Elizabeth Graeme Barbour, 1915). Written with Juliette Frantz were *History of Our Country* (1923), *Our Nation's Heritage* (1925), *Founders of Our Nation* (1929), *Makers of Our Nation* (1930), and *Our United States* (1935). He was an advisory editor to *School Review*.

A member of a number of professional and learned societies, Halleck was a fellow of the American Association for the Advancement of Science, a member of the National Society for the Scientific Study of Education (president, 1906–07), and was active in the National Educational Association as president of the department of secondary education (1904) and chairman of the Committee of Seventeen to consider professional preparation of secondary school teachers. He was awarded an honorary degree by the University of Kentucky in 1912.

REFERENCES: *AC; LE* (I); *NCAB* (27:79); *WWW* (I); Pat Bolling, "Reuben Post Halleck : A Biography" (Master's thesis, University of Louisville, 1968); Charles Carpenter, *History of American School Books* (Philadelphia: University of Pennsylvania Press, 1963); I. L. Kandel *(q.v.),* *A History of Secondary Education* (Boston: Houghton Mifflin, 1930).

Frank H. Stallings

HALLOWELL, Anna. B. November 1, 1831, Philadelphia, Pennsylvania, to Morris Longstreth and Hannah Smith (Penrose) Hallowell. M. no. D. April 6, 1905, Philadelphia, Pennsylvania.

Anna Hallowell attended a Quaker school as a child in Philadelphia, Pennsylvania. As a young woman, she became a board member and secretary of the Home for Destitute Colored Children. During the Civil War, she converted the family home into a hospital, where she treated wounded Union soldiers, including her brothers.

After the Civil War, Hallowell engaged in relief work for refugee freedmen who had escaped to Philadelphia. With others, she organized a group that came to be known as the Society for Organizing Charity and was chartered in 1883 as the Children's Aid Society. Hallowell was active as a member of the society's committee in the care and education of dependent children. The society later became the Public Education Association, a force for reform of the Philadelphia schools.

Hallowell served on the first board of directors of the Children's Aid Society (1885–97). She was active in the Public Education Association and supported incorporation of domestic science and manual training into the school curriculum.

In 1879 Hallowell began to establish free kindergartens for Philadelphia's poor and established the Sub-Primary School Society. The kindergartens were given public financing in 1882 and taken over by the Philadelphia board of education in 1887. Hallowell was the first woman member of the Philadelphia board of education (1887–1901).

Through her position on the school board, she effected the training of teachers in home economics and manual arts and worked to improve the condition of slum schools. She supported the Woman's Medical College of Pennsylvania and efforts to improve the quality of private girls' schools.

REFERENCES: *NAW;* Anna W. Williams, "Kindergarten Movement in Philadelphia," *Kindergarten Review* (January 1905).

Barbara Ruth Peltzman

HALSTED, George Bruce. B. November 25, 1853, Newark, New Jersey, to Oliver Spencer, Jr., and Adela (Meeker) Halsted. M. June 17, 1886, to Margaret Swearingen. Ch. three. D. March 16, 1922, New York, New York.

Distinguished for introducing non-Euclidian geometry to the English-speaking world, George Bruce Halsted was the fourth generation of Halsteds to enter the College of New Jersey (later, Princeton University) in 1871. He established himself as a mathematician by winning a mathematical fellowship before receiving the A.B. degree in 1875 and the A.M. degree (1879). He studied at Columbia University College of Mines and for a short time in Berlin, Germany. He became one of the first fellows at the new Johns Hopkins University, where he received the Ph.D. degree (1879).

Halsted had a long teaching career as a tutor and instructor in post-graduate mathematics at Princeton (1879–84) and as professor of pure and applied mathematics at the University of Texas in Austin (1884–1902). He was head of the mathematics department at St. John's College in Annapolis, Maryland (1903–04), and professor at Kenyon College in Gambier, Ohio (1904–06), and Colorado State Normal School (later, University of Northern Colorado) in Greeley (1906–12). His last ten years were spent in electrical engineering, continuing to translate mathematical classics, and suffering ill health.

Halsted's most productive years were his nearly two decades at the University of Texas. He translated the works of many eminent European mathematicians from German, French, Italian, Latin and Russian. He wrote *Bibliography of Hyper-Space and Non-Euclidian Geometry* (1878), *Metrical Geometry: An Elementary Treatise of Mensuration* (1881), *Elements of Geometry* (1885), *Elementary Synthetic Geometry* (1892), *Pure Projective Geometry* (1895), *Non-Euclidian Geometry for Teachers* (1900), *Synthetic Projective Geometry* (1906), *On the Foundation and Technique of Arithmetic* (1911), *The Foundations of Science* (1913), and *Euclid Freed of Every Fleck* (1919). He was a collaborator in mathematics for *The Century Dictionary and Cyclopedia.*

He was an active member of numerous American and foreign mathematical and scientific organizations.

REFERENCES: *AC; DAB; DSB; NCAB* (3:518); *TC; WWW* (I); Leonard E. Dickson, "Biography: Dr. George Bruce Halsted," *American Mathematical Monthly* 1 (October 1894): 337–40; Arthur M. Humphreys, "George Bruce Halsted," *Science* 56 (August 11, 1922): 160–61.

D. Richard Bowles

HALSTED, William Stewart. B. September 23, 1852, New York, New York, to William Mills, Jr., and Mary Louisa (Haines) Halsted. M. June 4, 1890, to Caroline Hampton. Ch. none. D. September 7, 1922, Baltimore, Maryland.

William Stewart Halsted, a great American surgeon, prepared for college at Phillips Academy in Andover, Massachusetts, and was graduated from Yale College with the A.B. degree (1874). He distinguished himself at Yale as an athlete and captain of the football team rather than as a scholar. He received the M.D. degree (1877) from the College of Physicians and Surgeons of Columbia University, where he led the graduating class and received a prize for scholarship. He served as a surgical intern at Bellevue Hospital and as house physician for several months at the New York Hospital. In the fall of 1878 Halsted traveled to Europe for two years of study in Vienna, Austria, and Wurzburg, Leipzig, and Halle, Germany.

Halsted returned to New York from Europe in 1880 and started an active surgical practice, serving on the staffs of six widely separated hospitals. Using himself as an experimental subject in 1885, he became addicted to cocaine, which brought to an end his clinical career in New York; after two long periods of hospitalization, Halsted overcame the addiction.

In December 1886 Halsted went to Baltimore and worked in William H. Welch's *(q.v.)* laboratory. He was part of the group that started Johns Hopkins Medical School in 1899 and became professor of surgery in the university and chief of the surgical service in the hospital. He held these positions until his death in 1922.

Halsted's most significant contributions to medical progress were in the field of surgery. He developed a process emphasizing cleanliness and deliberate procedures with special care in the handling of tissues. He discovered the procedure for anesthetizing a region of the body by injecting cocaine into a nerve. He developed surgical procedures for breast cancer, hernia, and thyroid gland, and blood vessels. As an educator, Halsted introduced the concept of surgical residencies, which is now the established norm in American surgical clinics. He believed that competent surgeons could be trained only by years of experience under the guidance of more experienced surgeons.

A fellow of the American Surgical Association, the American Association for the Advancement of Science, and the American Society of Experimental Pathology, Halsted was a member of many other American and foreign professional associations. He received several honorary degrees and the gold medal of the National Dental Association in 1922.

REFERENCES: *DAB; DSB; EB; NCAB* (20:209); *WWW* (I); W. G. Mac-Callum, *William Stewart Halsted–Surgeon* (Baltimore: The Johns Hopkins Press, 1930); John H. Talbott, *A Biographical History of Medicine* (New York: Grune and Stratton, 1970).   *Richard M. Coger*

HAMERSCHLAG, Arthur Acton. B. November 22, 1869, Omaha, Nebraska, to William and Francesca H. (Brummel) Hamerschlag. M. December 23, 1901, to Elizabeth Ann Lollast. Ch. one. D. July 20, 1927, New York, New York.

Arthur Acton Hamerschlag was educated in public schools in Omaha, Nebraska, and New York City and under private tutors. He did engineering fieldwork in the United States, Cuba, and Mexico (1888–92).

Hamerschlag was a consulting engineer in New York City and engaged in experiments that led to developments in cathode rays and induction coils, and he invented a front-wheel drive motor. He was an instructor of mechanical drawing (1892) and superintendent (1893–1904) at St. George's Evening School in New York City. From 1903 he organized and directed the establishment of Carnegie Technical Schools in Pittsburgh, Pennsylvania. The College of Industries was organized in 1905, followed by colleges of engineering and fine arts and the Margaret Morrison Carnegie College for Women. The name was changed to the Carnegie Institute of Technology in 1912, and a state charter and authority to award academic degrees were granted. A division of general studies, a bureau of metallurgical research, and the Langley Laboratory of Aeronautics were added.

An innovative administrator, Hamerschlag supported training students to engage in practical application of their studies and established a professionally equipped School of Dramatic Arts where students gained experience in play production. He opened one of the first student health departments. By his retirement from Carnegie Institute (later, Carnegie-Mellon University) in 1922, about four thousand students were enrolled instructed by about 280 faculty members. Hamerschlag served as president of the Research Corporation in New York City (1922–27) and also was an industrial consultant.

Hamerschlag was a member of many professional organizations. He was a member of the Pittsburgh City Planning Commission and president of the Smoke and Dust Abatement League of Pittsburgh (1914–22). He was the recipient of several honorary degrees.

REFERENCES: *NCAB* (23:52); *NYT,* July 21, 1927, p. 21; *WWW* (I).
John F. Ohles

HAMLIN, Cyrus. B. January 5, 1811, Waterford, Maine, to Hannibal and Susan (Faulkner) Hamlin. M. September 3, 1838, to Henrietta Loraine Jackson. M. May 18, 1852, to Harriet Martha Lovell. M. November 5,

1859, to Mary Eliza Tenney. Ch. six. D. August 8, 1900, Portland, Maine.

Cyrus Hamlin attended Bowdoin College in Brunswick, Maine, receiving the bachelor's (1834) and A.M. (1837) degrees. He was graduated from Bangor (Maine) Theological Seminary in 1837. Hamlin worked for the American Board of Commissioners for Foreign Missions. His first missionary and teaching assignment was in Constantinople, Turkey, and led to his founding of Bebek Seminary on the Bosporus Sea in 1840.

While serving as director of Bebek Seminary to 1860, Hamlin translated textbooks for use in Armenian schools and founded workshops and manufacturing sites to provide employment for needy Armenian students and persecuted Armenian Protestants. During the 1850s, as the suffering and malnutrition of soldiers of the Crimean War intensified, Hamlin was called upon to aid Florence Nightingale by securing needed supplies, building washing machines, and establishing sanitary bread-baking facilities. With the funds Hamlin earned from such efforts, he founded several churches and made an initial unsuccessful attempt to establish a college in the Middle East.

Resigning from Bebek Seminary in 1860 after a series of disagreements with the American Board of Commissioners for Foreign Missions, Hamlin returned to the United States where he met a wealthy New Yorker, Christopher Rhinelander Robert, who was impressed with the minister's work in Turkey. In 1861 Robert provided funds with which Hamlin purchased Roumeli Hissar, the first site of Robert College. Hamlin presided over the administration of the school, campaigned internationally for funds, and supervised the later construction of the college on a permanent site at Bebek. After sixteen years, Hamlin was dismissed from the presidency by Robert in 1877 after a disagreement between the two men. Founded as a private American college, Robert College later became Bosporus University, a state-controlled institution.

Hamlin returned to New England in 1877 and spent the next several years teaching and writing. From 1881 through 1886 he distinguished himself as president of Middlebury (Vermont) College, seeing the institution through a difficult five-year period.

Hamlin was the author of *Among the Turks* (1878) and *My Life and Times* (1893). He received several honorary degrees.

REFERENCES: *AC; DAB; NCAB* (10:491); *NYT,* August 9, 1900, p. 7; *TC; WWW* (I); Cyrus Hamlin, *Among the Turks* (Boston: Congregational Sunday-School and Publishing Society, 1893).   *Patricia Kern McIntyre*

HAMMOND, William Gardiner. B. May 3, 1829, Newport, Rhode Island, to William Gardiner and Sarah Tillinghast (Bull) Hammond. M. May 26, 1852, to Lydia Bradford Torrey. M. May 3, 1865, to Juliet Martha Roberts. Ch. one. D. April 12, 1894, St. Louis, Missouri.

William Gardiner Hammond was educated formally at preparatory schools and informally by his father and the local Congregational minister. Entering Amherst (Massachusetts) College, he excelled in his studies and was graduated in 1849 as salutatorian. He considered a career as a scholar and teacher of literature but chose to study law in Samuel E. Johnson's Brooklyn, New York, office. He was admitted to the bar in 1851 and practiced law in Brooklyn. He spent three years in Europe (1856–59), recovering his health and studying comparative and historical law at Heidelberg (Germany) University.

On his return to the United States, Hammond resumed the practice of law in Anamosa, Iowa. He moved to Des Moines in 1866 and engaged in legal projects,completing a digest of Iowa supreme court reports, establishing and editing the *Western Jurist*, serving on a commission to recodify the laws of Iowa, and helping to found the Iowa Law School. When the school became the law department of Iowa University in 1869, Hammond moved to Iowa City as the university's first chancellor and head of the law department (1869–81). In 1881 he became dean of the Washington University Law School in St. Louis, Missouri, a position he held until his death in 1894.

Hammond was considered the most eminent American authority on the history of common law. A legal educator, he initiated a program using selected cases to develop the principles underlying the judicial process. Concerned with the quality of legal instruction, he consistently urged improved standards for law schools as chairman of the American Bar Association's committee on legal education (1889–94). He advocated a historical study of the natural development of law as the most productive approach to legal understanding.

Hammond prepared an introduction for Thomas Collett Sandar's *Institutes of Justinian* (1876), edited Francis Lieber's *Legal and Political Hermeneutics* (1880), and incorporated his research on common law history into an annotated edition of *Blackstone's Commentaries* (1890).

REFERENCES: *DAB; NCAB* (9:322); *TC; WWW* (H); Emlin McClain, "William G. Hammond," in William Draper Lewis, ed., *Great American Lawyers* (Philadelphia: John C. Winston Co., 1909), 8:189–237; Edward H. Stiles, *Recollections and Sketches of Notable Lawyers and Public Men of Early Iowa* (Des Moines: Homestead Publishing Co., 1916).

Ralph E. Glauert

HAMRIN, Shirley Austin. B. August 26, 1900, St. Paul, Minnesota, to Christopher and Sarah (Hays) Hamrin. M. August 15, 1924, to Margaret Hanson. M. February 21, 1934, to Hazel Sundell. Ch. three. D. March 15, 1958, Evanston, Illinois.

Shirley A. Hamrin, son of a Methodist minister, received his early

education in the public schools of Tracy, Minnesota. After receiving the
B.A. degree (1921) from Hamline University in St. Paul, Minnesota, he
earned the M.A. degree (1926) from the University of Chicago and the
Ph.D. degree (1931) from Northwestern University in Evanston, Illinois.

Upon graduation from Hamline, Hamrin served in Minnesota as a high
school teacher at Long Prairie, dean of a junior college in Winnebago, and
high school principal at Moorhead. In 1925 he joined the staff of Moorhead
State Teachers College (later, State College) in the department of education. Hamrin became a member of the faculty of Northwestern University
in 1929 and remained there until his death in 1958. He served the university
in various capacities, including director of summer session (1939–42) and
director of University College (1940–43).

During his tenure at Northwestern, Hamrin was active in the development and improvement of guidance programs for secondary schools. In
addition to numerous articles and book reviews, Hamrin authored a
number of books on educational topics and, particularly, the training of
guidance personnel. Among his books were *Organization and Administrative Control in High Schools* (1932), *Co-Curricular Activities in Elementary Schools* (with H. J. Otto, 1937), *Guidance in Secondary Schools*
(with C. E. Erickson, 1939), *Making Good in High School* (with L. McCul-
loch, 1939), *Guidance Manual for Teachers* (with Erickson, 1939), *Guidance Practices in Public High Schools* (with Erickson and M. O'Brien,
1940), *Teachers' Manual for Use of Occupational Materials* (1945), *Guidance Talks to Teachers* (1947), *Counseling Adolescents* (with B. Paulson,
1949), *Chats with Teachers About Counseling* (1950), *Initiating and Administering Guidance Services* (1953), and *Guidance Talks to Students*
(with Hubert W. Houghton, 1960). He also edited with F. S. Endicott
Improving Guidance and Personnel Services Through Research (1946).

He was a member of professional associations and received an honorary
degree from Hamline University.

REFERENCES: *LE* (III); *NCAB* (47:534); *WWAE* (XIV); *WWW* (III).

Donna H. Wernz

HANCHETT, Henry Granger. B. August 29, 1853, Syracuse, New York, to
Milton Waldo and Martha Anna (Huntington) Hanchett. M. June 22, 1886,
to Ophelia Murphy. M. February 22, 1896, to Grace Mather. D. August 19,
1918, Siasconset, Massachusetts.

Henry Granger Hanchett, physician, musician, and teacher, received his
grammar school education in the public schools of Syracuse, New York. At
the age of seven he played the piano and at sixteen was a church organist.
Hanchett studied medicine and received the M.D. degree (1884) from the
Homeopathic College in New York City. He practiced medicine for a short
time.

Hanchett directed the piano department at Martha Washington College in Abington, Virginia (1876–78), and Beethoven Conservatory in St. Louis, Missouri (1880–81). He was professor of musical analysis and history at Metropolitan College of Music in New York City (1890–94) and directed music departments at Adelphi College (later, University in Garden City) in Brooklyn, New York (1900–04) and National Park Seminary in Washington, D.C. (1907–10). He directed the normal department at Brenau Conservatory (later, College) in Gainesville, Florida (1913–15), and founded and directed the Orlando (Florida) School of Musical Art (1917–18).

Hanchett gave free lectures in New York City (1889–1909) and lectured at the Brooklyn Institute of Arts and Sciences (1895–1904), directed music at several Chautauqua schools, and was director of choral societies in New York and New Jersey. He was organist at the Church of the Ascension (1884–87) and Marble Collegiate Church (1889–93) in New York City and the Central Congregational Church in Brooklyn (1893–98).

Hanchett invented the sostenuto or third tone sustaining pedal for grand pianos and gave many lecture-recitals on Ludwig van Beethoven. He was the composer of "A Te Deumanda Benedictus for Chorus" and the author of *Teaching as a Science* (1882), *The Elements of Domestic Medicine, A Plain and Practical Handbook* (1887), *Sexual Health* (1887), and *The Art of the Musician* (1905).

REFERENCES: *DAB; WWW* (I).   *Joan Duff Kise*

HANCOCK, John. B. February 18, 1825, near Point Pleasant, Ohio, to David and n.a. (Roberts) Hancock. M. n.a. D. June 1, 1891, Columbus, Ohio.

John Hancock, prominent Ohio educator, was educated in the Clermont Academy and attended Farmer's College at College Hill near Cincinnati, Ohio. He began teaching at the age of nineteen in country schools in Clermont County and at schools in the Ohio villages of Amelia, Batavia, and New Richmond. Like other teachers of his time, he also supplemented teaching with farming.

In 1850 he met Joseph Ray *(q.v.)*, who encouraged him to go to Cincinnati as first assistant in Upper Race Street School. He was promoted to principal in 1853 and in 1854 became principal of the First Intermediate School of Cincinnati, a position he held to 1864. He served as the editor of the *Journal of Progress in Education, Social Economy and the Useful Arts,* published semimonthly in Cincinnati, which encouraged the promotion of the common school. Through the *Journal,* he promoted the science of phonography (shorthand). Many articles were written in shorthand.

Hancock attended Nelson's Business College, where he also edited the college magazine, *The News and Educator.* In 1866 he became assistant in the editor's department of a Cincinnati publishing firm but moved back into the educational field in 1867 as superintendent of the Cincinnati schools; he held this position for seven years. In 1874, he moved to the same position in Dayton, Ohio, for a ten-year period.

In 1886 he was appointed by the state to manage the Ohio education exhibit at the World's Fair in New Orleans. Following his return, he became superintendent of the Chillicothe schools. In 1888 he was appointed by Governor Joseph B. Foraker as state commissioner of common schools; he was elected for a three-year term in 1889. During his tenure, the first compulsory attendance law in Ohio was passed.

Hancock was active in professional organizations, serving as a member of the Ohio Teachers Association (president, 1859), the National Educational Association (president, 1879), and the National Council of Education from its establishment in 1881. He was a frequent contributor of articles to professional journals, particularly the *Ohio Educational Monthly*. He received an honorary degree from Wooster University (1876).

REFERENCES: *NCAB* (5:553); James J. Burns, *Educational History of Ohio* (Columbus, Ohio: Historical Publishing Co., 1905), pp. 411–13; *Journal of Progress in Education* (Cincinnati, Ohio, 1861).

Sally H. Wertheim

HAND, Harold Curtis. B. January 5, 1901, Piper City, Illinois, to Curtis Judd and Margaret (Adamson) Hand. M. May 18, 1923, to Kathryn Alice Guy. Ch. one. D. June 19, 1967, Rhinelander, Wisconsin.

Harold C. Hand received the B.A. degree (1924) from Macalester College in St. Paul, Minnesota, the M.A. degree (1930) from the University of Minnesota, and the Ph.D. degree (1933) from Columbia University. He studied at the London (England) School of Economics and Political Science (1937–38).

Hand was a high school teacher at Thief River Falls, Minnesota (1924), and high school principal at Monticello, Minnesota (1924–26), and at Thief River Falls (1926–30). He was an assistant in secondary education (1930–31) and an instructor at Teachers College, Columbia University (1931–33). He was an assistant and associate professor of education at Stanford (California) University (1933–40) and professor of education at the University of Maryland (1940–42), the University of Illinois (1946–64), and the University of South Florida (1964–67). Hand was a guest lecturer at the American University in Cairo, Egypt (1943–44), and served with the Army Air Corps during World War II (1943–46). He was a consultant to city and county school systems in the United States (1934–47).

Hand was the author or coauthor of many books, including *An Appraisal of the Occupations or Life-Career Course* (1934), *High School and You* (with Irwin T. Smiley, 1937), *Neutrality in Social Education* (1940), *Appraising Guidance in Secondary Schools* (with G. N. Kefauver, *q.v.*,

1941), *What People Think About Their Schools* (1948), *Principles of Secondary Education* (1958), *Curriculum Innovations* (1966), and *National Assessment: Pro and Con* (1966). He coauthored with Margaret E. Bennett *Problems of Self-Discovery and Self-Direction* (1935), *Group Guidance in High School* (1938), *Designs in Personality* (1938), and *Beyond High School* (1938). He was editor of *Campus Activities* (with others, 1938) and *Living in the Atomic Age* (with others, 1946). He contributed to the *Illinois Secondary School Curriculum Bulletin*. He was a member of many professional organizations.

REFERENCES: *LE* (III); *WWAE* (XIII); *WWW* (V).   *John F. Ohles*

HANNA, Delphine. B. December 2, 1854, Markeson, Wisconsin, to John Vacausan and Juliet (Chadwick) Hanna. M. no. D. April 16, 1941, Coral Gables, Florida.

Delphine Hanna, pioneer physical educator, was graduated in 1874 from the Brockport (New York) State Normal School (later, State University of New York College at Brockport). As a teacher in the public schools of New York and Kansas, she became concerned over the lack of stamina in her students. She enrolled in a summer course offered in Boston by Dio Lewis *(q.v.)* but was concerned about the lack of scientific basis for physical training. She received a certificate from Sargent Normal School (1885) and stayed in Boston to study orthopedic lateral spine curvature, as well as principles of poise, at Currie School of Expression. Hanna was a student at the first Harvard Summer School of Physical Education (1887) and also enrolled in Nils Posse's *(q.v.)* Swedish gymnastics course in 1893. She received the M.D. degree (1890) from the University of Michigan and the B.A. degree (1901) from Cornell University in Ithaca, New York.

Hanna accepted a position at Oberlin (Ohio) College in 1885, which afforded her an opportunity to develop her "scientifically founded" program of physical education. She began physical examinations and anthropometric measurements that were used as data for national research in orthopedics and medical science. Hanna was director of physical education of the women's department at Oberlin College (1887–1903) where she expanded a one-year course into a program leading to the A.B. degree. In 1903 she was appointed full professor, the first professorship held by a woman in physical education. She retired in 1920 and was the first woman to receive the Carnegie pension.

Hanna was an American Association of Health, Physical Education and Recreation Award recipient in 1931. She was selected as a member of the Michigan Hall of Fame. She received an honorary degree from Oberlin College.

REFERENCES: "Brief Outline of the Life and Work of Dr. Delphine Hanna," *Research Quarterly* 12 (October 1941, Supplement): 646; Ellen

W. Gerber, *Innovators and Institutions in Physical Education* (Philadelphia: Lea and Febiger, 1971); Minnie L. Lynn, "Delphine Hanna," *Journal of Health, Physical Education, and Recreation* 31 (April 1960): 51; Deobold B. Van Dalen, Elmer D. Mitchell *(q.v.)*, and Bruce L. Bennett, *A World History of Physical Education* (New York: Prentice-Hall, 1953).

Adelaide M. Cole

HANNA, Paul Robert. B. June 21, 1902, Sioux City, Iowa, to George Archibald and Regula (Figi) Hanna. M. August 20, 1926, to Jean Shuman. Ch. three.

Paul Robert Hanna was graduated from Hamline University in St. Paul, Minnesota (1924). He received the M.A. (1924) and Ph.D. (1929) degrees from Teachers College, Columbia University.

He was superintendent of schools in West Winfield, New York (1925–27). At Columbia University, he served as a research associate at the Lincoln School (1928–35) and as an assistant professor of education (1930–35). With James Mendenhall, Hanna created a supplement for social studies classes entitled *Building America,* which was published on a monthly basis. In 1935 he went to the new Stanford University School of Education under Elwood P. Cubberly *(q.v.).* Hanna was awarded an endowed chair, the Lee J. Jacks Professor of Childhood Education (1954–68).

Hanna's publications include *Arithmetic Problem Solving* (1929), *Wonder Flights of Long Ago* (with M. E. Barry, 1930), Everyday-life-Stories Series (with Genevieve Anderson and William S. Gray, 1935–39), *Pioneering in Ten Communities* (with I. James Quillen, *q.v.,* and Gladys L. Potter, 1940), *Making the Goods We Need* (with I. James Quillen and Paul B. Sears, 1943), *Cross-Country; Geography for Children* (with Clyde F. Kohn, 1950), *Building Spelling Power* (with Jean S. Hanna, 1956), *In the Neighborhood* (with Genevieve Anderson Hoyt, 1958), *In City, Town, and Country* (with others, 1959), *In All Our States* (with Clyde F. Kohn and Robert A. Lively, 1961), *In the Americas* (with Clyde F. Kohn and Robert A. Lively, 1962), *A Great Frank Lloyd Wright House* (with Jean Hanna, 1963), *Geography in the Teaching of Social Studies* (with others, 1965), and *Spelling: Structure and Strategies* (with Richard E. Hodges and Jean S. Hanna, 1971).

During World War II he served in planning and consulting roles for the War Department, State Department, and educational organizations. He was active in international education, was a United Nations Educational, Scientific, and Cultural Organization consultant in the Philippines (1949), director of education for the United States Mutual Security Agency Philippine Mission (1952–53), and a consultant on German and Panama Canal Zone education (1947). He founded the Stanford International Development Education Center and was director (1963–68). He was a member of many educational organizations.

REFERENCES: *CA* (45–48); *LE* (V); *WW* (XXXVI); *WWAE* (XXI).

Murry R. Nelson

HANSON, Howard Harold. B. October 28, 1896, Wahoo, Nebraska, to Hans and Hilma (Eckstrom) Hanson. M. July 24, 1946, to Margaret Elizabeth Nelson. Ch. none.

Howard Hanson's mother was his first music teacher. As a student at Luther College in Wahoo, Nebraska, he learned Swedish folk songs and Lutheran chorales. He studied music at the University of Nebraska, the Institute of Musical Art in New York, and Northwestern University in Evanston, Illinois, where he received the Bachelor of Music degree (1916).

Hanson became professor of theory and composition at the College of the Pacific in San Jose, California (1916), and was dean of the Conservatory of Fine Arts (1919–21). During study in Rome, Italy (1921–24), Hanson won the Prix de Rome of the American Academy and composed his first major musical works, including the symphony *Nordic.* In 1924 he was invited to Rochester, New York, to direct the *Nordic* with the Rochester Philharmonic Orchestra. He met George Eastman and Rush Rhees, then president of the University of Rochester, and agreed to become director of the newly organized Eastman School of Music, a post he held for forty years. Eastman became one of the largest and most prestigious music schools in the country; Hanson was one of America's foremost music educators.

At Eastman Hanson began a composers' laboratory, which allowed beginner and amateur composers to exhibit their work. The laboratory developed into the American Composer's Concerts, an annual festival of American chamber, choral, symphonic, and stage music. Hanson was particularly committed to American music. In 1958 he organized a student orchestra, the Eastman Philharmonia, which toured Europe, the Soviet Union, and the Middle East (1961–62). On his retirement from the Eastman School of Music (1964), Hanson assumed the directorship of the Institute of American Music.

In addition to *Nordic,* Hanson wrote other symphonies, including *Romantic* (1930), his most successful work, *Requiem* (1943), for which he received the Pulitzer Prize, and *Sinfonia Sacra* (1955). He wrote *Merry Mount* (1934), an opera commissioned by the Metropolitan Opera Company, an unusual distinction for an American composer. He composed many musical selections in a wide variety of forms. Hanson also wrote *Harmonic Materials of Modern Music* (1960), a text for advanced music students.

Hanson was active in professional associations, serving as president and chairman of the Commission of Graduate Study of the National Association of Schools of Music and a member of the examining jury of the American Academy in Rome. He received many honorary degrees and other honors, including the Pulitzer Prize (1944) and the George Foster Peabody (1946) and Huntington Hartford Foundation (1959) awards.

REFERENCES: *CB* (October 1941 and September 1966); *EB; LE* (III); *NCAB* (F: 73); *WW* (XXVIII); *WWAE* (XI); Eric Blom, ed., *Grove's Dictionary of Music and Musicians* (New York: St. Martin's Press, 1954), vol. 4; David Ewen, *The World of Twentieth Century Music* (Englewood Cliffs, N.J.: Prentice-Hall, 1968). *Barbara Braverman*

HANUS, Paul Henry. B. March 14, 1855, Hermsdorf, Upper Silesia, Prussia, to Gustav and Ida (Aust) Hanus. M. August 10, 1881, to Charlotte Hoskins. Ch. one. D. December 14, 1941, Cambridge, Massachusetts.

Paul Hanus came to the United States from Prussia in 1859 with his widowed mother, who went to Mineral Point, Wisconsin, to marry Robert George, a mining engineer. His stepfather supported him throughout school and helped him find jobs where he learned the pharmaceutical trade. Hanus attended public and Episcopal schools in Wisconsin, New York, and Colorado. He entered Platteville (Wisconsin) Normal School (later, University of Wisconsin—Platteville) but left in the third year before completing the course. He studied mathematics and sciences at the University of Michigan and received the B.S. degree (1878).

Hanus was a druggist in Denver, Colorado, for a year and taught mathematics and science (1878–86) and was principal (1886–90) in a Denver high school and a lecturer in teachers' institutes in Colorado. In 1890 he became the first professor of pedagogy at Colorado State Normal School (later, University of Northern Colorado) at Greeley.

Hanus organized Unitarian churches in several Colorado communities, including one where the pastor was Samuel Atkins Eliot, son of Charles W. Eliot *(q.v.),* president of Harvard University. Charles Eliot invited Hanus to organize a normal department at Harvard in 1891. Hanus continued at Harvard to his retirement in 1921. Despite doubts of some faculty at Harvard that education could be taught, Hanus established courses for credit in education, a separate education department, a cooperative program with Radcliffe College for teacher training, and the Harvard Graduate School of Education in 1920. He directed a number of school studies, including the New York City system (1911–12) and Hampton Institute (1917–20). The New York City study brought him to the notice of Abraham Flexner *(q.v.)* and the General Education Board, which donated half a million dollars to establish the Harvard Graduate School of Education.

Hanus was the author of *Elements of Determinants* (1886), *Geometry in the Grammar School* (1893), *Educational Aims and Educational Values*

(1899), *A Modern School* (1904), *Beginnings in Industrial Education and Other Educational Discussions* (1908), *School Efficiency: A Constructive Study Applied to Education* (1913), *School Administration and School Reports* (1920), *Opportunity and Accomplishment in Secondary Education* (1926), and his autobiography, *Adventuring in Education* (1937). He was on the editorial board of *School Review* (1906–15) and participated in editing *Educational Administration and Supervision* (1915–17).

He studied Georg Kerschensteiner's vocational continuation schools in Berlin and was chairman of the Massachusetts State Commission on Industrial Education (1906–09), chairman of the executive board of the Boston Vocational Bureau (1909–17), and a member of the Massachusetts State Board of Education (1909–19). Hanus founded the Harvard Teachers Association in 1891 and was the founder and president of the New England and the National Society of College Teachers of Education (1909–10), and vice-president of section L of the American Association for the Advancement of Science. He was the president of the Colorado Teachers Association (1889) and the Massachusetts Schoolmasters Club (1903–04). He was a trustee of Wellesley College (1916–36) and International College in Izmir, Turkey (1930–35). In 1914 he traveled to New Zealand with a group studying that country's educational system. He received honorary degrees from the universities of Michigan and Colorado.

REFERENCES: *DAB* (supp. 3); *LE* (I); *NCAB* (35:165); *WWAE* (II); *WWW* (I); Paul H. Hanus, *Adventuring in Education* (Cambridge: Harvard University Press, 1937); *NYT,* December 15, 1941, p. 19.

Robert R. Sherman

HARAP, Henry. B. November 29, 1893, Austria, to Moses and Yetta (Harap) Harap. M. August 2, 1929, to Joan Chater. Ch. four.

Henry Harap came to the United States from Austria with his parents in 1900. He received the B.S. degree (1916) from the City College of New York and the A.M. (1918) and Ph.D. (1923) degrees from Columbia University.

Harap taught in public and private schools in New York City (1916–18). He was director of boys' work at the Hudson Guild in New York City (1918–23) and director of Antioch School and associate professor of education at Antioch College in Yellow Springs, Ohio (1923–24). He taught at the Cleveland (Ohio) School of Education (1924–28) and was associate professor of education at Western Reserve University (later, Case Western Reserve University) from 1928, when the Cleveland School of Education became part of Western Reserve University. In 1936 he was professor of education and research associate with the Bureau of Educational Research at Ohio State University. In 1937 he joined the faculty of George Peabody College for Teachers in Nashville, Tennessee, with the division of surveys and field services, where he stayed to his retirement in 1959. Harap became a leading figure in the field of curriculum development.

Harap was the author of several books, including *The Education of the Consumer* (1924), *Economic Life and the Curriculum* (1927), *The Technique of Curriculum Making* (1928), *A College Course in Consumer Problems* (1950), *Preparation of Teachers in the Area of Curriculum and Instruction* (1951), *A Survey of Surveys* (1952), *Social Living in the Curriculum* (1952), and *The Improvement of Curriculum in Indian Schools* (1959), and he edited *The Changing Curriculum* (1937), *Consumer Education* (with James E. Mendenhall, 1943), and *Curriculum Trends at Mid-Century* (1953). He was editor of *Curriculum Journal* (1929–43).

Harap participated in a number of educational surveys and was a member of many organizations, including president of the Council on Consumer Information and a founder and executive secretary of the Society for Curriculum Study (1929–37). He was an adviser on curriculum for the Central Bureau for Improvement of Textbooks and Curricula for India (1957).

REFERENCES: *LE* (III); *WW* (XXXI). *John F. Ohles*

HARDEY, Mary Aloysia. B. December 8, 1809, Piscataway, Maryland, to Frederick William and Sarah (Spalding) Hardey. M. no. D. June 17, 1886, Paris, France.

Mary Aloysia Hardey was born in Maryland but was raised and spent most of her early adult life in Louisiana. She attended school at the Convent of the Sacred Heart at Grand Coteau, Louisiana, and entered the novitiate there in 1825. After she professed she was named superior at St. Michael's, Louisiana, in 1836. She developed a relationship with Philippine Duchesne *(q.v.)*, a leader of the Sacred Heart Order.

In 1841 Hardey moved to New York City where she founded the first house of the Sacred Heart Order on the East Coast. She was the founder of what became Manhattanville College in Purchase, New York. By 1844 she was named superior vicar of all the houses of the society in the eastern United States and Canada. She founded convents and schools in Albany, Buffalo, New York City, Detroit, Philadelphia, Cincinnati, Montreal, Halifax, and Havana. In 1871 she became assistant general of the British Empire and North America.

She spent much of her later life in travel in Europe and elsewhere furthering the cause of Catholic education for women.

REFERENCES: *AC; DAB; TC; WWW* (H); *New Catholic Encyclopedia* (New York: McGraw-Hill, 1967). *James M. Vosper*

HARKNESS, Albert. B. October 6, 1822, Mendon, Massachusetts, to Southwick and Phebe (Thayer) Harkness. M. May 28, 1849, to Maria

Aldrich Smith. Ch. two, including Albert Granger Harkness, professor of Latin at Brown University (1893–1923). D. May 27, 1907, Providence, Rhode Island.

Albert Harkness was graduated as valedictorian from Brown University in 1842 and studied in Germany at the universities of Berlin, Bonn, and Göttingen (1853–55). He received the Ph.D. degree (1854) from the University of Bonn. He was a high school teacher in Providence, Rhode Island (1843–53), and was professor of Greek language and literature at Brown University (1855–92). Upon his retirement, he was elected professor emeritus and in 1904 was elected to the board of fellows of Brown University, serving until his death in 1907.

Harkness wrote Latin textbooks, including the famous *Latin Grammar* (1865), *Caesar's Gallic Wars* (1870), *Selected Orations of Cicero* (1873), *Easy Latin Method* (1890), *Complete Latin Grammar* (1898), *Short Latin Grammar* (1898), and *Cicero's Select Orations* (with J. C. Kirkland, Jr., 1905).

Harkness was president of the Rhode Island Historical Society, a founder of the American Philological Association (vice-president, 1869–70 and president, 1875–76), a founder of the American School of Classical Studies in Athens, Greece, and a member of its managing committee, and a member of the Archaeological Institute of America. In 1902 the Albert Harkness Fund made the facilities of the American School of Classical Studies available to all graduates of Brown University. Harkness received an honorary degree from Brown University in 1869.

REFERENCES: *AC; DAB; NCAB* (6:23); *TC; WWW* (I); *NYT,* May 27, 1907, p. 7.   *Barbara Ruth Peltzman*

HARPER, William Rainey. B. July 26, 1856, New Concord, Ohio, to Samuel and Ellen Elizabeth (Rainey) Harper. M. November 18, 1875, to Ella Paul. Ch. four. D. January 10, 1906, Chicago, Illinois.

William Rainey Harper was graduated from Muskingum College (Ohio) before he was fifteen, delivering the commencement address in Hebrew (1870). Before entering graduate school in 1873, he studied privately at his home in New Concord, Ohio. Two years after his matriculation at Yale College, Harper earned the Ph.D. degree (1875) in Indo-Iranian and Semitic languages and philology.

Harper was principal of Masonic College in Macon, Tennessee (1875–76), and was tutor (1876–79) and principal of the preparatory department (1879–80) at Denison University in Granville, Ohio. He accepted a professorship in Hebrew at the Baptist Theological Seminary in Chicago, Illinois (1880–86). He became professor of Semitic languages at Yale (1886–91) and accepted an assignment as Woolsey Professor of Biblical Literature at the Yale Divinity School (1889–91). He was also principal of the Chautauqua (New York) Institution's college of liberal arts (1885–91).

In 1888 the American Baptist Society began to plan the establishment of an outstanding university. In 1891 Harper was selected to head the project. He was founding president of the University of Chicago and remained its president and teaching head of the department of Semitic languages until his death in 1906. When Harper met with the university trustees before his acceptance of the presidency, he submitted detailed proposals to create the most comprehensive and liberal university in the world. The plans included a university extension system, cooperative programs with other institutions, the division of the school year into four quarters with the summer quarter becoming an integral part, emphasis on graduate study and research, a university press, and intellectual freedom. Harper was able to secure the support of wealthy philanthropists (particularly John D. Rockefeller), and the university started with some of the most advanced ideas and finest instructors, equipment, and buildings in America.

Harper was the author of books, including *Elements of Hebrew* (1882), *Hebrew Vocabularies* (1882), *Elements of Hebrew Syntax* (1888), *Introductory New Testament Greek Method* (with Revere F. Weidner, 1889), *Elements of Latin* (with Isaac B. Burgess, 1900), *The Prospects of the Small College* (1900), *The Priestly Element in the Old Testament* (1902), *Religion and the Higher Life* (1904), *The Trend in Higher Education* (1905), *The Prophetic Elements in the Old Testament* (1905), and *A Critical Exegetical Commentary on Amos and Hosea* (1905).

Harper founded *The Hebrew Student* and *Hebraica;* he organized the American Institute of Hebrew. He served as editor of *The Biblical World, The American Journal of Theology,* and *The American Journal of Semitic Languages and Literature.* He was a member of the committee that selected and arranged for the editing of the Appleton series, the World's Great Books. Harper was a member of the Chicago board of education (1896–98). He received five honorary degrees.

REFERENCES: *AC; DAB; EB; NCAB* (11:65); *TC; WWW* (I); C. F. Thwing *(q.v.),* "Estimate," *Harper's Weekly* 50 (January 27, 1906):118; *NYT,* January 11, 1906, p. 9; "William Rainey Harper," *Outlook* 82 (January 20, 1906): 110-12.   David E. Luellen

HARRINGTON, Harry Franklin. B. July 25, 1882, Logan, Ohio, to Frank and Margaret (Walker) Harrington. M. July 15, 1913, to Frieda Poston. Ch. none. D. September 21, 1935, Evanston, Illinois.

Inspiring students to write well was the career-long aim of Harry Franklin Harrington. He studied at the University of Wooster in Ohio (1899–1901) and received the B.A. degree (1905) from Ohio State University and the M.A. degree (1909) from Columbia University.

Harrington gained newspaper experience with the *Ohio State Journal* in Columbus, Ohio, and the London, Ohio, *Times.* In 1909 he began teaching English at Ohio Wesleyan University in Delaware, Ohio. A year later he went to Ohio State where he remained for four years as assistant professor of English and director of journalism. In 1914 he became assistant professor of journalism at the University of Kansas, and the following year he went to the University of Illinois. He became director of the Medill School of Journalism of Northwestern University in Evanston, Illinois, in 1921, a post he held until his death.

Harrington served as an editorial writer for the *Christian Science Monitor* from 1929. He wrote a number of textbooks, including *Essentials to Journalism* (with T. T. Frankenberg, 1912), *Typical Newspaper Stories* (1915), *The Teaching of Journalism in a Natural Setting* (1919), *Writing for Print* (with Evaline Harrington, 1921), *Chats on Feature Writing* (1925), *The Newspaper Club* (with Evaline Harrington, 1927), *Pathways to Print* (with Lawrence Martin, 1931), and *The Copyreader's Workshop* (with R. E. Wolseley, 1934). He served as an editorial adviser to Harper & Row. Harrington believed that interest was a major factor in good writing. Understanding of the process of writing would benefit not only the writer but the reader.

He was a member of several civic and professional organizations, including the American Association of Teachers of Journalism (president, 1919–20). He received the L.H.D. degree from Oklahoma City University (1931).

REFERENCES: *WWW* (I); *Evanston Review,* September 26, 1935, p. 62; *Scholastic* 27 (October 12, 1935):20.

Darlene E. Fisher

HARRIS, Chapin Aaron. B. May 6, 1806, Pompey, New York, to John and Elizabeth (Brundage) Harris. M. January 11, 1826, to Lucinda Heath Hawley. Ch. nine. D. September 29, 1860, Baltimore, Maryland.

Chapin A. Harris received his early education in the public schools of Pompey, New York. He studied medicine with his brother John for two years in Madison, Ohio, and established a medical practice in Greenfield, Ohio (1827–28).

He moved to Baltimore, Maryland, and worked as a surgeon-dentist there and in other southern cities. He was licensed as a dentist in 1833. In 1839 Harris and Horace H. Hayden (*q.v.*) founded the Baltimore College of Dental Surgery, the first of its kind in the world. Harris was professor of dental surgery and the first dean, and he succeeded Hayden as president in 1844.

Harris was the first editor of the *American Journal of Dental Science* (1839–58). His book, *The Dental Art: A Practical Treatise on Dental Surgery* (1839), was used as a text, translated into French, and sold for fifty years. He also wrote *A Dictionary of Dental Science* (1849), later revised as *Dictionary of Medicine, Dental Surgery and Cocutural Sciences* (1854),

Characteristics of the Human Teeth (1841), and *Diseases of the Maxillary Sinus* (1842). He edited Fox's *Natural History and Diseases of Human Teeth* (1846) and translated several articles on dentistry from French.

Harris was a founder of the American Society of Dental Surgeons and was its second president (1844). He organized and was president of the American Dental Convention (1855–56).

REFERENCES: *AC; DAB; NCAB* (22:432). *Shirley M. Ohles*

HARRIS, Franklin Stewart. B. August 29, 1884, Benjamin, Utah, to Dennison Emer and Eunice (Stewart) Harris. M. June 18, 1908, to Estella Spilsbury. Ch. six. D. April 18, 1960, Salt Lake City, Utah.

Franklin Stewart Harris was a Utah educator, scientist, and humanitarian. A graduate of the Juarez (Mexico) State Academy in 1903, he received the B.S. degree (1907) from Brigham Young University in Provo, Utah, and the Ph.D. degree in soils (1911) from Cornell University in Ithaca, New York.

Harris was an instructor of science at Juarez State Academy (1904–05) and was an assistant in chemistry at the Utah Experiment Station (1907–08) and in soil technology at Cornell University (1909–10). He was an instructor (1910–11), professor of agronomy (1911–16), and director of the experimental station (1916–21) at Utah State Agricultural College (later, Utah State University). The next twenty-nine years were spent in service as president of Brigham Young University (1921–45) and Utah State Agricultural College (1945–50). Harris was credited with strengthening the institutions' academic offerings, raising standards of scholarship, and promoting the fine arts at the institutions. He also attained an international reputation as an agronomist, traveling worldwide to determine the agricultural possibilities in such countries as Japan, Korea, Manchuria, Burma, India, and Iran. He was an unsuccessful candidate for United States senator from Utah in 1938.

Harris was the author of over six hundred articles and *The Principles of Agronomy* (with George Stewart, 1915), *The Young Man and His Vocation* (1916), *The Sugar Beet in America* (1918), *Soil Alkali* (1920), *Scientific Research and Human Welfare* (1924), and *The Fruits of Mormonism* (1925).

Harris was appointed to international missions, including agricultural adviser to the Iranian government (1939–40), chairman of a mission in technical collaboration between the governments of Iran and the United States (1950), chairman and agriculturist of a Siberian colonizing project of the Jewish Colonization Organization of Russia (1929), chairman of a United States agricultural mission to the Middle East (1946), and chairman of a United Nations Food and Agricultural Organization mission to Greece (1946). He was a fellow of the American Association for the Advancement of Science and a member of the Utah Academy of Science (president) and the American Society of Agronomy (president, 1920–21). He was awarded an honorary degree by Brigham Young University in 1945; the fine arts center at Brigham Young was named in his honor in 1965.

REFERENCES: *LE* (III); *WWAE* (XIV); *WWW* (IV); *NYT*, April 20, 1960, p. 39; Office of University Publications, *Franklin Stewart Harris, Educator, Administrator, Father, Friend. Vignettes of His Life* (Provo, Utah: Brigham Young University, 1965); *Utah Since Statehood: Historical and Biographical* (Chicago: S. J. Clarke Publishing Co., 1920), 4: 254–55; E. L. Wilkinson and W. C. Skousen, *Brigham Young University: A School of Destiny* (Provo, Utah: BYU Press, 1976).

Harry P. Bluhm

HARRIS, Samuel. B. June 14, 1814, East Machias, Maine, to Josiah and Lucy (Talbot) Harris. M. April 30, 1839, to Deborah Robbins Dickinson. M. October 11, 1877, to Mary S. Fitch. Ch. none. D. June 25, 1899, Litchfield, Connecticut.

Samuel Harris was graduated from Bowdoin College in Brunswick, Maine, in 1833 and was principal of Limerick (Maine) Academy (1833–34) and Washington Academy in East Machias, Maine (1834–35). He studied at Andover (Massachusetts) Theological Seminary (1835–38) and was graduated in 1838.

He taught at East Machias (1838–41) and was pastor of Congregational churches at Conway (1841–51), and Pittsfield, Massachusetts (1851–55). In 1855 Harris became professor of systematic theology at Bangor (Maine) Theological Seminary, where he remained until 1867 when he was elected president and professor of mental and moral philosophy of Bowdoin College. He resigned his position in 1871 to become professor of systematic theology at Yale College.

Harris published many sermons and addresses and several theological and religious works of considerable length, including *Zaccheus: The Scriptural Plan of Benevolence* (1844), *Christ's Prayer for the Death of His Redeemed* (1863), *The Kingdom of Christ on Earth* (1874), *Self-Revelation of God* (1887), and *God: The Lord and Creator of All* (1896). His best-known work was *The Philosophical Basis of Theism* (1883).

Harris received honorary degrees from Williams (1855) and Bowdoin (1871) colleges.

REFERENCES: *AC; DAB; NCAB* (1:418); *NYT*, June 27, 1889, p. 7; *TC; WWW* (I).   *Donald C. Stephenson*

HARRIS, William Torrey. B. September 10, 1835, North Killingly, Connecticut, to William and Zilpah (Torrey) Harris. M. December 27,

1858, to Sarah T. Bugbee. Ch. none. D. November 5, 1909, Providence, Rhode Island.

William Torrey Harris received his education in Providence, Rhode Island, and at various academies, including Woodstock (Connecticut) Academy and Phillips Academy in Andover, Massachusetts. He entered Yale College in 1854 but left after two and one-half years.

Harris went to St. Louis, Missouri, in 1857, where he taught in a phonographic (shorthand) institute and also was a private tutor. In 1858 he was an assistant teacher in the St. Louis public schools and became a teacher, principal, and assistant superintendent. From 1867 to 1880 he was superintendent of St. Louis schools. He introduced new subjects into the curriculum, including art, music, science, and manual arts, added the kindergarten to the school system, and strengthened the high school. Harris resigned in 1880 and spent nine years in Concord, Massachusetts, where he assisted in establishing the Concord School of Philosophy, an unsuccessful enterprise. He had a particular interest in the German philosopher Georg W. F. Hegel. In 1889 Harris was appointed United States commissioner of education, serving to 1906. Harris exerted a strong influence as commissioner.

Harris wrote many articles, and his reports as superintendent in St. Louis attracted wide attention. He was the author of books, including *Hegel's Doctrine of Reflection* (1881), *The Spiritual Sense of Dante's Divina Commedia* (three volumes, 1889), *Introduction to the Study of Philosophy* (1889), *Hegel's Logic* (1890), and *Psychologic Foundations of Education* (1898). He collaborated with A. J. Rickoff *(q.v.)* and J. Mark Bailey on the Appleton School Readers (1877), edited Appleton's International Education Series, and was assistant editor of *Johnson's Cyclopaedia*. He founded and edited the *Journal of Speculative Philosophy* (1867–93). He was editor-in-chief of *Webster's International Dictionary* (1900).

Harris was active in professional and scholarly associations as founder of the Philosophical Society of St. Louis (1866) and member of the National Educational Association (life director and president, 1875), the National Association of School Superintendents (president, 1873), the American Social Science Association, and others. He represented the Bureau of Education at the International Congress of Education at Brussels, Belgium (1880), and the Paris Exposition (1889). He received awards from France (1889) and Italy (1894). He received honorary degrees from many American universities and from the University of Jena, Germany.

REFERENCES: *AC; DAB; NCAB* (15:1); *TC; WWW* (I); *NYT*, November 6, 1909, p. 9; Selwyn K. Troen, *The Public and the Schools* (Columbia: University of Missouri Press, 1975); Bernard J. Kohlbrenner, "William T. Harris, Superintendent of Schools" (Ed.D. diss., Harvard University, 1942).   *Robert House*

HARRISON, Elizabeth. B. September 1, 1849, Athens, Kentucky, to Isaac Webb and Elizabeth Thompson (Bullock) Harrison. M. no. D. October 31, 1927, San Antonio, Texas.

Elizabeth Harrison was educated in the Davenport, Iowa, public schools, where the family had moved when she was seven years old. She completed high school at seventeen and remained at home caring for her parents until she was thirty, when she went to Chicago and entered Alice Putnam's *(q.v.)* kindergarten training school. After graduation in 1880, she assisted Putnam for a year and then conducted a kindergarten of her own. During her career she studied under Susan E. Blow *(q.v.)* and Halsey Ives in St. Louis, Missouri, Maria Kraus-Boelté *(q.v.)* in New York, Henrietta Breyman Schrader in Berlin, Germany, Baroness Bertha von Marenholtz-Bulow in Dresden, Germany, and Maria Montessori in Rome, Italy.

Harrison founded the Chicago Kindergarten Club with Putnam in 1883 to help kindergarten teachers improve their teaching. With Mrs. John N. Crouse she lectured to mothers, sponsored lectures, and held national conferences for mothers in Chicago, which foreshadowed the Parent-Teachers Association. She and Mrs. Crouse established the Chicago Kindergarten Training School, which became successively the Chicago Kindergarten College, the National Kindergarten College, the National Kindergarten and Elementary College, and finally the National College of Education located in Evanston, Illinois. Harrison was president of this institution for thirty-three years. Enrolling high school graduates, the college provided a three-year program of studies and awarded the bachelor of education degree after four years of study.

Harrison's lectures for mothers and teachers were published as *A Study of Child-Nature from the Kindergarten Standpoint* (1890). Her other publications include *A List of Books for Children Recommended from the Kindergarten Standpoint* (1889), *The Root of the Temperance Question from a Kindergarten Standpoint* (1889), *The Influence of the Kindergarten on Modern Civilization* (1891), *Story of Christopher Columbus for Little Children* (1893), *In Story Land* (1895), *Two Children of the Foothills* (1900), *Some Silent Teachers* (1903), *The Kindergarten Gifts* (1903), *Bead Stringing, for Public Schools from First to Eighth Grades* (1904), *Misunderstood Children: Sketches Taken from Life* (1910), *The Montessori Method and the Kindergarten* (1914), *When Children Err: A Book for Young Mothers* (1916), and *The Unseen Side of Child Life, for the Guardians of Young Children* (1922).

Harrison was a member of many organizations, including the International Kindergarten Union (advisory committee, 1892–1910), the National Education Association, the American Child Welfare Association, and the National Board of Congress of Mothers.

After her retirement in 1920, she worked on her autobiography, *Sketches*

Along Life's Road, which was edited by Carolyn Sherwin Bailey and published posthumously in 1930. A collection of stories, *In the Story World; Best Legends for Boys and Girls,* was also published in 1931 after her death.

REFERENCES: *DAB; NAW; NCAB* (21:135); *WWW* (I); Agnes Snyder, *Dauntless Women in Childhood Education, 1856–1931* (Washington, D.C.: Association for Childhood Education International, 1972).

Doris Cruger Dale

HART, Albert Bushnell. B. July 1, 1854, Clarksville, Pennsylvania, to Albert Gaillard and Mary Crosby (Harrell) Hart. M. July 11, 1889, to Mary Hurd Putnam. Ch. three. D. June 16, 1943, Boston, Massachusetts.

Albert Bushnell Hart was educated in the Cleveland (Ohio) public schools and received the A.B. degree (1880) from Harvard University and the Ph.D. degree (1883) from the University of Freiburg, Germany. He also studied at the University of Berlin, Germany, and the Ecole des sciences politiques in Paris, France.

Before attending college, Hart had worked in Cleveland lumberyards for four years and as a government clerk on a Sioux reservation for two years. He joined the faculty of Harvard as first instructor of American history (1883), was Eaton Professor of the Science of Government (1912), and continued to his retirement in 1926. He maintained an office in Widener Library at Harvard after his retirement and continued his research and writing. He was a leader in the movement to improve the study and teaching of American history.

Hart was the author or coauthor of over a hundred books, including *Introduction to the Study of Federal Government* (1890), *Studies in American Education* (1891), *Formation of the Union* (1892), *Guide to the Study of American History* (with Edward Channing, *q.v.*, 1896), *Salmon Portland Chase* (1899), *Foundations of American Foreign Policy* (1901), *Essentials in American History* (1905), *Manual of American History, Diplomacy, and Government* (1908), *War in Europe* (1914), *Abraham Lincoln* (1914), *The Monroe Doctrine, an Interpretation* (1916), *New American History* (1917), and *George Washington* (1927). He edited *Epochs of American History* (four volumes, 1890–1926), *American History Told by Contemporaries* (five volumes, 1897–1920), *Source Readers of American History* (five volumes, 1900–27), *The American Nation, A History* (twenty-eight volumes, 1904–18), *American Year Book* (twelve volumes, 1911–20 and 1926–32), *American Leaflets* (1895–1913), and others. He was an editor of *Theodore Roosevelt Encyclopedia* (1927–43), *Harvard Advocate* (1879–80), and *Harvard Graduates Magazine* (1894–1902).

Hart was a member of the Massachusetts Constitutional Convention (chairman of the committee on amendment and codification, 1917–19), the Cambridge (Massachusetts) School Committee (1891–96), and the United States Commission of Public Archives and a member and historian of the United States Commission of the Celebration of the Two Hundreth Anniversary of the Birth of George Washington (1926–32). He was a trustee of Howard University (1930–37) and the Roosevelt Memorial Association. He was a member of professional associations, including the American Historical Association (president, 1909), and the American Political Science Association (president, 1912). He received honorary degrees from three American institutions and the University of Geneva (Switzerland) in 1909.

REFERENCES: *CB* (August 1943); *DAB* (supp. 3); *LE* (II); *NCAB* (47:146); *WWAE* (VIII); *WWW* (II); *NYT*, June 17, 1943, p. 21.

Donald O. Dewey

HART, John Seely. B. January 28, 1810, Stockbridge, Massachusetts, to Isaac and Abigail (Stone) Hart. M. April 21, 1836, to Amelia Caroline Morford. Ch. one, James Morgan Hart, philologist. D. March 26, 1877, Princeton, New Jersey.

When John Seely Hart was two years old, his family moved from Stockbridge, Massachusetts, to Wilkes-Barre, Pennsylvania. After preparation under Dr. Orton of Wilkes-Barre, he attended the College of New Jersey (later, Princeton University), from which he was graduated with high honors in 1830. After teaching one year in an academy at Natchez, Mississippi, Hart attended Princeton Theological Seminary, graduating in 1834.

He was a tutor in the College of New Jersey (1832–34). In 1836 Hart purchased the Edge Hill School, remaining as master until 1841. He was principal of Central High School in Philadelphia (1842–59). He left Central in 1859 to edit the publications of the American Sunday-school Union. In 1862 he moved to Trenton as head of the model school department of the New Jersey State Normal and Model Schools. He became principal of the State Normal School (later, Trenton State College) in 1863. In 1872 he returned to the College of New Jersey as professor of rhetoric and English literature and remained until 1874 when he retired to write textbooks and edit anthologies.

Hart was the author of *Class-Book of Poetry and Prose* (1844), *Elementary Grammar of the English Language* (1845), *Essay on the Life and Writings of Edmund Spenser* (1847), *Female Prose Writers of America* (1851), *In the School Room,* a popular pedagogical text (1868), *Manual of Composition and Rhetoric* (1870), *Manual of English Literature* (1873), and *Short Course in English and American Literature* (1874). He was editor of the *Pennsylvania Common School Journal* (1844) and coeditor of *Sartain's Union Magazine of Literature and Art* (1849–51). He was founder and first editor of the *Sunday School Times* (1859–71). He was awarded an honorarydegree by Miami University (Ohio).

REFERENCES: *AC; DAB; NCAB* (9:263); *TC; WWW* (H).

William W. West

HART, Joseph Kinmont. B. February 16, 1876, near Columbia City, Indiana, to David N. and Lucy (Kinmont) Hart. M. 1903 to Lulu A. Calvert. M. 1929 to Frances Stuyvesant Uhrig. Ch. none. D. March 10, 1949, Hudson, New York.

Joseph Kinmont Hart, a prominent educator and prolific author, received the A.B. degree (1900) from Franklin (Indiana) College and the Ph.D. degree (1909) from the University of Chicago.

He served as professor of philosophy and psychology at Baker University in Baldwin, Kansas (1900–10), assistant professor of education at the University of Washington (1910–15), professor of education at Reed College in Portland, Oregon (1916–19), editor of the school and community department for *The Survey* in New York City (1920–26), and professor of education at the University of Wisconsin (1927–30). In 1930 Hart became professor of education and head of the department of education at Vanderbilt University in Nashville, Tennessee. He joined the Teachers College, Columbia University, faculty as professor of education in 1934, where he remained until his retirement in 1940.

Hart was deeply interested in the organization, reorganization, and disorganization of social institutions. He emphasized the importance of the social community as the sustaining source and reason for education. He was also interested in studying the ridigity and prejudices of cultural patterns as they affect educational means and goals.

Among his works were *Educational Resources of Village and Rural Communities* (1913), *Democracy in Education* (1918), *Community Organization* (1920), *The Discovery of Intelligence* (1924), *Social Life and Institutions* (1924), *Inside Experience* (1927), *Light from the North* (1927), *Adult Education* (1927), *Prophet of a Nameless God* (1927), *A Social Interpretation of Education* (1929), *Creative Moment in Education* (1931), *Education for an Age of Power* (1935), *An Introduction to the Social Studies* (1937), *Mind in Transition* (1938), and *Education in the Humane Community* (1951).

Hart was a lecturer at the New School for Social Research and a director of the Pennsylvania School for Social Service. He served in the Spanish-American War (1898) and was an organizer of training courses for voluntary social workers with the National War Camp Community Service (1919–20). He was a member of the Legal Advisory Board under the Selective Service Act (1917–18).

REFERENCES: *LE* (I); *WWAE* (VI); *WWW* (II); *NYT,* March 11, 1949, p. 17; *School and Society* 69 (March 19, 1949): 208–09.   *Jerome E. Lord*

HART, William Richard. B. March 31, 1853, Greene County, Pennsylvania, to Jacob and Xaveria (Ross) Hart. M. August 14, 1884, to Mary Ella McCray. Ch. none. D. October 19, 1929, Santa Barbara, California.

William Richard Hart moved with his family to Iowa at the age of two. He attended Iowa Wesleyan University in Mount Pleasant, Iowa, for two years. After twenty years as a schoolteacher and administrator, he studied at the University of Nebraska and received the A.B. (1896) and A.M. (1901) degrees.

From 1874 Hart was a teacher in the rural schools of Illinois, Iowa, and Nebraska and was a superintendent of schools in Nebraska for ten years. He served as head of the Nebraska State Normal School at Peru (later, Peru State College) from 1901 to 1907 and went to the Massachusetts Agricultural College (later, University of Massachusetts) in Amherst, where he was the first professor in a department specifically organized to prepare teachers of agriculture.

Hart went to Massachusetts after a distinguished career in Iowa and in Nebraska where he had been a leader in establishing agricultural education in elementary schools as a natural foundation for educating country children. He believed that the child's own environment was the best means of promoting a broad education. He brought the club idea to Massachusetts and within three years after his arrival, two hundred thousand boys and girls were enrolled in garden clubs, potato clubs, corn clubs, pig clubs, and poultry clubs. In his classes he pioneered in applying educational psychology to the teaching of agriculture. He believed intellectual and cultural values should be stressed in the study of agriculture.

He was the author of *Agricultural Education* (1907), *Redirection of the Rural School* (n.d.), *Boys and Girls Clubs* (with Orion A. Morton, 1914), and a number of circulars published by the Massachusetts Agricultural College. He was an active member of professional organizations.

REFERENCES: *NCAB* (B:252); Harold W. Cary, *The University of Massachusetts: A History of One Hundred Years* (Amherst: University of Massachusetts, 1962); Frank Prentice Rand, *Yesterdays at Massachusetts State College* (Amherst: Massachusetts State College, 1933); Rufus W. Stimson (*q.v.*) and Frank W. Lathrop, *History of Agricultural Education of Less Than College Grade in the United States* (Washington, D.C.: U.S. Office of Education, 1942).   *William Kornegay*

HARTRANFT, Chester David. B. October 15, 1839, Frederick, Pennsylvania, to Samuel Engle and Salome (Stetler) Hartranft. M. June 20, 1864, to Anna Frances Berg. M. November 22, 1911, to Ida Thomas Berg. Ch. five. D. December 30, 1914, Wolfenbüttel, Germany.

The Hartranft family settled in Philadelphia, Pennsylvania, in 1846, and Chester David Hartranft was educated in the city schools. His talents in mathematics led to his nomination for a vacancy at the United States Military Academy at West Point, but he was rejected because he was too young. He was graduated with the A.B. (1856) and A.M. (1859) degrees from Central High School in Philadelphia and attended the University of Pennsylvania, from which he was graduated with the A.B. (1861) and A.M. (1864) degrees. He studied at the Theological Seminary of the Dutch Reformed Church in New Brunswick, New Jersey, graduating in 1864. He served as pastor in South Bushwick, New York (1864–66), and at a Dutch Reformed church in New Brunswick, New Jersey (1866–78).

Hartranft founded and was president of a conservatory of music in New Brunswick (1870–73). He promoted the Sunday school idea of systematic study and teaching in the church. He became Waldo Professor of Ecclesiastical History at the Theological Institute of Connecticut (later, Hartford Theological Seminary) in 1879. He was professor of biblical theology (1892–97) and ecclesiastical dogmatics (1897–1903) and president of the seminary from 1888 to 1903. Favoring reform of theological education, he was responsible for extensive curriculum reform and development of the institute on a nondenominational basis. He opened theological instruction to women. He retired as honorary president in 1903.

In 1887 he edited the *Anti-Donatist Writings of St. Augustine* and in 1890 the *Ecclesiastical History of Sozomenus* for the American series of the Post-Nicene Fathers.

Hartranft was president of the Conservatory of Music in New Brunswick, New Jersey, and was a founder of the National Academy of Theology in which professors of all denominations were brought together. He received two honorary degrees from Rutgers College and one from Williams College.

REFERENCES: *DAB; NCAB* (6:42); *TC; WWW* (I).   *Marilyn Meiss*

HARTWELL, Edward Mussey. B. May 29, 1850, Exeter, New Hampshire, to Josiah Shattuck and Catherine Stone (Mussey) Hartwell. M. July 25, 1889, to Mary Laetitia Brown. Ch. three. D. February 19, 1922, Jamaica Plain, Boston, Massachusetts.

Edward Hartwell was the first American physical education historian. He prepared for college by attending Lawrence Academy in Groton, Massachusetts, and Boston Latin School. He matriculated at Amherst (Massachusetts) College and received the A.B. (1873), and A.M. (1876) degrees. He was granted the Ph.D. degree in animal physiology from Johns Hopkins University in Baltimore, Maryland (1881). He was a member of the gymnasium staff as a student. In 1882 he earned the M.D. degree from Miami Medical College in Cincinnati, Ohio.

Hartwell taught in high schools in Orange, New Jersey (1873), and at the Boston Latin School (1874–77). He became an associate in physical training and director of the gymnasium at Johns Hopkins University in 1883, a position from which he resigned in 1890 to become director of physical training in the Boston public schools. In 1897 he became secretary of the department of municipal statistics in Boston and served in this capacity until his death.

After extensive study and travel in the United States and Europe, Hartwell wrote numerous learned reports concerning physical training and school hygiene. He was noted for "The Nature of Physical Training and the Best Means of Securing Its Ends," which he presented at the Boston Conference in 1889. He also was recognized for a report, *Physical Training in American Colleges and Universities* (1885), which he completed for the United States Bureau of Education.

Hartwell served as president and treasurer of the American Association for the Advancement of Physical Education and was a member of many professional organizations. He was honored for his work by being made a fellow in memoriam of the American Academy of Physical Education and was awarded an honorary degree by Amherst College.

REFERENCES: *NCAB* (20:131); *WWW* (I); Ellen W. Gerber, *Innovators and Institutions in Physical Education* (Philadelphia: Lea and Febiger, 1971); Fred E. Leonard and George B. Affleck, *A Guide to the History of Physical Education* (Philadelphia: Lea and Febiger, 1947); Emmet Rice and John Hutchinson, *A Brief History Of Physical Education,* 3d ed. (New York: A. S. Barnes and Co., 1952); Arthur Weston, *The Making of American Physical Education* (New York: Appleton-Century-Crofts, 1962).   *Adelaide M. Cole*

HARVEY, Lorenzo Dow. B. November 23, 1848, Deerfield, New Hampshire, to John S. and Mary (Sanborn) Harvey. M. December 24, 1874, to Lettie Brown. Ch. two. D. June 1, 1922, Menomonie, Wisconsin.

Lorenzo Dow Harvey moved to Wisconsin with his family from New Hampshire when he was two years old. He worked on a farm and attended local Rock County schools. He taught in district schools during the winter to finance his college studies, graduating from Milton (Wisconsin) College with the A.B. (1872) and A.M. (1876) degrees. He studied law and was admitted to the Wisconsin bar in 1877.

Harvey was principal of the Mazomanie (Wisconsin) high school (1873–75) and was high school principal and superintendent of the Sheboygan, Wisconsin, public schools from 1875 to 1885. He was a conductor of teachers' institutes and professor of political economy at the Oshkosh Normal School (later, University of Wisconsin—Oshkosh) from 1885 to 1892. He was appointed president of the Milwaukee State Normal School (later, University of Wisconsin at Milwaukee) in 1892.

Harvey was elected state superintendent of schools (1899–1902) and was superintendent of Menomonie (Wisconsin) public schools and the Stout Training Schools (1903–08). From 1908 to 1922 Harvey was president of the Stout Institute (later, Stout State University), where he furthered the idea of vocational and industrial education, demonstrating that talent can be expressed through practical skills as well as through academic knowledge.

Harvey was the author of *Practical Arithmetic* (two volumes, 1908) and *Essentials of Arithmetic* (two volumes, 1914). He was active in professional associations, serving as president of the Wisconsin Teachers' Association (1890–91), and he was a member of the National Educational Association (vice-president, 1897, president, 1908–09, president of the library department, 1898–99, and department of superintendence, 1900). He received an honorary degree from Milton College (1885).

REFERENCES: *NCAB* (14:87); *WWW* (I); *Industrial Arts Magazine* 11 (August 1922): 317; *Industrial Education* 24 (July 1922): 5.

Lee H. Smalley

HARVEY, Thomas Wadleigh. B. December 18, 1821, New London, New Hampshire, to Moses S. Harvey and his wife (n.a.). M. 1849 to Louisa O. Beebe. Ch. six. D. January 20, 1892, Painesville, Ohio.

Thomas Wadleigh Harvey moved with his family to Ohio from New Hampshire in 1833 and settled on a farm in Concord. Harvey attended local schools and was employed in the office of the *Painesville* (Ohio) *Republican* (1836–41). In 1845 Harvey enrolled in the Western Reserve Teachers' Seminary in Kirtland, Ohio, where he was instructed by Asa Dearborn Lord (*q.v.*).

Harvey received a teaching certificate in 1841 and first taught in a Mentor, Ohio, district school. Harvey established the Geauga High School at Chardon, Ohio (1845–48), and was principal of an academy at Republic (Seneca County), Ohio (1848–51). Harvey was superintendent of the Massillon, Ohio, public schools (1851–65) and at Painesville, Ohio (1865–71). In 1871 he was appointed state commissioner of common schools by Governor Rutherford B. Hayes; he was elected to the office for a full term later in 1871. In 1877 he returned to Painesville as school superintendent, serving to his retirement in 1883. From 1883 Harvey was engaged as an instructor of teachers' institutes, as a lecturer, and as a trustee of the Lake Erie Seminary and the Grand River Institute.

Harvey assisted in revising the McGuffey readers and preparing the Eclectic Series of Geographies. He was the author of *Harvey's English Grammar* (1868), *Harvey's Elementary Grammar* (1869), *First Lessons in the English Language* (1875), and *The Graded School Primary Speller* (1875).

A founder of the Ohio State Teachers' Association (1847), Harvey also was a founder and the first president of the Northeastern Ohio Teachers' Association (1869). He was the recipient of honorary degrees from the University of Wooster and Allegheny College.

REFERENCES: James J. Burns, *Educational History of Ohio* (Columbus, Ohio: Historical Publishing Co., 1905), pp. 413–15; John L. Clifton, *Ten Famous American Educators* (Columbus: R. G. Adams Co., 1933), pp. 123–66; E. F. Moulton, "Sketch of Thomas W. Harvey," *Ohio Educational Monthly* 41 (August 1892): 444–53.   *John F. Ohles*

HATCHER, Orie Latham. B. December 10, 1868, Petersburg, Virginia, to William Eldredge and Oranie Virginia (Snead) Hatcher. M. no. D. April 1, 1946, Richmond, Virginia.

Orie Latham Hatcher was graduated from Richmond (Virginia) Female Institute in 1884 and attended Vassar College, where she received the A.B. degree (1888); she received the Ph.D. degree from the University of Chicago (1903).

She joined the faculty of Bryn Mawr (Pennsylvania) College where she served as head of the department of comparative literature (1910–15). She was founder and president of the Virginia Bureau of Vocations for Women and resigned from Bryn Mawr in 1915 to head the organization that became the Southern Women's Educational Alliance in 1920 and the Alliance for Guidance of Rural Youth in 1937. The alliance first worked to open vocational and educational opportunities for women in the South and later emphasized the need for educational and occupational guidance for underprivileged boys and girls in rural areas.

Hatcher was the author of numerous publications, including *John Fletcher* (1904), *A Book of Shakespeare's Plays and Pageants* (1915), *Occupations for Women* (1927), *Guiding Rural Boys and Girls* (1930), *A Mountain School* (1930), *Articulation Through Vocational Guidance* (1930), *Experimentation in Simple Guidance Programs for Rural Schools* (1931), *Interrelations of City and Country Problems of Vocational Guidance* (1931), and *Child Development and Guidance in Rural Schools* (with Ruth Strang, *q.v.,* 1943), which was chosen for microfilming for use in China.

She served as chairman of the Rural Section (1928–29) and trustee (1933–37) of the National Vocational Guidance Association. In 1917 she was cofounder and a member of the executive board of the Richmond School of Social Work and Public Health. She participated in National Occupational Conferences (1933–39) and was a consultant to the Youth Conference of the Department of Interior (1934). She was a member of the Council of Guidance and Personnel Associations (board member, 1935), the White House Conference on Children in a Democracy (1940–41), and the White House Conference on Rural Education (1944) and was chairman of the Institute for Rural Youth Guidance in Washington, D.C. (1941–44) and the Monthly Luncheon Forum of the Washington Youth Serving Agencies (1942). She was technical director of the Pine Mountain Guidance Institute in Harlan County, Kentucky (1936–42).

REFERENCES: *DAB* (supp. 4); *LE* (II); *NAW; WWW* (II); *NYT*, April 3, 1946, p. 25.   *Fannie R. Cooley*

HAVIGHURST, Robert James. B. June 5, 1900, DePere, Wisconsin, to Freeman Alfred and Winifred (Weter) Havighurst. M. June 21, 1930, to Edythe D. McNeely. Ch. five.

Robert James Havighurst earned the A.B. degree (1921) from Ohio Wesleyan University in Delaware, Ohio, and the Ph.D. degree (1924) in chemistry from Ohio State University. He was a National Research Council Fellow at Harvard University (1924–26).

Havighurst taught physics and chemistry at Miami University in Ohio (1927–28) and taught physics at the University of Wisconsin, where he was an adviser in the experimental college (1928–32). He taught science education at Ohio State University (1932–34). Havighurst was assistant director (1934–37) and director (1937–41) of the Rockefeller Foundation's General Education Board. From 1941 until his retirement in 1965 he was professor of education and human development at the University of Chicago. He held Fulbright professorships in Argentina, Australia, New Zealand, and Brazil, where he directed the Center for Educational Research of the Brazilian government (1956–58).

Havighurst wrote many books, including *Developmental Tasks and Education* (1948), *Human Development and Education* (1953), *American Higher Education in the 1960's* (1960), *Sociedad y Educación en America Latina* (1962), *The Public Schools of Chicago* (1964), *The Educational Mission of the Church* (1965), *Education in Metropolitan Areas* (1966), *Comparative Perspectives on Education* (1968), and *Developmental Tasks in Education* (1972). He was the coauthor of *Who Should Be Educated* (1944), *Father of the Man* (1947), *Adolescent Character and Personality* (1949), *Personal Adjustment in Old Age* (1949), *Social History of a War Boom Community* (1951), *The American Veteran Back Home* (1951), *Intelligence and Cultural Differences* (1951), *Older People* (1953), *The Meaning of Work and Retirement* (1954), *American Indian and White Children* (1954), *Educating Gifted Children* (1957), *Psychology of Moral Character* (1960), *Up in River City* (1962), *Society and Education in Brazil* (1965), *Society and Education* (1967), *Adjustment to Retirement: A Cross-National Study* (1967), *Brazilian Secondary Education and Socio-economic Development* (1969), and *To Live on This Earth: American Indian Education* (1972). He edited *Leaders in American Education*

(1970). He also wrote articles on child development, human behavior, educational systems, and comparative education.

He was director of the National Study of American Indian Education (1968–70). He was a member of many professional associations, including the Gerontology Society (president, 1958), the American Psychological Association (chairman, division of maturity and old age, 1960), and the National Society for the Study of Education (member, board of directors (1957–63, 1964–67, and from 1968). He received many awards and honorary degrees from Adelphi University (1962) and Ohio Wesleyan University (1963).

REFERENCES: *CA* (23–24); *LE* (V); *WW* (XXXVIII); *WWAE* (XXIII).

Robert A. Waller

HAWLEY, Gideon. B. September 26, 1785, Huntington, Connecticut, to Gideon and Sarah (Curtiss) Hawley. M. October 19, 1814, to Margarita Lansing. Ch. two. D. July 17, 1870, Albany, New York.

Gideon Hawley was graduated with the B.A. degree (1809) from Union College in Schenectady, New York. He was appointed a tutor in the college for the following year. During this period of time, he began the study of law under Henry Yates of Schenectady. For a while he considered entering the Presbyterian ministry but resumed the study of law. He was admitted to the bar in May 1812 and began practicing in partnership with Philip S. Parker.

He served as a tutor at Union College while he studied law. He was appointed master of chancery (1812–30). In 1812 the New York State legislature provided for the first state educational office, and in 1813 Hawley was named the first superintendent of common schools. The superintendent was "to digest and prepare plans for the improvement and management of the common school fund, and for the better organization of common schools." From 1813 until 1821, when the office was abolished, he laid the foundation for the public elementary schools of the state. He organized the system, created an interest in public schools, and was largely instrumental in securing new school legislation. Hawley has been called Father of Common Schools in New York.

Hawley was appointed secretary of the board of regents of the University of the State of New York (the state department of education, 1814–21). After the office of the superintendent was abolished, he continued as secretary until 1841, for a total of twenty-seven years. In 1842, following his resignation as secretary to the board of regents, he was appointed by the legislature as a permanent member of the board and continued in that office until his death twenty-eight years later.

Hawley was largely responsible for the establishment of the first normal school in New York State at Albany (1843), and he served as a member of its executive committee until 1852. The Gideon Hawley Library at the

State University of New York in Albany commemorates his service to the state. Hawley was the author of *Essays on Truth and Knowledge* (1856). He served as one of the first trustees of the Smithsonian Institution in Washington, D.C. (1846–61).

REFERENCES: *AC; DAB; EB; NCAB* (13:443); *WWW* (H); Harlan Hoyt Horner, ed., *Education in New York State 1784–1954* (Albany: The University of the State of New York, State Education Department, 1954). *Norman J. Bauer*

HAYAKAWA, Samuel Ichiye. B. July 18, 1906, Vancouver, British Columbia, Canada, to Ichiro and Tora (Isono) Hayakawa. M. May 27, 1937, to Margedant Peters. Ch. three.

S. I. Hayakawa was graduated from a Winnipeg (Manitoba, Ontario, Canada) high school in 1923 and received the M.A. degree (1930) from McGill University in Montreal, Quebec, Canada. He was awarded the Ph.D. degree (1935) from the University of Wisconsin.

Hayakawa was an instructor in English with the extension division of the University of Wisconsin (1936–39) and was a member of the faculty of the Armour Institute of Technology (later, Illinois Institute of Technology) from 1939 to 1947. He lectured at the University of Chicago (1950–55) and joined the faculty of San Francisco State College in 1955 as professor of English, where he developed a reputation as a semanticist. In the late 1960s, student unrest and violence led to the closing of San Francisco State College and resignations of two presidents in 1968. Hayakawa, who supported reopening and maintaining operation of the college, was appointed acting president (1968–69) and president in 1969, serving to his retirement in 1973. Under his leadership, classes were resumed and maintained despite violence and confrontation between students and police. He gained national recognition for his stand. In 1976 he was elected to the United States Senate from California at the age of seventy.

Hayakawa was author of many articles and a number of books, including *Language in Action* (1941), *Language in Thought and Action* (1949), *Language, Meaning and Maturity* (1954), *Our Language and Our World* (1959), *Symbol, Status and Personality* (1963), and *Modern Guide to Synonyms and Related Works* (1968). He was editor of *ETC: A Review of General Semantics* (from 1943) and wrote newspaper columns for the Chicago *Defender* (1942–47) and for the Register and Tribune Syndicate (from 1970).

A fellow of the American Psychological Association and the American Association for the Advancement of Science, Hayakawa was a member of professional organizations, including the International Society for General Semantics (president, 1949–50). He served as a director of Consumers Union (1953–55) and the Institute of Jazz Studies. He received an award for excellence from the New York Council of Churches and honorary degrees from several colleges and universities.

REFERENCES: *CA* (13–16); *CB* (January 1977); *LE* (V); *WW* (XXXIX).

John F. Ohles

HAYDEN, Horace H. B. October 13, 1769, Windsor, Connecticut, to Thomas and Abigail (Parsons) Hayden. M. February 23, 1805, to Marie Antoinette Robinson. Ch. six. D. January 26, 1844, Baltimore, Maryland.

By his early twenties, Horace H. Hayden had worked as a seaman, an architect, and a schoolteacher. By 1800 he had settled in Baltimore and begun his own dental practice. His interest in dentistry was believed to have come from an encounter with a New York dentist, John Greenwood, perhaps as early as 1792. He established a reputation by publishing a number of articles on dentistry, the earliest in 1804 in the New York *Medical Repository*. In 1810 he received the first dental license from the Medical and Chirurgical Faculty of Maryland. He served as a surgeon in the War of 1812.

Hayden began to teach dentistry at night in his office and encouraged some of his students to study medicine at the University of Maryland. Eventually he devoted most of his time to improving the training facilities for potential dentists. He lectured at the University of Maryland (1819 and 1823–25); these lectures are considered the first in dentistry education. Working with one of his former students, Chapin A. Harris *(q.v.)*, Hayden conceived of the idea of a dental school. In 1840 the Baltimore College of Dental Surgery (later, part of the University of Maryland) was granted a charter. Hayden was the college's first president and the first professor of the principles of dental science; he was professor of dental physiology and pathology to his death in 1844.

Hayden's major contributions to dental education were achieved through Harris. Hayden held to the view that techniques that had been acquired through experience should not be made public and freely distributed, but Harris objected strongly to this idea. In 1838 Harris published *The Dental Art*, the first significant American dental textbook, which incorporated most of Hayden's ideas; it had been reprinted in a dozen English editions by 1900 and translated into several languages.

Hayden was secretary of the Baltimore Physical Association (1818) and vice-president of the Maryland Academy of Sciences and Literature (1826). He was a cofounder of the American Society of Dental Surgeons (1840), an organization that presaged the establishment of a professional dentistry.

REFERENCES: *AC; DAB; EB; NCAB* (13:525); *TC; WWW* (H); J. Ben Robinson, "Dr. Horace H. Hayden and His Influence on Dental Education," *Dental Cosmos* (August 1932): 783–87.   *Richard J. Cox*

HAYDON, Glen. B. December 9, 1896, Inman, Kansas, to William Leslie and Ursula Evelyn (Parker) Haydon. M. September 14, 1922, to Helen Bergfried. Ch. two. D. May 8, 1966, Chapel Hill, North Carolina.

Glen Haydon attended the University of California at Berkeley, where he received the A.B. (1918) and M.A. (1921) degrees. He was a student in Europe, studying composition with Eugene Cools and clarinet with Auguste Périer in Paris (1923–24) and at the University of Vienna, Austria, where he received the Ph.D. degree (1932).

Haydon was an instructor of instrumental music with the Berkeley (California) high schools (1920–25) and an associate in music (1920–23) and instructor of music (1925–28) at the University of California. He was assistant professor (1928–34) and chairman of the department of music at the University of California at Los Angeles (1928–31). He moved to the University of North Carolina at Chapel Hill, where he was professor of music and department chairman (1934–51) and Kenan Professor of Music, continuing as chairman at the same time (1951–66).

Haydon was the author of several books, including *A Graded Course of Clarinet Playing* (1927), *The Evolution of the Six-Four Chord* (1933), *Studies in the Fundamentals of Music* (1933), *Introduction to Musicology* (1941), and *Hymns for the Whole Year* (1959). He translated Knud Jeppesen's *Counterpoint* from Danish (1939). He was composer of musical works, including *The Druids Weed* (ballet, 1929) and *Mass* (1930).

Haydon was a veteran of World War I as an infantry sergeant and was part of General John J. Pershing's General Headquarters Band. He was a member of many organizations, including the Music Educators National Conference (national board, 1937–41), and was president of the Music Teachers National Association (1940–42), the North Carolina State Music Teachers Association (1937–40), and the American Musicological Society (1942–44). He was a member of many other groups, including the National Association of Schools of Music (graduate committee, 1942–47), the American Council of Learned Societies (committee on musicology, 1934–48; chairman, 1941–48), and the American Society for Aesthetics (trustee, 1946–47).

REFERENCES: *CA* (9–12); *NYT,* May 9, 1966, p. 39; *WWAE* (XXII); *WWW* (IV); Nicholas Slonimsky, *Baker's Biographical Dictionary of Musicians,* 5th ed. (New York: G. Schirmer, 1958).   *John F. Ohles*

HAYES, Carlton Joseph Huntley. B. May 16, 1882, Afton, New York, to Philetus Arthur and Pamela Mary (Huntley) Hayes. M. September 18, 1920, to Mary Evelyn Carroll. Ch. two. D. September 3, 1964, Afton, New York.

Carlton J. H. Hayes was noted for his seminal studies of nineteenth-century nationalism and his college and high school European history textbooks. He attended public schools and Columbia University, from which he received the A.B. (1904), A.M. (1905), and Ph.D. (1909) degrees.

Hayes remained at Columbia from 1907 as a professor of history and was Seth Low Professor from 1935 to his retirement in 1950. He served in the United States Army (1918–19) and was United States Ambassador to Spain (1942–45).

Two major influences in Hayes's life were his conversion to Catholicism and his exposure to the Columbia school of historians, particularly James Harvey Robinson's *(q.v.)* "new history," which used social science methods to help explain historical events. Hayes was the author of many history books, including *Sources Relating to the Germanic Invasions* (1909), *British Social Politics* (1913), *Political and Social History of Modern Europe* (two volumes, 1916), *League of Nations* (with S. P. Duggan, *q.v.*, 1919), *History and Nature of International Relations* (with E. Walsh, 1922), *Modern History* (with P. T. Moon, 1923), *Recent Political Theory* (with C. E. Merrian, *q.v.*, 1924), *These Eventful Years* (1924), *Essays on Nationalism* (1926), *Essays in Intellectual History* (1929), *Ancient and Medieval History* (with P. T. Moon, 1929), *Historical Evolution of Modern Nationalism* (1931), *A Quarter Century of Learning* (1931), *Political and Cultural History of Modern Europe* (two volumes, 1932 and 1936), *A Generation of Materialism, 1871–1900* (1941), *Spain* (1951), *Christianity and Western Civilization* (1954), *History of Europe* (with others, 1956), *Modern Europe to 1870* (1958), *Nationalism: A Religion* (1960), and *History of Western Civilization* (with others, 1962). He edited *Social and Economic Studies of Post-War France* (1929–36).

In 1930 Hayes became involved in a controversy over the use in New York City schools of his *Modern History,* which a Protestant clergyman claimed was pro-Catholic. The book was banned by the New York school board. Eventually, Hayes was cleared of the charges that his book was pro-Catholic, but thereafter he chose to write college rather than high school texts.

Hayes was active in professional associations, including the American Historical Association (president, 1945), the American Catholic Historical Association (president, 1930), and the American Philosophical Society. He was awarded many honorary degrees and received many other honors, including the Laetare (1946), Cardinal Gibbons (1949), Alexander Hamilton (1952), and Catholic Action (1956) medals and the Cardinal Newman Award (1957).

REFERENCES: *CA* (1–4); *CB* (June 1942 and November 1964); *LE* (II); *NCAB* (G:320); NYT, September 4, 1964, p. 29; *Catholic Historical Review* 50 (January 1965); 677–79; Edward Meade Earle, ed., *Nationalism and Internationalism: Essays Inscribed to Carlton J. H. Hayes* (New York: Columbia University Press, 1950); Carter Jefferson, "Carlton J. H.

Hayes," in *Historians of Modern Europe,* ed. Hans A. Schmitt (Baton Rouge: Louisiana State University, 1972); *New Catholic Encyclopedia* (New York: McGraw-Hill, 1967).   *Stuart B. Palonsky*

HAYGOOD, Atticus Green. B. November 19, 1839, Walkinsville, Georgia, to Green B. and Martha Ann (Askew) Haygood. M. 1859 to Mary F. Yarbrough. Ch. n.a. D. January 19, 1896, Oxford, Georgia.

Atticus Green Haygood was tutored for college by his mother, was graduated from Emory College (later, University) in Oxford, Georgia, and was licensed as a Methodist minister in 1859.

Haygood was chaplain to the Confederate army during the Civil War and, after the war, served as a pastor and presiding elder. He was elected Sunday school secretary of the Methodist Episcopal Church, South in 1870, where he was editor of the church Sunday school publications and supervised religious instruction.

Haygood was chosen president of Emory College (1875–84). The college grew in student body and physical plant, and the college financial problems were resolved under Haygood. He also served as editor of the *Wesleyan Christian Advocate* (1878–82), in which he expressed a moderate stance in favor of improved race relations in the South. In 1882 he was elected bishop of the church but declined the honor and became the first agent for the John F. Slater Fund, established to promote the education of blacks. In 1890 Haygood was again elected bishop, and this time he accepted the position. He moved to Los Angeles, California, in 1893, and he died three years later.

Haygood was the author of *Our Brother in Black: His Freedom and His Future* (1881) and *Pleas for Progress* (1889), which were sympathetic toward blacks and advocated cooperation of South and North to raise the status of blacks. He also wrote *Go or Send: An Essay on Missions* (1873), *Our Children* (1876), *Close the Saloons* (1882), *Sermons and Speeches* (1884), and *The Man of Galilee* (1889). Haygood was awarded honorary degrees by Emory College and Southwestern (Texas) University.

REFERENCES: *AC; DAB; NCAB* (1:520); *TC; WWW* (H); Dorothy Orr, *A History of Education in Georgia* (Chapel Hill; University of North Carolina Press, 1950).   *John F. Ohles*

HAYNES, Benjamin Rudolph. B. January 25, 1897, Plattsburgh, New York, to Benjamin Gale and Louise (Kempter) Haynes. M. August 29, 1925, to Edna Mae Young. Ch. none. D. March 4, 1962, Birmingham, Alabama.

Benjamin Rudolph Haynes was graduated from the Plattsburgh (New York) State Normal School (later, State University of New York) (1917) and received the B.S. (1928), M.A. (1929), and Ph.D. (1936) degrees from

New York University. He also studied at the University of Rochester, Albany (New York) State Teachers' College (later, State University of New York at Albany), and the University of Southern California.

During World War I he served as a civilian clerk and later was in the quartermaster corps. He became head of the commercial department of Amsterdam (New York) High School and principal of the evening high school (1919). He was chairman of the commercial department of Madison Junior High School in Rochester, New York (1922–27), and taught commercial subjects at the Packard School in New York City (1927–30). Haynes taught commercial education at New York University (1928–30) and was a member of the commerce and education department at the University of Southern California (1930–37), until he was appointed professor of business education at the University of Tennessee (1937). In 1948 he became president of Wheeler Business College in Birmingham, Alabama, a position he held until his death in 1962.

Haynes was the author or coauthor of numerous articles in professional journals and books. Among his books were *Elementary Business Training* (with Seth B. Carkin, 1924), *Problems of Teaching Elementary Business Training* (with Paul Lomax, *q.v.*, 1929), *Secretarial Problems* (1931), *Research in Business Education* (with Jessie Graham, 1932), *Problems in Business Education* (with Jessie Graham, 1933), *Study-Guide in Foundations of Business Education* (with Jessie Graham, 1935), *A History of Business Education in the United States* (with Harry P. Jackson, 1935), and *Collegiate Secretarial Training* (with Jessie Graham and Virginia H. Moses, 1937).

He served as contributing editor (1932–34) and associate editor (1934–36) of the *Journal of Business Education* and was a member of numerous professional organizations.

REFERENCES: *LE* (III); *NCAB* (E:357); *WWAE* (XI); *WWW* (IV).

S. S. Britt, Jr.

HAZARD, Caroline. B. June 10, 1856, Peace Dale, Rhode Island, to Howland and Margaret Anna (Rood) Hazard. M. no. D. March 19, 1945, Santa Barbara, California.

Caroline Hazard was educated by private tutors and at Mary A. Shaw's School in Providence, Rhode Island, and in Europe. She then assisted her father with his business interests and participated in social welfare work in Peace Dale where she taught children sewing. She also wrote and published poetry and established a reputation as an author and authority on Rhode Island colonial history.

Without a college degree or instructional or administrative experience, Hazard was elected president of Wellesley College in 1899, remaining in that position until 1910. While she was president of Wellesley, the enrollment doubled and the curriculum expanded. She added instruction in household economics, established the department of music as an academic unit, sponsored a college choir, and founded a department of hygiene and physical education. She built a president's home and raised funds for the erection of four dormitories.

Hazard was a prolific author; her works include *Life of J. L. Diman* (1886), *Thomas Hazard, Son of Robert* (1893), *Narragansett Ballads* (1894), *The Narragansett Friends Meeting* (three volumes, 1899), *Some Ideals in the Education of Women* (1900), *Scalop Shell of Quiet* (1908), *A Brief Pilgrimage in the Holy Land* (1909), *The College Year* (1910), *The Yosemite and Other Verse* (1917), *Anchors of Tradition* (1924), *From College Gates* (1925), *Songs in the Swing, Homing* (verse, 1929), *Threads from the Distaff* (1934), and *Introduction to an Academic Courtship* (1940). She edited the works of R. G. Hazard (fourteen volumes, 1889), *South Country Studies* by Esther Bernon Carpenter (1924), *John Safflin: His Book (1664–1707)* (1928), and *Nailer Tom's Diary, 1778–1840* (1930).

Hazard was active in community and charitable groups and was a member of scholarly associations. She was a recipient of several honorary degrees.

REFERENCES: NAW; NCAB (34:139); *WWW* (II); *NYT*, March 20, 1945, p. 19.   *Joan Duff Kise*

HEALD, Henry Townley. B. November 8, 1904, Chancellor, New York, to Frederick de Forest and Nellie (Townley) Heald. M. August 4, 1928, to Muriel Starcher. Ch. none. D. November 23, 1975, Winter Park, Florida.

Henry Townley Heald received the B.S. degree in civil engineering (1923) from Washington State College (later, University) in Pullman and the M.Sc. degree in civil engineering (1925) from the University of Illinois.

Heald was an assistant engineer with the United States Bureau of Reclamation at Pendleton, Oregon (1923–24), a designer for the bridge department of the Illinois Central Railroad in Chicago, Illinois (1925–26), and a structural engineer for the bureau of design for the Chicago Board of Local Improvements (1926–27). He joined the faculty of the Armour Institute of Technology teaching civil engineering (1927–38) and also was assistant to the dean (1931–33), dean of freshmen (1933–34), dean of engineering (1934–38), and president (1938–40). He was president of the Armour Research Foundation (1936–40). In 1940 the Armour Institute of Technology merged with the Lewis Institute of Technology of Chicago with Heald as president; he was also president of the Armour Research Foundation and the Institute of Gas Technology (1941–52). During Heald's tenure at Illinois Institute of Technology, the campus increased from seven to eighty-four acres, enrollment increased from over four hundred to over seven thousand students, and the school became a major engineering institution. In 1952 Heald became chancellor of New York University in New York City and served in that capacity to 1956. He was president and trustee of the Ford Foundation (1956–65) and then partner (1965–69) and chairman from 1969 of Heald, Hobson and Associates.

Heald wrote many articles for professional journals on engineering education and participated in professional activities, including the National Commission on Accrediting (chairman, 1950–56). He was a member of many organizations, including the American Society for Engineering Education (president, 1942–43), the Western Society of Engineers (president, 1945–46), and the American Association for the Advancement of Science (vice-president, 1946–47), and he was director of the George M. Pullman Foundation (1950–52). He was active on many civic committees and commissions. He was chairman of the New York State Committee on Higher Education that was influential in the development of higher education in the state (1960). He was director of several corporations and a member of the board of trustees of Rollins College. He received service awards from the Chicago Junior Association of Commerce and the Illinois Junior Chamber of Commerce (1940), a navy award for distinguished civilian service (1945), and the Washington Award (1952), and he was the recipient of many honorary degrees from American colleges and universities.

REFERENCES: *CB* (February 1952); *LE* (III); *NYT*, November 25, 1975, p. 40; *WW* (XXXVI); *WWAE* (XVI); *WWW* (VI).   *John F. Ohles*

HEATHCOTE, Charles William. B. April 19, 1882, Glen Rock, Pennsylvania, to William T. and Eva (Frey) Heathcote. M. June 15, 1909, to Emma Grace Bair. Ch. two. D. August 5, 1963, Philadelphia, Pennsylvania.

Charles William Heathcote received the A.B. (1905) and A.M. (1908) degrees from Pennsylvania (later, Gettysburg) College in Gettysburg, Pennsylvania, and was graduated from Gettysburg Theological Seminary in 1908. He was awarded the A.M. degree (1913) from the University of Pennsylvania, the S.T.D. degree (1910) from Temple University in Philadelphia, and the Ph.D. degree (1918) from George Washington University in Washington, D.C. He was ordained a Lutheran minister in 1908 and entered the Presbyterian ministry in 1923.

Heathcote was a tutor in Greek and history at the York County (Pennsylvania) Academy (1905–07) and served churches in Chambersburg, Pennsylvania (1908–11), and Philadelphia (1911–12). He was professor of church history and philosophy at Temple University in Philadelphia (1912–22) and professor of social service at Beechwood College for Young Women (1915–22). He was head of the department of social science at West Chester (Pennsylvania) State Normal School (later, West Chester State College) from 1922 to 1952.

Heathcote was the author of many books, including *The Seventy-fifth*

Year (1911), *The Essentials of Religious Education* (1916), *The Lutheran Church and the Civil War* (1919), *Pilgrimage to Oberammergau* (1922), *Battle of the Brandywine* (1923), *Outlines of Modern Government* (1923), *Essentials of Economics* (1923), *Teaching of History* (1924), *Son of the Morning* (1924), *Story of Valley Forge* (1924), *Essentials of United States History* (1925), *Luke's Gospel* (1925), *Story of the Declaration of Independence* (1926), *Story of St. John's Gospel* (1926), *Teaching the Social Studies* (1931), *Signers of the Declaration of Independence* (1932), *Lincoln in Pennsylvania* (1935), and *Origins—Mayan Civilization* (1936). He was the coauthor of *Decade of Compromise, 1850–1860* (1940).

A member of many organizations, Heathcote was president of the Franklin County (Pennsylvania) Sunday School Association (1908–11) and the Brandywine Battle Association (from 1933). He was president of the Colwyn-Philadelphia board of education (1921–22). He founded the Tri-State Historical Society in 1937. He received an award of merit from the Daughters of the American Revolution (1954). Heathcote was awarded several honorary degrees.

REFERENCES: *LE* (II); *NYT,* August 7, 1963, p. 33; *WWW* (IV).

John F. Ohles

HEBARD, Grace Raymond. B. July 2, 1861, Clinton, Iowa, to George Diah Alonzo and Margaret E. Dominick (Marven) Hebard. M. no. D. October 11, 1936, Laramie, Wyoming.

Grace Hebard received the B.S. degree in civil engineering (1882) and the M.A. degree (1885) from the State University of Iowa. In 1893 she received the Ph.D. degree by correspondence from Illinois Wesleyan University in Bloomington, Illinois.

Hebard became a draftsman for the land office of the United States surveyor general in Cheyenne, Wyoming, and remained in that position for nine years (1882–91). In 1891 she became a member of the board of trustees at the University of Wyoming and served as secretary of the board. In that position, she assumed many administrative duties. She left the board in 1903 but continued on as secretary until 1908. In 1906 Hebard became an associate professor of political economy at the University of Wyoming and at the end of her career was head of that department. She taught many subjects at the university and served in many capacities, including that of head librarian (1891–1919). In 1898 she became the first woman admitted to the Wyoming bar.

Hebard authored books on the American West, including *The History and Government of Wyoming* (1904), *Sacajawea: Pilot for Lewis and Clark* (1907), *The Pathbreaker from River to Ocean* (1911), *The First Woman Jury* (1913), *The Bozeman Trail* (with E. A. Brininstool, 1921), *Chief Washakie* (1929), *Sacajawea: A Guide and Interpreter of the Lewis and*

Clark Expedition (1933), and *The Pony Express and Telegraph Line in Wyoming* (1935).

A leader in the Wyoming women suffrage movement, Hebard was on a committee of three that drew up a petition in 1898 asking the constitutional convention of Wyoming to adopt a women's suffrage clause. She was a member of the Wyoming Child Health Commission, the American Association for the Advancement of Science, the Wyoming Historical Society (advisory board), the Wyoming Public Health Association (director), and other professional and civic organizations. She was a regent of the Daughters of the American Revolution, the state historian of Colonial Dames, and a state champion tennis player.

REFERENCES: *LE* (I); *NAW; WWW* (I).   *Karen Wertz*

HEDGES, Cornelius. B. October 28, 1831, Westfield, Massachusetts, to Dennis and Alvena (Noble) Hedges. M. July 7, 1856, to Edna Layette Smith. Ch. eight. D. April 29, 1907, Helena, Montana.

Cornelius Hedges attended local Westfield, Massachusetts, schools and academies and was graduated from Yale College in 1853. He studied law with Edward B. Gillette in Westfield and at the Harvard Law School. He completed the course in 1855 and was admitted to the bar.

Hedges had taught school while studying law and moved to Independence, Iowa, in 1857 where he opened a law office and was also publisher and editor of the *Independent Civilian*. In 1864 he joined a party that moved to Virginia City, Montana, and from there went to Helena, Montana, where he practiced law, was appointed United States district attorney in 1871, and was probate judge of Lewis and Clark County (1875–80). He was an unsuccessful candidate for congress (1874) and United States senator (1899).

Hedges was appointed territorial superintendent of public instruction in 1872 by Governor Benjamin F. Potts. He was preceded in office by seven others, one of whom had declined to serve and the others had served a year or less in the post. Hedges was responsible for the first effective functioning of the state office and establishing the basis on which the state educational system developed. Leaving the post in 1878, he continued his judgeship.

Hedges was instrumental in the founding of the Helena Public Library in 1868. He was active in the Masonic order, organizing the first lodge in Helena in 1865. He was a member of a group that explored the geyser region and led the movement to establish Yellowstone National Park. He was an organizer and first president of the Montana Historical Society (1895).

REFERENCES: *NCAB* (12:250); Helen F. Sanders, *History of Montana* (Chicago: Lewis Publishing Co., 1913), 2: 224–25.   *John F. Ohles*

HEDRICK, Earle Raymond. B. September 27, 1876, Union City, Indiana, to Simon and Amy Isabella (Vail) Hedrick. M. October 21, 1901, to Helen Breeden. Ch. eleven. D. February 3, 1943, Glendale, California.

Earle Raymond Hedrick obtained his higher education at the University of Michigan where he received the A.B. degree (1896), at Harvard University where he was awarded the A.M. degree (1898), and at the University of Göttingen, Germany, where he received the Ph.D. degree (1901). He also studied at l'Ecole normale supérieure in Paris, France (1901).

He was an instructor in mathematics at the Sheffield Scientific School at Yale University (1901–03) and was professor of mathematics at the University of Missouri (1903–24) and the University of California at Los Angeles (1924–37), where he became vice-president and provost (1937).

Hedrick was the author of *A Course in Mathematical Analysis* (with Edouard Goursat, 1904), *An Algebra for Secondary Schools* (1908), and *Applications of the Calculus to Mechanics* (with Oliver Dimon Kellogg, 1909) and also published numerous articles in mathematical and educational journals. He was editor-in-chief of the *Bulletin of the American Mathematical Society* (1921–27) and was editor for the Macmillan Company Series of Mathematical Texts and Engineering Science Series.

Hedrick was director of mathematics of the army educational corps of the American Expeditionary Force. In 1932 he was decorated as a French officier d'académie. He was a member of the American Mathematical Society (president, 1929–30), the Mathematical Association of America (president, 1916), the National Research Council (1921–24 and 1929–32), and many American and foreign learned and professional associations. He was awarded honorary degrees by the universities of Michigan and Missouri.

REFERENCES: *LE* (II); *NCAB* (F:460; 32:320); *NYT*, February 4, 1943, p. 23; *WWW* (II). *Walter J. Sanders*

HENDERSON, Algo Donmyer. B. April 26, 1897, Solomon, Kansas, to Calvert Columbus and Ella Cora (Donmyer) Henderson. M. June 7, 1923, to Anne Gillespy Cristy. M. 1963 to Jean Glidden. Ch. two.

Algo Donmyer Henderson attended Kansas Wesleyan School of Commerce (1914–15); he received the LL.B. degree from the University of Kansas (1922) and the M.B.A. degree (1929) from Harvard University.

Henderson was an instructor and assistant professor of economics at the University of Kansas (1920–24). He was at Antioch College, Yellow Springs, Ohio, for twenty-three years (1925–48) as professor, business manager, dean, executive vice-president, and president (1935–48). As president, Henderson introduced many innovations in liberal education, such as campus community government. The Antioch campus became a laboratory in living, and the Antioch tradition of work-study, involving alternations between instruction on campus and work experience in business, industry, agriculture, and the professions, was established.

Henderson served as a member of the President's Commission on Higher Education (1946–48) and helped delineate fresh goals for higher education in the postwar United States. As associate commissioner of higher education in the newly organized State University of New York (1948–50), he helped initiate the public community college law and the Fair Education Practices Act, the first in the nation. As a result of that legislation, education in New York State turned from an elitist to a populist base. From 1950 to 1966 Henderson served as director of the Center for Studies in Higher Education at the University of Michigan. There and at the Center for Research and Development of Higher Education at the University of California at Berkeley (from 1966), Henderson helped to stimulate research on the problems of higher education and train fresh leadership for colleges and universities.

Henderson's publications include *Vitalizing Liberal Education: A Study of the Liberal Arts Program* (1942), *Antioch College: Its Design for Liberal Education* (1946), *Policies and Practices in Higher Education* (1960), *Higher Education in Tomorrow's World* (1968), *The Innovative Spirit: Change in Higher Education* (1970), *Training University Administrators* (1970), *Admitting Black Students to Medical and Dental Schools* (1971), *Higher Education: Problems and Policies* (1974), and numerous articles in professional journals.

Henderson served with the United States Army in World War I. He was active in professional associations, serving as president of the Ohio College Association (1941–42) and Ohio College Presidents and Deans (1941–42), and he was a member of the commission of the North Central Association of Colleges and Secondary Schools (1947). He was associate director of the Temporary Committee on the Need for a State University (New York) in 1947–48 and was a trustee of the Ohio Civil Service Council and of Antioch College (1936–47). He served on the United States surgeon general's committee on medical school grants and aids in the 1950s. He was a member of the Michigan Commission on College Accreditation (1950–64) and a consultant to universities and the United Nations Educational, Scientific, and Cultural Organization. He received the University of Michigan's Sesqui-Centennial Medal and many honorary degrees.

REFERENCES: *CA* (1-4); *LE* (V); *NCAB* (H:93); *WW* (XXXVI); *WWAE* (VIII). *T. S. Geraty*

HENDERSON, Howard Andrew Millet. B. August 15, 1836, Paris, Kentucky, to Howard M. and Jane Elizabeth (Moor) Henderson. M. February 5, 1861, to Susan Watkins Vaughan. Ch. none. D. January 2, 1912, Cincinnati, Ohio.

Howard Andrew Millett Henderson received the LL.B. degree (1856) from Gundry's Commercial and Law School in Cincinnati, Ohio. Ohio Wesleyan University in Delaware, Ohio, awarded him the A.B. (1858) and M.A. (1876) degrees. He prepared to be a lawyer reading law in the office of United States Senator Garrett Davis at Paris, Kentucky.

Henderson was ordained in the Methodist ministry (1856). He served churches in Newberne and Demopolis, Alabama (1857–61). At the start of the Civil War, Henderson was the pastor of a Methodist church near Demopolis, Alabama. He organized and served as colonel of the Twenty-eighth Alabama Regiment. Although he served in the Confederacy and rose to the rank of brigadier general, both he and his wife were strong advocates of the abolishment of slavery. After the war, he became editor of *The New Era,* a newspaper in Demopolis, in which he advocated his readers to forget the war and promoted the idea of wiping out sectional lines and feelings. He was assistant commissioner of exchange of prisoners of war (1864–65).

Henderson returned to Kentucky and served churches at Frankfort (1866–70) and Lexington (1870–71) and taught at the Kentucky Military Institute (1867–68). He was state superintendent of public instruction (1871–79). During his administration, a system of schools for blacks was developed in Kentucky. Eager to undo as much of the damage as possible that had resulted from the war, Henderson founded a system of schools to educate the children of former slaves. While state superintendent, he was active in Kentucky education and wrote many papers and delivered numerous addresses on educational topics. He promoted the publication by his department of a work on school architecture that had a marked influence in bettering the physical plants of the schools of Kentucky.

After his terms as superintendent of public instruction, Henderson served churches in San Francisco, California (1879–80), Hannibal, Missouri (1881–83), Jersey City, New Jersey (1883–86), New York City (1886–88), and Cincinnati, Ohio (1888–1903).

Henderson was the author of *Wealth and Workmen* (1889), *Cremation* (1890), *Ethics of the Pulpit, Pew, and Parish* (1890), *Diomede, the Centurion* (1902), *Autumn Leaves* (1907), and *My Black Mammy* (1909).

He was active in fraternal and veterans' organizations and was a member of the American Institute of Christian Philosophy. He was chaplain for a number of military and fraternal groups. He received honorary degrees from Kentucky Military Institute and Kentucky College.

REFERENCES: *WW* (VII); *WWW* (I); "History of Education in Kentucky," *Bulletin of Kentucky Department of Education* 7 (July 1914): 119–20).
                                                                Roger H. Jones

HENDERSON, Lawrence Joseph. B. June 3, 1878, Lynn, Massachusetts, to Joseph and Mary Reed (Bosworth) Henderson. M. June 1, 1910, to Edith Lawrence Thayer. Ch. one. D. February 10, 1942, Boston, Massachusetts.

Lawrence Joseph Henderson, American chemist and sociologist, was the son of a ship chandler whose business interests were located in Salem, Massachusetts, and on the French Islands of Saint Pierre and Miquelon, off the coast of Canada. He attended Salem High School and was graduated with the A.B. degree (1898) from Harvard University and the M.D. degree (1902) from Harvard Medical School. He studied in Europe at the University of Strasbourg (1902–04).

Henderson began his academic career as a professor of biological chemistry at Harvard in 1904. He was an exchange professor at several American and European universities. At Harvard he designed and taught the first history of science course in 1911. He developed an interest in sociology late in his career and became director of the Fatigue Laboratory of the Harvard Graduate School of Business in 1926, where he studied the physiology of work.

Henderson's early research centered about mechanisms of neutrality regulation in animal organisms, leading to the development of a precise mathematical formulation of the acid-base equilibrium (1908). His later research was concerned with problems in the chemistry of the blood and became the basis for work on blood plasma. Henderson was one of the most original and distinguished biological chemists of his time.

Among Henderson's writings were *The Fitness of the Environment* (1913), *The Order of Nature* (1917), *Blood* (1928), and *Pareto's General Sociology* (1935). He also contributed to many scientific journals.

Henderson was the first chairman of Harvard's prestigious Society of Fellows (1933–42). He was foreign secretary of the National Academy of Sciences, a fellow of the Academy of Arts and Sciences, a member of several professional and scholarly associations, and a corresponding member of the Académie de médecine, Paris, and a member of the French Legion of Honor.

REFERENCES: *CB* (April 1942); *DAB* (supp. 3); *DSB; EB; WWW* (I); David L. Sills, ed., *International Encyclopedia of the Social Sciences* (New York: Macmillan Co. and the Free Press, 1968), vol. 6; *NYT,* February 11, 1942, p. 21.   *Rebecca L. Sparks*

HENDERSON, Lester Dale. B. April 13, 1886, Lenox, Iowa, to James Leander and Elizabeth (Hamilton) Henderson. M. December 10, 1920, to Blanche Rae Maskin. Ch. two. D. October 16, 1945, Burlingame, California.

Lester Dale Henderson received the A.B. degree (1911) from Tarkio (Missouri) College and studied on the postgraduate level at the University of California, Teachers College at Columbia University, and Stanford (California) University where he received the A.M. degree (1930).

Henderson was a teacher in Iowa district schools from 1906 and in charge of science instruction and athletics in Idaho high schools at Emmett (1911–12) and Coeur d'Alene (1912–14). Henderson was superintendent of schools in Juneau, Alaska (1914–17).

Appointed the first commissioner of education for Alaska (1917–29), Henderson was credited with the formation of the school laws, providing a plan of transportation of pupils, publishing the first courses of study, and establishing a system of reports and accounting. Henderson resigned as commissioner in 1929 and was superintendent of schools in Burlingame, California, in 1930, where he served until his death in 1945. He had been active in professional affairs, serving as Alaska director of the National Education Association (1918–27). He was president of the San Mateo (California) County board of education. He wrote articles, particularly for the *Alaska Yearbook* and *Alaska School Bulletin* (editor, 1917–19) and was the author of *Alaska, Its Scenic Features, Geography, History and Government* (1928).

REFERENCES: *LE* (II); *WW* (XVIII); *WWAE* (XI); *Alaska Press* (Juneau), October 18, 1945, p. 1; *Alaska School Bulletin* (January 1940): 11; "Commissioner of Education," *The Alaska Teacher* (November 1954): 3. *John F. Ohles*

HENDRIX, Herman Elert. B. April 8, 1880, Hauen, Germany, to Elert and Mauna (Bauman) Hendrix. M. June 30, 1901, to Elva Harter. M. July 30, 1918, to Elizabeth Love. M. 1941 to Ruth Oelke. Ch. three. D. April 19, 1948, Mesa, Arizona.

Herman Hendrix came to the United States from Germany with his family when he was a year old. He became a naturalized citizen in 1885 and grew up in Blue Earth, Minnesota, where he was graduated from high school (1896). He continued his education at North Central College in Naperville, Illinois, receiving the B.A. and Ph.B. degrees (1901). In 1909 he was graduated from the Erie College of Law in Chicago and received the M.A. degree from Stanford (California) University (1924). Hendrix received the Ph.D. degree from New York University (1929) with a major in school administration.

Hendrix enjoyed a varied educational career. After teaching high school in St. Peter, Minnesota, Hendrix and his wife homesteaded near McCluskey, North Dakota, where he taught in a one-room school. He was an elementary school principal in Everett, Washington (1909–17), and superintendent of schools in Miami, Arizona (1917–19). He joined the faculty of Northern Arizona Normal School (later, Northern Arizona University) in Flagstaff (1919–20).

Hendrix held the dual posts of superintendent of Mesa Union High School and superintendent of schools for the city of Mesa (1920–31). A court action forced him to relinquish one of these positions, and he continued as superintendent of schools solely until 1933, when he became state superintendent of public instruction.

During his state superintendency (1933–41), Hendrix presided over a growing Arizona educational program designed to upgrade all aspects of public education in the state. He organized conferences, hired educational consultants, published and circulated instructional bulletins, revised curricula, oversaw the development of adult and vocational education programs, and modified teacher certification requirements. Through in-service teacher training, he improved the preparation and professional development of elementary and secondary teachers. Hendrix did much to improve the general public's impression of the quality of state-supported education through articles in such periodicals as *Arizona* and *The Arizona Teacher and Home Journal*.

REFERENCES: *LE* (II); *WW* (XXII); *The Arizona Republic*, April 20, 1948; John C. Berry, *The Historical Role of Arizona's Superintendent of Public Instruction* (Flagstaff: Northern Arizona University, 1974); *Phoenix Republic*, April 19, 1948.   *Larry C. Thompson*

HENRI, Robert. B. June 25, 1865, Cincinnati, Ohio, to John and Theresa (Henri) Cozad. M. June 21, 1898, to Linda Craige. M. May 5, 1909, to Marjorie Organ. Ch. none. D. July 12, 1929, New York, New York.

Robert Henri (his original name, Robert Henry Cozad, was changed because his father had killed a man) has been ranked among the three most important figures in modern American art. He has been called the Teacher and Champion of American Art and could also be called the Father of Independent Painting in the United States.

Henri was educated in schools in Cincinnati, Ohio, Denver, Colorado, and New York City. He studied with Thomas P. Anschutz at the Pennsylvania Academy of the Fine Arts (1886–88). Later he studied at the Académie Julian and the Ecole des beaux-arts in Paris, France (1888–91). He taught painting in Philadelphia in the Women's School of Design (1891–95) and then engaged in independent work abroad (1895–97 and 1899). He opened a school in Paris, France, which he conducted until his return to the United States in 1900, when he opened a studio in New York City. He served for a time as an instructor in the New York School of Art. In 1909 he founded a school of art in New York City.

Henri was respected more as a teacher than as a painter. His style was often considered by critics to be slick, fast, and fluid. His portrait work revealed an instant vision of reality expressed in an almost abstract and general way. His manner of painting reflected the style of the Munich school.

He is especially remembered for his book *The Art Spirit* (1923), compiled from his scattered essays and classroom notes. He was instrumental in organizing the group of artists known as The Eight in 1908 for the purpose of holding exhibitions.

Henri was one of the three ranked in first place in a survey conducted by the Arts Council of New York in 1929 to identify the "hundred most important living artists." He was a member of the National Academy of Design, a leader of the Society of Independent Artists, and a member of other art organizations. He was represented in permanent collections in many American museums. He received many awards, including the silver medal of the Buffalo Exposition (1901) and the St. Louis Exposition (1904), the gold medal of the Philadelphia Art Club (1909), the Harris Prize of the Art Institution of Chicago (1905), the silver medal of the Panama Pacific Exposition (1915), and the portrait prize of the Wilmington Society of Fine Arts (1920).

REFERENCES: *DAB; NCAB* (15:146); *NYT,* July 13, 1929, p. 15; *WWW* (I); William Innes Homer, *Robert Henri and His Circle* (Ithaca: Cornell University Press, 1961).   *Roger H. Jones*

HENRY, David Dodds. B. October 21, 1905, East McKeesport, Pennsylvania, to Ferdinand William and Myrtle May (Byerly) Henry. M. May 6, 1927, to Sara Emily Koerper. Ch. one.

David Dodds Henry was graduated from Schenley High School in Pittsburgh, Pennsylvania, in 1922 and attended Pennsylvania State College (later, Pennsylvania State University) where he received the A.B. (1926), A.M. (1927), and Ph.D. (1931) degrees.

By 1926, Henry already had a year of part-time college teaching to his credit, having worked as an instructor of English during his senior year in college. He served as supervisor of the liberal arts extension program of Pennsylvania State University (1926–28) and as an instructor in English literature (1928–29). He joined the staff of Battle Creek (Michigan) College as professor of English and head of the department (1929–33) and served as dean of men (1930–31) and director of the school of liberal arts (1931–33). He served as assistant superintendent of public instruction for the state of Michigan (1933–35).

In 1935 Henry joined the faculty of Wayne University (later, Wayne State University) in Detroit, Michigan, as professor of English and assistant to the executive vice-president of the university. He served as executive vice-president (1939–45) and president (1945–52). In 1952 Henry resigned his position at Wayne University to accept the newly created post of executive vice-chancellor of New York University where he supervised the educational program of the University and assisted the chancellor. Henry's record at Wayne University was challenged when he was under consideration for appointment as president of the University of Illinois. An unsigned letter from a fictitious organization claimed that Henry had appointed persons alleged to be communists to the faculty and that he had been slow to ban the Wayne chapter of American Youth for Democracy after it was placed on the list of subversive organizations by the United States attorney general in 1947. The charges were proved to be false.

On September 1, 1955, Henry became the twelfth president of the University of Illinois. The university experienced a rapid period of growth during his administration. After his retirement in 1971, he continued teaching as a Distinguished Professor of Higher Education (1971–74).

Henry was the author of *What Priority for Education: The American People Must Decide* (1931), *William Vaughn Moody, A Study* (1934), and many articles for professional journals.

A member of many associations, Henry was president of the National Association of State Universities and Land Grant Colleges (1964–65), a member of the board of trustees of the Carnegie Foundation for the Advancement of Teaching (1960–70, and chairman, 1969–70), and on the advisory committee of the United States Agency for International Development, Commission on Educational Television of the Carnegie Corporation (1967–69), and Carnegie Commission on Higher Education (1967–73). He was the recipient of many honorary degrees.

REFERENCES: *CB* (June 1966); *LE* (V); *WWAE* (XI); *WW* (XXXVI).

Darlene E. Fisher

HENZLIK, Frank Ernest. B. January 11, 1893, Great Falls, Montana, to Frank John and Frances (Fisher) Henzlik. M. August 20, 1919, to Pearl May Moore. Ch. none. D. May 24, 1977, Coral Gables, Florida.

Frank Ernest Henzlik attended local Missouri public schools and received the B.S. degree (1916) from Central Missouri State Teachers College (later, Central Missouri State College) in Warrensburg. He was awarded the LL.B. degree (1920) from the University of Missouri and the M.S. (1923) and Ph.D. (1924) degrees from Teachers College, Columbia University.

A teacher in the Missouri public schools (1909–11), Henzlik was superintendent of Faucett (Missouri) consolidated schools (1911–14) and of the De Kalb (Missouri) public schools (1919–22). He was an instructor at the teachers' college of the University of Nebraska in the summers of 1923 and 1924 and professor of school administration (1924–58). He was department chairman (1924–31) and dean of the college (1931–58). He built the college into a major institution in the Midwest. After his retirement, he was professor of educational administration at the University of Miami, Florida.

Henzlik was the author of *Rights and Liabilities of Public School Boards* (1925) and was a contributor to educational periodicals. He was active in professional associations, serving as president of the North Central Association of Colleges and Secondary Schools (1944–46) and chairman of a committee on subject matter preparation for secondary schools (1935–38). He was a member of the 1939 yearbook committee of the American Association of School Administrators.

REFERENCES: *LE* (III); *WW* (XXIX); *WWAE* (XII); Erwin H. Goldenstein, "Leaders in Education, XLIV—Frank Henzlik," *Education* 82 (May 1962): 52. *Erwin H. Goldenstein*

HETHERINGTON, Clark Wilson. B. August 12, 1870, Lanesboro, Minnesota, to James W. and Aura Hetherington. M. to Daisy Alford. Ch. one. D. December 27, 1942, Palo Alto, California.

Clark W. Hetherington grew up in San Diego, California, where his family had moved from Minnesota. He enrolled in Stanford (California) University, where he was graduated with the pioneer class of 1895. He attended Clark University in Worcester, Massachusetts, studying under G. Stanley Hall (*q.v.*) (1898–1900), and spent a year of study at Zurich, Switzerland (1904–05).

He was an instructor in the Encina Gymnasium under Thomas D. Wood (*q.v.*). He served as statistician and director of recreation in the state juvenile reformatory at Whittier, California (1896–98). Hetherington was professor of physical training and director of gymnastics and athletics at the University of Missouri (1900–10). He pioneered in the establishment of recreational programs and playground facilities in Missouri and introduced Play Days for high school girls as substitute activities for organized competitive sports. He directed the program of the Fels Foundation (1910–12) and was a lecturer and professor of physical education at the University of Wisconsin (1913–18).

Hetherington was the first state supervisor of physical education in California (1918–21) and the second person to hold the position in the country. He organized a state program in physical education and came into conflict when he sought to increase the requirements for teacher education. He was an investigator for the Institute of Educational Research at Columbia University (1921–23) and accepted a position as professor of physical and recreational education at New York University, where he established the department of physical education and prepared undergraduate and graduate programs. He began a doctoral program in physical education in 1926, sharing with Columbia University the first two programs in the country.

In 1929 Hetherington returned to Stanford University, where he was professor of health and physical education, until his retirement in 1938. He was the author of many articles in professional and popular periodicals.

While at Missouri Hetherington launched a national crusade to clean up intercollegiate athletics by having all colleges adopt eligibility rules requiring players to be bona fide students and amateurs. His efforts led to the establishment of the Missouri Valley Conference (the Big Eight), and many of his ideas were incorporated into the policies of the National Collegiate Athletic Association when it was founded in 1906.

He made significant contributions to theories of play, governance of intercollegiate athletics, school physical education programs, women's sports, the Athletic Research Society, the playground movement, recreational leadership, and the professional education of teachers. He was a founder of the Athletic Research Society (president, 1907–13) and was president of the Middle West Society of Physical Education (1912) and the department of school health and physical education of the National Education Association (1910). He served as director of the School Hygiene Association (1907–15) and was active in other associations. He was the recipient of a special honor day award of the American Association of Health, Physical Education and Recreation (1939), the Posse Medal (1927), the Gulick Medal (1928), and an honorary degree from the University of Southern California. He was the first fellow of the American Academy of Physical Education; an annual award for scholarly achievement was created in his honor by the academy in 1953.

REFERENCES: *LE* (I); *WWAE* (II); Alice Oakes Bronson, *Clark W. Hetherington: Scientist and Philosopher* (Salt Lake City: University of Utah Press, 1958); R. B. Morland, "A Philosophical Interpretation of the Educational Views Held by Leaders in American Physical Education" (Ph.D. diss., New York University, 1958); R. B. Morland, "The Pragmatism of Clark Hetherington," *NCPEAM Proceedings* (1969).

Richard B. Morland

HETZEL, Ralph Dorn. B. December 31, 1882, Merrill, Wisconsin, to Henry Clayton and Sadie (Dorn) Hetzel. M. August 4, 1911, to Estelle Helene Heineman. Ch. five. D. October 3, 1947, State College, Pennsylvania.

Ralph Dorn Hetzel was a leader in the land-grant college movement. He received the A.B. (1906) and LL.B. (1908) degrees from the University of Wisconsin. He was an instructor and professor of public speaking and political science at Oregon Agricultural College (later, Oregon State University) at Corvallis (1908–13) and was director of extension (1913–17). He was president of New Hampshire College of Agriculture and Mechanic Arts (later, University of New Hampshire) in Durham (1917–26).

Hetzel arrived in New Hampshire to find a small school of 550 students. His administration was one of the most productive in the hundred-year history of the institution. Under Hetzel, the name was changed to the University of New Hampshire, and a tax basis of financial support for the university was established. The trustees of Pennsylvania State College offered Hetzel the presidency of that institution, a position he assumed on

January 1, 1927, and held until his death on October 3, 1947. During his years at Pennsylvania State, the institution evolved from a predominantly agricultural college of thirty-five hundred students to a diversified university of eleven thousand.

Hetzel received honorary degrees from seven American colleges and universities. He held office in several educational associations, including the National Association of State Universities (president, 1934) and the Association of Land-Grant Colleges and Universities (president, 1947).

REFERENCES: *LE* (II); *NCAB* (B:349); *WWAE* (VIII); *WWW* (II); Donald C. Babcock, *History of the University of New Hampshire: 1866–1941* (Rochester, N.H.: Record Press, 1941); *New Hampshire Alumnus* 24 (October 1947): 3; *NYT,* October 4, 1947, p. 17; Everett B. Sackett, *New Hampshire's University* (Somersworth: New Hampshire Publishing Co., 1974). *Edward J. Durnall*

HEWETT, Waterman Thomas. B. January 10, 1846, Miami, Missouri, to Waterman Thomas and Sarah (Parsons) Hewett. M. June 22, 1880, to Emma McChain. M. December 18, 1889, to Katherine Locke. Ch. one. D. September 13, 1921, London, England.

On the death of Waterman Thomas Hewett's father in 1850, the family moved from Missouri to Maine. Hewett was graduated from the Maine State Seminary (1864) and from Amherst (Massachusetts) College, from which he received the A.B. (1869) and A.M. (1872) degrees. He received the Ph.D. degree (1879) from Cornell University in Ithaca, New York. Interested in literature and classics, he studied modern Greek in Athens and attended lectures at the University of Heidelberg, Germany (1869–70).

Hewett was professor of German language and literature and head of the German department at Cornell University (1883–1910). During leaves of absence, he studied at the universities of Leipzig, Germany (1877–78), Leiden, the Netherlands (1877–78), and Berlin, Germany (1887–88). He resided in Europe, chiefly in Oxford, England (1913–17).

Hewett procured the extensive Zarncke library of German literature for the Cornell library, the largest collection that had been brought to America at that time. He founded at Cornell the students' guild for the relief of those who were ill and the alumni bureau to assist students in securing positions upon graduation. He was a delegate to several learned societies in Europe in 1907 and in 1909.

Among the books he wrote were *The Frisian Language: A Historical Study* (1879), *The University of Leiden* (1881), *University Administration* (1882), *The Aims and Methods of the Collegiate Study of the Modern Languages* (1884), *The Present Condition of Instruction in the Modern Languages in American Colleges* (1885), *The House of Orange* (1885), *Introduction to the Life and Genius of Goethe* (1886), *Wilhelm Scherer* (1887), *The Mutual Relations of Colleges and High Schools* (1887), *The*

Revised Constitution of the Netherlands (1887), *The Study of Modern European Literature in America* (1887), *Ministers and Sovereign in Germany* (1888), *Homes of the German Poets* (1889), *The History of Cornell University* (1894), *University Life in the Middle Ages* (1898), and *Cornell University, A History* (three volumes, 1905). He edited *A German Reader* (1889), Goethe's *Herman and Dorothea* (1891), and Uhland's *Poems* (1896). Hewett initiated the annual English and American bibliography of Goethe literature published in the *Goethe Jahrbuch* (1880–85). He contributed numerous articles on literature, history, and education to popular and scholarly periodicals in the United States and Germany. He was contributing editor to *Americana Germanica* (1896), general editor of Macmillan's *German Classics* (1895), and Berlin correspondent to the *New York Nation* (1887–88).

Hewett was considered one of the great scholars in classical German. He was a member of the Society of Frisian Language and Literature, the Society of Netherland Literature, the Royal Society of British Literature, and many American and European scholarly organizations. During World War I, Hewett was associated with the British Foreign Office in presenting the Allied cause in America (1914–16).

REFERENCES: *AC; DAB; NCAB* (8:419); *TC; WWW* (I); *NYT,* September 14, 1921, p. 19.   *Ralph M. Carter*

HIBBEN, John Grier. B. April 19, 1861, Peoria, Illinois, to Samuel and Elizabeth (Grier) Hibben. M. November 1887 to Jenny Davidson. Ch. one. D. May 16, 1933, Woodbridge, New Jersey.

John Grier Hibben entered Peoria (Illinois) High School at the age of thirteen; graduating at sixteen years of age, he entered the College of New Jersey (later, Princeton University). He distinguished himself in mathematics and upon graduation was awarded a fellowship in mathematics. He received the A.B. degree (1882) as valedictorian and the M.A. degree (1885) from the College of New Jersey. Following graduation, he studied a year at the University of Berlin. Upon his return he entered Princeton Theological Seminary, received the Bachelor of Divinity degree in 1887, and was ordained a Presbyterian minister. While enrolled in the seminary he also taught French and German at the Lawrenceville School.

Hibben's first regular charge was at the Falling Spring Presbyterian Church at Chambersburg, Pennsylvania, where he remained for four years. When a throat ailment forced him to give up the ministry in 1891, he reentered Princeton, completing studies for the Ph.D. degree (1893) and serving as an instructor in logic.

Hibben was made a professor of logic in 1897 following the publication of his *Inductive Logic* (1896). His other books were *The Problems of Phi-*

losophy (1898), *Hegel's Logic* (1902), *Deductive and Inductive Logic* (1905), and *The Philosophy of the Enlightenment* (1909). *A Defense of Prejudice and Other Essays* was published in 1911 and *The Higher Patriotism* in 1915. In 1907 he became Stuart Professor of Logic and in 1912 was named to the Stuart Chair of Philosophy, which he held to 1932.

When Princeton President Woodrow Wilson *(q.v.)* sought to eliminate the upper-class clubs and life of the dormitories by housing undergraduates in quadrangles presided over by faculty members, a storm of protest arose from alumni and trustees. After Wilson resigned the presidency in 1910 to become governor of New Jersey, there followed a period of agitation over his ideas. After an interim of eighteen months under a president pro tempore, Hibben was named to the presidency as the man best suited to bring about peace and harmony.

Under Hibben the faculty doubled in size, the four-course plan of study in the upper classes was initiated, and library holdings were doubled. Three new schools established were the school of architecture (1919), awarding a master of fine arts degree, the school of engineering (1920), offering training in chemical, mechanical, and mining engineering, and the school of public and international affairs (1930), coordinating the studies in the departments of history, politics, economics, and modern languages. A department of Oriental languages and literature was added. Greek and Latin requirements were eliminated. He discontinued appointing all the faculty committees and gave representation to students on the faculty committee involving discipline.

At the outbreak of World War I Hibben became active in the American preparedness campaign and publicly advocated American entry on the side of the Allies. He was named a member of the advisory board of the American Defense Society and a member of the advisory commission of the National Security League and the United States Junior Naval Reserve. He served as a member of the executive committee of the League to Enforce the Peace and was honorary chairman of the New Jersey branch of the League of Nations Non-Partisan Association. He was president of the Motion Picture Research Council the year before he died.

Hibben was named president of the American Philosophical Association and was made an officer of the French Legion of Honor, commander of the Order of the Crown of Belgium, and grand officer of the Serbian Order of St. Sava. He was given honorary degrees by eleven American and Canadian colleges and universities.

REFERENCES: *DAB* (supp. 1); *LE* (I); *NCAB* (33:4); *WWW* (I); Donald Drew and D. M. Lee, *Princeton Portraits* (Princeton, N.J.: Princeton University Press, 1947), pp. 79–82; *NYT,* May 17, 1933, p. 1.

Franklin Ross Jones

HICKENLOOPER, Lucy Mary Olga Agnes. See **SAMAROFF, Olga.**

HILGARD, Ernest Ropriequet. B. July 25, 1904, Belleville, Illinois, to George Engelmann and Laura (Ropriequet) Hilgard. M. September 19, 1931, to Josephine Rohrs. Ch. two.

Ernest Ropriequet Hilgard, twentieth-century psychologist, received the B.S. degree (1924) from the University of Illinois and the Ph.D. degree in psychology (1930) from Yale University.

He taught psychology at Yale (1928–33). From 1933 until his retirement in 1969, Hilgard was at Stanford (California) University teaching psychology and education. He was executive head of the department of psychology (1942–50), and dean of the graduate division (1951–55) and emeritus professor from 1969.

His books brought to the field of education current knowledge about learning, motivation, psychology, and learning and instructional theories; they include *Conditioning and Learning* (with Donald G. Marquis, 1940), *Theories of Learning* (1948), *Introduction to Psychology* (1953), *Hypnotic Suggestibility* (1965), and *The Experience of Hypnosis* (1968).

Hilgard worked with the division of child development and teacher personnel of the American Council on Education at the University of Chicago (1940–41), was a member of the national advisory mental health council of the Public Health Service (1952–56), a fellow at the Center for Advanced Study in Behavioral Sciences at Stanford University (1956–57), chairman of the Society for the Psychological Study of Social Issues (1944–45), and president of the American Psychological Association (1948–49).

He was awarded the Warren Medal of the Society of Experimental Psychologists (1940) and the Wilbur L. Cross Medal from Yale University (1971).

REFERENCES: *LE* (V); *NCAB* (I:272); *WW* (XXXIX); *WWAE* (XIII).   *Stratton F. Caldwell*

HILL, Clyde Milton. B. October 2, 1885, West Plains, Missouri, to Carrick Samuel and Eva (Arbogast) Hill. M. November 27, 1912, to Doris Knoerle. Ch. one. D. December 31, 1965, Hamden, Connecticut.

C. M. Hill received the A.B. degree (1910) from Drury College in Springfield, Missouri, and the A.M. (1915) and Ph.D. (1926) degrees from Columbia University.

Hill was superintendent of West Plains, Missouri, public schools (1902–06). He was professor of mathematics at the Missouri State Normal School (later, Southwest Missouri State College) from 1910 to 1916. He inaugurated and served as supervisor of a system of junior high schools for the state of Vermont (1916–19). He served as president of the Southwest Missouri State Teachers College (previously Missouri State Normal School) at Springfield (1918–26). He joined the faculty of Yale University as professor of secondary education (1926), was chairman of the department of education (1929–52), and was appointed Sterling Professor of Education (1938–52). He retired in 1952 and became director of the Yale-Fairfield Study of Elementary Teaching.

Hill was the author of *The Junior High School Movement* (1915), *The War Book* (with John Avery, 1918), *Vermont Junior High Schools* (1918), *A Decade of Progress in Teacher Training* (1926), *Making the Most of High School* (with R. M. Mosher, 1929), and *Public Education Under Criticism* (with C. Winfield Scott, 1929).

Hill participated in school surveys of several American cities. He was an adviser to the Connecticut Senate Investigation Committee on Education and the Governor's Commission on the Reorganization of State Government. He received a citation for distinguished service to Connecticut education by the state board of education (1951). He was a member of many professional organizations and received several honorary degrees.

REFERENCES: *LE* (II); *NYT,* January 2, 1966, p. 76; *WWAE* (XI); *WWW* (IV). *John F. Ohles*

HILL, Daniel Harvey. B. July 12, 1821, Hill's Iron Works, York District, South Carolina, to Solomon and Nancy (Cabeen) Hill. M. November 2, 1852, to Isabella Morrison. Ch. five, including Joseph M. Hill, chief justice of Arkansas. D. September 24, 1889, Charlotte, North Carolina.

Daniel Harvey Hill's father died in 1825 when young Daniel was four years old. Entering the United States Military Academy at West Point in 1837 at the age of sixteen, Hill was graduated (1842) in a class that was to give twelve generals to the Union army and eight generals to the Confederate army.

Upon graduation, he served in the Mexican War, fought in every major battle of the war, and earned promotion to the rank of brevet major. He resigned from the army in 1849 and taught mathematics in Washington College (later, Washington and Lee University) in Lexington, Virginia. He accepted an appointment to a similar chair at Davidson College in Charlotte, North Carolina (1854–59).

In the early days of the Civil War, Governor John Willis Ellis of North Carolina invited Hill to Raleigh to organize the first camp of military instruction in the state. Promoted to major general in 1862, Hill won military fame at the battle of South Mountain, or Boonesboro, and played a major role in the battle of Chickamauga and in other military actions. At the close of the war he returned to North Carolina and established a monthly magazine, *The Land We Love*, at Charlotte. Later, this magazine merged with the *New Eclectic Magazine* of Baltimore. Hill established a newspaper, the *Southern Home*.

Hill accepted the presidency of the University of Arkansas in 1877, and his administration achieved fiscal efficiency for the school. He personally taught mental and moral philosophy and political economy. He served at Arkansas until 1884, when he resigned for health reasons. He accepted the presidency of Middle Georgia Military and Agricultural College (later, Georgia Military College) in Milledgeville in 1885 and served to 1889, when failing health again forced him to resign. He returned to Charlotte, North Carolina, and died there.

Hill was the author of *Elements of Algebra* (1857), *A Consideration of the Sermon on the Mount* (1858), and *The Crucifixion of Christ* (1859).

REFERENCES: *AC; DAB; NCAB* (4:102); *TC; WWW* (H); John Hugh Reynolds and David Yancey Thomas, *History of the University of Arkansas* (Fayetteville: University of Arkansas, 1910).   *Bill W. Oldham*

HILL, David Spence. B. December 14, 1873, Nashville, Tennessee, to Felix Robertson and Martha Ordalia Macgregor (Mayes) Hill. M. June 14, 1902, to Julia (Payne) Miller. Ch. none. D. November 10, 1951, Louisville, Kentucky.

David Spence Hill received his preparatory education at Smith Academy in St. Louis, Missouri. He received the B.A. degree (1897) from Randolph-Macon College in Ashland, Virginia, and the Ph.D. degree (1907) from Clark University in Worcester, Massachusetts.

He was an instructor at Smith Academy (1897–1904) and professor of philosophy and education at Peabody College for Teachers in Nashville, Tennessee (1907–11). He was professor of psychology and education and director of the Newcomb School of Education at Tulane University in New Orleans, Louisiana, and also director of the Callender Laboratory of Psychology and Education (1911–13). He became director of the first Bureau of Educational Research under the Delgado Fund in New Orleans for the community council and school board (1913–16), organizing it to undertake sociological investigations of industries and public schools and psychological, medical, and social studies of exceptional children. He was at the University of Wisconsin as acting professor (1916–17) and at the University of Illinois as professor of educational psychology (1917–19).

In 1919 Hill was appointed president of the University of New Mexico, where he remained until 1927. He reorganized the school and put it on a sound financial basis. He constructed seven buildings, including the library, a home economics building, two resident halls, and buildings for a radio station. During his time the faculty increased and enrollment doubled.

He was research professor of education at the University of Alabama (1927–29) and engaged in research for the National Advisory Committee on Federal Relations to Education and the Carnegie Foundation in New York City (1931–34). He surveyed 269 libraries for the American Council on Education (1934–35) and became a member of the research staff for higher education of the Regent's Inquiry into Education of the State of New York. He conducted surveys for the Brookings Institution (1938–40).

He conducted a historical and industrial study of the Jeffersonville (Indiana) Quartermaster Depot for the United States Army in World War II. After the war he made surveys for industry and was visiting professor at the University of Louisville, Kentucky.

Hill was the author of *An Experimental Study of Delinquent and Destitute Boys* (1914), *Introduction to Vocational Education* (1920), *Federal Relations to Education: Basic Facts* (1931), *Economy in Higher Education* (with Fred Kelly, 1933), *Control of Tax-Supported Higher Education* (1934), and *Libraries of Washington, D.C.* (1937).

Hill was a fellow of the American Association for the Advancement of Science and a member of the National Association of State Universities (honorary), the American Psychological Association (life member), the New Mexico Association for Science (president, 1924), and the Southern Society for Philosophy and Psychology (president, 1915–16). He received honorary degrees from the universities of Kentucky and Arizona.

REFERNCES: *LE* (III); *NCAB* (40:335); *WWW* (III); *NYT,* November 12, 1951, p. 25.   *Nelson L. Haggerson*

HILL, Frank Alpine. B. October 12, 1841, Biddeford, Maine, to Joseph and Nancy (Hill) Hill. M. February 28, 1866, to Sarah Brochett. Ch. three. D. September 12, 1903, Brookline, Massachusetts.

Frank Alpine Hill entered Bowdoin (Maine) College at the age of sixteen and was graduated with honors in 1862. He taught during the long winter vacations and decided upon teaching as his life's career. He became principal of his home high school at Biddeford (Maine) in 1862 after one term at Limington (Maine) Academy. He became principal of the high school at Milford, Massachusetts (1865–70), and Chelsea (Massachusetts) High School (1870–86). After being headmaster of the new English High School at Cambridge, Massachusetts (1886–93), and serving a one-year term at the Mechanic Arts School in Boston (1894), he was appointed secretary to the Massachusetts Board of Education.

A successor to Horace Mann *(q.v.)* as secretary of the board, Hill carried on the tradition of Mann in striving for quality public education, improved teacher preparation, and better school supervision. His annual reports outlined his goals and helped establish a role for public high schools in the American educational ladder.

Hill worked to maintain local autonomy in school affairs while allowing the states to determine major aspects of educational policy. He insisted that local school districts provide a superintendent of schools. He established improved procedures for gathering school statistics, insisted on high standards for admission to normal schools, and strengthened school attendance laws.

A recognized authority in education by the time he became secretary, Hill was in demand as a lecturer and was prominent in various educational associations. He edited *Holmes Fourth Reader* (1888) and *Holmes Fifth Reader* (1889) and with John Fiske wrote *Civil Government in the United States* (1890) and *History of the United States for Schools* (1894).

REFERENCES: *DAB; NCAB* (23:292); *WWW* (I); *NYT,* September 13, 1903, p. 7.

David E. Koontz

HILL, Howard Copeland. B. December 20, 1878, St. Louis, Missouri, to James Renwick and Margaret Agnes (Kirkpatrick) Hill. M. November 26, 1908, to Hermione Ireland. Ch. six. D. June 25, 1940, Chicago, Illinois.

Howard Copeland Hill began his undergraduate training at Eastern Indiana Normal School (later, Ball State University) at Muncie, Indiana (1899–1901). He taught in several small, rural schools to make enough money to enter Indiana University, where he was graduated with the A.B. degree (1906). He earned the A.M. degree (1909) from the University of Wisconsin and the Ph.D. degree (1925) from the University of Chicago.

Hill taught history at Brazil (Indiana) High School (1907), Highland Park (Illinois) High School (1910–12), and the State Normal School (later, University of Wisconsin—Milwaukee) in Milwaukee, Wisconsin (1912–17). He was head of the department of social science at the University of Chicago High School (1917–36). He was also an assistant professor in the department of social sciences at the University of Chicago (1924–36).

He was a prolific writer. Some of his major works were *Community Life and Civic Problems* (1922), *Reading and Living* (with Rollo L. Lyman, two volumes in 1924, three volumes in 1930), *Literature and Living* (two volumes, with Rollo L. Lyman, 1925), *My Community* (with David H. Sellers, 1927), *Roosevelt and the Caribbean* (1927), *Tests in Civic Information and Civic Attitudes* (1927), *Community Civics* (1928), *Vocational Civics* (1928), *Readings in Community Life* (1930), *Readings in Vocational Life* (1930), *My Occupation* (with David H. Sellers, 1930), *Our United States* (with James A. Woodburn, 1930), *Tests in Community and Vocational Civics* (1931), *Historic Background of Our United States* (with James A. Woodburn, 1932), *United States History by Units* (with Robert B. Weaver, 1933), *Early America* (with James A. Woodburn, 1934), *Our Economic Society and Its Problems* (1934), and *Life and Work of the Citizen* (1935).

Hill was a member of many professional associations, including the National Council for the Social Studies (president, 1925–26).

REFERENCES: *LE* (I); *NCAB* (30:228); *WWW* (I); *NYT,* June 26, 1940, p. 23.

LeRoy Barney

HILL, Patty Smith. B. March 27, 1868, Louisville, Kentucky, to William Wallace and Martha J. (Smith) Hill. M. no. D. May 25, 1946, New York, New York.

Patty Smith Hill was graduated from the Louisville (Kentucky) Collegiate Institute (1887) and the Louisville Kindergarten Training School (1889).

She was the director of Model Kindergarten in Louisville from 1889 to 1893. She served as the principal of Louisville Kindergarten Training School and supervisor of public school kindergartens (1893–1905). Under the direction of Anna Bryan *(q.v.)* and Hill, the Louisville school gained a national reputation and was a frequent host to visiting educators.

Hill joined the faculty of Teachers College, Columbia University, as an instructor in kindergarten education (1905–10). Beginning in 1910, she was director of the kindergarten department and assistant professor of kindergarten education. She taught kindergarten education and was director of the department of lower primary education (1918–35).

Hill was particularly interested in experimentation and innovation in her work at Columbia. Her graduate students engaged in extensive observations and record keeping. She created materials and equipment, including the Patty Smith Hill blocks, which were large enough for pupils to use to construct buildings.

Hill was editor of the Childhood Education Series and *Experimental Studies in Kindergarten Education* (1915), and she wrote *Kindergarten Problems* (with John A. MacVannel, 1912). With her sister Mildred, Hill wrote *Song Stories for Children* (1896), including "Good Morning to You," which became popular as "Happy Birthday to You."

Hill was president of the International Kindergarten Union (1908–09) and served as a member of the Committee of Nineteen (originally Fifteen) of the National Education Association. She was the recipient of a medal from the Parents Association of Greater New York in 1928 and an honorary degree from Columbia University in 1929.

REFERENCES: *DAB* (supp. 4); *LE* (II); *NAW; WWW* (II); *NYT*, May 26, 1946, p. 32; Agnes Snyder, *Dauntless Women in Childhood Education, 1856–1931* (Washington, D.C.: Association for Childhood Education International, 1972).   *Dee Wyckoff*

HILL, Thomas. B. January 7, 1818, New Brunswick, New Jersey, to Thomas and Henrietta (Barker) Hill. M. 1845 to Ann Bellows. M. 1866 to Lucy Shepard. Ch. seven. D. November 21, 1891, Waltham, Massachusetts.

Thomas Hill, the youngest of nine children who had an impoverished childhood, became interested in theology. He received the A.B. degree (1843) from Harvard University. He was graduated from the Harvard Divinity School in 1845. While at Harvard he invented the occulator for calculating eclipses and was awarded the Scott Medal by the Franklin Institute.

Hill was a pastor in Walpole, Massachusetts (1845–59). He succeeded Horace Mann *(q.v.)* as president of Antioch College at Yellow Springs, Ohio (1859–62), and was president of Harvard University (1862–68). At Harvard, he initiated the academic council and introduced elective courses for students. He finished his active career as pastor of the First Church in Portland, Maine (1873–77).

Throughout his life his writings reflected his broad interests; they include *Christmas, and Poems on Slavery* (1843), *Elementary Treatise on Arithmetic* (1845), *Geometry and Faith* (1849), *Curvature* (1850), *First Lessons in Geometry* (1855), *Jesus, the Interpreter of Nature and Other Sermons* (1859), *Second Book in Geometry* (1862), *A Statement of the Natural Sources of Theology* (1877), and *A Practical Arithmetic* (with G. A. Wentworth, 1881). He wrote many papers and articles.

Hill was a member of the Massachusetts legislature from Waltham (1871) and accompanied Louis Agassiz *(q.v.)* on an expedition to South America. He was a fellow of the American Academy of Arts and Sciences. He was awarded honorary degrees from Harvard and Yale universities.

REFERENCES: *AC; DAB; NCAB* (6:420); *WWW* (H). *Robert McGinty*

HILLARD, George Stillman. B. September 22, 1808, Machias, Maine, to John and Sarah (Stillman) Hillard. M. 1835 to Susan T. Howe. Ch. one. D. January 21, 1879, Longwood, Massachusetts.

George Stillman Hillard was graduated from Harvard University with the A.B. degree (1828). After teaching for two years in the Round Hill School in Northampton, Massachusetts, he entered Harvard's Dane Law School and received the A.M. (1831) and LL.B. (1832) degrees.

Hillard was admitted to the bar in 1833 and maintained an extensive law practice. He and George Ripley edited *The Christian Register,* a weekly Unitarian paper. In 1833 he was associated with Charles Sumner in publishing *The Jurist.* He was part-owner and associate editor of the *Boston Courier* (1856–61).

Hillard was a member of the Massachusetts House of Representatives (1835) and Senate (1850). He was president of the Boston Common Council (1846–47) and city solicitor (1854–55). He was a delegate to the state constitutional convention of 1853. He was United States attorney for the Massachusetts district from 1866 to 1871.

Hillard was the author of many books, including *Six Months in Italy* (1853), *Memoir of James Brown* (1873), *Memoir of Jeremiah Mason* (1873), *Life of Captain John Smith* (1848), and *George B. McClellan* (1864), and he edited *Poetical Works of Edmund Spenser* (five volumes, 1839). He was an author of schoolbooks, including *A First Class Reader* (1855), *A Second Class Reader* (1857), *A Third Class Reader* (1857), *Third Primary Reader* (1858), *Fifth Reader* (1862), and *Sixth Reader* (1874). Hillard emphasized silent reading in his books but realized that the general public was not receptive to silent reading and prepared the Franklin Series, which included discussions on gesturing and facial expression. The series was written with Loomis Campbell, the author of the New Franklin Reader Series (1886).

Hillard was a member of the Massachusetts Historical Society and a fellow of the American Academy of Arts and Sciences. He was on the board of overseers of Harvard University (1871–75). He received honorary degrees from Harvard University and Trinity College.

REFERENCES: *AC; DAB; NCAB* (3:244); *TC; WWW* (H); John A. Nietz, *Old Textbooks* (Pittsburgh, Pa.: University of Pittsburgh Press, 1961).

Gina L. Randolph

HILLS, Elijah Clarence. B. July 2, 1867, Arlington, Illinois, to Elijah Justin and Mary E. (Larkin) Hills. M. June 22, 1898, to Meta Vergil Strough. Ch. four. D. April 21, 1932, Berkeley, California.

Elijah Hills obtained the A.B. degree (1892) from Cornell University in Ithaca, New York, studied at the University of Paris, France (1893–94), and was awarded the Ph.D. degree from the University of Colorado in 1906.

Hills taught at Rollins College in Winter Park, Florida (1896–1901), and Colorado College in Colorado Springs, Colorado (1902–18). He was chairman of the Romance languages department at Indiana University from 1918 to 1922 and was professor of Spanish (1922–24) and Romance philology (1924–32) at the University of California at Berkeley. He served briefly as acting president of Rollins College and for many years was a consultant for publications in modern languages for D. C. Heath and Company.

A prolific writer, Hills's articles on Spanish phonology appeared in a number of journals. His books include *Barbos Cubanos* (1901), *Spanish Grammar* (with J. D. M. Ford, *q.v.*, 1904), *Modern Spanish Lyrics* (1913), *First Spanish Course* (1917), *The Odes of Bello, Olmedo and Heredia* (1919), *Spanish Tales for Beginners* (1904), *Spanish Short Stories* (with Louise Reinhardt, 1910), *Fortuna and Jaragueta* (1920), *Cuentos y Leyendas* (1922), *A Portuguese Grammar* (1925), *Contes Dramatiques* (1927), and *French Short Stories* (with R. T. Holbrook, 1930). A collection of his writings entitled *Hispanic Studies* was published in 1929 at Stanford University under the auspices of the American Association of Teachers of Spanish.

Hills was a fellow of the American Academy of Arts and Sciences and a member of many scholarly and professional associations, and he was president of the modern language division of the Colorado Teachers Association. He was decorated as commander of the Royal Order of Queen Isabel by Spain and received an honorary degree from Rollins College.

REFERENCES: *DAB* (supp. 1); *LE* (I); *NCAB* (23:211); *WWW* (I).

C. Len Ainsworth

HIMES, Charles Francis. B. June 2, 1838, Lancaster County, Pennsylvania, to William D. and Magdalen (Lanius) Himes. M. January 2, 1868, to Mary Elizabeth Murray. Ch. two. D. December 6, 1918, Baltimore, Maryland.

Charles Francis Himes prepared for college in an academy in New Oxford, Pennsylvania, and entered Dickinson College in Carlisle, Pennsylvania, as a sophomore in 1853 at the age of fifteen. He was graduated with the A.B. (1855) and A.M. (1858) degrees. He attended the University of Giessen, Germany (1863–65), receiving the Ph.D. degree in 1865.

Himes taught mathematics and natural science in the Wyoming Conference Seminary in Wayne County, Pennsylvania (1855–56), and went west to Missouri to teach in public schools (1856–57). Himes taught at the Baltimore Female College for a year and was professor of mathematics at Troy (New York) University (1860–63). When Himes returned to the United States from Germany in 1865 he was elected to the chair of natural sciences at Dickinson College and remained for thirty-one years. In 1885 the natural sciences department was divided, and he was named professor of physics. He served as acting president of the college (1888). The organization and offering of elective laboratory courses started by Himes were among the first in the field of science at any institution of higher education.

He became interested in photography and soon was a recognized authority in certain areas of the science. He was appointed a member of a government expedition to observe the total eclipse of the sun in 1869, which led to the publication of an official report in the *Journal of the Franklin Institute,* "Some of the Methods and Results of Observation of the Total Eclipse of the Sun, August, 7th, 1869." From 1872 to 1879 he assisted the Smithsonian Institution in preparing books and the annual records of science and industry.

Himes published many articles and books of scientific and pedagogical interest, including *Tables for Qualitative Analysis* (1866), *Leaf Prints or Glimpses at Photography* (1868), *The Stereoscope* (1872), and *Historical Sketches of Dickinson College* (1879). Himes was a fellow of the American Philosophical Society and the American Association for the Advancement of Science.

REFERENCES: *AC; DAB; NCAB* (4:144); *TC; WWW* (III); *NYT,* December 8, 1918, p. 22.   *Gorman L. Miller*

HINE, Charles Daniel. B. February 26, 1845, Fair Haven, Vermont, to Orlo Daniel and Ellen Caroline (Whittelsey) Hine. M. March 29, 1880, to Mary Newell (Stark) Thomas. M. June 26, 1916, to Mabel Elizabeth Moston. Ch. three. D. August 27, 1923, Winsted, Connecticut.

Charles Daniel Hine attended Phillips Academy in Andover, Massachusetts, where he was valedictorian of the class of 1862. He received the

B.A. degree (1871) from Yale College, where he was editor of the *Yale Literary Magazine*. He attended law school at Iowa State University (later, University of Iowa) in 1876–78, receiving the LL.B. degree in 1878.

Hine served as superintendent of schools in Saginaw, Michigan (1871–74), and Norwich, Connecticut (1874–76). He was principal of a high school in Omaha, Nebraska (1880–83). Appointed secretary of the Connecticut State Board of Education in December 1882, Hine held that position longer than any other person, retiring in 1920. When he headed the state department of education, Hine continued the pioneering work of Henry Barnard *(q.v.)*, whom he followed as secretary.

From 1883 to 1920, Connecticut changed from a basically rural Yankee agricultural state with many small infant industries to a highly urban industrial state with a diverse ethnic immigrant population. Hine guided a significant amount of vital legislation through the legislature and then effectively managed it. He shared with the state board of education a belief in the need for the training of teachers and providing an environment stimulating to the child's learning. Three new facilities for training teachers were established, and state certification of teachers by examination was instituted. Supervisory districts were organized in the rural sections of the state with a corps of rural supervisors. Trade schools for vocational training in industrial centers were established, and compulsory attendance laws were enacted for all children up to the age of fourteen. To meet the needs of the large immigrant population, evening schools were opened for Americanization and adult education.

Hine was interested in providing reading material for rural communities where he was personally acquainted with the people and, as chairman of the Public Library Commission (1893–1920), secured library grants for the purchase of books for free public libraries and schools. The library at the Connecticut State Department of Education was named in his honor.

REFERENCES: *NCAB* (19: 257); *WWW* (I); D. C. Allen, "Tribute to a Pioneer," *Connecticut Teacher* (February 1950); "Charles D. Hine and His Public Service," manuscript, Hine Library, Connecticut State Department of Education. *Arthur E. Soderlind*

HINSDALE, Burke Aaron. B. March 31, 1837, Wadsworth, Ohio, to Albert and Clarinda (Eyles) Hinsdale. M. May 24, 1862, to Mary Turner. Ch. three. D. November 29, 1900, Atlanta, Georgia.

Burke Aaron Hinsdale enrolled in the Western Reserve Eclectic Institute in Hiram, Ohio, at the age of sixteen; in two years he completed his formal education at the institute. At Hiram he became a close friend of his teacher, James A. Garfield, and remained a principal confidant of Garfield's until the President's assassination in 1881.

Hinsdale taught school in several northeastern Ohio districts before he returned to Hiram, where he taught throughout the Civil War. He temporarily left Hiram to enter the ministry for the Disciples of Christ (1865–68) and preached to small congregations in Solon and Cleveland, Ohio, and Detroit, Michigan, before he decided to return to study and teaching. He accepted the professorship of history, English literature, and political science (1868) and was president (1870–82) of Hiram College (the former institute).

Leaving Hiram, Hinsdale became superintendent of schools in Cleveland, a post he held for six years (1882–88). Despite his unpopularity with the school board, which was involved in scandals in the conduct of the schools, Hinsdale improved the program of the city's normal school, led a campaign for free textbooks, and reorganized the system's school building program. The school board failed to renew his contract in 1888, and he accepted an offer to become the second holder of a chair in the science and art of teaching at the University of Michigan.

At Michigan (1888–1900), he completed several ambitious projects, including reports on education in the United States and in foreign nations that were published by the United States Bureau of Education. Hinsdale edited President Garfield's papers in two volumes, *Works* (1882), and wrote *Genuineness and Authenticity of the Gospel* (1872), *The Jewish Christian Church* (1878), *Ecclesiastical Tradition* (1879), *President Garfield and Education* (1882), *Schools and Studies,* a collection of his essays and addresses dedicated to Hiram students (1884), *The Old Northwest,* a pioneering work in American social history (1888), *The American Government* (1891), *How to Study and Teach History* (1894), *Teaching the Language-Arts* (1896), *Horace Mann and the Common School Revival in the United States* (1898), and *The Art of Study* (1900). *The History of the University of Michigan* was published posthumously in 1906.

Active in professional associations, he served as president of the National Council of Education (1897) and the Michigan State Teachers' Association (1900).

REFERENCES:*AC; DAB; NCAB* (10:471); *TC; WWW* (I); Harold Eugene Davis, *Hinsdale of Hiram: The Life of Burke Aaron Hinsdale, Pioneer Educator, 1837–1900* (Washington, D.C.: The University Press of Washington, D.C., 1971); Ida S. Susseles, "Burke Aaron Hinsdale as Educator" (Ph.D. diss., New York University, 1939); Harriet Taylor Upton, *History of the Western Reserve* (Chicago: The Lewis Publishing Co., 1910).

Kim Sebaly

HITCHCOCK, Edward. B. May 24, 1793, Deerfield, Massachusetts, to Justin and Mercy (Hoyt) Hitchcock. M. 1821 to Orra White. Ch. six, including Edward Hitchcock, Jr. *(q.v.),* educator, and Charles Henry Hitchcock, geologist. D. February 27, 1864, Amherst, Massachusetts.

Edward Hitchcock was a geologist, educator, and clergyman. He developed an early interest in school work with a special interest in natural history and mathematics. His youth was spent on a farm, and he engaged in surveying and in carpentry. He worked through the day and studied at night.

Hitchcock was principal of Deerfield (Massachusetts) Academy (1815–18). Through Amos Eaton *(q.v.)*, he became interested in botany and mineralogy. He entered the theological school at Yale College in New Haven, Connecticut, and formed a friendship with Professor Benjamin Silliman *(q.v.)*. He was graduated from Yale in 1820. He was pastor of the Congregational church in Conway, Massachusetts (1821–25). He was appointed professor of chemistry and natural history at Amherst (Massachusetts) College in 1825 and in 1845 became president of Amherst. He held that office until 1855 when he resigned to assume a professorship of theology and geology. While Hitchcock was president of Amherst, new buildings, apparatus, and funds were obtained, and the number of students doubled.

In 1830 Hitchcock was appointed state geologist for Massachusetts. He completed the first survey of an entire state conducted under governmental authority. The results were published in *Report on the Geology, Mineralogy, Botany, and Zoology of Massachusetts* (1833). In 1841 he published two volumes entitled *Final Report on the Geology of Massachusetts*. He was appointed geologist of the first district of the newly organized survey of New York (1836). He was among the first to study the fossil footprints of the Connecticut valley. In 1856 he assumed the position of state geologist of Vermont and in 1861 presented the *Report on the Geology of Vermont* in two volumes.

Hitchcock was a prolific writer. In addition to geological reports, he wrote *The Downfall of Bonaparte* (1815), *Elementary Geology* (1837), *Outline of the Geology of the Globe* (1850), *The Religion of Geology and Its Connected Sciences* (1851), *Illustrations of Surface Geology* (1857), *Elementary Anatomy and Physiology* (with Edward Hitchcock, Jr., 1860), and the autobiographical *Reminiscences of Amherst College* (1863).

Hitchcock was a founder of the American Association of Geologists in 1840 (later, American Association for the Advancement of Science in 1847) and was its first chairman. He was a charter member of the American Academy of Arts and Sciences. He received honorary degrees from Harvard University and Middlebury College.

REFERENCES: *AC; DAB; DSB; NCAB* (5:308); *TC; WWW* (H); *NYT*, March 6, 1864, p. 5. *Michael R. Cioffi*

HITCHCOCK, Edward. B. May 23, 1828, Amherst, Massachusetts, to Edward *(q.v.)* and Orra (White) Hitchcock. M. November 30, 1853, to

Mary Lewis Judson. Ch. ten. D. February 16, 1911, Amherst, Massachusetts.

Edward Hitchcock, son of the third president of Amherst (Massachusetts) College, was the first professor of physical education to have full faculty status in an American college. After completing his studies at Amherst (Massachusetts) Academy and Williston Seminary in Easthampton, Massachusetts, Hitchcock attended Amherst College, graduating with the A.B. (1849) and A.M. (1852) degrees. He studied at Harvard University (1852–53) and received the M.D. degree in 1853.

Hitchcock taught elocution and natural sciences at Williston Seminary (1850–60). He spent a year studying comparative anatomy in England under the direction of Sir Richard Owen of the British Museum. In 1861 on his return to the United States, Hitchcock was selected director of the new department of hygiene and physical education at Amherst College, a departmental connection he retained for almost fifty years. He is credited with the formation of the first organized departmental program of physical education in an American college. Hitchcock was acting president (1898–99) and dean of the faculty (1898–1910) at Amherst.

During the first year of the new physical education program, Hitchcock began a study of student physical norms and anthropometric measurements. This study continued for many years, and the results were published in *An Anthropometric Manual* (1887). He had earlier published a book with his father, *Elementary Anatomy and Physiology for Colleges, Academies and Other Schools* (1860). He wrote articles and reports on physical education, which included his *Report of Twenty Years' Experience in the Department of Physical Education and Hygiene in Amherst College* (1881).

Hitchcock was one of the founders of the American Association for the Advancement of Physical Education in 1885 and served as its first president (1885–88). He was a charter member (1897) and president of the Society of College Gymnasium Directors. He was a trustee of several institutions, including Mount Holyoke College and Williston Seminary.

REFERENCES: *AC; DAB; NCAB* (13:95); *TC; WWW* (I); Fred E. Leonard and George B. Affleck, *A Guide to the History of Physical Education* (Philadelphia: Lea and Febiger, 1947); Arthur Weston, *The Making of American Physical Education* (New York: Appleton-Century-Crofts, 1962); *NYT*, February 16, 1911, p. 11.   *Adelaide M. Cole*

HOCKING, William Ernest. B. August 10, 1873, Cleveland, Ohio, to William Francis and Julia Carpenter (Pratt) Hocking. M. June 28, 1905, to Agnes (Smiley) Boyle O'Reilly. Ch. three. D. June 12, 1966, Madison, New Hampshire.

Educator, philosopher, and writer, William Ernest Hocking early learned discipline and practical handiwork from his Canadian-born physician father. He was graduated from high school at the age of fifteen and took a job as a surveyor, specializing in mapmaking. He moved with his family in 1894 to Ames, Iowa, where he studied for two years at the State College of Agriculture and the Mechanical Arts (later, Iowa State University). In 1899 he spent the summer at the University of Chicago. There he was influenced by his reading of William James's *(q.v.) Principles of Psychology* and decided to attend Harvard University. Hocking was graduated with the A.B. (1901), A.M. (1902), and Ph.D. (1904) degrees from Harvard. He attended Göttingen, Berlin, and Heidelberg universities in Germany as a Walker Fellow in Philosophy (1902–03).

Hocking taught philosophy at Harvard and history and philosophy at the nearby Andover-Newton Theological Seminary (1904–06). He taught philosophy at the University of California at Berkeley (1906–08) and was assistant professor and professor at Yale University (1908–14). Hocking returned as professor of philosophy to Harvard in 1914 and continued to teach until his retirement in 1943. He was Alford Professor of Natural Religion, Moral Philosophy, and Civil Polity (1920–43).

Strongly committed to the importance of philosophy in human affairs, Hocking sought to reconcile, or synthesize, the realistic and idealistic points of view of William James and Josiah Royce and to apply philosophical insights to practical human affairs. His many books include *The Meaning of God in Human Experience: A Philosophical Study of Religion* (1912), *Human Nature and Its Remaking* (1918), *Morale and Its Enemies* (1918), *Man and the State* (1926), *Types of Philosophy* (1929), *The Spirit of World Politics: with Special Studies of the Near East* (1932), *Re-Thinking Missions* (1932), *Lasting Elements of Individualism* (1937), *Living Religions and a World Faith* (1940), *Recent Trends in American Philosophy* (1941), *Science, Value, and Religion* (1942), *What Man Can Make of Man* (1944), *Science and the Idea of God* (1944), *Experiment in Education* (1954), *The Coming World Civilization* (1956), *The Meaning of Immortality* (1957), and *Strength of Men and Nations: A Message to the U.S.A. vis-à-vis the U.S.S.R.* (1959).

Hocking was president of the Metaphysical Society of America and a member of other important scholarly organizations. With his wife he founded Shady Hill School, which developed a reputation as an experimental elementary school. He received nine honorary degrees from American and foreign colleges and universities and was decorated by the Federal Republic of Germany.

REFERENCES: *CA* (13–16); *CB* (March 1962); *LE* (II); *NCAB* (54:5, D:452); *WWAE* (XIII); *WWW* (IV); *NYT*, January 13, 1966, p. 39.

William W. West

HODGE, Oliver. B. September 24, 1901, Exeter, Missouri, to George W. and Cordie Lee (Antle) Hodge. M. June 8, 1924, to Faye Hall. Ch. none. D. January 14, 1968, Oklahoma City, Oklahoma.

Oliver Hodge attended school in Collinsville, Oklahoma. He received the A.B. degree from the University of Tulsa (Oklahoma) in 1929 and the M.E. (1933) and Ed.D. (1937) degrees from the University of Oklahoma.

Hodge was a teacher and principal in the Collinsville High School (1921–28). He was a member of the faculties of the University of Tulsa (1929–32) and University of Oklahoma (1932–37). From 1937 to 1947, he was Tulsa County superintendent of schools. He was elected Oklahoma state superintendent of public instruction in 1947 and was reelected five times, serving to his death in 1968.

As state superintendent, Hodge exerted a strong leadership during his twenty-one years, reducing by one-sixth the number of school districts in the state, improving procedures for the selection of textbooks, leading the state into compliance with the United States Supreme Court rulings on desegregation, and improving the standards for teacher certification. As an ex officio member of the board of regents for Oklahoma colleges, he exerted an influence in the development of the colleges and changed the appointment of presidents from a system of patronage to one based on qualifications.

Hodge was a member of a number of professional associations, including the Council of Chief State School Officers, for which he served a three-year term on the board of directors and was president (1959–60). He represented the council on the National Council for the Accreditation of Teacher Education (1963–66).

REFERENCES: *LE* (III); *WWAE* (XIV); *WWW* (IV); "Oklahoma Loses One of Its Greatest Stars," *The Oklahoma Teacher* (March 1968): 18–19.

John F. Ohles

HODGIN, Charles Elkanah. B. August 21, 1858, Lynn, Indiana, to Filnias and Rachel (Hinshaw) Hodgin. M. to Sarah Overmen. M. December 24, 1892, to Mary Ella Brooks. Ch. none. D. August 27, 1934, Pasadena, California.

Charles E. Hodgin was graduated from the State Normal School of Indiana (later, Indiana State University) in Terre Haute in 1881. He was a member of the first graduating class of the University of New Mexico, receiving the B.Pd. degree (1894). He studied at the University of California (1903–04) and traveled abroad (1911–12).

Hodgin was principal of the Trafalgar (Indiana) village schools (1881–83) and professor of pedagogy and secretary of Richmond (Indiana) Normal School (1883–85). He was a teacher at the Albuquerque (New Mexico) Academy (1885–87) and was principal of the school (1887–91).

He was named the first superintendent of the Albuquerque public schools in 1891 and served in that position until 1897, when he joined the faculty of the University of New Mexico as a professor in the education department. He was named dean of the school of education (1913) and dean of the university (1914). He became vice-president of the university (1917), a position he held until his retirement in 1925. Hodgin was active in the establishment of a model school for practice teaching, involving the University of New Mexico and Albuquerque High School.

He was editor of the *University News* and authored many papers. Hodgin was the author of a text, *A Study of Spoken Languages* (1909), which was adopted by the Territorial Board of Education in New Mexico for teacher institutes.

He was one of the organizers of the New Mexico Educational Association in 1886 and twice served as president. He was active in the National Educational Association and served as sixth vice-president. He was president of the University of New Mexico Alumni (1909). In 1927 he was awarded an honorary degree by the University of New Mexico. The first building on the University of New Mexico campus was renamed in his honor.

REFERENCES: *WWW* (IV); D. F. Hughes, *Pueblo on the Mesa* (Albuquerque: University of New Mexico Press, 1939).   *E. A. Scholer*

HOLBROOK, Alfred. B. February 17, 1816, Derby, Connecticut, to Josiah (*q.v.*) and Lucy (Swift) Holbrook. M. March 24, 1843, to Melissa Pierson. M. August 31, 1892, to Eason Thompson. Ch. six. D. April 16, 1909, Lebanon, Ohio.

Alfred Holbrook entered Groton (Massachusetts) Academy after attending local public schools. His formal education ended with his withdrawal at the age of fourteen after three years of attendance. He prepared himself for civil engineering by independent study and on-the-job training in the family factory.

Because of ill health he moved to Berea, Ohio, accepting an appointment as a teacher in John Baldwin's school (later, Baldwin-Wallace College). He also served as principal of the Western Reserve Teachers Seminary in Kirtland, Ohio.

Holbrook accepted an appointment as the first principal of the Southwestern State Normal School at Lebanon, Ohio (1855). Southwestern State (also called Southwestern Normal School and Lebanon University) opened on November 24, 1855, with ninety-five students and three teachers as a privately financed venture until state aid could be obtained. No state money was granted, and the school was turned over to Holbrook to operate as his private enterprise. Holbrook hired more staff and implemented a common school and a high school course of study; enrollment reached 1,600 in 1874–75. Holbrook's program provided for staggered terms of ten to eleven weeks throughout the year. Self-boarding by students and boarding clubs reduced expenses 50 percent. Holbrook required no special examinations, gave equal rights and responsibilities to all men and women students, and had no prescribed rules of conduct. He was condemned for lowering standards in American higher education. The school continued its growth with its fifty-week calendar, opened a business department, and offered more collegiate studies in 1864.

By 1870 Holbrook was president, and he changed the name to the National Normal University. The school offered courses in teacher training, business, engineering, and regular collegiate courses in addition to a preparatory department. Despite continued growth in enrollment, financial difficulties forced the university into receivership in 1895. In 1896 Holbrook moved to Tennessee, where he established the unsuccessful Alfred Holbrook Normal University. In 1897 Holbrook became chancellor of Southern Normal University in Huntington, Texas, where he remained to his retirement.

Holbrook wrote *The Normal: or Methods of Teaching the Common Branches* (1859), *School Management* (1871), *An English Grammar Conformed to Present Usage* (1873), and *Reminiscenses of the Happy Life of a Teacher* (1885).

REFERENCES: *AC; DAB; WWW* (I); James J. Burns, *Educational History of Ohio* (Columbus: Historical Publishing Co., 1905), pp. 503–04; The Gazette Publishing House, *A History of Education in the State of Ohio: A Centennial Volume* (Columbus: The Gazette Publishing House, 1876).   *Charles M. Dye*

HOLBROOK, Josiah. B. 1788, Derby, Connecticut, to Daniel and Ann (Hitchcock) Holbrook. M. May 1815 to Lucy Swift. Ch. two, including Alfred Holbrook *(q.v.)*, developer of the National Normal University at Lebanon, Ohio. D. June 17, 1854, Lynchburg, Virginia.

Josiah Holbrook was a creative educational reformer who established the lyceum movement of adult education. He was graduated from Yale College in 1810 after studying with the eminent professor of chemistry and mineralogy, Benjamin Silliman *(q.v.)*. Holbrook was active in popularizing scientific knowledge and the scientific method through itinerate lectures on scientific subjects.

Holbrook organized and administered a series of schools, including a private school at Derby, Connecticut (1810), an industrial school (1819), and an agricultural seminary (1842–49). In October 1826 Holbrook wrote "Association of Adults for Mutual Education" for the *American Journal of Education*. He wrote that public education should be organized in mutual learning associations in towns and villages in the Northeast. His plan, which became known as the American lyceum, was implemented one month later at Millbury, Massachusetts. The movement sought to promote mutual improvement of members through study and association, to establish libraries and museums of natural science, and to encourage and support the establishment of tax-supported common schools. The lyceum movement peaked in the mid-1830s with about 3,500 local lyceums organized in the northeastern states.

Holbrook built and supplied local lyceums with scientific apparatus needed to assist in conducting educational activities. He lived at Lyceum Village in Berea, Ohio, where he manufactured and sold equipment (1837–42).

Holbrook lived in New York City (1842–49) when he was executive secretary of the American Lyceum Association. He moved to Washington, D.C., in 1849, where he promoted the lyceum system until his death in 1854. Holbrook wrote many pamphlets on geology and education. He drowned in Blackwater Creek near Lynchburg, Virginia, on an outing to collect specimens of minerals and plants indigenous to the area.

Holbrook was the author of *Easy Lessons in Geometry* (1829), *First Lessons in Geology* (1833), *A Familiar Treatise on the Fine Arts, Painting, Sculpture, and Music* (1833), *First Lessons in Geometry* (1833), *Penny Tracts for Children* (1833), *Apparatus for Schools, Academies, and Lyceums* (183?), and *Agricultural Geology* (1851).

REFERENCES: *DAB; WWW* (H); Carl Bode, *The American Lyceum Town Meeting of the Mind* (New York: Oxford University Press, 1965); Hartley C. Grattan, *American Ideas about Adult Education, 1790–1951* (New York: Bureau of Publications, Teachers College, Columbia University, 1959).   *Carroll A. Londoner*

HOLLAND, Ernest Otto. B. February 4, 1874, Bennington, Indiana, to Philip C. and Ann A. (Chittenden) Holland. M. no. D. May 30, 1950, Westover Air Force Base, Massachusetts.

Ernest Otto Holland was graduated from Indiana University with the A.B. degree (1895). He earned the Ph.D. degree (1912) from Columbia University. He studied social and economic conditions in Europe during the summers of 1905 and 1909.

Holland taught high school in Rensselaer and Anderson, Indiana, between 1895 and 1900. He was head of the English department at Boy's High School in Louisville, Kentucky (1900–05). He was a professor of secondary education at Indiana University (1905–11) and superintendent of the Louisville (Kentucky) public schools (1911–16).

Holland was president of Washington State College (later, University) in Pullman, Washington (1916–45). He reorganized the college into colleges and schools and established divisions of physical education and general extension. Many new buildings were constructed, and student enrollment more than doubled. He was honored after his retirement when the state legislature named a new campus library for him.

Holland was the author of *Written and Oral English* (with Martin W. Sampson, 1907), *The Pennsylvania State Normal Schools and Public Education* (1912), and *College and University Administration* (with E. E. Lindsay, 1930).

He was a member of many organizations, including the Reconstruction Educational Alliance (advisory board), the Society of College Teachers of Education (secretary), and the Association of Land-Grant Colleges and Universities (president, 1931–32). He served as a member of the Washington State Board of Education and the selection committee of the Rhodes Scholarship Trust and was an elector to the Hall of Fame. He received honorary degrees from Indiana University and Whitman College of Walla Walla, Washington.

REFERENCES: *LE* (III); *NCAB* (39:280); *WWAE* (XI); *WWW* (III); *NYT,* June 1, 1950, p. 27.   *James M. Vosper*

HOLLEY, Horace. B. February 13, 1781, Salisbury, Connecticut, to Luther and Sarah (Dakin) Holley. M. January 1805 to Mary Austin. Ch. two. D. July 31, 1827, at sea.

Horace Holley, clergyman, educator, and university president, was trained primarily to be a minister in the Unitarian church, although he made his greatest contribution in the field of school administration.

Holley began his formal education at Williams College in Williamstown, Massachusetts, and was graduated from Yale College with the A.B. (1803) and A.M. (1806) degrees. He studied law in the New York office of Riggs and Radcliffe but returned to New Haven in 1804 to study theology under Timothy Dwight *(q.v.);* he was ordained on September 13, 1805. He served churches at Fairfield, Connecticut (1805–08), and Boston, Massachusetts (1809–18).

Holley became president of Transylvania University in Lexington, Kentucky, in 1818 and served to 1827. Under his administration, Transylvania gained in enrollment and prestige. At the time of Holley's election, the school had been the center of conflict between sectarian groups for control of the board of trustees and the institution.

Holley was influential in obtaining state funds for Transylvania. He recruited men of ability and reputation to the faculty and provided leadership for the development of law and medical schools, with particular success with the medical school. During Holley's tenure, Transylvania became known as the Athens of the West and played an influential role in the education and culture of the Mississippi Valley.

Groundless charges of infidelity were made against Holley by a sectarian opposition that regarded him as too liberal and too independent. He was also troubled by a lack of adequate assistance and encouragement from the state and resigned the presidency in 1827.

After leaving Transylvania and Lexington, he went to New Orleans, Louisiana, where he was asked to reestablish the College of New Orleans. Unable to adjust to the weather and climate of New Orleans, Holley could not continue his work. To restore his health, he took an ocean voyage from New Orleans to New York, contacted yellow fever, died on July 31, 1827, and was buried at sea.

He received an honorary degree from Cincinnati College.

REFERENCES: *AC; DAB; NCAB* (4:513); *TC; WWW* (H).

Roger H. Jones

HOLLINGSWORTH, Orlando Newton. B. April 5, 1836, Calhoun County, Alabama, to Benjamin and Joycie (Jones) Hollingsworth. M. to n.a. D. n.a.

Orlando Newton Hollingsworth was a soldier, teacher, lawyer, editor, state legislator, and officer of the state government. After the death of his father, he moved with his mother from Alabama to Rusk County, Texas, in 1845. He was graduated from the University of Virginia (1859) and entered the Confederate army in 1861.

After the war, he established and taught at a private academy in San Antonio, Texas. In 1868 he founded the Coronal Institute at San Marcos. While there he was admitted to the bar and practiced law. In 1872 he was elected on the Democratic ticket to the thirteenth legislature, where he was influential in matters relating to public education. The following year he was elected state superintendent of public instruction by an overwhelming majority.

This was a tumultuous period in Texas school history. In a reaction against the Republican Reconstructionist regime, the Texas Constitution of 1875 abolished state procedures for controlling public schools and eliminated the office of superintendent of public instruction. Hollingsworth was then appointed secretary of the board of education (1876) and continued to serve in this position until January 1883. Throughout his term, he was one of the leaders in a movement to build confidence in a state system of public education.

In 1880 Hollingsworth established and assumed editorship of the *Texas Journal of Education,* a monthly periodical. In 1882 he sold the *Journal* and in 1883 retired from public office. After serving as a receiving clerk at the General Land Office, he disappeared from public life.

REFERENCES: Frederick Eby *(q.v.), Education in Texas: Source Materials,* University of Texas Bulletin No. 1834 (Austin: University of Texas, April 1918); W. S. Speer and J. H. Brown, eds., *The Encyclopedia of the New West* (Marshall, Texas: The United States Biographical Printing Co., 1881); *Texas Public Schools: 1854–1954* (Austin: Texas Education Agency, 1954).

Mary Doyle

HOLLINGWORTH, Leta Anna Stetter. B. May 25, 1886, Chadron, Nebraska, to John G. and Margaret Elinor (Danley) Stetter. M. December 31, 1908, to Harry L. Hollingworth. Ch. none. D. November 27, 1939, New York, New York.

Born in an underground dugout, Leta Stetter Hollingworth lived in a sod house and attended school in a one-room log schoolhouse. She was graduated from the Valentine, Nebraska, high school in 1902 and attended the University of Nebraska. She received the A.B. degree and state teacher's certificate in 1906. She received the M.A. (1913) and Ph.D. (1916) degrees from Teachers College, Columbia University.

Hollingworth was a teacher in high schools at Dewitt (1906–07) and McCook (1907–08), Nebraska. She was a clinical psychologist in New York City hospitals (1913–16) and accepted an appointment teaching educational psychology at Teachers College (1916–19) and education (1919–39). An experimental school was established by the New York City Board of Education in 1936 with Hollingworth as director of research.

Hollingworth was interested in group and individual differences. She pioneered in the clinical study and testing of subnormal children and advocated study, testing, and care of the gifted child. She sought the recognition and training of the gifted child to utilize his intellect and help him develop a healthy personality. She was a leader in establishing standards for clinical psychologists and building their professional organizations.

She was the author or coauthor of *Functional Periodicity* (1914), *The Psychology of Special Disability in Spelling* (1918), *The Psychology of Subnormal Children* (1920), *Special Talents and Defects: Their Significance to Education* (1923), *Gifted Children* (1926), and *The Psychology of the Adolescent* (1928). A collection of poems, *Prairie Years,* and *Public Addresses* were published posthumously in 1940. She was an associate editor of the *Journal of Genetic Psychology.*

Hollingworth was presented an honorary degree by the University of Nebraska in 1937.

REFERENCES: *DAB* (supp. 2); *LE* (I); *WWW* (I); *American Journal of Psychology* 53 (April 1940): 299–301; *NYT,* November 28, 1939, p. 25; Arthur I. Gates (ed.), "Education and the Individual," *Teacher's College Record,* 42 (December 1940): 183–264; Harry L. Hollingworth, *Leta Stetter Hollingworth* (Lincoln: University of Nebraska Press, 1943).

Ned V. Schimizzi

HOLMES, George Frederick. B. August 21, 1820, Straebrock, British Guiana, to Joseph Henry Hendon and Mary Anne (Pemberton) Holmes. M. July 23, 1845, to Laetitia Floyd. Ch. six. D. November 4, 1897, Charlottesville, Virginia.

George Frederick Holmes was sent from British Guiana, where his father was proctor of vice-admiralty and judge advocate, to England to be educated. In 1836 he entered the University of Durham but left school and England a year later, sailing to Canada.

From 1838 to 1842, he moved about in the southern United States, was admitted to the South Carolina bar in 1842, and practiced law for a year in Orangeburg, South Carolina. In 1846 he accepted a position as professor of classical languages at Richmond (Virginia) College. He became a professor of political economy at William and Mary College in Williamsburg, Virginia (1847). He was elected president of the newly created University of Mississippi in 1848, where he remained less than a year after a serious accident in which he lost the sight of an eye. From 1849 to 1857, he resided on his wife's plantation in western Virginia where he farmed, wrote articles, and carried on an extensive correspondence.

In 1857 Holmes accepted a professorship in the school of history and literature at the University of Virginia, and he spent the remainder of his career there. As head of the University of Virginia's school of historical science, created in 1882, Holmes instituted inquiries into and criticisms of the teachings of modern economists and published his findings in *The Science of Society* (1883). He was an important critic of positivism, a pioneer in sociology, and a contributor to southern periodical literature.

After the Civil War, Holmes began to write school textbooks, for which he ultimately gained a reputation. These included the Southern University Series of readers (primer to high school), *The Southern Elementary Spelling Book* (1866), and *The Southern School Speaker* (1867). In 1870 he published his University Series of *Holmes' Readers* (first to third) and *A School History of the United States of America* (1870). He also wrote *A Grammar of the English Language* (1871), *An Elementary Grammar of the English Language* (1868), *First Lessons in English Grammar* (1877), and *New School History of the United States* (1882).

REFERENCES: *AC; DAB; NCAB* (13:209); *TC; WWW* (H); Leonidas J. Betts, "George Frederick Holmes: A Critical Biography of a Nineteenth-Century Southern Educator" (Ed.D. diss., Duke University, 1966). *Leonidas Betts*

HOLZINGER, Karl John. B. August 9, 1892, Washington, D.C., to John Michael and Sara (Ritchie) Holzinger. M. June 17, 1917, to Marion Stone. Ch. two. D. January 15, 1954, Chicago, Illinois.

Karl John Holzinger was graduated from the University of Minnesota, receiving the A.B. (1915) and M.A. (1917) degrees. In 1917 he became an instructor of mathematics at Minnesota.

Holzinger served in World War I as a psychologist for the United States Army. In 1920 he joined the faculty of the University of Chicago where he received the Ph.D. degree (1922). Holzinger collaborated with Charles Spearman and Karl Pearson at the University of London in the research on factor analysis and educational psychology from 1922 to 1925. He continued as a member of the University of Chicago faculty to his death in 1954.

Included in Holzinger's list of publications are *Statistical Tables for Students in Education and Psychology* (1925), *Statistical Methods* (1928), *Statistical Resumé of the Spearman Theory* (1930), *The Student Manual of Factor Analysis* (1935), *The Spearman-Holzinger Preliminary Reports (1–9) on Factor Analysis* (1935–40), *Factor Analysis: A Synthesis* (with Harry H. Harman, 1941), *Twins* (with Frank N. Freeman, *q.v.*, and Horatio H. Newman, 1937), *The Stability of a Bi-Factor Solution* (with Frances Swinford, 1939), and *The Reliability of a Bi-Factor Solution* (with Frances Swinford, 1942). Holzinger was editor of the *Journal of Educational Psychology* from 1949 to 1954.

He was vice-president of the American Statistical Association (1933) and president of the Psychometric Society (1941).

REFERENCES: *LE* (III); *WWW* (III); *NYT,* January 16, 1954, p. 15.   *Thomas Meighan*

HOMANS, Amy Morris. B. November 15, 1848, Vassalboro, Maine, to Harrison and Sarah Blish (Bradley) Homans. M. no. D. October 29, 1933, Wellesley, Massachusetts.

Amy Morris Homans, one of the early leaders in physical education, was educated at Vassalboro (Maine) Academy and Oak Grove Seminary, also in Maine, and was privately tutored in history, literature, and languages.

Homans became the preceptress of Oak Grove Seminary (1867–69). She went to Wilmington, North Carolina, to teach the poor and served from 1869 to 1877 as teacher in the Tileston Normal School and principal in Hemenway School and the McRae and Chapbourn School. Here she met Mary Hemenway, a wealthy philanthropist from Boston.

Homans returned to Boston as Hemenway's executive secretary, where they held a national conference to bring Swedish gymnastics to the attention of the public. They offered a free two-year course for twenty-eight selected teachers in 1888. In 1889 Hemenway and Homans founded the Boston Normal School of Gymnastics, which became the department of hygiene and physical education at Wellesley College in 1909. As a result of Homans's efforts, the department became one of the first in the country to offer a graduate program for students with a bachelor's degree in physical education in 1917. Homans retired from Wellesley in 1918.

Homans was a charter member of the American Academy of Physical Education and the founder and an honorary member of the Eastern Association of Physical Education for College Women. She was one of the leaders in the Boston Conference of the American Physical Education

Association (later, American Alliance of Health, Physical Education and Recreation or AAHPER), which awarded her the first Honor Award in 1931. In 1967 her contributions were recognized by the National Association of Physical Education for College Women, which established an annual Amy Homans lecture, to be given each year at the AAHPER national convention. She was the recipient of honorary degrees from Bates College and Russell Sage College.

REFERENCES: *WWW* (IV); Ellen W. Gerber, *Innovators and Institutions in Physical Education* (Philadelphia: Lea and Febiger, 1971); Elizabeth Halsey, *Women in Physical Education: Their Role in Work, Home, and History* (New York: G. P. Putnam's Sons, 1961); "In Memoriam," *Journal of Health and Physical Education* 4 (December 1933): 25; Josephine Rathbone, "Amy Morris Homans," *Journal of Health, Physical Education and Recreation* 31 (April 1960): 37.   *Adelaide M. Cole*

HOOK, Sidney. B. December 20, 1902, New York, New York, to Isaac and Jennie (Halpern) Hook. M. March 31, 1924, to Carrie Katz. M. May 25, 1935, to Ann Zinkern. Ch. three.

Sidney Hook received the B.S. degree (1923) from the College of the City of New York and the M.A. (1926) and Ph.D. (1927) degrees from Columbia University. He taught in the New York City public schools (1923–28) and joined the New York University philosophy department in 1927, serving as departmental chairman (1934–68). He was Regents Professor at the University of California at Santa Barbara (spring, 1968).

A philosopher, teacher, administrator, and author, Sidney Hook served New York University in a variety of instructional and administrative roles from 1927 to 1969. A student of John Dewey *(q.v.)*, Hook became one of Dewey's major interpreters. Early interested in Marxism, he helped organize the American Workers party and taught one of the first university courses on communism. Disenchantment followed, and he warned against communist attempts to dominate cultural and intellectual conferences in the late 1940s. In 1949 he organized Americans for Intellectual Freedom, which became the anti-communist American Committee for Cultural Freedom.

Later Hook remained a strong independent voice warning against student radicals of the late 1960s whom he called "gravediggers of academic freedom" and opposing quota systems in academic appointments as a form of racism. He was a founder and president of University Centers for Rational Alternatives.

Twice a Guggenheim Fellow (1928–29; 1961–62), visiting professor at several leading universities, organizer of many committees and conferences, member of numerous professional organizations, and senior research fellow at the Hoover Institute on War, Revolution, and Peace at Stanford University (1973–76), Hook wrote numerous articles and over thirty books, including *Education for Modern Man* (1946), *The Ambiguous Legacy: Marx and the Marxists* (1955), *Common Sense and the Fifth Amendment* (1957), *Religion in a Free Society* (1968), and *Academic Freedom and Academic Anarchy* (1970).

REFERENCES: *CA* (9–12); *CB* (October 1952); *LE* (V); *WW* (XXXIX); "Professor Out of Step," *Time* 101 (January 1, 1973): 39.

Carey W. Brush

HOOKER, Worthington. B. March 2, 1806, Springfield, Massachusetts, to John and Sarah (Dwight) Hooker. M. September 30, 1830, to Mary Ingersoll. M. January 31, 1855, to Henrietta Edwards. Ch. one. D. November 6, 1867, New Haven, Connecticut.

Worthington Hooker was a Connecticut physician and writer. He was graduated from Yale College in 1825 and received the M.D. degree (1829) from Harvard University. He established a medical practice in Norwich, Connecticut, where he was a physician and writer (1829–52).

In 1852 he was appointed professor of the theory and practice of medicine at Yale and held this post until his death in 1867. He was a writer and maintained an extensive medical practice.

Hooker's publications include an essay, "Dissertation on the Respect Due to the Medical Profession" (1844), which was later enlarged into a book, *Physician and Patient* (1849). He also wrote *Human Physiology* (1854), for use in colleges and high schools, *The Child's Book of Nature* (1857), *The Child's Book of Common Things* (1858), *Natural History* (1860), *First Book in Chemistry* (1862), *Natural Philosophy* (1863), *Chemistry* (1863), and *Mineralogy and Geology* (1865). "Rational Therapeutics" (1857) was an essay that received the hundred-dollar prize of the Massachusetts Medical Association. He also wrote for literary and religious newspapers and magazines.

Hooker was an attending physician and director of the Connecticut Hospital Society. In 1864 he was elected vice-president of the American Medical Association. A public school in New Haven, Connecticut, was named in his honor.

REFERENCES: *AC; DAB; NCAB* (13:552); *WWW* (H).   *C. Roy Rylander*

HOPE, John. B. June 2, 1868, Augusta, Georgia, to James and Mary Frances (Butts) Hope. M. December 29, 1897, to Lugenia D. Burns. Ch. two. D. February 20, 1936, Atlanta, Georgia.

John Hope was the son of a wealthy Scottish immigrant and a black woman from South Carolina. His early education was received in Augusta, Georgia, and at Worcester (Massachusetts) Academy, where he was graduated in 1890 with honors. He received the A.B. (1894) and M.A. (1907) degrees from Brown University in Providence, Rhode Island. He did further study at the University of Chicago during the summers of 1897 and 1898.

His career in higher education began as a teacher at Roger Williams University in Nashville, Tennessee (1894–98). He accepted a position in 1898 teaching Greek and Latin at Atlanta (Georgia) Baptist College (later, Morehouse College) and also served as assistant to President George Sale. Following Sale's resignation in 1907, Hope became president and served in that capacity until 1931. In June 1931 he was elected president of Atlanta University, an affiliation of Atlanta University, Morehouse College, and Spelman College.

Hope was a member of the Association for the Study of Negro Life and History (president, 1933–36), the Commission on Interracial Cooperation (president, 1932–33), and the Niagara Movement (which was devoted to obtaining political, civil, and social rights for free-born Americans). He was a board member of the National Association for the Advancement of Colored People, the National Urban League, and the Spingarn Medal Award Committee. He was an official of the local, National Council and the World's Committee of the Young Men's Christian Association, and he rendered service to black troops in France during World War I.

Hope received honorary degrees from six colleges and universities and was awarded the William E. Harmon Award in Education for outstanding achievement among Negroes (1929) and the Spingarn Medal (awarded posthumously in 1936). A camp, school, and community center were named in his honor.

REFERENCES: *DAB* (supp. 2); *LE* (I); *NCAB* (28:344); *WWAE* (I); *WWW* (I); *Afro-American Encyclopedia* (North Miami, Fla.: Educational Book Publishers, 1974), 4: 1228–29; *NYT*, February 21, 1936, p. 17; Dorothy Orr, *A History of Education in Georgia* (Chapel Hill: University of North Carolina Press, 1950); Ridgely Torrence, *The Story of John Hope* (New York: Macmillan Co., 1948); Thomas Yenser, ed., *Who's Who in Colored America*, 4th ed. (New York: Thomas Yenser, 1937), p. 262.

Octavia B. Knight

HOPKINS, Ernest Martin. B. November 6, 1877, Dunbarton, New Hampshire, to Adoniram Judson and Mary Cheney (Martin) Hopkins. M. February 2, 1911, to Celia Stone. M. December 14, 1951, to Grace Stone Tibbetts. Ch. one. D. August 13, 1964, Southwest Harbor, Maine.

Ernest Martin Hopkins attended the Academy of Worcester (Massachusetts). His father was a graduate of Harvard University and argued that his son should attend Harvard, but Ernest Hopkins chose to attend Dartmouth College in Hanover, New Hampshire. He first worked in a stone quarry for a year following prep school to earn money for college. He entered Dartmouth in the fall of 1897 but had to leave at midterm and returned to work in the quarry. A local resident of Hanover offered to provide him with room and board in his home and President William J. Tucker *(q.v.)* of Dartmouth gave him a scholarship to cover tuition.

He remained at Dartmouth following graduation (1901). He served as secretary to President Tucker for four years and was appointed college secretary (1905). He earned the A.M. degree from Dartmouth (1908) and studied in the new field of personnel management. In 1910 he accepted a position as manager of education and training with the Western Electric Company. Later he held positions in personnel management at William Filene's Sons, Curtis Publishing Company, and the New England Telephone Company.

On July 1, 1916, he became president of Dartmouth College, a position he held until his retirement on November 1, 1945. He was credited with making the institution an outstanding undergraduate college of liberal arts. During his administration, Dartmouth significantly increased its enrollment, library collection, faculty, and endowment. Hopkins was known as a defender of academic freedom. He encouraged educational experimentation in the college and established honors courses. Opposed to narrow subject matter specialization, he supported the belief that a student's character, personality, and interest should be given equal weight with scholastic achievement in admission to the college.

Hopkins gained a reputation as an able educational administrator and was asked to assume positions of leadership in education, business, and government. He served in both world wars as a senior administrator in the War Department and the Office of Production Management. He received honorary doctorates from over a dozen colleges and universities.

REFERENCES: *CB* (October 1944); *LE* (III); *NCAB* (F:60); *WWAE* (VIII); *WWW* (IV); *NYT,* August 14, 1964, p. 27.   *Edward J. Durnall*

HOPKINS, Mark. B. February 4, 1802, Stockbridge, Massachusetts, to Archibald and Mary (Curtis) Hopkins. M. December 25, 1832, to Mary Hubbell. Ch. ten. D. June 17, 1887, Williamstown, Massachusetts.

Mark Hopkins entered Williams College in Williamstown, Massachusetts, in 1821 after having taught school at Richmond, Massachusetts. He was graduated from Williams in 1824 and entered the medical school at Pittsfield, Massachusetts. He was called back to Williams as a tutor. In 1827 he resumed his medical studies, was graduated from the Berkshire Medical School in 1829, and prepared to be a New York City physician.

Williams College asked Hopkins to become professor of moral philosophy and rhetoric. In 1836 he was chosen president of Williams College and, despite offers from other institutions, remained in that position until 1872. He continued to teach at Williams until his death in 1887.

Hopkins never attended theological school, but the Berkshire Association of Congregational Ministers licensed him to preach in 1833, and he was ordained in 1836. He served the American Board of Commissioners for Foreign Missions as president (1857–87). At the end of his life he was trying to mediate theological differences and establish churches abroad.

Hopkins taught his philosophical beliefs to the senior class that in understanding the body one could make it better serve the mind. He discussed levels in nature and in man, each coordinated to serve the level above to the highest good of man's love of God and fellow man. He believed in the "gospel of wealth" that taught one should strive to possess property and should treat possessions with a responsible Christian stewardship.

Hopkins's books were compilations of his lectures and included *Lectures on the Evidences of Christianity* (1846), *Lectures on the Moral Science* (1862), *Baccalaureate Sermons and Occasional Discourses* (1862), *The Law of Love and Love as Law* (1869), *An Outline Study of Man* (1873), *Strength and Beauty* (1874), and *The Scriptural Idea of Man* (1883).

REFERENCES: *AC; DAB; EB; NCAB* (6:237); *TC; WWW* (H); Franklin Carter, *Mark Hopkins* (Boston: Houghton Mifflin, 1892); *NYT*, June 18, 1887, p. 1.   *Darlene E. Fisher*

HORNE, Herman Harrell. B. November 22, 1874, Clayton, North Carolina, to Hardee and Ida Caroline (Harrell) Horne. M. August 20, 1901, to Alice Elizabeth Herbert Worthington. M. April 9, 1944, to Mary Dowell W. Williamson. Ch. four. D. August 16, 1946, Leonia, New Jersey.

Herman Harrell Horne was educated in local public schools and the Davis Military Academy in Winston-Salem, North Carolina. He was graduated with the A.B. and A.M. degrees (1895) from the University of North Carolina and the A.M. (1897) and Ph.D. (1899) degrees from Harvard University. He also studied at the University of Berlin, Germany (1906–07).

Horne was an instructor of French at the University of North Carolina (1894–96) and was an instructor and professor of philosophy at Dartmouth College in Hanover, New Hampshire (1899–1909). He was professor of the philosophy of education at the school of pedagogy and graduate school at New York University (1909–22). In 1922 the school of pedagogy became the school of education, and Horne served as professor of the history of education, professor of the philosophy of education, and chairman of both departments to his retirement in 1942. He was the first university professor to present a classroom lecture by radio (1923).

Horne was the author of many articles and twenty-six books, including *The Philosophy of Education* (1904), *Psychological Principles of Education* (1906), *Idealism in Education* (1910), *Free Will and Human Responsibility* (1912), *Leadership of Bible Study Groups* (1912), *Story-Telling, Questioning and Studying* (1916), *The Teacher As Artist* (1917),

Jesus—Our Standard (1918), *Modern Problems as Jesus Saw Them* (1918), *Jesus as a Philosopher* (1927), *The Essentials of Leadership* (1931), *This New Education* (1931), *The Democratic Philosophy of Education* (1932), *The Philosophy of Christian Education* (1937), *Introduction of Modern Education* (with others, 1937), *Tomorrow in the Making* (with others, 1939), and *Shakespeare's Philosophy of Love* (1946).

Horne was a member of educational organizations and was a fellow of the American Association for the Advancement of Science and the Society for the Advancement of Education. He was the recipient of four honorary degrees.

REFERENCES: *LE* (I); *NCAB* (44:93); *NYT,* August 17, 1946, p. 13; *WWW* (II).   *Joseph C. Bronars, Jr.*

HOSIC, James Fleming. B. October 11, 1870, Henry, Illinois, to James W. and Dorothy Ellen (Hervey) Hosic. M. August 19, 1903, to Nellie Augusta Lovering. Ch. two. D. January 13, 1959, Royal Oak, Michigan.

James Fleming Hosic was educated in the public schools of Henry, Illinois, and Tecumseh, Nebraska, and was graduated from the State Normal School (later, Peru State College) at Peru, Nebraska (1891). He received the Ph.B. (1901) and Ph.M. (1902) degrees from the University of Chicago and the Ph.D. degree (1920) from Columbia University.

Hosic was principal of the Auburn (Nebraska) High School (1891–93) and superintendent of the Arapahoe (Nebraska) public schools (1894–96). He was head of the English department at the State Normal School at Peru (1896–1900) and at the Chicago (Illinois) Normal School (later, Chicago State University) from 1902 to 1921. He served as a special supervisor of English for the Chicago public schools (1918–21). He was associate professor of education and director of extension (1921–24) and professor of education (1924–36) at Teachers College, Columbia University. Hosic was one of the first to introduce the project method of instruction.

The author of many books, Hosic wrote *Elementary Course in English* (1909), *Practical English for High Schools* (with W. D. Lewis, 1916), *A Child's Composition Book* (with C. L. Hooper, 1916), *A Composition Grammar* (1916), *Empirical Studies in Reading* (1921), *A Brief Guide to the Project Method* (with Sara E. Chase, 1924), *Pathway to Reading* (with others, 1926), *Introductory Studies in Literature* (with W. W. Hatfield, 1927), *English for Junior High Schools* (with Claudia E. Crumpton, 1928), and the American Language Series (with C. L. Hooper, 1931). He was the founder and editor of the *English Journal* (1912–21) and the *Journal of Educational Method* (1921–37).

Hosic was a founder (1910) and president (1919–20) of the National Council of Teachers of English. He organized the National Conference on Educational Method (1921), was adviser to the American School in Mexico

City, Mexico (1928), and was a member of many professional associations.
REFERENCES: *LE* (III); *NCAB* (47:495); *NYT,* January 15, 1959, p. 33;
WWW (III). *John F. Ohles*

HOSTOS, Eugenio María de. B. January 11, 1839, Rio Cañas, Mayaguez,
Puerto Rico, to Eugenio de Hostos and María Hilaria de Bonilla. M. July 9,
1877, to Belinda Otila de Ayala. Ch. one. D. August 11, 1903, Santo
Domingo, Dominican Republic.

Eugenio María de Hostos fought for the abolition of slavery, independence and federation for the Antilles, the extension of education to
women, and the education of the masses.

Hostos developed into an excellent scholar and was sent from Puerto
Rico to Spain at the age of thirteen to study. He completed secondary
school at Bilbao and began studies at the Central University of Madrid Law
School in 1857. While in Spain, Hostos became dedicated to the ideals of
independence for Puerto Rico and the abolition of slavery.

In 1863 he wrote *El Peregrinación de Bayoan,* a visionary allegory
calling for independence and the federation of Puerto Rico, Cuba, Haiti,
and the Dominican Republic. The Spanish republic overthrew the monar-
chy in 1868 but refused to consider independence for Cuba and Puerto
Rico, and there was an armed rebellion on the island. Hostos rejected a
political post offered by the Spanish republic and moved to New York
where he produced scholarly and political writings seeking support for
Cuban and Puerto Rican independence.

Hostos traveled widely in the Americas during the next decade. He
founded a newspaper in Lima, Peru, and was instrumental in improving
conditions for Chinese mine workers. In Chile he campaigned for the rights
of Chilean women and eliminated barriers to the admission of women to the
university. He lobbied in Argentina for a railroad link with Chile; in 1910
the first locomotive to cross the Andes was named Eugenio María de
Hostos.

Hostos moved to the Dominican Republic in 1879 where he founded the
first normal school and taught at the Autonomous University of Santa
Domingo, the oldest institution of higher learning in the Americas. Hostos
spent fifteen years in Santo Domingo organizing and democratizing the
educational system. Called by Chilean President José Manuel Balmaceda,
Hostos went to Santiago where he taught at the university and founded the
Liceo Miguel Luis Amunáteui. He moved to Caracas, Venezuela, and
taught law at the university before returning to the Dominican Republic.
After 1898 he shuttled between Washington, D.C., and San Juan, frus-
trated at the turn of events that saw Puerto Rico become a possession.

Hostos was the author of *Ensayos Sobre Hamlet, America* (1873),
Tratado de Derecho Constitucionál (1887), and *Moral Social* (1888). He

was honored when the Organization of American States, meeting in Lima, Peru, in 1938, proclaimed Hostos the Citizen of the Americas. In 1939 the government of Puerto Rico published the complete works of Eugenio María de Hostos in twenty volumes.

REFERENCES: German Arciniegas, *Latin America: A Cultural History* (New York: Alfred A. Knopf, 1968); Enrique Anderson-Imbert, *Spanish-American Literature: A History (1492–1910)* (Detroit, Mich.: Wayne State University Press, 1963), *Obros Completas de Eugenio María de Hostos* (San Juan, P.R.: Government of Puerto Rico, 1939).

HOUSTON, Edwin James. B. July 9, 1847, Alexandria, Virginia, to John Mason and Mary (Lamour) Houston. M. no. D. March 1, 1914, Philadelphia, Pennsylvania.

Edwin James Houston was graduated from Central High School of Philadelphia, Pennsylvania, with the A.B. degree (1864). He taught at Girard College in Philadelphia (1865) and attended the universities of Berlin and Heidelberg, Germany. He studied at Princeton University with Elihu Thompson, receiving the Ph.D. degree in 1894.

In 1867 Houston returned to Philadelphia from Germany to accept the chairmanship of the newly established department of physical geography and natural philosophy at Central High School. Houston designed the courses and wrote most of the textbooks used. He was one of the first educators to see the value of laboratory instruction and developed a well-equipped laboratory at Central High School.

Particularly interested in the applied uses of electricity, Houston, with Elihu Thompson, invented the Thompson-Houston system of arc lighting in 1881 and formed a company to market the system. The development gained Houston world renown in the field of electricity. He was the first president of the electrical section of the Franklin Institute and editor of its *Journal*.

In 1894 Houston resigned from Central High School and began practice as an electrical engineering consultant in association with A. E. Kennelly. They produced the first elementary textbooks on electricity, Elementary Electro-Technical Series (ten volumes, 1895–1906), and also wrote Electrical Engineering Leaflets (three volumes, 1895) and *Recent Types of Dynamo-Electric Machinery* (1898). Houston wrote many other books, including *Elements of Physical Geography* (1875), *Elements of Natural Philosophy* (1879), *Dictionary of Electrical Words, Terms, and Phrases* (1889), and *Outlines of Forestry* (1893). In the later years of his life Houston became involved in boys' associations and wrote boys' adventure books, such as *The Search for the North Pole* (1907) and *Born an Electrician* (1912).

Houston was a charter member of the American Institute of Electrical

Engineers (president, 1893–94). He was awarded an honorary degree by Princeton University.

REFERENCES: *DAB; NCAB* (13:359); *TC; WWW* (I); *Electrical World*, March 7, 1914; *NYT*, March 2, 1914, p. 9.   *John E. Phillips*

HOVEY, Charles Edward. B. April 26, 1827, Thetford, Vermont, to Alfred and Abigail (Howard) Hovey. M. October 9, 1854, to Harriette Farnham Spofford. Ch. three. D. November 17, 1897, Washington, D.C.

Charles Edward Hovey was graduated from Dartmouth College in 1852. While reading the law, he became a teacher and was appointed principal of the Free High School in Framingham, Massachusetts (1852–54).

He moved to Peoria, Illinois, where he was appointed principal of the boys' high school (1854–56) and was superintendent of the Peoria public schools (1856–57). The Illinois legislature authorized the establishment of the State Normal University in 1857 in Normal, Illinois, and Hovey was appointed the first president of what became Illinois State University. Hovey established a training school at Normal that offered instruction in teaching grades one through twelve. Its purpose was to supplement the academic training in pedagogy with "training in how to teach through observation and practice in the model school." He remained president of the university to 1861.

After the Civil War broke out, Hovey joined the Union army with some two hundred of his students and faculty who elected him colonel of the Thirty-third Illinois, or Normal, regiment. He was promoted to the rank of brigadier general and was brevetted major general of volunteers. He was forced to resign from active service in 1865 because of ill health and a wound he received at Arkansas Post in 1863. After the war Hovey moved to Washington, D.C., where he was admitted to the bar and practiced law (1869–97).

Hovey was president of the Illinois State Teacher's Association (1856) and a member of the first Illinois Board of Education (1857). He edited the *Illinois Teacher* (1856–58), a monthly magazine established as the organ of the association.

REFERENCES: *AC; DAB; TC; WWW* (H); John W. Cook and James V. McHugh, *A History of the Illinois State Normal University* (Bloomington, Ill.: Pentagraph Printing and Binding, 1882); Homer Hurst, *Illinois State Normal University and the Public School Movement* (Nashville, Tenn.: George Peabody College for Teachers, 1948); *NYT*, July 6, 1897, p. 9; *Notable Men of Illinois and Their State* (Chicago: The Chicago Daily Journal, 1912).   *Abdul Samad*

HOWARD, Ada Lydia. B. December 19, 1829, Temple, New Hampshire, to William Hawkins and Lydia Adaline (Cowden) Howard. M. no. D. March 3, 1907, Brooklyn, New York.

Encouraged and educated by her father, Ada Lydia Howard attended the New Ipswich Academy, Lowell (Massachusetts) High School, and Mount Holyoke Seminary in South Hadley, Massachusetts, where she was graduated in 1853. After additional study with private teachers, she became a teacher.

Howard taught at Mount Holyoke (1858–61) and at the Western College for Women in Oxford, Ohio (1861–62). She was principal of the women's department at Knox College in Galesburg, Illinois (1862–69). In 1870 she leased and operated Ivy Hall in Bridgeton, New Jersey.

In 1875 Henry Durant *(q.v.)*, founder of Wellesley (Massachusetts) College, selected Ada Howard as the college's first president and as the first woman president of a college in the world. To Durant's death in 1881, Howard was able to work satisfactorily with Durant and his wife in establishing the college as a major institution for women. Shortly after Durant's death, ill health forced Howard to take a leave of absence, and she resigned in 1882.

She was awarded an honorary degree by Mount Holyoke College in 1900 and a scholarship was established in her honor at Wellesley College.

REFERENCES: *DAB; NCAB* (7: 328); *NYT,* March 7, 1907, p. 9; *TC; WWW* (I).   *John F. Ohles*

HOWE, Samuel Gridley. B. November 11, 1801, Boston, Massachusetts, to Joseph N. and Patty (Gridley) Howe. M. April 27, 1843, to Julia Ward. Ch. five. D. January 9, 1876, Boston, Massachusetts.

Samuel Gridley Howe was graduated from Brown University in 1821 and from Harvard Medical School in 1824. He went to Greece to help in the war against the Turks, where he fought and served as a surgeon and helped in the reconstruction. He spent six years in Greece (1824–30) and returned to America to obtain money and clothing for the Greek people.

In 1831 Howe was given the responsibility of opening and directing a school for the blind incorporated by the state of Massachusetts. He traveled to Europe to study schools for the blind. He started the Massachusetts Asylum for the Blind with six pupils, using his father's house for a school building. The school was donated the mansion of a Colonel Perkins, and Howe moved his school there as the Perkins Institution. He showed that blind persons could be assisted to become economically and socially competent. His annual reports were philosophic common sense and widely read. In the forty-four years of Howe's directorship of the Perkins Institution, it became the leading school of its type in the United States and one of the greatest in the world.

He visited seventeen states on behalf of the education of the blind and sent his teachers to London, England, to study under Francis Joseph Campbell. He taught Laura Bridgman, a deaf-blind child, an accomplishment that astounded educators and physicians throughout the world.

Howe was the author of *An Historical Sketch of the Greek Revolution* (1828), *Reader for the Blind* (1839), which was printed in raised characters, *The Refugees from Slavery in Canada West* (1864), and *The Education of Laura D. Bridgmen* (189?). His wife, Julia Ward Howe, edited *Memoir of Dr. Samuel Gridley Howe* (1876). He coedited an anti-slavery paper, *The Commonwealth,* with his wife (1851–53) and edited *The Cretan* (1868–71).

Howe also worked for the care of the feebleminded, convicts, and slaves. He helped Dorothea Dix *(q.v.)* through private and public support for her work with the insane. In South Boston he founded an experimental school in 1848 for the training of mental incompetents, which became the Massachusetts School for Idiotic and Feeble-Minded Youth in 1851. He was superintendent of the school (the first in the country) from 1848 to 1875. He served as chairman of the Massachusetts Board of State Charities (1865–74). He was a member of the Boston School Committee.

He was an unsuccessful candidate for Congress in 1846. During the Civil War he was a member of the Sanitary Commission. In 1866 he raised funds and clothing for the Cretans and went again to Greece to help distribute food and clothing. While at Athens he opened a school for Cretan refugees.

President Ulysses S. Grant appointed Howe to a commission to study the advisability of annexing Santo Domingo. He was given many honors and awards by foreign countries and was decorated by the Greek government. He received an honorary degree from Brown University.

REFERENCES: *AC; DAB; EB; NCAB* (8:372); *TC; WWW* (H); Franklin Benjamin Sanborn, *Dr. S. G. Howe, the Philanthropist* (New York: Funk & Wagnalls, 1891); Julia Ward Howe, *Memoir of Dr. Samuel Gridley Howe* (Boston: Howe Memorial Committee, 1876); *NYT,* January 10, 1876, p. 1.   *Thomas Meighan*

HOWISON, George Holmes. B. November 29, 1834, Montgomery County, Maryland, to Robert and Eliza (Holmes) Howison. M. November 25, 1863, to Lois Caswell. Ch. none. D. December 31, 1916, Berkeley, California.

George Holmes Howison attended Marietta (Ohio) College, where he earned the A.B. (1852) and M.A. (1855) degrees. He entered Lane Theological Seminary in Cincinnati, Ohio, and was graduated in 1855. He spent a year studying at the University of Berlin (1881–82).

Upon graduation from Lane, Howison became a teacher and principal in a school in Marietta. Washington University in St. Louis, Missouri, engaged him to teach English literature in 1864; he also taught differential and integral calculus, geometry, mechanics, astronomy, logic, political economy, and Latin. Howison went to the Massachusetts Institute of Technology in 1872 as professor of logic and the philosophy of science (1872–78). He lectured at Harvard University (1879–80) and at the Chestnut Club, delivered the Lowell lectures, and offered private classes. He was on the original faculty of the Concord (Massachusetts) School of Philosophy, founded in 1879.

Howison went to the University of Michigan as a lecturer in 1882. He was the first Mills Professor of Mental and Moral Philosophy and Civil Polity at the University of California in Berkeley (1884–1909) and was professor emeritus until his death. At Berkeley Howison established the Philosophical Union with former students and San Francisco Bay area intellectuals. From meetings of the union came the great debate of 1895, published as *The Conception of God* by Josiah Royce.

Howison was the author of *A Treatise on Analytic Geometry* (1869) and *Limits of Evolution and Other Essays* (1901). He was editor of publications of the Philosophical Union at the University of California, was coeditor of the *Psychological Review,* and was one of the American coeditors of the *Hibbert Journal.* He was a fellow of the Association for the Advancement of Science and received three honorary degrees. An endowed lectureship in his name was established at the University of California at Berkeley.

REFERENCES: *DAB; NCAB* (23:179); *TC; WWW* (I); John Wright Buckham and George Malcolm Stratton, *George Holmes Howison: Philosopher and Teacher* (Berkeley: University of California, 1934).

Joyce McDonnold

HOWLAND, Emily. B. November 20, 1827, Sherwood, New York, to Slocum and Hannah (Talcott) Howland. M. no. D. June 29, 1929, Sherwood, New York.

Emily Howland was the only daughter of a devout Quaker family, who dedicated her life to anti-slavery, women's rights, temperance, and peace. She attended a private school in Sherwood, New York, and a Friends' school in Philadelphia, Pennsylvania.

Howland read widely in anti-slavery literature and went to Washington, D.C., to teach at Myrtilla Miner's *(q.v.)* school for free black girls (1857–59). She returned to Washington in 1863 where she taught and gave medical assistance during a smallpox epidemic. In 1867 her father bought a large tract of land in Heathsville, Virginia, where she helped settle former slaves and taught school. She also assisted in the establishment of another school in Lottsburg, Virginia. In later years Howland contributed to over thirty industrial training schools for blacks in the South. In 1871 she helped found the Sherwood (New York) Select School, which was renamed the Emily Howland High School after she donated it to the state in 1927 as a public school.

Howland was a close friend of feminist Susan B. Anthony and was president of the county suffrage society. She gave many girls interest-free college loans and encouraged Ezra Cornell to introduce coeducation at Cornell University. She wrote *Early History of Friends in Cayuga County, N.Y.* (1880).

In 1890 she became director of the First National Bank of Aurora, New York, and, at the age of ninety-nine, she was awarded an honorary degree by the University of the State of New York, the first woman to achieve this honor. At her death in 1929, much of Howland's estate was left to the schools she supported during her lifetime.

REFERENCES: *DAB; NAW; NCAB* (25:306); *WC; WWW* (I); Jane A. Morton, "Emily Howland," *The Woman's Journal* 13 (December 1929): 25; Genevieve Parkhurst, "A Hundred Years of Living," *Pictorial Review* 29 (September 1928): 2; *Quarterly Journal of New York State Historical Association* 10 (October 1929): 346–47; *Sketches of Leading American Women* (Detroit: Gale Research Co., 1893), pp. 397–98.

Phyllis Appelbaum

HOWLAND, John. B. October 31, 1757, Newport, Rhode Island, to Joseph and Sarah (Barber) Howland. M. January 28, 1788, to Mary Carlisle. Ch. none. D. November 5, 1854, Providence, Rhode Island.

John Howland was apprenticed to a hairdresser in Providence, Rhode Island, in 1770. He was a member of the Rhode Island minutemen and served under George Washington at Trenton Bridge and Princeton, New Jersey, and under John Sullivan at Newport, Rhode Island.

Howland was Providence town auditor (1803–18) and treasurer (1818–32). He was active in founding the Rhode Island public school system and served as a member of the school committee for twenty years. A member of the Rhode Island Historical Society, Howland served as president from 1833 to his death in 1854. He was a founder of the Providence Association of Mechanics and Manufacturers, serving as secretary for eighteen years and president for six years. He was an honorary member of the Royal Society of Northern Antiquarians of Denmark (1835) and was awarded an honorary degree from Brown University (1835).

His life was commemorated by Edward B. Hall's *Discourse of the Life and Times of John Howland,* delivered to the historical society in 1855, and Edwin M. Stone's *Life and Recollections of John Howland* (1857).

REFERENCES: *AC; NCAB* (8:58); *TC.*   *J. K. Ward*

HOYT, John Wesley. B. October 13, 1831, near Worthington, Ohio, to Jack and Judith (Hawley) Hoyt. M. 1854 to Elizabeth Orpha Sampson. Ch. two. D. May 23, 1912, Washington, D.C.

John Wesley Hoyt was graduated from Ohio Wesleyan University in Delaware, Ohio, in 1849. He began to study law but took up medicine instead, receiving the M.D. degree (1853) from the Eclectic Medical Institute in Cincinnati, Ohio.

Hoyt taught medical jurisprudence and chemistry at the institute (1853–57). He also taught natural history and chemistry at the newly organized Antioch College in Yellow Springs, Ohio, lectured at the Cincinnati College of Medicine, and served as physician at the Yellow Springs Sanitarium.

Hoyt went to Wisconsin where he was a partner in publishing the *Wisconsin Farmer and Northwest Cultivator* (1857–67). He used the journal to support the Morrill Act of 1862 and to urge the establishment of a Wisconsin school of agriculture. While serving as commissioner to the Paris Universal Exposition (1867), Hoyt was hired by Secretary of State William Seward to study and report on education in Europe. Hoyt's *Report on Education* was published by the United States government in 1870. He was appointed Wisconsin railway commissioner (1874).

Hoyt was appointed governor of Wyoming Territory (1878–82). In Wyoming he helped create the position of territorial superintendent of public instruction, proposed better educational facilities and opportunities for Indians, and was the first governor to propose a territorial university. In 1886 Hoyt's successor as governor appointed him to the first board of trustees of the University of Wyoming. He was made president of the university (1887), serving until 1890.

Hoyt was interested for many years in the congressional establishment of a national university, an institution he first proposed at the National Teachers' Association (later, National Education Association) convention in Trenton, New Jersey, in 1869. Although a bill was favorably reported out of a congressional committee, it was never enacted. Hoyt urged Andrew Carnegie to endow a national university in 1899. In the first years of the twentieth century, he sought to reorganize existing universities in Washington, D.C., into a national university. He had made only preliminary arrangements before ill health ended his efforts.

Hoyt was United States commissioner of exhibitions in London (1866), Paris (1867), and Vienna (1873) and to the International Postal Congress in Korea (1897). He was secretary of the Wisconsin State Agricultural Society. Hoyt was decorated by the government of Austria and received an honorary degree from the University of Missouri.

REFERENCES: *AC; DAB; NCAB* (13:158); *TC; WWW* (I); Ichabod S. Bartlett, ed., *History of Wyoming* (Chicago: S. J. Clarke Publishing Co., 1918), vol. 1; Francis Birkhead Beard, *Wyoming From Territorial Days to the Present* (Chicago: The American Historical Society, 1933), vol. 1; *NYT*, May 24, 1912, p. 13.   *Everett D. Lantz*

HUGHES, John Joseph. B. June 24, 1797, County Tyrone, Ireland, to Patrick and Margaret (McKenna) Hughes. M. no. D. January 3, 1864, New York, New York.

John J. Hughes was a common laborer who came to head the largest Catholic diocese in the United States. A native of Ireland, Hughes joined his father and older brother in America in 1817. After working as a quarrier, road mender, and gardener in Pennsylvania and Maryland, he entered Mount St. Mary's Seminary at Emmitsburg, Maryland, in 1820 and was ordained in 1826.

Hughes was a successful pastor in several parishes in Philadelphia, Pennsylvania. He became embroiled in controversy early in his priestly career through a written debate with a Protestant clergyman, John Breckinridge. Hughes became a bishop coadjutor to Bishop John Dubois of New York in 1838. He was made a bishop of the see (1842) and archbishop (1850).

As prelate of New York City, he helped found Fordham University and began construction of St. Patrick's Cathedral. He was instrumental in founding the North American College in Rome. He gained prominence for insisting on public funds for Catholic-controlled schools in response to the Protestant orientation of the New York schools. The controversy ended with no help for Catholic schools and eventually led to a secularization of the public schools and the creation of a separate Catholic school system.

He founded the *Catholic Herald* (1833) and wrote *The Conversion and Edifying Death of Andrew Dunn* (1828) and *A Review of the Charge of Bishop Onderdonk on the Rule of Christ* (1833).

Hughes supported the union in the Civil War and visited Europe to represent President Abraham Lincoln in a successful effort to counteract the southern sympathy developing in European countries. He helped end the New York City draft riots in 1863.

REFERENCES: *AC; DAB; EB; NCAB* (1:193); *TC; WWW* (H); *New Catholic Encyclopedia* (New York: McGraw-Hill, 1967). *James M. Vosper*

HUGHES, Ray Osgood. B. November 13, 1879, Saxtons River, Vermont, to Thomas and Jennie C. (Osgood) Hughes. M. June 26, 1906, to Helene W. Hopkins. Ch. none. D. April 10, 1959, Pittsburgh, Pennsylvania.

Ray Osgood Hughes received the A.B. degree (1900) from Brown University in Providence, Rhode Island, and the A.M. degree (1924) from the University of Pittsburgh, Pennsylvania.

Hughes was an instructor at the Williston Seminary in Easthampton, Massachusetts (1901), Leland and Gray Seminary in Townshend, Vermont (1901–02), Wellesley (Massachusetts) Boys School (1903), Keystone Academy in Factoryville, Pennsylvania (1903–06), and Westbrook Seminary in Portland, Maine (1907). He was a teacher of high school social studies in West Chester, Pennsylvania (1907–11), and the Fifth Avenue High School (1911–13) and Peabody High School (1913–26) in Pittsburgh, Pennsylvania. He was vice-principal of Peabody High School (1926–29).

Hughes was assistant director of the department of curriculum study (1929–39) and director of citizenship and social studies (1939–45) for the Pittsburgh public schools. He retired in 1945.

Hughes was the author of many social studies textbooks, including *Community Civics* (1917), *Economic Civics* (1921), *Elementary Community Civics* (1922), *Problems of American Democracy* (1922), *Textbook in Citizenship* (1923), *New Community Civics* (1924), *The Making of Our United States* (1927), *American Citizenship Charts* (1929), *Fundamentals of Economics* (1929), *Building Citizenship* (1933), *The Making of Today's World* (1935), *Good Citizenship* (1940), *Today's Problems* (1942), *Pennsylvania, Past and Present* (1944), *Eastern Lands* (1954), and *Western Lands* (1954).

Hughes was a member of many professional associations, including the National Council for the Social Studies (president, 1936). He was moderator of the Junior Town Meetings (1944–47). Hughes was awarded an honorary degree by Brown University (1941).

REFERENCES: *LE* (III); *NYT*, April 12, 1959, p. 86; *WWAE* (XVI); *WWW* (III).

John F. Ohles

HUGHES, William Leonard. B. January 30, 1895, Edgar, Nebraska, to James Thomas and Amy (Wells) Hughes. M. June 16, 1921, to Mary Elizabeth Cave. Ch. three. D. February 20, 1957, Washington, D.C.

William Leonard Hughes attended the Ong, Nebraska, public schools and was graduated from Nebraska Wesleyan University in Lincoln with the B.A. degree (1919). He received the M.A. (1924) and Ph.D. (1932) degrees from Columbia University.

Hughes was director of physical education and athletics and high school coach at Beatrice, Nebraska (1919–23). He was assistant professor of physical education and football and basketball coach at Oberlin (Ohio) College (1924–25) and director of health, physical education, and athletics, professor, and football and basketball coach at DePauw University in Greencastle, Indiana (1925–30). He taught physical education (1930–45) and was acting chairman of the department of physical education (1942–44) at Columbia University. In 1945 he became director of health and physical education and professor at Temple University in Philadelphia, Pennsylvania, and served to his death in 1957.

Hughes was the author of *Administration of Health and Physical Education in Colleges* (1935), *Athletics in Education* (with J. F. Williams, *q.v.*, 1930), *Football* (with G. Killinger, 1939), *Basketball* (with C. Murphy, 1939), *Baseball* (with D. Jesse, 1939), *Track and Field* (with R. Conger, 1939), *Health Problems and How to Solve Them* (with others, 1942), *Being Alive* (1942), *Youth Faces Maturity* (1942), *Sports–Their Organization and Administration* (1944), and *Administration of Physical Education* (with Esther French, 1954). He was editor and collaborator of *The Book of Major Sports* (1939).

Hughes served in the United States Army in World War I. He was a consultant on physical education to many schools, colleges, and universities and to the United States military and air force academies. A member of many professional associations, Hughes was a fellow of the American Association for Health, Physical Education and Recreation and served in many posts, including president (1944–46). He was a member of the national advisory board of the Athletic Institute, a fellow of the American Public Health Association, and a member of the College Physical Education Association (president, 1934) and the American College of Sports Medicine (treasurer, 1954–56). He participated in conferences on physical education and was a member of federal and state groups. He was a member of the boards of education at Leonia, New Jersey (1941–45), and Abington, Pennsylvania (1949–51). He received the Luther H. Gulick Award and honorary degrees from Boston University (1949) and Springfield College (1955).

REFERENCES: *LE* (III); *NCAB* (47:518); *NYT,* February 21, 1957, p. 27; *WWAE* (XIV); *WWW* (III).   *John F. Ohles*

HULL, Clark Leonard. B. May 24, 1884, Akron, New York, to Leander Gilday and Florence (Trask) Hull. M. September 20, 1911, to Bertha Elizabeth Iutzi. Ch. two. D. May 10, 1952, New Haven, Connecticut.

Clark Leonard Hull was born in a log farmhouse near Akron, New York. His family moved to Michigan where he was graduated from Alma (Michigan) Academy in 1905. He enrolled at Alma College where he studied for two years to become a mining engineer. His plans were abandoned when he contracted poliomyelitis and was crippled, though he could walk with crutches. As soon as his health permitted, he entered the University of Michigan, where he majored in psychology, receiving the B.A. degree (1913). He taught for a year, began graduate study in psychology at the University of Wisconsin, and received the Ph.D. degree (1918).

Hull was a public-school principal in Sickels, Michigan (1909–11), and acting professor of psychology at Eastern Kentucky State Normal School (later, State University) in Richmond (1913–14). After completing the Ph.D. Hull remained at Wisconsin as a member of the department of psychology (1918–29). He moved to Yale University in 1929 as a research professor in the Institute of Human Relations and was appointed Sterling Professor of Psychology in 1947.

Hull developed standardized test batteries to measure special aptitudes. He designed and constructed a correlation machine that performed many of the calculations to determine product-moment correlations. From 1929 to 1943 Hull conducted research for his most important scientific contribution, *Principles of Behavior,* published in 1943, which was one of the most influential books on the theory of learning. He also wrote *The Evolution of Concepts* (1920), *Influence of Tobacco Smoking on Mental and Motor Efficiency* (1924), *Aptitude Testing* (1928), *Hypnosis and Suggesta-*

bility: An Experimental Approach (1933), *Mathematico-Deductive Theory of Rote Learning (with others, 1940), Essentials of Human Behavior* (1951), and *A Behavior System* (1952), which was published posthumously.

Hull was president of the American Psychological Association (1935–36) and a fellow of the National Academy of Sciences, the American Academy of Arts and Sciences, and the Society of Experimental Psychology, which awarded him its Warren Medal in 1945.

REFERENCES: *EB; LE* (III); *NCAB* (41:69); *WWW* (III); *NYT,* May 11, 1952, p. 52; H. J. Eysenck, W. Arnold, and R. Meili, *Encyclopedia of Psychology* (New York: Herder and Herder, 1972). *Harold G. MacDermot*

HULLFISH, Henry Gordon. B. January 3, 1894, Washington, D.C., to Harry and Anna (Skerett) Hullfish. M. September 19, 1922, to Lucile Margaret Barnett. Ch. three. D. June 15, 1962, Columbus, Ohio.

H. Gordon Hullfish received the A.B. degree from the University of Illinois in 1921. He was a university scholar at Ohio State University and received the M.A. (1922) and Ph.D. (1924) degrees.

He started teaching at Ohio State as a teaching assistant in 1922 and continued there for the rest of his career. He was a professor from 1933.

Hullfish was the author of *Aspects of Thorndike's Psychology in Their Relationships to Educational Theory and Practice* (1926), *The Educational Frontier* (with others, 1933), *Democracy in Transition* (with others, 1937), *Educational Freedom and Democracy,* the second yearbook of the John Dewey Society (with others, 1939), and *Reflective Thinking: The Method and Education* (with Phillip G. Smith, 1961) and editor of *Adventures in the Reconstruction of Education* (with Arthur J. Klein, 1941) and *Educational Freedom in the Age of Anxiety* (1953). He served on the advisory board of *Education Digest* (1957–60).

Hullfish was curriculum consultant to the Dalton, New York, public schools (1933–36). He attended the Pan-Pacific Conference of the New Education Fellowship in 1938 and served on the board of education in Upper Arlington, Ohio (1942–44). He was a Fulbright lecturer in Japan (1958–59).

A member of many professional associations, Hullfish was secretary-treasurer (1955–58) and president (1958–62) of the John Dewey Society, president of the Philosophy of Education Society (1948–49), and president of the Progressive Education Association (1951–55).

REFERENCES: *LE* (II); *WWW* (IV); *Educational Theory* 13 (July 1963): 161–252.   *Margaret W. Ryan*

HUMPHREY, George Duke. B. August 30, 1897, Dumas, Mississippi, to John Washington and Louise Isabel (Cheeves) Humphrey. M. April 15, 1925, to Josephine Robertson. Ch. one. D. September 10, 1973, Laramie, Wyoming.

George Duke Humphrey was graduated from State Teachers College (later, University of Southern Mississippi) at Hattiesburg, Mississippi (1922), and received the B.A. degree from Blue Mountain (Mississippi) College (1929), the M.A. degree from the University of Chicago (1931), and the Ph.D. degree from Ohio State University (1939).

Humphrey was a public school teacher, principal, and superintendent in Mississippi. By 1932 he was a high school supervisor for the state of Mississippi. Appointed president of Mississippi State College at Jackson in 1934, he served in that post until 1945, when he accepted the presidency of the University of Wyoming. He retired in July 1964.

Humphrey participated in professional activities and organizations, from the presidency of an athletic conference, the Southeastern Conference (1938–40), to the presidency of the Association of Land Grant Colleges and Universities (1956–57). Among other organizations he was active in were the Southern Association of Colleges and Secondary Schools (president, 1942–45), the Western Interstate Commission for Higher Education (chairman, 1954–55), the Mississippi Association of Colleges (president, 1940–41), the American Council of Education, the American Arbitration Association, and the American Association for Adult Education.

On April 10, 1976, Mississippi State University dedicated a new coliseum to him.

REFERENCES: *LE* (III); *NCAB* (I:398); *WW* (XXXVIII); *WWAE* (XXII); *WWW* (VI); *Casper Star Tribune,* September 11, 1973.

Everett D. Lantz

HUNT, Henry Alexander. B. October 10, 1866, Sparta, Georgia, to Henry Alexander and Maria (Hunt) Hunt. M. June 14, 1893, to Florence Johnson. Ch. three. D. October 1, 1938, Washington, D.C.

Henry Alexander Hunt was graduated with honors from Atlanta (Georgia) University in 1890. He was principal of the main public school for Negroes in Charlotte, North Carolina, for one year and director of trades, business manager, and proctor of boys at Biddle (later, Johnson C. Smith) University in Charlotte (1891–1904). At Biddle he organized the first farmers' conference held in the state of North Carolina. In 1904 Hunt accepted an invitation to become second principal of Fort Valley (Georgia) High and Industrial School. The school became Fort Valley Normal and Industrial School and, later, Fort Valley State College.

Hunt sought to erect a Tuskegee-Hampton type of school at Fort Valley, believing that agriculture was the only way out of distress for Georgia blacks. When he arrived at Fort Valley, there were a few rudely constructed buildings, scant equipment, no funds, and only a few pupils. At the time of this death he had built up the institution to a half-million dollar plant with fourteen modern buildings, a campus of over ninety acres, and more than a thousand students. Hunt's success was achieved with support of the Protestant Episcopal church, the General Education Board, the Interracial Commission, the Harkness, Harmon, and Rockefeller foundations, and the Rosenwald, Slater, and Phelps-Stokes funds. He was supported by progressive educators who were interested in the education of blacks.

Under Hunt's leadership the school became a junior college for the training of rural teachers (1927). With the opening of the junior college, the curriculum included a liberal arts course to prepare students for future study in colleges and advanced professions and vocational courses in agriculture, home economics, and building trades. The school cooperated with elementary schools; and health projects, home nursing, and community hygiene projects, farm demonstration work, community clubs, co-operatives, and home demonstration programs were instituted. The school became the center of the Jeanes Foundation activities for vocational and social service programs.

Hunt established the Flint River Farm (a government farm project near Montezuma, Georgia, occupied by more than a hundred families), helped blacks in obtaining assistance from the farm credit administration and credit unions, aided in the establishment of state colleges at Albany, Georgia, and Forsyth, Georgia, and established a cooperative community at Fort Valley.

Hunt advanced the education of blacks in the United States. He was president of the Georgia Teachers' and Educational Association, special assistant to the governor of the farm credit administration (1933–38), and was awarded the Spingarn Medal (1930), a gold medal from the Harmon Foundation (1931), and a Rosenwald traveling fellowship for the study of cooperative farming in Denmark.

REFERENCES: *NCAB* (27:31); *NYT*, October 4, 1938, p. 25; Dorothy Orr, *A History of Education in Georgia* (Chapel Hill: University of North Carolina Press, 1950); Willard Range, *The Rise and Progress of Negro Colleges in Georgia* (Athens: University of Georgia, 1951); Cornelius V. Troup, *Distinguished Negro Georgians* (Dallas: Royal Publishing Co., 1962).   *Anne R. Gayles*

HUNT, Mary Hannah Hanchett. B. June 4, 1830, (sometimes July 4, 1831), South Canaan, Connecticut, to Ephraim and Nancy (Swift) Hanchett. M. October 27, 1852, to Leander B. Hunt. Ch. one. D. April 24, 1906, Dorchester, Massachusetts.

Mary Hannah Hanchett Hunt was born into the family of an iron manufacturer who was an active reformer and vice-president of the first temperance society in the United States. She attended local schools and was a graduate of the Patapsco Female Institute near Baltimore. She taught chemistry and physiology at the institute and coauthored science texts with Almira Hart Lincoln Phelps *(q.v.)*, head of the school.

Assisting her son in an experiment with the properties of alcohol, she realized the possibility of introducing scientific instruction in temperance in the schools. The local Hyde Park, Massachusetts, schools were persuaded to become the first to include temperance instruction in the curriculum. Hunt extended her efforts to other Massachusetts communities and came to the conclusion that state laws would be required to accomplish her goals. In 1879 she presented a plan for the enactment of state and national legislation to the national convention of the Womens Christian Temperance Union (WCTU). The following year, the WCTU set up a department of scientific temperance instruction and Hunt was appointed national superintendent of the department.

In 1882 Vermont became the first state to pass a mandatory temperance instruction law; the rest of the states followed, with Georgia being the last in 1901. The need to provide instructional materials for the subject led Hunt to develop subject content and to promote the inclusion of materials in physiology and health texts. She edited the *Scientific Temperance Monthly Advices* (renamed *School Physiology Journal*) from 1882 until her death. The *Journal* became the base from which Mary Hunt countered the attacks of those opposing instruction about alcoholism in the schools, including a report from the Committee of Fifty, a prestigious alcohol-study group.

In 1890 Hunt was appointed to a post in the world's WCTU comparable to her national responsibilities; she extended efforts toward compulsory temperance education in England and other countries. Texts Hunt approved were translated into many languages. Some American texts contained imprimature-like approvals with Hunt's name ensuring the adequacy of the content on temperance.

REFERENCES: *DAB; NAW; NCAB* (9:156); *TC; WC; WWW* (I); *NYT,* April 25, 1906, p. 13.   *John F. Ohles*

HUNT, Thomas Forsyth. B. January 1, 1862, Ridott, Illinois, to Thomas Marshall and Mary H. (Kirk) Hunt. M. August 22, 1888, to Juniata G. Campbell. Ch. two. D. April 26, 1927, at sea.

Thomas Forsyth Hunt received the B.Sc. (1884) and M.Sc. (1892) degrees from the University of Illinois. He served as an assistant to the Illinois state entomologist (1885–86), and assistant in agriculture at the University of Illinois (1886–88), and an assistant agriculturist at the Illinois Agricultural Experiment Station (1888–91).

Hunt was professor of agriculture (1891–92), dean of the school of agriculture, and director of the Pennsylvania Agricultural Experiment Station (1907–12) at Pennsylvania State College (later, State University) and was professor of agriculture (1892–1903) and dean of the college of agriculture and domestic science (1896–1903) at Ohio State University. He was professor of agronomy at Cornell University in Ithaca, New York

(1903–07). Hunt was professor of agriculture (1912–27), director of the agricultural experiment station (1912–19), and dean of the college of agriculture (1912–23) at the University of California at Berkeley.

Hunt was the author of books on agriculture, including *Soils and Crops of the Farm* (with G. E. Morrow, 1895), *History of Agriculture and Rural Economics* (1899), *The Cereals of America* (1904), *How to Choose a Farm* (1906), *The Forage and Fiber Crops in America* (1907), *The Young Farmer* (1913), *Soil and Crops* (with Charles W. Burkett, 1913), and *Farm Animals* (with Charles W. Burkett, 1914).

A member of the Society for the Promotion of Agricultural Science (president, 1907–09) and other organizations, Hunt received honorary degrees from the University of Illinois (1904) and Michigan Agricultural College (1907).

REFERENCES: *WWW* (I).   *John F. Ohles*

HUNT, William Morris. B. March 31, 1824, Brattleboro, Vermont, to Jonathan and Jane Maria (Leavitt) Hunt. M. 1855 to Louisa Dumeresq Perkins. Ch. none. D. September 8, 1879, Isle of Shoals, New Hampshire.

William Morris Hunt was the first of five children born to a talented artistic mother and a successful jurist and congressman father. He entered Harvard University but left before graduation and toured France, Italy, and Germany with his mother. For a short time he was a student at Dusseldorf (Germany) Academy but disliked its rigid atmosphere and returned to Paris where he began his studies with Thomas Coutoure in 1846. He met Jean François Millet, and a friendship developed that was to have an influence on both of them.

In 1855 Hunt returned to America and opened a studio, first in Rhode Island and later in Vermont. After travel to the Azores he settled in Boston in 1862 where he became a leading figure in Boston society. He became the vigorous champion of the then unknown painters of the Barbizon school. Largely through his efforts and the assistance of society friends and students, he created admirers and a market for their work even before they were recognized in France. He conducted highly successful classes in art in Boston.

Hunt turned to portraiture and undertook some allegorical works, including two large murals for the New York State Assembly chamber in 1875, which were lost because of the dampness in the walls on which they were executed. He illustrated *Hints for Pupils in Drawing and Painting* by Helen M. Knowlton (1880) and wrote *Talks About Art* (1878).

REFERENCES: *AC; DAB; EB; NCAB* (3:288); *TC; WWW* (H); *NYT*, September 9, 1879, p. 2.   *James F. Warwick*

HUNTER, Frederick Maurice. B. March 24, 1879, Savannah, Missouri, to Theodore F. and Frances M. (Tatlock) Hunter. M. 1907 to Emma Estelle

Schreiber. Ch. two. D. May 15, 1964, Eugene, Oregon.

Frederick Maurice Hunter received the A.B. degree (1905) from the University of Nebraska, the A.M. degree (1919) from Columbia University, and the Ed.D. degree (1925) from the University of California.

A teacher in Marshall County (Kansas) rural schools (1897–99), Hunter was principal of rural schools at Oketo, Kansas (1899–1901), director of evening schools at the Young Men's Christian Association in Lincoln, Nebraska (1901–03), and high school teacher (1904–05) and superintendent of schools at Fairmont (1905–07), Ashland (1907–08), and Norfolk (1908–11), Nebraska. Professor of agricultural education and principal of the school of agriculture at the University of Nebraska (1911–12), Hunter was superintendent of schools of Lincoln, Nebraska (1912–17), and Oakland, California (1917–28). He was chancellor of the University of Denver, Colorado (1928–35), and served as chancellor of the Oregon State System of Higher Education from 1935 to his retirement in 1946.

President (1920–21) of the National Education Association, Hunter also served as chairman of the Committee of One Hundred to study teacher tenure in the United States (1923–28) and was a member of the Educational Policies Commission (1935–43). He was a member of other professional associations, including the California Teachers Association (director, 1923–28 and vice-president). He was active as a member of the Curriculum Commission of the California State Department of Education (1927–28) and the Oregon state advisory board of the National Youth Administration (1935–39). He was a trustee of the Foundation for Advancement of Social Sciences at the University of Denver. He was the recipient of several honorary degrees.

REFERENCES: *LE* (III); *WW* (XXVI); *WWW* (VI); "NEA, Defender and Advocate," *California Teacher Association Journal* 54 (January 1958): 16–17. *John F. Ohles*

HUNTER, Thomas. B. October 19, 1831, Ardglass, Ireland, to John and Mary Ewart (Norris) Hunter. M. November 2, 1854, to Annie McBride. Ch. four. D. October 14, 1915, New York, New York.

Thomas Hunter received his early education in the private schools of Ardglass, Ireland, and Dandalk Institute and Santry Science School, Anglican boarding schools in nearby towns. A good student, he did not enjoy boarding school, particularly at Dundalk where corporal punishment was freely practiced. Santry, where it was not permitted, was more to his liking.

He taught for seven months in 1849 in the Cellan School, which was under the supervision of the Ossary Diocesan Church Education. His position was terminated because he wrote a series of newspaper articles in support of the Young Ireland party and Irish independence.

Hunter came to the United States in 1850 and became a teacher of drawing in New York City's Public School No. 35. He was principal of the school (1857–69). The school prospered under his leadership and became noted for its scholarship, as well as for its constructive discipline, which he patterned after that of Santry. He built a strong evening school to serve adults who were employed during the day.

Hunter was interested in the education of women and in teacher education. He established the Female Normal and High School in 1869; it opened in 1870 as the Normal College of the City of New York. Hunter served as its president and employed a female superintendent and a faculty of four professors. The college conducted a model school and established the first free kindergarten supported at public expense in the United States. By 1874 the college had an enrollment of a thousand students. Hunter continued as president of the college until his retirement in 1906. In response to public demand, the board of education changed the name of the college in 1914 to Hunter College of the City of New York.

Hunter wrote an article on normal schools for the *Encyclopedia Britannica* and a textbook on plane geometry, and he was coauthor of *Home Culture, A Self-Instructor and Aid to Social Hours at Home* (1884) and *A Narrative History of the United States for the Use of Schools* (1896).

In 1897 graduates of Public School No. 35 organized the Thomas Hunter Association as a tribute to Hunter. He was awarded honorary degrees by Columbia University, Williams College, and New York University.

REFERENCES: *DAB; NCAB* (22:244); *WWW* (IV); *Harper's Weekly* 18 (July 25, 1874): 617–18; *NYT,* October 15, 1915, p. 11.

Erwin H. Goldenstein

HUNTINGTON, Ellsworth. B. September 16, 1876, Galesburg, Illinois, to Henry Strong and Mary Lawrence (Herbert) Huntington. M. December 22, 1917, to Rachel Slocum Brewer. Ch. three. D. October 17, 1947, New Haven, Connecticut.

Eldest son of a scholar and clergyman, Ellsworth Huntington lived in Illinois, Maine, and Milton, Massachusetts, where he was graduated from high school in 1893. He received the A.B. degree from Beloit (Wisconsin) College in 1897, when his first article was published in *The Transactions* of the Wisconsin Academy of Sciences. He received the M.A. degree (1902) from Harvard University and the Ph.D. degree (1909) from Yale University.

A teaching assistant (1897–1901) to the president of Euphrates College in Harpoot, Turkey, he mapped the Harpoot area and traveled down the Euphrates River on a raft of inflated sheepskins in the manner reported by Xenophon, a feat achieved before by only one European. He studied physiography at Harvard under William Morris Davis *(q.v.),* who took him as an assistant on an expedition to Turkestan and Persia (1903). Fourteen months later he joined Robert L. Barrett in a journey across the Himalayas into the Tarim Basin of Inner Asia (1905–06). In 1907 he became a geography instructor at Yale University. He engaged in climatic studies in Palestine (1909) and the United States, Mexico, and Central America (1910–14). Huntington served as a research associate at Yale from 1917 until his death. After 1919 he rarely lectured to more than a few students, but his textbooks greatly influenced the teaching of geography in the United States and abroad.

His geography textbooks include *Asia, a Geography Reader* (1912), *The Human Habitat* (1927), and *Principles of Economic Geography* (1940); he was coauthor of *The Geography of Europe* (1918), *Principles of Human Geography* (1920), *Business Geography* (1922), *Modern Business Geography* (1924), *Living Geography* (two volumes, 1933), *Economic and Social Geography* (1933), and *Geography of Europe* (1935).

Huntington held that climate was the greatest single influence on the development and decay of civilizations, and he studied contributions of racial factors and natural selection in human progress. His works on climatic themes include *The Pulse of Asia* (1907), *Palestine and Its Transformation* (1911), *Civilization and Climate* (1915), and *World Power and Evolution* (1919). On the quality-of-people theme, he wrote *The Character of Races* (1924), *The Builders of America* (with Leon Whitney, 1927), *Tomorrow's Children: The Goal of Eugenics* (1935), *After Three Centuries* (1935), and *Season of Birth: Its Relation to Human Abilities* (1938). Huntington began to synthesize his life's work in *Mainsprings of Civilization* (1945) but died before completion of the next volume, *The Pace of History*.

Huntington's honors included the Royal Geographical Society's Gill Memorial Award; medals from the Paris Geographical Society, the Philadelphia Geographical Society, and the Foundation for the Study of Cycles; and the Distinguished Service to Geography Award of the National Council of Geography Teachers (1942). He was recognized by the National Anesthesia Research Society for his investigation of the effect of temperature and humidity on postoperative death rates. He was president of the Ecological Society of America (1917), the Association of American Geographers (1923), and the American Eugenics Society (1934–38) and a member of several other associations. He was appointed a member of the National Research Council in both the geology and geography (1919–22) and biology and agriculture (1921–24) divisions.

REFERENCES: *DAB* (supp. 4); *LE* (I); *NCAB* (A:510, 37:43); *WWAE* (XIII); *WWW* (II); *NYT,* October 18, 1947, p. 15.   *M. Jane Dowd*

HUTCHINS, Robert Maynard. B. January 17, 1899, Brooklyn, New York, to William James and Anna Laura (Murch) Hutchins. M. September 10, 1921, to Maude Phelps McVeigh. M. May 10, 1949, to Vesta Sutton Orlick.

Ch. three. D. May 15, 1977, Santa Barbara, California.

Robert Maynard Hutchins attended Oberlin (Ohio) College (1915–17) and served in the United States Army in World War I (1917–19). He received the A.B. (1921) and LL.B. (1925) degrees from Yale University.

Hutchins served as master of English and history at Lake Placid (New York) School (1921–23) before returning to Yale as secretary of the university (1923–27), acting dean (1927–28), and dean (1928–29) of the law school.

At the age of thirty, Hutchins became president of the University of Chicago (1929–45) where he introduced many innovative educational concepts and practices. Believing that a university is a center for inspiring youth with a passion for independent thought and criticism, Hutchins permitted high school juniors to matriculate at Chicago and sometimes graduate after two years. He abolished the course credit system and compulsory class attendance. When a student thought he was ready, he asked his instructor for a comprehensive examination. Hutchins thought these innovations would break the academic lockstep, encourage students to study independently, and ensure honest learning.

Hutchins was chancellor of the university from 1945 to 1951 when he became associate director of the Ford Foundation (1951–54). In 1954 he was named president of the Fund for the Republic. He was also president of the Center for the Study of Democratic Institutions.

Included among his writings are *No Friendly Voice* (1936), *The Higher Learning in America* (1936), *Education for Freedom* (1943), *St. Thomas and the World State* (1949), *Morals, Religion, and Higher Education* (1950), *The Democratic Dilemma* (1951), *Some Questions about Education in North America* (1951), *The Great Conversation* (1951), *The Conflict in Education* (1953), *The University of Utopia* (1953), *Freedom, Education, and the Fund* (1956), *Some Observations on American Education* (1956), and *The Learning Society* (1968). He served on the board of editors of *Encyclopedia Britannica* from 1946.

Hutchins received the Croce de Guerra of Italy (1918) and was named an officer of the Legion of Honor of France (1938). He received the Goethe Medal (1948) and the Sidney Hillman Award (1959). He was awarded honorary degrees by many American and foreign colleges and universities.

REFERENCES: *CB* (February 1954); *EB*; *LE* (III); *NCAB* (C:54); *NYT*, May 16, 1977, p. 1; *WW* (XXXVIII); *WWAE* (VIII); Adolphe E. Meyer *(q.v.)*, *An Educational History of the American People* (New York: McGraw-Hill, 1967).   *Abraham Blinderman*

HYATT, Alpheus. B. April 5, 1838, Washington, D.C., to Alpheus and Harriet Randolph (King) Hyatt. M. January 7, 1867, to Audella Beebe. Ch. four. D. January 15, 1902, Cambridge, Massachusetts.

Alpheus Hyatt attended the Maryland Military Academy and Yale College. He was graduated with the S.B. degree (1862) from the Lawrence Scientific School at Harvard University. While at Harvard, where he came under the influence of the noted naturalist, Louis Agassiz *(q.v.)*, his interests centered on the study of natural history.

After serving as an officer in the Civil War, Hyatt returned to Harvard to renew his studies with Agassiz. He was appointed curator of the Essex Institute in Salem, Massachusetts, in 1867. With others at the institute, he helped found and was curator of the Peabody Academy of Science at Salem (1869). In 1870 he began a lifelong association with the Boston Society of Natural Science, first as custodian in 1870 and then as curator in 1881.

Hyatt was professor of zoology and paleontology at the Massachusetts Institute of Technology (1870–88) and also taught at Boston University from 1877 until his death in 1902. He was director from 1870 of the Teacher's School of Science to prepare local public school teachers to include elementary science instruction in their classrooms. He helped establish a marine biological laboratory of natural history at Annisquam, Massachusetts, with the support of the Women's Educational Society of Boston. This laboratory was later moved to Woods Hole, Massachusetts.

Hyatt was particularly interested in the study of fossils and marine life, and he had a philosophical interest in problems of biological evolution. He formulated a number of principles that became the basis for a new system of evolutionary research, and he was recognized for his painstaking scientific work.

Hyatt was the author of *Observations on Polyzoa* (1866), *Fossil Cephalods of the Museum of Comparative Zoology* (1867), *Revision of North American Porifera* (1875–77), *Genesis of Tertiary Species of Planorbis at Steinheim* (1880), *Genera of Fossil Cephalopoda* (1883), *Larval Theory of the Origin of Cellular Tissue* (1884), *Genesis of the Arietidae* (1889), and *Phylogemy of an Acquired Characteristic* (1894). He was the founder and editor (1867–71) of the *American Naturalist*.

The chief founder of the American Society of Naturalists (first president, 1883), Hyatt was elected a fellow of the American Academy of Arts and Sciences (1869) and the National Academy of Sciences (1875), and he was a member of many American and foreign scientific associations. He was awarded an honorary degree by Brown University in 1898.

REFERENCES: *AC; DAB; DSB; NCAB* (23:362); *TC; WWW* (I); *NYT*, January 16, 1902, p. 9.   *Harold D. Lehman*

HYDE, Grant Milnor. B. April 4, 1889, The Dalles, Oregon, to Will Henry and Georgia Mabel (Colvin) Hyde. M. August 29, 1957, to Helen M. Patterson. Ch. none. D. September 9, 1972, Tucson, Arizona.

Grant Milnor Hyde attended Beloit (Wisconsin) College (1906–08) and studied architecture at Yale University, from which he received the A.B. (1910) and M.A. (1913) degrees. He also received the M.A. degree (1912) from the University of Wisconsin.

As an instructor in journalism (1910) at Wisconsin, Hyde assisted Willard G. Bleyer *(q.v.)* in organizing what became the school of journalism in 1927 and developed courses and undergraduate and graduate curricula. Hyde was acting head of the department of journalism (1922–23), acting director of the school of journalism (1927–28, 1935–36), and director (1936–49) and continued as professor of journalism to 1959. He had worked as a part-time reporter for newspapers in Janesville (1905–06) and Beloit (1906–08), Wisconsin, critic for the *New Haven* (Connecticut) *Journal-Courier* (1908–10), associate editor of *Popular Mechanics Magazine,* feature editor of the *New York Evening Mail,* and managing editor of *Popular Science Monthly* (1915). He served as Wisconsin correspondent for the *Christian Science Monitor* of Boston, Massachusetts. He was a founder (1927) and president of the Campus Publishing Company and editor of the University of Wisconsin Press Service (1915–27). Late in his career (1957), Hyde married his long-time colleague and a professor of journalism, Helen Patterson.

Hyde was a pioneer author of journalism textbooks; among his works were *Newspaper Reporting and Correspondence* (1912), *Newspaper Editing* (1915), *Handbook for Newspaper Workers* (1921), *A Course in Journalistic Writing* (1922), *Journalistic Writing* (1929), and *Newspaper Handbook* (1941). He served as faculty adviser to the University of Wisconsin's *Daily Cardinal* (1914–39).

He was active in professional associations, including the American Association of Teachers of Journalism (charter member, president, 1928), the American Association of Schools and Departments of Journalism (president, 1936), the National Joint Committee on Newspaper Relations (chairman, 1935–41), and the National Council on Education for Journalism (member, 1935–40).

REFERENCES: *WWAE* (XIV); *WWW* (V); *Capitol Times* (Madison, Wisconsin), September 11, 1972; *Wisconsin State Journal* (Madison), September 9, 1972; Grant M. Hyde, "35 Years of Journalism," *The Wisconsin Alumnus* (November 1940): 13–15.   *John F. Ohles*

HYDE, William DeWitt. B. September 23, 1858, Winchendon, Massachusetts, to Joel and Eliza (DeWitt) Hyde. M. November 6, 1883, to Prudence M. Phillips. Ch. none. D. June 29, 1917, Brunswick, Maine.

William DeWitt Hyde was educated in public schools and Phillips (Exeter, New Hampshire) Academy (1872–75). He was graduated with the A.B. degree (1879) from Harvard University, completed a course in theology at Andover (Massachusetts) Theological Seminary in 1882, and was ordained to the Congregational ministry in 1883.

Hyde served a church in Paterson, New Jersey (1883–85), and was appointed president and professor of mental and moral philosophy at

Bowdoin College in Brunswick, Maine (1885–1917). Bowdoin prospered under Hyde's leadership; entrance requirements were liberalized and the curriculum was extended to permit a greater selection of courses.

Hyde was the author of many books, including *Practical Ethics* (1892), *Social Theology* (1895), *Practical Idealism* (1897), *God's Education of Man* (1899), *School Speaker and Reader* (1900), *Jesus' Way* (1902), *The New Ethics* (1903), *The College Man and the College Woman* (1906), *Self-Measurement* (1908), *The Teacher's Philosophy In and Out of School* (1910), and *The Five Great Philosophies of Life* (1911).

He was a fellow of the American Academy of Arts and Sciences. Active in church affairs, he took the lead in founding the Maine Interdenominational Commission in 1890. He received honorary degrees from Harvard and Syracuse universities and Bowdoin College.

REFERENCES: *AC; DAB; NCAB* (1:419); *TC; WWW* (I); *NYT,* June 30, 1917, p. 11.   *John F. Ohles*

HYER, Robert Stewart. B. October 18, 1860, Oxford, Georgia, to William L. and Laura (Stewart) Hyer. M. 1881 to Madge Jordan. M. February 24, 1888, to Margaret Lee Hudgins. Ch. three. D. May 29, 1929, Dallas, Texas.

Robert Stewart Hyer's mother was an invalid, and he attended school in Atlanta, Georgia, while living with an aunt. From 1874 to 1881, he lived with an uncle, Joseph S. Stewart, and attended Emory College in Oxford, Georgia, graduating with the A.B. (1881) and A.M. (1883) degrees.

Hyer was professor of sciences (1882–1911) and president (1897–1911) of Southwestern University, a Methodist institution in Georgetown, Texas. He was credited with the beginning of education in the physical sciences in the state and was active in experimenting with X rays and other waves. He designed the first wireless station in Texas in 1904. As president of Southwestern, he increased the student body, erected new buildings, obtained endowment money, and established a medical college in Dallas (1903).

Failing in his efforts to move the university, Hyer resigned in 1911 to become president and professor and head of the department of physics of Southern Methodist University at Dallas. He served as president to 1919 and continued as professor of physics to his death in 1929. Hyer planned the campus, selected the architectural design, directed the construction of the first buildings, and raised an endowment fund.

Active in church affairs, Hyer was a delegate to ecumenical conferences in London, England (1902), and Toronto, Canada (1912), and participated in merger negotiations of the Methodist Episcopal Church and the Methodist Episcopal Church, South (1906–18). He was a member of the Southern Methodist general commission on education (1900–18). He published papers in scientific and religious journals and contributed a Sunday school lesson for five years to the Dallas *News* and *Time-Herald.* He was

awarded honorary degrees by Central College and Baylor University.
REFERENCES: *DAB; NCAB* (24:294); *WWW* (I).   *John F. Ohles*

I

IMMEL, Ray Keeslar. B. October 31, 1885, West Gilead, Michigan, to
Daniel Aurelius and Jennie Sarah (Keeslar) Immel. M. June 24, 1910, to
Carrie Bell Barnard. Ch. four. D. April 11, 1945, Inglewood, California.

Ray Keeslar Immel was educated in the Gilead Township and Clear-
water, Michigan, schools and attended Albion (Michigan) College. He was
graduated from the University of Michigan, receiving the A.B. (1910),
A.M. (1913), and Ph.D. (1931) degrees.

A teacher in rural Branch County (Michigan) schools (1904–05 and
1906–07), Immel was professor of oratory and expression at Muskingum
College in New Concord, Ohio (1910–12). He was an assistant at the
University of Michigan (1909–10 and 1912–13) and continued there teaching speech classes to 1924. He assisted in organizing the school of speech at
the University of Southern California in Los Angeles and served as dean
(later, director) to his death in 1945. He devised instruments to analyze
speech.

Immel was the author of books on speech, including *The Delivery of a
Speech* (1921), *Debating for High Schools* (with Ruth Huston Whipple,
1928), *Public Speaking for High Schools* (1931), *Speech Improvement*
(with Helen Loree Ogg, 1936), and *Speech Making* (with W. Norwood
Brigance, *q.v.,* 1938). He was a consultant in pronunciation to *Webster's
Dictionary* (1934) and business manager of the *Quarterly Journal of Speech
Education* (1919–24).

A member of professional organizations, Immel was treasurer (1919–24)
and president (1925) of the National Association of Teachers of Speech and
president of the Western Association of Teachers of Speech (1932).

REFERENCES: *NCAB* (33:523); *NYT,* April 14, 1945, p. 15; *WWAE*
(VIII); *WWW* (II).   *John F. Ohles*

INGLIS, Alexander James. B. November 24, 1879, Middletown, Connecticut, to William Grey and Susan (Byers) Inglis. M. December 20, 1911, to
Antoinette Clark. Ch. none. D. April 12, 1924, Boston, Massachusetts.

Alexander James Inglis was graduated from Middletown (Connecticut)
High School and attended Wesleyan University in Middletown, where he
received the B.A. degree (1902). He was awarded the M.A. (1909) and
Ph.D. (1911) degrees from Columbia University. He studied at the Ameri-

can School of Classical Studies in Rome, Italy, under a Wesleyan fellowship (1902–03).

From 1903 to 1912 Inglis taught Latin in schools in New Jersey and at the Horace Mann School in New York City, and he was headmaster of the Belmont School in California. He was professor of education and director of the summer school and extension courses at Rutgers College (later, University) in New Brunswick, New Jersey (1912–14). He joined the education faculty at Harvard University in 1914 and continued there to his death in 1924. He was active in the survey movement in education and participated in many surveys of educational institutions and state systems of education.

The author of a number of books, Inglis wrote *First Book in Latin* (1906), *Exercise Book in Latin Composition* (1908), *High School Course in Latin Composition* (with C. McC. Baker, 1909), *The Rise of the High School in Massachusetts* (1911), *Principles of Secondary Education* (1918), *Virginia Public Schools* (1919), and *Intelligence Quotient Values* (1921). He contributed to *Cardinal Principles of Education* (1918).

A member of professional organizations, Inglis was president of the Society of College Teachers of Education (1921) and a fellow of the American Association for the Advancement of Science.

REFERENCES: *DAB; NCAB* (23:54); *NYT*, April 13, 1924, p. 27; *WWW* (I). *Robert Emans*

IRELAND, John. B. c. September 11, 1838, Burnchurch, County Kilkenny, Ireland, to Richard and Judith (Naughton) Ireland. M. no. D. September 25, 1918, St. Paul, Minnesota.

John Ireland, first archbishop of St. Paul, Minnesota, went to Minnesota by prairie schooner and steamboat as a boy of fourteen with his family in 1851. St. Paul's first bishop, Joseph Cretin, selected Ireland as a prospective priest for the struggling new diocese. With the help of French priests, Cretin sponsored the boy's seminary education in France for eight years.

Following ordination in 1861 and a brief period of service as a Civil War chaplain, Ireland became a frontier parish priest, traveling over wide areas of Minnesota to bring the sacraments and to teach Catholic settlers and Chippewa Indians. He was consecrated bishop in 1875, succeeded to the bishopric of St. Paul in 1884, and became archbishop of St. Paul in 1888.

Ireland made his mark as a theorist and administrator in American education. He insisted on professional qualifications for teachers and those engaged in charitable work. He spoke on the subject at the 1884 Baltimore, Maryland, Plenary Council. Addressing the National Educational Association (1890 and 1892), Ireland spoke on the right and obligation of the state to provide free schools and the obligation of the church to educate in matters of faith and morals. He proposed to fulfill these obligations through a single school system as in the short-lived Faribault-Stillwater (Minnesota) compromise school plan, which provided state support for parochial schools.

Under Ireland's leadership, the number of parish schools in the St. Paul diocese increased from 63 to 102. Religious communities of women were expanded, and the number of pupils taught in Catholic institutions increased nearly threefold. Ireland was involved in the establishment in St. Paul of St. Thomas College, St. Paul Seminary, and the College of St. Catherine. He played a crucial role in the founding of the Catholic University of America in Washington, D.C. He was a spokesman for women's rights to higher education, the value of the liberal arts, and a church educational policy adapted to the American political system.

Ireland was the author of *The Church and Modern Society* (two volumes, 1896). He received an honorary degree from Yale University in 1901.

REFERENCES: *AC; DAB; NCAB* (9:226); *TC; EB; WWW* (I); Sister Helen Angela Hurley, *On Good Ground* (Minneapolis: University of Minnesota Press, 1951); James H. Moynihan, *The Life of Archbishop John Ireland* (New York: Harper, 1953); *New Catholic Encyclopedia* (New York: McGraw-Hill, 1967); *NYT,* September 26, 1918, p. 13; James Michael Reardon, *The Catholic Church in the Diocese of St. Paul* (St. Paul: Norton Central Publishers, 1952).   *Karen Kennelly*

IRWIN, Robert Benjamin. B. June 2, 1883, Rockford, Iowa, to Robert Payne and Hattie (Chappell) Irwin. M. June 19, 1917, to Mary Janet Blanchard. Ch. one. D. December 12, 1951, Port Orchard, Washington.

Robert Benjamin Irwin was blinded by an attack of inflammatory rheumatism when he was five years old. His experience in the Washington State School for the Blind in Vancouver, of which he was the first graduate (1901), influenced his decision to develop public school classes so that the blind could live with their families. He received the B.A. degree (1906) from the University of Washington and the M.A. degree (1907) from Harvard University, where he remained until 1909 studying methods of education and care of the blind.

Irwin was superintendent of classes for the blind in Cleveland, Ohio (1909–23). By 1913 he organized the first sight-saving classes and in 1915 organized classes for the blind throughout Ohio. He organized the Howe Publishing Society to provide educational materials for the blind and the vision impaired, including the printing of braille books. The Clear Type Publishing Committee was set up to print books in twenty-four point type.

In 1923, Irwin was appointed director of research and education for the newly founded American Foundation for the Blind. He resigned as director in 1929 to become executive director of the foundation and continued efforts to make educational materials available for the blind, working on "talking books," developing a variety of proposals for vocational training for the blind, and providing leadership for legislation to aid the blind. He worked with blind war veterans and was executive vice-president of National Industries for the Blind in 1938 and executive director of the American Foundation for Overseas Blind (1947). On his retirement, he became consultant for life to the American Foundation for the Blind and consultant to the United Nations on work for the blind.

His autobiography, *As I Saw It,* was published posthumously in 1955. He also wrote *Blind Relief Laws: Their Theory and Practice* (1919) and *Sight-Saving Classes in the Public Schools* (1920) and was editor of textbooks for the blind.

Irwin was a Guggenheim Fellow (1951–52). He was president of the American Association of Workers for the Blind (1923–27). He was chairman of the subcommittee on the visually handicapped for the White House Conference on Child Health and Protection (1930) and the organizing committee for the New York World Conference on Work for the Blind (1931), and the American Uniform Type Committee, which arranged with British experts to adopt a uniform braille code for the blind in English. He served on many advisory committees and was a member of many organizations. He was decorated chevalier of the Legion of Honor by France, was honored by the University of Washington (1945), and received an honorary degree from Western Reserve University (1943).

REFERENCES: *CB* (March 1948 and January 1952); *LE* (III); *NCAB* (D:400); *WWAE* (VIII); *WWW* (III); P. Irvine, "Robert Benjamin Irwin," *Journal of Special Education* 4 (Winter 1970): 1-2; Robert Benjamin Irwin, *As I Saw It* (New York: American Foundation for the Blind, 1955); *NYT,* December 13, 1951, p. 34. *Joseph M. McCarthy*

J

JACKMAN, Wilbur Samuel. B. January 12, 1855, Mechanicstown, Ohio, to Barnard C. and Ruth (Lilley) Jackman. M. December 23, 1884, to Ellen Amelia Reis. Ch. two. D. January 28, 1907, Chicago, Illinois.

Wilbur Samuel Jackman was one of the early leaders of the nature study movement. He developed outlines of nature study techniques that became generally used in elementary schools. He had developed an early interest in nature study on the family farm near California, Pennsylvania.

His first job after graduation from the normal school in California, Pennsylvania (1877), was as a teacher of that school, a position he held until 1880 when he entered Allegheny College in Meadville, Pennsylvania. He enrolled at Harvard University in 1882 and was graduated with the B.A. degree in 1884.

He was employed as a teacher in charge of the natural science courses at Central High School in Pittsburgh, Pennsylvania. In 1889 Jackman was hired by Francis W. Parker *(q.v.),* principal of the Cook County (Illinois)

Normal School, to serve as an instructor in charge of the sciences. Through Parker's influence, Jackman became involved in the reform of the elementary school curriculum through the addition of new content areas and the reduction of the formality common in schools of the period. He remained at the normal school until 1900, when he was appointed dean of the new Chicago Institute. Jackman became dean of the college of education of the University of Chicago in 1901 on the reorganization of the Chicago Institute.

Jackman resigned the post in 1904 to become principal of the University Elementary School, a position he held until his death in 1907. He believed that direct contact of educational students with pupils was the most important phase of teacher training.

Jackman gained national recognition for his leadership and writings. Among his books were *Nature Study for the Common Schools* (1891), *Number Work in Nature Study* (1893), *Field Work in Nature Study* (1894), *Nature Study Record* (1895), *Nature Study for the Common Grades* (1898), *Nature Study and Related Subjects* (1898), and *Nature-Study* (National Society for the Scientific Study of Education, third yearbook, part 2, 1904). During the winter of 1899–1900, Jackman toured England, France, Holland, and Germany studying education. In 1904 he became the editor of *Elementary School Teacher,* which he used to promote his views of elementary school curriculum reform.

REFERENCES: *DAB; NCAB* (27:325); *WWW* (I); Orra E. Underhill, *The Origins and Developments of Elementary School Science* (Chicago: Scott, Foresman, and Co., 1941).   *Dennis M. Wint*

JACKSON, Sheldon. B. May 18, 1834, Minaville, New York, to Samuel Clinton and Delia (Sheldon) Jackson. M. May 18, 1858, to Mary Voorhees. Ch. none. D. May 2, 1909, Asheville, North Carolina.

Sheldon Jackson studied at the public schools of Esperance, New York, attended Union College in Schenectady, New York, in 1855, and received a degree in 1858 from Princeton (New Jersey) Seminary.

Jackson was interested in missionary work, applied to the Presbyterian Board of Missions for a position, and ministered for a year among Indians of the Choctaw nation. He served as district superintendent with headquarters in western Wisconsin, southern Minnesota, and Iowa from 1859 to 1870, when he became superintendent of Presbyterian missions in Denver, Colorado, for the area from Mexico to Canada and Nevada to Nebraska. During this time he served with the Union army of the Cumberland in Tennessee and Alabama hospitals (1863) and was principal of the Rochester (Minnesota) Female Institute (1864–69). By 1883 he had established over a hundred churches in the Midwest and West and Indian schools in New Mexico and Arizona.

Jackson's first interest in Alaska came while he was head of the Rocky

Mountain district of the Presbyterian church in 1877 when he visited Alaska, which had been added to his jurisdiction. He was instrumental in promoting the enactment of legislation establishing a limited territorial government for Alaska.

Jackson was appointed a member of a special governmental commission to investigate conditions of the natives of southeast Alaska (1879) and was appointed a special agent of the United States government to report on the agricultural potentials of the Yukon valley. In 1880 he founded the Industrial Training School for Native Children at Sitka. Jackson was appointed general agent for education under the United States Bureau of Education in 1885 and served to 1908. He established a public school system in the territory.

A major contribution of Jackson was the introduction of reindeer from Siberia to Alaska to alleviate food problems of the native Alaskans. He organized mail services by canoe (1883) and reindeer (1885) for the territory.

Jackson was editor of *Rocky Mountain Presbyterian* (1872–82) and the *Sitka North Star* (1887–94). His reports as education agent for Alaska are considered important documents on the development of Alaskan education. He was the author of *Education in Alaska* (1872), *Alaska and Missions on the North Pacific Coast* (1880), and *Facts About Alaska* (1894).

He was a member of many religious, education, and civic organizations. He was the principal founder of the Woman's Board of Home Missions of the Presbyterian church (1870–79), attended many of the church's general assemblies, and served as moderator of the general assembly in 1897. He represented Alaska at the International Exposition at Mexico City, Mexico (1896), and was honored at the World's Columbian Exposition at St. Louis, Missouri (1893), and the Pan-American Exposition at Buffalo, New York (1901). He organized the Alaskan Society of Natural History and Ethnology (1887). Jackson was the recipient of several honorary degrees by American colleges and universities.

REFERENCES: *AC; DAB; EB; NCAB* (9:251); *TC; WWW* (I); John Eaton (*q.v.*), "Sheldon Jackson, Alaska's Apostle and Pioneer," *The Review of Reviews* 13 (June 1896):691–96.   *Thomas R. Hopkins*

JACOBI, Mary Corinna Putnam. B. August 31, 1842, London, England, to George Palmer and Victorine (Haven) Putnam. M. July 22, 1873, to Abraham Jacobi. Ch. three. D. June 10, 1906, New York, New York.

Mary Corinna Putnam Jacobi was the daughter of the founder of the G. P. Putnam's Sons publishing firm. Returning to America from England in 1848, the family resided in Staten Island, New York. Determined to become a physician, Jacobi studied at the New York College of Pharmacy and earned the M.D. degree from the Female Medical College (later, Women's Medical College), while gaining practical experience through private study and hospital work in Boston and Philadelphia. She went to Paris in 1866 where she sought admission to the Ecole de Médecine. While waiting to be admitted she entered laboratories and clinics, attended lectures, and contributed articles to American newspapers, *Putnam's Magazine,* and *Scribner's Monthly.* Her persistence was rewarded in 1868 when she was the first woman admitted to the Ecole de médecine over objections of the faculty. Three years later she was graduated with honors (1871).

Jacobi returned to New York City in 1871 and became the United States' leading woman physician and worked for the right of women to become accepted in the medical profession. She joined the staff of the Woman's Medical College of the New York Infirmary (1871–77) founded by her friend Dr. Elizabeth Blackwell. She served for three years on the faculty of the New York Post-Graduate Medical School in New York City. She was the first woman elected to membership of the New York Academy of Medicine and to be a delegate to the State Medical Association. A member of the Medical Society of the County of New York, she married the president of the society in 1873.

The two physicians shared a common interest in social causes as well as medicine; he was active in civil-service reform, and she pioneered in the study of the contributions of environmental conditions to disease and participated in the establishment of the Working Women's Society, which became the New York Consumers' League in 1890. She was active in the suffrage movement and was a founder of the League for Political Education.

In 1896 Mary Jacobi developed the first symptoms of a meningeal tumor that rendered her a mute invalid. Documenting her own illness through those last years, she died in New York City in 1906.

She was the author of *The Question of Rest for Women during Menstruation* (1877), for which she won Harvard University's Boylston Prize (1876), *The Value of Life* (1879), *Essays on Hysteria* (1888), *Found and Lost* (1894), and *Stories and Sketches* (1907).

REFERENCES: *AC; DAB; NAW; NCAB* (8:219); *TC; WWW* (I); *NYT,* June 12, 1906, p. 9.   *Kathryn D. Lizzul*

JACOBY, Henry Sylvester. B. April 8, 1857, Springtown, Pennsylvania, to Peter Landis and Barbara (Shelly) Jacoby. M. May 18, 1888, to Laura Louise Saylor. Ch. three. D. August 1, 1955, Quakertown, Pennsylvania.

Henry Sylvester Jacoby was a student at the Excelsior Normal Institute in Carversville, Pennsylvania, and Lehigh University in Bethlehem, Pennsylvania, where he received the C.E. degree (1877).

Jacoby worked with the Lehigh geographical corps of the second geological survey of Pennsylvania and the United States Army Corps of Engineers, and he was chief draftsman for the United States engineers' office in Memphis, Tennessee (1879–85). He was an instructor of civil engineering at Lehigh University (1886–90) and joined the bridge engineering department at Cornell University in Ithaca, New York (1890–1922). He developed Jacoby's triangle for italic lettering (1895).

Jacoby was the author of a number of books, including *Text-Book on Roofs and Bridges* (four parts, with Mansfield Merriam, 1890–98), *Notes and Problems in Descriptive Geometry* (1892), *Text-Book on Plain Lettering* (1897), *Structural Details or Elements of Design in Timber Framing* (1909), *Foundations of Bridges and Buildings* (with Roland P. Davis, 1914), *Timber Design and Construction* (with Roland P. Davis, 1929), and *The Jacoby Family Genealogy* (1930).

Active in many professional, historical, and genealogical organizations, Jacoby was a fellow of the American Association for the Advancement of Science (vice-president and chairman of section D, 1901) and a member of the Society for the Promotion of Engineering Education (secretary, 1900–02, vice-president, 1913–14, and president, 1915–16) and the National Genealogical Society (president, 1930–34). He was awarded an honorary degree from Lehigh University (1941).

REFERENCES: *NCAB* (D:108); *NYT,* August 3, 1955, p. 23; *WWW* (III).   *John F. Ohles*

JAMES, Edmund Janes. B. May 21, 1855, Jacksonville, Illinois, to Colin Dew and Amanda (Casad) James. M. August 22, 1879, to Anna Margaret Lange. Ch. Six. D. June 17, 1925, Covina, California.

Edmund Janes James was a student at Illinois State Normal University, Northwestern University in Evanston, Illinois, and Harvard University. He studied in Germany at the universities of Leipzig, Berlin, and Halle, where he received the A.M. and Ph.D. degrees in 1877.

James returned to the United States to become principal of the Evanston (Illinois) high school (1877–79) and the model high school at Illinois State Normal University. He was professor in public administration and finance at the University of Pennsylvania's Wharton School of Finance and Economy (1883–95). His beliefs that collegiate education had to be modified to emphasize economics and finance for young men planning careers in business received praise from the business community. In 1892 he went to Europe to study commercial education on behalf of the American Bankers Association. James's views were criticized by conservative colleagues, and he was dismissed from the Wharton faculty in 1896.

James was professor of public administration and director of university extension at the University of Chicago (1896–1904). He was president of Northwestern University (1902–04) and president of the University of Illinois (1904–20). During his administration at Illinois, the university's research capacity was enlarged, several major buildings were added, and the faculty was increased significantly. Ill health forced his resignation and retirement in 1920.

James was a leader in American educational thought and reform. His model for commercial education was adopted by most of the leading American universities. He promoted the introduction of the kindergarten in public schools, expansion of the elective system in colleges and universities, and growth of the university extension movement.

James was the founder and editor of the *Illinois School Journal* (1881–83) and editor of the University of Pennsylvania's Political Economy and Public Law Series (1886–95) and the *Annals* of the American Academy of Political and Social Science (1890–95). He wrote many essays and delivered lectures that were published.

He was the founder and first president of the American Academy of Political and Social Science (1889–1901), a founder and vice-president of the American Economic Association (1885), president of the American Society for the Extension of University Teaching (1891–95), and first president of the Municipal League of Philadelphia. He was awarded honorary degrees from six American colleges and universities.

REFERENCES: *AC; DAB; NCAB* (11:67); *WWW* (I); *NYT,* June 20, 1925, p. 13.   *R. Samuel Baker*

JAMES, William. B. January 11, 1842, New York, New York, to Henry and Mary (Walsh) James. M. July 10, 1878, to Alice Howe Gibbens. Ch. five. D. August 26, 1910, Chocorua, New Hampshire.

William James's education was a mixture of tutored experiences in the United States and Europe because his father was determined that his children would experience their education rather than be molded by it. At eighteen, James entered Lawrence Scientific School at Harvard University after a brief period of studying art under William Hunt. He was graduated in 1863 with a degree in chemistry and physiology and studied at Harvard Medical School, where he received the M.D. degree in 1869.

After two years' studying scientific literature at his father's home, James began a long tenure at Harvard (1871–97) as professor of physiology and anatomy. Influenced by Hermann von Helmholtz, Wilhelm Wundt, and Charles Darwin, he introduced new courses into his physiology curriculum and opened the first psychology laboratory in America in 1879. In 1889 he became Harvard's first professor of psychology. In 1879 James began to write his famous *Principles of Psychology,* which took him until 1890 to complete; it was immediately accepted as the most definitive text on psychology at that time. As he was finishing *Principles,* James's interest turned again to philosophy and religion in an attempt to reconcile the positions of science and religion. He adopted pragmatism, a philosophy originally conceived by Charles Peirce *(q.v.).* In the last years of his life, James became the best-known prophet of this American philosophy.

James's main writings in psychology include *Principles of Psychology* (1890) and *Talks to Teachers on Psychology* (1899). Among his many publications on philosophy are *Collected Essays and Reviews* (1892), *The Will to Believe and Other Essays* (1897), *The Variety of Religious Experiences* (1902), *Pragmatism: A New Name for Some Old Ways of Thinking* (1907), *A Pluralistic Universe* (1909), and *The Meaning of Truth* (1909). James's desire to ensure all viewpoints an equal hearing prompted him to help found the American Society for Psychic Research in 1885. He received honorary degrees from seven American and European universities.

REFERENCES: *AC; DAB; EB; NCAB* (18:31); *TC; WWW* (I); Gay W. Allen, *William James: A Biography* (New York: Viking Press, 1967); *NYT,* August 27, 1910, p. 7.   *Morton Patrick Mabry, Jr.*

JAYNE, Clarence D. B. April 12, 1902, Edwall, Washington, to Washington Irving and Susie Jayne. M. June 27, 1924, to Ruth Elizabeth Horn. Ch. three. D. October 22, 1963, Laramie, Wyoming.

Clarence D. Jayne was graduated with the B.A. degree (1929) from the University of Washington and the M.A (1940) and Ph.D. (1942) degrees from the University of Wisconsin. He taught at Wisconsin Central State Teacher's College (later, University of Wisconsin—Stevens Point) in Stevens Point (1942–44), and at the Japanese Relocation Camp in Lamar, Colorado (1944–45). He moved to Laramie, Wyoming, and served one year as acting principal of the University of Wyoming laboratory school. He served as an audiovisual specialist and director of field summer schools (1946–53) for the university in the division of adult education, initiating in 1946 the first educational film library in Wyoming.

From 1953 until his death, he remained heavily involved in adult education, serving as a teacher in the college of education, visiting exchange scholar in adult education in Germany (1953), Fulbright lecturer in New Zealand (1956–57), and teacher trainer in Operation Crossroads, Liberia (1960–62). He was appointed professor of adult education in 1957.

He wrote many articles and *Adult Education: The Community Approach* (with Paul Sheats and Ralph Spence, 1953). The Clarence Jayne Media Center in the college of education was founded (1970), and an annual scholarship is awarded each year to a deserving student in adult education in his name.

REFERENCES: *Laramie* (Wyoming) *Daily Boomerang,* October 23, 1963; *The Wyoming Alumnews* (January-February, 1963): 6–8.   *Glenn Jensen*

JEFFERSON, Mark Sylvester William. B. March 1, 1863, Melrose, Massachusetts, to Daniel and Mary (Mantz) Jefferson. M. August 22, 1891, to Theodora A. Bohnstedt. M. June 17, 1915, to Clara Hopkins. Ch. three. D. August 8, 1949, Ypsilanti, Michigan.

Mark Sylvester William Jefferson journeyed to South America at the age of twenty to take a position as computer and assistant astronomer at the

Argentine National Observatory at Cordoba, Argentine Republic. In 1886 he was manager and treasurer of the La Providencia sugar estate near Tucumán, Argentine Republic.

Jefferson returned to the United States in 1889 and in that year received the A.B. degree from Boston University. He attended Harvard University where he studied under William Morris Davis *(q.v.)* and received the A.B. (1897) and A.M. (1898) degrees.

He was a teacher at the Mitchell Boys' School in Billerica, Massachusetts (1890–91), principal of the high school in Turners Falls, Massachusetts (1891–93), school superintendent in Lexington, Massachusetts (1893–96), and submaster of the high school in Brockton, Massachusetts (1898–1901). In 1901 he became a professor of geography at the State Normal School (later, Eastern Michigan University) in Ypsilanti, Michigan, and served until his retirement in 1939.

Jefferson was credited with building a geography program at Ypsilanti that gave the college the title "nursery of American geographers." He was influential in including man as an important aspect of geography in place of the earth science concept of the 1892 Committee of Ten of the National Educational Association. He was a pioneer in urban geography in the United States.

At the conclusion of World War I, Jefferson was chief cartographer with the American Peace Commission in Paris. During 1918 he also made a journey to study European colonization in Chile, Argentina, and Brazil.

Jefferson wrote many articles for geographic journals and presented a record twenty-five papers before the Association of American Geographers. He was the author of *Teachers' Geography* (1906), *Dodge's Geography of Michigan* (1910), *Recent Colonization of Chile* (1921), *Man in Europe* (1924), *Principles of Geography* (1926), and *Exercises in Human Geography* (1930).

Jefferson was active in professional associations, serving as president of the Association of American Geographers (1916) and the Michigan Academy of Science (1907). He was elected to memberships in foreign geography societies and received medals or awards from several professional organizations.

REFERENCES: *DAB* (supp. 4); *LE* (I); *WWW* (IV); I. Bowman, "Mark Jefferson," *Geographical Review* 40 (January 1950): 134–37; S. S. Visher, "Mark Jefferson, 1863–1949," Association of American Geographers *Annals* 39 (December 1949): 307–12.

Peter W. Keelin

JEFFERSON, Thomas. B. April 13, 1743, Shadwell, Virginia, to Peter and Jane (Randolph) Jefferson. M. January 24, 1772, to Martha (Wayles) Skelton. Ch. six. D. July 4, 1826, Monticello, Virginia.

Thomas Jefferson attended local small private schools and enrolled in the College of William and Mary in Williamsburg, Virginia, at the age of sixteen. He was graduated in 1762, studied law with George Wythe, and was admitted to the bar in 1767.

Jefferson practiced law (1767–74) and served as a justice of the peace and a member of the Virginia House of Burgesses (1769–75). He was a representative of Virginia in the Continental Congress (1775–76) and was author of the Declaration of Independence (1776). He served as governor of Virginia (1779–81). After the death of his wife in 1782, he returned to Philadelphia as a member of the second Continental Congress (1783–84). He was appointed by the congress in 1784 as a special envoy to assist Benjamin Franklin *(q.v.)* and John Adams in negotiating trade treaties in Europe. In 1785 he followed Franklin as minister to France (1785–89) and served as secretary of state in the administration of George Washington (1790–94) and as vice-president of the United States under John Adams (1797–1801). Jefferson served as President of the United States (1801–09). He returned to his home, Monticello, where he supervised his farms and engaged in the founding of the University of Virginia.

Jefferson's major educational plans concerned Virginia. In 1779 he drew up a bill for the Virginia general assembly that called for a system of elementary, secondary, and college education and free education for impoverished students. Although the bill was defeated, the proposal was one of the first attempts in the United States to establish a comprehensive state-supported education system. In 1817 he recommended a similar measure; rejecting the elementary and secondary schooling recommendations, the legislature accepted the plan for a public university. Jefferson designed buildings, planned the curriculum, founded the library, recruited the faculty, and served as first rector of the University of Virginia. He also proposed continuing education institutions in Virginia, a public library, local agricultural societies, a national university, and a national philosophical academy devoted to scholarly and scientific research.

REFERENCES: *AC; DAB; EB; NCAB* (3:1); *TC; WWW* (H); Stuart G. Brown, *Thomas Jefferson* (New York: Washington Square Press, 1963); Robert D. Heslep, *Thomas Jefferson and Education* (New York: Random House, 1969); Gordon C. Lee, ed., *Crusade Against Ignorance: Thomas Jefferson on Education* (New York: Bureau of Publications, Teachers College, Columbia University, 1962).   *Robert D. Heslep*

JENNE, James Nathaniel. B. December 21, 1859, Berkshire, Vermont, to John Gilbert and Charlotte (Woodworth) Jenne. M. September 19, 1883, to Abbie Cushman. Ch. none. D. September 9, 1937, Burlington, Vermont.

James Nathaniel Jenne attended school in Enosburg, Vermont, and received the M.D. degree in 1881 from the University of Vermont. From

1890 to 1895 he spent six weeks each year studying at the New York Post-Graduate School and Hospital (later, part of Columbia University) and in 1896 he studied in Paris, France, at the Ecole de médecine.

He began to practice medicine in Georgia in 1881. He later became chief surgeon of the Central Vermont Railroad (1891–1901). In 1891 he joined the University of Vermont medical faculty as adjunct professor of materia medica, and he was professor of therapeutic and clinical medicine (1900–31) and dean of the medical school from 1926 until his death in 1937. Under Jenne, the proctor system was instituted in which physicians would agree to permit medical students to accompany and assist them in their practice so that the students could gain practical experience. The college was recognized for its high standards of scholarship and the increasing services it was providing. He was director of the university dispensary and consulting surgeon to a number of hospitals.

Jenne was surgeon general of the state of Vermont (1894–96). He served in the Vermont National Guard and was on active duty with the United States Army during the Spanish-American War.

Jenne was a member of a number of honorary and professional organizations and president of the Vermont State Medical Association (1890) and the Chittenden County Medical Society. He was a trustee of the University of Vermont (1923–26). He received an honorary degree from the University of Vermont in 1924.

REFERENCES: *NCAB* (28:299); *WWAE* (VIII); *WWW* (I); *NYT,* September 10, 1937, p. 24.   *S. S. Britt, Jr.*

JERSILD, Arthur Thomas. B. November 12, 1902, Elk Horn, Iowa, to Thomas Nielsen and Anne (Bille) Jersild. M. February 22, 1930, to Catherine Livingston Thomas. Ch. four.

Arthur Thomas Jersild, mindful of his Danish heritage, enrolled at Dana College in Blair, Nebraska, after having attended local elementary and secondary schools. He continued his education at the University of Nebraska, from which he earned the A.B. degree (1924). He was awarded the Ph.D. degree from Columbia University (1927).

Jersild served as an assistant in the department of philosophy at the University of Nebraska (1922–24). He was appointed an instructor in psychology at Barnard College in New York City (1927–29), became an assistant professor of psychology at the University of Wisconsin (1929–30), and returned to Columbia University in 1930 where he served the remainder of his career teaching psychology and education. He was a pioneer in research dealing with the emotional development of children and adolescents.

Jersild made his contributions to psychology and education in a variety of ways. He was a research associate at the Child Development Institute (1930–36) and a consulting psychologist for the Columbia Broadcasting

System (1935–48). He was a research associate for the Horace Mann-Lincoln Institute for School Experimentation. He was appointed a visiting expert of the Department of Army's Civil Affairs Division, Reorientation Branch, with which he served in Japan (1948–49). He was a frequent lecturer at conferences, institutes, and universities.

Jersild was the author of *Child Psychology* (1933), *In Search of Self* (1952), *Psychology of Adolescence* (1957), and *When Teachers Face Themselves* (1957). In addition, he coauthored such books as *Educational Psychology* (1936), *Child Development and the Curriculum* (1946), and *Children's Interests and What They Suggest for the Curriculum* (1949). *Psychology of Adolescence* was translated into many foreign languages. Jersild was a frequent contributor to scholarly journals and monographs; he was editor of *Child Development Monographs* and a member of the editorial boards of *Child Development Abstracts and Bibliography* and the *Journal of Experimental Education.*

He received an honorary degree from the University of Nebraska and was active in many professional associations.

REFERENCES: *LE* (III); *WW* (XXXV); *WWAE* (XXII).

Erwin H. Goldenstein

JESSE, Richard Henry. B. March 1, 1853, Epping Forest, Lancaster County, Virginia, to William T. and Mary (Claybrook) Jesse. M. July 13, 1882, to Addie Henry Polk. Ch. six. D. January 21, 1921, Columbia, Missouri.

Richard Henry Jesse received his preparatory education in a Lancaster County, Virginia, academy, founded by his father. He then attended Hanover (Virginia) Academy, the oldest school of its kind in Virginia. In 1875 he was graduated with distinction from the University of Virginia. He studied in Europe (1885, 1890, and 1905–06). Jesse taught math and Latin at Hanover Academy (1875–77) and was a high school principal in Princess Anne, Maryland (1877–79). He studied law at the University of Virginia (1879–80) but left his studies to become dean of the academic department at the University of Louisiana.

Jesse was successful at the University of Louisiana, where he built up the academic department, effected the merger of Louisiana University with Tulane University (1884), and became senior professor of Latin at Tulane (1884–91). Jesse left Tulane to become president of the University of Missouri (1891–1908). During his tenure there, he oversaw the rebuilding and expansion of the university after a fire destroyed the campus in 1892. The rebuilt campus was organized into the graduate, law, medical, sanitary, architectural, and engineering departments and the college of agriculture and mechanical arts with an agricultural experimental station.

Jesse strongly supported the development of secondary education in Missouri. He belonged to the Committee of Ten of the National Educational Association and was chairman of the association's higher education committee in 1898. He was a member of many professional organizations.

Jesse edited *Missouri Literature* (with E. A. Allen, 1901). He was an original trustee of Howard Memorial Library at Tulane University. He received honorary degrees from six American colleges and universities. A hall was named in his honor at the University of Missouri.

REFERENCES: *DAB; NCAB* (8:188); *TC; WWW* (II); *NYT,* January 24, 1921, p. 11.   *James R. Layton*

JESSUP, Walter Albert. B. August 12, 1877, Richmond, Indiana, to Albert and Anna (Goodrich) Jessup. M. June 28, 1898, to Eleanor Hines. Ch. two. D. July 5, 1944, New York, New York.

Walter Albert Jessup grew up on a farm in the Quaker community of Richmond, Indiana. Years before, his grandfather had assisted in the establishment of a Friends' school there, which became Earlham College. Jessup was graduated from Earlham (1903) and for a period of ten years was a teacher, principal, and superintendent of public schools in Indiana. He pursued graduate studies, receiving the M.A. degree from Hanover (Indiana) College (1908) and the Ph.D. degree from Teachers College, Columbia University (1911).

Jessup accepted a position as professor and dean of the school of education at Indiana University (1911) and a year later took an equivalent post at the State University of Iowa. In 1916 he became president of the University of Iowa and, during the next eighteen years, directed a rapid expansion of the university. Among the innovations he introduced was the first center for the study of child development in the United States.

In 1934 Jessup became president of the Carnegie Foundation for the Advancement of Teaching with headquarters in New York. He was regarded as a spokesman for American educators and counselor-at-large for college and university presidents. He felt that colleges should concentrate on undergraduate teaching and deplored the rising development of government subsidy of higher education and research.

Jessup's professional contributions were widely felt. In 1941 he became president of the Carnegie Corporation. He was an active leader in professional organizations and was the recipient of nine honorary degrees from American colleges and universities.

REFERENCES: *DAB* (supp. 3); *LE* (I); *NCAB* (37:294); *WWAE* (VII); *WWW* (II); *NYT,* July 8, 1944, p. 11.   *Harold D. Lehman*

JEWETT, Milo Parker. B. April 27, 1808, St. Johnsbury, Vermont, to Calvin and Sally (Parker) Jewett. M. September 17, 1833, to Jane Augusta Russell. Ch. none. D. June 9, 1882, Milwaukee, Wisconsin.

Milo Parker Jewett was educated at Bradford (Vermont) Academy. He attended Dartmouth College in Hanover, New Hampshire, graduating in

1829. He studied law in Josiah Quincy's law office in Rumney, New Hampshire (1829–30). In 1830 he began his theological studies at Andover (Massachusetts) Theological Seminary, from which he was graduated in 1833. At the same time, Jewett gave lectures on the value of a common school system, which are thought to be the first popular lectures on the subject.

Jewett was the principal of Holmes Academy in Plymouth, Vermont (1828–29). He was a professor of rhetoric and political economy at Marietta (Ohio) Collegiate Institute (later, Marietta College) from 1833 to 1838, where he became interested in the subject of higher education for the general public. In 1834 Jewett and Calvin E. Stowe *(q.v.)* participated in a convention in Ohio that led to the establishment of the state common school system.

Jewett's views on baptism led to his uniting with the Baptist church, and he resigned his position at Marietta College. In 1839 he established the Judson Female Institute in Marion, Alabama, which became one of the most successful schools in the South.

In 1855 he returned to the North where he purchased Cotton Hill Seminary in Poughkeepsie, New York, and served as principal from 1855 to 1861. At Poughkeepsie Jewett became acquainted with Matthew Vassar and persuaded him to found and endow a college for young women with Jewett as president of the board of trustees. In 1862 Vassar College was established, and Jewett was its first president. At the request of Vassar trustees, Jewett visited Europe in 1862 to study and report upon university organization.

Jewett's near blindness and injudicious remarks about Matthew Vassar led to his resignation from the presidency of Vassar in 1864. He moved to Milwaukee, Wisconsin, where he engaged in educational activities.

Jewett was the author of *Jewett on Baptism* (1840), *Report of the President's Visit to Europe* (1863), *Report on the Organization of Vassar College* (1863), *Relations of Boards of Health to Intemperance* (1874), *A Plan for Academies* (1875), and *The Model Academy* (1875).

Jewett was honorary president and trustee of Milwaukee Female College (later, Milwaukee-Downer College), chairman of the board of visitors of the University of Wisconsin, and president of the Wisconsin State Temperance Society. Jewett Hall at Vassar College was named in his honor.

REFERENCES: *DAB; NCAB* (5:234); *TC; WWW* (H). *Sue C. Tenorio*

JOHNSON, Alvin Saunders. B. December 18, 1874, near Homer, Nebraska, to John and Edel Katrine Marie (Bille) Johnson. M. April 18, 1904, to Margaret Edith Henry. Ch. seven. D. June 7, 1971, Nyack, New York.

Alvin Saunders Johnson received the A.B. (1897) and M.A. (1898) degrees from the University of Nebraska. He studied economics at Bryn

Mawr (Pennsylvania) College (1901–02) and received the Ph.D. degree from Columbia University in 1902.

Johnson taught at Columbia (1902–06) before going to the University of Nebraska as professor of economics (1906–08). After leaving Nebraska, he taught at the University of Texas (1908–09), the University of Chicago (1909–11), Stanford (California) University (1911–12 and 1916–18), and Cornell University in Ithaca, New York (1912–16).

In 1919 he was a founder of the New School for Social Research in New York City. Johnson served the New School as director (1923–45) and chairman of the graduate faculty of political science (1933–45). He was president emeritus of the New School from his retirement in 1945 until his death in 1971. In the 1930s Johnson was instrumental in bringing to the New School European scholars persecuted by the Nazi government of Germany. He was also director of general studies in the graduate school of Yale University (1938–39).

Johnson was the author of many books, including *Rent in Modern Economic Theory* (1903), *Introduction to Economics* (1909), *The Professor and the Petticoat* (novel, 1914), *John Stuyvesant, Ancestor* (1919), *Deliver Us from Dogma* (1934), *Spring Storm* (novel, 1936), *The Public Library* (1938), *The Clock of History* (1946), *Pioneer's Progress: An Autobiography* (1952), *Essays in Social Economics* (1955), *The Battle of the Wild Turkey* (1961), and *A Touch of Color* (1963). He also wrote hundreds of articles.

Johnson was the editor of *The New Republic* from 1917 until 1923. He also did editorial work on the *Political Science Quarterly* (assistant editor, 1902–06), *The International Encyclopedia* (1902–04), the American edition of *Nelson's Encyclopedia,* the *Encyclopedia of the Social Sciences* (associate editor, 1927–34), and the *Yale Review* (editorial council, 1927–47).

Johnson was president of the American Economic Association (1936) and the American Association for Adult Education (1939), as well as chairman of the New York State Commission on Discrimination in Employment (1943–45) and vice-chairman of the New York State Commission Against Discrimination (1944).

He received honorary degrees from five universities in America, Europe, and Africa and was decorated by the governments of Belgium, Denmark, the Federal Republic of Germany, and France.

REFERENCES: *CB* (February 1942); *LE* (III); *NCAB* (G:380); *WWW* (V); *NYT,* June 9, 1971, p. 1.   *Lawrence S. Master*

JOHNSON, Charles Spurgeon. B. July 24, 1893, Bristol, Virginia, to Charles Haddon and Winifred (Branch) Johnson. M. November 6, 1920, to Marie Antoinette Burgette. Ch. four. D. October 27, 1956, Louisville, Kentucky.

Charles Spurgeon Johnson, sociologist, educator, and university president, received the B.A. degree from Virginia Union University (1916) and the Ph.B. degree from the University of Chicago (1918). He was greatly influenced at the University of Chicago by sociologist Robert E. Park.

Johnson was director of research for the National Urban League (1921–28). In 1923 he founded *Opportunity*, the league's journal, and edited it from 1923 until 1928 when he joined the faculty of Fisk University in Nashville, Tennessee. He served as professor of sociology and head of the department of social science at Fisk (1928–47) when he was named president of the university, the first black president of the school.

His published works include *The Negro in Chicago* (1922), *Ebony and Topaz* (1927), *The Negro in American Civilization* (1930), *Economic Status of the Negro* (1933), *Shadow of the Plantation* (1934), *Race Relations* (1934), *The Negro College Graduate* (1936), *Growing Up in the Black Belt* (1941), *Patterns of Negro Segregation* (1943), and *Culture and the Educational Process* (1943).

Johnson served as American representative on the League of Nations Commission to Study Forced Labor in Liberia (1930), member of the President's Committee on Farm Tenancy (1936), president of the Southern Sociological Society (1945), State Department team member to organize the Japanese educational system (1946), delegate to the first United Nations Educational, Scientific, and Cultural Organization Conference (1946), director of the southern rural division of Negro youth for the American Youth Commission of the Council on Education, executive committee member of the Southern Sociological Society commission to study lynching, and consultant to the division of higher education of the Ford Foundation. He was a member of numerous educational associations. He received seven honorary doctoral degrees from colleges and universities, including the University of Glasgow (Scotland).

REFERENCES: *CB* (November 1946); *LE* (III); *NCAB* (48:179); *WWAE* (XVI); *WWW* (III); *NYT,* October 28, 1956, p. 88; *Who's Who in Colored America,* 7th ed. (Brooklyn, N.Y.: Burckel & Associates, 1950).

Don C. Locke

JOHNSON, David Bancroft. B. January 10, 1856, La Grange, Tennessee, to David Bancroft and Margaret Emily (White) Johnson. M. August 6, 1902, to Mai Rutledge Smith. Ch. three. D. December 26, 1928, Rock Hill, South Carolina.

David Bancroft Johnson attended public schools in Memphis and Nashville, Tennessee. In 1871 at the age of fifteen, he entered the preparatory school of the University of Tennessee and was graduated with the A.B. (1877) and A.M. (1880) degrees.

He was principal of Boys High School in Knoxville, Tennessee, until 1879 when he became an assistant professor of mathematics at the University of Tennessee. Johnson organized and was principal of an elementary school in Abbeville, South Carolina (1880–82). He went to New Bern, North Carolina, in 1882 and organized a graded school system. From 1883 to 1895 he served as the first superintendent of schools in Columbia, South Carolina, organizing a school system that was copied in many other parts of the state and the country.

Johnson believed that the most pressing problem for public schools was obtaining qualified teachers. With the assistance of the Peabody Educational Foundation and its chairman, Robert C. Winthrop, Johnson organized and established the Winthrop Training School for Women (1886). The school opened on November 15, 1886, in a former stable on the grounds of the Columbia (South Carolina) Theological Seminary with one teacher and nineteen students.

The college was moved to Rock Hill, South Carolina, in 1895 and renamed the Winthrop Normal and Industrial College (later, Winthrop College). It opened with twenty instructors and three hundred students, with Johnson as president; he served until his death in 1928. For a number of years the college was the only teacher-training institution for women in South Carolina, North Carolina, Georgia, and Florida. The college flourished under Johnson's leadership.

Johnson was active in professional associations, serving as founder and first president of the South Carolina Association of School Superintendents (1889) and president of the South Carolina Teachers' Association (1884–88). He was active in the National Educational Association (vice-president, 1894 and 1906–07, president, 1915–16) and was president of the association's normal department (1908, 1911), department of elementary education (1909), and department of rural and agricultural education (1909). He was a member of the National Council of Education and other organizations. He was the recipient of two honorary degrees.

REFERENCES: *DAB; NCAB* (3:123); *TC; WWW* (I); J. C. Garlington, *Men of the Time* (Spartanburg, S.C.: Garlington Publishing Co., 1902); Ralph E. Grier, *South Carolina and Her Builders* (Columbia, S.C.: The Carolina Biographical Association, 1930); J. C. Hemphill, *Men of Mark in South Carolina* (Washington, D.C.: Men of Mark Publishing Co., 1907).   *Ishmael C. Benton*

JOHNSON, Earl Shepard. B. September 14, 1894, Stratford, Iowa, to Charles Frederick and Clara (Bridge) Johnson. M. June 7, 1923, to Esther Charlotte Bailey. Ch. none.

Earl S. Johnson, sociologist and leading social studies educator, was one of the architects of the new social studies of the 1960s and a strong advocate of an integrated social studies curriculum. He received his education in several small towns in Iowa and Kansas and was graduated from Iola (Kansas) High School in 1911. He received the A.B. degree (1918) from Baker University in Baldwin City, Kansas, and served in the United States Army (1918–19). He received the M.A. (1932) and Ph.D. (1941) degrees in sociology from the University of Chicago.

Johnson taught history, rhetoric, and literature at Sherman County High School in Goodland, Kansas (1919–20). In the fall of 1920 he became principal of the high school in Lincoln, Kansas, until October 1924 when he began graduate study at the University of Chicago in sociology and was also employed as a field house director in two parks on Chicago's South Side. He joined the faculty at Chicago as an instructor in sociology in 1932 and was on the faculty until 1959. From 1945 to 1959 he was chairman of the committee on the divisional master's degree in the social sciences, an interdisciplinary program that included several integrated social science courses, combining subjects traditionally taught separately.

After his retirement from Chicago, Johnson accepted an appointment in the school of education at the University of Wisconsin-Milwaukee and taught there for fourteen years (1959–73). He was a member of the faculty at Wichita (Kansas) State University (1976–77).

Johnson wrote many articles for a wide variety of journals. His most important contribution to social studies was *Theory and Practice of the Social Studies* (1956), one of the first theoretically oriented textbooks in the field of social studies education, which helped lay the foundation for new directions in the field.

Johnson was a research associate in the social sciences on the staff of the Twenty-two College Study in General Education (1939–41). He also served numerous government agencies and school systems, including being a consultant for the Los Angeles (California) County Schools (1962–67).

REFERENCES: *WW* (XXX); *American Men of Science: The Social Sciences,* 11th ed. (New York: R. R. Bowker, 1968).   *Harris L. Dante*

JOHNSON, Franklin. B. November 2, 1836, Frankfort, Ohio, to Hezekiah and Eliza Shepherd (Harris) Johnson. M. September 28, 1863, to Mary Alma Barton. M. June 29, 1886, to Persis Isabel Swett. Ch. two. D. October 9, 1916, Brookline, Massachusetts.

Franklin Johnson's parents helped found Denison University in Granville, Ohio (1831), and moved to Oregon City, Oregon, where they established the first Baptist church on the Pacific Coast and helped organize Oregon City College (later, Linfield College) at McMinnville. Johnson taught school at Dalles, Oregon, and assisted in the printing office of the *Argus* (his parents' newspaper at Oregon City). At the age of twenty-one, he went east to Colgate Theological Seminary in Hamilton, New York. He was graduated in 1861 and ordained in 1862. He traveled in Egypt and the Holy Land and studied at the University of Jena, Germany (1868–69), where he received the D.D. degree in 1869.

Johnson served as a missionary in Bay City, Michigan (1861–63), and as pastor of New Jersey churches at Lambertville (1864–66) and Passaic (1866–72). After a short pastorate in Newark, New Jersey (1872–74), he went to the Old Cambridge (Massachusetts) Baptist Church (1874–88), where he developed close friendships with Phillips Brooks, Henry Wadsworth Longfellow, James Russell Lowell, William James *(q.v.)*, and other eminent persons of the times.

In 1888 he resigned his pulpit in Cambridge and traveled in Europe, spending the winter in Greece. In 1889 he became president of Ottawa (Kansas) University, which he left in 1892 to join the faculty of the University of Chicago to teach church history and homiletics (1892–1908).

With George Lorimer, he served as coeditor of the *Watchman* (1876–80). He wrote three studies for Bible students that were published in the *International Sunday School Commentary* (1873–75). He provided excellent English translations of *Dies Irae* (1880), *The Stabat Mater Speciosa* (1886), and *The Stabat Mater Dolorosa* (1886). He also wrote *True Womanhood: Hints on the Formation of Womanly Character* (1882), *A Romance in Song: Heine's Lyrical Interlude* (1884), *The New Psychic Studies in Their Relation to Christian Thought* (1886), *The Quotations of the New Testament from the Old Considered in the Light of General Literature* (1896), which was his chief theological work, *The Home Missionaries* (1899), *Have We the Likeness of Christ?* (1901), and *The Christian's Relation to Evolution* (1904).

Johnson served as a trustee of the Newton (Massachusetts) Theological Seminary (1883–91) and was a member of the executive committee of the Baptist Foreign Mission Society (1885–88). In 1860 he attended the Republican National Convention in Chicago. After his retirement from the University of Chicago, he visited missions in Japan, China, India, and Palestine. He received an honorary degree from Ottawa University (1898).

REFERENCES: *DAB; NCAB* (16:274); *WWW* (I); *Boston Transcript,* October 9, 1916; *Cambridge* (Massachusetts) *Chronicle,* October 14, 1916; *Morning Oregonian* (Oregon City, Oregon), October 26, 1916; *University Record,* University of Chicago, January 1917.   *Lawrence S. Master*

JOHNSON, Henry. B. February 10, 1867, Norra Rörum, Sweden, to John and Christine (Engquist) Johnson. M. 1892 to Etta Elizabeth Bishop. M. to Helen Chapman Wilcox. Ch. two. D. October 3, 1953, New Rochelle, New York.

Henry Johnson came to the United States from Sweden with his parents in 1869. He received the B.Lit. degree (1889) from the University of Minnesota and the A.M. degree (1902) from Columbia University. He studied at the universities of Paris and Berlin (1904–05).

Johnson served in Minnesota as a secondary school teacher at Lutheran Academy in Albert Lea (1889–91) and at Northfield High School (1894–95) and as superintendent of schools at Rushford (1891–93). He was head of the department of history at Minnesota State Normal School (later, Moorhead State College) from 1895 to 1899 under Livingston Lord *(q.v.)*, whom he followed to Illinois State Normal School (later, Eastern Illinois University) at Charleston (1899–1906). Johnson was professor of history at Teachers College, Columbia University, from 1906 to his retirement in 1934. He was a major figure in teaching social studies.

Johnson was the author of *The Problem of Adapting History to Children* (1908), *Teaching of History in Elementary and Secondary Schools* (1915), *Introduction to the History of Social Sciences in the Schools* (1932), and *The Other Side of Main Street* (1943). He was a corresponding editor of the American Historical Association journal, *History Teacher's Magazine* (1900), and chairman of the editorial committee from 1911.

In 1916 Johnson was appointed to the New York Regents Committee on History in High Schools and the National Board for Historical Service. He was a member of the Commission on the Investigation of the Social Studies in the Schools. He was a member of the Illinois State History Commission (1906) and secretary (1906–12) and president (1914) of the Association of History Teachers of the Middle States and Maryland. He was a founder of the New York Conference of History Teachers (1909) and the National Council for the Social Studies (1921, vice-president, 1922–23). Johnson was awarded an honorary degree by the University of Minnesota (1937).

REFERENCES: *LE* (III); *NYT*, October 4, 1953, p. 88; *WW* (XVIII); *American Historical Review* 59 (January 1954): 510; *School and Society* 78 (October 17, 1953): 126; *Teachers College Record* 55 (February 1954): 168–70; Henry Johnson, *The Other Side of Main Street* (New York: Columbia University Press, 1943). *John F. Ohles*

JOHNSON, Joseph French. B. August 24, 1853, Hardwick, Massachusetts, to Gardner Nye and Eliza (French) Johnson. M. August 4, 1884, to Caroline Temperance Stolp. Ch. two. D. January 22, 1925, New Foundland, New Jersey.

Joseph French Johnson's family moved to Aurora, Illinois, in 1860 where he attended Aurora High School and was graduated from Clark Seminary, a Methodist academy (1872). He taught at Rockport Female Collegiate Institute for one year, entered Northwestern University in Evanston, Illinois, in 1873, transferred to Harvard University, from which he was graduated with the A.B. degree (1878). He also studied for a year in Halle, Germany (1875–76).

After teaching for three years in the Harvard School in Chicago and traveling to Europe as tutor to Marshall Field, Jr., he turned to journalism. He worked under Samuel Bowles on the *Springfield Republican* (1881–84) and became financial editor of the *Chicago Tribune* in 1887. He briefly interrupted his journalism career, serving for one year as superintendent of schools in Yazoo City, Mississippi, and working two years with Investors Agency in Chicago. He founded the *Spokesman* in Spokane, Washington, in 1890 and sold the paper in 1893.

In 1893 he became associate professor of business practice at the Wharton School of Finance of the University of Pennsylvania. He developed practical courses in finance and was professor of journalism (1895–1901). He was professor of political economy at the New York University school of commerce, accounts, and finance (1901–25) and was dean (1903–25). The enrollment of the school increased from fewer than one hundred to more than five thousand students, and he arranged for students to work during the day and attend classes in the evening. Johnson helped to organize and served as president of the Alexander Hamilton Institute to provide business and finance training by correspondence (1909–25).

In addition to editing publications of the Alexander Hamilton Institute, Johnson wrote for the institute *Business and the Man* (1917) and *Economics, the Science of Business* (1924). He also wrote *Syllabus of Money and Banking* (1899), *Money and Currency* (1905), *The Canadian Banking System* (1916), *We and Our Work* (1922), and *Organized Business Knowledge* (1923). He edited the *Journal of Accountancy* and the Modern Business Series.

Johnson was active in state and national financial reform. He served as secretary of the special currency committee of the New York Chamber of Commerce (1906), was a member of Mayor William Jay Gaynor's Commission on New Sources of Revenue for New York City (1912), and was a member of the George C. Van Tuyl, Jr., Commission to Revise the Banking Law of the State of New York (1913). He was influential in promoting the federal reserve system.

Johnson was responsible for revolutionizing education for business. He believed that the traditional classical content of the college curriculum was not adequate and that the study of business should be related to society. He introduced and interpreted business materials in the classroom that led to new courses of study, textbooks, college departments, and degrees.

He received honorary degrees from Union and Hobart colleges.

REFERENCES: *DAB; TC; WWW* (I); *NYT,* January 23, 1925, p. 19.   *Elizabeth S. Oelrich*
                                                    Edward B. Goellner

JOHNSON, Marietta Louise Pierce. B. 1864, St. Paul, Minnesota, to Clarence D. and Rhoda Matilda (Morton) Pierce. M. June 6, 1897, to John Franklin Johnson. Ch. two. D. December 23, 1938, Fairhope, Alabama.

Marietta Louise Pierce Johnson was graduated in 1885 from the State Normal School (later, St. Cloud State College) in St. Cloud, Minnesota. A schoolteacher, she served in Minnesota as a critic and model teacher at the St. Paul Teachers' Training School (1890–92), critic teacher and department supervisor at Moorhead at the State Teachers College (later, Moorhead State College) from 1892 to 1895, and department supervisor at the State Teachers College (later, Mankato State College) from 1896 to 1899.

Johnson moved to Alabama, where she founded (1907) and served as director (1907–38) of the School of Organic Education in Fairhope. The school was based on progressive educational ideas, enrolling a maximum of two hundred students in a program in which there were no examinations, grades, report cards, or punishment. Books were not used in classes until the ninth grade; children learned to read as they became interested in reading. No tuition was charged, and no public funds were used to support the school; the institution was supported by donations. When serious consideration was given to closing the school in 1937, parents raised funds to continue the school. Johnson also was director of the Edgewood School in Greenwich, Connecticut. She conducted summer schools for teachers, parents, social workers, and children in Greenwich (1913–16 and 1919–21) and Fairhope (1917 and 1918).

Johnson was one of the founders of the Progressive Education Association and was honorary vice-president at the time of her death.

REFERENCES: *WWAE* (VIII); *WWW* (I); "Marietta Johnson and Fairhope," *Progressive Education* 16 (February 1939): 117–18.

John F. Ohles

JOHNSON, Mordecai Wyatt. B. January 12, 1890, Paris, Tennessee, to Wyatt and Carolyn (Freeman) Johnson. M. to Alice King. M. December 25, 1916, to Anna Ethelyn Gardner. Ch. five. D. September 10, 1976, Washington, D.C.

Mordecai Wyatt Johnson, first black president of the largest predominantly black university in the United States, attended local Paris, Tennessee, public schools and the high school of Roger Williams University in Nashville, Tennessee (1903–04). When the school was destroyed by fire, he enrolled in Howe Institute in Memphis, Tennessee (1904–05). He attended Atlanta (Georgia) Baptist College (later, Morehouse College) where he received the B.A. degree (1911). He received the A.B. degree (1913) from the University of Chicago and the B.D. degree (1921) from Rochester (New York) Theological Seminary. He attended Harvard University, where he was awarded the S.T.M. degree (1922).

Johnson was a professor of English and economics and history at Morehouse College (1911–13) and was a student pastor of a Baptist church in Mumford, New York. He was ordained into the Baptist ministry in 1916 and served as pastor of the First Baptist Church in Charleston, West Virginia (1917–26). He became president of Howard University in Washington, D.C., serving from 1926 to his retirement in 1960. At Howard he tripled the size of the faculty and student body, directed the construction of twenty buildings, and strengthened the academic program. All schools and colleges received accreditation. Johnson was effective in lobbying for funds for Howard from the United States Congress.

While at Charleston, West Virginia, Johnson was founder of the local branch of the National Association for the Advancement of Colored People and organized a cooperative society and a cooperative grocery. He was a member of advisory councils for the Virgin Islands, the National Youth Administration, and the National Youth Commission. He was a director of the national council of the United Negro College Fund and the National Conference of Christians and Jews, a member of the general executive board of the National Religion and Labor Foundation, and vice-chairman of the National Council for the Prevention of War. He was a member of the District of Columbia Board of Education (1962–65). He received the Spingarn Medal in 1929. Johnson was decorated by the governments of Ethiopia, Haiti, Liberia, and Panama and was the recipient of nine honorary degrees from American and foreign colleges and universities.

REFERENCES: *CB* (April 1941); *LE* (III); *NYT*, September 11, 1976, p. 22; *WW* (XXXI); *WWW* (VI); *Washington Post*, September 11, 1976, sec. B, p. 6; Benjamin Brawley *(q.v.)*, *Negro Builders and Heroes* (Chapel Hill: University of North Carolina Press, 1937).   *John F. Ohles*

JOHNSON, Palmer Oliver. B. September 3, 1901, Eagle Grove, Iowa, to Nels Andrew and Elizabeth Ann (Osmundsen) Johnson. M. August 20, 1936, to Hildegard Binder. Ch. two. D. January 25, 1960, Minneapolis, Minnesota.

Palmer O. Johnson attended the University of Wisconsin, where he received the A.B. degree (1912). He also was graduated from the University of Minnesota with the B.S. (1921), M.S. (1926), and Ph.D. (1928) degrees. He engaged in study and research at the Galton Laboratory of the University of London, England (1934–35).

Johnson was a high school teacher of agriculture, biology, and chemistry at Dassel, Minnesota (1913–16), superintendent of animal breeding farms (1917), and high school biology teacher at Quincy, Illinois (1921–26). He joined the faculty of the University of Minnesota in 1926 and served as head of science education and statistics. At his death in 1960, he was chairman of the statistics department (from 1958) and professor of educational psychology. He was a pioneer in the uses of statistics in the social sciences.

The author of many articles for professional journals, Johnson wrote *Curricular Problems in Science at the College Level* (1930), *Aspects of Land-Grant College Education* (1934), *The Effective General College Curriculum* (with others, 1937), *The National Youth Administration* (with O. L. Harvey, 1938), *An Evaluation of Modern Education* (with others, 1942), *Statistical Methods in Research* (1949), *Education Research and Appraisal* (with others, 1953), *Introduction to Statistical Methods* (with R. W. B. Jackson, 1953), *Modern Statistical Methods: Descriptive and Inductive* (with R. W. B. Jackson, 1957), and *Modern Sampling Methods* (1959). He was statistical editor for the *Journal of Experimental Education Research* and collaborator of the *Journal of the American Statistical Association*.

Johnson was a member of many professional associations; he was a fellow of the American Association for the Advancement of Science (chairman of sections L and Q; vice-president, 1950–51) and the American Statistical Association (council member, 1951–53), and a member of the

Minnesota Academy of Science (vice-president, 1946–47). He directed the Land-Grant College Survey for Minnesota (1928–30), was a member of the survey commission of Oregon's Higher Education Institutions for the United States Office of Education (1929), and a consultant to President Franklin D. Roosevelt's Advisory Committee on Education (1937–38) and the Educational Policies Commission (1939–60).

REFERENCES: *LE* (III); *NYT,* January 26, 1960, p. 33; *WWW* (III); *Science Education* 44 (April 1960): 168–70.   *John F. Ohles*

JOHNSON, Samuel. B. October 14, 1696, Guilford, Connecticut, to Samuel and Mary (Sage) Johnson. M. September 26, 1725, to Charity (Floyd) Nicoll. M. June 18, 1761, to Sarah (Hull) Beach. Ch. three, including William Samuel Johnson, statesman and jurist. D. June 6, 1772, Stratford, Connecticut.

Samuel Johnson was a teacher, clergyman, and first president of King's College (later, Columbia University) in New York City (1754–63). He was graduated with the A.B. degree (1714) from Yale College and was appointed a tutor in 1716 when the college moved from Saybrook, Connecticut, to New Haven. He studied theology and resigned from Yale in 1719. He was ordained as a Congregational minister in 1720 and served a church in West Haven, Connecticut.

He began to doubt his church affiliation and was ordained in England as a priest in the Protestant Episcopal church (1723) and became rector of the church at Stratford, Connecticut. Throughout his life, he was involved in religious controversies.

Johnson was offered the position of first president of the University of Pennsylvania in 1749, but he declined. In 1754 he resigned his ministry in Stratford and moved to New York City, where he accepted the position as first president of King's College. He taught the first class of eight students; the class was conducted in the schoolhouse attached to Trinity Church. In 1760 he moved into the first college building. During his term of office, he directed the institution through smallpox epidemics in which he lost his wife, a son, and a stepdaughter. He established a course of study, set policy, and solicited financial support.

Johnson was an important philosophical student and writer, ranking with Jonathan Edwards as one of the two most important exponents of idealistic philosophy in colonial America. He was the author of *Introduction to Philosophy* (1731), *Ethics Elementa* (1746), *An English and Hebrew Grammar* (1767), and three works published by Benjamin Franklin*(q.v.)* in 1752: *Elementa Philosophica, Ethica,* and *Noetica.*

He received honorary M.A. degrees in 1723 from Oxford and Cambridge universities in England and an honorary D.D. from Oxford in 1743.

REFERENCES:*AC; DAB; NCAB* (6: 341); *TC; WWW* (H).

Michael R. Cioffi

JOHNSON, William Woolsey. B. June 23, 1841, near Owego, New York, to Charles Frederick and Sarah Dwight (Woolsey) Johnson. M. August 12, 1869, to Susannah Leverett Batcheller. Ch. two. D. May 14, 1927, Baltimore, Maryland.

William Woolsey Johnson was graduated from Yale College with the A.B. degree (1862) at the age of twenty-one and received the A.M. degree from Yale in 1868.

He worked at the United States Nautical Almanac office at Cambridge, Massachusetts (1862–64). He was an instructor in mathematics in 1864 at the United States Naval Academy, then located at Newport, Rhode Island. The academy was moved the following year to Annapolis, Maryland, and Johnson served on the faculty there until 1870.

Johnson taught for two years at Kenyon College in Gambier, Ohio (1870–71), and at St. John's College in Annapolis, Maryland (1872–81). He returned to the naval academy in 1881 and remained there the rest of his active life.

Johnson was one of the best known of the expository mathematicians of his time because his numerous contributions to the mathematical literature helped arouse interest in mathematical studies. He wrote many textbooks, including *An Elementary Treatise on Analytical Geometry* (1869), *The Elements of Differential and Integral Calculus Founded on the Methods of Rates or Fluxions* (three volumes, 1874–76), *An Elementary Treatise on the Integral Calculus Founded on the Methods of Rates or Fluxions* (1881), *Curve Tracing in Cartesian Coordinates* (1884), *A Treatise of Ordinary and Partial Differential Equations* (1889), *The Theory of Errors and Methods of Least Squares* (1890), *An Elementary Treatise on Theoretical Mechanics* (two volumes, 1900–01), *Treatise on Differential Calculus* (1904), *Differential Equations* (1906), *Treatise on Integral Calculus* (1907), and *An Elementary Treatise on the Differential Calculus* (1908).

Johnson was one of the founders of the New York Mathematical Society (later, the American Mathematical Society) and was a member of the London Mathematical Society and the British Association for the Advancement of Science. In 1913, through a special act of Congress, he was commissioned a lieutenant in the United States Navy, and when he retired from the academy in 1921, he was given the rank of commodore. He was awarded an honorary degree by St. John's College in 1915.

REFERENCES: *DAB; NCAB* (23:237); *TC; WWW* (I).   *Daniel S. Yates*

JOHNSTON, Richard Malcolm. B. March 18, 1822, Hancock County, Georgia, to Malcolm and Catherine (Davenport) Johnston. M. November 1844 to Mary Frances Mansfield. Ch. several. D. September 23, 1898, Baltimore, Maryland.

Richard Malcolm Johnston was graduated from Mercer University in Penfield (later, Macon), Georgia, in 1841. He read law and was admitted to the Georgia bar in 1843.

Johnston taught school in Penfield (1841–42). In 1844 he accepted a position at the well-known academy at Mount Zion, Georgia, founded by the Beman brothers. From 1846 to 1857 he worked in law partnerships at Sparta, Georgia. In 1857 he was offered a judgeship of the northern Georgia circuit and the presidency of Mercer University, but accepted a professorship of belle lettres at the University of Georgia, which he held from 1858 to 1862.

He served with the Confederate forces during the Civil War with the rank of colonel and was active in the organization of the Georgia state militia. He established a select classical boys' school at Rockby, near Sparta, Georgia, in 1862 and served as principal until 1868. He moved to Chestnut Hill near Baltimore, Maryland, in 1868, where he established the Pen Lucy Institute. The school prospered for a number of years; Johnston employed methods incorporating features of the honor system in place of the usual methods of corporal punishment.

He left the classroom to write and lecture (1882–95) and lectured at the Catholic Summer School in Plattsburg, New York. He was appointed to the United States Bureau of Education as a clerk (1895–98).

Johnston was an author noted for his humorous stories, sometimes writing under the pseudonym Philemon Perch. Among his books were *English Classics* (1860), *Georgia Sketches* (1864), *Historical Sketch of English Literature* (with W. H. Brown, 1872), *Life of Alexander H. Stephens* (with W. H. Brown, 1878), and *Studies Literary and Social* (1891–92). The *Autobiography of Col. Richard Malcolm Johnston* was published posthumously in 1900. He received an honorary degree from St. Mary's University in Baltimore, Maryland (1895).

REFERENCES: *AC; DAB; EB; NCAB* (1:440); *TC; WWW* (H); William F. Northern, ed., *Men of Mark in Georgia, 1733 to 1911* (Atlanta: A. B. Caldwell, Publisher, 1911), 3:469.   *Donald C. Stephenson*

JOHNSTONE, Edward Ransom. B. December 27, 1870, Galt, Ontario, Canada, to William and Jane (Ransom) Johnstone. M. June 17, 1898, to Olive Lehmann. Ch. four. D. December 29, 1946, Vineland, New Jersey.

Edward Ransom Johnstone was educated in the public schools in Cincinnati, Ohio, where he was graduated from Woodward High School (1885). He attended Fort Wayne (Indiana) College of Medicine for three years.

Johnstone was an officer of the Cincinnati House of Refuge (reformatory) for a short time (1889) and became a teacher in the public schools of Hamilton County, Ohio, and Cincinnati (1889–93). He was employed as a teacher and principal of the Indiana School for Feeble-Minded Youth in Fort Wayne (1893–98).

He assumed the position of assistant superintendent of the Vineland

(New Jersey) Training School in 1898, becoming superintendent in 1900. He implemented a psychology laboratory to investigate the causes and effects of mental deficiency. Annual summer courses for teachers of special classes laid the groundwork for later development of special training on college and university campuses. *The Training School Bulletin,* which he edited during his years at Vineland, was his contribution to the professional literature in this field. In 1922 he was made executive director, a position he held until his retirement in 1944.

Johnstone established a research department to study the psychology of the mentally retarded, established colonies for outdoor work programs for older boys, and promoted the establishment of the state-operated Woodbine colony. He provided training courses for teachers of the mentally retarded and supported legislation providing for special classes for retarded youngsters. He wrote *The Study of Human Heredity* (with others, 1911) and *Dear Robinson: Some Letters on Getting Along with Folks* (1923).

Johnstone served in the educational corps of the American Expeditionary Force in World War I and on the American Commission to Serbia in 1919. His scientific interests included research in agriculture and horticulture, and he was cited for distinguished service to agriculture by the New Jersey State Board of Agriculture in 1920.

He was a member of many associations, including the American Association on Mental Deficiency (president, 1902 and 1927), the National Conference of Social Work, the New Jersey State Conference on Social Welfare (president, 1903), the State Prison and Parole Board (president 1927–46), the New Jersey Crime Commission (chairman, committee on education, 1935), and the American Association for the Advancement of Science. He was awarded the Order of St. Sava of Serbia (1920) and received honorary degrees from Princeton and Rutgers universities.

REFERENCES: *DAB (supp. 4); LE* (I); *WWW* (II); *NYT,* December 30, 1946, p. 19; "Honoring of Edward Ransom Johnstone, 1870–1946," *Training School Bulletin* 44 (May 1947): 32–58; *Journal of Criminal Law and Criminology* 37 (January 1947): 355–56.   *Bruce D. Mattson*

JONES, Arthur Julius. B. May 21, 1871, Grinnell, Iowa, to Publius Vergilius and Lavinia (Burton) Jones. M. June 26, 1899, to Ethel Louise Rounds. Ch. two. D. August 27, 1963, Eaglesmere, Pennsylvania.

Arthur Julius Jones was educated in Grinnell, Iowa, in public schools, Iowa College Academy, and Grinnell College, where he received the A.B. degree (1893). He was a student at the University of Chicago (1894) and Teachers College, Columbia University, where he was awarded the Ph.D. degree (1907).

Jones was an instructor in biology at Grinnell College (1893–95), teacher of Greek, Latin, and biology at Central High School in Minneapolis,

Minnesota (1895–98), superintendent of schools in Redwood Falls, Minnesota (1898–1904), and a teacher at the Charlton School in New York City (1905–06). He was head of the department of education at the Rhode Island State Normal School (later, Rhode Island College) from 1907 to 1911 and at the University of Maine (1911–15). He joined the faculty of the University of Pennsylvania in 1915 and was professor of secondary education from 1919, director of the appointment bureau (1919–26), and a part-time professor from his retirement in 1941 to 1945. He was influential in the development of the guidance movement.

Jones was the author of articles for professional journals and *Education and the Individual* (1926), *Principles of Guidance* (1930), *The Education of Youth for Leadership* (1938), and *Principles of Unit Construction* (with others, 1939). He was active in professional organizations, including the American Personnel and Guidance Association (archivist), the National Vocational Guidance Association (president, 1936), and the Society of College Teachers of Education (secretary, 1922–41). He received citations from B'nai B'rith (1956) and the National Vocational Guidance Association (1958) and an honorary degree from Grinnell College (1963).

REFERENCES: *LE* (III); *NCAB* (51:302); *WWAE* (XV); *WWW* (V).

John F. Ohles

JONES, Gilbert Haven. B. August 23, 1883, Fort Mott, South Carolina, to Joshua H. and Lizzie (Martin) Jones. M. June 10, 1910, to Rachel Gladys Coverdale. Ch. four. D. June 1966, Wilberforce, Ohio.

Gilbert Haven Jones was graduated from Central High School in Columbus, Ohio, and attended Ohio State University. He was graduated from Wilberforce (Ohio) University with the A.B. (1902) and B.S. (1903) degrees. He attended Dickinson College in Carlisle, Pennsylvania, where he received the Ph.B. (1906) and A.M. (1907) degrees. He studied in Germany at the universities of Göttingen and Jena (1908–09) and received the Ph.D. degree from Jena in 1909.

Jones was the principal of Lincoln High School in Carlisle, Pennsylvania (1903–05), professor of philosophy and education (1909–10) at St. Augustine's Collegiate Institute (later, St. Augustine's College) in Raleigh, North Carolina, and professor of ancient languages at the Colored Agricultural and Normal University (later, Langston University) in Langston, Oklahoma (1910–14). In 1914 Jones joined the faculty at Wilberforce University, where he served as dean of the college of liberal arts and sciences (1914–24) and president (1924–32), professor of economics (1932–36), vice-president (1936–37), and professor of the philosophy of education and dean of the College of Education (1937–56).

The author of *Education in Theory and Practice* (1919), he was active in professional organizations, a delegate to an ecumenical conference in Paris, France, and a member of the National Advisory Council to the

United States Department of Health, Education and Welfare and the advisory board of the Northeast Life Insurance Company. He was awarded an honorary degree by Howard University (1925).

REFERENCES: *LE* (III); *NCAB* (D: 201); *WW* (XXVI); *WWAE* (XVII).

Anne R. Gayles

JONES, Lawrence Clifton. B. November 21, 1884, St. Joseph, Missouri, to John Q. and Lydia (Foster) Jones. M. June 29, 1912, to Grace Morris Allen. Ch. two. D. July 13, 1975, Jackson, Mississippi.

Lawrence Clifton Jones, pioneer educator of blacks in Mississippi, was graduated from Marshalltown (Iowa) High School (1903), and received the Ph.B. degree (1907) from the State University of Iowa.

He left Iowa and settled in the Piney Woods area near Braxton, Mississippi, in 1909. He started the Piney Woods Country Life School for Education of Boys and Girls in the Black Belt. The school was started without funds in a sheep shed located on forty acres of land donated to the school by a black farmer. The school later developed into a sixteen-hundred acre campus with five hundred students and a staff of forty teachers. The school, whose initial enrollment was twelve students, was chartered by the state of Mississippi in 1913. Jones appeared on a "This Is Your Life" television program and, following his appearance, received more than $600,000 in contributions from the viewing audience.

Jones was in charge of the Thrift Stamp Campaign among black people in Mississippi during World War I and was assistant director of the Armenian Relief Campaign in Mississippi. His published works include *Up Thru Difficulties* (1910), *Piney Woods and Its Story* (1923), *The Spirit of Piney Woods* (1931), *The Bottom Rail* (1933), and numerous articles on the racial issue. In January 1955 Governor Hugh White acclaimed Jones Mississippi's First Citizen.

REFERENCES: *LE* (III); *WW* (XXXVIII); *WWAE* (VIII); *WWW* (VI); Beth Day, *The Little Professor of Piney Woods* (New York: Julian Messner, 1955); *NYT,* July 15, 1975, p. 36.   *Don C. Locke*

JONES, Thomas Jesse. B. August 4, 1873, Llanfacthraeth, Wales, United Kingdom, to Benjamin and Sarah B. (Williams) Jones. M. August 18, 1901, to Carrie Schlaegel. Ch. two. D. January 5, 1950, New York, New York.

Thomas Jesse Jones came to the United States from Wales in 1884. He was a student at Washington and Lee University in Lexington, Virginia (1891–92), and received the A.B. degree (1897) from Marietta (Ohio) College and the A.M. (1899) and Ph.D. (1904) degrees from Columbia University. He attended Union Theological Seminary in New York City, where he received the B.D. degree (1900).

Jones was acting head of the University Social Settlement in New York City (1901–02) and director of the research department at Hampton (Virginia) Institute (1902–09), where he developed an interest in the problems of blacks. He worked for the federal government as a statistician with the Census Bureau (1909–12) and as a specialist in education for the United States Bureau of Education (1912–19). Educational director for the Phelps Stokes Fund in 1913, he was appointed director of the fund in 1917 and served in that post to his retirement in 1946.

He wrote many books, including *The Sociology of a New York City Block* (1904), *Negro Education in the United States* (1917), *Educational Adaptations* (1920), *Education in Africa* (1922), *Education in East Africa* (1925), *Four Essentials of Education* (1926), and *Essentials of Civilization* (1929).

During World War I, Jones visited the fighting front for the Young Men's Christian Association to seek to improve the conditions of black soldiers. On his return, he was instrumental in establishing the Commission on Interracial Cooperation, which was designed to help black soldiers returning after the war to be accepted by society. Jones headed the Phelps Stokes Fund Education Commission to West, South, and Equatorial Africa to study conditions of Africans (1920). He headed similar groups to the Near East (1929), South Africa (1932), and the Navaho Indians (1937). He was a member of professional associations and served as chairman of the committee on social studies in secondary schools for the National Education Association. He received the Gold Cross of the Order of the Savior from the government of Greece.

REFERENCES: *NYT,* January 6, 1950, p. 21; *WWW* (II).

John F. Ohles

JORDAN, David Starr. B. January 19, 1851, Gainesville, New York, to Hiram and Huldah (Hawley) Jordan. M. May 10, 1875, to Susan Bowen. M. August 10, 1887, to Jessie L. Knight. Ch. six. D. September 19, 1931, Palo Alto, California.

At fourteen years of age, David Starr Jordan was permitted to enroll as a student in the Gainesville (New York) Female Seminary. He taught school in South Warsaw, New York, at the age of seventeen and received a scholarship to study at Cornell University in Ithaca, New York, where he was graduated with the M.S. degree (1872). He received the M.D. degree (1875) from Indiana Medical School in Indianapolis.

Jordan taught several subjects at Lombard University (later, College) in Galesburg, Illinois (1872–73), before becoming principal and teacher at the Collegiate Institute and Scientific School in Appleton, Wisconsin (1873–74). He taught in a high school in Indianapolis, Indiana (1874–75).

Jordan was professor of natural history at North Western Christian University (later, Butler University) in Indianapolis (1875–79) before going to Indiana University as head of the natural science department (1879–85). He became president of Indiana University in 1885. During his tenure, legislative appropriations to the university were increased, allowing the construction of a new building; the curriculum was expanded; and the choosing of major subjects by students with major advisers was introduced.

Jordan left Indiana to become the first president of Stanford (California) University in 1891, where he guided the university through its difficult first two decades. He retired from Stanford in 1913.

A scientist by training, Jordan gave his name to Jordan's law on the geographical distribution of species and was the author of more than fifty books, including *Manual of the Vertebrates of the Northern U.S.* (1876), *Animal Life* (1900), *Animal Forms* (1902), *American Food and Game Fishes* (1902), *Fishes* (1907), and many notes and descriptions of fish. Among his other books were *Care and Culture of Men* (1896), *Imperial Democracy* (1899), *The Heredity of Richard Roe* (1911), *Unseen Empire* (1912), *War and Waste* (1914), *A Study in Conquest* (1915), *Democracy and World Relations* (1918), *The Days of a Man* (1922), and *The Trend of the American University* (1929).

Jordan was an early conservationist and supporter of the arbitration of international disputes. He believed militarism brought survival of the unfittest; he opposed football at Stanford as more war than sport. He was vice-president of the Anti-Imperialist League (1899), chief director of the World Peace Foundation, and president of the World's Peace Congress (1915). In 1925 he won the twenty-five-thousand-dollar Raphael Herman Prize for "A Plan to Develop International Justice and Friendship."

Jordan wrote the constitution of the Association of American Universities. He was an initial member of the Carnegie Foundation for the Advancement of Teaching and president of the National Education Association (1915), the American Association for the Advancement of Science (1909–10), and the California Academy of Science (1896–1904 and 1908). He received many awards and honorary degrees.

REFERENCES: *AC; DAB; EB; NCAB* (22:68); *TC; WWAE* (I); *WWW* (I); David Starr Jordan, *The Days of a Man* (Yonkers-on-Hudson, N.Y.: World Book Co., 1922); *NYT*, September 20, 1931, Sec. II, p. 6.

Jack K. Campbell

JOYNER, James Yadkin. B. August 7, 1862, Davidson County, North Carolina, to John and Sallie (Wooten) Joyner. M. December 1887 to Effie E. Rouse. Ch. two. D. January 25, 1954, La Grange, North Carolina.

James Yadkin Joyner was orphaned at fourteen months of age and was taken into the family of his grandfather, Council Wooten. When Joyner was ten years old, his grandfather died, and the boy was reared in the family of his uncle, Shadrach I. Wooten.

Joyner attended La Grange (North Carolina) Academy and entered the University of North Carolina in 1878, where he received the Ph.B. degree (1881). He studied law at the Law School of Dick and Dillard, was admitted to the bar, and practiced law in Goldsboro, North Carolina (1886–89).

His career was spent in the state of North Carolina, where he was principal of La Grange Academy (1882–83) and superintendent of public schools of Lenoir County (1884–85). He gave up his law practice in 1889 to become superintendent of the Goldsboro graded schools and resigned in 1893 to become professor of English in the State Normal and Industrial College (later, University of North Carolina at Greensboro) at Greensboro. He remained there until 1902, when he was appointed state superintendent of public instruction.

As state superintendent, Joyner supervised the construction of many new school buildings, established the first public high schools and the first State Literary Fund as an aid in building school houses, initiated vocational education, enacted compulsory attendance laws, and began statewide certification of teachers. The first state administration and consolidation of rural schools was begun. In 1918 a six-month school term was adopted on a statewide basis. In 1919 ill health forced Joyner to leave his state post and return to the farm. In 1922 he became president of the Tobacco Growers Cooperative Association in Raleigh, North Carolina.

Joyner was an alderman in Greensboro, North Carolina (1899–1902), and was chairman of the state textbook commission (1901). He was president of the National Education Association (1909–10) and the Association of State Superintendents of the Southern States (1903–05).

REFERENCES: *LE* (I); *NCAB* (A:307); *WWW* (III); Samuel A. Ashe, Stephen B. Weeks, and Charles L. Van Noppen, *Biographical History of North Carolina* (Greensboro, N.C.: Charles L. Van Noppen, Publisher, 1907), vol. 6; *Greensboro News,* January 26, 1954.   *Linda C. Gardner*

JOYNES, Edward Southey. B. March 2, 1834, Accomack County, Virginia, to Thomas Robinson and Anne Bell (Satchell) Joynes. M. December 14, 1859, to Eliza Waller West. Ch. four. D. June 18, 1917, Columbia, South Carolina.

Edward Southey Joynes prepared for college at the local school near his home, at Delaware College (later, University of Delaware) in Newark, Delaware, and at Concord Academy in Fredericksburg, Virginia. The principal teacher of Concord Academy, Frederick Coleman, inspired Joynes to study languages, especially Latin and Greek, and Joynes spent his life studying and teaching languages.

Joynes enrolled in the University of Virginia in 1850 and received the B.A. (1852) and M.A. (1853) degrees. From 1853 to 1856 he served as assistant professor of ancient languages at Virginia. He studied with some of the best-known scholars of the day at the University of Berlin (1856–58).

William and Mary College in Williamsburg, Virginia, elected Joynes professor of Greek and German in 1858, where he remained until the Civil War began in 1861 and the college was closed. Joynes became chief clerk in the Confederate War Department in Richmond, Virginia, until 1864 when he became professor of modern languages and English at Hollins Institute (later, College) in Hollins College, Virginia. In 1866 he was a professor of modern languages at Washington College (later, Washington and Lee) in Lexington, Virginia, where he insisted on teaching English also. He was an early advocate of English as a separate and distinct branch of study in college work, and Washington College became the first college in Virginia to offer English as a principal study.

Joynes left Virginia in 1875 to accept the faculty chair of modern languages and English in the newly organized Vanderbilt University in Nashville, Tennessee. Three years later, he joined the faculty of the University of Tennessee and in 1882 moved to South Carolina College in Columbia as professor of modern languages and English. The position was divided in 1888, and Joynes continued until his retirement in 1908 as professor of modern languages.

Joynes was widely known for his work to improve schools and colleges. He consistently recommended better trained teachers at all levels, more public schools, and more efficient and effective methods of teaching in the schools of Virginia, Tennessee, and South Carolina. He worked to establish schools for black children as well as white.

His writings, chiefly textbooks for language classes, especially French and German, include *Joynes-Otto German Course* (with Emil Otto, 1869–70), *Joynes-Otto French Course* (1870), *First Book of French* (1874), *Joynes-Meissner German Grammar* (1887), *German Reader Exercises* (1890), *Minimum French Grammar and Reader* (1892), and *German Lesson Grammar* (with E. C. Wesselhoeft, 1907). His only book related to the teaching of English was a collection of lectures entitled *Notes on Lectures on English Language* (1916).

Upon his retirement after fifty-five years of teaching, the Carnegie Foundation awarded him a pension for "unusual and distinguished service as a professor of modern languages." Joynes received honorary degrees from Delaware College and William and Mary College.

REFERENCES: *AC; DAB; NCAB* (11:37); *WWW* (I).   *Earl W. Thomas*

JUDD, Charles Hubbard. B. February 20, 1873, Bareilly, British India, to Charles Wesley and Sarah (Hubbard) Judd. M. August 23, 1898, to Ella Le Compte. M. August 28, 1937, to May Diehl. Ch. one. D. July 18, 1946, Santa Barbara, California.

Born in India, Charles Judd was brought to the United States in 1879 by his parents, who were Methodist missionaries. He was graduated from Wesleyan University in Middletown, Connecticut, with the A.B. degree (1894). He continued his studies at Leipzig, Germany, where he studied under Wilhelm Wundt and received the Ph.D. degree (1896).

Judd served as an instructor in psychology at Wesleyan University (1896–98), professor of psychology at New York University (1898–1901), and professor of psychology and pedagogy at the University of Cincinnati, Ohio (1901–02). In 1902 he received an appointment to teach psychology at Yale University and was director of the psychological laboratory (1907–09). In 1909 he became professor and head of the department of education at the University of Chicago and was chairman of the department of psychology (1920–25). He retired as professor emeritus in 1938.

Judd is best known for his educational surveys, research studies, editing services to educational and psychological journals, and textbooks. He was influential in American education as a pioneer in the use of scientific methods in the study and resolution of educational problems. He edited the *Psychological Review* and Studies from the Yale Psychological Laboratory (1905–09). He was the author of many books, including *Genetic Psychology for Teachers* (1903), *General Introduction to Psychology* (1907), *Psychology of High School Subjects* (1915), *Measuring the Work of the Public Schools* (1916), *Introduction to the Scientific Study of Education* (1918), *Reading, Its Nature and Development* (1918), *Psychology of Social Institutions* (1926), *Psychology of Secondary Education* (1927), *Education and Social Progress* (1934), *Education as Cultivation of the Higher Mental Processes* (1936), and *Educational Psychology* (1938). He translated from the German Wilhelm Wundt's *Outlines of Psychology* (1907) and edited publications for federal bureaus, institutions, and associations.

A fellow of the American Association for the Advancement of Science, Judd was president of the American Psychological Association (1909), the National Society of College Teachers of Education (1911 and 1915), and the North Central Association of Colleges and Secondary Schools (1923). He was chairman of the American Council on Education (1929–30) and a member of the advisory committee of the National Youth Administration (1935–40), the International Inquiry on School and University Examinations (1935), and the Educational Policies Commission of the National Education Association (1935–37). He was a consultant to the War Department (1942–43), a member of the National Resources Planning Board (1937–40), and a member of many professional organizations. He was awarded five honorary degrees.

REFERENCES: *CB* (September 1946); *DAB* (supp. 4); *EB; LE* (I); *NCAB* (A:252, 42: 678): *WWW* (II); Frank N. Freeman *(q.v.)*, "Reflections on the Personality and Professional Leadership of Charles Hubbard Judd," *The Elementary School Journal* 47 (January 1947): 266–70; *NYT,* July 19, 1946, p. 19.   Paul L. Ward

JUDSON, Harry Pratt. B. December 20, 1849, Jamestown, New York, to Lyman Parsons and Abigail Cook (Pratt) Judson. M. January 14, 1879, to Rebecca Anna Gilbert. Ch. two. D. March 4, 1927, Chicago, Illinois.

Harry Pratt Judson, second president of the University of Chicago, was educated at the Geneva (New York) Classical Union School and the Lansingburg (New York) Academy. He received the A.B. (1870) and A.M. (1883) degrees from Williams College in Williamstown, Massachusetts.

He was teacher and principal of Troy (New York) High School (1870–85) and accepted a professorship in history at the University of Minnesota, where he taught from 1885 to 1892.

Judson joined the faculty of the University of Chicago in 1892 as professor of political science and dean of the colleges. He was dean of the faculties of arts, literature, and science and head of the department of political science (1894–1907), and he assumed many of the day-to-day administrative duties of the president's office. With the onset of William Rainey Harper's (q.v.) illness in 1903, the trustees of the university asked Judson to assume the responsibilities of the president's office. When Harper died in 1906, Judson was appointed acting president and was elected president of the university in 1907, serving until his retirement in 1923.

When Judson assumed the presidency, the university had fewer than five thousand students; when he retired, more than eight thousand were enrolled, and university finances were stabilized.

Judson was the author of *History of Troy's Citizens Corps* (1884), *Caesar's Army* (1885), *Europe in the Nineteenth Century* (1894), *The Growth of the American Nation* (1895), *The Latin in English* (1896), *The Young American* (1897), *The Government of Illinois* (1900), and *Our Federal Republic* (1925). He coedited *Caesar's Commentaries* (1885), and *Graded Literature Readers* (with Ida C. Bender, eight volumes, 1899–1901), and was coeditor of the *American Historical Review* (1895–1902).

Judson was a member of the General Education Board (1906) and the Rockefeller Foundation (1913–24). He went to China in 1914 as chairman of the Rockefeller Foundation's China Medical Mission and directed the American Relief Commission in Persia (1918). He was chairman of the trustees of the American University Union in Europe (1921–27). He was awarded honorary degrees by nine American and foreign universities.

REFERENCES: *DAB; NCAB* (20:24); *TC; WWW* (I); Thomas Wakefield Goodspeed, *The Story of the University of Chicago 1890–1925* (Chicago: University of Chicago Press, 1925); *NYT,* March 5, 1927, p. 15; Richard J. Storr, *Harper's University, the Beginnings: A History of the University of Chicago* (Chicago: University of Chicago Press, 1966).   *Erika Hugo*

JUNKIN, George. B. November 1, 1790, near Carlisle, Pennsylvania, to Joseph and Eleanor (Cochran) Junkin. M. June 1, 1819, to Julia Miller. Ch. three. D. May 20, 1868, Philadelphia, Pennsylvania.

George Junkin received his first education in a primitive schoolhouse on the Pennsylvania frontier. He was graduated from Jefferson College in Canonsburg, Pennsylvania, in 1813. He studied theology with John Mason at the Theological Seminary of the Associate Reformed Church in New York City, was licensed to preach in 1816, and was ordained in 1818 by the Associated Reformed Presbytery of Philadelphia.

Junkin served as pastor of the Presbyterian church in Milton, Pennsylvania (1819–30), and helped establish Milton Academy (1819–22). He became principal of the Manual Labor Academy of Pennsylvania at Germantown (1830–32).

He was one of the founders and first president of Lafayette College at Easton, Pennsylvania (1832–41). Junkin used the manual-labor system with former students from his Germantown academy to establish the college. In 1834 a permanent site for the college was purchased, and the first building, constructed by the students, was opened in May 1834. The manual-labor system was discontinued in 1839. Junkin served as president of Lafayette College as the student body grew and new physical facilities and courses were added. In 1841 he became president of Miami (Oxford, Ohio) University but ran into conflict as an opponent of abolitionism and an advocate of compensated slavery. He returned to the presidency of Lafayette College in 1844.

In 1848 he again resigned from Lafayette and became president of Washington College (later, Washington and Lee University) in Lexington, Virginia. His loyalty to the Union resulted in conflict with students who advocated secession, and he resigned from Washington College in 1861. Junkin spent the rest of his life in Philadelphia in study and writing.

He was the author of *The Vindication, Containing a History of the Trial of Rev. Albert Barness* (1836), *The Integrity of American National Union vs. Abolitionism* (1843), *Political Fallacies: An Examination of False Assumptions in Refutation of the Sophistical Reasoning Which Have Brought on This Civil War* (1863), *A Treatise on Sanctification* (1864), *The Tabernacle, or the Gospel According to Moses* (1865); and *Sabatismos* (1866). A week before his death, he completed *A Commentary upon the Epistle to the Hebrews*, which was published posthumously in 1873.

Junkin served as moderator of the general assembly of the Presbyterian church in 1844. He was the recipient of three honorary degrees.

REFERENCES: *AC; DAB; NCAB* (11:240); *TC; WWW* (H).

Gorman L. Miller

K

KANDEL, Isaac Leon. B. January 22, 1881, Botoshani, Rumania, to Abraham and Fanny (Manales) Kandel. M. July 27, 1915, to Jessie Sarah Davis. Ch. two. D. June 14, 1965, Geneva, Switzerland.

I. L. Kandel's elementary schooling (1887–92) was followed by a classical education at Manchester (England) Grammar School. He won highest honors in the classics and the B.A. degree (1902) at the University of Manchester, which also granted him the M.A. degree in education and the teacher's diploma in 1906. He taught at the Royal Academical Institute of Belfast, Ireland (1906–08) before obtaining the Ph.D. degree (1910) from Teachers College, Columbia University.

Kandel was an assistant editor of *Monroe's Cyclopedia of Education* (1909-13) and taught the history of education and comparative education at Teachers College (1913-47). He was also a research specialist for the Carnegie Foundation for the Advancement of Teaching (1914-23). In this capacity, he published several important monographs, particularly one on the American system of examinations.

As professor of education at Teachers College (1923-47), Kandel gained a reputation as the leader of the field of comparative education in the United States and as one of the outstanding specialists of the world. Kandel was a frequent and outspoken critic of the extreme tendencies of progressive education and often debated publicly with its proponents. He stressed the importance of the historical and international dimensions of all educational questions. A masterly reader and translator of many languages, Kandel was in demand as a visiting professor, guest lecturer, consultant, and writer in various parts of the world.

After retiring from Teachers College, Kandel inaugurated the professorship of American studies at the University of Manchester, England (1948-50).

Kandel made many significant contributions to the advancement of the fields of the history and philosophy of education, comparative education, and international education. His most influential book was *Comparative Education* (1933). Among his other writings were *Training of Elementary School Teachers in Germany* (1910), *Elementary Education in England* (1914), *Training of Elementary School Teachers in Mathematics* (1915), *Federal Aid for Vocational Education* (1917), *Pensions for Public School Teachers* (with Clyde Furst, 1918), *History of Secondary Education* (1930), *Conflicting Theories of Education* (1938), *The End of an Era* (1941), *Intellectual Cooperation: National and International* (1944), *The New Era in Education* (1955), and *American Education in the Twentieth Century* (1957). Of particular significance was his documented analysis of the principles and practices of education in National Socialist Germany, *The Making of Nazis* (1934). He was editor of the *Educational Yearbook* of the International Institute of Teachers College (1924-47), *School and Society* (1946-53), *Universities Quarterly* (1947-49), *Twenty-five Years of American Education* (1924), the Nelson Education Series, and the Professional Aptitude Tests (1940).

Kandel was active in many professional associations as a member of the Society of the American Friends Field Service Fellowship for French Universities (secretary, 1919-24), the Committee for a Free Europe (staff member), the American Association of University Professors (council member), and the American Council of Learned Societies (advisory board). He was a trustee of Finch Junior College. He was the recipient of honorary degrees and the French Legion of Honor.

REFERENCES: *CA* (1-4); *LE* (III); *NCAB* (51:86); *WWAE* (XIII); *WWW*

(IV); *NYT,* June 15, 1965, p. 41; William W. Brickman *(q.v.),* "I. L. Kandel," *School and Society* 93 (October 30, 1965): 387; Robert Ulich *(q.v.),* "In Memory of Isaac L. Kandel, 1881–1965," *Comparative Education Review* 9 (October 1965): 255–57. **William W. Brickman**

KAUFFMAN, Treva Erdine. B. September 23, 1889, Osborn, Ohio, to Theodore and Anna Laura (Hershey) Kauffman. M. no.

Treva Erdine Kauffman received the B.S. degree (1911) from Ohio State University and the M.A. degree (1931) from Columbia University. She also studied at the University of Chicago (1916) and the University of Montreal, Canada (1946). She studied folk schools and homes in Denmark and Sweden in 1929.

Kauffman was a teacher of home economics in the Hamilton (Ohio) public schools (1911–13) and an instructor in the Ohio State University Extension Service (1913–15). She organized the school lunch program in rural and centralized schools in Ohio (1915–16) and was the state leader of Ohio Girls Clubs. From 1917 to 1920, she was assistant professor of home economics at Ohio State University, and she also was state supervisor of home economics education for the state of Ohio (1918–20).

Kauffman joined the New York State Department of Education in 1920 as state supervisor of home economics and was acting chief of the bureau of home economics education (1944–47). She retired from the state position in 1959.

Kauffman wrote articles and bulletins on home economics and *Teaching Problems in Home Economics* (1930), *Homemaking Course in Training Girls for Household Service* (1935), *Young Folks at Home* (1948), and *Development and History of Home Economics in New York State* (1959). She was home economics editor of *The High School Teacher* (1926–35), a member of the advisory council of *Practical Home Economics Magazine* (from 1928), and on the advisory board of *The Forecast Magazine* (from 1936).

A member of many professional associations, Kauffman was vice-president of the New York State Home Economics Association (1930–34) and vice-president of the Council of Women of the New York State Education Department (1931–32), and she organized and directed adult education programs in homemaking in New York for federal and state Temporary Emergency Relief Administrations (1932–35). She was a member of the White House Conference on Child Health and Protection (1930), the President's Conference on Home Building and Ownership (1931), and many other state and federal bodies. She received a citation for twenty-five years of service to the American Red Cross and citations for service to the New York State Vocational Education Association, the American Home Economics Association (1972), and the *Knickerbocker News* (Albany, New York) for civic service (1972).

REFERENCES: *LE* (III); *WW* (XXXI); *WWAE* (XIX); *Who's Who of American Women*, 9th ed. (Chicago: Marquis, 1975).   *John F. Ohles*

KEANE, John Joseph. B. September 12, 1839, Ballyshannon, County Donegal, Ireland, to Hugh and Fannie (Connolly) Keane. M. no. D. June 22, 1918, Dubuque, Iowa.

John Joseph Keane arrived with his family in Baltimore, Maryland, from Ireland in 1848. He studied at Calvert Hall, St. Charles' College, and St. Mary's Seminary in Baltimore, where he received the A.B. (1864), A.M. (1865), and S.T.B. (1866) degrees.

After his ordination in 1866, he developed skills as an orator and an organizer during his twelve years at St. Patrick's Church in Washington, D.C. (1866–78). In 1878 he became bishop of Richmond, Virginia, where he supported temperance and charitable societies and schools for white and black pupils. He was transferred to the titular see of Jasso in 1888 and was elevated to archbishop of Damascus in 1897.

Keane's activities at the Third Plenary Council of Baltimore (1884) caused him to be named first rector of the Catholic University of America (1889). He selected the first staff of professors, wrote the university's statutes, raised funds, visited other American and European universities, supervised the erection of the first building, and lectured widely.

In 1896 Pope Leo XIII dismissed Keane from his post. Keane's reputed liberalism, especially his support for the Knights of Labor, lost him the confidence of conservative prelates, notably Archbishop Michael Corrigan of New York and Bishop Bernard McQuaid *(q.v.)* of Rochester. He chose to live in Rome where he became an archbishop and a consultor to two congregations. He also served as spokesman for such moderate American prelates as Bishop John Spalding *(q.v.)*, Bishop John Ireland *(q.v.)*, and James Cardinal Gibbons during the controversy over Americanism.

He became archbishop of Dubuque, Iowa, in 1900, where he fostered Loras College and established eleven academies for girls and two high schools for boys. Ill health forced his resignation in 1911.

Keane published many articles, particularly on higher education in religious and professional journals. In retirement he published a book of pious reflections, *Emmanuel* (1915). His most representative style is found in his journal articles and in his papers, *The Providential Mission of Pius IX* (1878) and *The Providential Mission of Leo XIII* (1888), and in *Onward and Upward* (1902), which contains extracts from sermons and addresses compiled by Maurice Francis Egan. He helped found the Catholic Total Abstinence Union of America (1872), and Catholic Young Men's National Union (1875), Carroll Institute (1873), and the Tabernacle Society.

REFERENCES: *AC; DAB; NCAB* (6:285); *TC; WWW* (I); *New Catholic Encyclopedia* (New York: McGraw-Hill, 1967); Patrick Henry Ahern, *The Life of John J. Keane* (Milwaukee: Bruce Publishing Co., 1955).
                                                                    David Delahanty

KEEN, William Williams. B. January 19, 1837, Philadelphia, Pennsylvania, to William Williams and Susan (Budd) Keen. M. December 11, 1867, to Emma Corinna Borden. Ch. four. D. June 7, 1932, Philadelphia, Pennsylvania.

William Williams Keen, a teacher, surgeon, and writer, attended Central High School in Philadelphia and received the A.M. degree from Brown University in Providence, Rhode Island (1859). He was graduated from Jefferson Medical College in Philadelphia, Pennsylvania (1862). His medical studies were interrupted in 1861 when he served as assistant surgeon of the Fifth Massachusetts Regiment during the Civil War. After he received the M.D. degree in 1862, he served as acting assistant surgeon of the United States Army (1862–64).

After two years of postgraduate studies in Berlin and Paris (1864–66), Keen started practicing medicine in Philadelphia and headed the Philadelphia School of Anatomy (1866–75). He taught at Jefferson Medical College (1866–75 and 1889–1907). From 1866 to 1869, he taught at Woman's Medical College in Philadelphia. It was during his teaching career that he gained an international reputation.

Keen was among the first surgeons in America to adopt Lister's method of antisepsis, and he performed what is said to have been the first successful operation for brain tumor in America (1877). The patient survived the operation, and lived for thirty more years. In 1893 he assisted Joseph D. Bryant of New York in removing the left upper jaw of President Grover Cleveland for a sarcoma. A specialist in the surgery of the brain and the nervous system, Keen was a pioneer in successfully performing new and difficult operations.

Keen was the editor of a number of well-known works, including *System of Surgery* (eight volumes, 1906–1921), *Gray's Anatomy* (1887), and *American Text-Book of Surgery* (1892). He was the author of *The Surgical Complications and Sequels of Typhoid Fever* (1898), *Animal Experimentation and Medical Progress* (1914), *I Believe in God and Evolution* (1922), and *The Surgical Operations on President Cleveland in 1893* (1928).

Keen served as president of a number of organizations, including the American Surgical Association (1899), the American Medical Association (1900), the International Congress of Surgery, Paris (1920), the Congress of American Physicians and Surgeons (1903), and the American Philosophical Society (1907–17). He was an honorary fellow of national associations of England, Italy, and Ireland. The recipient of honorary degrees from many American and foreign universities, he was awarded medals by the Boston Surgical Society and the Pennsylvania Society of New York and received the Colver-Rosenberger Medal of Honor of Brown University. He was granted honors by the governments of France and Belgium.

REFERENCES: *AC; DAB* (supp. 1); *EB; NCAB* (11:367); *TC; WWW* (I); Ralph H. Major, *A History of Medicine* (Springfield, Ill.: Charles C.

Thomas Publisher, 1954), p. 1037; *NYT,* June 8, 1932, p. 19.
                                                            Richard M. Coger

KEFAUVER, Grayson Neikirk. B. August 31, 1900, Middletown, Maryland, to Oliver Henry and Lillie May (Neikirk) Kefauver. M. December 25, 1922, to Anna Elizabeth Skinner. Ch. three. D. January 4, 1946, Los Angeles, California.

Grayson Neikirk Kefauver was graduated from Middletown (Maryland) High School with a commercial diploma in 1917, attended Franklin and Marshall College in Lancaster, Pennsylvania, for one year, and transferred to Heidelberg College in Tiffin, Ohio, in 1918. When a chronic throat ailment forced him to move to a warm, dry climate, he enrolled in the University of Texas and later transferred to the University of Arizona, where he was graduated with the A.B. degree (1921). He received the M.A. degree (1925) from Stanford (California) University and the Ph.D. degree (1928) from the University of Minnesota.

Kefauver began his teaching career in Tucson, Arizona (1921), as a high school teacher and vice-principal. In 1923 he moved to Fresno, California, where he held several administrative positions. He was an instructor in secondary education at the University of Minnesota (1926–28) and taught at Teachers College, Columbia University (1929–32). He joined the education faculty at Stanford University in 1932 and was appointed dean in 1933, serving to 1943.

Kefauver was the author of *Guidance in Secondary Education* (with Leonard V. Koos, *q.v.,* 1933) and *Appraising Guidance in Secondary Schools* (with Harold C. Hand, *q.v.,* 1941). He was a joint editor of *Best-liked Literature* (with others, 1944) and, with Holland D. Roberts and Walter V. Kaulfers, wrote *English for Social Living* (1943) and *Foreign Languages and Cultures in American Education* (1942).

On leave from Stanford from 1943 until his death in 1946, Kefauver worked for the organization of an international educational agency. He participated in the creation of the United Nations Educational, Scientific, and Cultural Organization and ensured United States participation in the organization. In 1945 he was appointed United States delegate with the rank of minister to the preparatory commission, which established UNESCO.

REFERENCES: *DAB* (supp. 4); *LE* (I); *NCAB* (D: 299, 35: 36); *WWAE* (VIII); *WWW* (II); Harold John Bienvenu, "The Educational Career of Grayson Neikirk Kefauver" (Ed.D. diss., Stanford University, 1955); *NYT,* January 6, 1946, p. 40.   *Marvin Gerber*

KELLAS, Eliza. B. October 4, 1864, Mooers Forks, New York, to Alexander and Elizabeth Jane (Perry) Kellas. M. no. D. April 10, 1943, Troy, New York.

Eliza Kellas began her formal education in a one-room district school in Mooers, New York. She attended Franklin Academy in Malone, New

York, and at age sixteen started her teaching career in her home district. In 1887 she entered Potsdam (New York) Normal School (later, State University of New York College) and was graduated in 1889. She completed her education at Radcliffe College in Cambridge, Massachusetts, where she enrolled at the age of forty, and received the B.A. degree in 1910. She engaged in graduate study at Radcliffe (1910–11).

She taught at Potsdam Normal School (1890–91). When the new State Normal School (later, State University of New York College at Plattsburgh) was opened in Plattsburgh, New York, in 1891 Kellas was asked to become principal of the practice school and was preceptress of the normal school (1895–1901). In 1901 she resigned her post to become a salaried adviser in the household of Mrs. Charles P. Cheney, niece of Andrew S. Draper *(q.v.)*, New York commissioner of education. Mrs. Cheney married Professor William Henry Schofield of Harvard University, and Kellas moved with them to Cambridge, Massachusetts.

In February 1911 Kellas was asked to become principal of the Emma Willard School in Troy, New York. The school was in serious financial difficulty, but under Kellas it became one of the leading preparatory institutions in the United States. The students were encouraged to use the resources of Troy and Albany, New York, and attend lectures and concerts there; Kellas brought frequent guest lecturers on campus. Athletics were emphasized, and a stable and riding ring were built. School dramatics, self-discipline, patriotism, and academic rigor became part of the Emma Willard tradition. Kellas worked individually with each student and faculty member to instill a feeling of moral and intellectual responsibility.

When the Russell Sage College of Practical Arts was opened in old Emma Willard School buildings in Troy in September 1916, Kellas became its first president while continuing to be principal of the Emma Willard School. A separate charter was granted to the college in 1927, authorizing it to issue academic degrees. Russell Sage College grew under Kellas in size, program, and reputation. On February 6, 1928, at the age of sixty-three, Kellas announced her resignation as president of the college. She continued as principal of the Emma Willard School until she retired at the age of seventy-seven in 1942. She received several honorary degrees.

REFERENCES: *CB* (May 1943); *LE* (II); *WWAE* (I); *NAW; WWW* (II); *NYT,* April 11, 1943, p. 49; Elizabeth B. Potwine, *Faithfully Yours, Eliza Kellas* (Troy, N.Y.: Emma Willard School, 1960). *Gertrude Langsam*

KELLEY, Truman Lee. B. May 25, 1884, Whitehall, Michigan, to Marshall Charles and Mary Strong (Smith) Kelley. M. August 26, 1911, to Lura Osgood. M. August 4, 1936, to Grace Winifred (Cookney) Madge. Ch. two. D. May 2, 1961, Santa Barbara, California.

Truman L. Kelley received the B.A. degree in mathematics (1909) and the M.A. degree in psychology (1911) from the University of Illinois, where he was a cofounder of the education honorary society Kappa Delta Pi. He received the Ph.D. degree (1914) at Columbia University as a student of Edward L. Thorndike *(q.v.)*.

Kelley taught mathematics at the Georgia Institute of Technology in Atlanta (1909–10) and at a high school and junior college in Fresno, California (1911–12), and he was consulting psychologist at Culver Military Academy (1913–14). He taught educational psychology at the University of Texas (1914–17) and went to Teachers College, Columbia University, in 1917 where he worked with Thorndike developing classification tests used by the army in World War I. He was appointed professor of education and psychology at Stanford (California) University in 1920, where he collaborated with L. M. Terman *(q.v.)* in refining the Stanford-Binet IQ test and the Stanford Achievement Test (1923). In 1931 he went to Harvard University, where he taught to his retirement in 1950.

Kelley was the nation's leading statistical psychologist in the 1920s. His *Statistical Method* (1923) and *Interpretation of Educational Measurements* (1927) were highly influential and quickly recognized as milestones in the advance of psychometrics. He also wrote *Educational Guidance* (1914), *Mental Aspects of Delinquency* (1917), *The Influence of Nurture upon Native Differences* (1926), and a pioneering work in factor analysis and the first major alternative to Spearman's approach, *Crossroads in the Mind of Man* (1928), *Scientific Method* (1929), *Tests and Measurement in the Social Sciences* (with A. C. Krey, *q.v.*, 1934), *Essential Traits of Mental Life* (1935), *The Kelley Statistical Tables* (1938), *Talents and Tasks* (1940), and the monumental *Fundamentals of Statistics* (1947).

Kelley was president of the Psychometric Society (1938–39) and a fellow of the American Statistical Association (vice-president, 1926), the American Association for the Advancement of Science (vice-president, section Q, 1928), and the American Academy of Arts and Sciences. He was president of the Educational Research Corporation (1946–48), director of the American Institute for Research (1946–61), and a member of other professional and scientific groups.

REFERENCES: *LE* (III); *NCAB* (49:443); *WWW* (IV); J. C. Flanagan, *Psychometrika* 26 (December 1961): 343–45; *NYT,* May 3, 1961, p. 37; David L. Sills, ed., *International Encyclopedia of Social Science* (New York: Macmillan, 1968).   *Ronald D. Szoke*

KENDALL, Calvin Noyes. B. February 9, 1858, Augusta, New York, to Leonard J. and Sarah M. Kendall. M. June 30, 1891, to Alla P. Field. Ch. one. D. September 2, 1921, Knoxboro, New York.

Calvin Noyes Kendall was graduated from Hamilton College in Clinton, New York, with the A.B. degree (1882).

Kendall taught in rural New York schools for two years, and he was high school principal (1885–86) and superintendent (1886–90) of the Jackson

(Michigan) public schools. He was superintendent of schools in Saginaw, Michigan (1890–92), New Haven, Connecticut (1895–1900), and Indianapolis, Indiana (1900–11). He spent three years in business enterprises (1892–95). In Indiana he was a member of the state board of education (1900–11). Kendall was appointed New Jersey commissioner of education in 1911 by Governor Woodrow Wilson *(q.v.)* and continued to be reappointed to 1921, when he retired due to ill health.

Kendall was the joint author of several books, including *History of the United States for Grammar Schools* (with Reuben G. Thwaites, n.d.), *How to Teach the Fundamental Subjects* (with George A. Mirick, 1915), *How to Teach History in the Elementary Schools* (with Florence A. Stryker, 1918), *How to Teach the Special Subjects* (with George A. Mirick, 1918), and the Kendall Series of Readers with Caroline E. Townsend and Marion Paine Stevens. He was editor-in-chief of *Pictured Knowledge: The New Method of Visual Instruction Applied to Child Interest, School Subjects and Character Training,* published in 1935.

Kendall was active in professional organizations, serving as president of the Connecticut Council of Education (1897–98), the Connecticut State Teachers Association (1899–1900), the Southern Indiana Teachers Association (1904–05), the Indiana State Teachers Association (1910–11), the Department of Superintendence of the National Education Association (1920), and the New Jersey Council of Education (1914–15). He was appointed a member of the advisory committee on federal tubercular schools. He was the recipient of several honorary degrees.

REFERENCES: *WWW* (I); Thomas F. Fitzgerald, *Manual of the Legislature of New Jersey* (Trenton: State of New Jersey, 1921); *NYT*, September 3, 1921, p. 9.   *John F. Ohles*

KENDRICK, Asahel Clark. B. December 7, 1809, Poultney, Vermont, to Clark and Esther (Thompson) Kendrick. M. 1838 to Ann E. Hopkins. M. 1857 to Helen Morris Hooker. Ch. none. D. October 21, 1895, Rochester, New York.

Asahel Clark Kendrick was graduated from Hamilton College in Clinton, New York, in 1831 and was appointed tutor in the literary and theological institution at Hamilton. He was elected professor of Greek and Latin in 1832 but was relieved from Latin duties several years later, continuing as professor of Greek until he was appointed professor of Greek in the newly organized University of Rochester in 1850.

He traveled to Greece in 1852 to perfect his knowledge of Greek at the University of Athens. He studied antiquities at Rome and Athens and visited several Italian and German universities to study their educational methods. Kendrick returned to the University of Rochester in 1854, where he also taught Hebrew and New Testament interpretation at Rochester

Theological Seminary (1865–68). He was among the most noted scholars of the Greek language and literature.

Kendrick was an ordained Baptist minister, but he never held a pastorate. He was the author of *Introduction to the Greek Language* (1841), *A Child's Book in Greek* (1847), *Greek Ollendorf* (1851), *Echoes* (1855), *The Life and Letters of Mrs. Emily C. Judson* (1860), *Principles of Greek Grammar* (1868), *Greek Exercises* (1869), *Our Poetical Favorites* (1871), *The Moral Conflict of Humanity* (1894), and *Martin B. Anderson* (with Florence K. Cooper, 1895). He translated and revised Hermann Olshausen's *Commentary on the New Testament* in six volumes.

Kendrick was a member of the committee to revise the New Testament (1872–80) and was president of the American Philological Association (1872–73). He was the recipient of two honorary degrees.

REFERENCES:*AC; DAB; NCAB* (12:245); *WWW* (H).   *Norman J. Bauer*

KENT, Raymond Asa. B. July 21, 1883, Plymouth, Iowa, to Thomas Oliver and Ellen C. (Stephens) Kent. M. December 23, 1911, to Frances Stanton Morey. Ch. three. D. February 26, 1943, on a train en route from Washington, D.C., to Louisville, Kentucky.

Raymond Asa Kent was graduated with the A.B. degree (1903) from Cornell College in Mount Vernon, Iowa. He studied at Drew Theological Seminary in Madison, New Jersey (1902–04 and 1907–08), and at Columbia University, where he received the A.M. (1910) and Ph.D. (1917) degrees.

In Minnesota, he served as principal of graded schools in Fountain (1904–05), superintendent of schools in Mabel (1905–07) and Lanesboro (1908–09), instructor in mathematics at the state normal school (later, Winona State College) at Winona (1909–11), superintendent of schools in Winona (1911–13), secretary of the State Education Commission in St. Paul (1913–14), and principal of the University High School and assistant professor of education at the University of Minnesota (1914–16). He was superintendent of schools in Lawrence, Kansas, and professor of education at the University of Kansas (1916–20); superintendent of schools in Duluth, Minnesota (1920–21); and dean of the University of Kansas school of education and director of summer sessions (1921–23). Kent was dean of the college of liberal arts and professor of education at Northwestern University in Evanston, Illinois (1923–29).

From 1929 until his death in 1943 he was president of the University of Louisville (Kentucky). In 1932 the school of music was opened, and the university added its well-known Little Theatre Company. He added a division of adult education (1935) and a graduate division of social administration (1936). The Raymond A. Kent School of Social Work is named in his honor.

His published works include *Bobbs-Merrill Arithmetics* (three volumes,

1927) and *Foreign Language Equipment of 2325 Doctors of Philosophy* (with George H. Betts,*q.v.,* 1929). He edited *Higher Education in America* (1930) and George H. Betts's *Foundations of Character and Personality* (1937).

Kent was a member of the Federal Committee on Emergency Aid in Education (1934), was on several committees of the American Council on Education, and was president of the Kentucky Association of Colleges and Universities (1933–34) and the Association of Urban Universities (1933–34). He was on the executive committee of the American Printing House for the Blind in Louisville (1937) and a member of the board of consultants for the National Youth Administration (1937). He was a member of the Kentucky State Textbook Commission (1936–43) and chairman of the committee on college standards of the Kentucky Association of Colleges and Secondary Schools. He was the recipient of three honorary degrees.

REFERENCES: *LE* (II); *NCAB* (32:436); *WWAE* (XI); *WWW* (II); *NYT,* February 27, 1943, p. 13. *Lawrence S. Master*

KENT, Roland Grubb. B. February 24, 1877, Wilmington, Delaware, to Lindley C. and Anna (Grubb) Kent. M. July 12, 1904, to Gertrude Freeman Hall. Ch. none. D. June 27, 1952, Bryn Mawr, Pennsylvania.

Roland Grubb Kent acquired his early education in the Friends' School of Wilmington, Delaware. He attended Swarthmore (Pennsylvania) College, from which he received the A.B. (1895), B.L. (1896), and A.M. (1898) degrees. He received the Ph.D. degree (1903) from the University of Pennsylvania.

Kent began his professional career as a secondary school teacher at Lower Marion High School in Ardmore, Pennsylvania. In 1899 he went to Europe where he studied classical languages, literature, and archaeology at the American School of Classics in Athens, Greece, and at the universities of Berlin and Munich in Germany. After returning to the United States he became a Harrison Fellow in the classics and subsequently Harrison Research Fellow at the University of Pennsylvania. He was appointed to the faculty of the University of Pennsylvania in 1904 as an instructor of Greek and Latin. He remained there until retirement as professor emeritus of Indo-European linguistics in 1947.

Kent developed an international reputation as an educator, philologist, scholar, and author. He taught Greek, Latin, Sanskrit, and comparative philology. He was a contributor to French, English, German, and American periodicals on technical and semipopular topics. He also authored or edited many books, including *Folk Tales of India* (1916), *Language and Philology* (1923), *The Cipher of Roger Bacon* (1928), *The Sounds of Latin* (1932), and *Old Persian Grammar* (1950). He was the translator and editor of *Varro de Lingua Latina* (two volumes, 1938).

He was a fellow of the American Association for the Advancement of

Science, a charter member of the American Association of University Professors, founder of the Linguistic Society of America (secretary-treasurer, 1925–40, and president, 1941), and a member of the Oriental Society (president, 1934–35), the Philological Society of London (vice-president), and many other American and foreign organizations. The French government presented him the award de l'instruction publique (1926) and made him a chevalier in the Legion of Honor (1934). He received an honorary degree from the University of Pennsylvania.

REFERENCES: *EB; LE* (III); *NCAB* (47:496); *WWW* (III); *NYT,* June 28, 1952, p. 20; *School and Society* 76 (July 5, 1952): 14; *Wilson Library Bulletin* 27 (September 1952): 28.   *Samuel A. Farmerie*

KEPPEL, Frederick Paul. B. July 2, 1875, Staten Island, New York, to Frederick and Frances Matilda (Vickery) Keppel. M. January 31, 1906, to Helen Tracy Brown. Ch. five, including Francis Keppel, United States Commissioner of Education. D. September 8, 1943, New York, New York.

Frederick Paul Keppel was educated in public schools and entered Columbia University in 1894, graduating with the A.B. degree in 1898.

He was an editor with the publishing house of Harper & Brothers (1898–1900). He returned to Columbia University as assistant secretary in 1900 and was secretary by 1902. In 1910, when Keppel became dean of Columbia College at the age of thirty-five, he was the youngest ever named to that office. He encouraged the adoption of policies and the hiring of faculty that supported an openness and accessibility to students.

Keppel took a leave of absence from Columbia in 1918 to become an aide to the United States secretary of war and was promoted to the post of third assistant secretary of war in charge of all nonmilitary matters concerning soldiers. At the conclusion of World War I, Keppel became vice-chairman of the American Red Cross and assumed the directorship of its foreign operations (1919–20). He was appointed the American delegate in Paris to the International Chamber of Commerce (1920–22). In 1922 he became secretary of a New York City planning body funded by the Russell Sage Foundation and in 1923 was appointed president of the Carnegie Corporation of New York.

Until 1941 Keppel presided over the formative stages of the Carnegie Foundation. His administration of the foundation was characterized by imagination, creativity, and diversification in projects undertaken. Among many areas supported by the foundation was the general education movement to which Keppel gave his personal attention in the promotion of the concept of lifelong learning. To foster activities in support of this view, Keppel encouraged the adult education movement. After an initial conference in 1924, the Carnegie Corporation supported the formation of the American Association for Adult Education in 1926.

Keppel authored a number of articles and several books, including

Columbia University (1913), *The Undergraduate and His College* (1917), *Some War Time Lessons* (1920), *Education for Adults* (1926), *The Foundation* (1930), *The Arts in America* (with Robert L. Duffus, 1933), and *Philanthropy and Learning* (1936). He set a model for the role of philanthropy in America.

He was a member of a number of societies and associations. He was the secretary of the American Association for International Conciliation (1908–18), a member of the National Gallery of Art Commission, and secretary for the Plan of New York (1922–23). He was a member of the President's Committee on War Relief Agencies (1941) and the State Department's Board of Appeals on Visa Cases. He was awarded the French Legion of Honor (1911) and a number of honorary degrees from American and foreign colleges and universities.

REFERENCES: *DAB* (supp. 3); *LE* (II); *NCAB* (E:473, 32:391); *WWW* (II); *NYT,* September 9, 1943, p. 25.   *Gary C. Ensign*

KEPPEL, Mark. B. April 11, 1867, Butte County, California, to Garret and Rebecca (Hurlburt) Keppel. M. April 15, 1893, to Mae Hubbard. Ch. one. D. June 16, 1928, Los Angeles, California.

Mark Keppel was graduated from the San Joaquin (California) Valley College with the Ph.B. degree (1892) and taught there from 1892 to 1893. He was a teacher in the Los Angeles city schools (1893–1903) and was elected superintendent of schools for Los Angeles County in 1903, continuing in that office to his death in 1928. During his administration of the county schools, the number of students rose from forty thousand to five hundred thousand, the teaching staff from twelve hundred to fourteen thousand five hundred, and the number of high schools increased from fifteen to one hundred.

Keppel was particularly influential in professional organizations, including the National Education Association and the California State Teachers Association (chairman of committees and president, 1922–28). He contributed many articles to professional journals and was the author of *Lessons in California History* (with Harr Wagner, 1922) and *History of California* (with Harr Wagner, 1929). He was awarded an honorary degree by Philomath College.

REFERENCES: *NCAB* (22:344); Roy W. Cloud, *Education in California* (Stanford, Cal.: Stanford University Press, 1952).   *John F. Ohles*

KERR, Clark. B. May 17, 1911, Stony Creek, Pennsylvania, to Samuel William and Caroline (Clark) Kerr. M. December 25, 1934, to Catherine Spaulding. Ch. three.

Clark Kerr attended Swarthmore (Pennsylvania) College where he was graduated with the B.A. degree (1932). He received the M.A. degree (1933) from Stanford (California) University and the Ph.D. degree (1939) from the University of California. His specialty was labor economics. Kerr was a traveling fellow of the American Friends Service Committee (1935–36) and a teaching fellow at the University of California (1937–38).

Kerr taught at Antioch College in Yellow Springs, Ohio (1936–37), Stanford University (1939–40), and the University of Washington at Seattle (1940–45). While at Seattle, he developed skills as an arbitrator and for a time was the busiest arbitrator on the West Coast. He moved to head the Industrial Relations Institute at the University of California at Berkeley in 1945 where his involvement in faculty government led quickly to his appointment as the first chancellor of the university in 1952 and the eighth president of the University of California system in 1958.

Under his leadership the University of California became one of the outstanding universities in the world. Its graduate program was called by the American Council of Education "the best balanced" United States graduate school. The student body enrollment doubled, and the budget tripled in size. In 1967, under Governor Ronald Reagan's administration, Kerr was fired by the University of California Board of Regents for his handling of student unrest.

Upon leaving the presidency of the University of California, Kerr was appointed chairman of the Carnegie Commission for the Study of Higher Education in 1967. The commission issued a number of reports calling for an overhaul of the higher education system in the United States.

Kerr was the author of the controversial *The Uses of the University* (1963), *Migration of the Seattle Labor Market Area* (1942), *Unions, Management and the Public* (with E. W. Bakke, 1948), *Unions and Union Leaders of Their Own Choosing* (1957), *Industrialism and Industrial Man* (with others, 1960), *Labor and Management in Industrial Society* (1964), and *Marshall, Marx and Modern Times* (1969), as well as many scholarly articles.

Kerr was first vice-chairman of the American Council on Education (1953–54) and a member of the board of directors of the Center for Advanced Study in the Behavioral Sciences of the Ford Foundation (1953–61). He was a public member of the Wage Stabilization Board (1950–51), on the advisory panel of Social Science Research of the National Science Foundation (1953–57), and a trustee of the Rockefeller Foundation. He belonged to many professional associations and was the recipient of several honorary degrees.

REFERENCES: *CA* (45–48); *CB* (April 1961); *LE* (IV); *WW* (XXXVIII); *WWAE* (XIII); Mary H. Hall, "Clark Kerr," *Psychology Today* (October 1967): 25–31; "Master Planner," *Time* 76 (October 17, 1960): 58–69; "Failure of a Peacemaker," *Time* 89 (January 27, 1967): 60; "The Wounded Are Many," *Newsweek* 69 (January 30, 1967): 87–88.

Dennis Rittenmeyer

KERR, William Jasper. B. November 17, 1863, Richmond, Utah, to Robert Marion and Nancy Jane (Rawlins) Kerr. M. July 8, 1885, to Leonora Hamilton. Ch. six. D. April 15, 1947, Portland, Oregon.

William Jasper Kerr attended the University of Utah, where he received the B.S. degree (1885). He studied at Cornell University in Ithaca, New York (1890–91 and summers, 1891–93).

Kerr was superintendent of Smithfield (Utah) public schools (1885–87). He taught science (1887–88) and mathematics (1888–90 and 1891–92) at Brigham Young College (later, University) in Provo, Utah, and was professor of mathematics and astronomy at the University of Utah (1892–94). Kerr served as president of Brigham Young College (1894–1900), Utah State Agricultural College (later, State University) in Logan (1900–07), and Oregon State Agricultural College (later, State University) in Corvallis (1907–34). An able university administrator, Kerr led Oregon State to a period of expansion in which academic divisions were organized into schools in 1908, and he established schools of forestry and mining (1913), pharmacy (1917), and vocational education (1918). The school of basic arts and sciences was organized in 1922 and the school of health and physical education in 1929; nine branch agricultural experiment stations were also established. The size of the student body, faculty, and physical plant grew enormously.

In 1932 Kerr was appointed chancellor of higher education in Oregon, presiding over a state government department established in 1929 to reorganize and unify the University of Oregon, Oregon State College, the University of Oregon Medical School, and three state normal schools. He retired in 1935 and served as chairman of the board of directors of the Northwestern Portland Cement Company.

Kerr was active in professional organizations, including the National Education Association (vice-president, 1909–10) and the Land Grant College Association (first vice-president, 1909–10 and president, 1910–11); he was chairman of the Oregon committee of the National Student Forum. He was a delegate to the Utah constitutional convention in 1887 and 1895. He was the recipient of two honorary degrees.

REFERENCES: *LE* (III); *NCAB* (E:133); *WWW* (II); *Oregonian,* April 16, 1947, p. 1. *John F. Ohles*

KEYES, Charles Henry. B. September 6, 1858, Banfield, Wisconsin, to Henry and Joan (Murphy) Keyes. M. April 12, 1881, to Nellie Elmira Brown. Ch. six. D. January 16, 1925, New York, New York.

Charles Henry Keyes attended rural schools and a local academy. He was graduated from St. John's College in Annapolis, Maryland (1878), studied law (1878–80), and was admitted to the bar in 1880. He studied pedagogy and philosophy at the University of California in Berkeley (1896–97), Clark University in Worcester, Massachusetts (1897–99), and Columbia University (1910–11), where he received a doctor's diploma in education and the Ph.D. degree (1911).

Keyes was principal of the River Falls (Wisconsin) High School (1880–82), professor of the Fourth State Normal School (later, University of Wisconsin—River Falls) in River Falls (1882–84), and superintendent of the Janesville (Wisconsin) public schools (1884–89). He also conducted teachers' institutes during the summers from 1882 to 1889. He was superintendent of schools at Riverside, California (1889–91).

In 1891 Keyes was selected president of Throop Polytechnic Institute (later, California Institute of Technology), where he reorganized the institution. In 1896 he left Throop to engage in advanced study at the University of California, Clark University (where he also served as headmaster of Holyoke High School), and Columbia University. He served as supervisor of South District schools of Hartford, Connecticut (1899–1910). The first president of Skidmore School of Arts (later, Skidmore College) in Saratoga Springs, New York, from 1910 to his death in 1925, he moved the institution from a school of fine and applied arts to one of degree-granting status.

The author of many articles in professional journals, Keyes was active in professional organizations. He was treasurer (1901–02) of the National Educational Association and president of its manual training department (1896 and 1899–1900). He was president of the Southern California Teachers' Association (1893–96), the American Institute of Instruction (1903–06), and the National Council of Education (1911–13).

REFERENCES: *NCAB* (20:386); *NYT,* January 17, 1925, p. 15; *WWW* (I).   *John F. Ohles*

KIDDLE, Henry. B. January 15, 1824, Bath, England, to n.a. M. no. D. September 25, 1891, New York, New York.

Henry Kiddle emigrated to New York City from England with his parents at nine years of age. He studied under private tutors and at a normal school. At the age of thirteen he was a monitor teacher in a school operated by the Public School Society of the City of New York. The society established schools in the wards of the city, and Kiddle was appointed the first principal of a ward school in 1843. He studied law in the office of Samuel J. Tilden and was admitted to the bar in 1848.

In 1856 Kiddle was appointed assistant superintendent of the New York public schools and also was principal of the Saturday Normal School. He was superintendent of the public schools (1870–79). He resigned this position in 1879, following publication of a book that contained his beliefs about spiritualism.

After his resignation, Kiddle engaged in writing and revising many educational and other works and lecturing on spiritualism. He published in pamphlet form various addresses on education, modern spiritualism, and religious topics. He edited several revisions of Goold Brown's *(q.v.) Eng-*

lish Grammar. He wrote *A Manual of Astronomy* (1852), *New Elementary Astronomy* (1868), *A Short Course in Astronomy* (1871), *How to Teach* (1874), *Spiritual Communications* (1879), *The Dictionary of Education* (1881), and *A Text-Book on Physics* (1883). He was editor of *The Year-Book of Education* (1878, 1879), and *The Cyclopedia of Education* (with Alexander J. Schem, 1877).

During the last year of his life he continued his literary work while suffering from almost total blindness. Kiddle received an honorary degree from Union College in 1854 and was made an officer of the French Academy by the University of France (1878).

REFERENCES: *AC; NCAB* (2:512); *TC; WWW* (H).   *Michael R. Cioffi*

KIEHLE, David Litchard. B. February 7, 1837, Danville, New York, to James and Elizabeth (Litchard) Kiehle. M. July 16 or 25, 1864. Ch. three. D. April 7, 1918, Portland, Oregon.

David Litchard Kiehle was graduated from the State Normal School (later, State University of New York at Albany) at Albany, New York (1856), and received the A.B. (1861) and A.M. (1864) degrees from Hamilton College in Clinton, New York. He was graduated from Union Theological Seminary in New York City and was ordained to the Presbyterian ministry (1865).

Kiehle taught in rural schools in New York from the age of sixteen and in Canandaigua (New York) Academy (1856–59), a Monroe (Michigan) graded school (1862), and the Polytechnic and Collegiate Institute of Brooklyn, New York. He organized and served as pastor to the Presbyterian church in Preston, Minnesota (1865–75 and 1902–10). He was superintendent of Fillmore County (Minnesota) schools (1869–75) and served on the Minnesota state normal school board (1870–75). Kiehle served as principal of the St. Cloud (Minnesota) Normal School (later, St. Cloud State College) from 1875 to 1881.

Appointed by Governor John S. Pillsbury as Minnesota's state superintendent of public instruction in 1881, Kiehle was reappointed six times by succeeding governors, serving to 1893, when he resigned to accept the chair of pedagogy at the University of Minnesota.

As state superintendent, Kiehle organized the high school system under a law originally drawn by William Watts Folwell *(q.v.)* and organized a system of teachers' institutes and summer schools. As ex officio member of the board of regents of the University of Minnesota (1881–93), he was instrumental in the establishment of the school of agriculture at the university.

Kiehle served as professor of pedagogy to 1902 and established the department of education in 1893. Previously staffed by one professor, the department developed rapidly and was made the college of education in 1905. He conducted the university summer school two years and organized a teachers' school of home study and correspondence that was later affiliated with the University of Minnesota. Kiehle served the Preston church to 1910, when he retired and moved to Portland, Oregon.

He was the author of *Education in Minnesota* (1903) and was active in professional associations, serving as president of the department of superintendence of the National Educational Association in 1895. He received an honorary degree from Hamilton College in 1887.

REFERENCES: *TC; WWW* (IV); James Douglas Carr, "The University of Minnesota and the Men Who Have Made It," *Minneapolis Star,* August 29, 1927; Jeremiah Clemens, *The United States Biographical Dictionary,* Minnesota Volume (New York: American Biographical Publishing Co., 1879), pp. 247–48; *The Gopher* (Minneapolis: University of Minnesota, 1895), p. 243; *St. Paul* (Minnesota) *Pioneer Press,* April 9, 1918, p. 1.

John F. Ohles

KILPATRICK, William Heard. B. November 20, 1871, White Plains, Georgia, to James Hines and Edna Perrin (Heard) Kilpatrick. M. December 27, 1898, to Marie Beman Guyton. M. November 26, 1908, to Margaret Marigault Pinckney. M. May 8, 1940, to Marion Y. Ostrander. Ch. two. D. February 13, 1965, New York, New York.

William Heard Kilpatrick received the A.B. (1891) and A.M. (1892) degrees from Mercer University in Macon, Georgia, and the Ph.D. degree (1912) from Columbia University.

Kilpatrick was a teacher and principal in Georgia public schools (1892–97). He returned to Mercer University as professor of mathematics (1897–1906) and served as acting president (1903–05). He went to Teachers College, Columbia University, in 1909 and taught there until his retirement in 1938.

Kilpatrick originated the project method of education, a rejection of traditional subjects as the curriculum pattern. He wrote many books, including *The Dutch Schools of New Netherland and Colonial New York* (1912), *The Montessori System Examined* (1914), *Froebel's Kindergarten Principles Critically Examined* (1916), *Source Book in the Philosophy of Education* (1923), *Foundations of Method* (1925), *Education for a Changing Civilization* (1926), *How We Learn* (with Mason Olcott, 1928), *Our Educational Task* (1930), *Education and the Social Crisis* (1932), *Remaking the Curriculum* (1936), *Group Education for a Democracy* (1940), *Selfhood and Civilization* (1941), and *Philosophy of Education* (1951), and he was editor and coauthor of *The Educational Frontier* (1933), *The Teacher and Society* (1937), *Intercultural Attitudes in the Making* (1947) and a founder of *The Social Frontier.*

He helped found Bennington (Vermont) College, a leading progressive college, and was president of its board of trustees (1931–38). He was a fellow of the American Association for the Advancement of Science and the American Physical Education Association, a member of the board of the Progressive Education Association, and president of the New York Urban League (1941–51). He was chairman of the Bureau of Intercultural Education (1946–54) and the board of American Youth for World Youth (1946–51). He received the Brandeis Award (1953) and four honorary degrees.

REFERENCES: *LE* (III); *NYT*, February 14, 1965, p. 92; *WWAE* (XIV); *WWW* (IV); "Memorial Issue on William Heard Kilpatrick," *Educational Theory* 16 (January 1966); *New Catholic Encyclopedia* (New York: McGraw-Hill, 1967); Leslie R. Perry, ed., *Bertrand Russell, A. S. Neill, Homer Lane, W. H. Kilpatrick: Four Progressive Educators* (New York: Macmillan, 1967); Samuel Tenenbaum, *William Heard Kilpatrick* (New York: Harper, 1951). *Joseph C. Bronars, Jr.*

KIMBALL, Dexter Simpson. B. October 21, 1865, New River, New Brunswick, Canada, to William Henry and Jane (Paterson) Kimball. M. May 10, 1898, to Clara Evelyn Woolner. Ch. three. D. November 1, 1952, Ithaca, New York.

Dexter Simpson Kimball was educated at local schools and Stanford (California) University, from which he received the A.B. (1896) and M.E. (1913) degrees. He worked in industry until September 1898, when he was appointed assistant professor of machine design at Sibley College of Engineering, Cornell University, Ithaca, New York. From 1901 to 1904 he again worked in industry and then returned to Sibley, where he was professor of machine construction (1904–05), machine design and construction (1905–15), and industrial engineering (1915–36). From 1920 until his retirement with emeritus rank in 1936, he also served as dean of the college of engineering at Cornell and twice as acting president of the university.

Kimball's greatest contribution to education was in the field of engineering economics; in 1904 he gave the first lectures on that subject delivered at an American university. He introduced a senior option in industrial engineering, one of the first efforts to combine technical engineering with engineering and industrial economics in an efficient manner.

His book *Principles of Industrial Organization* (1913) was recognized as authoritative. His other writings include *Elements of Machine Design* (with John H. Barr, 1909), *Industrial Education* (1911), *Elementary Cost Finding* (1914), *Plant Management* (1916), *Industrial Economics* (1929), and *I Remember* (1953). He edited *The Book of Popular Science* (1945) and contributed more than 225 articles to technical journals.

Kimball was a member of a number of education and business boards and commissions. He was appointed chairman of the Second Pan-American Conference on Standardization in 1927. During World War I he directed the school for training army mechanics at Cornell and during World War II served as chairman of the priority committee on machine tools and equipment of the Office of Production Management and chief of the priority section of the machine tools division of the War Production Board.

Kimball was a member of many professional associations, including the American Society of Mechanical Engineers (president, 1921–22), the American Engineering Council (president, 1926–28), the Federated American Engineering Societies (vice-president, 1920–22), and the Society for the Promotion of Engineering Education (vice-president, 1922–23, president, 1929). He was honored with the Lamme Medal of the Society for the Promotion of Engineering Education (1933), the Worcester Reed Warner Medal of the American Society of Mechanical Engineers (1933), the H. L. Gandt Gold Medal of the American Management Association and the American Society of Mechanical Engineers (1943), and the Fred Winslow Taylor Key of the Society for the Advancement of Management (1948). He received honorary degrees from several universities.

REFERENCES: *LE* (III); *NCAB* (D:343, 42:23); *WWAE* (XIII); *WWW* (III); *NYT*, November 2, 1952, p. 88.   *J. Franklin Hunt*

KING, Charles Francis. B. January 30, 1843, Wilton, New Hampshire, to Sanford and Susan (Burnham) King. M. August 1, 1867, to Elizabeth Boardman. M. July 6, 1897, to Gratia Cobb. Ch. six. D. May 22, 1924, Boston, Massachusetts.

Charles Francis King became interested in teaching early in life, accepting his first assignment in 1864. He pursued his formal education, receiving the A.B. degree (1867) from Dartmouth College in Hanover, New Hampshire.

After graduation he accepted a position in a New Bedford (Massachusetts) grammar school, moving in 1870 to a larger, more prestigious school in Gloucester, Massachusetts, and then was elected submaster of the Lewis School in Boston. His growing reputation as scholar and leader led to his appointment in 1884 as principal of Dearborn Grammar School in Roxbury, Massachusetts, where he served until his retirement in 1913.

King was a leader in educational organization and methodology. He earned a reputation as a reformer in the methods of teaching geography. He organized the National School of Methods in Saratoga Springs, New York, in 1885. It was the first methods-of-teaching summer school and was quickly recognized and imitated. His later Glens Falls Summer School and the National School of Methods at Glens Falls, New York, were extensions and refinements of the Saratoga school.

King was the author of many books on geography, of which the most notable were *Methods and Aids in Geography* (1888), *Picturesque Geographical Readers for Home and School* (1889), *This Continent of Ours* (1890), *The Land We Live In* (three volumes, 1892), *Rocky Mountains*

(1894), *Northern Europe* (1896), *Round About Rambles* (1898), *Elementary Geography* (1903), *Advanced Geography* (1906), *New England Supplement of Geography* (1909), and *Suggested Lessons in Geography* (1909).

REFERENCES: *NCAB* (20:225); *WWW* (I).   *Kenneth L. Burrett*

KING, William Fletcher. B. December 20, 1830, near Zanesville, Ohio, to James Johnson and Mariam (Coffman) King. M. August 3, 1865, to Margaret McKell. Ch. none. D. October 23, 1921, Mount Vernon, Iowa.

William Fletcher King attended Zanesville (Ohio) High School and was graduated from Ohio Wesleyan University in Delaware, Ohio, with the A.B. (1857) and A.M. (1860) degrees.

King was principal of Unionville (Tennessee) Academy (1853–54) and a tutor at Ohio Wesleyan University (1857–62). He joined the faculty of Cornell College in Mount Vernon, Iowa, in 1862 and continued there as professor of Latin and Greek (1862–63), acting president (1863–65), and president (1865–1908). During his long tenure as president, the college increased in the size of its physical plant, more than doubled the number of students, and increased the faculty from six to thirty instructors. Women were admitted on equal terms with men when the college was first opened, and it was said to be the first college in the country where a woman was hired at the same rank and salary as male instructors.

The author of many papers and addresses, King was active in professional organizations, including the Iowa State Teachers' Association (president), the educational council of the National Educational Association (1886–1900), and the National Council of Education. King was appointed by President Benjamin Harrison to membership on the national commission of the World's Columbian Exposition in 1890. He was active in the Methodist Episcopal church as an Iowa delegate to General Conferences in 1888, 1896, 1904, and 1908 and was a member of the church board of education. He attended the Ecumenical Conference in London, England, in 1901. He was the recipient of honorary degrees from Illinois Wesleyan and Ohio Wesleyan universities and the State University of Iowa.

REFERENCES: *NCAB* (7:79); *NYT,* October 25, 1921, p. 17; *TC; WWW* (I).   *John F. Ohles*

KINGSBURY, John. B. May 26, 1801, South Coventry, Connecticut, to John and Dorothy (Leavens) Kingsbury. M. August 19, 1834, to Mary Mackie Burgess. Ch. nine. D. December 21, 1874, Providence, Rhode Island.

As innovator in girls' secondary education when most affluent females went abroad for schooling, John Kingsbury demonstrated that such education was effective and desirable. Kingsbury alternated winter school attendance with working on the family farm until the age of fifteen; he taught winters in a local school and farmed in the summers. In 1822 he entered Brown University in Providence, Rhode Island, and continued teaching to pay his college expenses. He was graduated from Brown in 1826.

Kingsbury became associate principal of Providence High School, a private boys' school (1826–28). He established the Young Ladies' High School as a department in the same school in 1828; it later became a separate and independent school without patronage, or public or other financial support.

Kingsbury introduced in his school several features that were innovative for girls' schools. He added Latin, algebra, geometry, and "higher English" to the curriculum. He changed the annual vacation from July Fourth, Thanksgiving Day, and four Fridays in the year to an eight-week recess. He built a new school with papered walls, carpeted floors, and comfortable and attractive furniture. Kingsbury eliminated periodic oral examinations and insisted on high standards of attendance and conduct. His efforts were successful, and he maintained his announced maximum enrollment of forty-three students despite a more than doubling of the quarterly tuition. He conducted the school for thirty years until his retirement in 1858.

Kingsbury was a promoter of public education in Rhode Island. He was a founder of the American Institute of Instruction (state president, 1845–56, and national president, 1855–57). He was Rhode Island commissioner of public education (1857–58) and was active in civic and academic affairs. He served on the board of Brown University and received an honorary degree from Brown (1856). After his retirement in 1858 he was president of the Washington Insurance Company of Providence until his death.

REFERENCES: *DAB; NCAB* (9:417); *WWW* (H); Henry Barnard *(q.v.)*, *American Educational Biography: Memoirs of Teachers, Educators, and Promotors and Benefactors of Education, Science and Literature* (Syracuse, N.Y.: C. W. Bardeen, 1859); Henry Barnard, "John Kingsbury, and the Young Ladies' High School, Providence, R.I.," *American Journal of Education* 5 (June 1858): 9–34.   *D. Richard Bowles*

KINGSLEY, Clarence Darwin. B. July 12, 1874, Syracuse, New York, to Edwin A. and Emma Howell (Garnsey) Kingsley. M. June 26, 1914, to H. Elizabeth Seelman. Ch. none. D. December 31, 1926, Cincinnati, Ohio.

Clarence Darwin Kingsley studied at Syracuse (New York) High School (1889–92). He received the B.S. degree from Colgate University in Hamilton, New York (1897), and the M.A. degree from Teachers College, Columbia University (1904).

Kingsley taught mathematics at Colgate (1898–1902) and was a teacher at Manual Training High School in Brooklyn, New York (1904–12). In 1912 he accepted a position as state supervisor of high schools in Massachusetts under David Snedden *(q.v.)*.

Kingsley was active in professional organizations. He gained prominence as the chairman of the National Education Association (NEA) Committee of Nine on the Articulation of High School and College (1910), and he also chaired the NEA Commission on the Reorganization of Secondary Education (1912–23). In the latter chairmanship, he edited fifteen separate reports, including *Cardinal Principles of Secondary Education* (1918). During this period, Kingsley served on five of the nine standing committees of the New York High School Teachers Association.

In 1923 Kingsley resigned from the position of Massachusetts high school supervisor and chairman of the Commission on the Reorganization of Secondary Education to engage in a private practice as a consultant in school construction. A brilliant career was cut short when he died at the age of fifty-two.

REFERENCES: *NCAB* (20:93); *NYT,* January 1, 1927, p. 13; *WWW* (I); Walter H. Drost, "Clarence Kingsley—'The New York Years,' " *History of Education Quarterly* 6 (Fall 1966): 18–34.   *Michael R. Cioffi*

KINGSLEY, James Luce. B. August 28, 1778, Scotland, Connecticut, to Jonathan and Zillah (Cary) Kingsley. M. September 23, 1811, to Lydia Coit. Ch. four. D. August 31, 1852, New Haven, Connecticut.

James L. Kingsley was the son of a prominent citizen, who was fond of reading and the founder of a local society for the circulation of books. Young Kingsley showed an unusual interest in the study of books and preferred books to play activities as a child. He attended Yale College and was graduated with the B.A. degree (1799). After his graduation he spent a year at Wethersfield, Connecticut, as principal of a select school.

He was appointed a tutor at Yale, teaching a group of students in all the required studies to the end of the junior year (1801–12). Competent in Hebrew, Greek, and Latin, he was appointed the first professor of languages at Yale in 1805. He also served as librarian from 1805 to 1824 and traveled to Europe at his own expense to purchase books for the college library. He was credited with introducing the *Iliad, Graeca Minora,* and *Majora* as textbooks in classical studies.

Kingsley was recognized for a breadth of intellectual interest and accuracy of scholarship. His scholarly interest first centered on mathematics, particularly astronomical calculations. He was also interested in the study of science and was an authority on the history of Connecticut and New England.

He was a frequent contributor, sometimes anonymously, to popular and scholarly journals. He was the author of a biography of Ezra Stiles *(q.v.)* in *The Library of American Biography,* compiled by Jared Sparks *(q.v.)*.

REFERENCES: *AC; DAB; NCAB* (10:121); *TC; WWW* (H).

Edward B. Goellner

KINLEY, David. B. August 2, 1861, Dundee, Scotland, to David and Jessie Preston (Shepherd) Kinley. M. June 22, 1897, to Kate Ruth Neal. Ch. two. D. December 3, 1944, Urbana, Illinois.

David Kinley's family came to the United States from Scotland in 1872. He attended preparatory school and Yale College, where he received the A.B. degree (1884). He studied at Johns Hopkins University in Baltimore, Maryland (1890–92), and at the University of Wisconsin, where he received the Ph.D. degree (1893).

He became principal of a high school in North Andover, Massachusetts (1884–90). While studying at Johns Hopkins he was an instructor in the Woman's College in Baltimore. He joined the faculty of the University of Illinois as an assistant professor in economics (1893–94) and was the dean of the college of literature and arts (1894–1906). He was dean of the graduate school (1906–14) and vice-president (1914–19), acting president (1919–20), and president (1920–30). During his tenure, the student body, faculty, budget, and physical plant increased greatly. The college of law was made a graduate school in 1928.

Kinley's books include *Independent Treasury of the United States* (1893), *Trusts: A Monograph* (1899), *Money: A Study of the Theory of the Medium of Exchange* (1904), *Government Control of Economic Life and Other Essays* (1936), and reports prepared for the National Monetary Commission. He was editor of *Preliminary Studies of the War* (twenty-five volumes, 1913–22) published by the Carnegie Foundation.

Kinley was a member of the Illinois commissions on industrial insurance (1906–07), taxes (1910), and state salaries (1919). He was president of the National Association of State Universities (1923–24) and a member of many other professional and scholarly organizations. He served as a delegate to the Fourth International Conference on American States at Buenos Aires, Argentina (1910), and as minister plenipotentiary and envoy on a special mission to Chile on the centennial of Chilean independence (1910). He was a delegate to the Second Pan-American Scientific Congress at Washington, D.C. (1915), and was a member of the permanent group committee of the Pan-American Conference assigned to Chile. He was awarded the Newman Medal in 1930 and received four honorary degrees.

REFERENCES: *NCAB* (E:109); *TC; WWW* (II); *NYT*, December 4, 1944, p. 23.   *Joan Duff Kise*

KIRBY-SMITH, Edmund. B. May 16, 1824, St. Augustine, Florida, to Joseph Lee and Frances (Kirby) Smith. M. September 24, 1861, to Cassie Selden. Ch. eleven. D. March 28, 1893, Sewanee, Tennessee.

Edmund Kirby-Smith chose to enter a military career early in his life, graduating from the United States Military Academy at West Point (1845).

Kirby-Smith fought in the Mexican War and returned to the academy as an assistant professor of mathematics (1849–52). Rejoining his regiment (1852) he served for three years as commander of a military escort for the Mexican Boundary Commission and as botanist for the expedition. The report of his observations was published by the Smithsonian Institution. When Florida seceded from the Union, he entered the Confederate army. He commanded the trans-Mississippi forces, was promoted to lieutenant general, and surrendered the last military force of the Confederacy in 1865.

After the war, Kirby-Smith served as president of an insurance company and a telegraph company (1866–68). He opened a military academy at New Castle, Kentucky (1868). The school was destroyed by fire in 1870, and he and Bushrod R. Johnson reopened the literary department of the University of Nashville and the Montgomery Bell Academy as the university preparatory school. A collegiate department was organized with six professors offering a variety of subjects; Kirby-Smith taught mental philosophy, political economy, natural history and geology, and agriculture and served as president.

The school did not prosper and received assistance from the Peabody Fund. The institution became the State Normal School (1875) and later was Peabody Normal School and then the George Peabody College for Teachers. Kirby-Smith became professor of mathematics at the University of the South in Sewanee, Tennessee (1875). He joined Bishop Charles Todd Quintard in deemphasizing the military department and in establishing a liberal arts curriculum with a close association with the Protestant Episcopal church. He continued at the University of the South to his death in 1893. He had been the last surviving general of either side from the Civil War.

REFERENCES: *DAB; EB; WWW* (H); George R. Fairbanks, *History of the University of the South* (Jacksonville, Fla.: The H. & W. B. Drew Co., 1905); Moultrie Guerry, *Men Who Made Sewanee: Biographical Sketches* (Sewanee, Tenn.: University Press, University of the South, 1932); Joseph Howard Parks, *General Edmund Kirby Smith, C.S.A.* (Baton Rouge: Louisiana State University Press, 1954).   *Leon W. Brownlee*

KIRK, John Robert. B. January 23, 1851, Bureau County, Illinois, to George W. and Mary K. Kirk. M. July 1875 to Rebecca I. Burns. Ch. six. D. November 7, 1937, Kirksville, Missouri.

John R. Kirk was graduated from the State Normal School (later, Northeast Missouri State College) in Kirksville, Missouri, in 1878 and studied in the extension divisions of the universities of Kansas and Missouri (1889–92), the summer of 1899 at the University of Missouri, and in Paris, France, and London, England, in the summer of 1902. He received the B.S. in

Educ. degree (1926) from the then-named State Teachers College in Kirksville, Missouri, and the A.M. degree (1930) from George Peabody College for Teachers in Nashville, Tennessee.

Kirk began teaching in Missouri rural schools in 1871. Admitted to the bar in 1884, he practiced law in Iowa and Missouri (1884–88) and was city attorney for Bethany, Missouri (1883). He was superintendent of Harrison County schools and Bethany public schools, an elementary school principal and high school teacher in Kansas City, Missouri (1888–92), and superintendent of schools in Westport, Missouri, and Kansas City (1892–94). From 1895 to 1899, Kirk was state superintendent of public schools and inspector of schools for the University of Missouri in 1899. Appointed president of the State Normal School in Kirksville, Missouri (1899–1919), he continued as head of the institution (1919–25) after it became the State Teachers College. He continued as professor of psychology and the philosophy of education after he retired as president. While at Kirksville, he designed a demonstration rural school (1907) and a demonstration farm cottage (1915).

Active in professional associations, Kirk was a life member of the National Education Association and served the association as president of the normal school (1905–07 and 1919–20) and the library (1907–08) departments, member of the Committee of Eleven on rural education (1911–13) and on the committee on character education (1918–24), state director (1895–99, 1907–09, and 1911–12), and a member of the council from 1905. Kirk was president of the Missouri State Teachers' Association (1897), the North Central Council of Normal School Presidents (1906–07), and the American Association of Teachers Colleges (1920–21). He received honorary degrees from Missouri Wesleyan (1907) and Park (1907) colleges.

REFERENCES: *LE* (III); *NYT,* November 8, 1937, p. 23; *WWW* (I).

John F. Ohles

KIRK, Samuel Alexander. B. September 1, 1904, Rugby, North Dakota, to Richard B. and Nellie (Boussard) Kirk. M. June 25, 1933, to Winifred Eloise Day. Ch. two.

Samuel Alexander Kirk received the Ph.B. (1929) and M.S. (1931) degrees from the University of Chicago. He was a resident teacher at the Oaks School for mentally retarded children from 1929 to 1931 and developed a lifelong interest in the psycho-social-educational problems of the retarded. For the next five years he served as a resident psychologist at Wayne County Training School in Northville, Michigan, while he earned the Ph.D. degree (1935) in psychology from the University of Michigan.

Kirk moved to Milwaukee (Wisconsin) State Teachers College (later, University of Wisconsin-Milwaukee) where he served as director of the division of education of exceptional children until he accepted a commission in the United States Army in 1942 to become chief of educational rehabilitation at Walter Reed Hospital in Washington, D.C. Following his release from active duty in 1946, he returned to Milwaukee (1946–47) and then joined the faculty of the University of Illinois, where he remained for twenty-one years (1947–67). Following retirement in 1967 he taught at the University of Arizona at Tucson. At Illinois he established the Institute for Research on Exceptional Children, drawing faculty from various departments and colleges, to encourage multidisciplinary research efforts toward solving problems of exceptional children. Kirk made a substantial contribution to the research literature in mental retardation and the field of learning disabilities.

He wrote *Remedial Reading Drills* (with T. G. Hegge, 1940), *Educating the Retarded Child* (with G. Orville Johnson, 1951), *Teaching Reading to Slow-Learning Children* (1951), *You and Your Retarded Child* (1955), *Educating Exceptional Children* (1962), *The Diagnosis and Remediation of Psycholinguistic Disabilities* (1963), and *The Organization and Implementation of Programs for Handicapped Children and Youth* (1964). He developed the Illinois Test of Psycholinguistic Abilities (ITPA) with James C. McCarthy. It provided a means of differential diagnosis of language-related academic problems in schoolchildren that could lead to a specific remedial program of instruction.

Kirk was consultant to the United States high commissioner for Germany (1950–51), chairman of the 1950 yearbook of the National Society for the Study of Education, vice-president of the American Association on Mental Deficiency (1951), member of the mission to the Soviet Union for President John Kennedy's Panel on Mental Retardation (1962), chairman of the Advisory Board to the Association for Children with Learning Disabilities (1964), and chairman of the National Advisory Committee on Handicapped Children to the United States Office of Education (1966–69). He received the first international award for professional services in mental retardation from the Joseph P. Kennedy, Jr., Foundation, and he was named honorary vice-president of the British Association for Special Education. He received the J. E. Wallace Wallin Award from the council for Exceptional Children in 1966. Lesley College awarded him an honorary degree (1969).

REFERENCES: *CA* (45–48); *LE* (IV); *WW* (XXXVIII).

Robert A. Henderson

KIRKLAND, James Hampton. B. September 9, 1859, Spartanburg, South Carolina, to William Clarke and Virginia Lawson (Galluchat) Kirkland. M. November 21, 1895, to Mary Henderson. Ch. one. D. August 5, 1939, Magnetawan, Ontario, Canada.

James H. Kirkland was graduated from Wofford College in Spartanburg,

South Carolina, with the A.B. (1877) and M.A. (1878) degrees. He studied in Germany from 1883 to 1886 and received the Ph.D. degree (1885) from the University of Leipzig. He stayed in Germany to study at the University of Berlin.

Kirkland taught the classics, Greek, Latin, and German at Wofford College (1878–83) and joined the faculty of Vanderbilt University in Nashville, Tennessee (1886), becoming its second chancellor in 1893. He remained to his retirement in 1937.

During his tenure as chancellor, Kirkland was able to establish full control under his administration of all departments of the university. He improved the faculty, teaching standards, and physical facilities. In 1914 the general conference of the Methodist Episcopal Church, South, severed all relations with Vanderbilt after an unfavorable court decision on the control of the university. Kirkland was highly successful in raising money from Andrew Carnegie and the Carnegie and Rockefeller foundations and from general subscriptions, which was used to establish and maintain a medical school and teaching hospital and endow the college of liberal arts and sciences.

Kirkland edited *Horace: Satires and Epistles* (1901) and wrote articles and monographs. He founded the Southern Association of Colleges and Secondary Schools in 1895, serving as its secretary (1895–1909) and president (1911–12 and 1920–21). He was a leader in the organization of the Southern University Conference in 1935 and was a trustee (1917–37) and chairman of the board (1922–23) of the Carnegie Foundation for the Advancement of Teaching. Honorary degrees were conferred on him by eight universities.

REFERENCES: *DAB* (supp. 2); *LE* (I); *NCAB* (29:491); *WWW* (I); *NYT*, August 6, 1939, p. 37.   *J. Stewart Allen*

KIRKLAND, John Thornton. B. August 17, 1770, Little Falls, New York, to Samuel and Jerusha (Bingham) Kirkland. M. September 1, 1827, to Elizabeth Cabot. Ch. none. D. April 26, 1840, Boston, Massachusetts.

John Thornton Kirkland studied at Phillips Academy, Andover, Massachusetts, where he boarded in the home of Judge Samuel Phillips. In 1786 he entered Harvard University, where his study was interrupted by brief military service with General Benjamin Lincoln in the suppression of Shays's rebellion in January 1787. He was graduated with the B.A. degree in 1789. He studied theology and was ordained in 1794.

Kirkland taught at Phillips Academy (1789–90). He was a tutor in logic and metaphysics at Harvard (1792–94) and served as pastor of New South Church in Boston (1794–1810).

Kirkland became president of Harvard in 1810. Under his administration schools of law, medicine, and divinity were established. The undergraduate arts and science college became a national rather than a regional institution. The lecture method was introduced and the curriculum widened.

After 1823 conditions began to change as Harvard lost its yearly grant from the state of Massachusetts. Attacks on the liberality of the college appeared in the press. Enrollment declined, and a deficit was reported. Kirkland suffered a mild stroke in 1827. He tendered his resignation in March 1828 after critical remarks were made about his administration by Nathaniel Bowditch, a member of the Harvard Corporation. His administration was called the Augustan Age of Harvard.

He was the author of *Eulogy on Washington* (1799), *Biography of Fisher Ames* (1809), and *Discourse on the Death of Hon. George Cabot* (1823). He was a member of the Massachusetts Historical Society and vice-president of the American Academy of Arts and Sciences. He was a founder of the *Monthly Anthology* and the Boston Athenaeum. He received four honorary degrees.

REFERENCES: *AC; DAB; NCAB* (6:417); *TC; WWW* (H); Claude M. Fuess, *Men of Andover* (New Haven: Yale University Press, 1928); Samuel E. Morison, *Three Centuries of Harvard* (Cambridge: Harvard University Press, 1936). *Richard G. Durnin*

KIRKPATRICK, Edwin Asbury. B. September 29, 1862, Peoria, Iowa, to Francis Asbury and Catharine (Bradbury) Kirkpatrick. M. August 29, 1895, to Florence May Clifford. M. May 2, 1927, to Annis Louise Kindman. Ch. four. D. January 4, 1937, DeLand, Florida.

The son of a pioneer Iowa preacher, Edwin Asbury Kirkpatrick attended rural schools and received the B.S. (1887) and M.Ph. (1889) degrees from Iowa State College (later, University). He pursued further study at Clark and Harvard universities. He was an assistant in mathematics and English at Iowa State (1887–89), an instructor in psychology at Winona (Minnesota) State Normal School (later, Winona State College) from 1892 to 1897, and director of the child study department of Fitchburg (Massachusetts) State Teachers' College (later, Fitchburg State College) from 1898 to 1928.

A pioneer in child psychology, Kirkpatrick published *Inductive Psychology* (1895), *Fundamentals of Child Study* (1903, revised 1929), *Genetic Psychology* (1909), *Studies in Development and Learning* (1909), *The Individual in the Making* (1911), *The Use of Money* (1915), *Fundamentals of Sociology* (1916), *Studies in Psychology* (1918), *Imagination and Its Place in Education* (1919), *Conduct Problems* (1930 and 1931), *The Sciences of Man in the Making* (1932), and *Mental Hygiene for Effective Living* (1934).

He was a fellow of the American Association for the Advancement of

Science and a member of other professional and civic associations. At the Louisiana Purchase Exposition (1904) Kirkpatrick received a gold medal for a child study exhibit.

REFERENCES: *LE* (I); *NCAB* (37:245); *WWW* (I); *NYT,* January 5, 1937, p. 23.   *M. Jane Dowd*

KITSON, Harry Dexter. B. August 11, 1886, Mishawaka, Indiana, to Clarence and Nellie (Hamblin) Kitson. M. June 14, 1922, to Angeline S. Freeman. Ch. one. D. September 25, 1959, Mishawaka, Indiana.

Harry Dexter Kitson, pioneer psychologist in occupational choice and adjustment, received the A.B. degree (1909) from Hiram (Ohio) College, the A.M. degree (1913) from the University of Minnesota, and the Ph.D. degree (1915) from the University of Chicago.

While a student, Kitson was an assistant in psychology at Minnesota (1912–13) and a fellow at Chicago (1913–14). He served with the American Expeditionary Force in World War I. He joined the faculty of the University of Indiana (1919–25) where he lectured in psychology over an Indianapolis radio station and was the first to broadcast a series about psychological tests. He moved to New York City, where he was professor of education at Teachers College, Columbia University. He introduced vocational guidance programs for the Columbia Broadcasting System's American School of the Air and for several years supervised the preparation of dramatic sketches for the program. He organized an instructional program to train people in vocational guidance and student personnel work.

Kitson was the author of *How to Use Your Mind* (1916), *The Scientific Study of the College Student* (1917), *Manual for the Study of the Psychology of Advertising and Selling* (1920), *The Mind of the Buyer* (1921), *The Psychology of Vocational Adjustment* (1925), *How to Find the Right Vocation* (1929), *I Find My Vocation* (1931), *Vocations for Girls* (with Mary R. Lingenfelter, 1939), *Vocations for Boys* (with Mary R. Lingenfelter, 1942), and *Helping People Find Jobs* (with Juna B. Newton, 1950). He edited the Kitson Career Series and was editor of *Occupations: The Vocational Guidance Magazine* for fourteen years.

Kitson was active in the National Vocation Guidance Association and the American Council of Guidance and Personnel Associations.

REFERENCES: *CB* (April 1951); *LE* (III); *NCAB* (52:152); *WWW* (III); *NYT,* September 26, 1959, p. 23.   *Vernon Lee Sheeley*

KLAPPER, Paul. B. July 17, 1885, Jassy, Rumania, to Louis and Rachel (Halpern) Klapper. M. June 25, 1911, to Flora Eydenberg. Ch. one. D. March 25, 1952, New York, New York.

Paul Klapper emigrated from Rumania to New York in 1892. Taking advantage of the free City College, he mastered English and earned the

A.B. degree in 1904. He taught in the public schools and pursued graduate work at New York University, where he earned the M.A. (1907) and Ph.D. (1909) degrees.

He was a tutor in the new department of education at City College in 1907, director of the summer sessions (1917–22), and first dean of the school of education. Klapper resigned in 1937 to become the first president of Queens College in New York City, where he served to his retirement in 1948. He selected the first faculty and the first class of four hundred students. Queens College developed into one of the major public institutions in New York. For a short time he acted as dean of teacher education for the four city colleges. He was a visiting professor of education at the University of Chicago (1949–50).

Klapper was a versatile author; his publications include *Principles of Educational Practice* (1912), *Teaching Children to Read* (1914), *The Teaching of English: Teaching the Art and the Science of Language* (1915), *The Teaching of Arithmetic* (1916), *College Teaching: Studies in Methods of Teaching in the College* (editor, 1920), *Modern English* (with Abraham London, 1923), *The Teaching of History* (1926), *Contemporary Education: Its Principles and Practices* (1929), *Childhood Readers* (with others, 1932), and *Reading for Appreciation* (with William E. Grady, 1936). He was the editor of the Appleton Series in Methods of Teaching.

Klapper served on the New York Council of the State Commission Against Discrimination and the New York State Commission on the Need for a State University. He was a fellow of the American Association for the Advancement of Science and belonged to professional organizations. He received honorary degrees from Yeshiva University, Queens College, and Columbia University. He was a trustee of the State University of New York and Brandeis University.

REFERENCES: *LE* (III); *WWAE* (XIII); *WWW* (III); *NYT,* March 26, 1952, p. 29; S. Willis Rudy, *The College of the City of New York: A History, 1847–1947* (New York: City College Press, 1949).

Richard G. Durnin

KNAPP, Seaman Asahel. B. December 16, 1833, Schroon Lake, New York, to Bradford and Rhoda (Seaman) Knapp. M. August 16, 1856, to Maria Elizabeth Hotchkiss. Ch. five. D. April 1, 1911, Washington, D.C.

Seaman Asahel Knapp was graduated from Union College in Schenectady, New York, with the A.B. degree (1856) and became a teacher of Greek and Latin and associate manager at Fort Edward Collegiate Institute in New York until 1863. He was associate manager of Ripley (Vermont) Female College (1863–65). An incapacitating leg injury forced him to give up teaching, and he went to Iowa, where he was a farmer, Methodist clergyman, and the superintendent of the Iowa State College for the Blind (1869–75). Knapp was professor of agriculture (1879–86) and president

(1883–84) of Iowa State Agricultural College (later, State University).

In 1882 Knapp petitioned Congress to provide federal aid to establish experimental stations at agricultural colleges; the Hatch Act carried out the proposal. He began the farmers' cooperative demonstration movement and was the major promoter for the continued education of farmers through the use of agricultural extension programs that sent county agents to farms to demonstrate improved techniques to farmers. He began home demonstration programs and organized clubs that were forerunners of the 4-H Club. He was an associate of agricultural leaders, including James Wilson (later secretary of agriculture) and Henry Wallace.

Knapp went to Lake Charles, Louisiana, where he introduced a colonization plan for better methods for the production of rice. As a special agent of the United States Department of Agriculture, he was sent to Japan, China, and the Philippines (1898–99) to investigate rice varieties and production and to Puerto Rico in 1900. When the boll weevil became a threat to the cotton crops in Texas, Knapp introduced improved methods of farming and, despite the boll weevil, increased production. He worked in the South for the United States Department of Agriculture from 1902 to 1910.

Knapp introduced scientific farming and stock breeding and was the cofounder and first president of the Iowa Improved Stock Breeders' Association. He founded the *Western Stock Journal and Farmer* at Cedar Rapids, Iowa. He was the author of many farmers' bulletins issued by the United States Department of Agriculture and numerous articles. Seaman A. Knapp School of Country Life, associated with George Peabody College for Teachers in Nashville, Tennessee, was named for him. His radical educational innovations played an important role in the improvement of agricultural techniques throughout the world. He received several honorary degrees.

REFERENCES: *DAB; EB; NCAB* (28:401); *NYT,* April 3, 1911, p. 9; *TC; WWW* (I).   *S. E. Russell*

KNIGHT, Edgar Wallace. B. April 9, 1886, Northampton County, North Carolina, to John Washington and Margaret (Davis) Knight. M. June 28, 1916, to Annie Mozelle Turner. Ch. two. D. August 7, 1953, Chapel Hill, North Carolina.

Edgar Wallace Knight was educated in the schools of Durham, North Carolina, and earned the B.A. (1909) and M.A. (1911) degrees from Trinity College (later, Duke University) and the Ph.D. degree (1913) from Columbia University.

Knight taught at Trinity College (1913–18), spent one year as superintendent of schools in Wake County (Raleigh), North Carolina (1917–18), and was assistant educational director for the War Department in the southeast states (1918–19). He was professor of education at the University of North Carolina in 1919 and Kenan Professor of Educational

History from 1934 until his death in 1953. He directed summer sessions at North Carolina (1934–37) and was a visiting professor at other institutions.

Knight was an advisory editor of *School Management* (1938–53) and an associate editor of *High School Journal* (1919–53). An authority on educational history, he published many studies of education and culture in North Carolina, the South, the United States, and in foreign countries. His books discussed the making and training of citizens, state government, studies of the national and state constitutions, principles of teaching, educational administration, and commentaries on education. They include *The Influence of Reconstruction on Education in the South* (1913), *Some Principles of Teaching* (1915), *Public School Education in North Carolina* (1916), *Reconstruction and Education in Virginia* (1916), *Reconstruction and Education in South Carolina* (1920), *Public Education in the South* (1921), *Training for Citizenship* (with J. G. deR. Hamilton, 1922), *Our Constitutions—National and State* (with A. J. Clowd, 1924), *Our State Government* (1926), *Among the Danes* (1927), *Notes on Education* (1927), *Education in the United States* (1929), *Reports on European Education* (1930), *Culture in the South* (with others, 1934), *What College Presidents Say* (1940), *Twenty Centuries of Education* (1941), *Progress and Educational Perspective* (1942), *The Graduate School: Research and Publication* (with Agatha B. Adams, 1947), *A Documentary History of Education in the South before 1860* (volumes one to five, 1949–53), *Readings in American Educational History* (with Clifton L. Hall, 1951), *Fifty Years of American Education* (1952), and *Readings in Educational Administration* (1953).

As an educational consultant, Knight studied the rural and folk schools of Scandinavia (1925–26) and educational conditions in China (1930–31), and he helped prepare a public school system for Iraq (1931–32). He served on the Florida Educational Survey and directed a study of higher education for blacks in Alabama. He was a consultant to Hampton Institute in Virginia and a trustee of North Carolina College at Durham.

During World War II, he was regional director of testing in the Southeast for army and navy college training programs. He was a member of the Chapel Hill (North Carolina) school board (1922–52), the North Carolina High School Textbook Commission (1923), and the North Carolina Library Commission (1927–39). He was president of the North Carolina Education Association (1926–27) and the National Society of College Teachers of Education (1935–36) and a member of many other professional, fraternal, and civic organizations. He received an honorary degree from Duke University.

REFERENCES: *LE* (III); *NCAB* (40:77); *WWW* (III); *NYT*, August 8, 1953, p. 11; C. L. Hall, "Edgar Wallace Knight: 1886–1953," *School and Society* 79 (March 6, 1954): 67–69; *Teachers College Record* 55 (February 1954): 271–77. *Robert R. Sherman*

KNOX, Samuel. B. 1756, County Armagh, Ireland, to Samuel Knox and his wife (n.a.). M. to Grace Gilmour. M. to Zeraiah McCleery. Ch. four. D. August 31, 1832, Frederick, Maryland.

Samuel Knox may have immigrated to Maryland from Ireland as a schoolmaster in 1786, but he was in Scotland from 1789 to 1792, where he received the M.A. degree at the University of Glasgow. He prepared for the ministry, was licensed by the presbytery of Belfast, Ireland, and in 1795 received a pastorate at Bladensburg, Maryland. He served as a supply minister at Frederick, Maryland (1797–1803), and Soldiers' Delight, Maryland (1804–09).

Knox taught in Bladensburg (1788–89). He was the first principal of Frederick (Maryland) Academy (1797–1803) and principal of a private academy in Baltimore, Maryland, that participated in a merger in 1808 into Baltimore College. Knox was principal of the college (1808–20). He returned to Frederick Academy (1823–27) as principal and taught at a private school and had a book shop.

He engaged in preaching, pedagogy, and politics as he sought to make education a matter for serious public policy. In 1797 he won a prize offered by the American Philosophical Society for a proposal that would establish the best system of liberal education adapted to the "genius of the Government of the United States." This tract was published in *Essays on Education* (1799). He argued for a national school system that would provide social solidarity for a mixed and decentralized society, equality of opportunity, and responsibility for democratic citizenship. He was more specific in his proposals for implementation than many of his contemporaries; he indicated how "teaching halls" should be "pewed" and how all levels should be graded in terms of purposes and practices.

Knox feared religious bias in education and wrote *A Vindication of the Religion of Mr. Jefferson and a Statement of His Services in the Cause of Religious Liberty* (1800). His interest in state certification of teachers and a program for teacher welfare and security was stated in *Essay on the Means of Improving Public Instruction* (1803). Thomas Jefferson *(q.v.)* offered him the first professorship of languages and belles lettres at the University of Virginia, but he declined. The author of many pamphlets, his last *Essay on Education* (1826) was an attempt to apply monitorial methods of instruction to higher education.

REFERENCES: *DAB; NCAB* (24:155); *WWW* (H); Ashley Foster, "The Educational Views and Influence of Samuel Knox" (Ph.D. diss., New York University, 1952); Allen Oscar Hansen, *Liberalism and American Education in the Eighteenth Century* (New York: Macmillan Co., 1926), pp. 110–39; Adolphe E. Meyer *(q.v.)*, *Grandmasters of Educational Thought* (New York: McGraw-Hill, 1975), pp. 191–99.   *Jack K. Campbell*

KOOS, Leonard Vincent. B. March 9, 1881, Chicago, Illinois, to Adam and Mary (Zimmerman) Koos. M. June 14, 1916, to Hazel Byrd Smith. Ch. three.

Leonard Vincent Koos was an early leader in the junior high school and the community and junior college movements. He was educated at Oberlin (Ohio) College, receiving the B.A. degree (1907). He was awarded the M.A. (1915) and Ph.D. (1916) degrees from the University of Chicago.

He taught in rural and elementary schools in Illinois (1900–04) and was superintendent of schools in Illinois and Minnesota (1907–14). He was professor of secondary education at the universities of Washington (1916–19) and Minnesota (1919–29). He was on the faculty of the University of Chicago from 1929 to his retirement in 1946.

Koos was the author or coauthor of many books and articles, and he was editor of special reports and yearbooks on education. His books include *Administration of Secondary School Units* (1917), *The Junior High School* (1920), *The Junior College* (two volumes, 1924), *The High School Principal* (1924), *The Junior College Movement* (1925), *The American Secondary School* (1926), *Secondary Education in California* (1929), *Private and Public Secondary Education* (1931), *Guidance in Secondary Schools* (with Grayson N. Kefauver, *q.v.,* 1933), *Integrating High School and College: The Six-Four-Four Plan at Work* (1946), and *Junior High School Trends* (1955). He was editor of *The School Review* (1930–49) and *Junior College Journal* (1946–49). Koos authored several of the United States Bureau of Education bulletins and served as editor of the *Yearbook on Extra-Curricular Activities* of the National Society for the Study of Education (1926).

Active in educational organizations, Koos was a member of the National Education Association (chairman of the board), the National Society for the Study of Education (chairman of the board, 1926–31), and the Minnesota Education Association (president, 1928–29). He was a fellow of the American Association for the Advancement of Science (vice-president, 1930). He was an associate director of the National Survey of Secondary Education, as well as a member of local and state surveys. He was a consultant to states and communities to aid their development of junior colleges.

REFERENCES: *LE* (III); *WW* (XXII); *WWAE* (II); *WWW* (VI); Michael Brick, *Forum and Focus for the Junior College Movement* (New York: Bureau of Publications, Teachers College, Columbia University, 1964); George Conger and Raymond Schultz, "Leonard V. Koos: Patriarch of the Junior College," *The Junior College Journal* 40 (March 1970); 26–31; "Emphasis: Leonard Vincent Koos," *The Junior College Journal* 34 (March 1964): 1.   *S. V. Martorana*

KRAUS, John. B. February 2, 1815, Nassau, Germany, to Jacob and Margaretha (Herbst) Kraus. M. 1873 to Maria Boelté *(q.v.),* Ch. none. D. March 4, 1896, New York, New York.

John Kraus, an effective disciple of Friedrich Froebel in promoting the kindergarten movement in the United States, finished military training at the age of twenty and entered the teachers' seminary at Idstein, Germany. He met Froebel in 1844, became a convert to his beliefs, and began to spread his ideas in Germany.

In 1851 he emigrated to the United States where he established schools based on Froebel's principles and was one of the first writers on the kindergarten. He was engaged by Henry Barnard *(q.v.)* in 1867 at the United States Bureau of Education as an expert on the kindergarten. Kraus provided information to Congress on the kindergarten and contributed to a favorable National Teachers' Association committee report in 1872. He resigned from the bureau in 1873.

In 1873 Kraus married Maria Boelté (who became known as Kraus-Boelté, *q.v.*), another kindergarten expert from Germany. They established the Kraus Seminary for Kindergartners in New York City, which they operated to his death. They wrote *The Kindergarten Guide* (two volumes, 1877), which discussed Froebelian principles and practices. Kraus continued to write and give seminars for teachers; his last lecture was given a few days before his death in 1896. He was credited with playing a major role in establishing the Froebelian kindergarten in America.

REFERENCES: *DAB; NCAB* (13:466); *WWW* (H).*Joseph C. Bronars, Jr.*

KRAUS, Mother M. Seraphine (Mary Katharine). B. June 12, 1854, Mary-town, Wisconsin, to Peter and Anna Mary (Burg) Kraus. M. no. D. January 3, 1954, La Crosse, Wisconsin.

Mary Katharine Kraus received her early education at Marytown and Mount Calvary, Wisconsin. After graduating from St. Mary Institute in Milwaukee, Wisconsin, she taught school in Kenosha County. Kraus entered St. Rose Convent, La Crosse, Wisconsin, in 1872 and received the name Sister M. Seraphine. She was a teacher in elementary and secondary schools and continued her studies, earning the class A diploma from Boston Home Study College in 1891.

From 1888 to 1910 and again from 1919 to 1921, Sister Seraphine directed the education of the Franciscan Sisters of Perpetual Adoration. In 1890 she organized St. Rose Normal School, the forerunner of Viterbo College in La Crosse, Wisconsin. As first assistant to the superior general of the Franciscan Sisters of Perpetual Adoration (1910–28) and mother general (1928–40), Mother Seraphine encouraged the development of the St. Rose normal training program into a collegiate curriculum. With Sister Rose Kreibich, the dean, she became cofounder of Viterbo College, later a coeducational, four-year Christian liberal arts institution.

She was the author of *Manual and Graded Course of Study for Use in the Schools Conducted by the Franciscan Sisters of Perpetual Adoration* (1902) and two textbooks, *Forty Lessons in English* (1909) and *Sixty Lessons in English* (1915), and she collaborated in several widely used textbooks for Catholic schools: *Geography Briefly Told* (1904), *American History Briefly Told* (four volumes, 1909–12), *A History of the United States for Catholic Schools* (1914), and *Our Country in Story* (1917). The history texts were the first in the United States to emphasize Catholic backgrounds and foundations in American history and point out contributions of Catholicism in building the United States.

Mother Seraphine became an authority on ornithology and an expert taxidermist. Viterbo College Museum is indebted to her for its original collections of biological and geological specimens, rare coins, historical relics, and cultural artifacts.

REFERENCES: *American Catholic Who's Who* (Grosse Pointe, Mich.: Walter Romig, 1934), vol. 11; *La Crosse* (Wisconsin) *Tribune*, January 5, 1954, p. 1; Sister M. Francile Meyer, "Valiant Woman," *Touchstone* 3 (Spring 1951): 5–7. *M. Theodine Sebold*

KRAUS-BOELTÉ, Maria. B. November 8, 1836, Mecklenburg-Schwerin, Germany, to Johann Ludwig Ernest and Louise (Ehlers) Boelté. M. 1873 to John Kraus *(q.v.)*. Ch. one. D. November 1, 1918, Atlantic City, New Jersey.

Maria Kraus-Boelté was educated by tutors as a young girl and studied in Hamburg, Germany, with Louise Lewis Froebel, widow of Friedrich Froebel, and Wichard Langé, and she attended the local teachers' seminary.

Kraus-Boelté went to London, England, and taught with Bertha Rongé, a pupil of Froebel's, in her kindergarten and school for poor youngsters. She taught German and Swedish gymnastics and kindergarten methods to a group of twenty or thirty youngsters and adults using the study of plants and animals, garden work, and excursions to study nature. She exhibited work by her pupils at the London International Exhibition in 1862. In 1867 she resigned from her work to study at South Kensington (London) School of Art and later in 1867 went to Hamburg to teach in the Froebel Union and to observe in the city's kindergartens. After a period of ill health, she organized a successful tuition kindergarten school at Lübeck and worked out and conducted a program for preparing kindergarten teachers. She went to England in 1870 and to the United States in 1872, where she began her kindergarten work in New York City under the sponsorship of Henrietta B. Haines, whom she had met in England.

Married in 1873 to John Kraus, an expert on the kindergarten with the United States Bureau of Education, she and her husband organized the Normal Training Kindergarten and model schools in New York City in October 1873. The institution gained national recognition. Kraus died in

1896, and Kraus-Boelté continued to manage the school until she retired in 1913, when she engaged in lecturing and writing.

Kraus-Boelté wrote several monographs and articles and was author, with John Kraus, of *The Kindergarten Guide* (two volumes, 1877). She was active in national and international kindergarten associations, serving as president of the kindergarten department of the National Educational Association (1899–1900).

REFERENCES: *DAB; NAW; NCAB* (13:467); *NYT,* November 3, 1918, p. 21; *WWW* (IV).   *Wilma J. Pyle*

KREY, August Charles. B. June 29, 1887, Germany, to August F. and Albertina (Konig) Krey. M. August 20, 1913, to Laura Lettie Smith. Ch. two. D. July 28, 1961, Houston, Texas.

August Charles Krey received the A.B. (1907), A.M. (1908), and Ph.D. (1914) degrees from the University of Wisconsin.

Between 1908 and 1913 he taught at a Milwaukee (Wisconsin) high school, the University of Texas, and the University of Illinois. In 1913 he went to the University of Minnesota as a history professor; he became chairman of the department of history in 1944, a position he held until his retirement in 1955.

Krey's publications include *A City That Art Built* (1936), *The Meaning of the Humanities* (1938), *A Regional Program for the Social Studies* (1938), and *History and the Social Webb* (1955). He edited *First Crusade* (1921) and coauthored several studies, including *Founding of Western Civilization* (with G. C. Sellery, 1929), *Tests and Measurements in the Social Sciences* (with Truman L. Kelley, *q.v.*, 1934), and *William of Tyre: History of the Crusades,* an annotated translation (two volumes, with Emily Waters Babcock, 1944). In addition, Krey made numerous contributions to historical and educational publications. He was a member of the editorial boards of *Social Studies, Journal of Higher Education,* and *American Historical Review.*

During his years at Minnesota, Krey was active in a number of scholarly and educational organizations. He was a member of the Committee on Social Studies in the Schools (chairman, 1929–34), the executive council of the Minnesota Historical Society (vice-president from 1947), the Committee on Public Information, Washington, D.C. (1917), and the American Historical Association (chairman of the committee on history in the schools, 1925–29, and a member of the council from 1946). Krey was president of the National Council for Social Studies and the Folk Arts Foundation (from 1946).

REFERENCES: *WWW* (IV); *NYT,* July 31, 1961, p. 19.

Winifred Wandersee Bolin

KRÜSI, Johann Heinrich Hermann. B. June 24, 1817, Yverdon, Switzerland, to Hermann and Catherine (Egger) Krüsi. M. November 26, 1856, to Caroline W. Dunham. Ch. three. D. January 28, 1903, Alameda, California.

Hermann Krüsi, Jr., son of Johann Heinrich Pestalozzi's first associate, was a major figure in the Oswego movement and contributed to popularizing object teaching in the United States. He was a student in the Cantonal School at Trogen, which his father directed, and at the normal school at Gais, Switzerland, to which his father had been assigned.

Krüsi began teaching in 1841 at his father's normal school in Gais and moved to the Home and Colonial Society School in London, England, in 1847. He moved to the United States in 1853, where he taught in a normal school in Lancaster, Massachusetts (1853–55), lectured in teachers' institutes in New England, engaged in private instruction, and taught at a normal school in Trenton, New Jersey (1857–59). Through a former London colleague, Krüsi was invited in 1862 to teach at Edward Sheldon's *(q.v.)* Oswego Normal School (later, State University of New York College at Oswego) in New York. During his twenty-five years at Oswego, Krüsi taught drawing, geometry, philosophy, and modern languages.

At Oswego, Krüsi influenced many students who later worked in normal schools throughout America. He was firmly committed to Pestalozzi's objective method and emphasized understanding and reason against the excessive formalism he saw in American object teaching. Objects were occasions for developing intellectual skills rather than ends in themselves. He was opposed to the widespread practice of conducting verbatim reenactments of model object lessons. Krüsi's greatest contribution was his inventive drawing course based on Pestalozzian principles, which followed a synthetic-to-analytic sequence and stressed combining known elements to construct complex forms.

Krüsi was the author of *A Progressive Course of Inventive Drawing on the Principles of Pestalozzi* (1852), *Krüsi's Drawing* (1873), and other books of Krüsi's Graded Drawing Course. He also wrote *Pestalozzi: His Life, Work and Influence* (1875). *Recollections of My Life* (edited by Elizabeth Sheldon Alling, 1907), a biographical sketch and collection of his writings, was published posthumously. He received an honorary degree from Yale College in 1871.

REFERENCES: *DAB;* Hermann Krüsi, *Recollections of My Life,* ed. Elizabeth Sheldon Alling (New York: Grafton Press, 1907); Dorothy Rogers, *Oswego: Fountainhead of Teacher Education* (New York: Appleton-Century-Crofts, 1961). *Walter Doyle*

L

LADD, Azel Parkhurst. B. September 5, 1811, Haverhill, New Hampshire, to William and Abigail (Spaulding) Ladd. M. 1845 to Louise M. Burril. Ch. four. D. July 27, 1854, Shullsburg, Wisconsin.

Azel Parkhurst Ladd was both a physician and an educator. He taught school in Massachusetts at Westport and New Bedford and studied medicine before migrating to Shullsburg, Wisconsin, about 1845, where he practiced medicine. He was active in the organization of the Mining Region Teachers' Association in 1848. He was a founder of the State Historical Society of Wisconsin (1849) and served as vice-president (1852).

He was elected the second Wisconsin state superintendent of schools in 1851. Through regional meetings, he organized the Wisconsin Teachers' Association and called the first state teachers' convention for Wisconsin at Madison in 1853. Well known for his school reform program, he frequently advocated better management of school funds and a profitable disposition of the state's school lands. He worked for higher teachers' salaries, better schoolroom equipment, and more adequate school libraries.

Ladd felt that town high schools were not suited to the sparse population of Wisconsin. He thus proposed establishing county high schools. He conducted institutes in several parts of Wisconsin and assisted in organizing county teachers' associations. He and other authorities who recognized that a large proportion of Wisconsin teachers had an inadequate training were confident that five-day institutes could produce a well-trained and competent teaching corps. Instruction in the content of the common school curriculum was one of the functions of the institute.

He was not renominated for reelection in the fall of 1853 and returned to Shullsburg where he resumed practice of medicine. A cholera epidemic broke out in 1854, and while treating patients, Ladd contracted the disease and died.

REFERENCES: *Daily State Journal* (Madison, Wisconsin), July 29, 1854; *Dictionary of Wisconsin Biography* (Madison: State Historical Society of Wisconsin, 1960), p. 217; Lloyd P. Jorgenson, *The Founding of Public Education in Wisconsin* (Madison: State Historical Society of Wisconsin, 1956); *Wisconsin Patriot* (Madison), August 5, 1854.

Lawrence S. Master

LADD, George Trumbull. B. January 19, 1842, Painesville, Ohio, to Silas T. and Elizabeth (Williams) Ladd. M. December 8, 1869, to Cornelia A. Tallman. M. December 9, 1895, to Frances Stevens. Ch. four. D. August 8, 1921, New Haven, Connecticut.

George Trumbull Ladd attended a private school in Painesville, Ohio, and was graduated with the A.B. (1864) and A.M. (1867) degrees from Western Reserve College in Hudson, Ohio (later, Case Western Reserve University in Cleveland). He completed his studies at Andover (Massachusetts) Theological Seminary in 1869.

Ladd was a minister at Edinburgh, Ohio (1869–71), and at the Spring Street Congregational Church in Milwaukee, Wisconsin (1871–79). He taught philosophy at Bowdoin College in Brunswick, Maine (1879–81) and was professor of philosophy at Yale University from 1881 to 1905. Ladd taught metaphysics and other philosophy courses at Yale and lectured at colleges and universities in the United States, India, and Japan.

Ladd sought to reconcile the contributions of idealists and realists in philosophy and psychology. He contributed comprehensive and encyclopedic presentations of a new experimental science of physiological psychology. He cooperated with William James *(q.v.)*, J. McKeen Cattell *(q.v.)*, J. Mark Baldwin *(q.v.)*, G. Stanley Hall *(q.v.)*, and Joseph Jastrow and founded with them the American Psychological Association in 1892.

Among Ladd's writings were *Principles of Church Polity* (1882), *Doctrine of Sacred Scripture* (two volumes, 1884), *The Elements of Physiological Psychology* (1887), *Psychology, Descriptive and Explanatory* (1894), *Philosophy of Mind* (1894), *A Theory of Reality* (1899), *Essays on the Higher Education* (1899), *Philosophy of Conduct* (1902), *The Philosophy of Religion* (1905), *Knowledge, Life and Reality* (1909), *What Can I Know?* (1914), *What Ought I to Do?* (1915), *What Should I Believe?* (1915), *What May I Hope?* (1915), and *The Secret of Personality* (1918).

Ladd was active in professional associations and was president of the American Psychological Association (1893). He was decorated by the emperor of Japan and received the Imperial Educational Society of Japan's gold medal. He was an adviser to Prince Ito in Korea. He was a delegate to the World's Congress of Psychologists in Paris, France (1900). He received honorary degrees from Western Reserve College and Princeton and Yale universities.

REFERENCES: *AC; DAB; NCAB* (33:561); *NYT,* August 9, 1921, p. 9; *TC; WWW* (I); *New Haven Journal-Courier,* August 9, 1921; *The Philosophical Review* 30 (November 1921): 639; *Science* 54 (September 16, 1921): 242. *Thomas Meighan*

LAIRD, Warren Powers. B. August 8, 1861, Winona, Minnesota, to Matthew James and Lydia (Powers) Laird. M. November 15, 1893, to Clara Elizabeth Tuller. Ch. two. D. February 18, 1948, Bryn Mawr, Pennsylvania.

Warren Powers Laird was educated in the Winona (Minnesota) public schools and the local state normal school. He studied a special course in architecture at Cornell University in Ithaca, New York (1885–87). He practiced and studied with architects in Minnesota, Boston, and New York

City, and spent time traveling and studying architecture in Europe between 1882 and 1890.

Laird was an instructor of architecture at Cornell (1887–88) and at the University of Pennsylvania (1890–91). He was professor of architecture at Pennsylvania (1891–1932) and was dean of the school of fine arts from its founding in 1920 to his retirement in 1932. He was a lecturer at Princeton University (1932–33). He served as a consulting architect for municipal, state, and other public and private agencies in many states and Canada.

Laird served on many public bodies, including the Pennsylvania State Art Commission (1928–36 and 1938–41), the Tri-State Regional Planning Federation of Philadelphia (director), and the Philadelphia Zoning Commission (1929). He was a fellow of the American Institute of Architects, an organizer of the Association of Collegiate Schools of Architecture (president, 1912–21), and a member of the permanent committee of the International Congress of Architects (1925–35).

He was an honorary member of associations of architects of many foreign countries and was a delegate to the third Pan-American Congress of Architects in Buenos Aires, Argentina (1927). He was a member of the advisory board of Lingnan University of Canton, China, and served as a trustee (1909–26). He received two honorary degrees from the University of Pennsylvania (1911 and 1932).

REFERENCES: *LE* (II); *WWW* (II); *NYT,* February 19, 1948, p. 23.

John F. Ohles

LANCOUR, Adlore Harold. B. June 27, 1908, Duluth, Minnesota, to Adlore Dealor and Mary Mino (Hoffer) Lancour. M. October 1, 1936, to Marie Antoinette McClellan. Ch. one.

Harold Lancour was introduced to library work while attending the University of Washington. Immediately after graduating with the A.B. degree (1931) from Washington, he was the owner-proprietor of the Windjammer Book Shop in Seattle until 1935. He earned the B.S. (1936), M.S. (1940), and Ed.D. (1947) degrees from Columbia University. He worked as a reference assistant with the New York Public Library from 1936 to 1938, when he became head of the museum library at the Cooper Union. He was named head librarian of the Cooper Union (1941–47).

As head librarian Lancour's job was to reorganize and consolidate library operations. He produced a lively and vital organization of several departmental libraries under a strong central structure. In 1947 he was appointed professor and associate director of the graduate library school at the University of Illinois, where he served until 1961.

At Illinois, Lancour achieved national and international prominence in the field of library education. He was an instructor in the Army Library Schools in Paris and Oberammergau (1950–51), director of the United States Information Service Libraries in France (1952–53), a member of the United Nations Educational, Scientific, and Cultural Organization's International Committee for Social Sciences Documentation (1953–57), and conductor of a survey of libraries in West Africa for the Carnegie Corporation (1957) and in Liberia for the Ford Foundation (1959). Lancour served as dean of the new school of librarianship at the University of Pittsburgh (1961–72). From 1973 he was director of the International Summer School of Librarianship in Wales.

Lancour's editorial assignments have included *Library Trends, University of Illinois Occasional Papers,* and the *Journal of Education for Librarianship.* His publications include *Issues in Library Education* (1949), *The School Library Supervisor* (1956), *Libraries in British West Africa* (1958), *Nebraska Libraries Face the Future* (1962), and a checklist, *American Art Auction Catalogs, 1785 to 1941* (1944), which remains a standard work in the field. From 1968 he was coeditor with Allen Kent of the *Encyclopedia of Library and Information Science,* the first attempt to provide encyclopedic coverage of the field of library science in English and projected to number eighteen volumes.

Active in professional associations, Lancour was president of the Association of American Library Schools (1954–56) and was a member of the American Library Association (chairman of the board of education for librarianship, 1954–56, and the commission on accreditation, 1956–57), and the Association of College and Reference Libraries (director, 1946–49). He was a Fulbright Scholar to England (1950–51) and was a trustee of the Bibliothèque Française de Pittsburgh and the Western College for Women.

REFERENCES: *LE* (IV); *WW* (XXXI); *WWAE* (XVI); *College and Research Libraries* 8 (October 1947): 458–59; *College and Research Libraries* 22 (November 1961): 471–72; *Library Quarterly* 31 (October 1961): 401–02.   *Gary D. Barber*

LANEY, Lucy Craft. B. April 13, 1854, Macon, Georgia, to David and Louisa Laney. M. no. D. October 23, 1933, Augusta, Georgia.

Lucy Craft Laney was graduated from Lewis High School (later Ballard Normal School) in 1869 and from Atlanta (Georgia) University (1873) as one of four members in the first class. She later took summer courses at the University of Chicago.

Laney taught in Georgia public schools of Macon, Milledgeville, Augusta, and Savannah for ten years. In 1883 she opened a school in a rented room in the basement of Christ Presbyterian Church in Augusta. On January 6, 1886, the school received a charter from the state of Georgia. In 1887 Laney traveled to Minneapolis where she successfully requested financial assistance from the general assembly of the Presbyterian church. One influential person, Mrs. Francina E. H. Haines, persuaded others to help, and the rapidly growing school was named for her.

In the early 1890s Laney established Augusta's first kindergarten and a nurses' training department. The nursing program soon evolved into the school of nursing at Augusta's University Hospital. By 1917 the Haines Normal and Industrial Institute had about nine hundred pupils and twenty-five teachers. Mary McLeod Bethune *(q.v.)*, founder of Bethune-Cookman College in Florida, began her teaching career at Haines.

Lucy Laney died in 1933. In 1949 the Haines Normal and Industrial Institute was closed and its buildings razed. The Lucy C. Laney High School, a modern structure, now stands on the site.

REFERENCES: *NAW;* Benjamin Brawley *(q.v.)*, *Negro Builders and Heroes* (Chapel Hill: University of North Carolina Press, 1937); Kelley Miller *(q.v.)* and Joseph R. Gay, *Progress and Achievements of the Colored People* (Washington, D.C.: Austin Jenkins Co., 1917).

Don C. Locke

LANGDELL, Christopher Columbus. B. May 22, 1826, New Boston, New Hampshire, to John and Lydia (Beard) Langdell. M. September 22, 1880, to Margaret Ellen Huson. Ch. none. D. July 6, 1906, Cambridge, Massachusetts.

Christopher Langdell attended the local New Boston, New Hampshire, district school before working his way through Phillips Academy in Exeter, New Hampshire. He entered Harvard University as a sophomore in 1848, but financial difficulties forced him to leave without graduating. He tutored briefly before becoming a clerk and student in the law firm of Stickney and Tuck in Exeter. In 1851 he entered Harvard Law School and was graduated in 1853. The following year the school awarded Langdell the A.M. honoris causa. While a student, he had worked as a librarian and assisted T. Parsons prepare *The Law of Contracts* (1871).

Langdell spent the next sixteen years in relative obscurity, practicing in New York City, seldom appearing in court. However, he gained a reputation in the bar for his mastery of the principles of the law. Charles Eliot *(q.v.)* invited Langdell to become Dane Professor of Law at Harvard (1870–1900). He was the school's first dean from 1871 until 1895 when failing health forced him to retire as dean.

Langdell believed that law is a science and that legal principles should be induced from a thorough study of the basic case materials; he thus evolved case-study method. Under Langdell's leadership, the law school experienced an increase in enrollment, introduced rigid scholastic requirements, extended the course to three years, expanded the curriculum, increased the size of the faculty, and improved library resources.

His publications, largely works intended for use in legal instruction, include *Selection of Cases of the Laws of Contracts* (1871), *A Selection of Cases on Sales of Personal Property* (1872), *Cases on Equity Pleading* (1875), *A Summary of Equity Pleading* (1877), *A Summary of the Law of Contracts* (1879), and *A Brief Survey of Equity Jurisdiction* (1904). He received an honorary degree from Harvard University.

REFERENCES: *AC; DAB; EB; NCAB* (6:423); *TC; WWW* (I); James Barr Ames *(q.v.)*, "Christopher Columbus Langdell," in William Draper Lewis, ed., *Great American Lawyers* (Philadelphia: The John C. Winston Co.,

1909), 7: 465–89; Joseph H. Beale, "Professor Langdell—His Later Teaching Days," *Harvard Law Review* 20 (November 1906): 9–11; Arthur E. Sutherland, *The Law at Harvard* (Cambridge, Mass.: Belknap Press of Harvard University Press, 1967), pp. 162–205; Eugene Wambaugh, "Professor Langdell—A View of His Career," *Harvard Law Review* 20 (November 1906): 1–4.   *Robert H. Truman*

LANGE, Alexis Frederick. B. April 23, 1862, Lafayette County, Missouri, to Alexander and Caroline (Schnegelslepen) Lange. M. September 8, 1891, to Caroline Crosby Penny. Ch. one. D. August 28, 1924, Berkeley, California.

Alexis Lange began his education in the local elementary and high schools in Lafayette County, Missouri. At the University of Michigan he received the B.A. and M.A. degrees in 1885. Lange spent 1886–87 as a student in Germany, first at the University of Marburg, then at the University of Berlin. After returning to the United States and the University of Michigan, he became an instructor in English and professor of German and Anglo-Saxon. He received the Ph.D. degree from the University of Michigan.

Lange joined the faculty of the University of California in 1890 as assistant professor of English and later taught English and Scandinavian philology. He was dean of the college of letters (1897–1909), dean of the graduate division (1909–10), and acting dean of the faculty (1913), a position similar to that of vice-president in many other universities. When the University of California organized the school of education in 1913, he was made director and, in 1922, dean.

Lange was one of the originators of the junior high school movement and, with David Starr Jordan (*q.v.*), originated the junior college movement. His main interest as an administrator of the school of education was in preparing high school teachers. The teacher-training program developed into one of the best in the country.

Lange and Charles De Garmo (*q.v.*) translated from the works of Johann Freidrich Herbart, *Outlines of Educational Doctrine* (1901), and edited *The Gentle Craft* by Thomas Deloney (1903). After his death in 1924, his most important papers were collected by A. H. Chamberlain as *The Lange Book: The Collected Writings of a Great Educational Philosopher* (1927). Lange helped reorganize the California Teachers Association (1908) and belonged to other professional associations.

REFERENCES: *DAB; NCAB* (25:329); *WWW* (I); *NYT*, August 30, 1924, p. 9.   *Larry Froehlich*

LANGSTON, John Mercer. B. December 14, 1829, Louisa County, Virginia, to Ralph Quarles and Lucy Langston. M. October 1854 to Caroline M. Wall. Ch. five. D. December 15, 1897, Washington, D.C.

John Mercer Langston, son of a slave owner and his slave, was a slave at birth. He was freed at six years of age by the terms of his father's will. He moved with his two older brothers to Chillicothe, Ohio, after the death of their parents in 1834. Their father had requested in his will that Langston live with his good friend, William D. Gooch, in Chillicothe. He lived with the Gooch family until they moved to Missouri, a slave state. Langston went to Cincinnati with his older brother Gideon and studied in a private school in the basement of the Baker Street Baptist Church. Returning to Chillicothe, he attended the Chillicothe Colored School until the winter of 1844.

He went to Oberlin (Ohio) College, where his brothers had studied, and took college preparatory courses for one year. The following winter (1844–45) he taught in Hicks Settlement near Chillicothe and at the Colored School he had attended. He enrolled in Oberlin in the spring of 1845, graduating with high honors in 1849. At the college he established himself as an outstanding orator.

Langston intended to study law but was refused admission to law schools and offices. He returned to Oberlin to study theology, received the M.A. degree in 1852, and completed his course work in theology in 1853. He was accepted as a law student in the office of Judge Philemon Bliss, an anti-slavery activist in Elyria, Ohio. He was admitted to the Ohio bar on September 13, 1854, and won his first case the next month. He was the first black admitted to the bar in the United States.

Langston was elected township clerk in Brownhelm, Ohio, the first black popularly elected to public office in the United States. He moved to Oberlin in 1856 and remained there until 1871. He was elected clerk of Russia Township, served as secretary to the board of education, was a school visitor (1856), and sat on the Oberlin city council (1857–60) and the board of education (1860). He recruited black troops for the Union army and made his first trip to Washington, D.C., on official business in 1863. In Oberlin, Langston took young blacks into his home to be educated.

Langston was appointed general inspector of the Bureau of Refugees, Freedmen and Abandoned Lands in the South (1867–69) and worked to establish educational facilities for blacks. He organized the law school at Howard University and served as its dean from 1869 to 1876. He was acting president of the university in 1872. He was a member of the board of health for the District of Columbia and its attorney for seven years. He was minister-resident to Haiti (1877–85) and president of Virginia Normal and Collegiate Institute (later, Virginia State College) in Petersburg (1885–88). He served one term in the United States House of Representatives from Virginia (1889–91), one of the last blacks elected to that body for many years.

Langston addressed the American Anti-Slavery Society in 1855 and was president of the National Equal Rights League in 1865. A selection of his addresses was published as *Freedom and Citizenship* (1863). He wrote an autobiography, *From the Virginia Plantation to the National Capitol* (1894).

REFERENCES: *AC; DAB; NCAB* (3:328); *TC; WWW* (H); John Mercer Langston, *From the Virginia Plantation to the National Capitol* (New York: Arno Press and the New York Times, 1969); Harry A. Ploski, Otto J. Lindenmeyer, and Ernest Kaiser, *Reference Library of Black America* (New York: Bellwether Publishing Co., 1971), vol. 5; Wilhelmena S. Robinson, *International Library of Negro Life and History: Historical Negro Biographies* (New York: Publishers Company, 1967), pp. 93–94.

Francine C. Childs

LANMAN, Charles Rockwell. B. July 8, 1850, Norwich, Connecticut, to Peter and Catharine (Cook) Lanman. M. July 18, 1888, to Mary Billings Hinckley. Ch. six. D. February 20, 1941, Boston, Massachusetts.

Charles Rockwell Lanman received the A.B. (1871) and Ph.D. (1873) degrees from Yale College. He studied languages in Leipzig, Germany (1873–76).

Lanman taught Sanskrit at Johns Hopkins University in Baltimore, Maryland (1876–80), and Harvard University from 1880, where he was later Wales Professor of Sanskrit (1903–26). He was Percy Trumbull Lecturer on Poetry of India at Johns Hopkins (1898) and also lectured at the Lowell Institute in Boston (1898).

Lanman was a major American contributor to the literature in Sanskrit studies; among his writings were *Noun-Inflection in the Veda* (1880), *Sanskrit Reader* (1884), and *Beginnings of Hindu Pantheism* (1890). He was editor with others of many collections and translations of Sanskrit. He was editor of Harvard Oriental Series, under which over thirty titles were published and the proceedings and *Transactions* of the American Philological Association (1879–83), and he was joint editor of the *Journal* of the American Oriental Society and its proceedings.

A member of philological and scholarly organizations, Lanman was president of the American Philological Association (1890), the American Oriental Society (1907 and 1919, vice-president, 1897–1907) and the Omar Khayyam Club of America (1921). He was an honorary or corresponding member of many foreign scholarly societies. The Research Society of Bihar (Buddha's native land) granted him honorary membership.

He was one of eight non-Japanese scholars to be awarded the Japanese Medal on the 2,500th anniversary celebration of the birth of Buddha. Lanman was the recipient of honorary degrees from Yale University and the University of Aberdeen, Scotland. An oarsman, he was said to have rowed over ten thousand miles on the Charles River (Massachusetts).

REFERENCES: *DAB* (supp. 3); *EB; NCAB* (11:96); *TC; WWW* (I); *NYT,* February 21, 1941, p. 19.

Lew E. Wise

LARRABEE, William Clark. B. December 23, 1802, Cape Elizabeth, Maine, to n.a. M. September 28, 1828, to Harriet Dunn. Ch. four. D. May 4, 1859, Greencastle, Indiana.

William Larrabee's father, a sea captain, died soon after the boy's birth, and, at six years of age, young William was taken to live with his grandparents and uncle at Durham, Maine, where he grew up, working on the farm and going to school. Converted to Methodism at the age of fourteen, he received a license to preach at the age of nineteen. He attended New Market Academy in New Hampshire, Farmingham (Maine) Academy, and Bowdoin College in Brunswick, Maine, from which he was graduated in 1828.

He was principal of Alfred (Maine) Academy (1828–30) and tutor at a school in Middletown, Connecticut, that later became Wesleyan University (1831). Larrabee was principal of Oneida Conference Seminary in Cazenovia, New York (1831–35), and principal of Maine Wesleyan Seminary at Kent's Hill, Maine (1835–41). Larrabee moved to Indiana, where he was professor at Indiana Asbury (later, DePauw) University (1841–52). He was the first state superintendent of public instruction of Indiana (1853–54). Defeated for reelection in 1854, he was successful in the election of 1856 and served a second term (1857–58).

As first state superintendent, Larrabee was confronted with the challenge of founding the school system from sketchy provisions of Indiana's 1851 constitution. His effectiveness in studying the laws and constitution, traveling throughout the state, and meeting with educators and citizens did much to promote uniform schools in the state. During his second term of office (1856–58), he reconstructed the school system because the former school laws had been declared unconstitutional.

Larrabee was the author of *Lectures on the Scientific Evidences of Natural and Revealed Religion* (1850), *Wesley and His Coadjutors* (two volumes, 1851), *Asbury and His Coadjutors* (two volumes, 1853), and *Rosabower* (1854). He was editor of *Ladies' Repository* (1852). He was awarded honorary degrees by McKendree College and Indiana State University.

REFERENCES: *AC; DAB; NCAB* (25:308); *TC; WWW* (H); Claude Chambers, "The Life and Contribution of William C. Larrabee to Education in Indiana" (Master's thesis, Indiana State Teachers College, 1936).   *Benjamin F. Walker*

LARSEN, Peter Laurentius. B. August 10, 1833, Oslo, Norway, to Herman and Ellen Else Marie (Oftedahl) Larsen. M. July 23, 1855, to Karen Radine Neuberg. M. August 20, 1872, to Ingeborg Astrup. Ch. twelve. D. March 1, 1915, Decorah, Iowa.

Laur Larsen was graduated from the University of Christiania (later, University of Oslo), Norway, in 1850, completed the theological course at the university in 1855, and studied French, German, and Hebrew (1855–57). He was ordained in the Lutheran church in 1857.

Larsen emigrated to the United States and served a church in Rush River, Wisconsin (1857–59). He established other churches and was professor of Norwegian at Concordia College and Seminary in St. Louis, Missouri (1859–61). He returned to Halfway Creek (near La Crosse), Wisconsin, in 1861 and became president of the newly established Luther College. In 1862 the college was moved to Decorah, Iowa. Despite the poverty of the immigrant families from which his students came, a limited enrollment, and a fire in 1889, Larsen directed the college. He resigned as president in 1902 and continued as professor of Hebrew to 1911.

Larsen was active in the Norwegian Lutheran church as editor of *Kirkelig Maanedstidende* (1868–69) and its successor *Evangelisk Luthersk Kirketidende* (1902–12). He worked unsuccessfully for establishment of churches serving Norwegian–Swedish congregations. He served on church committees and was vice-president of the Iowa district of the Norwegian Lutheran Church (1876–79), vice-president of the Norwegian Synod (1876–93), and chairman of the Lutheran Synodical Conference (1881–83). He received an honorary degree from Concordia Seminary in 1903 and was decorated by the Norwegian government (1908).

REFERENCES: *DAB; NCAB* (25:304); *TC; WWW* (I). *John F. Ohles*

LARSON, Lars Moore. B. August 20, 1856, Vernon County, Wisconsin, to Michael and Rachel Larson. M. December 1882 to Belle E. Porter. M. 1893 to Cora Gunn. Ch. three. D. June 30, 1931, Dundas, Minnesota.

A pioneer in education for the deaf, Lars Moore Larson, lost his hearing as a result of sickness at the age of one. He spent his early years on a farm in Wisconsin and at the age of thirteen was sent to the Wisconsin School for the Deaf in Delavan. He was graduated as valedictorian of his class in 1876 and attended Gallaudet National College for the Deaf in Washington, D.C., graduating with the A.B. degree (1882). He represented the Chicago Young Men's Christian Association as a special delegate for deaf-mute members at the Milwaukee, Wisconsin, convention in 1883.

After graduation, Larson took a position in the Chicago deaf-mute day schools and was a lecturer on popular and religious topics to the adult deaf of Chicago. In 1884 he resigned his position in Chicago and went to New Mexico where he established the New Mexico School for the Deaf, which opened in 1885 with five pupils. His school was privately supported at first, but the school was incorporated by the territorial legislature as a public institution in 1887. While the school was under the jurisdiction of the territory, Larson was appointed superintendent and instructor. As the school grew Larson erected a new building at his own expense. The building was rented to the territory of New Mexico and was officially opened in 1891. Larson used a combined system of instruction in the school, making signs subordinate to the use of the manual alphabet and writing.

On his retirement, Larson moved to Minnesota to live with a daughter and taught in the department for the deaf at St. Olaf College in Northfield, Minnesota.

REFERENCES: *NCAB* (3:67); *WWW* (III); *Northfield* (Minnesota) *News,* July 3, 1931, p. 8.   *Nelson L. Haggerson*

LATHROP, John Hiram. B. January 22, 1799, Sherburne, New York, to John and Prudence Elizabeth (Hatch) Lathrop. M. 1833 to Frances E. Lothrop. Ch. one. D. August 2, 1866, Columbia, Missouri.

John Hiram Lathrop attended Hamilton College in Clinton, New York (1815–17), and entered Yale College in 1817, graduating in 1819. He taught in a grammar school in Farmington, Connecticut, and Monroe Academy in Weston, Connecticut (1819–22). He returned to Yale as a tutor and law student (1822–26) and was admitted to the bar in 1826.

He soon abandoned law to return to teaching at Military Academy in Norwich, Vermont, and was principal at Gardiner (Maine) Academy. In 1829 he was professor of mathematics and natural philosophy at Hamilton College, where he became Maynard Professor of Law, Civil Polity, and Political Economy.

In 1840 Lathrop left Hamilton to become president of the newly organized University of Missouri. Despite difficulties, he established an institution modeled on traditional eastern colleges. Appointment of a hostile board of curators and the increasing controversy over slavery prompted him to accept the position as chancellor at the recently founded University of Wisconsin in 1849.

At Wisconsin Lathrop received an enthusiastic response to his proposals for a university having both classical and utilitarian aims. He guided Wisconsin through the first ten formative years. In response to two invitations, Lathrop resigned as chancellor and left Wisconsin to become president of Indiana University (1859–60).

He returned to the University of Missouri as professor of English literature. When the Civil War required suspension of classes in 1862, the president's office was abolished, and the university reopened with Lathrop as chairman of the faculty and professor of moral, mental, and political philosophy. With the war's end in 1865, Lathrop was again made president of the university and served to his death in 1866.

Lathrop was a member and secretary of the board of examiners of the United States Military Academy (1851) and was president of the African Colonization Society.

REFERENCES: *AC; DAB; NCAB* (5:178); *TC; WWW* (H); *NYT,* August 10, 1866, p. 2; Merle Curti *(q.v.)* and Vernon Carstensen, *The University of Wisconsin: A History, 1848–1925* (Madison: University of Wisconsin Press, 1949); Frank F. Stephens, *A History of the University of Missouri* (Columbia: University of Missouri Press, 1962); Jonas Viles, *The University of Missouri: A Centennial History* (Columbia: University of Missouri, 1939). *Ralph E. Glauert*

LAUBACH, Frank Charles. B. September 2, 1884, Benton, Pennsylvania, to John and Harriet (Derr) Laubach. M. May 15, 1912, to Effa Seely. Ch. one. D. June 11, 1970, Benton, Pennsylvania.

After graduating from Bloomsburg (Pennsylvania) State Normal School (later, State College) (1901) and attending Perkiomen Seminary (1904–05), Frank Charles Laubach received the A.B. degree (1909) from Princeton University and the A.M. and Ph.D. (1915) degrees from Columbia University. He was a student at Union Theological Seminary in New York City (1911–14).

He taught in Pennsylvania and moved to New York City, where he was an associate in the Spring Street Community House (1910) and secretary of the Charity Organization Society (1914). He went to the Philippine Islands as a missionary in Cagayan, Misamis (1915–19), served as dean of Union College in Manila (1922–26), and was director in 1930 of the Maranaw Folk Schools in Lanao, a position he held for most of his professional life. He conducted literacy tours through scores of countries.

Founder of the "each one teach one" technique for teaching reading, Laubach spent thirty years in an effort to eradicate illiteracy throughout the world. After developing a system of drawings that represented letters and words, he coauthored over 250 primers for illiterate adults in some 165 languages and produced writing systems for languages previously not written. In addition he was interested in the revisions of English spelling.

In addition to preprimers and primers, Laubach authored or edited *Why There Are Vagrants* (1915), *People of the Philippines* (1924), *Seven Thousand Emeralds* (1929), *Rizal, Man and Martyr* (1936), *Letters of Modern Mystic* (1937), *English Maranaw Dictionary* (1937), *Toward a Literate World* (1939), *Moro Folklore* (1939), *India Shall Be Literate* (1940), *You Are My Friends* (1942), *The Silent Billion* (1943), *Streamlined English Lessons* (1945), *Prayer: The Mightiest Force in the World* (1946), *Story of Jesus* (1946), *Making Everybody's World Safe* (1947), *Teaching the World to Read* (1947), *Clear Horizons* (1947), *Pray for Others* (1948), *Wake Up or*

Blow Up (1951), *The Wise Man* (1951), and *Thirty Years with the Silent Billion* (1960).

Laubach was the chairman of the board of trustees of Silliman University (1939–41) and received honorary degrees from Princeton University and Wooster College.

REFERENCES: *CB* (February 1950 and September 1970); *WWW* (V); Frank C. Laubach, *Thirty Years with the Silent Billion* (Westwood, N.J.: Fleming H. Revell Co., 1960); *NYT,* June 12, 1970, p. 39. *Robert Emans*

LAWS, Samuel Spahr. B. March 23, 1824, Ohio County, Virginia, to James and Rachel (Spahr) Laws. M. January 19, 1860, to Ann Maria Broadwell. Ch. none. D. January 9, 1921, Asheville, North Carolina.

Samuel Spahr Laws was graduated from Miami University in Oxford, Ohio, with the A.B. (1848) and A.M. (1851) degrees and from Princeton (New Jersey) Theological Seminary (1851). He received the LL.B. degree (1869) from Columbia College (later, University) and the M.D. degree (1875) from Bellevue Hospital Medical College in New York City.

Ordained a Presbyterian minister in 1851, Laws served the West Church in St. Louis, Missouri (1851–53). He was associated with Westminster College in Fulton, Missouri, as professor of physical science (1854–55) and became president (1855–61). He resigned as a southern sympathizer in the Civil War and was imprisoned on his refusal to pledge allegiance to the Union government. He studied in Europe (1861–62) and returned to the United States, settling in New York City. He was vice-president of the New York Gold Exchange and invented the stock market ticker.

Laws returned to Missouri in 1876 as president of the University of Missouri in Columbia and professor of mental and moral philosophy. Under his administration, the enrollment doubled, new departments were added, and improved financial support was obtained from the state. He resigned from the university in 1889 and served as professor of Christian apologetics at the Presbyterian Theological Seminary in Columbia, South Carolina (1893–98).

Laws was the author of several books, including *Polygamy and Citizenship in Church and State* (1906) and *The Atonement of the Christian Trinity* (1919). He was a delegate to the Pan-Presbyterian Council in Washington, D.C. (1899). He was appointed a visitor to the United States Military Academy at West Point, New York (1882). He received honorary degrees from Washington and Lee University, Miami University, and Westminster College.

REFERENCES: *DAB; NCAB* (8:186); *NYT,* January 10, 1921, p. 11; *TC; WWW* (I).   *John F. Ohles*

LAWSON, Andrew Cowper. B. July 25, 1861, Anstruther, Scotland, to William and Jessie (Kerr) Lawson. M. November 30, 1889, to Ludovika

Von Jantsch. M. January 5, 1931, to Isabel R. Collins. Ch. five. D. June 16, 1952, San Leandro, California.

Andrew Cowper Lawson, geologist and educator, received the A.B. degree (1883) from the University of Toronto, Canada, and the A.M. (1885) and Ph.D. (1888) degrees from Johns Hopkins University in Baltimore, Maryland.

Lawson was with the Geological Survey of Canada (1882–90) during which time he surveyed northwestern Canada and examined pre-Cambrian deposits in the Lake Superior region. He joined the faculty of the University of California in 1890 to teach geology and mineralogy and remained there until his retirement as professor emeritus in 1928. He served as dean of the college of mining (1914–18). While chairman of the department of geology at the university for two decades, Lawson vigorously directed its growth. As dean of the college of mining he established the first program in petroleum engineering in the United States.

Lawson made structural and stratigraphic studies in numerous countries in Europe, Central America, Mexico, Alaska, and the United States. He presented new information about pre-Cambrian rocks and did extensive research into the geology of the western coastal area. His activity in the area of seismology resulted in the organization of the Seismological Society of America, and the development of the most extensive seismographic station in the United States in Berkeley (California) in 1911.

Lawson was the author of numerous geological papers and monographs. He established the bulletin of the Department of Geology (University of California) and the bulletin of the Seismological Society of California.

He was a delegate to geological congresses in London, England (1888), St. Petersburg, Russia (1897), Toronto, Canada (1913), and Madrid, Spain (1926). He was chairman of the California Earthquake Investigation Commission (1906). He was president of the Seismological Society of America (1909–10) and the Geological Society of America (1926). He was awarded the Hayden Medal of the Academy of Natural Sciences (1935) and the Penrose Medal of the Geographical Society of America (1938). He received honorary degrees from the universities of Toronto, Canada, and California and Harvard University.

REFERENCES: *DSB; LE* (II); *NCAB* (41:48); *WWW* (III); *NYT,* June 18, 1952, p. 27; *Time* 59 (June 30, 1952): 80.   *Stratton F. Caldwell*

LEACH, Daniel Dyer. B. June 12, 1806, Bridgewater, Massachusetts, to Apollos and Chloe (Dyer) Leach. M. May 1834, to Mary H. Lawton, Ch. three. D. March 16, 1891, Providence, Rhode Island.

Daniel Dyer Leach, a pioneer in school administration, was educated in the district school at Bridgewater, Massachusetts. He entered Brown University in Providence, Rhode Island, to study for the ministry and was graduated in 1830. He continued his theological studies at Andover, Massachusetts, and was ordained in 1833.

After five years as an Episcopal minister (1833–38), he decided to go into teaching. Leach was appointed principal of the Classical School in Roxbury, Massachusetts (1838–42). He conducted a successful private school from 1842 to 1848. Appointed an agent to the Massachusetts state board of education (1848–55), he was charged with improving the physical facilities of the schoolhouses. One of his notable achievements was the development of a better ventilation system to increase the comfort of pupils.

He became superintendent of schools in Providence, Rhode Island, where he wrote widely on teaching and discipline (1855–70). He was elected to the Rhode Island Board of Education in 1870, holding the position to 1890.

Leach was the author of schoolbooks, including *The Primary School Arithmetic* (1850), *A Theoretical and Practical Arithmetic* (1851), *An Elementary Intellectual Arithmetic* (1853), *The Complete Spelling Book* (1856), *First Lessons in Arithmetic* (1857), and *Directions to Teachers* (1873).

Leach was a trustee of Brown University (1877–91) and vice-president and director of the Rhode Island Institute of Education for over twenty years. He was awarded an honorary degree by Brown University in 1875.

REFERENCES: *DAB; NCAB* (8:467); *WWW* (H).   *George Lucht*

LEE, James Melvin. B. May 16, 1878, Port Crane, New York, to James Newell and Emma (White) Lee. M. May 17, 1908, to Helen Olga Wellner. Ch. one. D. November 9, 1929, New York, New York.

James Melvin Lee, who combined the careers of editor, author, and educator with success in each, was one of the most ardent defenders of modern journalism. He was graduated from Wyoming Seminary in Kingston, Pennsylvania (1896), and entered Wesleyan University in Middletown, Connecticut, where he received the A.B. degree (1900). At college he was largely self-supporting, writing a series of articles for newspapers about student employment, a series that he later used in a book, *How to Be Self-Supporting at College* (1903).

After his graduation, he joined the staff of the *Springfield* (Massachusetts) *Union.* He taught English at Western Reserve Seminary in West Farmington, Ohio (1901), and returned to newspaper work as circulation manager of the *Oneonta* (New York) *Star.* Beginning in 1905, he was affiliated with magazines, including *Outing, Bohemian Magazine, Circle, Leslie's Weekly,* and *Judge.* While with *Judge,* he became a pioneer in the teaching of journalism as a lecturer (1910) and director of the department of journalism (1911–29) at New York University.

He was active in writing books and articles, principally on topics dealing with journalism. He was the author of *Wordless Journalism in America* (a book of cartoons, 1915), *Newspaper Ethics* (1915), *History of American Journalism* (1917), *Instruction in Journalism in Institutions of Higher Learning* (1918), *America's Oldest Daily Newspaper* (1918), *Opportunities in the Newspaper Business* (1919), and *Business Ethics* (1926), and he was editor of *Business Writing* (1920). He served in editorial positions with *Blue Pencil, Administration* (editor-in-chief, 1921–23), *Editor and Publisher,* and *Three Em Dash.*

Lee took a leading role in defending American journalism against critics. He established scholarships in journalism, including some as memorials to journalists, among them William Bradford, publisher of the first newspaper in New York. He collected early periodicals and first editions in American literature, particularly works of James Fenimore Cooper and Edgar Allan Poe. He was active in professional associations, serving as secretary of the International Association of Schools of Journalism and the American Association of Teachers of Journalism (1913–14, and president, 1916–17). He received an honorary degree from Washington and Lee University.

REFERENCES: *DAB; NCAB* (23:20); *WWW* (I); *NYT,* November 9, 1929, p. 31. *Albert S. Weston*

LEE, Mabel. B. August 18, 1886, Clearfield, Iowa, to David Alexander and Jennie (Aikman) Lee. M. no.

Mabel Lee, a leader in women's physical education, spent her early life in Iowa. She attended public school and was graduated from high school in Centerville. She was graduated magna cum laude (1908) from Coe College in Cedar Rapids, Iowa, with majors in psychology and philosophy. She attended Boston Normal School of Gymnastics and Wellesley (Massachusetts) College, where she received a certificate in physical education in 1910. She attended Chalif School of Dance and the Vestoff-Serova School of Dance in New York City.

Lee taught at Coe College, Oregon Agricultural College (later, Oregon State University) in Corvallis, and Beloit (Wisconsin) College. Most of her academic career was spent at the University of Nebraska in Lincoln, where she served as professor and director of physical education for women (1924–52).

She authored *The Conduct of Physical Education* (1927), *History of the Middle West Society of Physical Education* (1963), *History of the Central Association of Health, Physical Education and Recreation* (1964), and parts one and two of *Seventy Five Years of Professional Preparation in Physical Education for Women at the University of Nebraska-Lincoln, 1898–1973* (1973), and she coauthored *The Fundamentals of Body Me-*

chanics and Conditioning (1949), *Brief History of Physical Education*
(1958), and *Seventy-Five Year History of the American Association for
Health, Physical Education, and Recreation* (1960). In her retirement, Lee
worked on an autobiography supported by an Amy Morris Homans
Fellowship Award from Wellesley College. She contributed many articles
to professional journals and lectured frequently on physical education and
sports for women.

Lee was the first woman president of the American Physical Education
Association (1931) and the American Academy of Physical Education
(1940–42), and she was also president of the National Association of
Physical Education for College Women (1926). During World War II she
was regional director of the division of physical fitness for the United
States Seventh Army Service Command. She was a Fulbright scholar in
Iraq as a consultant to the Ministry of Education (1952–53). She served on
the national council of the American Youth Hostel Association, the board
of directors of the women's division of the National Amateur Athletic
Federation, the chief of staff's National Civilian Advisory Committee for
the Women's Army Corps, and the board of directors of the American Folk
Arts Society.

Lee was honored with the Luther Halsey Gulick Award (1948) and the R.
Tait McKenzie Award (1968) of the American Association for Health,
Physical Education and Recreation and the Hetherington Award (1957) of
the American Academy of Physical Education. In 1975 an annual award
bearing her name was established by the American Association for Health,
Physical Education and Recreation. She received honorary degrees from
Coe and George Williams colleges.

REFERENCES: *LE* (III); *American Women 1939–40* (Los Angeles:
American Publications, 1939); Henry and Vera Bradshaw, "Dr. Phys.
Ed.," *NRTA Journal* (January-February 1977):19–20.

James M. Vosper

LEE, Stephen Dill. B. September 22, 1833, Charleston, South Carolina, to
Thomas and Caroline (Allison) Lee. M. February 9, 1865, to Regina Harrison. Ch. one. D. May 28, 1908, Vicksburg, Mississippi.

Stephen Dill Lee was graduated from the United States Military Academy at West Point, New York, in 1854. He resigned from the United States
Army in February 1861 and was soon recommissioned in the Confederate
army, where he rose to the rank of lieutenant general.

After the Civil War he moved to Mississippi, where for almost twelve
years he operated a plantation in Noxumbee County. While he was there,
he learned the importance of applying scientific principles to agriculture,
and he recognized the need for an institution to teach those principles to
farmers.

Lee was elected to a seat in the Mississippi Senate in 1877 and worked for the passage of a bill to create an agricultural and mechanical college. The bill passed, and in 1880 he became the first president of the Mississippi Agricultural and Mechanical College (later, Mississippi State University). He used established schools as models for his school and actively recruited a competent and experienced faculty. Lee was known as the Father of Industrial Education in the South.

Lee resigned as president of Mississippi Agricultural and Mechanical College in 1889 when President William McKinley appointed him a member of the commission to organize Vicksburg Military Park. He was a delegate to the Mississippi Constitutional Convention of 1890.

The Mississippi State legislature chartered the Mississippi Historical Commission in 1890. Lee was president of the Mississippi Historical Society and was then president of the commission. He wrote important articles about the Civil War, which appeared in the publications of the Mississippi Historical Society. He was awarded an honorary degree by Tulane University. Lee was elected commander-in-chief of the United Confederate Veterans in 1904, a position for which he traveled extensively and spoke frequently.

REFERENCES: *AC; DAB; NCAB* (5:414); *NYT,* May 29, 1908, p. 7; *TC; WWW* (I); John K. Bettersworth, *People's College: A History of Mississippi State* (Birmingham: University of Alabama Press, 1953).

Ronnie W. Clayton

LEESER, Isaac. B. December 12, 1806, Neuenkirchen, Westphalia, Germany, to Uri Leeser and his wife (n.a.). M. no. D. February 1, 1868, Philadelphia, Pennsylvania.

Isaac Leeser was raised by his grandmother after his mother died when he was eight years old. He began his formal education under Rabbi Benjamin Cohen and Rabbi Abraham Sutro, the chief rabbi of Münster and Mark, in Dulmen, Germany. He received his secular education at the gymnasium in Münster.

In 1824 Leeser emigrated to Richmond, Virginia, to live and work with his uncle, Zalma Rehine, a merchant. He gained recognition for essays he published and was appointed a hazzan in Mikveb Israel (a Sephardic congregation) in Philadelphia in 1829. These essays were later published as *The Jews and The Mosiac* (1833).

He founded and edited *The Occident and Jewish Advocate,* a monthly Jewish magazine (1843), and founded the Jewish Publication Society of America (1845), the first Jewish communal religious school (1839), the first Hebrew high school (1849), the board of delegates of American Israelites, a Jewish representative and defense organization (1859), and Maimonides College, the first American Jewish rabbinical school (1867–73). He translated into English Joseph Johlson's *Instruction in the Mosaic Religion*

(1830), Joseph Schwartz's *Descriptive Geography of Palestine* (1850), the Sephardic prayer book (1848), and the Ashkenazic prayer book. He wrote the first American translation of the Hebrew Bible (1853). He introduced the first regular English sermon into the synagogue service as an educational tool.

Among Leeser's other books were *Discourses, Argumentative, and Devotional in the Subject of the Jewish Religion* (1836), *Catechism for Jewish Children* (1839), the first Hebrew primer, and *Claims of the Jews to Equality of Rights* (1840), a collection of letters to the editor of the *Philadelphia Gazette*.

REFERENCES: *AC; DAB; NCAB* (10:393); *WWW* (H); Moske Davis, *The Emergence of Conservative Judaism* (Philadelphia: Jewish Publication Society of America, 1963); *Jewish Encyclopedia* (New York: Funk and Wagnalls, 1904); B. W. Korn, "Isaac Leeser: Centennial Reflections," *American Jewish Archives* 19 (November 1967): 127–141; Herbert Parzen, *Architects of Conservative Judaism* (New York: Jonathan David, 1964).   *David E. Kapel*

LEFFINGWELL, William Henry. B. June 14, 1876, Woodstock, Ontario, Canada, to Wendell Phillips and Mary Catherine (Edwards) Leffingwell. M. February 12, 1900, to Anna Short. Ch. three. D. December 19, 1934, Westfield, New Jersey.

William Henry Leffingwell was born in Canada of American parents, who soon moved to Michigan. He attended Union High School in Grand Rapids for two years. At the age of seventeen he worked as a stenographer for six months without pay for the experience, and later he was the private secretary to the superintendent of the McCormick Harvester Works in Chicago. He was office manager of a large Chicago advertising agency and general manager of a mail order publication in New York City. He spent several years in England, France, and Germany establishing branches for American companies.

About 1907 Leffingwell became interested in Frederick Taylor's principles of scientific management. He was one of the first to adapt Taylor's methods to the office and wrote books on the applications of these principles to office organization and operation.

In 1918 Leffingwell started the W. H. Leffingwell Company in Chicago, an office-management consulting firm. He invented the first posture chair for office clerks and the Leffingwell-Ream scale for measuring typists' production, and he instituted a bonus plan relating salary to clerical output.

In 1925 he wrote the first office management textbook, *Office Management, Principles and Practices*. Others of his writings include *Scientific*

Office Management (1917), *Making the Office Pay* (1918), and *The Automatic Letter Writer* (1918). In 1932 he coauthored *Textbook of Office Management* with Edwin Robinson. He edited *The Office Appliance Manual* for the National Association of Office Appliance Manufacturers in 1926.

Leffingwell was considered a pioneer and one of the country's leading experts in the field of office management. He belonged to many professional associations, including the National Office Management Association (president, 1930-32). At the time of Leffingwell's death in 1934 he was president of the Taylor Society and still active in management engineering and working to organize the Federated Management Societies.

REFERENCES: *NYT,* December 20, 1934, p. 23; *WWW* (I); *Bulletin of Taylor Society and the Society of Industrial Engineers* 1 (January 1935): 86.   *Elizabeth S. Oelrich*

LEIDY, Joseph. B. September 9, 1823, Philadelphia, Pennsylvania, to Philip and Catherine (Mellick) Leidy. M. August 1864 to Anna Harden. Ch. one. D. April 29, 1891, Philadelphia, Pennsylvania.

Joseph Leidy displayed a marked talent for drawing in school. His father withdrew him from school at the age of sixteen with the intention of having him become a sign painter. He decided instead to become a draftsman. Later he began his scientific career studying on his own mineralogy, botany, and comparative anatomy while working as a clerk in a drugstore. Encouraged by his stepmother, he began the study of medicine in 1840, and in 1844 he received the M.D. degree from the University of Pennsylvania.

After a short period in the practice of medicine, Leidy decided to teach. He was appointed to the chair of anatomy at the University of Pennsylvania (1845). In 1848 he toured museums and hospitals in England, France, and Germany with W. E. Horner, and in 1850 he accompanied George B. Wood *(q.v.)* to Europe to collect specimens for use in courses at Pennsylvania. Leidy succeeded Horner in the chair of anatomy at the University of Pennsylvania in 1853, holding the post until his death in 1891. He became recognized as the foremost American anatomist of his time. During the Civil War he served as surgeon in the Satterlee United States Army General Hospital (1861–65). Leidy also was professor of natural history at Swarthmore (Pennsylvania) college (1870–85) and director of the department of biology at the University of Pennsylvania (1884–91).

Leidy was the author of *The Ancient Fauna of Nebraska* (1853), *An Elementary Treatise on Human Anatomy* (1860), *The Extinct Mammalian Fauna of Dakota and Nebraska* (1869), and *Researches in Helminthology and Parasitology* (published posthumously and edited by his son, 1904).

Leidy also edited Jones Quains's *Human Anatomy* (1849), and he wrote many bulletins and reports published by the Smithsonian Institution.

He was a member of the National Academy of Sciences, the Boston Society of Natural History, and the Academy of Natural Sciences of Philadelphia (president, 1881–91). He was awarded the Walker Prize from the Boston Society of Natural History (1880), the Lyell Medal from the Geological Society of London (1884), and the Cuvier Medal from the Institute of France (1888). He received an honorary degree from Harvard University in 1886.

REFERENCES:*AC; DAB; DSB; NCAB* (5:220); *WWW* (H).

C. Roy Rylander

LEIGH, Edwin. B. September 10, 1815, South Berwick, Maine, to Thomas and Nancy (Baker) Leigh. M. April 10, 1839, to Susan Scollay. Ch. nine. D. April 9, 1890, Kerr County, Texas.

Edwin Leigh was educated at South Berwick (Maine) Academy and at Bowdoin College in Brunswick, Maine. He was graduated with the A.B. degree (1835) from Bowdoin and entered Andover (Massachusetts) Theological Seminary. In 1838 his course of study was completed, and he was ordained to the Congregational ministry in 1839. He studied medicine at Harvard University and received the M.D. degree (1850). He worked as an assistant to Louis Agassiz *(q.v.)* in Cambridge, Massachusetts, for two years.

Leigh served churches at Kennebunk, Maine, Winchendon, Massachusetts, and Woonsocket, Rhode Island, and he taught school in Bristol, Rhode Island. He practiced medicine in Townsend, Massachusetts (1851–54), and then spent several years in commercial pursuits in St. Louis, Missouri.

Leigh taught in the high school and at St. Louis City University for seven years. He designed a transitional phonetic system, described in his book, *Pronouncing Orthography* (1864). The system was designed to improve primary instruction in reading and assist in teaching English to foreigners. The system was introduced in the Clay School in St. Louis in 1866 by the principal, William Torrey Harris *(q.v.)*. Leigh's program was later adopted in all St. Louis schools. He also wrote *Bird's-Eye Views of Slavery in Missouri* (1862) and *New Guide to Modern Conversation* (1872). He edited many school readers in pronouncing orthography, including those of William H. McGuffey *(q.v.)*, G. S. Hillard *(q.v.)*, Epes Sargent *(q.v.)*, J. M. Watson *(q.v.)*, and Charles W. Sanders *(q.v.)*. An essay he wrote in 1849, "The Philosophy of Medical Science," was awarded the Boylston Prize for essays.

REFERENCES: *NCAB* (20:406); Lee C. Deighton, ed., *The Encyclopedia of Education* (New York: Macmillan, 1971), 5:90. *Jerry L. Johns*

LEIGH, Robert Devore. B. September 13, 1890, Nelson, Nebraska, to Charles Pascal and Olivia Belle (Thompson) Leigh. M. June 23, 1916, to Mildred Adelaide Boardman. M. October 22, 1960, to Carma Russell Zimmerman. Ch. two. D. January 31, 1961, Chicago, Illinois.

Robert D. Leigh received his preparatory education at the public schools in Seattle, Washington. He was graduated from Bowdoin College in Brunswick, Maine, with the A.B. degree (1914) and received the A.M. (1915) and Ph.D. (1927) degrees from Columbia University.

He taught government at Reed College in Portland, Oregon (1914–19). During World War I he was assistant educational director in the United States Public Health Service in Washington, D.C. (1917–18). He lectured in government at Columbia University (1919–22) and was A. Barton Hepburn Professor of Government at Williams College (1922–28) in Williamstown, Massachusetts.

Leigh became the first president of Bennington (Vermont) College, a progressive college for women. He was largely responsible for the educational plan for Bennington College (1929), which proposed innovations, including abolishing required courses for students, having students plan their own course of study according to their interests, and providing a large amount of time for independent study. A long winter recess allowed students to travel or participate in fieldwork in the community. Believing that there should be a regular change of college presidents at or near the point of the president's highest usefulness, Leigh resigned in 1941.

After leaving Bennington, Leigh accepted a temporary position with the school of economics and politics of the Institute for Advanced Study at Princeton University (1941) and conducted a survey of instruction in social studies in high schools. He served as special adviser to the National Resources Planning Board (1941–42) and was director of the Foreign Broadcast Intelligence Service of the Federal Communications Commission (1942–44). He was director of the Commission of Freedom of the Press at the University of Chicago (1944–46) and was visiting professor of political science. He was director of the nationwide Public Library Inquiry for the Social Science Research Council (1946–49). In 1950 Leigh was appointed visiting professor of library science at Columbia University and later served the university as acting dean (1954–56) and dean (1956–59) of the school of library services.

Leigh was the author of *Federal Health Administration in the United States* (1927), *Group Leadership* (1936), *Modern Rules of Parliamentary Procedure* (1937), *Peoples Speaking to Peoples* (with Llewellyn White, 1946), and *The Public Library in the United States* (1950), and he was editor of *Major Problems in the Education of Librarians* (1954). He also contributed numerous articles to magazines.

Leigh was an active member of various organizations and was clerk (1932–38) and moderator (1938–41) of the village of Bennington, Vermont. He received honorary degrees from Bowdoin College and Colgate University.

REFERENCES: *CB* (June 1947); *LE* (III); *NCAB* (51:455); *WWAE* (XIV); *WWW* (IV); *NYT,* February 1, 1961, p. 35.   *Edward B. Goellner*

LEIPZIGER, Henry Marcus. B. December 29, 1854, Manchester, England, to Marcus and Martha (Samuel) Leipziger. M. no. D. December 1, 1917, New York, New York.

Henry Marcus Leipziger's family emigrated to the United States from Manchester, England, and settled in New York City. He attended the public schools there and entered the College of the City of New York, from which he received the A.B. and B.S. degrees in 1873. He enrolled in the law school of Columbia College, received the LL.B. degree (1875), and was admitted to the bar. He opened a law office but decided to return to teaching, a profession he had been following in the evening schools of New York while pursuing his law studies.

Leipziger suffered a nervous breakdown in 1881 and traveled widely and read extensively to 1883. He persuaded a group of Jewish philanthropists to establish the Hebrew Technical Institute in 1884 and became the superintendent. He organized courses to train Jewish youths in trades and crafts to fit them for skilled jobs. The school brought him recognition that led to his appointment in 1891 as assistant superintendent of the public schools in New York City, a position he held until 1896. He laid the plans for a system of public lectures to be given in the evenings in different school centers under the auspices of the board of education. A small experiment at first, it soon grew into one of the largest organized lecture systems in the country. Leipziger called it "The People's University." Hundreds of lecturers were employed, thousands of lectures were given, and audiences numbering more than a million a year were in attendance. A special position of supervisor of public lectures was created, which Leipziger filled to his death in 1917. The program later fell victim to extension courses in colleges and schools and the phonograph and motion pictures. It was one of the greatest forces for adult education in New York City for twenty years.

Outside of his regular work, Leipziger was active in Hebrew charities, libraries, and historical societies. For seventeen years he was chairman of the committee of the Aguilar Free Library, which became part of the New York Public Library in 1903. He was vice-president of the Dickens Fellowship and the American Scenic and Historic Preservation Society. He received honorary degrees from Columbia University and Union College.

REFERENCES: *DAB; NCAB* (14:366); *WWW* (I); "Apostle of the Open Schoolhouse," *Independent* (New York), August 19, 1915; *NYT,* December 2, 1917, p. 5.   *Paul J. Schafer*

LEONARD, Levi Washburn. B. June 1, 1790, Bridgewater, Massachusetts, to Jacob and Mary (Swift) Leonard. M. September 8, 1830, to Elizabeth Morison Smith. M. March 25, 1851, to Elizabeth (Dow) Smith. Ch. two. D. December 12, 1864, Exeter, New Hampshire.

Levi Washburn Leonard was graduated from Harvard University in 1815 and the Harvard Divinity School in 1818. He taught for two years at Bridgewater (Massachusetts) Academy (1818–20) and was ordained in September 1820 as pastor of the First Congregational (Unitarian) Society of Dublin, New Hampshire. He continued as pastor to his death in 1864. After he moved to Exeter, New Hampshire, the congregation continued his relationship, while engaging a "colleague" pastor to provide daily pastoral services.

In 1822 Leonard established a children's library in his home, the first free public library in the country. In 1833 he established the first free library supported by taxation in Peterboro, New Hampshire.

He was chairman of the school committee in Dublin (1821–52) and was Cheshire County superintendent of schools. He introduced a number of innovations in the local schools, including nature study as a course of instruction, and he published a number of texts on the subject. He organized local lyceum lecture programs, founded the first high school in Dublin (1823), and helped organize the Cheshire teachers' institute for the training of schoolteachers (1836). School buildings he designed were used as models throughout the state.

Leonard was the author of *The Literary and Scientific Class Book* (1826), *Sequel to Essay Lessons* (1830), *Selections of Reading Lessons for Common Schools* (1830), *North American Spelling Book* (1835), *Modes of Instruction in Common Schools* (1844), *An Analysis of Elementary Sounds of the English Language* (1848), and *History of Dublin, New Hampshire* (1855). He also wrote many essays and hymns and was the chief compiler of *Christian Hymns.* He was editor of the Exeter *Newsletter* (1854–63). He received an honorary degree from Harvard University in 1849.

REFERENCES: *AC; DAB; NCAB* (26:228); *WWW* (H).   *Kenneth Sipser*

LEONARD, Robert Josselyn. B. February 5, 1885, San Jose, California, to Joseph Howland and Ella Isabelle (Clark) Leonard. M. August 13, 1913, to Eugenie Ann Andruss. Ch. two. D. February 9, 1929, New York, New York.

Robert Josselyn Leonard attended San Jose High School and the State

Normal School (later, California State University, San Jose), from which he was graduated in 1904. He attended Columbia University, where he received the B.S. (1912), M.A. (1914), and Ph.D. (1922) degrees.

Leonard taught in California at Belmont and Fresno. He introduced vocational education in the Berkeley (California) schools and the Horace Mann School at Columbia University. He studied the paper box industry for the New York Factory Investigation Commission (1914) to determine the education that was needed by workers in the industry; it was the first study of its kind in the country. He was the first professor of vocational education in the United States at Indiana University (1914–17). He worked for the Federal Board for Vocational Education (1917–18) administering in the Midwest the Smith-Hughes Act, which provided federal funds for vocational programs in high schools. He was professor of education (1918–23), university representative in educational affairs (1921–23), and acting dean of the school of education (1922–23) at the University of California at Berkeley. He was professor of education and director of the school of education at Teachers College, Columbia University (1923–29). He organized the first course in the United States on the administration of institutions of higher education.

Leonard was the author of several survey reports and books in the field of vocational education, including *An Investigation of the Paper Box Industry to Determine the Possibility of Vocational Training* (1915), *A Study of the People of Indiana and Their Occupations* (1915), *Some Facts Concerning the People, Industries and Schools of Hammond, Indiana* (1915), *Vocational Education Survey of Richmond, Indiana* (1916), *An Introductory Course on Part-time Education* (with others, 1920), and *The Coordination of State Institutions for Higher Education Through Supplementary Curricula Boards* (1923). His addresses were published posthumously as *An Outlook on Education* (1930).

Leonard was a frequent consultant to institutions of higher education and a conductor of surveys of American colleges and universities. He was a member of professional associations and a director of the National Junior Personnel Service, the Child Study Association of America, and the American Association for Adult Education.

REFERENCES: *DAB; NCAB* (25:251); *WWAE* (I); *WWW* (I).

John F. Ohles

LEONARD, Sterling Andrus. B. April 23, 1888, National City, California, to Cyreno N. and Eva (Andrus) Leonard. M. December 27, 1913, to Minetta F. Sammis. Ch. one. D. May 15, 1931, Madison, Wisconsin.

Sterling Andrus Leonard began his education at Simpson College in Indianola, Iowa (1904–07). He received the A.B. (1908) and A.M. (1909) degrees from the University of Michigan and the Ph.D. degree (1928) from Columbia University.

His early work was in experimental pedagogy, first at the Milwaukee Normal School and then at the Horace Mann School at Columbia University. He was an exchange teacher at the Gymnasium of Danzig, Germany (1911–12). In 1920 he went to the University of Wisconsin where he taught in the department of English until his untimely death by drowning in 1931.

Two of his most widely used books on the teaching of English were *English Composition as a Social Problem* (1917) and *Essential Principles of Teaching Reading and Literature* (1922). He also wrote *General Language* (with Riah Fagan Cox, 1925) and *The Doctrine of Correctness in English Usage, 1700–1800* (1928) and edited *Poems of the War and the Peace* (1920), *Atlantic Book of Modern Plays* (1922), and Melville's *Typee* (1922). He produced a graded series of school readers with W. W. Theisen.

Leonard was president of the National Council of Teachers of English (1926) and for a number of years was chairman of its committee on essentials. As chairman he prompted investigations of curriculum methods and materials and took the lead in the council's studies on usage.

REFERENCES: *DAB; NCAB* (26:64); *WWW* (I); *Washington, D.C., Evening Star,* February 9, 1929.

Lawrence S. Master

LESSENBERRY, David Daniel. B. September 7, 1896, Barren County, Kentucky, to James David and Martha Bell (Sanders) Lessenberry. M. August 28, 1926, to Elona J. Spence. M. December 26, 1945, to Bess McCain Dahlinger. Ch. none.

David Daniel Lessenberry was graduated from Colorado Springs (Colorado) High School and received the B.C.S. degree from Bowling Green (Kentucky) Business University, the B.S. degree (1928) from Duquesne University in Pittsburgh, Pennsylvania, and the A.M. degree (1934) from New York University.

In Pittsburgh, Lessenberry was a teacher of typewriting and shorthand in Allegheny High School (1919–27), principal of the Allegheny Evening High School (1923–27), and vice-principal (1927–29) and principal (1929–30) of the Business High School. Lessenberry was professor of education (1930–62) and director of courses in business education (1930–55) at the University of Pittsburgh.

Lessenberry was the author of many articles published in professional journals and of *20th Century Typewriting* (1927) and *College Typewriting* (1930); both of these texts were republished in many editions. He was a contributor to and editor of yearbooks of the Eastern Commercial Teachers Association and the National Business Teachers Association and was sponsor of *The Journal of Business Education.*

A member of many professional associations, he was president of the National Business Teachers Association (1935), the Eastern Business Teachers Association (1944 and member of the board of directors, 1930–35), and the Tri-State Business Education Association (1942). He received the John Robert Gregg Award in 1955 and an honorary degree from Westminster College in 1943.

REFERENCES: *LE* (III); *WW* (XXXI); *WWAE* (XIV).   *John F. Ohles*

LEVY, Florence Nightingale. B. August 13, 1870, New York, New York, to Joseph Arthur and Pauline (Goodheim) Levy. M. no. D. November 15, 1947, New York, New York.

Florence Nightingale Levy was educated in private New York City schools and attended the National Academy of Design in New York City, where she first studied painting and, later, art history and writing. She studied under Gaston Lafenestre at the Ecole du Louvre in Paris, France (1894–95), and in Italy, and she continued her studies on her return to the United States.

Levy was a staff member of the Metropolitan Museum of Art (1909–17), manager of the Art Alliance of America (1917–20), and director of the Baltimore Museum of Art (1922–27). She was executive secretary of the New York Regional Arts Council (1927–32) and supervisor of the National Alliance of Art and Industry (1932–34) and the Federated Council on Art Education (later, Art Education Council) from 1934 to 1937. She was director of the Art Guidance Council of the National Association for Art Education in 1937. She was a major promoter of art education in the schools.

In 1898 Levy founded the *American Art Annual,* which was divided into *American Art Directory* and *Who's Who in American Art* in 1948. She served as editor (1898–1918 and 1944) and advisory editor (1946) of the *Annual.* She was editor of *A Guide to the Works of Art in New York City* (1916–39), *New York Art Calendar, The New York Art Bulletin,* and *Art Education in the City of New York* (1938). A trustee for the Federation of the Arts (1913–47), she was secretary of the School Art League (1909–45). She was one of the first women elected to the American Institute of Graphic Arts (1925).

REFERENCES: LE (II); *NAW; NCAB* (B: 488); *NYT,* November 17, 1947, p. 22; "Florence Levy Dies," *Art Digest* 22 (December 1, 1947): 18; Dorothy E. Gilbert, ed., *American Art Annual, 1948* (Washington, D.C.: American Federation of the Arts, 1949), pp. 31–32; *Magazine of Art* 41 (January 1948): 32.   *James F. Warwick*

LEWIS, Dioclesian. B. March 3, 1823, near Auburn, New York, to John C. and Delecta (Barbour) Lewis. M. July 11, 1849, to Helen Cecelia Clark. Ch. none. D. May 21, 1886, Yonkers, New York.

As a youth Dio Lewis was well regarded for his inquisitiveness and his ability to speak, frequently engaging in debates and talking on temperance.

He began teaching in Auburn, New York, at the age of fifteen and became well known locally for his teaching methods. When he was eighteen years old, he moved to Lower Sandusky (now Fremont), Ohio, and organized a private school named the Dioclesian Institute. Shortly before the end of the school year, an illness forced him to return to New York, and he abandoned the school.

Lewis studied medicine with a local physician and at the Harvard Medical School (1845–46). He left Harvard, without obtaining a degree, to practice medicine in Port Byron, New York, where he became a believer in homoeopathy. In 1851 the Homoeopathic Hospital College in Cleveland, Ohio, awarded him an honorary M.D. degree.

Lewis moved his private practice to Buffalo, New York, in 1848, where he began stressing the importance of hygiene in the prevention of disease. In the early 1850s, Lewis embarked on a six-year speaking tour throughout the middle and northern United States and Canada. Realizing the necessity for physical culture, especially in the schools, he established the Boston Normal Institute of Physical Education (1861–88), where he taught his new gymnastics, an eclectic system based primarily on the Swedish system of light gymnastics. Lewis established the Sanatorium and Gymnasium for girls in Lexington, Massachusetts, in 1864. The school building was destroyed by fire in 1868, and the school operated for one more year in a summer hotel on Spy Pond, five miles from Boston. From 1868 until his death, Lewis devoted most of his time to writing and lecturing on hygiene, physical education, and temperance. Because of his emphasis on health and fitness and because of his belief that physical culture should be a part of the school curriculum, he is regarded as a pioneer in the field of physical education.

His best-received work was *New Gymnastics for Men, Women and Children* published in 1862. He also wrote *Weak Lungs and How to Make Them Strong* (1864), *Talks About People's Stomachs* (1870), *Talks About Health* (1871), *Our Girls* (1871), *Our Digestion* (1872), *Chastity; or Our Secret Sins* (1874), *Prohibition a Failure* (1875), *Gypsies* (1881), *Curious Fashions* (1883), *In a Nutshell* (1883), and *The Dio Lewis Treasury* (1886). He also edited *Today* (1871–72), *Dio Lewis's Monthly,* and *Dio Lewis Nuggets.* He received an honorary degree from Amherst College.

REFERENCES: *AC; DAB; NCAB* (10:381); *TC; WWW* (H); Mary Eastman, *The Biography of Dio Lewis, A.M., M.D.* (New York; Fowler and Wells Co., 1891); Alanson Lester Fish, "Life, Work, and Influence of Dio Lewis, A.M., M.D." (thesis, Springfield College, 1898); *NYT,* May 22, 1886, p. 5; Alfred Albert Smith, "Dio Lewis and His Contribution to Physical Education" (thesis, Springfield College, 1914).

William J. Sullivan

LEWIS, Enoch. B. January 29, 1776, Radnor, Pennsylvania, to Evan and Jane Lewis. M. May 9, 1799, to Alice Jackson. M. May 11, 1815, to Lydia Jackson. Ch. n.a. (at least one). D. July 14, 1856, Philadelphia, Pennsylvania.

Enoch Lewis attended the Radnor (Pennsylvania) School, and Friends Academy in Philadelphia, Pennsylvania.

Lewis taught at the Radnor School (1793–94) and at Friends Academy (1794–98). He was head of the mathematics department at Friends Westtown boarding school (1799–1808). He established a boarding school in New Garden, Pennsylvania, in 1808 and later moved it to Wilmington, Delaware, where he retired from teaching in 1827. He also served as a surveyor and laid out several towns, including West Chester, Wilmington, and Pottsville, and was a regulator of Philadelphia.

Lewis was the author of *Observations on the Military System* (1821), *The Arithmetical Expositor* (1824), *A View of the Present State of the African Slave Trade* (1824), *The Practical Analyst* (1826), *Vindication of the Society of Friends* (1834), *A Dissertation on Oaths* (1838), *Observations on Baptism* (1839), *Memoirs of the Life of William Penn* (1841), *A Treatise on Plane and Spherical Trigonometry* (1844), and *A Treatise on Algebra* (1844). He was founder and editor of the *African Observer* (1827–28) and *Friends Review* (1847–56). He produced almanacs for 1800 and 1806.

REFERENCES: *AC; DAB; NCAB* (10:112); *WWW* (H).

Robert McGinty

LEWIS, Samuel. B. March 17, 1799, Falmouth, Massachusetts, to Samuel and Abigail (Tolman) Lewis. M. 1823 to Charlotte E. Goforth. Ch. two. D. July 28, 1854, Cincinnati, Ohio.

Samuel Lewis, a founder of the free public school system in Ohio and the first Ohio state superintendent of common schools, was self-educated. His father was a ship's captain who moved his family to Cincinnati, Ohio, in 1813. Samuel Lewis was employed in farming and carpentry until 1819 when he became a court clerk. He was admitted to the bar in 1822 and licensed to preach in 1824.

Lewis became interested in the local Cincinnati schools and persuaded clients to establish endowments for the support of Woodward and Hughes high schools in Cincinnati. In 1831 he helped organize the Western Literary Institute and College of Professional Teachers, an organization to promote education. Elected state senator in 1825, he secured passage of the common school law allowing local communities to levy and collect taxes for schools. In 1837 the Ohio legislature created the office of state super-intendent of common schools and appointed Lewis to the post. Although he resigned the position in 1839 because of poor health, he continued his interest in education.

Lewis ran unsuccessfully for Congress (1843 and 1848) as a candidate of the Liberty party he had helped to organize with Salmon P. Chase. He failed as a Liberty party candidate for governor (1846, 1851, and 1853). He advocated free public education and supported the establishment of public elementary schools in Cincinnati.

In the 1850s Lewis became interested in secondary education, noting that the state was able to extend the public support of education to that level. He proposed combining the resources of the Hughes and Woodward funds, over which he exercised some control, with other resources, and a financial base was laid in Cincinnati that enabled the city to provide at public expense a limited secondary curriculum for all qualified applicants.

Lewis's long career in support of free education for the people of Ohio earned him the title Father of the Free School System in Ohio. He was instrumental in the William Woodward bequest that provided funds for the Woodward High School in Cincinnati and was a trustee of the Woodward Fund from its inception to his death in 1854.

REFERENCES: *AC; DAB; NCAB* (25:439); *WWW* (H); James J. Burns, *Educational History of Ohio* (Columbus, Ohio: Historical Publishing Co., 1905); William G. W. Lewis, *Biography of Samuel Lewis* (Cincinnati: Printed at the Methodist Book Concern, R. P. Thompson, Printer, 1857); John B. Shotwell, *A History of the Schools of Cincinnati* (Cincinnati: The School Life Company, 1902).

Marjorie Muntz

LIEBER, Francis. B. March 18, 1800, Berlin, Germany, to Friedrich Wilhelm Lieber and his wife (n.a.) M. September 21, 1829, to Matilda Oppenheimer. Ch. four, including Guido Norman Lieber, judge advocate general of the United States. D. October 2, 1872, New York, New York.

Francis Lieber grew up in an atmosphere of German nationalism and liberalism. He studied at the universities of Jena, Halle, and Dresden, interrupting his studies to take part in the last campaign of the Napoleonic wars at Waterloo (1815). He received the Ph.D. degree (1820) from the University of Jena.

Lieber was a leader in Friedrich L. Jahn's nationalist Turner movement and was imprisoned for his liberal political views in 1819 and 1824. He lived in Rome (1822–23) and was influenced by the German diplomat-historian B. G. Niebuhr. He went to England in 1826 and served for a year as a tutor, emigrating to the United States in 1827. Lieber founded and edited the *Encyclopedia Americana* (1829–33). In 1835 he accepted a professorship in political theory at South Carolina College (later, the University of South Carolina). He remained there for twenty-one years, establishing a reputation as a leading political theorist and developing a rigorous and systematic philosophy of political science. He moved to Columbia College (later, University) in 1857 to teach history and political science. He joined the faculty of Columbia Law School in 1865, a position he held for the rest of his life.

After the outbreak of the Civil War Lieber was consulted often by the Union government. At the request of the War Department he wrote *Instructions for the Government of the Armies of the United States in the Field* (1863), the first code of military law for any country. He was chief of the Bureau of Rebel Archives in charge of Confederate records captured during the war. Lieber was umpire of the Mexican Claims Commission (1870–72).

Lieber was the author of *German Anacharsis* (1823), *Letters to a Gentleman in Germany* (1834), *Reminscences of Niebuhr* (1835), *Manual of Political Ethics* (two volumes, 1838), *Legal and Political Hermeneutics* (1839), *Essay on Property and Labor* (1842), *Great Events Described by Great Historians* (1847), *On Civil Liberty and Self-Government* (two volumes, 1853), and *Guerilla Parties Considered with Reference to the Laws and Usages of War* (1862).

A member of many American and European learned societies, Lieber was a fellow of the American Academy of Arts and Sciences and a corresponding member of the Institut de France. He received an honorary degree from Harvard University (1850).

REFERENCES: *AC; DAB; NCAB* (5:116); *TC; WWW* (H); Bernard Edward Brown, *American Conservatives: The Political Thought of Francis Lieber and John W. Burgess* (New York: Columbia University Press, 1951), pp. 13–25; *NYT,* October 3, 1872, p. 10.

Dennis G. Wiseman

LILLIE, Frank Rattray. B. June 27, 1870, Toronto, Ontario, Canada, to George Waddell and Emily Ann (Rattray) Lillie. M. June 29, 1895, to Frances Crane. Ch. seven. D. November 5, 1947, Chicago, Illinois.

Frank Rattray Lillie was an indifferent student in grammar school; however, in high school he became interested in religion and in the natural sciences. Believing science to be a threat to religion, he entered the University of Toronto, Canada, to study for the ministry. Attempting to resolve the conflict involved him deeply in the study of both science and religion; by his senior year, the differences were resolved, and science had completely captured his career interests. He was awarded the A.B. degree with honors from the University of Toronto (1891). He accepted a fellowship for the summer session of 1891 at the Marine Biological Laboratory at Woods Hole, Massachusetts, then in its fourth year of operation. There he developed an enduring interest in embryology.

Lillie studied for one year at Clark University and completed his studies at the University of Chicago, where he received the Ph.D. degree (1894). His first teaching position was as an instructor at the University of Michigan (1894–99); he later became professor of biology at Vassar College (1899–1900). In 1900 he returned to the University of Chicago, becoming chairman of the biology department in 1910. He was appointed Andrew MacLeish Distinguished Professor of Embryology and dean of the newly established division of biological sciences (1931). He retired in 1935.

Lillie taught at the Marine Biological Laboratory at Woods Hole and was chairman of the department of zoology at the laboratory (1893–1907), assistant director (1907), director (1908), and president of the corporation and the board of trustees (1926). He became president emeritus in 1942. Lillie contributed much toward the growth and development of the democratic academic consortium into which the laboratory evolved. He was largely responsible for the building of the Oceanographic Institution, of which he was the first president (1930–39).

Lillie was a contributor to scientific journals. He was managing editor of the *Biological Bulletin* (1912–26) and associate editor of several other professional periodicals. He was chairman of the National Research Council (1935–36), a fellow in the American Association for the Advancement of Science and the Philadelphia Academy of Natural Science, and president of the American Society of Zoologists (1905–08) and the American Society of Naturalists (1914). He held memberships and leadership positions in many other societies in the United States and abroad. He received several honorary degrees.

REFERENCES: *DAB* (supp. 4); *DSB; LE* (II); *NCAB* (36:32); *WWW* (II); *NYT,* November 6, 1947, p. 27; "Frank Rattray Lillie," *Science* 107 (January 9, 1948): 33–35.   *Isadore L. Sonnier*

LINCOLN, Almira Hart. See PHELPS, Almira Hart Lincoln.

LINDLEY, Ernest Hiram. B. October 2, 1869, Paoli, Indiana, to Hiram and Laura (White) Lindley. M. September 18, 1895, to Elizabeth Kidder. Ch. two, including Ernest K. Lindley, columnist. D. August 21, 1940, at sea.

Ernest Hiram Lindley was educated in the schools of Bloomington, Indiana; he received the A.B. degree from Indiana University (1893) and the A.M. (1894) and Ph.D. (1897) degrees from Clark University in Worcester, Massachusetts. He also studied in Germany at the universities of Heidelberg, Leipzig, and Jena (1897–98) and at Harvard University (1904–05).

Lindley taught at Indiana University (1893–1917) and rose from the rank of instructor to full professor and head of the department of philosophy and psychology. He was president of the University of Idaho (1917–20) and chancellor of the University of Kansas (1920–39).

While at Kansas, he was involved in raising scholastic standards, enforcing regulations, and supervising an extensive building program. In 1924 the Ku Klux Klan brought pressure on the governor to remove Lindley, who obtained a court injunction that prohibited the governor and the board of administration from removing him from office. The state supreme court ruled that the chancellor held office at the pleasure of the board and the governor, but the incoming governor aided in getting a law enacted for the following year that separated the control of the state educational institutions from other state agencies. A nonsalaried board of nine was appointed to govern educational institutions.

Lindley authored *Ueber Arbeit und Ruhe* (1900) and coauthored *Compte-rendu du quatrième congres international* (with William L. Bryan, 1900).

A fellow of the American Association for the Advancement of Science, Lindley was also a trustee of the Carnegie Foundation for the Advancement of Teaching. He was president of the National Association of State Universities (1924–25). He received several honorary degrees.

REFERENCES: *CB* (1940); *LE* (I); *NCAB* (E: 451, 42:628); *WWAE* (VIII); *WWW* (I); *NYT,* August 22, 1940, p. 19.   *S. S. Britt, Jr.*

LINDQUIST, Everet Franklin. B. June 4, 1901, Gowrie, Iowa, to Jonas Algot and Hannah Olivia (Anderson) Lindquist. M. August 31, 1927, to Marguerite Liebig. Ch. one.

E. F. Lindquist received the A.B. degree (1922) from Augustana College in Rock Island, Illinois. He studied at the University of Chicago and the State University of Iowa, where he received the Ph.D. degree (1927).

Lindquist was a high school teacher at Macoutah, Illinois (1922), and a professor of education at the State University of Iowa in Iowa City (1927–69). He served as the director of the Iowa Testing Programs (1929–69). He was in charge of the construction and standardization of tests of General Educational Development for the United States Armed Forces Institute (1942–44). He was founder and president of the Measurement Research Center at Iowa City from 1953 to 1968, when he became president of the Iowa Measurement Research Foundation.

Lindquist was cofounder and general test constructor of the American College Testing Program and originator of the Iowa Educational Information Center. In 1967 he received the Phi Delta Kappa Educational Research Association Award and, in 1970, the Educational Testing Service Award for distinguished service to measurement. He belonged to many professional associations and was a fellow of the American Statistical Association.

He was editor of the *Iowa Tests of Basic Skills* and *Iowa Tests of Educational Development.* He edited *The Construction and Use of Achievement Exams* (1936) and *Educational Measurement* (1952). He was the author of *A First Course in Statistics* (1938), *Statistical Analysis in Educational Research* (1940), and *Design and Analysis of Experiments in Psychology and Education* (1953), and he coauthored *Statistics for Economics and Business* (with Donald W. Paden, 1951) and *Elementary Statistical Methods* (with Paul Blommers, 1960). He invented an electronic test scoring machine in 1953.

REFERENCES: *LE* (III); *WW* (XXXIX); *WWAE* (XVI); R. H. Beck, "Educational Leadership, 1906–1956," *Phi Delta Kappan* 37 (January 1956): 159-65.   *Lawrence S. Master*

LINDSLEY, John Berrien. B. October 24, 1822, Princeton, New Jersey, to Philip *(q.v.)* and Margaret Elizabeth (Lawrence) Lindsley. M. February 9, 1857, to Sarah McGavock. Ch. six. D. December 7, 1897, Nashville, Tennessee.

John Berrien Lindsley received the A.B. (1839) and A.M. (1841) degrees from the University of Nashville, where his father was president. He received the M.D. degree (1843) from the University of Pennsylvania and practiced medicine in the Nashville, Tennessee, area (1843–50).

Lindsley was ordained in the Presbyterian church in 1846, served as a supply pastor, and preached to slaves in the Nashville area for a year. In 1850 he helped organize a medical school at the University of Nashville and was elected dean of the faculty. He became chancellor of the university in 1855 and remained in that post until 1870. In 1855 he arranged for a merger of the Western Military Institute with the university and thus reopened the collegiate department that had been closed in 1850. Through his personal efforts, the university medical school remained open during the Civil War. He served as post surgeon of Confederate hospitals in Nashville (1861–62).

He devised the plan for the creation of a normal school within the university structure to be financed by the Peabody Fund. First a state normal school, the institution later became the George Peabody College for Teachers. He organized the Montgomery Bell Academy in 1867 and served as president to 1870, when he resigned to assist in founding the Tennessee College of Pharmacy, where he served as professor of materia medica (1876–97). He also served as professor of chemistry and state medicine at the University of Tennessee (1880–97).

In 1851 Lindsley began working on behalf of the public schools of Tennessee and he became a member of the Nashville City Board of Education (1856–60). He was elected superintendent in 1866. He prepared the legislative bill creating the first state board of education in Tennessee (1875) and served as secretary of the board (1875–87). He helped organize the Tennessee State Teachers' Association and was a strong advocate of the establishment of normal schools at a time when the concept of professional education for teachers was not popular in the South.

Lindsley became interested in the cause of public health and served in various capacities with the Tennessee State Board of Health (1877–97). He wrote on a variety of subjects. Among his works were *On Medical Colleges* (1858), *African Colonization and Christian Missions* (1873), and *The History of the Law School of Cumberland University at Lebanon* (1876). He edited the *Confederate Military Annals of Tennessee* (1886) and the Nashville *Journal of Medicine and Surgery*.

Lindsley was a member of many organizations, including the American Public Health Association (treasurer, 1879–97), the National Prison Association (director), and the Royal Historical Society of London, England. He received an honorary degree from the College of New Jersey (later, Princeton University).

REFERENCES: *AC; DAB; NCAB* (8:131); *TC; WWW* (H); Robert H. White, *Development of the Tennessee Educational Organization,* Contribution to Education, No. 62 (Nashville: George Peabody College for Teachers, 1929); John Edwin Windrow, *John Berrien Lindsley* (Chapel Hill: University of North Carolina Press, 1938).   *Jerry B. Ayers*

LINDSLEY, Philip. B. December 21, 1786, near Morristown, New Jersey, to Isaac and Phoebe (Condict) Lindsley. M. October 14, 1813, to Margaret Elizabeth Lawrence. M. April 19, 1849, to Mary Ann (Silliman) Ayers. Ch. five, including John Berrien Lindsley *(q.v.)*, medical educator. D. May 25, 1855, Nashville, Tennessee.

Philip Lindsley entered Robert Finley's school at Basking Ridge, New Jersey, at the age of thirteen. He entered the junior class of the College of New Jersey (later, Princeton University), graduating in 1804. After teaching in Morristown, New Jersey, and at Mr. Finley's school, he returned to the college (1807) as junior tutor and studied theology, primarily under President Samuel Stanhope Smith *(q.v.)*. He was licensed to preach in 1810 and ordained in 1817 by the presbytery of New Brunswick. He continued his theological studies during the next two years, preached at home and in adjoining states, and returned to the college at Princeton as a senior tutor in 1812.

In 1813 Lindsley was transferred from the tutorship to professor of languages and was chosen secretary of the board of trustees; he was later made the college librarian. He was elected vice-president of the college(1817) and served one year as acting president (1822), but he refused an offer to become president in 1823. In 1824 Lindsley accepted a second offer to become president of Cumberland College, which was then being reorganized as the University of Nashville. He found that the financial backing necessary for a university was not forthcoming and decided to make the University of Nashville a good undergraduate college. He selected a quality faculty and increased the student enrollment. He resigned the presidency of the University of Nashville in 1850 to become professor in New Albany (Indiana) Theological Seminary (1850–53).

In 1866 his complete writings were published in three volumes, *Works,* edited by L. J. Halsey. Lindsley was active in the Presbyterian church; he was chosen moderator in 1834 and commissioner of the presbytery to the general assembly of 1855. He received an honorary degree from Dickinson College in 1825.

REFERENCES: *AC; DAB; NCAB* (8:131); *TC; WWW* (H); W. W. Clayton, *History of Davidson County, Tennessee, with Illustrations and Biographical Sketches of Its Prominent Men and Pioneers* (Nashville, Tenn.: C. Elder, 1971), pp. 388-92; L. J. Halsey, ed., *The Works of Philip Lindsley, D. D.* (Philadelphia: J. B. Lippincott & Co., 1866).

Leon W. Brownlee

LINVILLE, Henry Richardson. B. August 12, 1866, St. Joseph, Missouri, to Richard Baxter and Emma (Richardson) Linville. M. June 9, 1908, to Adele Miln. M. December 26, 1931, to Laura Branson. Ch. four. D. October 1, 1941, Linville, North Carolina.

Henry Richardson Linville spent the first twenty years of his life in Mill Grove, Missouri, and Ness County, Kansas. At the age of sixteen, he entered the University of Kansas preparatory school in Lawrence and continued at the university, where he received the A.B. degree (1893). In 1894 he entered Harvard University, where he assisted in the zoology department and received the A.B. (1894), A.M. (1895), and Ph.D. (1897) degrees.

Linville joined the New York City school system where he was chairman of the biology departments at DeWitt Clinton (1897–1908) and Jamaica (1908–21) high schools. He believed that education should serve the welfare of mankind. He considered organized labor a critical socially oriented organization. He played an important role in organizing the Teachers' Union of New York City and the American Federation of Teachers in 1916. He served as president and later executive director of the Teachers' Union (1916–35). During the early years of the national organization, he served as editor of *The American Teacher*. He resigned from the New York public schools in 1921 to devote the remainder of his career to teacher unionism.

In 1931 Linville was elected president of the American Federation of Teachers, a post he held until 1935 when he returned to New York City as president of the New York Teachers Guild. He participated in the factional fight within the New York teachers' union and national organization during the 1930s.

Linville authored several books and articles, including *A Textbook in General Zoology* (with Henry A. Kelly, 1906) and *The Biology of Man and Other Organisms* (1923). He wrote many articles advocating and explaining the principles of teacher unionism.

REFERENCES: *LE* (II); *WWW* (II); Solon De Leon, ed., *The American Labor Who's Who* (New York: Vanguard, 1925).   *Dennis East II*

LLOYD-JONES, Esther McDonald. B. January 11, 1901, Lockport, Illinois, to Leon and Clara A. (Rudd) McDonald. M. June 12, 1924, to Silas Lloyd-Jones. Ch. two.

Esther McDonald Lloyd-Jones received the A.B. degree (1923) from Northwestern University in Evanston, Illinois, and was a fellow at Columbia University (1923–24), where she received the A.M. (1924) and Ph.D. (1929) degrees.

Assistant director of personnel at Northwestern University (1924–26) and conductor of research for the American Council on Education (1929–30), Lloyd-Jones spent her career at Columbia University, beginning as an instructor in the department of student personnel administration (1928–30). She was an assistant professor (1931) and professor (1941–66) with the department of student personnel administration and was acting chairman (1939–41) and chairman (1941–66). She was head of the guidance laboratory (1933–63) and associate director of personnel (1939–46). After her retirement in 1966, she became professor of human behavior with the graduate school of human behavior at the United States International University in San Diego, California (1967).

Lloyd-Jones wrote several books, including *Student Personnel Work at Northwestern University* (1929), *A Student Personnel Program for Higher Education* (with M. R. Smith, 1938), *Re-directing Teacher Education* (with G. Watson and D. P. Cottrell, 1938), *Social Competence and College Students* (1940), *Coming of Age* (with R. Fedder, 1941), and *Student Personnel as Deeper Teaching* (with Margaret Ruth Smith, 1954). She edited *Case Studies in College Student-Staff Relationships* (1956), *Case Studies in Human Relationships in Secondary Schools* (with others, 1956), and *Guidance in Elementary Education* (1958). She was associate editor of *Understanding the Child* (1938–58).

A member of many professional associations, Lloyd-Jones was active in the American Council on Education (chairman of the commission on education of women, 1953–58), the Hazen Foundation (chairman, counseling committee, 1941–54), the American Council of Guidance and Personnel

Associations (secretary-treasurer, 1938–39), the American Psychological Association (diplomate in counseling and guidance), the National Council on Religion in Higher Education (director, 1941–46), and the American Association of University Women (New York City director, 1937–39). She served as president of the American College Personnel Association (1935–37 and secretary, 1933–35) and the New York State Association of Deans (1943–45). She was active in the Girl Scouts of the U.S.A. (member, national personnel committee, 1939–45) and the Young Women's Christian Association (board and council member, 1931–36, and chairman of the national student council, 1923–24 and 1928–31). She received awards of merit from Northwestern University (1945) and the University of Arizona (1960) and honorary degrees from Elmira College (1955), Boston University (1961), and Long Island University (1963).

REFERENCES: *CA* (13–16); *LE* (III); *WW* (XXXIV); *WWAE* (XIV); "Esther Lloyd-Jones Given 1966 Nancy C. Wimmer Award," *Personnel and Guidance Journal* 44 (June 1966): 1109-10.   *John F. Ohles*

LOCKE, Alain LeRoy. B. September 13, 1886, Philadelphia, Pennsylvania, to Pliny L. and Mary (Hawkins) Locke. M. no. D. June 9, 1954, New York, New York.

Alain LeRoy Locke was graduated from Central High School in Philadelphia, Pennsylvania, receiving the A.B. degree in 1902. He was graduated from the Philadelphia School of Pedagogy in 1904 and was a student at Harvard University, where he received the A.B. (1907) and Ph.D. (1918) degrees. He was the first black to be a Rhodes Scholar, studying at Oxford, (England) University (1907–10), and he also studied at the University of Berlin, Germany.

Locke was assistant professor of philosophy and education at Howard University in Washington, D.C. (1912–17), and headed the department of philosophy (1917–53). He was an exchange professor to Fisk University in Nashville, Tennessee (1927–28), and Inter-American Exchange Professor to Haiti in 1943. He was a visiting professor at the University of Wisconsin (1945–46), the New School for Social Research (1947), and the College of the City of New York (1948).

Locke was a major interpreter of black culture and racial relations on the national and international levels. He was the author of several important books, including *Race Contacts and Inter-racial Relations* (1916), *The New Negro* (1925), *The Negro in America* (1933), *The Negro and His Music* (1936), *Negro Art—Past and Present* (1937), *The Negro in Art* (1941), and *When Peoples Meet* (with Bernhard Stern, 1941). He was contributing editor of *Survey Graphic* and editor of *Plays of Negro Life* (with Montgomery Gregory, 1927) and the Bronze Booklet Series of the Associates in Negro Folk Education (1937).

Locke was a member of the Associates in Negro Life Education (secretary) and of many ethnic and scholarly organizations. He was a founding member of the Conference on Science, Philosophy, and Religion.

REFERENCES: *CB* (January 1944, September 1954); *LE* (II); *WWW* (III); *NYT,* June 10, 1954, p. 31; Wilhelmena S. Robinson, *International Library of Negro Life and History: Historical Negro Biographies* (New York: Publishers Co., 1967), pp. 222-23.   *John F. Ohles*

LODGE, Gonzalez. B. February 19, 1863, Fort Littleton, Pennsylvania, to William J. and Virginia H. (Cockey) Lodge. M. June 10, 1909, to Ida B. Stanwood, Ch. none. D. December 23, 1942, New Canaan, Connecticut.

Gonzalez Lodge was educated in the Baltimore (Maryland) public schools, at Baltimore City College, and at Johns Hopkins University in Baltimore, where he received the A.B. (1883) and Ph.D. (1886) degrees. He studied in Germany and Greece (1888–89).

Lodge was professor of Greek at Davidson (North Carolina) College (1886–88) and professor of Latin at Bryn Mawr (Pennsylvania) College (1889–1900). In 1900 he became a professor of Latin and Greek at Teachers College, Columbia University, where he introduced the oral method of instruction in Greek and Latin. He retired in 1929.

The author of textbooks in Latin, he wrote *The Gildersleeve-Lodge Latin Grammar and Latin Composition* (with Basil L. Gildersleeve, *q.v.,* 1894), *Lexicon Plautinum* (volume 1, ten parts, 1901–24; and volume 2, ten parts, 1925–23), and *Vocabulary of High School Latin* (1907). He was managing editor of the Gildersleeve-Lodge Latin Series (sixteen volumes, 1894–1908) and editor of *The Gorgias of Plato* (1890). He was editor-in-chief of the *Classical Weekly* (1907–13).

Lodge was a member of professional and scholarly organizations. He was awarded honorary degrees by Franklin and Marshall College (1901) and Columbia University (1929).

REFERENCES: *LE* (II); *NCAB* (31:59); *NYT,* December 25, 1942, p. 17; *WWW* (IV).

John F. Ohles

LOMAX, Paul Sanford. B. May 3, 1890, Laclede, Missouri, to James Wesley and Alsina Arabella (Artlip) Lomax. M. December 25, 1919, to Emily Bertha Tschann. M. August 15, 1929, to Beatrice Marie Loyer. Ch. three. D. February 6, 1975, Maplewood, New Jersey.

Paul Sanford Lomax, leader in business education, received the B.S. degree (1917) from the University of Missouri. He studied at the University of Dijon, France (1919), and at Harvard University during the summers of 1922 and 1923. He received the Ph.D. degree (1927) from New York University.

Lomax taught in the Missouri public schools (1908–13) and at the University of Missouri high school (1914–16). He was professor of commerce at New Mexico Normal University (1916–18). After serving in World War I, he was a specialist in commercial education with the Federal Board for Vocational Education (1919–20) and with the New York State Department of Education (1920–21). He was director of business education with the Trenton, New Jersey, public schools (1921–24). Joining the faculty at New York University in 1924, he was chairman of the department of business education from 1926, retiring in 1956. He was recognized for his contributions to graduate studies in the field of business education.

The author of many articles in professional journals, he also wrote *Commercial Teaching Problems* (1928), *Problems of Teaching Elementary Business Training* (with B. R. Haynes, 1929), *Problems of Teaching Bookkeeping* (with P. L. Agnew, 1930), *Problems of Teaching Shorthand* (with J. V. Walsh, 1930), *Problems of Teaching Economics* (with H. A. Tonne, *q.v.*, 1932), *Problems of Teaching Arithmetic* (with J. J. W. Neuna, 1932), *Teaching Principles and Procedures for Gregg Shorthand* (with others, 1932), and *Problems of Teaching Typewriting* (with others, 1935). He was editor of yearbooks of the Eastern Commercial Teachers Association (1928, 1929, 1930) and *Journal of Business Education* (1929–38) and a contributing editor to *Journal of Educational Sociology* and *Clearing House.*

Lomax was active in professional associations, serving as president of the business education department of the National Education Association, and he was a cofounder and president of the National Council of Business Education (later, merged into the National Business Education Association). He received the John Robert Gregg Award in Business Education (1953) and other forms of recognition for his contributions to his profession. He was the recipient of honorary degrees from Bryant and Rider colleges.

REFERENCES: *LE* (III); *WW* (XXVIII); *WWAE* (XV); *WWW* (VI); *Business Education Forum* 29 (April 1975): 43; *NYT*, February 8, 1975, p. 28. *John F. Ohles*

LONDON, Hoyt Hobson. B. October 12, 1900, Fannin County, Texas, to William H. and Mary (Jones) London. M. August 27, 1930, to Ova L. Payne. M. June 10, 1961, to Virginia Mace Carlson. Ch. four.

Hoyt H. London earned the B.S. degree (1924) from North Texas State University, the M.A. degree (1929) from the University of Missouri, and the Ph.D. degree (1934) from Ohio State University.

London was an instructor in industrial arts at Muskogee (Oklahoma) High School (1922–23) and taught industrial education at Arlington (Texas) State College (later, University of Texas at Arlington) (1923–26), West Texas State University (later, University of Texas at El Paso) (1926–27),

North Texas State University at Denton (1927–28 and 1929–31), and Ohio State University (1931–34). He was an educational adviser with the Civilian Conservation Corps in San Antonio (1934–35). In 1935 he became professor of industrial education at Georgia Southern College at Statesboro, moving to Mississippi State University at State College in 1937. He was professor of industrial education at the University of Missouri from 1938 until his retirement in 1971. He established the graduate program in industrial education there.

London was a founder of the Missouri Industrial Education Association. He was secretary-treasurer of the Missouri Vocational Association (1948–58) and chairman of its legislative committee (1954–64). He was a trustee, vice-president, and president (1954) of the National Association of Industrial and Technical Teacher Educators, president of the American Vocational Association (1959), and chairman of the Mississippi Valley Industrial Arts Conference (1961–71).

He served on international educational study commissions, led a United States government-sponsored delegation to the Soviet Union (1961) to study technical education programs there, and helped revise educational programs and establish vocational schools in Nigeria in 1969. He was the author of many articles published in professional journals and *Principles and Techniques of Vocational Guidance* (1973).

He was honored by the state of Kentucky, the University of Missouri, and the American Vocational Association, which presented him with its distinguished service award.

REFERENCES: *CA* (49–52); *LE* (V); *WWAE* (VIII); William T. Sargent, "The Dedication to Hoyt H. London," *Journal of Industrial Teacher Education,* 8 (Winter 1971): 66-68; *Who's Who in Industrial Arts Teacher Education* (American Council on Industrial Arts Teacher Education, 1969). *Claude A. Bell*

LONG, Oren Ethelbirt. B. March 4, 1889, Altoona, Kansas, to George Rile and Melissa Jeanette (Johnson) Long. M. June 28, 1917, to Ida Geneva Rule. Ch. none. D. May 6, 1965, Honolulu, Hawaii.

Oren E. Long attended local Kansas schools and continued his education in Kimberlin Heights, Tennessee, where he was graduated from Johnson Academy (1909) and Johnson Bible College with the B.A. degree (1912). He received the M.A. degree (1916) in economics and literature from the University of Michigan and a second M.A. (1922) in education from Columbia University. He studied at the universities of Tennessee and Pennsylvania.

A history teacher (1912–14) and principal (1914–17) at Johnson Academy, Long moved to the Territory of Hawaii in 1917 and began a forty-eight-year career serving the islands. He was a social settlement worker at Hilo, Hawaii (1917–18), educational director of the Young Men's Christian Association program serving the United States Army (1918–19), vice-principal at McKinley High School in Honolulu (1919–20), and personnel director for the Kohala Sugar Company (1920–21). He returned to the United States mainland as Church Farm School principal in Glen Loch, Pennsylvania (1921–23). He returned to Hawaii and began a nine-year tenure as deputy superintendent of public instruction (1925–34) and superintendent of public instruction (1934–46). He strengthened the quality of the state's educational program, increased qualifications for teachers, and extended educational opportunities to the rural areas of the territory.

In 1946 Long was named secretary of Hawaii, a position similar to that of lieutenant-governor, and he served as governor of the territory (1951–53), vice-chairman of the Statehood Commission (1954–56), a member of the territorial senate (1956–59), and first United States Senator from the State of Hawaii (1959–63).

Long was a member of professional organizations and served as director of public welfare for the Territory of Hawaii (1946), chairman of the advisory committee on education for trust territories for the United States Navy (1946), Boy Scouts of America local commissioner, and chairman of the board of the Investors Equity Life Insurance Company. He was a delegate to the World Federation of Education Association Conventions in Toronto, Canada (1929), Denver, Colorado (1931), and Tokyo, Japan (1937). He was a regent of the University of Hawaii (1935–46), chairman of the board of trustees of the Hawaii School of Religion (1944–51), and president of the Pan-Pacific Union (1936–40). He was editor of *Hawaii Educational Review* (1925–34). He received an honorary degree from the University of Hawaii (1951).

REFERENCES: *CB* (September 1951); *LE* (III); *NCAB* (J: 593); *NYT*, May 7, 1965, p. 41; *WW* (XXXII); *WWW* (IV).   *J. K. Ward*

LORD, Asa Dearborn. B. June 17, 1816, Madrid, New York, to Asa and Lucretia (Dearborn) Lord. M. July 21, 1842, to Elizabeth W. Russell. Ch. none. D. March 7, 1875, Batavia, New York.

Asa Dearborn Lord received his education from his mother, in local district schools, and at an academy at Potsdam, New York. He studied at the Western Reserve College (later, Case Western Reserve University in Cleveland, Ohio) in Hudson, Ohio, and received a medical diploma from Willoughby (Ohio) University in 1846. He studied theology and was licensed to preach in the Presbyterian church in 1863.

Lord taught in a private school in Willoughby, Ohio (1837–39), and became head of the Western Reserve Teachers' Seminary in Kirtland, Ohio, in 1839. The Columbus, Ohio, schools, under the influence of Henry

Barnard *(q.v.)* , created the first superintendent of schools position in the Midwest, and Lord was appointed to the post in 1847. He organized one of the first high schools in the state and served as principal as well as superintendent. He initiated the first graded school system in the state.

Lord resigned from the Columbus superintendency in 1856 and assumed the leadership over the Ohio Institution for the Education of the Blind in Columbus. He moved to Batavia, New York, in 1868 to head the new state school for the blind, and he remained there to his death in 1875. Elizabeth Lord, his wife, succeeded him as superintendent of the school.

Lord was extremely active in professional affairs. While at Kirtland, Ohio, he had organized and conducted the first teachers' institutes in Ohio in 1843. He was an organizer of the Ohio State Teachers' Association in 1847 and took a leave of absence as Columbus superintendent of schools in 1854 to act as the association's agent. He edited and published the *Ohio School Journal* from 1846 to 1849, when it was merged with *The School Friend.* He also published *The Public School Advocate* while he was Columbus superintendent, and he served as resident editor (1852–55) of the teachers' association journal, *The Ohio Journal of Education.*

REFERENCES: *DAB; NCAB* (12:313); *WWW* (H); James J. Burns, *Educational History of Ohio* (Columbus: Historical Publishing Co., 1905).   *Bruce D. Mattson*

LORD, Livingston Chester. B. August 27, 1851, Killingworth, Connecticut, to Benjamin and Antoinette (Case) Lord. M. 1874 to Mary E. Cook. Ch. five. D. May 15, 1933, Charleston, Illinois.

Livingston Chester Lord was educated in local country schools and worked in a spool shop in Tolland, Connecticut, at the age of sixteen. In 1869 he entered the New Britain (Connecticut) State Normal School (later, Central Connecticut State College), from which he was graduated in 1871.

Lord was a high school principal in Terryville, Connecticut (1871–74). He moved with his bride to Minnesota in 1874 where he was the principal of Winnebago City schools (1874–78) and the Union School in Mankato (1878–79). He served as superintendent of the St. Peter schools (1879–88). Lord became principal of the newly established State Normal School (later, Moorhead State College) in Moorhead, Minnesota (1888–99). His success in establishing the school led to offers to assume leadership over other normal schools, which he declined until he was offered the position of president in the normal school recently established in Charleston, Illinois. Succeeding to the position on the death of the first president of the school, Lord moved to Illinois, bringing with him from Moorhead John Paul Goode *(q.v.)*, Henry Johnson *(q.v.)* and later, Ellen Ford. Lord served as president of Eastern Illinois State Normal School (later, Eastern Illinois University) from 1899 to his death in 1933. He received honorary degrees from

Harvard and Miami universities and the University of Illinois.

REFERENCES: *LE* (I); *NYT,* May 16, 1933, p. 17; *WWAE* (I); *WWW* (I); Isabel McKinney, "An American Scholar," *American Scholar* 4 (January 1935): 4-16; Isabel McKinney, *Mr. Lord* (Urbana: University of Illinois Press, 1937).   *John F. Ohles*

LORD, Nathan. B. November 28, 1792, South Berwick, Maine, to John and Mehitabel (Perkins) Lord. M. July 24, 1816, to Elizabeth King Leland. Ch. n.a. (at least eight). D. September 9, 1870, Hanover, New Hampshire.

Nathan Lord attended a local academy and Bowdoin College in Brunswick, Maine, where he received the A.B. (1809) and A.M. (1812) degrees. He was graduated from Andover (Massachusetts) Theological Seminary in 1815 and was ordained in 1816.

Lord taught at Phillips Academy in Exeter, New Hampshire, under Benjamin Abbot (*q.v.*) in 1810-11 and was pastor of the Amherst, New Hampshire, Congregational church (1816–28). He was elected a trustee of Dartmouth College in Hanover, New Hampshire, in 1821 and became president of the college in 1828 and taught courses in ethics and theology. Under Lord, the curriculum was enlarged, several new professorships were established, the physical plant was expanded, and the Chandler scientific department was established.

Lord was a strong supporter of slavery, yet Dartmouth was for many years the only college to admit blacks. They were treated equally with white students. His views led to his retirement in 1863, after college trustees expressed disapproval over publication of Lord's *A True Picture of Abolition* (1863).

Other works of Lord were *Letters to Rev. Daniel Dana, D. D., on Park's Theology of New England* (1852), *An Essay on Millennium* (1854), and *Two Letters to the Ministers of All Denominations on Slavery* (1854–55). He also edited the selected sermons of his son, John King Lord, in 1850. Lord was the recipient of honorary degrees from Dartmouth and Bowdoin colleges.

REFERENCES: *AC; DAB; NCAB* (9:88); *NYT*, September 10, 1870, p. 5; *TC; WWW* (H).   *Barbara Ruth Peltzman*

LOUGHRIDGE, Robert McGill. B. December 24, 1809, Laurensville, South Carolina, to James and Deborah Ann (McGill) Loughridge. M. December 6, 1842, to Olivia Hills. M. December 4, 1846, to Mary Avery. M. October 15, 1853, to Harriett Johnson. Ch. one, Robert Hills Loughridge, agricultural chemist and geologist. D. July 8, 1900, Waco, Texas.

Robert McGill Loughridge's family moved from South Carolina to Eutaw, Alabama, where he went to school and studied theology with a tutor at Mesopotomia Academy. He was graduated from Miami University

(Ohio) in 1837 and then attended Princeton Theological Seminary for a year, but he returned to Alabama on his father's death. He taught school and continued his theological studies in Alabama.

Loughridge was licensed to preach in 1841 and was ordained a Presbyterian minister in 1842. He went to Indian Territory (Oklahoma) in 1841 as a missionary to the Creek Indians. He was accepted only grudgingly by the Creeks, who had expelled all missionaries from their territory in Alabama in 1836 and who had been moved from Alabama and Georgia to the Indian Territory. Loughridge opened a school in Coweta, Indian Territory, in 1843. The school and the mission prospered. The Creeks considered him their friend and agreed, with Presbyterian help, to support the school and to establish a manual training boarding school in Tullahassee, Indian Territory. Loughridge became superintendent of the Tullahassee school in 1850 but, with other missionaries, was expelled from the Creek Nation at the outbreak of the Civil War. He served Presbyterian churches in eastern Texas until 1881, when he returned to the mission and took charge of the Tullahassee school, located in a new building at Wealaka, to 1885. He worked with the Creeks until 1888. He was a minister in Presbyterian churches in Tulsa (1888–92) and Red Fork (1889–92), Indian Territory, and in Waco, Texas (1892–95).

Loughridge was a noted translator and writer of books for Indian religious instruction. He wrote and published school books and other literature in Muskokee, the principal Creek dialect, including *Muskokee Hymns* (1845), based on the earlier work of the Reverend John Fleming, and *Translation of the Introduction to the Shorter Catechism* (1846). He translated the *Gospel According to Matthew* (1855) and published the *English and Muskokee Dictionary* (with David M. Hodge, 1890), also based on earlier work of Fleming.

REFERENCES: *DAB; NCAB* (19:127); *WWW* (H).   *Robert R. Sherman*

LOVELL, John Epy. B. April 23, 1795, Colne, Lancashire, England, to John and Elizabeth (Epy) Lovell. M. 1835 to Harriet Fletcher. M. March 29, 1845, to Minerva Camp. Ch. three. D. May 3, 1892, Milwaukee, Wisconsin.

John Epy Lovell attended a private boarding school at St. Ives, England, and served as tutor to the family of the Duke of Bedford (1811–13). He became acquainted with Joseph Lancaster, originator of the Lancastrian (or monitorial) method of instruction. He became principal of a Lancastrian school at Burr Rose, England.

Lovell emigrated to the United States in 1815 and unsuccessfully attempted to establish schools in Philadelphia, Pennsylvania, and Baltimore, Maryland. In 1822, he founded a Lancastrian school in New Haven, Connecticut, and served as principal to 1827, when he accepted a position as a teacher of elocution in the Mount Pleasant Classical Institute in Amherst, Massachusetts. He returned to the New Haven school in 1830 and continued there to 1857, when he engaged in writing textbooks and private tutoring (1857–82). Lovell's greatest talents were in the field of elocution. The author of school textbooks, Lovell wrote *Introductory Arithmetic* (1827), *The United States Speaker* (1833), *Rhetorical Dialogues* (1839), and the Lovell Progressive Reader Series of five volumes (1855–59).

He moved to Waterbury, Connecticut, in 1882 and to Milwaukee, Wisconsin, in 1890.

REFERENCES: *DAB; WWW* (H); *New Haven Daily Palladium,* May 4, 1892; *New Haven Evening Register,* May 4, 1892; *New Haven Leader,* May 4, 1892.   *Thomas Meighan*

LOWELL, Abbott Lawrence. B. December 13, 1856, Boston, Massachusetts, to Augustus and Katharine Bigelow (Lawrence) Lowell. M. June 19, 1879, to Anna Parker Lowell. Ch. none. D. January 6, 1943, Boston, Massachusetts.

A. Lawrence Lowell was a student at George W. C. Noble's private classical school. He was graduated with honors, receiving the A.B. (1877) and LL.B. (1880) degrees from Harvard University.

Lowell practiced law, managed the family trust, and served on the Boston School Committee (1895–97). His early publications, *The Transfer of Stock in Private Corporations* (1884), *Essays on Government* (1889), and *Governments and Parties in Continental Europe* (1896), won him a lectureship at Harvard in 1897. He became a popular professor in government, and his reputation as a scholar grew with *The Government of Dependencies* (1899), *Colonial Civil Service* (with H. Morse Stephens, 1900), *The Government of England* (1908), and articles in the *Harvard Law Review.*

Lowell's interest in academic reform led to his appointment as Harvard president in 1909. During his twenty-four-year tenure, student enrollment more than doubled, teachers and staff tripled, and the endowment increased fivefold. His chief interest was the undergraduate program where he required students to concentrate within a field of specialization and to distribute their courses over a broad range. A gift to Harvard from Edward S. Harkness allowed Lowell to reorganize the residences into the house plan, which followed the English university model of self-contained units of dormitory, dining hall, study room, and library. Each house included tutors and a resident master.

A frequent lecturer, Lowell also was the author of *Public Opinion and Popular Government* (1913), *Public Opinion in War and Peace* (1923), *Conflicts of Principle* (1923), *At War with Academic Traditions in America*

(1934), and *What a University President Has Learned* (1938).

After retiring as president in 1933, he maintained an active interest in the Society of Fellows, which he had founded and endowed. He was the sole trustee of the Lowell Institute of Boston, Massachusetts, from 1900, chairman of the executive committee of the League to Enforce Peace, and a member of scholarly associations. He was awarded the French Legion of Honor and the Belgian Order of the Crown. He received many honorary degrees from American and foreign colleges and universities.

REFERENCES: *DAB* (supp. 3); *LE* (II); *NCAB* (31:1); *NYT*, January 6, 1943, p. 19; *WWW* (II); Henry Aaron Yeomans, *Abbott Lawrence Lowell, 1856–1943* (Cambridge: Harvard University Press, 1948).

David Delahanty

LOZIER, Clemence Sophia Harned. B. December 11, 1813, Plainfield, New Jersey, to David and Hannah (Walker) Harned. M. 1829 to Abraham Wilton Lozier. Ch. one. D. April 26, 1888, New York, New York.

Clemence Harned Lozier, youngest of thirteen children, was orphaned at the age of twelve. She studied at the Plainfield (New Jersey) Academy and was married when she was sixteen to Abraham Lozier.

Lozier opened a girls' school in her home in New York City; it was in existence for eleven years (1832–43) and she was one of the first to teach hygiene, physiology, and anatomy. She engaged in welfare work and studied medicine under her brother, William Harned. Her husband died in 1837, and she later moved to Rochester, New York, where she studied medicine. She received the M.D. degree from Syracuse (New York) Medical College (1853). Returning to New York City, Lozier practiced medicine, particularly surgery, and also taught in her home.

In 1863 the New York Medical College and Hospital for Women was chartered. It later became the New York Homeopathic Medical College and in 1918 the New York Medical College. Lozier toured Europe in 1867 and on her return reorganized the school; she was dean and professor of surgery for more than twenty years.

Lozier wrote for general readers rather than for medical specialists, for example, a pamphlet *Childbirth Made Easy* (1870). She was president of the New York Women's Suffrage Society (1873–86), the National Suffrage Association (1877–78), the Moral Education Society, and the Women's American Temperance League.

REFERENCES: *AC; DAB; NAW; NCAB* (25:281); *NYT, April 28, 1888, p. 8; TC; WWW* (H).   *Shirley M. Ohles*

LUCKEY, George Washington Andrew. B. February 11, 1855, Decatur, Indiana, to George W. and Druzilla (Arnold) Luckey. M. December 26, 1882, to Bertha M. Musson. Ch. two. D. March 30, 1933, Lincoln, Nebraska.

George Washington Andrew Luckey received the B.S. degree (1883) from Northern Indiana Normal School and the A.B. degree (1894) from Stanford (California) University. He received the M.A. degree (1895) from Clark University in Worcester, Massachusetts, and the Ph.D. degree (1900) from Columbia University. He studied biology at Hopkins Seaside Laboratory at Pacific Grove, California, during the summers of 1893 and 1894, and he was a fellow in psychology at Clark University (1894–95) and a fellow in education at Teachers College, Columbia University (1899–1900). He studied at Göttingen (Germany) University (1912–13).

Luckey taught in rural and village schools in Indiana (1872–79) and was superintendent of Adams County (Indiana) schools (1879–83). He served in the dual capacity of city superintendent of schools and high school principal in Decatur, Indiana (1883–87). In 1887 he went to California to serve as supervisory principal for the Beaumont, California, schools, a position he held until 1892. He accepted an appointment to the University of Nebraska in 1895 to organize a newly created department of pedagogy. Promoted to professor the following year, Luckey remained at the University of Nebraska until 1918.

At the University of Nebraska, Luckey served as head professor of education (1906–18) and dean of the graduate school of education (1914–18). He left Nebraska in 1918 because of criticism of his questions about the United States' entry into World War I and his period of study in Germany. He joined the United States Bureau of Education in 1920 as a specialist of foreign educational systems, a position he held until his retirement in 1925.

Luckey was a regular contributor to educational and psychological journals. His books and monographs include *The Professional Training of Secondary School Teachers in the United States* (1902), *Outlines of Child Study* (1912), *The Essentials of Child Study* (1917), *Education, Democracy, and the League of Nations* (1919), *Outlines of Education Systems and School Conditions in Latin America* (1923), *The International Education Research Council and World Bureau of Education* (1925), *Longevity of Eminent Individuals* (1929), and *Longevity of Eminent Poets, Scientists, and Educators Compared* (1931). He was child study editor for the *Northwestern Monthly* (1896–99).

Luckey was active in professional and scholarly groups. He was chairman of the executive committee of the Nebraska Child Study Association (1896–1907) and a fellow of the American Association for the Advancement of Science. He was president of the Indiana County Superintendents' Association (1882), vice-president of the California State Teachers' Association (1891), president of the Nebraska State Teachers' Association (1915), and delegate to the Peace Congress held in Geneva, Switzerland, in 1912.

REFERENCES: *LE* (I); *WWW* (I); Erwin H. Goldenstein, *The University of Nebraska Teachers College—The First Fifty Years* (Lincoln: University of Nebraska Press, 1958); *Nebraska Educational Journal* 13 (April 1933): 117; F. W. Smith, "Tribute to Dr. G. W. A. Luckey," *School and Society* 37 (May 20, 1933): 656–57.   *Erwin H. Goldenstein*

LUTKIN, Peter Christian. B. March 27, 1858, Thompsonville, Wisconsin, to Peter Christian and Hannah Susanna (Olivarius) Lutkin. M. October 27, 1885, to Nancy Lelah Carman. Ch. one. D. December 27, 1931, Evanston, Illinois.

Peter Christian Lutkin's family moved to Chicago in 1869, where both of his parents died in 1871. Lutkin received his education in the Chicago public schools and in the choir school of the Episcopal Cathedral of Sts. Peter and Paul. In 1881 he went to Berlin, Germany, to study organ, piano, and music theory at the Hochischule für Musik, and in 1882 he won a scholarship at the Königliche Meisterschule für Composition. He was at the Leschetizky Piano School in Vienna, Austria, and at Paris, France, studying piano under Moritz Moszkowski during 1882.

Lutkin became the organist at the Cathedral of Sts. Peter and Paul at the age of fourteen and served there from 1871 to 1881. In 1879 he was appointed instructor of piano at Northwestern University in Evanston, Illinois (1879–81). He returned to Chicago in 1884 as choirmaster at St. Clement's Church and was choirmaster in St. James Church in Chicago in 1891. He was director of the music department of the American Conservatory of Music (1888–96). He was appointed professor of music at Northwestern University (1891) and served as dean of the school of music (1897–1928). During his deanship, Northwestern became one of the most important schools of music in the country. In 1906 he founded the a cappella choir of Northwestern University for which he wrote most of his original compositions and choral units. He founded the Chicago North Shore Festival Association in 1908 and remained its choral conductor until 1930. He lectured on church music at the Western Theological Seminary in Chicago and the Garrett Bible Institute in Evanston.

Lutkin's lectures were published in 1910 as *Music in the Church*. He was joint music editor of the official hymnal of the Methodist Episcopal church and the Methodist Episcopal church, South, musical editor of *Methodist Sunday School Hymnal,* and a member of the commission for revision of the hymnal of the Protestant Episcopal church. He composed church music and part songs.

Lutkin was one of the founders of the American Guild of Organists and was twice president of the Music Teachers National Association (1911–12, 1919–20). He received an honorary degree from Syracuse University (1900).

REFERENCES: *DAB; NCAB* (26:480); *NYT,* December 28, 1931, p. 17; *WWW* (I); Carl Beecher, "Peter Christian Lutkin," *Northwestern Alumni News* (1932); *Chicago Tribune,* December 28, 1931.   *Thomas Meighan*

LYON, Mary Mason. B. February 28, 1797, Buckland, Massachusetts, to Aaron and Jemima (Shepard) Lyon. M. no. D. March 5, 1849, South Hadley, Massachusetts.

Mary Lyon's father died when she was a child, leaving the family of seven children in difficult financial circumstances. She attended the local district schools and financed her attendance at Sanderson Academy in Ashland, Massachusetts, by teaching. She was graduated from Sanderson Academy, studied with Joseph Emerson *(q.v.)*, and was tutored in science in Amherst, Massachusetts.

Lyon taught school in Shelburne Falls, Massachusetts, at the age of eighteen and taught in private and public schools (1821–34), including Miss Grant's (Zilpah Polly Grant Banister, *q.v.*) school in Ipswich, Massachusetts. Determined to establish a women's college, she solicited funds in Ipswich and throughout Massachusetts and Connecticut. She was aided by Edward Hitchcock *(q.v.)*, famed geologist, in raising funds for the seminary. Selecting a site in South Hadley, Massachusetts, Lyon opened the Mount Holyoke Female Seminary on November 8, 1837, with one hundred students. She established high academic standards and set up a curriculum of science, mathematics, and languages, as well as philosophy and the arts. Students and teachers were required to share in housework. The school grew in enrollment and reputation.

Lyon served as principal of the seminary from 1837 to her death in 1849. The institution was incorporated as a college in 1888. Mary Lyon was enshrined in the Hall of Fame of New York University in 1905.

REFERENCES: *AC; DAB; EB; NAW; NCAB* (4:462); *TC; WWW* (H); Arthur C. Cole, *A Hundred Years of Mount Holyoke College* (New Haven: Yale University Press, 1940); Fidelia Fisk, *Recollections of Mary Lyon* (Boston: American Tract Society, 1866); Beth Bradford Gilchrist, *The Life of Mary Lyon* (Boston: Houghton Mifflin, 1910). *Robert C. Morris*

LYTE, Eliphalet Oram. B. June 29, 1842, Bird-in-Hand, Pennsylvania, to Louis Clarkson and Rebecca (Martin) Lyte. M. March 26, 1872, to Mary McJunkin. Ch. two. D. January 3, 1913, Lancaster, Pennsylvania.

E. Oram Lyte spent his early years working in his father's nursery in the spring and summer and attending public school in the winter. He left school to join the federal army in the Civil War, where he served for almost three years. For two years after returning from the war, he continued his studies and taught in a local middle school.

He entered the Pennsylvania State Normal School at Millersville (later, Millersville State College) receiving the B.S. degree (1868) and later completing the scientific course, for which he was granted the M.S. degree (1876). He was elected a member of the faculty of the normal school, his first position being that of a teacher of rhetoric and bookkeeping. He later taught pedagogy and English grammar for many years and was appointed principal. He made improvements in all departments of the normal school; enrollment increased, and courses of study were broadened. Many buildings were erected.

Lyte's special interests were in the area of language, philosophy, and pedagogics. Some of his books include *Grammar and Composition for Common Schools* (1870), *Institute Songs for Institutes and Schools* (1876), *School Room Songs* (1878), *The Institute Glee Book for Institutes and Schools* (1878), *Forms of Parsing and Analysis, Oral and Written with Forms for Correcting Syntax* (1879), *Practical Bookkeeping* (1880), *Advance Pages of an English Grammar for the Use of the Schools, Based on the Inductive Method* (1883), *The School Bell* (1883), *The School Song Book* (1883), *School Song Annual* (1885), *Elementary English* (1898), *Elements of Grammar and Composition* (1898), *Advanced Grammar and Composition* (1899), *Song Hour for Institutes and Schools* (1899), *Some Recent Public School Legislation* (1901), *State Normal Schools of the United States* (1904), and *What Is an Ideal Course for a Normal School?* (1908).

In 1891 he was elected president of the Pennsylvania State Teachers' Association. He was a life member of the National Educational Association (president, 1899) and served several years as its director for Pennsylvania. Lyte was a member of the Council of Education and the American Academy of Political and Social Science. He received two honorary degrees from Franklin and Marshall College.

REFERENCES: *AC; NCAB* (5:227); *TC; WWW* (I); Sarah H. Gilbert, "Dr. E. Oram Lyte," *The Millersvillian* 26 (February 1913): 14–19.

William S. O'Bruba

M

MacALISTER, James. B. April 26, 1840, Glasgow, Scotland, to John and Agnes (Robertson) MacAlister. M. June 24, 1866, to Helen Lucretia Brayton. Ch. one. D. December 11, 1913, at sea.

Following the death of his father and grandfather, James MacAlister's family emigrated from Scotland to Wisconsin in 1850. MacAlister was graduated from Brown University in Providence, Rhode Island, with the A.B. degree (1856). He taught school in Milwaukee, Wisconsin, and then entered Albany (New York) Law School, where he received the LL.B. degree (1864).

MacAlister practiced law from 1866 until 1873, when he was appointed superintendent of schools in Milwaukee. After ten years in Milwaukee, he was appointed the first superintendent of the Philadelphia, Pennsylvania, public schools (1883–91). He changed a conservative school system into one with progressive attitudes and programs. He introduced modern classics and a program of manual training in the schools.

In 1891 MacAlister was appointed president of the new Drexel Institute of Art, Science and Industry in Philadelphia. The successes of Drexel Institute gained international recognition for innovative programs and generated financial support from Andrew Carnegie, J. Pierpont Morgan, and Thomas A. Edison. Following a productive career as the Drexel president, poor health forced MacAlister's resignation in 1913.

MacAlister was the author of *Manual of Primary Instruction* (1884), *Manual of Instruction in United States History and Civil Government* (1887), *Manual Training in the Public Schools of Philadelphia* (1890), and *Art Education in the Public Schools* (1893).

A fellow of the American Association for the Advancement of Science, Mac Alister was a regent of the Wisconsin normal schools (1878–83) and a trustee of the University of Pennsylvania (1885–97), and he was awarded the officier d'académie by France in 1890 and honorary degrees by Brown University and Albany Law School.

REFERENCES: *AC; DAB; NCAB* (13:79); *NYT*, December 13, 1913, p. 13; *TC; WWW* (I).   *Richard T. Rees*

MacCAUGHEY, Vaughan. B. July 7, 1887, Huron, South Dakota, to William Franklyn and Matilda (Vaughan) MacCaughey. M. November 25, 1909, to Janet H. Brooker. Ch. six. D. March 24, 1954, San Francisco, California.

Vaughan MacCaughey received the B.S.Agr. degree (1908) from Cornell University in Ithaca, New York, and the B.Ed. degree from San Francisco (California) State College. He studied at the University of Chicago (1916–17).

MacCaughey was a teaching assistant at Cornell University (1905–08) and head of the department of natural science and vice-president of the Territorial Normal School of Hawaii (1908–09). He was professor of botany at the College (later, University) of Hawaii from 1910 to 1919.

He served as superintendent of public instruction for Hawaii (1919–23). During his administration, a survey was made of the territorial schools by the federal Bureau of Education, and the recommendations from that survey structured the future development of the Hawaiian schools. He was on the extension staff of the University of California in 1923 and was a visiting professor at colleges and universities. He was a frequent participant in Chautauqua Institute lecture tours.

MacCaughey was the author of *The Natural History of Chautauqua* (1917), *The Schools of Hawaii: Race-Mixtures in Hawaii,* and several other monographs. He was founder and editor of the *Hawaii Educational Review* (1913–16) and the *Sierra Education News* (1923–52).

MacCaughey was active in civic and professional organizations. He served the Boy Scouts of America as special field commissioner for California, director of region twelve, and dean of the San Francisco School for Scout Officers. He was a member of the National Education Association (Hawaii director, 1916–23, and member of the National Editorial Council, 1922–23). He was chairman of the executive committee for the Pan-American Educational Conference (1921) and a delegate to the World Conference on Education in San Francisco, California (1923). He was a fellow of the American Association for the Advancement of Science.

REFERENCES: *LE* (II); *WW* (XII); *WWW* (III); *Berkeley* (California) *Daily Gazette,* March 29, 1954, p. 16; *Honolulu* (Hawaii) *Star-Bulletin,* March 24, 1954, p. 1.   *John F. Ohles*

McCLELLAN, Henry Brainerd. B. October 17, 1840, Philadelphia, Pennsylvania, to Samuel and Margaret (Ely) McClellan. M. December 31, 1863, to Katherine Miller Matthews. Ch. six. D. October 1, 1904, Lexington, Kentucky.

Henry Brainerd McClellan was graduated with the A.B. (1858) and A.M. (1869) degrees from Williams College in Williamstown, Massachusetts. He taught school in Cumberland County, Virginia (1858–61).

In 1861 McClellan enlisted in the Confederate army and served in the Civil War as chief of staff to J. E. B. Stuart and Wade Hampton. After the war he lived in Lexington, Kentucky, where he was assistant principal and professor of music at the Sayre Female Institute (1869–70). In 1870 McClellan became principal of the institute and served to his death in 1904. The school gained a reputation for excellence under his leadership. It was one of the first in the region to offer college courses for women. Later the institution became a high school and junior college, and in 1950 it became a private elementary and secondary school.

McClellan was the author of *The Life and Campaigns of Major-General J. E. B. Stuart* (1866). He was awarded an honorary degree by Central University of Richmond, Kentucky (1900).

REFERENCES: *AC; DAB; NCAB* (4:140); *TC; WWW* (I); J. Winston Coleman, Jr., *History of Sayre School* (Lexington, Ky.: Wilburn Press, 1954).   *Thomas D. Myers*

McCLOY, Charles Harold. B. March 30, 1886, Marietta, Ohio, to William Alexander and Emma Maria (Langley) McCloy. M. December 20, 1907, to Anna Florence Fisher. Ch. five. D. September 18, 1959, Iowa City, Iowa.

Charles Harold McCloy completed his undergraduate studies for the Ph.B. degree (1907) at Marietta (Ohio) College. He earned the M.A. degree from Marietta (1910) through an external program. He received the Ph.D. degree (1932) from Teachers College, Columbia University. He studied in the new field of physical education at Harvard University Summer School of Physical Education (1905–07) under Dudley Sargent *(q.v.)*.

McCloy was first employed as a coach and physical education instructor at Marietta while a college sophomore and continued to his graduation. He was coach of football, basketball, and baseball and teacher of biology at Yankton (South Dakota) College (1907–08) and physical director of the Young Men's Christian Association (YMCA) in Danville, Virginia (1908–11). He enrolled in the Johns Hopkins University program of medical studies, where he spent two years studying human physiology.

McCloy went to China in 1913, where he spent the next thirteen years as director of the school of physical education at the National Southeastern University in Nanking. He wrote fourteen monographs in Chinese about health and physical education. On his return to the United States in 1926, he taught for a year at Detroit Teachers College (later, Wayne State University) and was secretary of research for the National Council of the YMCA in New York City (1927–30). He was appointed research professor of physical education at the State University of Iowa in 1930, a position he held to his retirement in 1954. During World War II McCloy developed tests and scales that were used by the armed forces to measure the physical fitness of recruits and the effects of training programs.

He was the author of many books, including *The Physiology of Exercise* (1915), *A Syllabus of Anthropometry* (1917), *A Manual of Marching* (1917), *Biology and Physical Education* (1921), *A Textbook of Physical Examinations* (1923), all in Chinese, and in English *The Measurement of Athletic Power* (1932), *Appraising Physical Status: The Selection of Measurements* (1936), *Appraising Physical Status: Methods and Norms* (1938), *Philosophical Bases for Physical Education* (1940), and *Physical Education* (with Aileen Carpenter, 1941).

McCloy was president of the American Association of Physical Education when it became the American Association for Health and Physical Education in 1938, the Central District Physical Education Association (1933), the Pan-American Institute of Physical Education (1946–54), and the American Academy of Physical Education (1947–49). He was the recipient of the Research Award of the American Academy of Physical Education (1938) and the Gulick (1944) and Hetherington (1944) awards. He was awarded four honorary degrees.

REFERENCES: *LE* (III); *WWAE* (XVI); *WWW* (III); Ellen W. Gerber, "The Ideas and Influence of McCloy, Nash, and Williams," in Earle F. Zeigler, *A History of Physical Education and Sport in the United States and Canada* (Champaign, Ill.: Stipes Publishing Co., 1975), pp. 319–38; J. R. Little, "Charles Harold McCloy: His Professional Preparation and Early Work Experiences," *NCPEAM Proceedings* (1969), pp. 91–99; *NYT,* September 20, 1959, p. 87.   *Richard B. Morland*

McCONATHY, Osbourne. B. January 15, 1875, Bullitt County, Kentucky, to William Jacob and Cynthia (Osbourne) McConathy. M. July 9, 1907, to Alice Mary Brown. Ch. three. D. April 2, 1947, Pattenburg, New Jersey.

Osbourne McConathy was educated in the Louisville, Kentucky, public schools and studied music with private tutors, including Luther Mason (*q.v.*), his instructor in school music.

His career in music education began at the age of nineteen when he became supervisor of music in the Louisville public schools (1893–1903). He held a supervisory position in the public schools of Chelsea, Massachusetts (1903–13). He conducted choral and orchestral concerts, which led him to edit a series of choruses for general and school use. During 1912 he was managing editor for Silver Burdett Company in Boston, preparing a series of school music books.

Northwestern University in Evanston, Illinois, named McConathy professor of music methods and director of the department of public school and community music in 1913. He remained at Northwestern until he joined Silver Burdett Company in New York in 1925 as chief editor of music publications, which became his lifelong work.

McConathy was an advocate of high school academic credit for outside music study. He tried to adapt public school music instruction to the individual abilities of pupils and to the social program, other subjects, and the interests of students. In 1931 he conducted weekly afternoon piano lessons on WEAF radio station in New York City. McConathy was superintendent of the eastern session of the American Institute of Normal Methods in Boston, Massachusetts (1908–18), and directed both the eastern and western sessions from 1918 until his death in 1947.

He wrote many books, including the Progressive Music Series (fourteen volumes, with others, 1914), *Music in Secondary Schools* (1917), *An Approach to Harmony* (1927), *The Catholic Music Hour* (1929), *Music in the Junior High School* (1930), *Music of Many Lands and Peoples* (1932), *Music in Rural Education* (1933), *Music Highways and Byways* (1936), *Music, the Universal Language* (1941), *Music in the Senior High School* (1941), and *New Music Horizons,* (1944) and he edited *The School Songbook* (1909).

McConathy was a member of professional associations and president of the Music Teachers National Association (1922), the Illinois State Music Teachers Association (1924–25), the music section of the National Education Association (three terms), and the Music Educators National Conference (1919). He received an honorary degree from the American Conservatory of Music in Chicago (1937).

REFERENCES: *LE* (II); *NCAB* (39:105); *WWW* (II); *NYT*, April 3, 1947. p. 25.   *Darlene E. Fisher*

McCONNELL, Thomas Raymond. B. May 25, 1901, Mediapolis, Iowa, to William John and Nell (Cox) McConnell. M. June 20, 1925, to Ruth Kegley. Ch. two.

T. R. McConnell, leader in the study and development of twentieth-century American higher education, attended Cornell College in Mount Vernon, Iowa, and received the A.B. (1924), A.M. (1928), and Ph.D. (1933) degrees from the University of Iowa.

McConnell was a faculty member at Cornell College at Mount Vernon, Iowa (1925–39), serving as instructor of English and journalism, college dean, and professor of education and psychology. He was professor of educational psychology (1936–50) and associate dean, acting dean, and dean (1940–50) of the college of science, literature, and arts at the University of Minnesota. After four years as chancellor of the University of Buffalo (later, State University of New York at Buffalo) (1950–54), McConnell was professor of higher education at the University of California at Berkeley, from 1954 until his retirement in 1968. Later he was emeritus professor and research director at the Center for Research and Development in Higher Education at the University of California at Berkeley.

McConnell served as a member of President Harry Truman's Commission on Higher Education, presidents John F. Kennedy's and Lyndon Johnson's commissions on public higher education, and the Carnegie Commission on Higher Education. He was a consultant in higher education to various colleges, universities, and state agencies.

McConnell wrote *Psychology in Everyday Living* (with others, 1938), *Educational Psychology* (with others, 1948), *A Restudy of the Needs of California in Higher Education* (with T. C. Holy and H. H. Semans, 1962), *A General Pattern for American Public Higher Education* (1962), *Governments and the University: A Comparative Analysis* (1966), *Training for Educational Research* (with others, 1968), *The Faculty in University Governance* (with K. P. Mortimer, 1971), *The Redistribution of Power in Higher Education* (1971), *Students and Colleges: Interaction and Change* (with others, 1972), and *From Elite to Mass to Universal Higher Education: The British and American Tranformations* (with R. O. Berdahl and M. A. Fay, 1973). He was a member of the board of editors of the *Encyclopedia of Educational Research* (1957–59).

He was a member of professional associations and was president of the American Educational Research Association (1941–42) and chairman of the National Society for Study of Education (1948–49). McConnell received awards from Phi Delta Kappa (1966), the University of California at Berkeley (1968), and the Carnegie Commission on Higher Education (1971). He received an honorary degree from Syracuse University (1952).

REFERENCES: *LE* (III); *WW* (XXXIX); *WWAE* (XVI).

Stratton F. Caldwell

McCONNELL, Wallace Robert. B. October 4, 1881, Mount Sterling, Illinois, to James and Mary Ann (Gabbert) McConnell. M. June 26, 1918, to Della Bennett. Ch. one. D. February 18, 1960, Redlands, California.

Educated in the public schools of Brown County, Illinois, Wallace Robert McConnell began his professional career in education at the age of eighteen as a teacher in local rural schools (1900–06). He attended the Maccomb (Illinois) Normal School (later, Western Illinois University) (1906–08) and the University of Illinois, where he received the A.B. degree (1912). He received the M.A. degree (1917) from the University of Wisconsin. He held a fellowship at Clark University in Worcester, Massachusetts (1924–25), where he received the Ph.D. degree (1925).

McConnell was a teacher on the staff of the Oshkosh (Wisconsin) State Teachers' College (later, University of Wisconsin—Oshkosh) in 1914–15. He moved to Platteville, Wisconsin, serving as professor of geography at the State Teachers College (later, University of Wisconsin—Platteville) from 1915 to 1917. He was appointed professor of geography at Miami University in Oxford, Ohio, a position he held from 1918 to 1952.

McConnell wrote many textbooks and produced a series of industrial outline maps in 1926. His books include *Mineral Resources of Southwestern Wisconsin* (1916), *Problems in the Geography of Europe* (1925), *Appleton Modern School Atlas* (edited with George Philip, 1928), *Geography of Ohio* (1929), *Study Guides in Geography* (1931), *The United States in the Modern World* (1932), *Living in the Americas* (1934), *Living Across the Seas* (1934), *Living in Different Lands* (1936), *Living in Country and City* (1937), *Experiences in Geography* (a five-book series, 1940), *Geography of the Americas* (1945), *Geography Around the World* (1945), *Geography of Lands Overseas* (1946), *Geography of American Peoples* (1950), and *Geography of World Peoples* (1952).

McConnell was a popular lecturer at county educational institutes and before city and state teachers' association meetings. He was president of the geography section of the Central Association of Science and Mathematics Teachers (1917) and the National Council of Geography Teachers (1924–25), and he was a member of many other professional organizations. He was involved in educational radio as a teacher on the Ohio School of the Air (1928–32).

REFERENCES: *LE* (II); *NCAB* (51:156); *WWAE* (VIII); *WWW* (IV).

Charles M. Dye

McCORKLE, Samuel Eusebius. B. August 23, 1746, near Harris's Ferry, Lancaster County, Pennsylvania, to Alexander and Agnes Montgomery

McCorkle. M. July 2, 1776, to Margaret Gillespie. Ch. ten. D. June 21, 1811, Rowan County, North Carolina.

Samuel Eusebius McCorkle started school at the age of four and moved with his family from Pennsylvania to North Carolina in search of richer farm lands. Because there were no schools in the area, he started teaching the younger members of his family when he was only nine. At the age of twenty, he began his classical education in a school conducted in Guilford County by David Caldwell (*q.v.*), who made a lasting impression on McCorkle. When he was twenty-two, he decided to enter the ministry and attended the College of New Jersey (later, Princeton University); he was graduated in September 1772. He began theological studies in the New Castle (Pennsylvania) presbytery, received a license to preach from the New York presbytery (1774), and for the next two years was an itinerant preacher in Virginia. At the age of thirty he returned to North Carolina to preach at the Thyatira Church in Rowan County.

He opened the Zion-Parnassus Academy (c. 1785) modeled after the classical school of David Caldwell. McCorkle added a special department for teacher training, thus establishing the first normal school in the country.

McCorkle was a founding trustee of the University of North Carolina. He delivered the cornerstone address on December 12, 1793, and was made chairman of the committee to report on a "plan for education"; he also served on the financial committee. He influenced the educational and financial plans and the building designs of the university. He declined an appointment as professor of moral and political philosophy, the stepping-stone to the presidency, and returned to his church and the Zion-Parnassus Academy.

McCorkle wrote sermons, discourses, and essays. He received an honorary degree from Dickinson (Pennsylvania) College in 1792.

REFERENCES: *AC; NCAB* (7: 223); James F. Hurley and Julia Goode Eagan, *The Prophet of Zion-Parnassus, Samuel Eusebius McCorkle* (Richmond, Va: Whittet and Shepperson, 1934).   *Linda C. Gardner*

McCORMICK, Samuel Black. B. May 6, 1858, Irwin, Pennsylvania, to James Irwin and Rachel L. (Black) McCormick. M. September 29, 1882, to Ida May Steep. Ch. four. D. April 18, 1928, Coropolis Heights, Pennsylvania.

Samuel Black McCormick was graduated from Washington and Jefferson College in Washington, Pennsylvania, receiving the A.B. degree (1880) with highest honors and the A.M. degree (1883). He taught in Canonsburg (Pennsylvania) Academy (1880) and at Washington and Jefferson College (1881–82), and he studied law with Henry H. McCormick, an uncle. He was admitted to the bar in 1882 and practiced law in Pittsburgh, Pennsylvania (1882–83), and Denver, Colorado, where he went into practice with R. D. Thompson (1883–87).

Dissatisfied with the practice of law, he returned to Pennsylvania to enter the ministry. He attended the Western Theological Seminary in Allegheny (later, Pittsburgh), was graduated in 1890, and was ordained by the presbytery of Allegheny. He served the Central Presbyterian Church in Allegheny, and moved to the First Presbyterian Church of Omaha, Nebraska, in 1894. He was elected president of Coe College in Cedar Rapids, Iowa, in 1897, where he served for seven years and gained a reputation as a college administrator. He was invited to assume the position of chancellor of the Western University of Pennsylvania and served for the next seventeen years. He transformed the college into a modern university, changing the name to the University of Pittsburgh in 1908. A research institution was affiliated with the university in 1910, and a graduate school was organized in 1912. The student population grew from eight hundred to six thousand by the time of his retirement in 1920.

McCormick was a member of the American Association for the Advancement of Science, the American Academy of Political and Social Science, and other organizations, and he was a trustee of the Carnegie Foundation for the Advancement of Teaching and a director of the Western Theological Seminary. He received two honorary degrees from Washington and Jefferson College and honorary degrees from five other institutions.

REFERENCES: *DAB; NCAB* (24:141); *TC; WWW* (I).   *William J. Parente*

McCOSH, James. B. April 1, 1811, Carskoech, Ayrshire, Scotland, to Andrew and Jean (Carson) McCosh. M. September 29, 1845, to Isabella Guthrie. Ch. one, Andrew James McCosh, eminent surgeon. D. November 16, 1894, Princeton, New Jersey.

James McCosh studied at Glasgow (Scotland) University from the age of thirteen (1824–29) and received the M.A. degree (1833) from the University of Edinburgh, Scotland, where he studied theology (1829–34).

Ordained a minister in the church of Scotland in 1835, McCosh served the Abbey Church in Arboath (1835–38) and was appointed to a church in Breslin (1838). He was a founder of the Free Church of Scotland (1843) and served as a minister until 1852, when he was appointed professor of logic and metaphysics at Queens College in Belfast, Ulster, Ireland.

In 1868 McCosh accepted the position as president and professor of biblical instruction, psychology, and history of philosophy at the College of New Jersey (later, Princeton University). Serving to his retirement in 1888, he restored the college from its depressed condition during the Civil War by recruiting a competent faculty and doubling the enrollment. The schools of science, philosophy, and art were established, and the physical plant was enlarged during his term of office.

McCosh was the author of important works, including *The Wheat and the Chaff* (1843), *The Method of the Divine Government, Physical and Moral* (1850), *Typical Forms and Special Ends in Creation* (with George Dickie, 1855), *The Intuitions of the Minds Inductively Investigated* (1860), *The Supernatural in Relation to the Natural* (1862), *Examination of Mill's Philosophy* (1866), *The Laws of Discursive Thought* (1869), *Christianity and Positivism* (1871), *The Scottish Philosophy* (1874), *Ideas in Nature Overlooked by Dr. Tyndall* (1875), *The Development Hypothesis* (1876), *The Emotions* (1880), *Realistic Philosophy Defended in a Philosophic Series* (two volumes, 1887), *Psychology: the Cognitive Powers* (1886), *Psychology: the Motive Powers* (1887), *The Religious Aspect of Evolution* (1888), *First and Fundamental Truths* (1889), *The Tests of Various Kinds of Truth* (1889), *The Prevailing Types of Philosophy* (1890), *Our Moral Nature* (1892), and *Philosophy of Reality* (1894).

He was the recipient of several honorary degrees from American and foreign universities.

REFERENCES: *AC; DAB; NCAB* (5:468); *NYT,* November 17, 1894, p. 5; *TC; WWW* (H); George P. Schmidt, *Princeton and Rutgers* (Princeton, N.J.: D. Van Nostrand Co., 1964), pp. 72-80; Thomas Jefferson Wertenbaker, *Princeton 1746–1896* (Princeton, N.J.: Princeton University Press, 1946).   *Franklin Ross Jones*

MacCRACKEN, Henry Mitchell. B. September 28, 1840, Oxford, Ohio, to John Steele and Eliza (Hawkins-Dougherty) Welch MacCracken. M. July 2, 1872, to Catherine Almira Hubbard. Ch. four, including George Gere MacCracken, president of Lafayette College, and Henry Noble MacCracken, president of Vassar College. D. December 24, 1918, Orlando, Florida.

Henry Mitchell MacCracken received the A.B. degree (1857) from Miami University in Oxford, Ohio. He studied theology at the United Presbyterian Seminary in Xenia, Ohio (1860–62), completed his work at the Princeton (New Jersey) Seminary (1862–63), and studied in Germany at the universities of Tübingen and Berlin (1867–68).

MacCracken taught the classics at Grove Academy in Cedarville, Ohio (1857–58), and in Xenia, Ohio (1860–62), and was superintendent of schools in Charleston, Ohio (1858–60). He was pastor of the Westminster Church in Columbus, Ohio (1863–67). In 1867 he went to Europe as a deputy of the Free Church Assembly but resigned his position to engage in study in Germany. He served as pastor of the First Presbyterian Church in Toledo, Ohio, from 1868 to 1881.

In 1881 MacCracken was elected chancellor and professor of philosophy at the Western University of Pennsylvania (later, University of Pittsburgh). He moved the university to Allegheny (later, Pittsburgh) in 1882. In 1884 he became the first professor of philosophy at the University of the City of New York (later, New York University), was vice-chancellor in 1885, and succeeded John Hall as chancellor in 1891.

As chancellor MacCracken opened the graduate seminary, founded the school of pedagogy, and affiliated the university with the Union Theological Seminary. In 1892 he purchased land for a new campus between Morris Heights and Fordham Heights and moved the university there in 1894. College halls and a library and academic buildings for schools of law and pedagogy were constructed at Washington Square. The school of commerce, accounts, and finance was organized, and the school of medicine and the Bellevue Medical College were merged into University and Bellevue Hospital Medical College. In 1900 he founded the Hall of Fame at the university library to pay tribute to famous American men and women.

Among MacCracken's publications were *Tercentenary of Presbyterianism* (1870), *Leaders of the Church Universal* (three volumes, 1879), *Cities and Universities* (1882), *The Scotch-Irish in America* (1884), *John Calvin* (1888), *A Metropolitan University* (1892), *Educational Progress in the U.S.* (1893), *The Three Essentials* (1901), *The Hall of Fame* (1901), *The Urgent Eastern Question* (1912), and *A Propaganda of Philosophy* (1914).

MacCracken served as vice-president of the Society for the Prevention of Crime (1891), was moderator of the New York presbytery (1914–15), represented the Scandinavian Society of New York in Europe (1908), and was president of the American Institute of Christian Philosophy. He was a member of the committee that founded the University of Wooster (later, College of Wooster) in Wooster, Ohio (1865–66). He was a delegate to general assemblies of the Free Church of Scotland (1867) and the Irish Presbyterian church (1884). He received honorary degrees from Wittenberg College and Miami and New York universities.

REFERENCES: *AC; DAB; NCAB* (6:324); *TC; WWW* (I); *NYT*, December 25, 1918, p. 15.   *Barbara Ruth Peltzman*

McCROREY, Henry Lawrence. B. March 2, 1863, Fairfield County, South Carolina, to James and Nancy (Denton) McCrorey. M. December 27, 1897, to Karie Novella Hughes. M. September 19, 1916, to Mary Catherine Jackson. Ch. four. D. July 13, 1951, Charlotte, North Carolina.

Henry L. McCrorey received the A.B. (1892), B.D. (1895), and D. D. (1902) degrees from Biddle (later, Johnson C. Smith) University in Charlotte, North Carolina. He studied on the graduate level at the University of Chicago (1895–96 and 1930).

McCrorey was ordained a minister in the Presbyterian church (1895) and was a teacher and principal at Biddle University (1895–1900). He taught Latin in the Biddle college of liberal arts (1900–01) and Greek and Hebrew in the theological seminary (1901–07). He became president of Biddle University in 1907 and served in that capacity until 1947, when he became emeritus president.

The university experienced a period of growth from fifty to nine hundred and fifty students and from fifteen to sixty faculty members during McCrorey's administration. Biddle University became Johnson C. Smith University on March 1, 1923, after Mrs. Johnson C. Smith donated over $700,000 to the institution. McCrorey also obtained financial aid from the James B. Duke Foundation; the endowment increased from $40,000 in 1907 to over $1.3 million in 1947.

McCrorey served as editor of the *Quarterly Review of Higher Education Among Negroes* (1933–51) and the *Afro-American Presbyterian*. He was a delegate from North Carolina to the Negro Education Congress held in St. Paul, Minnesota (1912), and the Southern Sociological Congress in Houston, Texas (1915). He was a member of the National Association of Teachers in Colored Schools (president, 1921–22 and trustee, 1932–37). He was active in the Presbyterian Church of the U.S.A. as a delegate to quadrennial meetings of the World Alliance of Reformed Churches, commissioner at the Church's general assembly, and member of the board of Christian education, and president of the college union of the Presbyterian Church of the U.S.A. (1940). He was a member of the Fraternal Council of Negro Churches of America (executive committee), the Southern Council on International Relations, and the North Carolina State Interracial Commission. He received a certificate for distinguished service to Christian education from the Presbyterian church and was the recipient of honorary degrees.

REFERENCES: *LE* (III); *NCAB* (42:45); *WWAE* (VIII); *WWW* (III); *NYT,* July 14, 1951, p. 13.   *Anne R. Gayles*

McCURDY, James Huff. B. December 2, 1866, Princeton, Maine, to John and Augusta Evelyn (Heath) McCurdy. M. July 17, 1895, to Persis Baker Harlow. Ch. two. D. September 4, 1940, Springfield, Massachusetts.

James Huff McCurdy, physician and physical education director, was graduated from Princeton (Maine) High School (1885) and received the M.D. degree (1893) from the University Medical College of New York University. He served as physical education director in Maine at the Bangor (1887) and Auburn (1888) Young Men's Christian Associations (YMCA). He attended the International YMCA College at Springfield, Massachusetts (1888–90), and studied the physiology of exercise at Harvard Medical School (1896 and 1900). In 1890 he entered the four-year program at New York University and was graduated in three years (1893). He had been the athletic and aquatic director of the New York YMCA while he was a student.

In 1895 McCurdy became instructor of physical education at the International YMCA College. He was promoted to professor (1900) and then to medical director and director of the physical education department (1906). He received the M.P.E. degree (1907) from the International YMCA College and the M.A. degree (1909) from Clark University in Worcester, Massachusetts.

At the International YMCA College McCurdy organized a football team on which he played and acted as coach and trainer. His team and department were among the finest in the country. He was credited with being the first person to develop and use the forward pass and spiral pass from center.

In 1915 he was special consultant for hygiene and physical education to the United States Bureau of Education. In 1917 he accompanied the American Expeditionary Force to France as director of the YMCA division of athletics, social hygiene, and recreation and served in the same capacity with the French army. He reorganized physical education teaching in the French schools (1918–19).

McCurdy wrote *Bibliography of Physical Training* (1905), *Calisthenic Nomenclature* (1916), and *Physiology of Exercise* (1939) and coauthored *Decimal Classification of Physical Training* (with J. T. Bowne, 1902). He was editor of the *American Physical Education Review* (1906–29).

He was secretary-treasurer of the American Physical Education Association and served as a member of the board of the National Recreation Association and on the committee on physical education of the national YMCA.

REFERENCES: *LE* (I); *NCAB* (30:185); *WWW* (I); *NYT*, September 5, 1940, p. 23; Laurence Locke Doggett, *Man and a School* (New York: Association Press, 1943).   *C. Roy Rylander*

MacDONALD, Arthur. B. July 4, 1856, Caledonia, New York, to Angus and Virginia (Dibble) MacDonald. M. September 29, 1904, to Margaret Jane Porterfield. Ch. none. D. January 17, 1936, Washington, D.C.

Upon completion of the A.B. degree (1879) at the University of Rochester (New York), Arthur MacDonald began the study of law, his father's aspiration for him. Changing to theology, he entered Princeton (New Jersey) Theological Seminary, from which he received the A.M. degree (1883). Graduate school at Harvard University involved specialized course work in philosophy, metaphysics, and religious subjects during the period 1883 to 1885. Declining a fellowship in psychology, he studied medicine in European universities in Berlin and Leipzig, Germany, Paris, France, and Zurich, Switzerland. He also studied insanity, criminology, hypnotism, and related subjects, such as psychophysics.

MacDonald was appointed docent in applied ethics and criminology at Clark University in Worcester, Massachusetts, in 1889, a role he filled until 1891, when he became a specialist in the education of abnormal and handicapped persons for the United States Bureau of Education. As a pioneer special educator, he conducted studies of subjects in slums, prisons, and insane asylums in the United States and abroad, the results of which were significant to both educational science and anthropology. After 1904 his major activity was the conduct of anthropological research involving numerous observations of abnormal and normal people, especially school-age children. His studies of the relative dimensions of the brain and cranium led to the need to develop delicate measuring and recording instruments.

A pioneer in the scientific study of abnormal man, MacDonald's writings include *Criminology* (1894), *Abnormal Man* (1895), *Le Criminel-Type* (1895), *Educational and Pathosocial Studies* (1896), *Emile Zola* (1896), *Experimental Study of Children* (1899), *Plan for Study of Man* (1902), *Statistics of Crime, Suicide, and Insanity* (1903), *Man and Abnormal Man* (1905), and *Juvenile Crime and Reformation* (1908). He wrote many articles for professional journals in the United States and Europe.

MacDonald was an American delegate to three international psychological and criminological congresses and was honorary president of the Third Congress. At his request, his brain was sent to the anatomical laboratory of Western Reserve University in Cleveland, Ohio, for scientific study upon his death.

REFERENCES: *NCAB* (26:260); *NYT*, January 18, 1936, p. 15; *WWW* (I).

Bruce D. Mattson

McDOUGALL, William. B. June 22, 1871, Chadderton, Lancashire, England, to Isaac Shimwell and Rebekah (Smalley) McDougall. M. 1900 to Anne Aurelia Hickmore. Ch. five. D. November 28, 1938, Durham, North Carolina.

At the age of fourteen William McDougall was sent to Real-Gymnasium at Weimar, Germany. He was graduated in science from Owen's College in Manchester, England, at the age of seventeen with highest honors. He entered St. John's College of Cambridge (England) University and studied physiology, anatomy, and anthropology. In 1844 he received the university scholarship at St. Thomas Hospital, London, where he completed the medical courses. Because of a strong interest in research and an appointment as a fellow of St. John's College in 1898, he decided against continuing a medical career. He spent two years with the Cambridge Anthropological Expedition to the Torres Straits and was tempted to make field anthropology his life work; he turned instead to the field of psychology. He received the B.A. degree (1894) from Cambridge University and the M.A. degree (1897) from Oxford (England) University and studied at the University of Göttingen, Germany.

From 1900 to 1920 McDougall was a reader at University College in London, England, where he lectured and conducted demonstrations in psychology, built a laboratory, and for four years engaged in extensive research in scientific psychology. He accepted an offer to become a professor of psychology at Harvard University (1920–27) and was professor of psychology at Duke University in Durham, North Carolina, from 1927. He was one of the most original and productive twentieth-century psychologists.

McDougall's two most important books were *Outline of Psychology* (1923) and *Outline of Abnormal Psychology* (1926). His other writings include *Physiological Psychology* (1905), *Social Psychology* (1908), *Pagan Tribes of Borneo* (1911), *Psychology* (1912), *Body and Mind* (1912), *Group Mind* (1920), *Is America Safe for Democracy?* (1921), *Outline of Psychology* (1923), *Ethics and Some Modern World Problems* (1924), *Outline of Abnormal Psychology* (1926), *Janus* (1927), *Character and Conduct of Life* (1927), *Modern Materialism and Emergent Evolution* (1929), *World Chaos—The Responsibility of Science* (1931), *Energies of Man* (1933), and *Psycho-Analysis and Social Psychology* (1936).

He was president of the British Society for Psychical Research, a fellow of the Royal Society of London, and a member of other professional and scholarly organizations. He was awarded the Dc.Sc. by the British Society for Psychical Science.

REFERENCES: *DAB* (supp. 2); *LE* (I); *WWW* (I); *NYT*, November 29, 1938, p. 23.   *John W. Schifani*

MACE, William Harrison. B. August 27, 1852, near Lexington, Indiana, to Ira and Nancy S. (Johnson) Mace. M. September 10, 1878, to Ida Dodson. Ch. one. D. August 10, 1938, Gananoque, Quebec, Canada.

William Harrison Mace was graduated from the State Normal School (later, Indiana State University) in Terre Haute, Indiana, in 1876, where he developed his interest in historical study. He studied at the University of Michigan, where he received the B.L. and M.L. degrees (1883), and the University of Indiana, where he was awarded the A.M. degree (1889). He was a graduate student at Cornell University in Ithaca, New York (1890–91), and studied in Germany at the University of Berlin and at the University of Jena, where he received the Ph.D. degree in 1897.

Mace served as principal of a ward school in Logansport, Indiana (1876–77), and as superintendent of schools in Winamack, Indiana (1877–79), and McGregor, Iowa (1883–85).

From 1885 to 1890 Mace was professor of history at DePauw University Normal School in Greencastle, Indiana. On his return from Europe in 1891, he was appointed William Griffin Professor of History and Political Science at Syracuse (New York) University, where he served to his death in 1938. He opened the first university extension center under the auspices of the University of the State of New York at Watertown in January 1892 and taught many classes there. He received an invitation from Cambridge

(England) University to lecture on the English and American constitutions in 1893, a significant compliment to American scholarship in the field. He also was a university extension lecturer on American history to the American Society (1899) and the summer school of South Knoxville, Tennessee (1903–04).

Mace was the author of *A Working Manual of American History* (1895), *Method of History* (1897), *A School History of the United States* (1904), *Stories of Heroism* (1907), *Old Europe and Young America* (with E. P. Tanner, 1919), *American History for Schools* (with George Petrie, *q.v.,* 1919), *History of the United States* (with Frank S. Bogardus, 1921), and *American History for High Schools* (1925). He contributed *Lincoln, the Man of the People* and *Washington, a Virginia Cavalier* to the Little Lives of Great Men Series (1933).

He received honorary degrees from Syracuse University and Indiana University.

REFERENCES: *NCAB* (4:407); *TC; WWW* (I); *NYT,* August 11, 1938, p. 17.   *Kenneth Sipser*

McGRATH, Earl James. B. November 16, 1902, Buffalo, New York, to John and Martha Carolyn (Schottin) McGrath. M. May 12, 1944, to Dorothy Anne Leemon. Ch. none.

Earl McGrath received the A.B. (1928) and M.A. (1930) degrees from the University of Buffalo, New York (later, State University of New York at Buffalo). He held a fellowship at the University of Chicago (1933–35), where he received the Ph.D. degree in 1936.

McGrath was employed at the University of Buffalo as associate director of personnel research (1928–29), lecturer in psychology (1928–33), assistant dean of the evening session (1929–30), assistant to the chancellor (1930–33), professor of education (1935–38, 1940–42), and administrative dean (1940–45). He served as a specialist in higher education for the American Council on Education (1938-40). During World War II, McGrath took a leave of absence from Buffalo and served in educational administrative posts in the United States Navy. He became dean of the college of liberal arts at the State University of Iowa (1945-48).

McGrath was appointed United States commissioner of education (1949–53). He was president and chancellor at the University of Kansas City, Missouri (1953–56), professor of higher education and director of the Institute of Higher Education at Teachers College, Columbia University (1956–68), director of the Higher Education Center at Temple University in Philadelphia, Pennsylvania (1968–73), and chancellor of Eisenhower College in Seneca Falls, New York (1965–69), and he has been emeritus chancellor from 1969. He was also senior educational adviser for the Lilly Endowment (1973).

McGrath served as a member of the staff of the Regents Inquiry into the Character and Cost of Education in the State of New York (1937), the committee to survey German education in the American occupied zone of the United States State Department (1946), and the President's Commission on Higher Education (1946), and he was a consultant to a number of colleges and universities.

He wrote many articles for professional journals and served as editor of the *Journal of General Education.* He was coauthor of *Cooperation in General Education* (1948), *Toward General Education* (1948), *The Changing Mission of Home Economics* (1968), and *Should Students Share the Power* (1969) and author of *Education—the Wellspring of Democracy* (1951) and *The Predominantly Negro Colleges and Universities in Transition* (1965). He received many honorary degrees.

REFERENCES: *CA* (19–20); *CB* (April 1949); *LE* (III); *WWAE* (XIV); *WW* (XXVIII). *Paul J. Schafer*

McGROARTY, Susan (Sister Julia). B. February 13, 1827, Inver, Donegal County, Ireland, to Neil and Catherine (Bonner) McGroarty. M. no. D. November 12, 1901, Peabody, Massachusetts.

Susan McGroarty was brought to America shortly after her fourth birthday, and the family settled in Cincinnati, Ohio. In 1840 the sisters of Notre Dame from Namur, Belgium, opened a small school that McGroarty attended. She became a postulant to the sisters on January 1, 1846, and on August 3, 1848, she was professed as Sister Julia.

Upon entering the convent she began to teach and was placed in charge of the day school. In September 1854 she became mistress of boarders at the Academy of Notre Dame in Roxbury, Massachusetts, and in 1860 superior of the sisters' house in Philadelphia. In 1877 she opened a free school for black children, which was closed in 1880 with the passage of a law admitting black children to public schools.

In 1885 Sister Julia returned to Cincinnati. In 1886 she was appointed superior of Notre Dame de Namur houses east of the Rocky Mountains, to which those of the California province were added in 1892. During her tenure as superior, Sister Julia founded fourteen convents and schools. She sought to improve the quality of education offered by members of the community by preparing outlines of studies and generalized examinations for all grades.

In 1897, while considering opening a house outside of Washington, D.C., the order consulted with the rector of Catholic University. He and his advisers requested that the sisters found a college for women because there was none in the area. In 1898, with assistance from the faculty of Catholic University, selected sisters began development of a curriculum for the college, and ground was broken for the first building in June 1899. Students arrived in October, 1900, and Trinity College was formally dedicated the following November.

REFERENCES: *DAB; NAW; WWW* (H); *The Cincinnati Enquirer,* November 13, 16, 1901; *New Catholic Encyclopedia* (New York: McGraw-Hill, 1967); Helen Louise Nugent, *Sister Julia* (New York: Binziger Brothers, 1928). *Anne E. Scheerer*

McGUFFEY, William Holmes. B. September 23, 1800, Washington County, Pennsylvania, to Alexander and Anna (Holmes) McGuffey. M. April 3, 1827, to Harriet Spinning. M. 1857 to Laura Howard. Ch. six. D. May 4, 1873, Charlottesville, Virginia.

William Holmes McGuffey moved to Trumbull County, Ohio, with his parents in 1802. He was largely self-educated and taught in rural subscription schools as a teenager. He continued his education at Greersburg Academy in Pennsylvania and taught in Ohio and Kentucky. He was graduated in 1826 from Washington (Pennsylvania) College, where he was influenced by the college president, Andrew Wylie *(q.v.).*

While teaching at Paris, Kentucky, McGuffey met Robert H. Bishop *(q.v.),* president of Miami University in Oxford, Ohio. Prior to his graduation from Washington College, Bishop offered McGuffey a teaching position at Miami. He taught ancient languages (1826–32) and mental philosophy (1832–36). Licensed a Presbyterian minister in 1829, he served as pastor of the Presbyterian church at Darrtown, Ohio, for four years, and became a popular public speaker.

Elected president in 1836 of Cincinnati (Ohio) College, a struggling institution, McGuffey accepted the presidency of Ohio University at Athens. He remained there to 1843, when conflict arose over reappraisal of the lands from which Ohio University derived its financial support. McGuffey resigned his position in 1843 and Ohio University was closed for five years.

From 1843 to 1845, McGuffey taught at Woodward High School in Cincinnati, where he, Samuel Lewis *(q.v.),* and others were successful in persuading the legislature to adopt a law establishing a public school system in Ohio. He accepted a position as professor of philosophy at the University of Virginia in 1845 and remained there to his death in 1873.

While at Miami University, McGuffey began compiling the readers for which he became famous. He arranged with Winthrop B. Smith of Cincinnati for their publication. The first, published in 1836, were the *First Reader* and *Second Reader,* followed by the *Third Reader* and *Fourth Reader* in 1837. McGuffey's brother Alexander wrote the *Fifth Reader* in 1844, and the *Sixth Reader* and *High School Reader* were published in 1857. The McGuffey Readers dominated the textbook field for many years, were published in many editions, and sold 122 million copies.

REFERENCES: *AC; DAB; EB; NCAB* (4:443); *TC; WWW* (H); Benjamin F. Crawford, *William Holmes McGuffey: The Schoolmaster to our Nation* (Delaware, Ohio: Carnegie Church Press, 1963); Mildred S. Fenner and Jean C. Soule, "William Holmes McGuffey and His Common School Readers," *Journal of the National Education Association* 35 (September 1946): 300-01; Walter Havighurst, "Primer from a Green World," *American Heritage* 8 (August 1957); 10-11; John A. Nietz, *Old Textbooks* (Pittsburgh, Pa.: University of Pittsburgh Press, 1961).

Robert H. Hoexter

McHUGH, Anna (Sister Antonia). B. May 17, 1873, Omaha, Nebraska, to Patrick and Rose (Welch) McHugh. M. no. D. October 11, 1944, St. Paul, Minnesota.

Anna McHugh grew up on the frontier, her parents having moved from Omaha, Nebraska, to Deadwood, South Dakota, in 1876, three years after the Custer massacre. The family then settled in Langdon, North Dakota, where her father established a successful land-deeds office and became a prominent state legislator. She learned to read at the age of four from a Deadwood public school teacher who boarded at the McHugh hotel. She studied in public schools at Custer, South Dakota, and Grafton, North Dakota. She developed an interest in teaching and the religious life as a student of a woman who later joined the Gray Nuns at Montreal, Canada, and from boarding school contacts from the ages of twelve to sixteen with the Gray Nuns and the Sisters of St. Joseph.

McHugh lived with the Sisters of St. Joseph in St. Paul in 1891. Deciding to join the order and teach, she took the name of Sister Antonia. She earned the Ed.B. (1908), B.A. (1908), and M.A. (1909) degrees from the University of Chicago. She returned to St. Paul and the College of St. Catherine, which had been founded by the St. Joseph Sisters in 1905.

An outspoken advocate of women's right to and need for higher education, Sister Antonia collaborated with other religious and lay educators of her time in improving women's college standards and in encouraging women to pursue professional goals.

Sister Antonia served as dean (1914–18) and president (1918–37) of the College of St. Catherine. She guided the institution into a status as a fully accredited liberal arts college with a distinguished faculty, an outstanding library, six major buildings, and a chapter of Phi Beta Kappa.

Active in professional organizations, she participated in the White House Conference on Child Health and Protection (1930) and served as president of the Minnesota Association of Colleges and in executive positions in the National Catholic Educational Association and the American Association of Colleges. She received the University of Chicago Distinguished Alumnae citation and the Pro Ecclesia et Pontifice decoration for outstanding work in education (1931). She received an honorary doctorate from the University of Minnesota (1936).

REFERENCES: *LE* (I); *WWAE* (III); *American Women* (New Jersey, Zephyrus Press, 1939), 3:593.   *Karen Kennelly*

McIVER, Charles Duncan. B. September 27, 1860, Moore County, North Carolina, to Matthew Henry and Sarah (Harrington) McIver. M. 1885 to Lula V. Martin. Ch. five. D. September 17, 1906, Greensboro, North Carolina.

Charles Duncan McIver was graduated from the University of North Carolina in 1881 and began teaching in private and public schools. An advocate of public education, he participated in the establishment of public school systems in Durham and Winston, North Carolina.

The University of North Carolina was a male institution, and McIver sought the establishment of a college for women. He argued that more women than men were elementary and high school teachers, and the state should provide educational institutions both for the preparation of teachers and for the equally important function of motherhood.

McIver was appointed by the teachers' assembly of North Carolina in 1889 to serve as chairman of a group to appear before the legislature to urge adoption of a bill for the establishment of a training school for teachers. The bill did not pass, but the state board of education transferred its appropriation from short-term summer normal schools to a system of county institutes. McIver and Edwin Alderman *(q.v.)* were appointed coconductors of the institutes (1889–92).

In 1891 his request for the establishment of a college for women passed the legislature. McIver organized the North Carolina State Normal and Industrial College (later, North Carolina College for Women) in Greensboro in 1892 and was elected president at the first meeting of the board of directors. He continued in that position for the rest of his life.

McIver was an organizer of the Conference for Education in the South. He served as secretary of the Southern Education Board and was president of the Southern Education Association (1905) and the North Carolina Teachers' Assembly. He served on the council of the National Educational Association. McIver received two honorary degrees from the University of North Carolina.

REFERENCES: *DAB; NCAB* (25:113); *TC; WWW* (I); *NYT,* September 18, 1906, p. 9.   *Jill Holland*

MACKENZIE, James Cameron. B. August 5, 1852, Aberdeen, Scotland, to Alexander and Catherine (Cameron) Mackenzie. M. October 5, 1880, to Ella Smith. Ch. eight. D. May 10, 1931, Staten Island, New York.

When James Mackenzie was three years old, his father died of cholera and his mother took the family to Wilkes-Barre, Pennsylvania. Mackenzie was educated at the Millersville (Pennsylvania) State Normal School (later, Millersville State College), Phillips Academy in Exeter, New Hampshire, and Lafayette College in Easton, Pennsylvania, where he received the A.B. (1878) and Ph.D. (1882) degrees. He studied at Princeton (New Jersey) Theological Seminary (1882) and was ordained in the Presbyterian church in 1885.

From 1882 until his retirement Mackenzie served as founder, organizer, reorganizer, headmaster, and adviser to independent preparatory schools in Pennsylvania, New Jersey, Maryland, New York, and Connecticut. He organized and was first headmaster of the Lawrenceville (New Jersey) School (1882–99) and reorganized and was director of the Tome Institute in Port Deposit, Maryland (1899-1901). In 1901 he founded the Mackenzie School in Monroe, New York, and headed the school to 1926, when he engaged in writing and preaching.

Mackenzie sought to model his schools on those at Eton and Rugby, England. He established the English house system and honor system and emphasized athletics.

Mackenzie was a founder and president of the Headmasters Association (1897), a member of the National Educational Association's Committee of Ten (1891), chairman of the International Congress of Secondary Education (1892), president of the Middle Atlantic Association of Colleges and Secondary Schools (1898), and a member of the advisory board of St. Luke's school in New Canaan, Connecticut.

REFERENCES: *DAB; NCAB* (43: 508); *TC; WWW* (I); Oscar J. Harvey, *A History of Wilkes-Barre and Wyoming Valley, Pennsylvania* (Wilkes-Barre: The author, 1909), vol. 3; *NYT*, May 11, 1931, p. 19.

Samuel A. Farmerie

McKENZIE, Robert Tait. B. May 26, 1867, Almonte, Ontario, Canada, to William and Catherine (Shiells) McKenzie. M. August 18, 1907, to Ethel O'Neil. Ch. none. D. April 28, 1938, Philadelphia, Pennsylvania.

R. Tait McKenzie, educator, physical educator, physician, and sculptor, attended the Ottawa (Ontario, Canada) Collegiate Institute and McGill University in Montreal, Quebec, Canada, where he received the A.B. (1889) and M.D. (1892) degrees. He attended the Harvard Summer School of Physical Education and received the diploma in 1901.

McKenzie practiced medicine in Canada as house physician at the Montreal General Hospital (1893), surgeon on the Beaver Line steamer between Liverpool, England, and Montreal (1893), and house physician to the governor-general of Canada (1895). He was lecturer in anatomy (1895–1904) and was North America's first medical director of physical training (1896–1904) at McGill University.

McKenzie went to the University of Pennsylvania as director of the department of physical education from 1904 until 1931. Through his influence physical education and athletics were recognized as integral parts of the university curriculum. McKenzie was a leader in the new and rapidly expanding profession of physical education, contributing to the formulation of a basic philosophy and the redirection of the profession. He developed an outstanding program of physical education at the University of Pennsylvania.

While at Pennsylvania, he also was appointed professor of physiotherapy (1907) on the medical faculty, the first appointment as professor of this subject in an American university. During World War I, McKenzie served in the British army and organized and conducted a program of physical therapy for training camps and hospitals in England and Canada. On his retirement in 1931, he served as Research Professor of Physical Education, heading the divisions of student health, physical instruction, and intercollegiate atheletics.

McKenzie wrote in the field of physical medicine; his books include *A System of Gymnastic Exercises and a System of Fencing* (n.d.), *A System of Physical Education* (n.d.), *Exercise in Education and Medicine* (1909), *Reclaiming the Maimed* (1918), and *Physiology of Exercise* (n.d.).

McKenzie's reputation as an artist was more firmly established abroad than was his professional status in education or medicine. He executed over two hundred works of art, which included twenty-five war and other memorials and twenty-one athletic bronzes. Among his best-known works were "Young Franklin," "The Call," "Reverend George Whitefield," the "General Wolfe Statue," and the official seal of the American Alliance of Health, Physical Education and Recreation.

McKenzie was active in professional associations, serving as president of the American Physical Education Association (1912–15), the Society of Directors of Physical Education in Colleges (1901, 1904, and 1909), the Academy of Physical Medicine, and as a charter member and first president of the American Academy of Physical Education (1930–38). The R. Tait McKenzie Award was established in his honor by the American Alliance of Health, Physical Education and Recreation in 1968, and he was awarded several honorary degrees.

REFERENCES: *DAB* (supp. 2); *LE* (III); *NCAB* (C:357); *WWW* (I); Ellen W. Gerber, *Innovators and Institutions in Physical Education* (Philadelphia: Lea & Febiger, 1971); Adelaide M. Hunter, "R. Tait McKenzie: Pioneer in Physical Education" (Ed.D. diss. Teachers College, Columbia University, 1950); Christopher Hussey, *Tait McKenzie, A Sculptor of Youth* (London, 1929); *NYT*, April 29, 1938, p. 21; E. Leroy Mercer, "R. Tait McKenzie—34 Years at the University of Pennsylvania," *Journal of Health and Physical Education* 15 (February 1944): 58.

Adelaide M. Cole

McKOWN, Harry Charles. B. January 11, 1892, Peoria, Illinois, to Charles Wesley and Rebecca Catherine (Traxler) McKown. M. August 17, 1926, to Ruth Irene Hord. Ch. one. D. September 5, 1963, Gilson, Illinois.

Harry Charles McKown was graduated from Knox College in Galesburg, Illinois, with the B.S. degree (1913) and received the M.A. degree (1917) from the University of Illinois. He also studied at the University of Chicago in the summer of 1917 and at Iowa State University in the summer of 1920. He received the M.A. (1922) and Ph.D. (1923) degrees from Columbia University.

McKown was a secretary with the Young Men's Christian Association at Chicago (1913–15) and Galesburg, Illinois (1915–16), and a high school teacher in Ottumwa, Iowa (1917–21). He was professor of secondary education at the University of Pittsburgh, Pennsylvania (1923–33). He was a leader in the development of extracurricular programs in schools. From 1933 to his death in 1963, McKown engaged in writing and lecturing and was a visiting professor and conductor of workshops at many major colleges and universities across the country. He was a specialist with the United States Department of State in 1950–51.

He wrote *Trend of College Entrance Requirements* (1924), *Extracurricular Activities* (1927), *School Clubs* (1929), *Assembly and Auditorium Activities* (1930), *Commencement Activities* (1931), *Home Room Guidance* (1934), *Character Education* (1935), *Activities in the Elementary School* (1938), *The Junior Citizen* (1939), *A Boy Grows Up* (1940), *Audio Visual Aids to Instruction* (with Alvin B. Roberts, 1940), *Fools and Foolishness* (1943), *How to Pass a Written Examination* (1943), *The Student Council* (1944), *Adventures in Thrift* (1946), and *So You Were Elected* (with Virginia Ballard, 1946). He was an editor and adviser to the McGraw-Hill Book Company, editor of *School Activities* magazine from 1935, and president of School Activities Publishing Company from 1942.

A veteran of World War I, McKown was active in professional associations. He was president of the National Conference on Student Participation and Control, a committee member of the National Student Forum on the Paris Pact, and a member of the national council of the National Honor Society. He received the Knox College Alumnae Award in 1955 and received the Award for Service and Contribution to the United States from President John F. Kennedy.

REFERENCES: *LE* (III); *NCAB* (52:278); *WWAE* (XVI); *WWW* (IV); *NYT,* September 6, 1963, p. 29.   *James V. Sandrin*

MACLEAN, John. B. March 1, 1771, Glasgow, Scotland, to John and Agnes (Lang) Maclean. M. November 7, 1798, to Phebe Bainbridge. Ch. six, including John Maclean *(q.v.),* president of Princeton University. D. February 17, 1814, Princeton, New Jersey.

John Maclean was orphaned at an early age and was raised by George Macintosh. He attended the Glasgow, Scotland, Grammar School and first entered the University of Glasgow at the age of twelve. He left in 1787 to study in Edinburgh, Scotland, London, England, and Paris, France, and returned to Glasgow to resume his studies in 1790. On August 1, 1791, he received a diploma granting him the right to practice surgery and pharmacy. He was appointed a member of the faculty of physicians and surgeons at the University of Glasgow at the age of twenty-one. In 1797 he was awarded the M.D. degree by Glasgow.

Sympathetic to the American political climate, Maclean emigrated to the United States in 1795, where he met Dr. Benjamin Rush *(q.v.)* who persuaded him to settle at Princeton, New Jersey. In the fall of 1795, he became the first professor of chemistry and natural history at the College of New Jersey (later, Princeton University), the first professor of chemistry in an American college (other than in medical schools).

Dating from his stay in Paris, Maclean was enthusiastic about the theories and teachings of Antoine Lavoisier and taught them at Princeton. He was among the first to adopt and teach Lavoisier's antiphlogiston theory, which correctly held that instead of emitting phlogiston into the air, burning materials combine with oxygen. In 1797 he wrote *Two Lectures on Combustion: Supplementary to a Course of Lectures on Chemistry Read at Nassau Hall; Containing an Examination of Dr. Priestley's Considerations on the Doctrine of Phlogiston, and the Decomposition of Water.* Discussion of the subject was continued between Maclean, Joseph Priestley, James Woodhouse *(q.v.)*, and Samuel Mitchell in the New York *Medical Repository.*

Maclean was elected a member of the American Philosophical Society in 1805. He joined the faculty of the College of William and Mary in 1812 but returned to Princeton a year later.

REFERENCES: *AC; DAB; DSB; TC; WWW* (H). *B. Richard Siebring*

MACLEAN, John. B. March 3, 1800, Princeton, New Jersey, to John *(q.v.)* and Phebe (Bainbridge) Maclean. M. no. D. August 10, 1886, Princeton, New Jersey.

John Maclean's father was professor of natural philosophy (first professor of chemistry) at the College of New Jersey (later, Princeton University). The younger Maclean was graduated from the College of New Jersey in 1816, at the age of sixteen, the youngest in his class.

Maclean taught for a year at the nearby Lawrenceville (New Jersey) School before he entered Princeton Theological Seminary, where he studied for a year. In 1818 he returned to the college as a tutor. Two years later he was an instructor in mathematics and natural philosophy, and in 1823 he was named professor of mathematics. He moved to the department of ancient languages and literature in 1829 and was promoted to professor of Greek in 1847. In 1828 he was ordained in the Presbyterian church but never held a pastorate. During his last years at the college (1866–68) he taught biblical studies.

During the administration of President James Carnahan, Maclean was appointed to the post of vice-president of the college (1829). Through Maclean's efforts funds were raised, new faculty members added, and two new buildings erected. Upon Carnahan's retirement in 1854, Maclean was elected to head the College of New Jersey.

During Maclean's tenure the college's enrollment dropped severely when the Civil War deprived it of the many students formerly drawn from the South. His presidency ended in June 1868 when he was succeeded by James McCosh *(q.v.)*. Maclean served as vice-president of Princeton Theological Seminary (1882–86).

In addition to several sermons and addresses, Maclean was the author of *Lectures on a School System for New Jersey* (1829), in which he recommended a board of education for the state, a state superintendent of schools, and public support for teacher training, *Letters on the True Relations of the Church and the State to Schools and Colleges* (1853), *A Memoir of John Maclean, M.D., the First Professor of Chemistry in the College of New Jersey* (1876), a biography of his father, and his largest and most important work, *History of the College of New Jersey* (two volumes, 1877), which remained the definitive source on the institution until 1946.

The Alumni Association of the college was formed in 1826, and John Maclean served as its secretary for over fifty years; the group helped in the secularizing of Princeton. Maclean was a member of the board of directors of Princeton Theological Seminary (1861–68) and was a regent of the Smithsonian Institution in Washington, D.C. (1868–86). He received honorary degrees from Washington and Jefferson College and the University of the State of New York.

REFERENCES: *AC; DAB; NCAB* (5: 467); *NYT,* August 11, 1886, p. 5; *TC; WWW* (H); Varnum L. Collins, *Princeton* (New York: Oxford University Press, 1914); John Maclean, *History of the College of New Jersey* (Philadelphia: J. B. Lippincott, 1877); Thomas Jefferson Wertenbaker, *Princeton, 1746–1896* (Princeton: Princeton University Press, 1946).

Richard G. Durnin

McMASTER, John Bach. B. June 29, 1852, Brooklyn, New York, to James and Julia (Bach) McMaster. M. April 14, 1887, to Gertrude Stevenson. Ch. three. D. May 22, 1932, Darien, Connecticut.

John Bach McMaster received his early education in the New York City public schools. He was graduated from the City College of New York with the A.B. degree in 1872 and served that institution as an instructor of

English grammar while pursuing studies in civil engineering. He completed his studies in civil engineering in 1873.

McMaster became instructor of civil engineering at the City College. From 1877 to 1883 he was instructor of civil engineering at the College of New Jersey (later, Princeton University). In 1883 the first volume of his *History of the American People* was published, and he was appointed professor of history at the University of Pennsylvania.

During his thirty-seven-year tenure at the University of Pennsylvania, he continued to publish history books and in 1913 the eighth volume completed the series. He retired as professor emeritus in June 1920. Through the *History of the American People,* he is cited as the leader of a movement to bring about a shift in the historical point of view from military and political to social and economic history. He is also credited with being the first professor of American history in the United States to combine research and writing with teaching.

In addition to *History of the American People* (eight volumes, 1883–1913) and numerous magazine and review articles, he wrote *Benjamin Franklin as a Man of Letters* (1887), *With the Fathers* (1893), *Origin, Meaning, and Application of the Monroe Doctrine* (1893), *A School History of the United States* (1897), *Primary School History of the United States* (1901), *Daniel Webster* (1902), *Brief History of the United States* (1907), *Life and Times of Stephen Girard* (1917), *The United States in the World War* (two volumes, 1918–20), and *A History of the People in the United States during the Administration of Abraham Lincoln* (1927). He was an associate editor of *American Historical Review* (1896–99).

McMaster was a member of the American Historical Association (vice-president, 1904, and president, 1905) and a member of historical societies of Massachusetts, Pennsylvania, Delaware, and Minnesota. He received honorary degrees from Washington and Jefferson College and the universities of Pennsylvania and Toronto, Canada.

REFERENCES: *AC; DAB; NCAB* (11:445); *NYT,* May 25, 1932, p. 19; *TC; WWW* (I). *C. Kenneth Murray*

McMURRIN, Sterling Moss. B. January 12, 1914, Woods Cross, Utah, to Joseph W., Jr., and Gertrude (Moss) McMurrin. M. June 8, 1938, to Natalie Barbara Cotterel. Ch. five.

Sterling Moss McMurrin was graduated from Manual Arts High School in Los Angeles, California, in 1931. He studied at the University of California and the University of Utah, where he was graduated with the B.A. (1936) and M.A. (1937) degrees. He earned the Ph.D. degree from the University of Southern California (1946).

McMurrin served with the department of education of the Church of Jesus Christ of Latter-day Saints (1937–45), including two years (1943–45) as director of its institute of religion at the University of Arizona. He was assistant professor of philosophy at the University of Southern California (1946–48), professor of philosophy at the University of Utah (1948–61), dean of Utah's college of letters and science (1954–60), and academic vice-president (1960–61).

In 1961 President John F. Kennedy appointed McMurrin United States commissioner of education. Resigning in 1962, he returned to the University of Utah where he was Eriksen Distinguished Professor of Philosophy and became provost (1965), dean of the graduate school (1966), and professor of history (1970).

A lecturer and conductor of seminars at the Aspen (Colorado) Institute for Humanistic Studies (from 1955), McMurrin was adviser to the University of Tehran (Iran) for one year (1958–59). He revised the third edition of Benjamin A. G. Fuller's *A History of Philosophy* (two volumes, 1955) and edited *Contemporary Philosophy* (with James L. Jarrett, 1954). He wrote many articles and reviews published in scholarly journals.

McMurrin was a Ford Fellow (1962–63) and visiting professor at several universities. He was United States delegate to the Policy Conference on Economic Growth and Investment in Education in Washington, D.C. (1961), the United Nations Educational, Scientific, and Cultural Organization Conference on Latin American Education in Santiago, Chile (1962), vice-president of the Twenty-fifth International Congress on Education at Geneva, Switzerland (1962), and delegate to other international meetings. He was chairman of the Federal Commission on Instructional Technology, chairman of the mountain states and midcontinent manpower advisory commissions of the United States Department of Labor (1965–68), senior commissioner of the Western Association of Schools and Colleges (from 1974), member of the Graduate Record Examination Board (from 1974), and member of the board of directors of the Agency for Instructional Television (from 1974). He was a member of professional organizations and was awarded many honorary degrees.

REFERENCES: *CA* (29–32); *CB* (June 1961); *LE* (V); WW (XXXIX); Dorsey Baynham, "Sterling McMurrin: New U.S. Commissioner of Education," *Saturday Review* 44 (February 18, 1961); 66.

                                                            Lawrence S. Master

McMURRY, Charles Alexander. B. February 18, 1857, Crawfordsville, Indiana, to Franklin Morton and Charlotte (Underwood) McMurry. M. July 19, 1888, to Emily K. La Crone. Ch. five. D. March 24, 1929, Nashville, Tennessee.

Charles Alexander McMurray, older brother of Frank Morton McMurry (*q.v.*), received his elementary, high school, and first professional education in the training school of the Illinois State Normal University (later,

Illinois State University). He attended the university and was graduated in 1876. He attended the University of Michigan from 1876 to 1880.

He taught in country schools in Illinois and Colorado and for one year was principal of a school in Denver, Colorado. He spent two years in graduate study at the University of Halle, Germany, and a year as principal of the high school at Pueblo, Colorado. He returned to Halle where he received the Ph.D. degree (1887). He went to Jena, Germany, for a year to study Herbartian pedagogy with Professor William Rein and became a Herbartian enthusiast.

Returning to the United States, he was principal of a grammar school at South Evanston, Illinois, and spent three years as head of the training school and teacher of education at Winona (Minnesota) Normal School (later, Winona State University). He joined the faculty of the Illinois State Normal School in 1900 and, when John Williston Cook *(q.v.)* left Illinois Normal to become president of the newly established Northern Illinois Normal School (later, Northern Illinois University) at De Kalb, in 1899, McMurry went with him as a faculty member. He remained at De Kalb until 1915, when he became professor of elementary education at George Peabody College for Teachers in Nashville, Tennessee. He served at Peabody until his death in 1929.

While at Illinois State Normal, McMurry was a founder of the American Herbartian movement. For eight years he was secretary of the National Herbart Society, which was organized in 1892. He was editor of its yearbooks and also editor of the first two yearbooks of the successor organization, the National Society for the Scientific Study of Education. McMurry was the author of numerous publications on teaching methods. He became known for his type studies in geography. Over a period of thirty-six years he lectured at teachers' institutes in more than forty states.

Among his books were *Special Method in Geography* (1894), *Special Method in Natural Science* (1896), *Method of the Recitation* (with Frank M. McMurry, 1898), *Special Method in Reading* (1898), *Special Method in Literature and History* (1898), *Special Method in Arithmetic* (1905), *Special Method in Language* (1905), *Conflicting Principles in Education* (1914), *Teaching by Projects* (1919), and *How to Organize the Curriculum* (1923). He edited *Type Studies in Geography and Practical Teaching* (three volumes, 1904).

REFERENCES: *TC; WWW* (I); Earl W. Hayter, *Education in Transition: The History of Northern Illinois University* (De Kalb: Northern Illinois University Press, 1974); Mary L. Seguel, *The Curriculum Field* (New York: Teachers College Press, 1966).   *Leo J. Alilunas*

McMURRY, Frank Morton. B. July 2, 1862, Crawfordsville, Indiana, to Franklin Morton and Charlotte (Underwood) McMurry. M. December 20,

1894, to Elizabeth Lindley. Ch. two. D. August 1, 1936, Quaker Hill, New York.

Frank M. McMurry was five years younger than his brother, Charles Alexander McMurry (*q.v.*), with whom he teamed up later as the McMurry brothers, introducing American educators to Johann Friedrich Herbart's educational programs. When their father died in 1866, their mother moved to Normal, Illinois, where she opened a boarding house for students at the Illinois State Normal School. McMurray taught in country schools in order to attend the University of Michigan (1881–82), and after a few more years of itinerant teaching, traveled to Germany and studied at the universities of Halle and Jena (1886–89). He received the Ph.D. degree (1889) from Jena.

McMurry returned to the United States and served as principal of a school in Chicago, where he was influenced by Francis W. Parker *(q.v.)*. He was professor of pedagogics at the State Normal School in Normal, Illinois (later, Illinois State University) in 1891.

After another year in Europe (1892–93), he joined the faculty at the University of Illinois (1893–94) and served as principal of the Franklin School in Buffalo, New York (1894–95). In 1895 he was appointed professor of pedagogics and dean of the teachers' college at the University of Buffalo (later State University of New York at Buffalo). He was professor of elementary education at Teachers College, Columbia University (1898–1926), where he stressed values and motives. He became more experimentalist and supported John Dewey *(q.v.)* on most of the educational issues of the day.

McMurry was the author of *Tarr and McMurry Common School Geographies* (with Ralph S. Tarr, 1900), *Method of the Recitation* (with Charles A. McMurry, 1903), *How to Study* (1909), *Teaching How to Study* (1909), *Elementary School Standards* (1914), *McMurry and Parkins Common School Geographies* (with A. E. Parkins, 1921), and *Living Geography* (with E. Huntington and C. B. Benson, 1932). He edited McMurry and Benson Social Arithmetics (1926) and was associate editor of *The Students Reference Work* (1909).

McMurry was a founder of the National Herbart Society for the Scientific Study of Education (later, National Society for the Study of Education) in 1895.

REFERENCES: *DAB* (supp. 2); *LE* (I); *NYT,* August 2, 1936, sec. II, p. 7; *WWW* (I); Mary L. Seguel, *The Curriculum Field* (New York: Teachers College Press, 1966). *Jack K. Campbell*

McMYNN, John Gibson. B. July 9, 1824, Palatine Ridge, New York to n.a. M. n.a. D. June 5, 1900, Madison, Wisconsin.

John Gibson McMynn was graduated from Williams College in Williamstown, Massachusetts, in 1848 and moved to Southport (later,

Kenosha), Wisconsin, where he was principal of the north ward school. He was instrumental in organizing the first public school system in Wisconsin in Southport. He lived in Racine, Wisconsin, where he helped organize the public school system and was superintendent of public instruction and principal of the high school (1853–57).

McMynn traveled and studied educational systems in Europe in 1858. He returned to Racine in 1859 and became the president of Minnesota's first normal school at Winona in 1861. He left at the outbreak of the Civil War and served as an officer with the Tenth Wisconsin Volunteer Infantry (1861–63). He resigned his commission in 1863 and returned to Wisconsin. In 1864 he was elected state superintendent of public instruction to replace Josiah L. Pickard *(q.v.)* and served to January 1868. He was employed by the J. I. Case Company from 1868 to 1875. He established the Racine Academy in 1875 and headed the institution until he retired in 1882.

McMynn was a regent of the University of Wisconsin in 1857 and served four terms (1857-63, 1864-68, 1868-70, and 1880-89) and was president (1865-66) and vice-president (1887-88) of the board of regents. He was an organizer of the Wisconsin State Teachers' Association and served as its president (1853). He was editor of the *Wisconsin Journal of Education* (1856-57).

REFERENCES: *Dictionary of Wisconsin Biography* (Madison: State Historical Society of Wisconsin, 1960), p. 249; *Milwaukee Journal,* June 5, 1900; *Racine Daily Journal,* November 28, 1891; William C. Whitford, *Historical Sketch of Education in Wisconsin* (Madison, Wisconsin, 1876).

Lawrence S. Master

McQUAID, Bernard John. B. December 15, 1823, New York, New York, to Bernard and Mary (Maguire) McQuaid. M. no. D. January 8, 1909, Rochester, New York.

Bernard John McQuaid, founder of Seton Hall University, was orphaned at the age of nine and raised in the St. Patrick's Orphan Home for Boys in New York City. He attended Chambly College near Montreal, Canada, and was graduated in 1843 from St. John's College (later, Fordham University) at Fordham, New York.

Ordained as a Catholic priest in 1848, McQuaid was pastor of St. Vincent's Church in Madison, New Jersey (1848–53), and built churches at Morristown and Springfield, New Jersey, and planned a third in Mendham, New Jersey. He started two parochial schools and taught for six months at St. Vincent's School in Madison, the first parochial school in New Jersey. He served in Newark, New Jersey, as rector and vicar-general of the diocese. He founded Seton Hall College and Seminary in Madison (later, South Orange), New Jersey, and served as president (1856–57) and was president and professor of rhetoric (1859–68).

In 1868, McQuaid was consecrated first bishop of the Rochester, New York, diocese. He established many schools and institutions and founded sixty-nine parishes. He was a major influence in Catholic education in the United States. He established the Sisters of St. Joseph in Rochester as a teaching order. He was instrumental in founding St. Andrews (1870) and St. Bernard's (1893) seminaries. He engaged in controversies with Bishop John Ireland *(q.v.)* over the relation of church schools to the state.

McQuaid was a participant in the Fourth Provincial Council of New York (1883), the Third Plenary Council of Baltimore (1884), and Vatican Council I (1869–70).

REFERENCES: *AC; DAB; NCAB* (12: 141); *NYT*, January 14, 1909, p. 7; *TC; WWW* (I); *New Catholic Encyclopedia* (New York: McGraw-Hill, 1967).   *John F. Ohles*

McVEY, Frank LeRond. B. November 10, 1869, Wilmington, Ohio, to Alfred Henry and Anna (Holmes) McVey. M. September 21, 1898, to Mabel Moore Sawyer. M. 1923 to Frances Jewell. Ch. three. D. January 4, 1953, Lexington, Kentucky.

Frank Le Rond McVey, president of the University of Kentucky, received his early education in the public elementary and high schools in Toledo, Ohio, and Des Moines, Iowa. He received the B.A. degree (1893) from Ohio Wesleyan University in Delaware, Ohio. He entered graduate school at Yale University, where he specialized in economics and received the Ph.D. degree in 1895.

McVey began his teaching career as an instructor in history at Teachers College, Columbia University (1895–96). While at Teachers College, McVey wrote editorials for the *New York Times*. He taught economics at the University of Minnesota (1896–1907) and took a leave from teaching in 1898 to study in England. He served as chairman of the Minnesota Tax Commission (1907–09). He was elected president of the University of North Dakota in 1909, a post that he held until 1917, when he became president of the University of Kentucky. McVey served the University of Kentucky as president until 1940 and was president emeritus until his death.

The University of Kentucky became a major university under McVey, with major growth in physical plant and scholastic standing. Twenty-two new buildings were added; the main campus and experiment-station farm were enlarged; and subexperiment stations were established at Quicksand and Princeton. All graduate work in state-maintained institutions of higher learning was centered at the University of Kentucky.

McVey was the author of *The Populist Movement* (1896), *History and Government of Minnesota* (1901), *Modern Industrialism* (1904), *Railroad Transportation* (1910), *The Making of a Town* (1913), *Applied Economics*

(1916), *Financial History of Great Britain, 1914–18* (1918), *A University is a Place—a Spirit* (1944), *History of Education in Kentucky* (1948), and *Gates Open Slowly* (1949). He wrote many reports and articles and served as editor for the papers of the Minnesota Academy of Social Sciences (1908–09) and Social Science Series (twenty-five volumes, 1914–23).

McVey was a member of a number of professional associations. He was president of the Minneapolis Associated Charities (1898–1907), secretary of the Minnesota Academy of Social Sciences (1898–1907), vice-president of the American Economic Association (1910, 1928), and secretary (1916–22) and president (1923) of the National Association of State Universities. He was president of the Southeast Conference (1933), the Southern Association of Schools and Colleges (1934), the Association of Land Grant Colleges (1935), and the Kentucky Education Association (1937). He was a member of educational surveys of many states and was an adviser to Venezuela (1943). He was a chairman of national conferences on marketing and farm credits in 1914, 1915, and 1916.

McVey was the recipient of many awards and honors and honorary degrees from seven colleges and universities.

REFERENCES: *LE* (III); *NCAB* (13:316); *NYT,* January 6, 1953, p. 29; *WWAE* (VIII); *WWW* (III); *Louisville* (Kentucky) *Courier-Journal,* January 5, 1953.   *Roger H. Jones*

MacVICAR, Malcolm. B. September 30, 1829, Dunglass, Argyleshire, Scotland, to John and Janet (MacTavish) MacVicar. M. January 1, 1865, to Isabella McKay. Ch. four. D. May 18, 1904, Cato, New York.

Malcolm MacVicar left Scotland with his parents for Canada at the age of six. His early education by a local Presbyterian pastor was directed toward preparation for the ministry. In 1850 he entered Knox College, Ontario, Canada, but left after two years. He joined the Baptist church and was ordained in 1856, but he never held a pastorate. He went to the United States and entered the University of Rochester, New York, graduating in 1859.

He became a teacher and later principal of the Brockport (New York) Collegiate Institute, remaining there until 1868 except for a year at Buffalo (New York) Central High School. He was appointed chairman of a committee to report on the recently instituted regents' programs. MacVicar believed classroom instruction neeeded to be improved through teacher training. He was instrumental in securing legislation in 1866 for four new normal schools and was appointed principal of the first normal school established at Brockport (later, State University of New York College at Brockport).

In 1868 MacVicar took a year's leave because of failing health. Upon his return, he was assigned to organize and administer the Potsdam Normal

School (later, State University of New York College at Potsdam), where he remained for the next twelve years. In 1880 MacVicar taught at the Michigan State Normal School (later, Eastern Michigan University) at Ypsilanti. In 1881 he was appointed to the faculty of the Toronto (Ontario, Canada) Baptist College; the college became the theology department of McMaster University, with MacVicar as its first chancellor (1887–90). He resigned to superintend the educational work of the American Baptist Home Mission Society (1890–1900). He served as president of Virginia Union University in Richmond from 1900 to his death in 1904.

MacVicar wrote *A Complete Arithmetic* (1876), *A Primary Arithmetic* (1877), *Hand-book of Drill Exercises in Arithmetic* (1878), *Teacher's Manual of Elementary Arithmetic* (1880), and *Principles of Education* (1892). He developed aids for classroom instruction, including the tellurian globe.

REFERENCES:*AC; DAB; NCAB* (4:57); *NYT,* May 19, 1904, p. 9; *TC.*

Marilyn Meiss

McVICAR, Peter. B. June 15, 1829, St. George, New Brunswick, Canada, to George and Christina McVicar. M. September 10, 1863, to Martha Porter Dana. Ch. two. D. June 5, 1903, Topeka, Kansas.

At the age of fourteen, Peter McVicar moved with his family to a homestead near Waukesha, Wisconsin. He was graduated from Beloit (Wisconsin) College with the A.B. (1856) and A.M.(1859) degrees. He studied at the Union Theological Seminary in New York City in 1857. He received a doctorate from Andover (Massachusetts) Theological Seminary in 1860.

McVicar was an instructor of mathematics at Beloit College (1856–57). He was sent to Topeka, Kansas, in 1860 as a missionary for the American Home Missionary Society. He organized the First Congregational Church in Topeka and served as pastor (1861–67). He was also superintendent of the Shawnee County schools (1861–65). From 1867 to 1871 he served as Kansas state superintendent of public instruction. McVicar fought to preserve the use of public lands for schools against railroads' claims and state and federal legislation that would have diverted lands to various noneducational purposes.

He was a founder and president of Washburn College in Topeka (1871–96). Under McVicar a new college site was obtained, instructional program organized, and buildings erected. He was active in professional organizations, serving as president of the Kansas State Teachers' Association (1867) and was an editor of the *Kansas Educational Journal.* He was on the first board of trustees of Lincoln College (1865–66). He received an honorary degree from Beloit College (1871).

REFERENCES: *TC;* D. L. McEachron, "Peter McVicar, The 'Grand Old

Man' of Washburn College," *Washburn College Bulletin* 18 (October 1933); C. O. Wright, *100 Years in Kansas Education* (Topeka: Kansas State Teachers Association, 1963).   *John F. Ohles*

MADDY, Joseph Edgar. B. October 14, 1891, near Wellington, Kansas, to William Henry and Mary Elizabeth (Harrington) Maddy. M. April 25, 1938, to Fay Pettit. Ch. three. D. April 18, 1966, Traverse City, Michigan.

Joseph Edgar Maddy was a student at Bethany College in Lindsborg, Kansas (1906–07), and the Wichita (Kansas) College of Music (1907–08).

Maddy joined the Minneapolis (Minnesota) Symphony Orchestra in 1909 as the youngest member at the age of eighteen and continued there to 1914. He met Thaddeus P. Giddings, music supervisor of the Minneapolis public schools, who persuaded Maddy to become a music teacher. He was director of the Wichita Falls (Texas) College of Music (1915–17) and teacher of wind instruments at the Metropolitan School of Music in Chicago, Illinois (1917–18). He was supervisor of instrumental music for the Rochester (New York) public schools (1918–20), supervisor of music and director of civic music in Richmond, Indiana (1920–24), and supervisor of the Ann Arbor (Michigan) public schools (1924–27).

Maddy joined the University of Michigan as professor of music (1924–66). In 1928 he and Thaddeus Giddings founded the famous National Music Camp at Interlochen, Michigan. Maddy served as president of the camp and was cofounder of the National Arts Academy at Interlochen (1962) and founder and president of the Interlochen Press in 1957. In 1931 he instituted educational radio instruction from the University of Michigan, teaching instrumental and vocal music, and conducted music lessons over the National Broadcasting System (1935–39). Maddy was the organizer and conductor of the first national high school orchestra in Detroit, Michigan, in 1926 and the second national orchestra that performed for a convention of school superintendents in Dallas, Texas (1927); he continued to organize similar groups. He invented the aluminum violin and string bass. He took part in a struggle with a union over the control of educational broadcasting.

Maddy was the coauthor of music books, including *All-American Song Book* (with W. O. Miessner, 1942), and he wrote with T. P. Giddings programs for the instruction of school bands and orchestras, including *The Universal Teacher for Orchestra and Band Instruments* (1923), *Instrumental Technique for Orchestra and Band* (1926), *Instrumental Class Teaching* (1928), and *Fun in Music* (1937).

Maddy was active in professional organizations as a life member of the Music Educators National Conference (president, 1936–38), charter member of the Association for Education by Radio, chairman of the Michigan Cultural Commission, and a member of the Michigan Arts Council (1963–66) and many other groups. He received honorary degrees from seven American colleges and universities.

REFERENCES: *CB* (April 1946); *LE* (III); *WWW* (IV); *NYT,* April 19, 1966, p. 41; "Dr. Joseph E. Maddy Receives Medal of Honor for 1965 at Mid-West Clinic," *School Musician* 37 (January 1966): 70-71, and 37 (June 1966): 3.   *John F. Ohles*

MADELEVA, Sister Mary (Mary Evaline Wolff). B. May 24, 1887, Cumberland, Wisconsin, to August and Lucy (Arntz) Wolff. M. no. D. July 25, 1964, Boston, Massachusetts.

Sister Madeleva, born Mary Evaline Wolff, received her early schooling in Wisconsin public schools. She enrolled in St. Mary's College in Notre Dame, Indiana, and, while still a student, joined the Congregation of the Holy Cross in 1908. She was graduated with A.B. degree (1909) and received the A.M. degree (1918) from the University of Notre Dame, Indiana, and the Ph.D. degree (1925) from the University of California. She was the first woman religious to receive a doctorate from the University of California. She was a student at Oxford (England) University (1933–34).

Sister Madeleva began teaching in the St. Mary's College English department in 1910. She became principal of Sacred Heart Academy in Ogden, Utah (1919–22), and at Holy Rosary Academy in Woodland, California (1922–24), while she studied at the University of California.

Sister Madeleva went to the newly founded College of St. Mary-of-the-Wasatch in Salt Lake City, Utah, as its first dean and president in 1925; she remained there until 1933. In 1934 she returned to St. Mary's College, Notre Dame, as president and served until her retirement in 1961. During her presidency, student enrollment and the faculty tripled in size, and the campus was greatly enlarged. In 1944, the graduate school of sacred theology was established, the first school of its kind for women.

Sister Madeleva contributed many articles and poems to secular and Catholic journals and published books of verse and essays, particularly on medieval subjects. She was the author of many books, including *Knights Errant and Other Poems* (1923), *Chaucer's Nuns and Other Essays* (1925), *Pearl—A Study in Spiritual Dryness* (1925), *Penelope and Other Poems* (1927), *A Question of Lovers and Other Poems* (1935), *The Happy Christmas Wind* (1936), *Gates and Other Poems* (1938), *Selected Poems* (1939), *Four Girls* (1941), *Lost Language and Other Essays* (1951), *American Twelfth Night* (1955), *My First Seventy Years* (1959), *The Four Last Things* (1959), and *Conversations with Cassandra* (1961).

She was vice-president of the Indiana Conference on Higher Education, Indiana director of the National Conference of Christians and Jews, and a member of the Catholic Commission on Intellectual and Cultural Affairs, the Catholic Poetry Society of America (president), and many other associations. She received several awards—including the Siena Medal, the

Cum Laude Poets' Corner Medal, and the Campion Award of the Catholic Book Club (1959)—and seven honorary degrees.

REFERENCES: *CB* (February 1942); *NCAB* (51:202); *WWAE* (XVI); *WWW* (IV); Matthew Hoehn, *Catholic Authors: Contemporary Biographical Sketches, 1930–1942* (Newark: St. Mary's Abby, 1948); *South Bend* (Indiana) *Tribune,* July 25, 1964, p. 1; *NYT,* July 26, 1964, p. 57; *New Catholic Encyclopedia* (New York: McGraw-Hill, 1967); Sister M. Madeleva, *My First Seventy Years* (New York: Macmillan, 1959).

Anne E. Scheerer

MAGILL, Edward Hicks. B. September 24, 1825, Bucks County, Pennsylvania, to Jonathan Paxson and Mary (Watson) Magill. M. 1852 to Sarah Warner Beans. M. April 24, 1902, to Sarah Elizabeth (Sutton) Gardner. Ch. five. D. December 10, 1907, New York, New York.

Edward Hicks Magill attended local Friends' schools. He taught school (1841–48) and was an assistant to Benjamin Hallowell at Hallowell's school in Alexandria, Virginia (1848–49). He attended Williston Seminary in Easthampton, Massachusetts (1849–50), Yale College (1850–51), and Brown University in Providence, Rhode Island, from which he received the A.B. (1852) and A.M. (1855) degrees.

Magill was principal of the classical department of the Providence High School (1852–59) and submaster of the Boston (Massachusetts) Latin School (1859–67). He traveled in Europe (1867–68). He helped found Swarthmore (Pennsylvania) College and served at its opening in 1869 as principal of the preparatory department. He served as president of Swarthmore (1871–89) and continued as professor of French language and literature from 1889 to his retirement in 1900.

Swarthmore was the first coeducational college in the eastern states. Magill initiated a letter exchange between French and American students to assist in their learning each other's languages. He was the author of *French Grammer* (1865), *Coeducation of the Sexes* (1867), *Introductory French Reader* (1867), *Methods of Teaching Modern Language* (1871), *History of Education in the Religious Society of Friends* (1884), *Short Method of Learning to Read French* (1892), and the autobiographical *Sixty-five Years in the Life of a Teacher* (1907). He also edited *French Prose and Poetry* (1867) and the Modern French Series (1879).

Magill was a founder of the Association of Pennsylvania Colleges (later, Middle States Association of Colleges and Secondary Schools) in 1887. He received an honorary degree from Haverford College (1886).

REFERENCES: *AC; DAB; NCAB* (6:354); *TC; WWW* (I); Edward H. Magill, *Sixty-five Years in the Life of a Teacher* (Boston: Houghton Mifflin, 1907). *John F. Ohles*

MAGRUDER, Frank Abbott. B. May 6, 1882, Woodstock, Virginia, to John Williams and Lucretia (Donaldson) Magruder. M. September 1, 1915, to Louise Southgate Taylor. M. 1930 to Clara Taylor Gainor. Ch. two. D. December 2, 1949, Corvallis, Oregon.

Known principally as an author of political science textbooks, Frank Abbot Magruder received the bachelor's degree from Washington and Lee College in Lexington, Virginia (1905). He attended Johns Hopkins University in Baltimore, Maryland, where he earned the Ph.D. degree (1911).

Magruder was the principal of the Rockton (South Carolina) high school (1905–06) and a teacher of English and civics at Millersburg (Kentucky) Military Academy (1906–08). He was an instructor of political science at Princeton University (1911–17). In 1917 he went to the Pacific Coast and began more than three decades of teaching political science at Oregon State College (later, University) at Corvallis, Oregon. He served as temporary head of the department of political science at the University of Maryland (1935–36).

Magruder's published works include *Recent Administration in Virginia* (1911), *The American Government* (1917), *Moral Teachings of the Bible* (1925), *Our Nation's Government* (1929), *National Government and International Relations* (1929), *The Constitution* (1933), *The American Government Today* (1936), and *Our Government at Work* (1940).

REFERENCES: *LE* (III); *WWAE* (XI); *WWW* (III).   *James M. Vosper*

MAHAN, Asa. B. November 9, 1799, Vernon, New York, to Samuel and Anna (Dana) Mahan. M. May 9, 1828, to Mary H. Dix. M. 1866 to Mary E. Chase. Ch. none. D. April 4, 1889, Eastbourne, England.

Asa Mahan was graduated from Hamilton College in Clinton, New York, in 1824 and Andover (Massachusetts) Theological Seminary in 1827. He was ordained a Congregational minister in 1829.

Mahan taught in a local district school at the age of seventeen and continued to teach during the winter months to finance his college education. He served churches in Pittsford, New York (1829–31), and Cincinnati, Ohio (1831–33). He was a trustee of Lane Theological Seminary in Cincinnati and became embroiled in the controversy over slavery that split the seminary. In 1835 Mahan became the first president of Oberlin (Ohio) College, bringing with him eighty Lane students, who formed the basis for the establishment of a department of theology at Oberlin. Under his leadership, Oberlin admitted students without regard to color or sex; Mahan was the first college president to award degrees to women on the same conditions as men.

President and professor of theology of the short-lived Cleveland (Ohio) University (1850–54), Mahan was pastor of Michigan Congregational churches at Jackson (1855–57) and Adrian (1857–60). He served Adrian (Michigan) College as a professor and was president from 1860 to 1871. He retired to England in 1871 where he completed his chief work, *A Critical History of Philosophy* (1883), and engaged in preaching and editing *The Divine Life,* a monthly periodical.

Mahan wrote many books, including *Scripture Doctrine of Christian Perfection* (1839), *System of Intellectual Philosophy* (1845), *The Doctrine of the Will* (1846), *The True Believer* (1847), *The Science of Moral Philosophy* (1848), *Election and the Influence of the Holy Spirit* (1851), *Modern Mysteries Explained and Exposed* (1855), *The Science of Logic* (1857), *Science of Natural Theology* (1867), *Theism and Anti-Theism in Their Relations to Science* (1872), *The Phenomena of Spiritualism Scientifically Explained and Exposed* (1876), *Critical History of the Late American War* (1877), and *A System of Mental Philosophy* (1882). He received honorary degrees from Hillsdale and Adrian colleges.

REFERENCES:*AC; DAB; NCAB* (2:461); *TC; WWW* (H).

Abdul A. Al-Rubaiy

MAHAN, Dennis Hart. B. April 2, 1802, New York New York, to John and Mary (Cleary) Mahan. M. June 25, 1839, to Mary Helena Okill. Ch. five, including Alfred Thayer Mahan, naval historian. D. September 16, 1871, New York, New York.

Dennis Hart Mahan entered West Point at the age of eighteen and devoted the rest of his life to the United States Military Academy there, committing suicide at the age of sixty-nine rather than face retirement.

Singled out almost at once by Superintendent Sylvanus Thayer *(q.v.),* Mahan was groomed for his career by two years of travel and study, bringing back the best science and military arts of Europe to West Point. During his almost fifty years there as teacher, writer, dean of faculty, and defender of the academy, he not only helped to build the academy into a pioneer institution of scientific education but also contributed to the change and reform of higher education in the United States.

As a teacher of both engineering and military tactics and strategy, he insisted on adding "and the art of war" to his title "professor of civil and military engineering." Mahan's students became engineers, and many became the teachers of other engineers.

His textbook, *Advanced Guard, Outpost and Detachment Service of Troops with the Essential Principles of Strategy* (1863), was used by both North and South during the Civil War. The most famous of his other books was *An Elementary Course of Civil Engineering* (1837), a leading textbook in the United States for several decades. He also wrote *A Complete Treatise on Field Fortification* (1836), *Summary of the Course of Permanent Fortification* (1850), *Industrial Drawing* (1852), *Descriptive Geography* (1864), and *An Elementary Course of Military Engineering* (two volumes, 1866–67).

As dean of the academic board, Mahan had a principal role in ensuring the intellectual vigor of West Point by choosing and retaining well-qualified faculty members. As a vigorous spokesman against congressional and other critics, he helped ensure survival of the academy. His defense of West Point helped to secure the continuation of the systematic study of science and engineering in American higher education that he had pioneered.

REFERENCES: *AC; DAB; NCAB* (10:440); *NYT* September 17, 1871, p. 5; *TC; WWW* (H); Thomas J. Fleming, *West Point: The Men and Times of the U.S.M.A.* (New York: Morrow, 1969); K. Bruce Galloway and Robert Bowie Johnson, Jr., *West Point: America's Power Fraternity* (New York: Simon & Schuster, 1973); John W. Masland and Laurence I. Radway, *Soldiers and Scholars: Military Education and National Policy* (Princeton, N.J.: Princeton University Press, 1975).   *Joseph C. Bronars, Jr.*

MAHONEY, John Joseph. B. December 2, 1880, Lawrence, Massachusetts, to John D. and Ellen E. (Regan) Mahoney. M. June 27, 1923, to Mildred Hodgman. Ch. none. D. August 26, 1964, Winchester, Massachusetts.

John J. Mahoney was graduated from Phillips Academy in Andover, Massachusetts, in 1899 and received the A.B. (1903), Ed.M. (1922), and Ed.D (1944) degrees from Harvard University. He supported himself in college by tutoring students.

Mahoney was a high school English instructor (1903–04), master of the elementary school (1904–12), and director of evening schools (1907–12) at Lawrence, Massachusetts. He was assistant superintendent of schools in Cambridge, Massachusetts (1912–15), and principal of the State Normal School (later, Lowell University) from 1915 to 1922. In 1922 he was appointed professor of education at Boston University, where he headed the Harvard-Boston University extension program for teachers for twenty-five years.

His early work in extension and evening courses for immigrants led to an interest in education for citizenship. He developed the Lawrence Plan for education in citizenship and was appointed supervisor for Americanization Studies in Massachusetts. With Henry W. Holmes, he established the Lincoln Filene Center for Citizenship and Public Affairs at Tufts University in Medford, Massachusetts (1954–57), and was the first Lincoln Filene Professor of Civic Education (1955–57).

Mahoney wrote *Standards in English* (1917), *First Steps in Americanization* (1919), *Self-Help English Series* (1921), and *For Us the Living* (1945).

He was a member of many professional organizations and received numerous awards including the Lt. Hirxhel L. Guteman Foundation Award from Temple Israel Brotherhood (Boston), B'nai B'rith awards, and an honorary degree from Tufts University.

REFERENCES: *LE* (III); *NCAB* (52:488); *WWW* (IV).   *John Mahoney*

MANLY, John Matthews. B. September 2, 1865, Sumter County, Alabama, to Charles and Mary (Matthews) Manly. M. no. D. April 2, 1940, Tucson, Arizona.

John Matthews Manly was the son of a president of Furman University in Greenville, South Carolina, and grandson of a president of the University of Alabama. He attended the Staunton (Virginia) Military Academy and Greenville (South Carolina) Military Institute before going to Furman, where he earned the M.A. degree (1883). He attended Harvard University, where he received the A.M. (1889) and Ph.D. (1890) degrees in philology.

Manly was acting principal of the high school at Greer, South Carolina, and teacher of mathematics and an assistant in the preparatory department of William Jewell College in Liberty, Missouri (1884–91). He joined the English department at Brown University in Providence, Rhode Island, in 1891 and became a professor within the year. He became the first head of the English department at the University of Chicago and held that position from 1898 to 1933. He was granted a leave of absence to serve in the United States Army during World War I.

Manly's greatest literary research work was on *Piers Plowman* and the works of Chaucer. *The Text of the Canterbury Tales,* which was fourteen years in the preparation and eight volumes in length, represented the greatest breakthrough in research on Chaucer and was published in 1940, a few months before Manly died. His other writings include *Lessons in English* (with E. R. Bailey, 1912), *A Manual for Writers* (with J. A. Powell, 1914), *The Writing of English* (with Edith Rickert, 1919), *Contemporary American Literature* (with Edith Rickert, 1922), *Some New Lights on Chaucer* (1926), *Chaucer and the Rhetoricians* (1926), and *Better Business Letters* (1926). He edited *Macbeth* (1896), *Specimens of the Pre-Shakespearean Drama* (1897), *English Poetry* (1907), *English Prose* (1909), and *English Prose and Poetry* (1916). He was the general editor of *Modern Philology.*

Manly was a fellow of the Royal Society of Literature (British) and the Medieval Academy of America (president, 1929–30) and a member of the Modern Language Association of America (president 1920–21), the Modern Humanities Research Association (president, 1922–23), and other scholarly and professional groups in the United States and England. He received several honorary degrees.

REFERENCES: *DAB* (supp. 2); *LE* (I); *NCAB* (48:196); *TC; WWW* (I); *NYT,* April 3, 1940, p. 23.   *Thomas Meighan*

MANN, Horace. B. May 4, 1796, Franklin, Massachusetts, to Thomas and Rebecca (Stanley) Mann. M. September 12, 1830, to Charlotte Messer. M. May 1, 1843, to Mary Peabody. Ch. three. D. August 2, 1859, Yellow Springs, Ohio.

Horace Mann, father of American Public Education, entered Brown University in Providence, Rhode Island, in 1816 and was graduated in 1819. He served as a tutor at Brown (1819–21), began the study of law at Litchfield, Connecticut, and was admitted to the bar of Norfolk County, Massachusetts, in 1823.

Mann practiced law in Massachusetts at Dedham (1823–33) and Boston (1833–37) and served in the Massachusetts House of Representatives (1827–33) and Senate (1833–37). As a legislator, he was instrumental in the creation of the state board of education; he became its secretary (chief executive officer) and served from 1837 to 1848.

In 1848 Mann succeeded John Quincy Adams in the United States House of Representatives where he served for five eventful years. He was appointed the first president of Antioch College at Yellow Springs, Ohio, in 1853, a position he held until his death in 1859.

Mann utilized the popular lyceum movement to mobilize general sentiment for public education. He was assisted by many public figures of the day who joined in the crusade. The result was a series of landmark legislative acts in Massachusetts that set the pace for public education across the nation. With the advent of the common schools came the need for trained teachers. Mann and his supporters pioneered in the organization of teachers' institutes and the establishment of state-supported normal schools.

Mann collected and published information concerning public education's history, conditions, and prospects. His most significant writings are the twelve annual reports that were issued during his tenure as secretary of the Massachusetts state board. Mann also wrote numerous articles published in the *Common School Journal,* which he established in 1838 and edited to 1848. He also wrote many articles for the *American Journal of Education* and the *Proceedings* of the American Institute of Instruction, and he was the author of *Lectures on Education* (1845), *A Few Thoughts for a Young Man* (1850), and *Powers and Duties of Woman* (1853).

Mann was a fellow of the American Academy of Arts and Sciences and received an honorary degree from Harvard University (1869). He was the first educator elected to the New York University Hall of Fame for Great Americans in 1900.

REFERENCES: *AC; DAB; EB; NCAB* (3:78); *NYT,* August 3, 1859, p. 8; *TC; WWW* (H); Lawrence A. Cremin, ed. *The Republic and the School: Horace Mann on the Education of Free Men* (New York: Teachers College Press, 1957); Robert E. Downs, *Horace Mann: Champion of Public Schools* (New York: Twayne Publishers, 1974); Mary Peabody Mann, *Life of Horace Mann* (Washington D.C.: National Education Association, 1937); Jonathan Messerli, *Horace Mann: A Biography* (New York: Alfred A. Knopf, 1972); E. I. E. Williams, *Horace Mann: Educational Statesman* (New York: The Macmillan Co., 1937).   *Joe L. Green*

MANNES, Clara Damrosch. B. December 12, 1869, Breslau, Silesia, Germany, to Leopold and Helene (von Heimburg) Damrosch. M. June 4, 1898, to David Mannes *(q.v.)*. Ch. two: Leopold Damrosch Mannes, pianist and inventor, and Marya Mannes, author and critic. D. March 16, 1948, New York, New York.

Clara Damrosch Mannes was born into a musical dynasty headed by her father Leopold, a pianist and conductor. Her brother Walter Damrosch became a conductor of the New York Symphony Orchestra; another brother, Frank Heino Damrosch *(q.v.)*, was an organist, musician, and music educator.

The Damrosch family moved to the United States in 1871. At the age of six, Clara Damrosch began to study piano. During the next twelve years, she studied with Clara Gross, Jessie Pinney, and Clara Schumann. She made her debut as a chamber music performer at the age of eighteen. Following a year of musical and artistic studies in Germany, she returned to New York in 1889 to pursue a career as a piano teacher, both privately and in settlement houses.

In 1897 Damrosch returned to Europe to study with Ferruccio Busoni in Berlin. Her marriage in 1898 to David Mannes *(q.v.)*, first violinist and later concertmaster of the New York Symphony Orchestra, began a new phase of her music career. From 1901 to 1913, Clara and David Mannes made concert tours throughout the United States and in London, England. After they founded the Mannes School of Music in New York in 1916, Clara Mannes ended her performing career to devote full time to administration and teaching in the school.

The Mannes School of Music was open to all ages. Not limited to the highly talented elite, instruction was provided to all who were interested in acquiring a musical education. This approach was primarily based on David Mannes's experiences at the Music School Settlement (founded in New York City in 1894 by Emilie Wagner); Clara Mannes had served on the settlement board.

In 1926 Clara Damrosch Mannes received from the French government the title of officier de l'instruction publique in recognition of her music teaching. In 1928 she and David Mannes published, with Louis Untermeyer, a collection of children's songs, *New Songs for New Voices*. The Mannes School was incorporated in 1934 and in 1953 became the Mannes College of Music, offering a five-year course leading to the B.S. degree in music.

Clara Damrosch Mannes was important as a performer and a music educator. She was particularly interested in and adept at music education for children and believed that music should be a part of the total environment in the home as well as school. Her unfinished autobiography is located in the music division of the Library of Congress.

REFERENCES: *DAB* (supp. 4); *NAW;* Rose Heylbut, "Building Musicianship," *The Etude Music Magazine* 62 (April 1944): 201; *NYT,* March 18, 1948, p. 27.   *Lorraine M. Zinn*

MANNES, David. B. February 16, 1866, New York, New York, to Henry and Nathalia (Wittkowsky) Mannes. M. June 4, 1898, to Clara Damrosch *(q.v.).* Ch. two: Leopold Damrosch Mannes, pianist and inventor, and Marya Mannes, author and critic. D. April 24, 1959, New York, New York.

Health problems limited David Mannes's formal education, but his parents encouraged him in his study of the violin at an early age. Limited family resources resulted in interruptions in his studies, but he was determined to play the violin professionally. He managed to study with a number of competent New York teachers and to enter the New York College of Music for a term. In 1897 he studied with noted European musicians in Berlin, Germany, and in 1903 in Brussels, Belgium.

In 1881, at the age of fifteen, he began his professional career as an apprentice violinist at the Union Square Theatre in New York City, and for the next few years he played at theaters and clubs with several bands, orchestras, and quartets, gaining recognition as a competent first violinist and concertmaster. By 1891 he had played two concerts with the New York Philharmonic Orchestra and had acquired several private pupils. Walter Damrosch invited him to play with the New York Symphony Orchestra in 1891. He was concertmaster in 1899 and assistant conductor; he resigned from the orchestra in 1912.

About 1896, Mannes and his wife, the former Clara Damrosch, began to give concert recitals in New York City and toured the United States and abroad. Mannes organized a string quartet that performed at private subscription concerts (1900–04). He established a children's orchestra in 1898 and directed it in private concerts. He worked with the group, gave private lessons to the children, and it became known as the Symphony Club. The club gave concerts for charitable purposes from 1904 to 1917.

Mannes became a music educator in the 1890s when he organized a violin class at the Music School Settlement on New York's Lower East Side. He obtained outside support to purchase instruments, established scholarships, and remodeled the settlement buildings. He was head of the string department until 1901, when he became director of the school, a position he held until 1916. He founded the Music Settlement for Colored People in Harlem (1910) and was a cofounder of the National Federation of Music School Settlements.

In 1916 he and his wife became codirectors of the David Mannes School of Music in New York City. They sought to establish a music school to prepare potential professional musicians, and also to provide an education for those who wished to receive a general music education. They raised capital and attracted distinguished teachers; the school grew from modest beginnings to an enrollment of over six hundred students. Mannes continued as codirector of the college until his retirement in 1947. In 1953 the school was authorized by the regents of the University of the State of New York to give courses leading to an academic degree and was renamed the Mannes College of Music.

Mannes conducted a series of free orchestral concerts at the Metropolitan Museum of Art in 1917, a series underwritten by John D. Rockefeller, Jr., which proved so popular that it continued for thirty years. He was the author of *Music Is My Faith* (1938), an autobiography, and coeditor with his wife and Louis Untermeyer of *New Songs for New Voices* (1928).

He was an adviser to the music department and a trustee of Fisk University in Nashville, Tennessee, and a consultant to the music department of the Laurel School in Cleveland, Ohio. He received an honorary degree from Oberlin College in 1942, was decorated Knight of the Crown of Italy, and was named officier de l'instruction publique de France.

REFERENCES: *NCAB* (47:14); *WWAE* (VIII); *WWW* (III); David Mannes, *Music Is My Faith* (New York: W. W. Norton and Co., 1938); *NYT*, April 25, 1959, p. 21.   *J. Franklin Hunt*

MANNING, James. B. October 22, 1738, Piscataway, New Jersey, to James and Grace (Fitz-Randolph) Manning. M. March 29, 1763, to Margaret Stites. Ch. none. D. July 29, 1791, Providence, Rhode Island.

James Manning attended the Baptist Latin School at Hopewell, New Jersey, before entering the College of New Jersey (later, Princeton University) in 1758. He was graduated second in his class of twenty-one with the A.B. degree (1762) and received the A.M. degree in 1765.

Manning was ordained a Baptist minister in 1763, and the following year he founded a church and a Latin school at Warren, Rhode Island. He was elected first president of Rhode Island College (later, Brown University), the first Baptist college in America (1765). He served as pastor, teacher, and president until the college was moved to Providence, Rhode Island, in 1770.

Manning continued to serve as president of the college and professor of languages, and he also was pastor of the first Baptist church in Providence. His Latin school became the University Grammar School. He was an able administrator, and, although the college was temporarily closed during the Revolutionary War, it was fairly well established by his death in 1791.

Manning was deeply interested in education and served as chairman of the Providence School Committee. In 1791 he authored *A Report in Favor of the Establishment of Free Schools in the Town of Providence*, which formed the basis of the school system.

In 1767 he organized the Warren Association, the first Baptist association in New England. He was also active politically and during 1785–86 was a delegate to the Continental Congress. Largely through his efforts Rhode Island accepted the Constitution. He received an honorary degree from the University of Pennsylvania (1785).

REFERENCES: *AC; DAB; EB; NCAB* (8:20); *TC; WWW* (H).

Robert H. Truman

MARBLE, Albert Prescott. B. May 21, 1836, Vassalboro, Maine, to John and Emeline (Prescott) Marble. M. 1861 to Louise Wells Marston. Ch. one. D. March 25, 1906, New York, New York.

Albert Prescott Marble worked on the family farm earning money to attend Yarmouth (Maine) Academy and Waterville (Maine) Academy, and he matriculated at Waterville (later, Colby) College when he was twenty-one. He was graduated in 1861. During his undergraduate studies, he taught in elementary and secondary schools and served as principal of an Eastport (Maine) public school and a Stockbridge (Massachusetts) private school.

On graduation, Marble taught briefly in Maine. Moving to Beaverton, Wisconsin, in 1862, he was professor of mathematics in Wayland University, where he served as recruiting officer for the northern army during the Civil War. He returned to Maine, and then he became principal of Worcester (Massachusetts) Academy, which in two years he led from a rundown institution to an outstandingly successful one (1866–68). His success led to his appointment as superintendent of the Worcester schools in 1868. The Worcester schools gained a national reputation under Marble. He served as superintendent of Omaha (Nebraska) schools (1894–96) and then became an assistant superintendent in New York City in charge of the system's first three high schools. Marble continued in the position through changing administrations, until failing health forced his resignation shortly before his death in 1906.

Marble was a fine speaker and effective writer. The United States Bureau of Education published his *Sanitary Conditions for School Houses* (1891). He was a member of the board of visitors at Wellesley College, served three terms as president of the Massachusetts State Teachers Association, and was secretary and president (1889) of the National Educational Association.

REFERENCES: *DAB; NCAB* (13:581); *NYT,* March 26, 1906, p. 11.

M. Jane Dowd

MARCH, Francis Andrew. B. October 25, 1825, Sutton (later Millbury), Massachusetts, to Andrew Patch and Nancy (Parker) March. M. August 12, 1860, to Margaret Mildred Stone Conway. Ch. nine, including Francis Andrew March, lexicographer, and Peyton Conway March, United States Army officer and chief of staff. D. September 9, 1911, Easton, Pennsylvania.

Francis Andrew March attended the public schools of Worcester, Massachusetts. He was graduated from Amherst (Massachusetts) College with the A.B. (1845) and A.M. (1848) degrees.

March taught in academies at Swanzy, New Hampshire, and Leicester, Massachusetts (1845–47), and was a tutor at Amherst (1847–49). He went to New York to study law (1849–50) and was admitted to the bar in 1850. Following two years of law practice he traveled south for health reasons and taught in a private school at Fredericksburg, Virginia (1852–55).

From 1857 March taught at Lafayette College in Easton, Pennsylvania, and was professor of the English language and comparative philology, the first position of its kind in America or Europe. He held this position until he retired in 1906. He taught classes in French, German, Latin, Greek, philosophy, political economy, law, and botany, but he was best known for raising the study of English to an intellectual discipline. He was first to apply exegesis to the classroom study of the English language; his exegetical method spread through American universities and was studied by scholars in Europe.

March spent ten years on research that was published as *Comparative Grammar of the Anglo-Saxon Language* (1870), an exhaustive analysis of the relationship between English and the other Indo-European languages. He also wrote *Method of Philological Study of the English Language* (1865), *A Parser and Analyser for Beginners* (1869), and *Introduction to Anglo-Saxon: An Anglo-Saxon Reader* (1870) and he directed American workers for *The Oxford English Dictionary*. He helped prepare *The Standard Dictionary* (two volumes, 1893–95), wrote *The Spelling Reform* (1881), and edited four volumes of Latin and Greek Christian classics (*Latin Hymns, Euselius, The Select Work of Tertullian,* and *Athengorecs*). He wrote *Thesaurus Dictionary of the English Language* (with F. A. March, Jr., 1903).

March was president of the American Philological Association (1873–74 and 1895–96), the Spelling Reform Association (1876–1905), and the Modern Language Association of America (1891–93), vice-president of the New Shakespeare Study of London, England, and a member of other American and foreign associations.

REFERENCES: *AC; DAB; EB; NCAB* (11:244); *TC; WWW* (I); *NYT,* September 10, 1911, sec. 2, p. 13.   *John E. Phillips*

MARKHAM, Walter Tipton. B. October 22, 1885, Ewing, Virginia, to George Washington and Amanda Morrison (Robinson) Markham. M. August 16, 1910, to Daisy Ella Murphy. Ch. two. D. January 18, 1946, Dodge City, Kansas.

W. T. Markham was a student at Marionville (Missouri) College (1905–11) and received the A.B. degree (1914) from Campbell College in Holton,

Kansas. He studied at Harvard University (1923) and was awarded the A.M. degree (1926) from the University of Kansas.

A teacher in Missouri rural schools from 1905 to 1908, Markham taught at the University of Kansas (1908–09). He was superintendent of schools in the Kansas communities of Oneida (1910–14), Spring Hill (1914–17), Wetmore (1918–22), and Yates Center (1922–32). Markham was the first Democrat elected state superintendent of the public schools (1932–39). He was an outstanding state superintendent and promoted curriculum reform and the reorganization of school districts. He was state supervisor of occupational information and guidance for the state board for vocational education (1939–46).

Markham devised a vocabulary test for high school and college students. He was a member of the state board of regents (1939–43) and chairman of the Kansas State Board of Education (1932–39).

REFERENCES: *LE* (II); *WWW* (II); *Industrial Arts and Vocational Education* 35 (April 1946): 20A. *John F. Ohles*

MARLATT, Abby Lillian. B. March 7, 1869, Manhattan, Kansas, to Washington and Julia Ann (Bailey) Marlatt. M. no. D. June 23, 1943, Madison, Wisconsin.

Abby Lillian Marlatt studied at Kansas State Agricultural College (later, Kansas State University) in Manhattan, where she received the B.S. (1888) and M.S. (1890) degrees. She was a graduate student at Clark University in Worcester, Massachusetts, and Brown University in Providence, Rhode Island.

Marlatt began her professional career in 1890 as a professor of home economics at Utah Agricultural College (later, Utah State University) in Logan. She was an instructor of home economics at Technical High School in Providence, Rhode Island (1894–1909), and went to the University of Wisconsin as first director of the home economics department in 1909. She served in that capacity until her retirement as emeritus professor in 1939. Under Marlatt's leadership, a curriculum was designed and established, specialized work was introduced, and teaching and extension work were emphasized. She advocated broad training, including work in the sciences and liberal arts. During World War I, she assisted in drawing up a plan for state cooperation in the food-conservation program.

She wrote several pamphlets on foods. She was president of the American Home Economics Association and belonged to many other professional organizations. She received an honorary degree from Kansas State Agricultural College in 1925.

REFERENCES: *DAB* (supp. 3); *LE* (II); *WWW* (V); *NYT,* June 25, 1943, p. 17; *Dictionary of Wisconsin Biography* (Madison: State Historical Society of Wisconsin, 1960); *State Journal* (Madison, Wisconsin,) June 24, 1943.

Lawrence S. Master

MARSHALL, Charles. B. May 8, 1744, Philadelphia, Pennsylvania, to Christopher Marshall and n.a. M. n.a. D. August 25, 1825, Philadelphia, Pennsylvania.

Charles Marshall's father was one of Philadelphia's earliest chemists and druggists and established one of the American colonies' largest pharmacies, supplying medicines and drugs to the Continental army in Pennsylvania, New Jersey, and Delaware. Charles Marshall received a classical education, joined his father and brother in the drug business, and became sole proprietor when they both retired.

In the early nineteenth century the University of Pennsylvania began to grant a diploma in pharmacy, setting standards for its issuance. The pharmacists of Philadelphia believed the course was an infringement on their rights. Marshall and other prominent pharmacists founded the Philadelphia College of Pharmacy in 1821, the first school of its kind in the United States. Marshall became the school's first president, serving until his death in 1825.

Marshall served on the Philadelphia Committee on Safety during the Revolutionary War.

REFERENCES:*AC; NCAB* (5:343). *M. Jane Dowd*

MARSHALL, Leon Carroll. B. March 15, 1879, Zanesville, Ohio, to John Wesley and Rachel Ann (Tanner) Marshall. M. September 1, 1903, to Mary Brown Keen. Ch. four. D. March 18, 1966, Chevy Chase, Maryland.

Leon Carroll Marshall was graduated with the A.B. degree (1900) from Ohio Wesleyan University in Delaware, Ohio, and received the A.B. (1901) and A.M. (1902) degrees from Harvard University. He was Henry Lee Fellow and assistant in economics at Harvard from 1902 to 1903.

He was professor of economics at Ohio Wesleyan University (1903–07). He joined the faculty of the University of Chicago in 1907, where he taught political economy and served successively as dean of the college of commerce and administration, senior colleges, and school of social service administration and as chairman of the department of political economy and director of work in economics and business.

He left the University of Chicago in 1928 and went to Johns Hopkins University (in Baltimore, Maryland), where he was professor at the institute of law (1928–33) and visiting professor of education (1935–39). He was professor of political economy at the American University in Washington, D.C. (1936).

Marshall was editor of *Material for the Study of Business* (forty volumes), publications issued by the National Recovery Administration Division Review (150 volumes), and *Textbooks in the Social Studies* (thirteen volumes). In 1918 he was a joint editor of *Lessons in Community and National Life*. He was the author of *Outlines of Economics* (1910), *Bibliography of Economics* (1910), *Materials for the Study of Economics* (1913), *Readings in Industrial Society* (1918), *Our Economic Organization* (1920), *Business Administration* (1921), *Social Studies in Secondary Schools* (1922), *The Study of Human Progress* (1925), *Modern Business* (1926), *Collegiate Education for Business* (1928), *Outlines of the Economic Order, The Emergence of the Modern Order* (1929), *The Coordination of Specialists through the Market* (1929), *Judicial Statistics* (1930), *Comparative Judicial Criminal Statistics, Six States* (1932), *Judicial Criminal Statistics* (1932), *The Divorce Court* (two volumes, 1932), *Expenditures of Public Monies for the Administration of Justice in Ohio* (1933), *Unlocking the Treasuries of the Trial Courts* (1933), *National Crisis Series* (1934), *Wages and Hours Provisions in N.R.A. Codes* (1935), *The National Recovery Administration—An Analysis and Appraisal* (1935), *Curriculum Making in Social Studies* (1936), and *Understanding Yourself and Your World* (1954).

Marshall was a member of many professional and scholarly organizations. During World War I, Marshall was secretary of the Advisory Council of the Department of Labor, director of industrial relations of the Emergency Fleet Corporations, and economic adviser to the War Labor Policies Board. He was a deputy assistant administrator on matters of policy for the National Recovery Administration. He received an honorary degree from Ohio Wesleyan University.

REFERENCES: *NCAB* (F:154); *WWW* (IV); *NYT,* March 19, 1966, p. 29.   *Lawrence S. Master*

MARTIN, Alexander. B. January 24, 1882, Nairn, Scotland, to n.a. M. June 1853 to Caroline M. Hursey. Ch. four. D. December 16, 1893, Greencastle, Indiana.

In 1836 when Alexander Martin was fourteen years old, his family moved from Scotland to Jefferson County, Ohio, where he was educated. He served a three-year apprenticeship as a tanner and leather dresser. While attending college he served in Virginia as a teaching principal of Kingwood (later, West Virginia) Academy and a teaching assistant-principal of the Northwestern Virginia Academy at Clarksburg (later, West Virginia). He was graduated with honors from Allegheny College in Meadville, Pennsylvania, in 1847.

As a licensed preacher, Martin became minister of the Methodist Episcopal church in Charleston, where he was assigned for three years. He left Charleston to return to Clarksburg as principal of the Northwestern Virginia Academy in 1851 and also served as minister of a church. In 1852 he accepted a two-year assignment as minister at Moundsville, (West) Virginia. Martin went to Allegheny College as professor of Greek but returned to West Virginia in 1863 as minister of the Fourth Street Church of Wheeling, where he served for three years.

During the Civil War, he was elected president of the West Virginia branch of the Christian Commission and took charge of the hospital work of the commission from Maryland to Tennessee and from Harper's Ferry to the Ohio River. The commission served both Union and Confederate soldiers. He established a structure for the public free school system in West Virginia, which resulted in passage of the Public Free School Act of December 10, 1863.

Martin was inaugurated as the first president of the Agricultural College of West Virginia on June 27, 1867. The name of the college was changed on his recommendation to West Virginia University by an act of the legislature on December 4, 1868. As president of West Virginia University, he helped organize the West Virginia Historical Society (1869).

Because of sectional differences that arose during Reconstruction, Martin was discharged from office in 1875 and accepted the presidency of Indiana Asbury University at Greencastle, where he served until 1889. During his tenure, the name was changed to DePauw University. He resigned the presidency of DePauw in 1889, but remained as professor of philosophy until his death in 1893.

Martin was the recipient of honorary degrees from Ohio Wesleyan University (1863) and Allegheny College (1878).

REFERENCES: *NCAB* (7:383); Charles H. Ambler, *A History of Education in West Virginia, from Early Colonial Times to 1949* (Huntington, W.Va.: Standard Printing & Publishing Co., 1951); George W. Atkinson and Alvaro F. Gibbens, *Prominent Men of West Virginia* (Wheeling, W.Va.: W. L. Callin, 1890). *Ellis Ivey II*

MARVIN, John Gage. B. 1815, LaRaysville, Pennsylvania, to William and Lucienda Marvin. M. no. D. December 10, 1857, Honolulu, Hawaii.

John Gage Marvin studied Latin in a preparatory school and Greek and liberal arts at Wesleyan University in Middletown, Connecticut, graduating in 1841. He read law and attended Harvard Law School where he studied with Joseph Story *(q.v.)*, Simon Greenleaf *(q.v.)*, and Charles Sumner. Among his classmates were Rutherford B. Hayes and Francis Parkman. He was awarded the LL.B. degree (1844).

Marvin was principal of the Athens (Pennsylvania) Academy (1840–42); among his students was Stephen Collins Foster, who played his first composition at the 1841 commencement when he was fourteen. Marvin was law librarian at Harvard (1844–46). He resigned to write *Legal Bibliography, or a Thesaurus of American, English, Irish, and Scotch Law Books. Together with Some Continental Treatises. Interspersed with Critical Observations upon Their Various Editions and Authority. To Which Is Prefixed a Copious List of Abbreviations.* (1847). He was the founder of legal bibliography in the United States.

At the time of the gold rush, he traveled to California, where he was said to have engaged in selling gold mining equipment and the "sidewalk practice of law" drawing contracts for miners and saloon-keepers and handling gambling debts. He engaged in land speculation and was a founder of Empire City, California, where he served as justice of the peace. In 1849 he was editor and publisher of the *Sonora Herald.*

In 1850 Marvin ran successfully for the office of state superintendent of public instruction, receiving fewer than four thousand of eighteen thousand votes in a field of ten candidates. Marvin played an important role in the form of the organization and the division of power over the schools of the state while he was superintendent. He prepared the California School Act of 1852, which dealt with details of school organization. It reflected his views that education was a state function rather than a local or national one and that schools should be administered by a strong central agency. He has been called the Father of California School Law.

Marvin was defeated in his bid for reelection in 1853. He returned to Sonora and moved to Hawaii, where he died in 1857.

REFERENCES: Roy W. Cloud, *Education in California* (Stanford, Cal.: Stanford University Press, 1952); David F. Ferris, *Judge Marvin and the Founding of the California Public School System* (Berkeley: University of California Press, 1962); Howard Jay Graham, "John G. Marvin and the Founding of American Legal Bibliography," *Law Library Journal* 48 (August 1955): 194; L. H. Johnson, *The Development of the Central Agency for Public Education in California, 1849–1949* (Albuquerque: University of New Mexico Press, 1952); Margaret C. Klingelsmith, "J. G. Marvin: An Appreciation," *Law Library Journal* 15 (January 1923): 71; John Swett (*q.v.*), *History of the Public School System of California* (San Francisco: American Book Co., 1876).   *John C. Hogan*

MARWEDEL, Emma Jacobina Christiana. B. February 27, 1818, Münden, Germany, to Heinrich Ludwig and Jacobina Carolina Christiana Maria (Brokmann) Marwedel. M. no. D. November 17, 1893, San Francisco, California.

Emma Jacobina Christiana Marwedel was self-educated in Germany and became active in education as an exponent of the principles of Friedrich Froebel. She was elected a member of the board of directors of an association to promote public education in Leipzig, Germany, in 1864 and joined the first German association for the advancement of women in 1865.

Marwedel was director of the Girls' Industrial School in Hamburg, Germany (1867–68), and also conducted a kindergarten. Elizabeth Peabody *(q.v.)* visited the kindergarten in 1867 and later credited the experience with inspiring her to establish a similar institution in the United States. In 1869 Peabody invited Marwedel to go to the United States, where she established a short-lived women's cooperative industrial training school in Brentwood, Long Island, New York (1870), and was successful in establishing a kindergarten, kindergarten normal school, and school for industrial arts in Washington, D.C. (1870–74).

Persuaded to move to California, Marwedel established the first kindergarten normal school in the state in Los Angeles (1876). She started the Pacific Kindergarten Normal School with twenty-five children and three students; her first graduate was Kate Douglas Wiggin *(q.v.)*. She later moved the school to Oakland (1878), Berkeley (1879), and San Francisco (1880). In 1878 she founded the Silver Street Kindergarten in San Francisco.

Marwedel investigated women's working conditions in Europe and the need for female industrial schools; her findings were published in Germany in 1868. She was also the author of *Conscious Motherhood* (1887), *Children's Poetry and Studies in the Life, Forms and Colours of Nature* (1888), *The Connecting Link* (1891), and two undated pamphlets, *An Appeal for Justice to Childhood* and *Games and Studies in Life Forms*. She was founder and first president of the California Kindergarten Union (1879).

REFERENCES: *DAB; NAW; WWW* (H).   *E. Robert LaCrosse*

MASLOW, Abraham Harold. B. April 1, 1908, Brooklyn, New York, to Samuel and Rose (Schilofsky) Maslow. M. December 31, 1928, to Bertha Goodman. Ch. two. D. June 8, 1970, Menlo Park, California.

Abraham Harold Maslow attended New York City College, Cornell University, and the University of Wisconsin, from which he received the B.A. (1930), M.A. (1931), and Ph.D. (1934) degrees. He taught at Wisconsin (1930–35) and was a Carnegie Fellow at Teachers College, Columbia University, for two years (1935–37).

Maslow taught psychology at Brooklyn College (1937–51) and Brandeis University in Waltham, Massachusetts (1951–69), where he was department chairman from 1951 to 1961. In 1969 he left Brandeis to accept a fellowship at the Laughlin Foundation in Menlo Park, California. He died there the following year.

Maslow was a principal exponent of humanistic or third-force psychology, a departure from Freudian and behaviorist psychologies. His work stressed healthy rather than unhealthy persons. He was especially interested in creative persons and their self-actualization, the highest stage in his hierarchy of needs. Maslow believed that education should neither pamper nor restrain children but encourage them to be creative and responsibly free. He wrote a number of articles on creativity and education published in scholarly journals.

He was the author of *Principles of Abnormal Psychology* (with Beta Mittelmann, 1941), *Motivation and Personality* (1954), *Toward a Psychology of Being* (1962), *Religion, Values and Peak-Experiences* (1964), *Eupsychian Management: A Journal* (1965), *The Psychology of Science: A Reconnaissance* (with H. M. Chiang, 1966), and *Farther Reaches of Human Nature* (published posthumously, 1971), and he was editor of *New Knowledge in Human Values* (1959) and *The Healthy Personality: Readings* (1969).

He was often a member of the councils of the Society for the Psychological Study of Social Issues and the American Psychological Association (president, 1967) and was named Humanist of the Year by the American Humanist Association in 1967. He was awarded an honorary degree by Xavier University in Cincinnati, Ohio.

REFERENCES: *CA* (1–4); *WWW* (V); *NYT,* June 10, 1970, p. 47; Frank G. Goble, *The Third Force: The Psychology of Abraham Maslow* (New York: Grossman Publishers, 1970); Willard B. Frick, *Humanistic Psychology: Interviews with Maslow, Murphy and Rogers* (Columbus, Ohio: Merrill, 1971).   *Frederik F. Ohles*

MASON, John Mitchell. B. March 19, 1770, New York, New York, to John and Catherine (Van Wyck) Mason. M. May 13, 1793, to Ann Lefferts. Ch. seven. D. December 26, 1829, New York, New York.

John Mitchell Mason received most of his early education from his father, the Reverend John Mason. The son was graduated from Columbia College in 1789. His theological training was received from his father and at the University of Edinburgh, Scotland, where he was graduated in 1792. He was ordained in 1793 and installed as a pastor of the Associate Reformed church of North America.

Mason believed that the educational standards of the American ministry were not sufficient, and he outlined a plan to establish a theological seminary; it was opened in New York City in 1804 with Mason as its first professor. It was the forerunner of Union Theological Seminary.

Mason was a trustee of Columbia College (1795–1811 and 1812–24) and was a member of a committee on raising standards for college admission in 1809. The trustees evolved a new curriculum in 1811 and created the office of provost. Mason was elected provost to supervise the president and serve as president in his absence. Mason also taught the classics to the senior class. His work on the committee and as provost helped to strengthen the college.

The strain of his many duties in college, seminary, church, and public affairs affected Mason's health, and he resigned as provost in 1816. In 1821 Mason accepted the presidency of Dickinson College in Carlisle, Pennsylvania. He was the outstanding preacher in America and was said to have been one of the greatest pulpit orators in all the English-speaking world.

Mason founded *Christian's Magazine* in 1866 and wrote much of it for several years. He wrote *A Plea for Sacramental Communion on Catholic Principles* (1816), a book that aroused much interest in America and abroad.

REFERENCES: *AC; DAB; NCAB* (6:462); *TC; WWW* (H).

Michael R. Cioffi

MASON, Lowell. B. January 8, 1792, Medfield, Massachusetts, to Johnson and Catharine (Hartshorn) Mason. M. September 3, 1817, to Abigail Gregory. Ch. four, including William Mason *(q.v.)*. D. August 11, 1872, Orange, New Jersey.

Lowell Mason, Father of American Church Music and Father of Singing Among Children, first learned to play musical instruments as a child from George W. Adams, a Medfield, Massachusetts, neighbor and organ builder, and he studied music with Amos Aldrich. At the age of eighteen, Mason was a leader of the parish choir and a local band.

He went to Savannah, Georgia, in 1812, where he worked in a bank and also led a choir, gave singing lessons, and was superintendent of Savannah's first Sunday school. Invited by a committee of representatives of several Boston, Massachusetts, churches, he moved to Boston in 1827 and was engaged as a teller in the Columbian Bank and worked with the local churches. In the early 1830s, he conducted a free singing school for children in Boston churches. In 1832 Mason and George James Webb organized the Boston Academy of Music, which continued to 1847. In 1836 the Boston School Committee responded to a public petition and authorized the introduction of Mason's system of music instruction in the grammar schools. The Boston City Council refused to pass an appropriation to finance the instruction, and Mason instructed without charge for a year. He visited Europe to study music instruction in 1837 and was engaged to teach music in Boston schools in 1838.

In 1833 Mason aided Samuel G. Howe *(q.v.)* by organizing instruction at the Perkins Institute for the Blind. For seven years he taught music to the blind, developing instructional techniques that substituted for methods suitable to sighted students. He pioneered in music instruction to teachers' institutes in Massachusetts. In 1851 Mason and George F. Root *(q.v.)* held classes for three months in North Reading, Massachusetts. He visited Europe a second time (1851–52) and returned to New York City where he taught at the New York Musical Institute. From 1854 he retired to an estate located on Orange Mountain in New Jersey, where he continued his writing.

Mason compiled and wrote over fifty volumes, including *Boston Handel and Haydn Society Collection of Church Music* (1822), which was compiled in Savannah, Georgia, with G. K. Jackson, and *Juvenile Lyre* (1830), the first book of school songs published in the United States. He also produced *Juvenile Psalmist* (1829), *The Choir or Union Collection* (1832), *Manual of Instruction in Vocal Music* (1834), *Boston Academy Collections of Church Music* (with G. J. Webb, 1834), *Sabbath School Songs* (1836), *Lyra Sacra* (1837), *Occasional Psalmody* (1837), *Songs of Asaph* (1838), *The Seraph* (1838), *Boston Anthem Book* (1839), *The Gentleman's Glee Book* (1841), *American Sabbath Singing Book* (1843), *Boston Academy Collection of Choruses* (1844), *Song Book of the School Room* (1845), *Primary School Song Book* (1846), *The National Psalmodist* (with G. J. Webb, 1848), *The Hand Book of Psalmody* (1852), *The Normal Singer* (1856), *Mammoth Musical Exercises* (1857), *Collections of Psalms and Hymns for Public Worship* (with others, 1858), and *The Song Garland* (1866).

Mason was president of the Handel and Haydn Society of Boston (1827–32). He received the first honorary Doctor of Music degree awarded in the United States from New York University in 1855.

REFERENCES: *AC; DAB; NCAB* (7:422); *NYT*, August 13, 1872, p. 5; *TC; WWW* (H); Edward B. Birge *(q.v.)*, *History of Public School Music in the United States* (Philadelphia: Oliver Ditson Co., 1927); John T. Howard, *Our American Music* (New York: Thomas Y. Crowell, 1931), pp. 142–48; Arthur L. Rich, *Lowell Mason, the Father of Singing Among the Children* (Chapel Hill: University of North Carolina Press, 1946); Nicholas Slonimsky, ed., *Baker's Biographical Dictionary of Musicians*, 5th ed. (New York: G. Schirmer, 1958); Albert E. Wier, *The Macmillan Encyclopedia of Music and Musicians* (New York: Macmillan, 1938).

Thomas A. Barlow

MASON, Luther Whiting. B. April 3, 1828, Turner, Maine, to Willard and Mary (Whiting) Mason. M. no. D. July 14, 1896, Buckfield, Maine.

Luther Whiting Mason, orphaned in 1838, was self-taught in music. He earned his tuition in an academy by teaching music and became supervisor of music in the public schools of Louisville, Kentucky, and Cincinnati, Ohio (1853–61). He was a drum major in the United States Army (1861–65) and supervisor of music in the Boston, Massachusetts, public schools (1865–80 and again 1883).

Mason demonstrated his method of music instruction utilizing graded books and charts to the Centennial Exposition in Philadelphia, Pennsylvania, in 1876. Mason was invited by the Japanese government to Japan where he supervised music instruction in the schools, directed a school of music, and gave private lessons to the nobility (1880–83). He returned to his position in Boston in 1883 and compiled the *National Music Course* (four volumes, with George A. Veazie, Jr., 1887–97). He spent several months in Berlin and Leipzig, Germany, studying music methods to improve his system and his music course was approved by the faculty of the University of Leipzig for publication in a German edition.

Mason was honored by the Japanese government and received the first honorary degree awarded to a musician by Tokyo University (1882). He was feted by a public reception in Boston on May 25, 1895.

REFERENCES: *DAB; TC; WWW* (H); Nicholas Slonimsky, ed., *Baker's Biographical Dictionary of Musicians,* 5th ed. (New York: G. Schirmer, 1958); Albert E. Wier, *The Macmillan Encyclopedia of Music and Musicians* (New York: Macmillan, 1938); Kenneth Ray Hartley, "The Life and Works of Luther Whiting Mason" (Ed.D. diss., Florida State University, 1959).   *Darlene E. Fisher*

MASON, William. B. January 24, 1829, Boston, Massachusetts, to Lowell (*q.v.*) and Abigail (Gregory) Mason. M. March 12, 1857, to Mary Isabella Webb. Ch. three. D. July 14, 1908, New York, New York.

William Mason's father, Lowell Mason, was a pioneering teacher of music who provided a background for the development at an early age of his son's musical talent. William Mason studied piano with Henry Schmidt in Boston. He made his debut at the Boston Academy of Music at the age of seventeen and made frequent public appearances. He traveled to Europe in 1849 to complete his musical education and studied in Leipzig, Germany, under Ignaz Moscheles, Moritz Hauptmann, and Ernst Friedrich Richter and in Prague, Czechoslovakia, with Alexander Dreyschock. He was particularly influenced as a student of Franz Liszt in Weimar, Germany (1853–54). He traveled widely in Germany, meeting musicians and performing in public.

Mason returned to the United States in 1854 and successfully toured major cities from Boston to Chicago. He settled in New York City in 1855 where he taught and performed. In the winter of 1855–56, he was a founder of the Mason-Thomas Soirees of Chamber Music, a series of quality concerts given until 1868. Thereafter he devoted himself principally to teaching.

Though he found concert giving distasteful, Mason was perhaps the first pianist to tour the United States performing piano recitals exclusively and was the first to introduce the *Hungarian Rhapsodies* and other Liszt compositions to American audiences. His compositions include *Silver Spring* (opus 6), *Danse Rustique, Spring Dawn* (opus 20), and *Reverie Poetique* (opus 24). He was the author of *A Method for the Pianoforte*

(1867), *A System for Beginners in the Art of Playing upon the Pianoforte* (1871), *A System of Technical Exercises for the Pianoforte* (with W. S. B. Mathews, 1876), and *Touch and Technic* (four volumes, 1889–92).

REFERENCES: *AC; DAB; NCAB* (7: 423); *TC; WWW* (V); Nicholas Slonimsky, ed., *Baker's Biographical Dictionary of Musicians,* 5th ed. (New York: G. Schirmer, 1958); Albert E. Wier, *The Macmillan Encyclopedia of Music and Musicians* (New York: Macmillan, 1938).

Joseph P. Cangemi
Thomas E. Kesler

MATHER, Frank Jewett, Jr. B. July 6, 1868, Deep River, Connecticut, to Frank Jewett and Caroline Arms (Graves) Mather. M. February 20, 1905, to Ellen Suydam Mills. Ch. two. D. November 11, 1953, Princeton, New Jersey.

Frank Jewett Mather was graduated from Williams College in Williamstown, Massachusetts, with the A.B. degree (1889). He received the Ph.D. degree (1892) in literature and philology from Johns Hopkins University in Baltimore, Maryland, and later studied at the University of Berlin, Germany, and the Ecole des hautes études in Paris, France.

Early in his career Mather taught Anglo-Saxon and Romanic languages at Williams College (1893–1900) and spent several years as a journalist. From 1901 to 1910 he was an editorial writer and art critic for the *New York Evening Post,* assistant editor of *The Nation,* and American editor for *Burlington Magazine.* He taught at Princeton University from 1910 until he retired in 1933. He was director of the art museum at Princeton from 1920 to 1948. After leaving Princeton he taught at Cornell University, the University of Wisconsin, Union College in Schenectady, New York, and the Metropolitan Museum of Art in New York City.

Mather was a prolific writer. His books include *Homer Martin, Poet in Landscape* (1912), *The Collectors* (short stories, 1912), *Estimates in Art* (1916), *The Portraits of Dante* (1921), *A History of Italian Painting* (1923), *Ulysses in Ithaca* (1926), *Modern Painting* (1927), *Estimates in Art* (series two, 1931), *Concerning Beauty* (1935), *Venetian Painters* (1936), *Western European Painting of the Renaissance* (1939), and several monographs. He was joint editor of *Art Studies* (from 1923).

Mather was a member of many professional and scholarly associations and received an honorary degree from Williams College.

REFERENCES: *LE* (II); *WWW* (III); *Art Digest* 28 (December 15, 1953):4; S. Lane Faison, Jr., "Frank J. Mather, Jr." *College Art Journal* 13 (Spring 1954): 222–23; *Wilson Library Bulletin* 28 (January 1954): 398.

Roger H. Jones

MATHER, Increase. B. June 21, 1639, Dorchester, Massachusetts, to Richard and Katherine (Holt) Mather. M. 1662 to Maria Cotton. M. 1717 to

Ann (Lake) Cotton. Ch. ten, including Cotton Mather, American Puritan religious leader. D. August 23, 1723, Boston, Massachusetts.

Increase Mather, Puritan religious leader of colonial Massachusetts and president of Harvard College, grew up in Dorchester, Massachusetts, near Boston, where his father, the Reverend Richard Mather, was the minister. He was prepared for college by his father, who tutored him in Latin and Greek. He entered Harvard College at the age of twelve and was graduated in 1656. Within a year, he preached his first sermon near Dorchester and later at his father's church. He went to Ireland in 1657, where he studied at Trinity College and received the M.A. degree (1658). Mather preached at several locations in England, but Puritanism was becoming increasingly unpopular, and he sailed for home in 1661.

He studied and preached itinerantly until called to the Second Church of Boston as its minister in 1664. Mather became associated with Harvard College when he was elected to the Fellows (the corporation that governed the college) in March 1675. Elected president of Harvard in 1681, his church in Boston refused to release him and he declined. He presided at commencement and made weekly visits to the institution until 1683 when John Rogers was inaugurated president. He became president of Harvard in 1685, received the title of rector in 1686, and served as head of the college to 1701.

Provincial politics took up increasing amounts of his time. When the Massachusetts charter was annulled and royal governors were appointed by the Crown, Mather was selected a leader of the opposition and was sent to England to 1688 to petition the king to restore the charter. He was successful in obtaining favorable provisions in the charter of 1691 and returned to America in 1692.

Mather was one of the most prolific writers of colonial America. His bibliography of 175 items (sermons, history, biography, natural philosophy, witchcraft, theological subjects, prefaces and attestations) includes *Brief History of the Warr with the Indians* (1676), *A Testimony Against Several Prophane and Superstitious Customs* (1687), *A Brief Relation of the State of New England* (1689), and *Cases of Conscience Concerning Evil Spirits* (1693).

Mather was the first American-born president of Harvard College and the first to be awarded an honorary doctorate by an American college, a Doctor of Sacred Theology degree from Harvard in 1692.

REFERENCES: *AC; DAB; EB; NCAB* (6:412); *TC; WWW* (H); Kenneth B. Murdock, *Increase Mather: The Foremost American* (Cambridge: Harvard University Press, 1925); John L. Sibley, *Biographical Sketches of Graduates of Harvard University* (Cambridge: Charles W. Sever, 1873), 1: 410–70.   *Richard G. Durnin*

MATTHEWS, James Brander. B. February 21, 1852, New Orleans, Louisiana, to Edward and Virginia (Brander) Matthews. M. May 10, 1873, to Ada S. Smith. Ch. one. D. March 31, 1929, New York, New York.

Brander Matthews, though born in New Orleans, Louisiana, spent most of his life in New York City and was a cosmopolitan visitor of London and Paris. He received the A.B. (1871), LL.B. (1873), and A.M. (1874) degrees from Columbia University. He was admitted to the bar in 1873 but never practiced law.

His appointment as professor of dramatics at Columbia University in 1900 is regarded as the first such appointment in American higher education. He remained at Columbia to his retirement in 1924. He was recognized as a contributor to the development of the short story as a literary form. Through his teaching at Columbia and as drama critic for the *New York Times,* he was influential in the development of the American theater.

Matthews was noted as a writer of short stories, novels, successfully staged plays, drama criticism, and other essays. He was the author of over forty books, including *Introduction to the Study of American Literature* (1896), *Development of the Drama* (1903), *A Study of the Drama* (1910), *A Study of Versification* (1911), *Shakespeare as a Playwright* (1913), *A Book About the Theater* (1916), *Principles of Playmaking* (1919), *Essays on English* (1921), *Playwrights on Playmaking* (1923), and the autobiographical *These Many Years* (1917).

Matthews was a trustee of Columbia University Press, an organizer of the American Copyright League and the Dunlop Society (president, 1914), a founder of Authors and Players Clubs, and a member of other associations, including the American Academy of Arts and Letters (chancellor, 1922–24), the Modern Language Association (president, 1910), and the National Institute of Arts and Letters (president, 1914). He received the Legion of Honor from the French government (1907) and several honorary degrees from American universities. The Brander Matthews Dramatic Museum was established at Columbia University to house a collection of theater models and costumes.

REFERENCES: *AC; DAB; EB; NYT,* April 1, 1929, p. 1; *TC; WWW* (I); Stanley T. Kunitz and Howard Haycraft, *American Authors, 1600–1900* (New York: H. W. Wilson Co., 1938), pp. 519–20; Brander Matthews, *These Many Years* (New York: Charles Scribner's Sons, 1917).

Joseph C. Bronars, Jr.

MAUPIN, Socrates. B. November 12, 1808, Albemarle County, Virginia, to Chapman White and Mary (Spencer) Maupin. M. 1833 to Sally Travers Hay. Ch. ten. D. October 19, 1871, Charlottesville, Virginia.

Socrates Maupin received the A.B. degree (1828) from Washington (later, Washington and Lee) College in Lexington, Virginia. He studied medicine at the University of Virginia, graduating in 1830, and received the

A.M. degree (1833) in general literary and scientific studies.

Maupin was appointed to the chair of ancient languages at Hampden-Sydney (Virginia) College (1833–35). He was principal of Richmond (Virginia) Academy (1835–38) and organized and conducted a private school in Richmond (1838–53). He became a professor of medicine in 1838 and helped found the Richmond Medical College in 1846, where he was professor of chemistry. He taught there until 1853 when he returned to the University of Virginia as professor of chemistry. He became chairman of the faculty in 1854 and held that office for sixteen years, the longest tenure in the university's history.

Maupin helped to preserve the university during and after the Civil War and with other faculty put up money for the reconstruction of the campus. The student body grew rapidly after the war. Under Maupin's direction the school of applied mathematics was established in 1867 and the school of agriculture in 1869. He resigned in 1870 and died the next year.

REFERENCES: *NCAB* (13:134); *TC;* Thomas Abernathy, *A Sketch of the University of Virginia* (Richmond: Whittet & Shepperson, 1885).

Franklin Ross Jones

MAXCY, Jonathan. B. September 2, 1768, Attleboro, Massachusetts, to Levi and Ruth (Newell) Maxcy. M. August 22, 1791, to Susan Hopkins. Ch. six. D. June 4, 1820, Columbia, South Carolina.

Jonathan Maxcy attended Wrentham (Massachusetts) Academy, a well-known college preparatory school, and at the age of fifteen entered Rhode Island College (later, Brown University). He was graduated in 1787 with highest honors and as valedictorian of the class; upon graduation, he accepted a tutorship at the college.

He studied theology and on April 1, 1790, was ordained a Baptist minister. He acted as supply pastor during the next year for the First Baptist Church in Providence, Rhode Island, and was appointed minister of the church on September 8, 1791. On the same day, he was appointed trustee of Rhode Island College and professor of divinity. In 1792 Maxcy resigned his pastoral assignment and was inaugurated as the second president, pro tempore, of Rhode Island College at the age of twenty-four. After serving five years as president pro tempore, he was named president in 1797.

In 1802 he became the third president of Union College in Schenectady, New York, where he came into conflict with several trustees over his theological beliefs. Faced with continued disagreement with trustees and in failing health, Maxcy accepted the nomination in 1804 to become the first president of South Carolina College (later, the University of South Carolina) in Columbia.

The first months of his presidency at South Carolina were spent organizing the institution, preparing a curriculum, establishing the course of study, setting entrance requirements, and recruiting the faculty. In January 1805 the college began with Maxcy and one professor offering the traditional classical curriculum; the first commencement was held in 1807. During Maxcy's tenure the curriculum was enlarged to include chemistry, mineralogy, and natural philosophy. From 1808 to 1814 his administration was interrupted by student uprisings and rioting. In addition to turmoil and the struggle to establish the college, Maxcy's health began to fail. From 1815 to his death in 1820, he was frequently unable to attend faculty meetings and maintain the office of the president. He received an honorary degree from Harvard University (1801).

REFERENCES: *AC; DAB; NCAB* (8:21, 11:30); TC; WWW (H); Daniel Hollis, *University of South Carolina* (Columbia: University of South Carolina Press, 1951); J. C. Hungerpiller, *A Sketch of the Life and Character of Jonathan Maxcy, D.D.* (Columbia: University of South Carolina Bulletin, No. 58, July 1917).   *Fred L. Splittgerber*

MAXWELL, William Henry. B. March 5, 1852, Stewartstown, County Tyrone, Ireland, to John and Maria (Jackson) Maxwell. M. December 1, 1877, to Marie Antoinette Polk. Ch. two. D. May 3, 1920, Flushing, Queens, New York.

William Henry Maxwell attended local Irish national schools, was tutored in the classics by his father, and completed the honors course at the Royal Academical Institution at Belfast. He earned the bachelor's degree (1872) and the master's degree (1874) with honors from Queen's College in Galway. While completing the master's degree he taught at the Royal Academical Institution and the Ladies Collegiate Institute. He was unable to pursue plans to study law because of financial problems.

In 1874 Maxwell emigrated to New York City where, unable to secure a teaching position, he decided to become a journalist and worked as a reporter for the *New York Tribune* and *New York Herald*. He was assistant editor of the *Metropolitan Weekly* and for five years was managing editor of the *Brooklyn Times*. A series of articles on Brooklyn schools helped Maxwell obtain a teaching position in the evening schools of Brooklyn (1880–81).

Maxwell was associate superintendent (1882–87) and was elected superintendent of the Brooklyn schools (1887–98). When New York and Brooklyn were consolidated and the City of New York was chartered, Maxwell was elected the first city superintendent of schools. During his twenty years as superintendent, Maxwell worked to remove partisan influence from the schools. He established vocational education, kindergartens, a summer school, and a continuation school. He provided enrichment of the elementary school curriculum and for education of a typical pupil. He experimented with the intermediate school, playgrounds, and free meals and eyeglasses for poor children. Financial independence for the city schools was achieved by legislation providing for direct school taxes on real and personal property. Teachers' salaries were standardized and a pension system created. Maxwell improved the quality of teachers in the system by requiring high school and normal school training and established a merit system of appointment and promotion of teachers.

Maxwell was the author of Maxwell's English Series (1886–1902), *Writing in English* (with G. S. Smith, 1900), *Elementary Grammar* (1904), and *School Grammar* (1907). With Nicholas Murray Butler *(q.v.)* and others, he was a founder (1891) and an editor (1891–97) of the *Educational Review*.

Maxwell was active in regional, state, and national educational organizations and was president of the National Educational Association (1905) and its department of superintendence (1895) and the State Council of Superintendents (1895) and a member of the advisory board of the Simplified Spelling Board. He received honorary degrees from St. Lawrence and Columbia universities.

REFERENCES: *AC; DAB; NCAB* (13:218); TC; WWW (I); *NYT,* May 4, 1920, p. 11; *Educational Review* 60 (June 1920): 87–88.

Barbara Ruth Peltzman

MAYO, Amory Dwight. B. January 31, 1823, Warwick, Massachusetts, to Amory and Sophronia (Cobb) Mayo. M. July 28, 1846, to Sarah Carter Edgarton. M. June 7, 1853, to Lucy Caroline Clarke. Ch. one. D. April 8, 1907, Washington, D.C.

Amory Dwight Mayo's early childhood education was received at public schools in Massachusetts and his college preparatory studies were at Deerfield (Massachusetts) Academy. He enrolled in Amherst (Massachusetts) College, but was forced to withdraw at the end of his first year of studies (1844) because of ill health. He received the A.M. degree from Amherst College, studied theology, and was ordained a Unitarian minister in 1846.

Mayo taught in Massachusetts common schools (1839–44). His first two pastoral assignments were in Gloucester, Massachusetts (1846–54), and Cleveland, Ohio (1854–56). It was not until his next assignment in Albany, New York, that he became involved in education, serving on the local school board (1856–63).

Serving churches in Cincinnati (1863–72) and Springfield (1872–80), Ohio, he also served on those local city school boards (1863–80). Mayo was increasingly involved with public education and the training of Unitarian seminarians. As a promoter of public education, he wrote and worked toward the Christian Amendment Movement, an attempt to incorporate into the United States Constitution a provision that would guarantee Bible instruction a place in public education. He was concerned with the education of blacks of the United States, especially in the South. He was a forceful advocate of integrated and equal educational opportunities for black children.

Mayo was appointed chief editorial writer (1880–86) for the *Journal of Education* and moved to Boston. For the next twenty years Mayo visited schools in thirty states, particularly in the South, conferring and speaking freely with school committees and state legislatures. At the encouragement of William T. Harris *(q.v.)*, commissioner of education, Mayo began to write a history of public education in the United States. Although the project was never completed, Harris incorporated much of this writing into his annual reports.

Mayo published government documents, including *Building for the Children of the South* (1884), *Industrial Education in the South* (1888), and *Southern Women in the Recent Educational Movement in the South* (1892), and he also wrote *The Moral Argument of Universalism* (1847), *Biography and Writings of Mrs. S. C. Edgarton Mayo* (1849), *Graces and Powers of the Christian Life* (1852), *Symbols of the Capitol* (1859), and *Talks with Teachers* (1881).

Mayo was awarded honorary degrees by Amherst (1874) and Berea (1897) colleges.

REFERENCES: *AC; DAB; NCAB* (25:330); TC; WWW (I).

Isadore L. Sonnier

MAYS, Benjamin Elijah. B. August 1, 1895, Epworth, South Carolina, to Hezekiah and Louvenia (Carter) Mays. M. 1920 to Ellen Harvin. M. August 9, 1926, to Sadie Gray, Ch. none.

The son of slave parents, Benjamin E. Mays was the youngest of eight children. He attended the high school of South Carolina State College and was graduated from Bates College in Lewiston, Maine, with the A.B. degree (1920). He earned the M.A. (1925) and the Ph.D. (1935) degrees from the University of Chicago.

Mays began his career in Atlanta, Georgia, as professor of mathematics at Morehouse College (1921–24) and pastor of the Shiloh Baptist Church (1922–25). He was professor of English at South Carolina State College at Orangeburg (1925–26). From 1926 to 1928, he was the executive secretary of the Tampa (Florida) Urban League and national student secretary of the Young Men's Christian Association (YMCA) from 1928 to 1930. He was the director of the Study of Negro Churches in the United States for the Institute of Social and Religious Research (New York) from 1930 to 1932 and was coauthor of *The Negro's Church* (with J. W. Nicholson, 1933).

He was dean of the school of religion at Howard University in Washington, D.C. (1934–40). He accepted the presidency of Morehouse College in 1940 and held that position until his retirement in 1967. Mays advocated that blacks should work in the existing society and viewed black separatism as an "impractical goal." He was a dominant force in higher education and religious and civic affairs for more than fifty years. He had a talent for relating to persons of different racial and ethnic backgrounds. Like *The Negro's Church,* his other books reflected his religious orientation, including *The Negro's God* (1938), and *Seeking to be Christian in Race Relations* (1946). He was editor and compiler of *A Gospel for Social Awakening* (1950). His autobiography, *Born to Rebel* (1971), was an account of his career as an educator, clergyman, and author. Mays was a weekly columnist for the *Pittsburgh* (Pennsylvania) *Courier.*

Active in religious and educational organizations, Mays was a member of the World Commission and the board of the National Council of the YMCA. He attended the Oxford (England) Conference on Church, Community and State (1937) and world conferences of the YMCA in Mysore, India (1937), and Stockholm, Sweden (1938). He was a delegate to the first and second assemblies of the World Council of Churches (1948 and 1954). He was the first black to be elected vice-president of the Federal Council of the Churches of Christ in America (1944–46). He was president of the United Negro College Fund and a member of the national committee of the Mid-Century White House Conference on Children and Youth.

Awarded many honorary degrees, Mays was the recipient of awards for his work in the area of race relations.

REFERENCES: *CA* (45–48); *CB* (May 1945); *LE* (III); *WWAE* (XVI); *Afro-American Encyclopedia* (North Miami, Fla.: Educational Book Publishers, 1974), 6: 1618–19; Benjamin E. Mays, *Born to Rebel* (New York: Charles Scribner's Sons, 1971); *The Negro Handbook* (Chicago: Johnson Publishing Co., 1966), p. 408; Ann A. Shockley and Sue P. Chandler, *Living Black American Authors* (New York: R. R. Bowker Co., 1973).

Octavia B. Knight

MEARNS, William Hughes. B. September 28, 1875, Philadelphia, Pennsylvania, to William Hughes and Lelia Cora (Evans) Mearns. M. December 22, 1904, to Mabel Fagley. Ch. one. D. March 13, 1965, New York, New York.

(William) Hughes Mearns was graduated from Philadelphia's Central High School (1893) and the Philadelphia School of Pedagogy (1894). He received the B.S. degree from Harvard University (1902) and studied at the University of Pennsylvania Graduate School (1902–08).

Mearns's main interest was writing for the stage, but he accepted a teaching position to earn money. He taught English at the Philadelphia School of Pedagogy (1902–20) and was a director of the Shady Hill Day School in Philadelphia (1914–17). At Shady Hill School he experimented with the creative processes of children from three to eight years of age. He kept records of their conversations and came upon a "hidden individual spirit of surprising keenness and of stubborn honesty."

Mearns was a staff member of the Lincoln School and the Institute of Educational Research of Teachers College, Columbia University (1920–25). Mearns spent the remainder of his career at New York University as associate professor and professor of education (1925–46). He served as chairman of the department of creative education from 1926 to 1946.

He was the author of textbooks, novels, and verse, including "The Little Man Who Wasn't There," which was set to music and tagged as a hit parade tune in early 1940. His other works include *Richard, Richard* (1916), *The Vinegar Saint* (1919), *I Ride in My Coach* (1923), *Creative Youth* (1925), *Creative Power* (1929), and *The Creative Adult* (1940).

Mearns was an active member of professional associations, serving on the board of directors of Plays and Players, as director of the American Society for Extension University Teaching, and as president of the Philadelphia Teachers Association (1906–08).

REFERENCES: *CB* (January–February 1940 and April 1965); *LE* (III); NYT, March 14, 1965, p. 87; *WWAE* (XI); *WWW* (IV); J. C. Duff, "Hughes Mearns: Pioneer in Creative Education," *Clearing House* 40 (March 1966): 419–20.   *Paul J. Schafer*

MECHEM, Floyd Russell. B. May 9, 1858, Nunda, New York, to Isaac J. and Celestia (Russell) Mechem. M. December 4, 1884, to Jessie P. Collier. Ch. two. D. December 11, 1928, Chicago, Illinois.

Floyd Russell Mechem began his training in the high schools of Titusville, Pennsylvania, and Battle Creek, Michigan. Financially unable to attend law school, he was admitted to the Michigan bar (1879) without the benefit of an earned degree. He began to practice law in Battle Creek (1879–87) and later moved to Detroit (1887–93). Four years later he was one of the founders of the Detroit College of Law, where he served as professor and dean for one year. He was Tappan Professor of Law at the University of Michigan (1892–1903) and joined the law faculty at the University of Chicago in 1903. He was a popular summer lecturer at several universities.

Mechem's most notable work was *Treatise on the Law of Agency* (1889), which shaped the law of agency in the United States and earned him an international reputation. His *Treatise on the Law of Sale of Personal Property* (two volumes, 1901) was frequently cited by the courts. His other works include *A Treatise on the Law of Public Offices and Officers* (1890), the 1891 edition of Robert Hutchison's *Treatise on the Law of Carriers*, and *Elements in the Law of Partnership* (1896). His writings exerted a strong influence in shaping contemporary legal education.

Although he never received an earned degree, the University of Michi-

gan conferred upon him honorary A.M. (1894) and LL.D. (1912) degrees.
REFERENCES: *DAB; NCAB* (23:361); *WWW* (I); *NYT,* December 12, 1928, p. 31. *LeRoy Barney*

MEIKLEJOHN, Alexander. B. February 3, 1872, Rochdale, England, to James and Elizabeth (France) Meiklejohn. M. June 14, 1902, to Nannine A. La Villa. M. June 9, 1926, to Helen Everett. Ch. four. D. December 16, 1964, Berkeley, California.

Alexander Meiklejohn came to the United States from England with his parents in 1880. He was educated in the Pawtucket, Rhode Island, public schools, at Brown University in Providence, Rhode Island, where he received the B.A. (1893) and M.A. (1895) degrees, and at Cornell University in Ithaca, New York, where he received the Ph.D. degree (1897).

Meiklejohn began his teaching career as an instructor in philosophy at Brown in 1897. In 1901 he was appointed dean, an office that had been created only a year earlier. In 1912 he was chosen president of Amherst (Massachusetts) College, the first nonalumnus and first nonclergyman to hold that position. Meiklejohn shifted the emphasis at Amherst from training the well-rounded man of good, Christian character to developing intelligence, seeing this as a moral obligation of the college. He believed in the necessity of the use of intelligence for a democratic society to continue. He led Amherst in developing a curriculum designed to train students to make reasonable decisions in a complex world. He introduced the first survey course in the social sciences and transformed the school into a place of academic excellence. Under severe pressure and conflict with alumni and some of the older faculty, he refused on principle to resign and was fired in 1923.

He went to the University of Wisconsin in 1925 and in 1928 organized the experimental college. The college had one course for each of the first two years: fifth-century Athens and modern America. Students pursued their vocational interests in the regular curriculum of the university during their last two years. The college was discontinued in 1933 because of objections from university faculty. Meiklejohn continued on the Wisconsin faculty teaching half-time until his retirement in 1938. He organized a pioneer adult study institution, the School of Social Studies, in San Francisco, California, which closed during World War II. Meiklejohn continued to be an active lecturer and writer until his death in 1964. During his latter years he became one of America's leading lay experts on the First Amendment and academic freedom

Meiklejohn was the author of *The Liberal College* (1920), *Freedom and the College* (1923), *The Experimental College* (1932), *What Does America Mean?* (1935), *Education Between Two Worlds* (1942), and *Free Speech and Its Relation to Self-government* (1948).

Meiklejohn was a founder of the American Civil Liberties Union (1920) and vice-chairman of the League for Industrial Democracy. He was president of the American Philosophical Association (1923) and the American Association of Adult Education (1942). He belonged to many professional organizations, received numerous honorary degrees and other awards, and was a recipient of the presidential Medal of Freedom in 1963.

REFERENCES: *LE* (II); *NCAB* (51:632); *WWW* (IV); *NYT,* December 17, 1964, p. 41; *Nation* 199 (December 28, 1964): 506.   *James M. Green*

MELBY, Ernest Oscar. B. August 16, 1891, Lake Park, Minnesota, to Ole and Ellen Caroline (Stakke) Melby. M. December 29, 1914, to Aurora M. Herbert. Ch. one.

Ernest O. Melby received the B.A. degree (1913) from St. Olaf College in Northfield, Minnesota, and the M.A. (1926) and Ph.D. (1928) degrees from the University of Minnesota.

Melby served in Minnesota as a science teacher at Alexandria (1913–14), a principal at Breckenridge (1914–15), and superintendent of schools at Brewster (1915–17), Blackduck (1917–20), and Long Prairie (1920–26). He was an instructor of education at the University of Minnesota (1926–27) and assistant director of the Bureau of Educational Research (1927–28).

From 1928 to 1934 Melby was a member of the education faculty at Northwestern University in Evanston, Illinois, and served as dean of the school of education (1934–41). He was president of Montana State University at Bozeman (1941–45) and was chancellor of the six units under the University of Montana (1943–45). He left Montana to become dean of the school of education at New York University (1945) and served there to his retirement in 1956, when he became Distinguished Professor of Education at Michigan State University.

Melby was the author of many articles and books, including *The Organization and Administration of Supervision* (1930), *Diagnostic and Remedial Teaching* (with Leo J. Brueckner *q.v.*, 1931), *Supervision of High Schools* (1931), *Effective Instructional Leadership* (1933), *New Schools for a New Culture* (with Charles M. MacConnell and Christian O. Arndt, 1943), *American Education Under Fire* (1951), *Israel: Problems of Nation Building* (with Emil Lengyel, 1951), *Administering Community Education* (1955), *The Education of Free Men* (1955), *Education for Renewed Faith in Freedom* (1959), *The Role of the School in Community Education* (1963), *The Teacher and Learning* (1963), and *Education II—The Social Imperative* (with Vasil M. Kerensby, 1971) and was editor of *Mobilizing Educational Resources for Winning the War* (1943) and *Freedom and Public Education* (with Morton Piner, 1953).

Active in professional associations, Melby was secretary of the American Council on Education (1937–40), chairman of the National Commission on the Defense of Democracy through Education of the National Education Association (1947–48), director of the National Society for the Study of Education (1944–47), and president of the John Dewey Society (1947–48). He received honorary degrees from several colleges and universities.

REFERENCES: *LE* (III); *WW* (XXXVII); *WWAE* (XVI); Robert John Alfonso, "Ernest O. Melby: Evangelist for Education" (Ph.D. diss., Michigan State University, 1962).   *Edward T. Marquardt*

MEMMINGER, Christopher Gustavus. B. January 9, 1803, Nayhingen, Duchy of Wurtemberg, Germany, to Christopher Godfrey and Eberhardina (Kohler) Memminger. M. 1832 to Mary Wilkinson. M. 1878 to Sarah A. Wilkinson. Ch. eight. D. March 7, 1888, Charleston, South Carolina.

Soon after Christopher Gustavus Memminger was born, his father was killed, and his mother and maternal grandparents emigrated to Charleston, South Carolina. Orphaned at the age of four, Memminger was placed in the Charleston Orphan House, where he remained until the age of nine, when he was placed in the home of Thomas Bennett, later governor of South Carolina. He attended South Carolina College, graduating in 1820. He studied law and was admitted to the bar in 1825.

Active in politics, Memminger opposed the doctrine of nullification in a pamphlet, *The Book of Nullification* (1830). He served in the South Carolina legislature (1836–52 and from 1854). He supported slavery and was a member of the secession convention of South Carolina and a delegate to the convention at Montgomery, Alabama, where he served as chairman of the committee that drafted the provisional Confederate constitution. He served as secretary of the treasury for the Confederate government (1861–64).

In 1834 Memminger and W. J. Bennett began the reorganization of the public schools of South Carolina. From 1855 to 1888 he served as commissioner of the public schools of Charleston, South Carolina. He also served on the board of South Carolina College (later, University of South Carolina) for thirty-two years.

REFERENCES: *AC; DAB; NCAB* (4:200); *TC; WWW* (H).

Jaclyn S. Cohen

MERIAM, Junius Lathrop. B. October 28, 1872, Randolph, Ohio, to Theodore Frelinghuysen and Sarah (Adams) Meriam. M. July 30, 1907, to Mary McCoy Bone. Ch. two. D. June 29, 1960, Los Altos, California.

Junius L. Meriam was graduated with the A.B. degree (1895) from Oberlin (Ohio) College, the Pd.B. degree (1898) from New York State Normal College at Albany (later, State University of New York at Albany), the A.M. degree (1902) from Harvard University, and the Ph.D. degree (1905) from Columbia University.

Meriam was a township superintendent of schools and high school principal in Wakeman, Ohio, and was principal of the Spicer Elementary School in Akron, Ohio (1898–99). He was a critic teacher at the New York State Normal College (1899–1901), taught philosophy and education at Harvard University (1902–03), and was assistant in education at Columbia University (1903–04).

In 1904 he became professor of education and superintendent of university schools at the University of Missouri (1905–24). He also served as director of the Francis W. Parker School in San Diego, California (1921–22), and as director of the Glendora (California) Foothills School (1924). He was professor of education at the University of California at Los Angeles from 1924 to his retirement in 1943.

Meriam gained recognition through his writing, teaching, and work in experimental schools in elementary education. He was a critic of many practices of progressive schools and encouraged changing the traditional methods of teaching reading, writing, and arithmetic to instruction using activities appropriate to the interests of children.

Meriam was the author of *Normal School Education and Efficiency in Teaching* (1905), *Child Life and the Curriculum* (1920), *Catalog: Units of Work, Activities, Projects, etc. to 1932* (compiler with Alice E. Carey and Paul R. Hanna, *q.v.*, 1932), *Activities, Projects, Units of Work Cataloged, 1932–1939* (1943), and *The Traditional and Modern Curriculum, An Emerging Philosophy* (1960). He was a member of many professional associations.

REFERENCES: *LE* (III); *NCAB* (47:339).   *Walter J. Sanders*

MERRIAM, Charles Edward. B. November 15, 1874, Hopkinton, Iowa, to Charles Edward and Margaret Campbell (Kirkwood) Merriam. M. August 3, 1901, to Elizabeth Hilda Doyle. Ch. four. D. January 8, 1953, Rockville, Maryland.

Charles Edward Merriam's mother had been a schoolteacher in Scotland. Merriam was graduated from Lenox College in Hopkinton, Iowa, with the A.B. degree (1893) and the University of Iowa with the B.A. degree (1895) in economics and political science. He taught for a year at Lenox College and studied political theory at Columbia University where he received the M.A. (1897) and Ph.D. (1900) degrees. His thesis was published in 1900 as *The History of the Theory of Sovereignty since Rousseau*. He studied in Berlin, Germany, and Paris, France (1899–1900).

Merriam began teaching in the department of political science at the University of Chicago in 1900 and was chairman of the department from 1923 to his retirement in 1940. He was active in Chicago politics. He was a member of the charter convention in 1905 and helped to draft a new charter for the city. He investigated and reported on Chicago's revenues, served as secretary of the harbor commission, and was a member of the city council (1909–11 and 1913–17). He was instrumental in creating a commission that exposed large-scale graft in Chicago. Merriam won the Republican nomination for the mayoralty race in 1911 but lost the election the following year. He was important in the establishment of the city Bureau of Public Efficiency.

Merriam became vice-chairman of President Herbert Hoover's Research Committee on Social Trends in 1929 and served in Franklin Roosevelt's administration on the National Resources Board from 1933 until the board was discontinued in 1943.

He was the author of *A History of American Political Theories* (1903), *Primary Elections* (1909), *American Political Ideas: 1865–1917* (1921), *The American Party System* (1922), *Non-Voting* (with H. F. Gosnell, 1924), *New Aspects of Politics* (1925), *Four American Party Leaders* (1926), *Chicago: A More Intimate View of Urban Politics* (1929), *The Making of Citizens* (1931), *Political Power* (1934), *What Is Democracy?* (1941), *On the Agenda of Democracy* (1941), *Public and Private Government* (1944), and *Systematic Politics* (1945). He was the editor of *History of Political Theories* (with others, 1924), *Chicago* (1926), *The Written Constitution* (1931), *Metropolitan Region of Chicago* (with others, 1933), *Civic Education in the United States* (1934), *Role of Politics in Social Change* (1936), *The New Democracy and the New Despotism* (1939), *Prologue to Politics* (1939), and *The American Government* (with Robert E. Merriam, 1954).

Merriam was a member of the Social Science Research Council (president, 1924–27), the American Political Science Association (president, 1924–25), and other organizations. He was awarded the Commendatore della Corona from Italy and received five honorary degrees from American universities. He was a brother of John Campbell Merriam *(q.v.)*.

REFERENCES: *CB* (February 1947); *LE* (II); *NCAB* (D:435); *WWW* (III); *NYT*, January 9, 1953, p. 21.   *Thomas Meighan*

MERRIAM, John Campbell. B. October 20, 1869, Hopkinton, Iowa, to Charles Edward and Margaret Campbell (Kirkwood) Merriam. M. December 22, 1896, to Ada Gertrude Little. M. February 20, 1941, to Margaret Louise Webb. Ch. three. D. October 30, 1945, Oakland, California.

John Campbell Merriam received the B.S. (1887) degree from Lenox College in Hopkinton, Iowa, and the Ph.D. degree (1893) from the University of Munich, Germany. He taught paleontology and historical geology at the University of California (1894–1920) and served as dean of faculties at California in 1920. He was chairman of the National Research

Council (1919) and president of the Carnegie Institution in Washington, D.C. (1920–38).

Merriam was a prolific writer whose publications include works on paleontology, geology, and scientific research and subjects in education, including *Function of Educational Institutions in the Development of Research* (1920), *The Research Spirit in the Everyday Life of the Average Man* (1920), *Common Aims of Culture and Research in the University* (1922), *The Place of Education in a Research Institution* (1925), *The Responsibility of the Federal and State Governments for Recreation* (1926), *International Cooperation in Historical Research* (1926), *The Place of Geology among the Sciences* (1929), *Natural Phenomena as Sources of Inspiration and Education* (1929), *Significance of the Border Area between the Natural and the Social Sciences* (1930), *Responsibility of Science to Government* (1934), *Science and Human Values: Time and Change in History* (1936), and *The Most Important Methods of Promoting Research, as Seen by Research Foundations and Institutions* (1937).

Merriam was a regent of the Smithsonian Institution (1928–45), a fellow of the American Association for the Advancement of Science (president, Pacific Division, 1919–20), the Geological Society of America (president, 1910), and the American Paleontology Society (president, 1917), and a member of many other scientific and professional organizations. He was a member of the Presidential Science Advisory Board (1933–35), corresponding member of the London Zoological Society, and chairman of Michelsens Institute in Bergen, Norway. He was an honorary member of the Society of Geography and History of Guatemala and of several societies in Mexico. He was president of the executive committee of the Pan-American Institute of Geography and History (1935–38). He received honorary degrees from many colleges and universities. He was a brother of Charles Edward Merriam *(q.v.)*.

REFERENCES: *CB* (December 1945); *DAB;* (supp. 3); *DSB; LE* (II); *NCAB* (A:485); *WWW* (II); *NYT,* October 31, 1945, p. 23.

Lawrence S. Master

MERRIFIELD, Webster. B. July 27, 1852, Williamsville, Vermont, to John A. and Louisa W. Merrifield. M. June 26, 1902, to Elizabeth (McBride) Bull. Ch. none. D. January 2, 1916, Pasadena, California.

Webster Merrifield received his early education at Cushman Academy in Bernardston, Vermont, and Wilbraham (Massachusetts) Academy. He attended Yale College where he received the B.A. degree (1877).

Merrifield was a teacher in a private school at Newburgh, New York (1877–79). He was a tutor at Yale College (1879–83). He moved to Grand Forks, North Dakota, and the University of North Dakota in 1883, where he helped to organize the institution and became professor of Latin and

Greek and later professor of political and social science. The first students were admitted to the university in 1888. In 1891 he became president of the University of North Dakota and professor of economics. While he was president, the student enrollment tripled, the faculty increased from thirteen to sixty-one members, and the budget was greatly increased. He was a founder of the state high school board, and he initiated state examinations for North Dakota high schools.

Merrifield was a member of the American Economic Association, the American Academy of Political and Social Science, and the National Association of State University Presidents. He received honorary degrees from Yale University and the University of North Dakota.

REFERENCES: *NCAB* (17:278); *WWW* (I); *NYT,* January 23, 1916, p. 17. *Joan Duff Kise*

MERRILL, George Arthur. B. September 9, 1866, South Portland, Maine, to Henry Franklin and Aurelia Maria (Grant) Merrill. M. June 11, 1895, to Sarah Elizabeth McKie. Ch. three. D. November 30, 1944, Redwood City, California.

George A. Merrill completed his preparatory education at Boys' High School in San Francisco, California. He received the B.S. degree (1888) from the University of California and also spent a year of postgraduate study there (1893–94).

He was an instructor of science in 1888 at Cogswell Polytechnical College in San Francisco, the first institution of its kind west of Chicago, Illinois. He became head of the department of science (1890), vice-principal of the college (1890–92), and principal (1892–93).

He was asked by the regents of the University of California to plan the curriculum and to organize a school of mechanical arts in San Francisco. He was appointed president of the Lick School of Mechanical Arts in 1894, the Wilmerding School of Industrial Arts in 1900, the Lux School of Industrial Training in 1913, and the Dey Endowment in 1925, called the Lick-Wilmerding-Lux Schools. The Wilmerding School combined vocational training with academic studies and was the fourth of its kind in the United States. The Lux School was established in 1913 under the direction of Mrs. Charles Lux, widow of a California cattle raiser and financed by a bequest on her death. He retired as head of the schools in 1939.

Merrill was active in the California Teachers Association, was credited with early advocacy of the junior high school, and was said to have coined the term "junior high school" at a meeting of the association in 1908. He proposed a school of seventh and eighth grades where exploratory courses would be given to determine youngsters' capabilities for advanced work; the fundamental instruction would have been completed in the sixth grade.

His books include *An Introductory Course of Physical Measurements*

(1897), *Elementary Textbook of Theoretical Mechanics* (1899), *Electricity and Magnetism* (1905), and *Educating Youth in and Through the Practical Arts of Life* (1937).

Merrill was mayor of Redwood City, California (1908–16), and president of the draft board in San Mateo County, California, from July 1917 to March 1919. He was a member of several professional associations and was president of the Institute of Pacific Relations and the Commonwealth Club of California.

REFERENCES: *NCAB* (E:341); *WWAE* (I); *WWW* (IV); Roy W. Cloud, *Education in California* (Stanford, Cal.: Stanford University Press, 1952); *San Francisco Examiner,* December 1, 1944, p. 13.

Edward B. Goellner

MERRILL, Helen Abbot. B. March 30, 1864, Orange, New Jersey, to George and Emily Dodge (Abbot) Merrill. M. no. D. May 1, 1949, Wellesley, Massachusetts.

Helen Abbot Merrill attended public schools in Newburyport, Massachusetts, and New Brunswick, New Jersey. She entered Wellesley (Massachusetts) College and received the B.A. degree (1886). She studied at the University of Chicago, University of Göttingen, Germany, and Yale University, where she received the Ph.D. degree (1903).

She taught at Classon School for Girls in New York City (1886–91) and at Walnut Lane School in Philadelphia (1891–93). In 1893 she joined the Wellesley College faculty as an instructor of mathematics and taught there until she retired in 1932. She was chairman of the mathematics department (1916–32) and in 1931 was made Lewis Atterbury Stimson Professor.

Merrill was the author of *The Elements of the Theory of Functions* (n.d.) and *Mathematical Excursions* (1933), which presents mathematics in popular form, and she coauthored with Clara E. Smith *Selected Topics from College Algebra* (1914) and *First Course in Higher Algebra* (1917). She was a member of professional associations, including the American Association for the Advancement of Science, the Mathematical Association of America (vice-president and trustee), and the American Mathematical Society (vice-president, 1919).

REFERENCES: *NAW; NCAB* (42:171); *NYT,* May 3, 1949, p. 25.

Janet Durand Thomas

MESERVE, Charles Francis. B. July 15, 1850, North Abington, Massachusetts, to Charles and Susanna (Blanchard) Meserve. M. December 19, 1878, to Abbie Mary Whittier. M. May 16, 1900, to Julia Frances Philbrick. Ch. two. D. April 20, 1936, Raleigh, North Carolina.

Charles Francis Meserve attended local public schools and worked as a shoemaker with his father (1864–69). He attended the Classical Institute in

Waterville, Maine, and Colby University (later, College) in Waterville, where he received the A.B. (1877) and A.M. (1880) degrees.

Meserve was principal of the high school at Rockland, Massachusetts (1877–85), and the Oak Street School in Springfield, Massachusetts (1885–89). He was superintendent of Haskell Institute (1889–94), a federal government Indian industrial training school at Lawrence, Kansas. In 1894 he became president of Shaw University at Raleigh, North Carolina, serving to his retirement in 1920.

In 1896 Meserve was a special agent for the National Indian Rights Association of Philadelphia. He made an investigation for the Dawes Commission with the Indians in the Indian Territory and reported favorably on his studies. Meserve was a frequent public speaker on problems of Indians and blacks. He served as a trustee of Shaw University and was recording secretary of the Lake Mohawk Conference of Friends of the Indians and Other Dependent People. He was awarded an honorary degree by Colby University in 1899.

REFERENCES: *LE* (I); *NCAB* (26: 355); *NYT*, April 22, 1936, p. 23; *TC; WWW* (I).

John F. Ohles

MESSER, Asa. B. May 31, 1769, Methuen, Massachusetts, to Asa and Abiah (Whittier) Messer. M. May 11, 1797, to Deborah Angell. Ch. four. D. October 11, 1836, Providence, Rhode Island.

Asa Messer grew up on his father's farm and at the age of thirteen became a clerk in a wholesale grocery in Haverhill, Massachusetts. He prepared for college at an academy in Windham, New Hampshire, and under the Reverend Hezekiah Smith, pastor of the Baptist church in Haverhill, and the Reverend William Williams of Wrentham, Massachusetts. He entered Rhode Island College as a sophomore in June 1788 and was graduated with honors in 1790. He was licensed to preach by the First Baptist Church of Providence in 1792 and was ordained in 1801; he occasionally engaged in preaching.

Messer was chosen tutor of Rhode Island College in 1791. He became professor of the learned languages (1798) and of mathematics and natural philosophy in 1799. On September 2, 1802, at the age of thirty-three, Messer was made acting president of the college and became president in 1804, the year that the institution took the name of Brown University from Nicholas Brown, college treasurer and benefactor. He resigned the presidency in 1826 and lived on a farm near Providence.

Messer was a capable college president and a leading citizen of the state. He was an excellent financial manager, and the college progressed under his administration. After 1826 he was an alderman in Providence for many years and an unsuccessful gubernatorial candidate in 1830.

Messer received two patents for inventions on mill parts. He was awarded honorary degrees from Harvard and Yale universities and the University of Vermont.

REFERENCES: AC; DAB; NCAB (8:21); *TC; WWW* (H).

Joseph P. Cangemi
Thomas E. Kesler

MEYER, Adolf. B. September 13, 1866, Niederwenigen, Switzerland, to Rudolf and Anna (Walder) Meyer. M. September 15, 1902, to Mary Potter Brooks. Ch. one. D. March 17, 1950, Baltimore, Maryland.

After graduation from the Zurich (Switzerland) Gymnasium, Adolf Meyer studied medicine at the University of Zurich. He was licensed as a physician in 1890 and studied with leading European neurologists and psychiatrists (1890–92). Meyer was awarded the M.D. degree (1892) from the University of Zurich.

Meyer emigrated to the United States in 1892, where he settled in Chicago, Illinois. He was appointed a fellow and lecturer in neurology at the University of Chicago. After serving as a pathologist at Illinois Eastern Hospital for the Insane, he was appointed pathologist at Worcester (Massachusetts) Insane Hospital and was a docent in psychiatry at Clark University in Worcester.

He improved the Worcester hospital's clinical efficiency and found he could not satisfactorily study pathology without including the living patient. He wrote *Critical Review of Data and General Methods and Deductions of Modern Neurology* (1898), which became the basis for teaching functional anatomy of the nervous system. He was director of the Pathology Institute of the New York State Hospital Service at Woods Island, where he organized the facility as a psychiatric institute and training center for clinical psychiatry.

Meyer taught psychiatry using a person-oriented case-study method; it became the model for case records. He was professor of psychiatry at Cornell University Medical College (1904–09) and was recognized as the foremost American scientific student of psychiatry.

Meyer was appointed professor of psychiatry (1910) and director (1913) of the new Henry Phipps Psychiatric Clinic of the Johns Hopkins University Hospital in Baltimore, Maryland, serving to his retirement in 1941. He instituted a curriculum that included psychiatric study and treatment apprenticeship. His method was based on the belief that diagnosis and understanding of psychopathological disease processes requires traditional clinical investigation and a complete review of the patient's life experiences. He introduced concepts of personality functions that focus on child development into undergraduate medical education and established rationale and methods for teaching care of the person, not just the disease.

Meyer pioneered in the use of audiovisual materials, including glass and plasticine nervous system models, for psychiatric education. Active in many professional societies and editor of several journals, he promoted psychiatric social services and coined the term "mental hygiene."

Meyer wrote many journal articles. His *Collected Papers* (four volumes, 1950–52) and *Psychobiology* (1957) were published posthumously. He was president of the American Neurology Association (1922), the American Psychiatric Association (1927), and the American Psychopathology Association (1912 and 1916) and was a member of the Academie der Naturforscher zu Halle and corresponding member of several societies in France and the Sociedad Neurologia y Psiquiatria in Buenos Aires, Argentina. He received honorary degrees from American and European universities.

REFERENCES: *EB; DAB* (supp. 4); *LE* (I); *NCAB* (38:45, E:26); *WWW* (II), *NYT,* March 18, 1950, p. 13. *Daniel J. Delaney*

MEYER, Adolphe Erich. B. October 15, 1897, New York, New York, to Adolphe and Frieda (Schelker) Meyer. M. 1924 to Margaret Holt McDonald. M. 1942 to Jesse Bryant. Ch. two.

Adolphe E. Meyer attended New York University in New York City, where he received the B.S. (1921), A.M. (1922), and Ph.D. (1926) degrees.

Meyer was an instructor of German at New York University (1922–28) and continued there instructing in education from 1928 to his retirement in 1963. He was a visiting professor of education at the University of Illinois (1965–67) and Distinguished Professor of Education at Old Dominion University in Norfolk, Virginia (1967–68).

A noted educational historian, Meyer wrote *Public Education in Modern Europe* (1927), *Education in Modern Times* (1931), *John Dewey and Modern Education* (1932), *Modern European Educators* (1934), *Development of Education in the Twentieth Century* (1939), *Voltaire—Man of Justice* (1945), *An Educational History of the American People* (1957), and *An Educational History of the Western World* (1965), and he coauthored *Becoming an Educator* (1963) and *Grandmasters of Educational Thought* (1975). He translated with H. Bernstein *Phantom Lover* by Georg Kaiser (1929) and was a contributor in history to the *Encyclopaedia Britannica* (1958–59).

REFERENCES: *LE* (III); *WW* (XXXVIII); *Directory of American Scholars* 3d ed. (New York: R. R. Bowker, 1957). *Abraham Blinderman*

MEZES, Sidney Edward. B. September 23, 1863, Belmont, California, to Simon Monserrate and Juliet Janin (Johnson) Mezes. M. December 10, 1896, to Annie Olive Hunter. Ch. none. D. September 10, 1931, Altadena, California.

Sidney Edward Mezes was an accomplished linguist during his early years. He attended St. Matthews Hall in San Mateo, California, and was graduated with the B.S. degree (1884) from the University of California. He enrolled at Harvard University and received the A.B. (1890), A.M. (1891), and Ph.D. (1893) degrees.

He taught at both Bryn Mawr (Pennsylvania) College and the University of Chicago (1893–94) before accepting a teaching position in philosophy at the University of Texas at Austin in 1894. He was dean of the college of arts (1902–08). He served as president of the University of Texas (1902–14). In 1914 Mezes was selected as president of the College of the City of New York (CCNY), a position he held until his retirement in March 1927.

In his early years as a teacher, Mezes was recognized as one of the ablest philosophic thinkers in the nation, but he made his greatest contribution as a college administrator. Under his leadership both the University of Texas and CCNY experienced improved internal organization, expanded programs, improved physical plant, and increased student enrollment. At the request of his brother-in-law, Edward House, Mezes was appointed by President Woodrow Wilson in 1917 director of a large task force of experts to collect data to be used at the peace conference at the conclusion of World War I. He served as chief of the territorial division of the American commission to negotiate the peace in 1919.

Mezes was the author of portions of *The Conception of God* (by Josiah Royce, 1897) and wrote *Ethics: Descriptive and Explanatory* (1901). His observations and impressions of the Paris Peace Conference are included in *What Really Happened at Paris* (1921). He was a fellow of the American Association for the Advancement of Science and received the French Legion of Honor and several honorary degrees.

REFERENCES: *DAB; NCAB* (15:206, 30:346); *WWW* (I); *NYT,* September 12, 1931, p. 17.   *Fred W. Tanner*

MIES VAN DER ROHE, Ludwig. B. March 27, 1886, Aachen, Germany, to n.a. M. no. D. August 17, 1969, Chicago, Illinois.

Ludwig Mies van der Rohe was educated at the Cathedral School in Aachen, Germany (1897–1900), and also attended a trade school for two years. He did not receive a formal education in architecture, but was apprenticed at the age of fifteen and worked as a draftsman for designers and architects.

Mies moved to Berlin, Germany, in 1905 and worked for a short time as an architect designing in wood and served as an apprentice to the leading furniture designer Bruno Paul (1905–07). He designed and built his first house in 1907 and was apprenticed to architect Peter Behrens (1908–11). From 1912 to 1914, he worked in The Hague, the Netherlands, and served in the German army in World War I (1914–18). After the war, he was engaged in the design of buildings that attracted international attention. He was director of the Bauhaus School of Modern Design in Dessau, Germany, in 1930 and, under pressure from the Nazis, moved the school to Berlin in 1932 and closed it in 1933.

Mies visited the United States in 1937 and returned in 1938 as professor of architecture and director of the architecture department at the Armour Institute of Technology in Chicago, Illinois. He continued in his position with the merger of the Armour Institute and Lewis Institute into the Illinois Institute of Technology and exerted a major influence on architecture with his urban structures.

A fellow of the American Institute of Architects and the American Academy of Arts and Sciences, Mies was a member of many other American and foreign organizations. He received many awards, including the medal of honor of the Seventh Congress of Pan-American Architects, the award of merit of the Ruskin Society of America, and the Feltrinelli International Prize for Architecture in Rome, Italy. He was awarded the presidential Medal of Freedom and several honorary degrees from American and foreign colleges and universities.

REFERENCES: *CB* (October 1951); *EB; NYT,* August 19, 1969, p. 1; *WWW* (V); "Ludwig Mies van der Rohe: 1886–1969," *Architectural Record* 146 (September 1969): 9; *Time,* August 29, 1969, pp. 46–47.

John F. Ohles

MILES, Manly. B. July 20, 1826, Homer, New York, to Manly and Mary (Cushman) Miles. M. February 15, 1851, to Mary E. Dodge. Ch. none. D. February 15, 1898, Lansing, Michigan.

At the age of eleven, Manly Miles moved with his family to Flint, Michigan, where he attended the common schools. He was graduated from Rush Medical College in Chicago, Illinois, with the M.D. degree (1850).

Miles practiced medicine in Flint, Michigan, to 1859 when he became the assistant state geologist and in 1861 was appointed the first professor of animal physiology and zoology at Michigan State Agricultural College (later, Michigan State University) in Lansing. He became the first professor of practical agriculture in the country in 1865, when the college established a course in agriculture with Miles as the professor. He was professor of agriculture at the University of Illinois (1875–78), conducted research at the Houghton Farm in Mountainville, New York (1878–80), and was professor of agriculture at Massachusetts Agricultural College (later, University of Massachusetts) at Amherst (1880–86). He returned to Lansing, Michigan, in 1886, where he studied, wrote, and conducted experiments to his death in 1898.

Manly was the author of several books, including *Stock-Breeding* (1879), *Experiments with Indian Corn* (1882), *Silos, Ensilage, and Silage* (1889), and *Land Draining* (1892). He was a fellow of the American Association for the Advancement of Science and the Royal Microscopical Society, and a member of other organizations.

REFERENCES: *DAB; NCAB* (15:243); *Popular Science* 54 (April 1899): 834–41.   *John F. Ohles*

MILLER, Edwin Lillie. B. January 9, 1868, Aurora, Illinois, to Robert and Mary (Lillie) Miller. M. July 19, 1920, to Gertrude Margaret Doyle. Ch. none. D. August 21, 1934, Detroit, Michigan.

Edwin L. Miller was graduated from the University of Michigan with the A.B. (1890) and A.M. (1891) degrees. He was principal of the high school in Hancock, Michigan (1891–92), and an English teacher in Englewood High School in Chicago, Illinois (1891–1907). He moved to Detroit, Michigan, in 1907 as head of the English department and assistant principal of the Detroit Central High School, where he remained to 1914.

Miller was the principal of Detroit's Northwestern (1914–20) and Northern (1920–22) high schools. From 1922 to 1925 he was supervising principal of Detroit high schools and in 1925 became assistant superintendent of schools; he remained in the position until his death. Throughout his career, Miller was interested in the study and teaching of English and worked to improve both.

Miller published extensively. His best-known books were English textbooks, including *Practical English Composition* (books 1-4, 1914–16), *English Literature—A Guide to the Best Reading* (1917), *New English Composition* (books 1-4, 1927–30), and *Explorations in Literature: American Writers* (1933). He contributed to various yearbooks and published in many professional journals. He was general editor of Lippincott's English Classics Series.

A member of professional associations, Miller was an organizer of the Chicago English Club and active in the Middle-Western Association of Teachers of English, both of which were forerunners of the National Council of Teachers of English (NCTE). Miller was a founder (1911) and president (1917–19) of NCTE and also president of the Michigan State Federation of Teachers' Clubs (1915–19), the Michigan State Teachers' Association (1923), and the North Central Association of Colleges and Secondary Schools (1924–25).

REFERENCES: *LE* (I); *NCAB* (25:54); *NYT,* August 22, 1934, p. 17; *WWAE* (III); *WWW* (I); "In Memory of Edwin L. Miller," *English Journal* 24 (February 1935): 140.   *Earl W. Thomas*

MILLER, Kelly. B. July 23, 1863, Winnsboro, South Carolina, to Kelly and Elizabeth (Roberts) Miller. M. July 17, 1894, to Annie May Butler. Ch. five. D. December 29, 1939, Washington, D.C.

Kelly Miller's mother was a slave and his father was a free black and a tenant farmer who served in the Confederate army during the Civil War. Miller was educated in a one-room school and at Fairfield Institute in

Winnsboro, South Carolina. He was awarded a scholarship to Howard University in Washington, D.C., where he attended the academy and was graduated from the university in 1886 and received the A.M. degree (1901). He engaged in postgraduate studies at Johns Hopkins University in Baltimore, Maryland (1887–89).

He taught mathematics in a Washington (D.C.) high school and joined the faculty at Howard University as a teacher of mathematics and, from 1918, sociology. He was dean of the college of arts and sciences (1907–18). He was the author of many pamphlets and books on racial issues, including *The Education of the Negro* (1902), *Forty Years of Negro Education* (1908), *Race Adjustment* (1908), *Progress and Achievements of the Colored People* (with Joseph R. Gay, 1913), *Out of the House of Bondage* (1914), *An Appeal to Conscience* (1918), *Our War for Human Rights* (1919), *Education of the Negro in the North* (1921), and *The Everlasting Stain* (1924). He assisted W. E. B. Du Bois *(q.v.)* in editing *Crisis* and was the first black academician to write a weekly column in black newspapers. He unsuccessfully sought to unify black organizations during the 1920s.

A member of many scholarly and professional organizations, Miller received honorary degrees from Howard, Wilberforce, and Virginia Union universities.

REFERENCES: *DAB* (supp. 2); *NYT,* December 30, 1939, p. 15; *WWW* (II); *Journal of Negro Education* 9 (October 1940): 647–48; Harry A. Ploski and Ernest Kaiser, eds., *AFRO-USA* (New York: Bellwether, 1971).

John F. Ohles

MILLER, Leslie William. B. August 5, 1848, Brattleboro, Vermont, to Nathan and Hannah (Works) Miller. M. October 29, 1874, to Maria Persons. Ch. two. D. March 7, 1931, Martha's Vineyard, Massachusetts.

While working at his father's harness shop from the age of twelve, Leslie William Miller acquired a knowledge of Latin and other high school subjects through self-instruction. He worked in a japanning factory in Orange, Massachusetts, painting baby carriages and sewing machines. Because of an interest in art, he moved to Boston to attend a drawing school at night. He was a student in the first classes held in the School of Drawing and Painting in the Museum of Fine Arts. He attended the Massachusetts Normal Art School, from which he was graduated in 1875.

He taught in the Salem (Massachusetts) Normal School and at Adams Academy in Quincy, Massachusetts. He taught painting at the Summer Institute in Martha's Vineyard in 1879. Miller became acquainted with Walter Smith, who had established a school of industrial art for the state of Massachusetts. Smith recommended Miller to reorganize the School of Industrial Art in Philadelphia (1880–1920). Miller assumed leadership of the institution with a handful of students and little equipment, and he guided the school to become one of the leading institutions in the field. He was a lecturer on art at Swarthmore (Pennsylvania) College.

Miller was the author of *Essentials of Perspective* (1887) and many articles on art and industrial education. He was active in the Municipal Art Jury of Philadelphia (secretary and vice-president, 1912–20). He was a member of many other organizations and served as secretary and vice-president of the Art Club of Philadelphia. He received the gold medal from the Art Club of Philadelphia (1920) and received honorary degrees from the University of Pennsylvania and Temple University.

REFERENCES: *DAB; WWW* (I); *NYT*, March 8, 1931, sec. 2, p. 8.

Bruce D. Mattson

MILLER, Paul Gerard. B. January 23, 1875, Pickett, Wisconsin, to John and Julia Anne Miller. M. November 9, 1899, to Ella A. Rasmussen. Ch. three. D. May 21, 1952, Winneconne, Wisconsin.

Paul Miller was graduated from the teacher preparation course at the State Normal School (later, University of Wisconsin—Oshkosh) in Oshkosh, Wisconsin, and attended the University of Wisconsin where he received the B.A. (1910), M.A. (1911), and Ph.D. (1914) degrees.

In 1898 Miller fought in the Spanish-American War and participated in a Puerto Rican expedition. He remained in Puerto Rico until 1908, serving as supervisor of the San German schools (1899–1902), superintendent of schools in San Juan (1902), and chief of the division of supervision of the Puerto Rico Department of Education (1903–08). He was principal of the Insular Normal School (1903–08).

On his return to the United States, Miller taught Romance languages at the University of Wisconsin (1908–10 and 1911–15) and was professor of education at Carleton College in Northfield, Minnesota (1910–11). Miller returned to Puerto Rico to serve as the commissioner of education from 1915 until 1921 and played an important role in the development of the island's schools. He worked for Rand McNally & Company (1921–47).

Miller edited several Spanish-American editions of literary classics and was the author of *Historia de Puerto Rico* (1922), *Spanish-American Readers,* and six annual reports, *Education in Puerto Rico.*

Miller was a member of the Executive Council of Puerto Rico (1915–21) and the Public Service Commission (1917–21), president of the Teachers' Pension Fund Board (1917–21), president of the board of trustees of the University of Puerto Rico, and a delegate from Puerto Rico to the Second Pan-American Scientific Congress in Washington, D.C. (1915–16). He received an honorary degree from the University of Puerto Rico in 1940.

REFERENCES: *LE* (III); *WWW* (III); *NYT*, May 22, 1952, p. 27; *School and Society* 75 (May 31, 1952): 351.   *Audrey Potter*

MILLIKAN, Robert Andrews. B. March 22, 1868, Morrison, Illinois, to Silas Franklin and Mary Jane (Andrews) Millikan. M. April 10, 1902, to Greta Irvin Blanchard. Ch. three. D. December 19, 1953, Pasadena, California.

Robert Andrews Millikan grew up on a farm at Maquoketa, Iowa, where his family had moved in 1873. He was graduated from high school in 1885 and attended Oberlin (Ohio) College, where he received the A.B. (1891) and M.A. (1893) degrees. He received the Ph.D. degree (1895) from Columbia University. He traveled to Europe, where he contacted scientists who were making the fundamental discoveries that laid the foundations of modern physics.

Millikan taught physics at Oberlin College from his junior year and became an assistant in physics at the University of Chicago on his return from Europe in 1896. He served at Chicago until 1921, when he became director of the Norman Bridge Institute and chairman of the executive council (equivalent of president) of the California Institute of Technology (formerly, Throop College of Technology) at Pasadena, California. Millikan's organizational efforts served as a model for engineering education. He established an endowment for the institute and introduced fundamental science and humanities courses as the basis of the engineering programs of study. He developed the Norman Bridge Laboratory of Physics and the Jet Propulsion Laboratory.

An outstanding research scientist, Millikan isolated and measured the electron and studied the nature of the photoelectric effect that had been discovered and described by Albert Einstein. He was awarded the Nobel Prize for Physics in 1923. In California he opened the cosmic radiation field of study.

Millikan was the author of *A Course of College Experiments in Physics* (1898), *Mechanics, Molecular Physics and Heat* (1903), *A First Course in Physics* (1906), *A Laboratory Course in Physics for Secondary Schools* (with Henry Gale, 1906), *Electricity, Sound and Light* (with John Mills, 1908), *The Electron* (1917), *Science and Life* (1923), *Evolution of Science and Religion* (1927), *A First Course in Physics for Colleges* (1928), *Science and the New Civilization* (1930), *Time, Matter, and Values* (1932), *Electrons, Protons, Photons, Neutrons and Cosmic Rays* (1935), *New Elementary Physics* (1936), *Mechanics, Molecular Physics, Heat and Sound* (1937), *Cosmic Rays* (1939), and *Autobiography* (1950). He became editor of the *Proceedings of the National Academy of Sciences* in 1916 and was associate editor of the *Physical Review* (1903–16).

A fellow of the American Academy of Arts and Sciences and the American Association for the Advancement of Science (president, 1929), Millikan was a member of many American and over twenty foreign honorary societies and was decorated by the governments of France, China, and

Chile, and received the United States Medal of Merit (1947). He was the recipient of many awards and medals and of twenty-five honorary degrees from American and foreign colleges and universities.

REFERENCES: *CB* (June 1952); *DSB; NCAB* (42:1); *NYT,* December 20, 1953, p. 1; *WWW* (III); L. A. DuBridge, "Robert Andrews Millikan: 1868–1953," *Science* 119 (February 26, 1954): 272–74; Lee A. DuBridge and Paul S. Epstein, "Robert Andrews Millikan," *Biographical Memoirs of the National Academy of Sciences* 33 (1959): 241–82; Robert A. Millikan, *The Autobiography of Robert A. Millikan* (New York: Prentice-Hall, 1950).   *Kim Sebaly*

MILLS, Caleb. B. July 29, 1806, Dunbarton, New Hampshire, to Caleb and Tamar (Cheney) Mills. M. September 13, 1833, to Sarah Marshall. Ch. seven. D. October 17, 1879, Crawfordsville, Indiana.

Caleb Mills grew up on a farm, attended Pembroke (New Hampshire) Academy, and was graduated from Dartmouth College in Hanover, New Hampshire, with the A.B. degree (1828). He was graduated from Andover (Massachusetts) Theological Seminary in 1833 and was ordained in the Presbyterian church in 1835.

With his wife and four teachers he moved from New Hampshire to Crawfordsville, Indiana, in 1833 where he founded Wabash College. Mills was principal of the preparatory and normal schools at Wabash (1835–41 and 1857–58), professor of Greek (1841–54 and 1858–76), and librarian (1839–55 and 1876–79).

Mills was the author of a series of anonymous messages in 1846 to the state legislature pointing out the widespread illiteracy in the state and outlining plans for the establishment, support, and operation of free public schools. Because of these efforts, he is called the Father of Public School Education in Indiana. The first law for public schools in the state was passed in 1848. In 1854 Mills was elected the second state superintendent of public instruction in Indiana. During his two-year term, he stressed the need for better teacher training and for the creation of normal schools to train teachers.

He received honorary degrees from Franklin and Dartmouth colleges.

REFERENCES: *NCAB* (38:500); Fassett A. Cotton *(q.v.), Education in Indiana (1793 to 1934)* (Bluffton, Ind.: Progress Publishing Co., 1934); Ralph L. Worley, "Caleb Mills and the Indiana School System" (Thesis, Indiana State University, 1934); Charles W. Moores, *Caleb Mills and the Indiana School System* (Indianapolis: Wood-Weaver, 1905).

David Alan Gilman

MILLS, Susan Lincoln Tolman. B. November 18, 1825, Enosburg, Vermont, to John and Elizabeth (Nichols) Tolman. M. September 11, 1848, to Cyrus Taggert Mills. Ch. none. D. December 12, 1912, Oakland, California.

Susan Lincoln Tolman Mills attended the public schools in Ware, Massachusetts, and a seminary in West Brookfield, Massachusetts. She was graduated from Mount Holyoke Seminary (later, College) in South Hadley, Massachusetts (1845), and remained there as a teacher under Mary Lyon *(q.v.)* for three years (1845–48).

In 1848 she married Cyrus Mills and went with him on a missionary tour in Ceylon where he was head of the Batticotta College in Jaffna, a school for boys, and she taught domestic science to local girls. Health problems and lack of help led to frustration and their return to the United States in 1854. Reverend Mills lectured, served as a pastor in Berkshire, New York, and engaged in business while his wife recovered her health.

In 1860 they went to Hawaii to teach. Mills's husband became president of Oahu College in Honolulu where she taught geography, geology, chemistry, and botany. In 1864 they returned to the United States and bought the Young Ladies Seminary in Benicia, California, in 1865 with Cyrus Mills serving as head of the institution and Susan Mills as his assistant. When he died in 1884, she took over as president and treasurer. The school grew and in 1871 was moved to Seminary Park, a new campus outside of Oakland, California. The institution was incorporated in 1877 and was renamed Mills College and chartered in 1885 with Homer Baxter Sprague as president and Susan Mills as treasurer and principal of the seminary. In 1887 Charles Carroll Sprague was chosen president. In 1890 Mills assumed the presidency, and the college gradually recovered from internal problems that had arisen in the transition from a seminary. From 1906 the seminary was systematically phased out. For a time, Mills College was the only women's college on the West Coast. Mills retired from the presidency in 1909.

Susan Mills was active in educational, missionary, and other organizations. She received an honorary degree from Mount Holyoke College in 1901.

REFERENCES: *DAB; NAW; NCAB* (19:438); *TC; WWW* (I); Elias O. James, *The Story of Cyrus and Susan Mills* (Stanford, Cal.: Stanford University Press, 1953); *NYT*, December 14, 1912, p. 15.   *Karen Wertz*

MINER, Myrtilla. B. March 4, 1815, Brookfield, New York, to Seth and Eleanor (Smith) Miner. M. no. D. December 17, 1864, Washington, D.C.

Myrtilla Miner, white promoter of education for black women prior to the Civil War, overcame poor health and poverty to receive an education and become a teacher. In 1844 she attended school and taught at the Female Domestic Seminary in Clinton, New York, where she promised to pay her tuition after she began teaching. Her first experience with blacks may have been with three young black girls especially enrolled at the school by the principal.

Miner taught at the Clover Street Seminary in Rochester, New York, and the Richmond Street School in Providence, Rhode Island (1844–46). She moved to Whiteville, Mississippi, where she taught at a slaveholders' school, the Newton Female Institute. This first experience with slavery shocked her.

For three years, she developed a plan to open a school for blacks, enlisting the support of two noted abolitionists, Harriet Beecher Stowe and her brother Henry Ward Beecher. A small group of abolitionist ministers and a Quaker philanthropist urged her to open the school in Washington, D.C., a stronghold of pro-slavery sentiment. Frederick Douglass opposed the school on the grounds that it might mean danger and possibly death for Miner.

Miss Miner's Colored Girls' School opened in 1851 in a small apartment in Washington with a capital fund of one hundred dollars. Enrollment grew from six to forty students in six months. Miner was placed under fierce criticism, threatened, and was almost burned out during the first ten years of the school. The school attracted national attention and many visitors, including President Millard Fillmore and his family, who visited regularly. Mary (Mrs. Horace) Mann taught grammar, and her niece taught art at the school.

The United States Congress incorporated Miner's school in 1863 as the Institution for the Education of Colored Youth in the District of Columbia. Miner died the following year. The school merged with Howard University in 1871, but was separated in 1876. In 1879, it came under the District of Columbia public school system as Miners Teachers College.

REFERENCES: *AC; DAB; NAW; NCAB* (12:185); *WWW* (H); Lillian Dabney, *The History of the Schools for Negroes in the District of Columbia 1807–1947* (Washington, D.C.: Catholic University of America, 1949); Ellen M. O'Connor, *Myrtilla Miner: A Memoir* (Boston: Houghton Mifflin, 1885); Lester G. Wells, "Myrtilla Miner," *New York History* 243 (July 1943): 358–75; G. Smith Wormley, "Myrtilla Miner," *Journal of Negro History* 5 (October 1920): 448–57.   *George J. Michel*

MINOR, John Barbee. B. June 2, 1813, Louisa County, Virginia, to Lancelot and Mary Overton (Thompkins) Minor. M. 1837 to Martha Macon Davis. M. 1859 to Anne Jacqueline Fisher Colston. M. to Ellen Temple Hill. Ch. nine. D. July 29, 1895, Charlottesville, Virginia.

At an early age, John Barbee Minor traveled through Virginia as a correspondent for Richmond newspapers and made acquaintance with some of the state's most distinguished citizens, including James Madison and James Monroe. After studying one year at Kenyon College (Ohio), Minor entered the academic department of the University of Virginia, where he received the LL.B. degree (1834).

Minor practiced law for six years in Buchanan, Virginia. In 1840 he moved back to Charlottesville, Virginia, and formed a law partnership with his brother Lucien, who was later a professor of law at the College of William and Mary. He taught law at the University of Virginia (1845–95), starting as the only member of the department. He led the law school to improved standards and attracted students and hired new faculty. He was a distinguished teacher and authority on common and statute law.

Minor was a supporter of the Union prior to the Civil War but sided with the Confederacy when President Abraham Lincoln issued a call for volunteers from Virginia. As a member of the home guard, he helped in receiving from Union army commanders guarantees that the university would not be destroyed when General Philip Sheridan passed through Charlottesville from his devastating valley campaign. Minor personally borrowed money to prepare for the reopening of the university in 1865.

Minor was the author of the monumental and authoritative *Institutes of Common and Statute Law* (1875–95), *The Virginia Report, 1799–1800* (1850), and *Exposition of the Law of Crimes and Punishments* (1894).

REFERENCES:*AC; DAB; NCAB* (20:144), *TC; WWW* (H); *NYT*, July 30, 1895, p. 3.   *Harold D. Lehman*

MINOT, Charles Sedgwick. B. December 23, 1852, West Roxbury, Massachusetts, to William and Katharine Maria (Sedgwick) Minot. M. June 1, 1889, to Lucy Fosdick. Ch. none. D. November 19, 1914, Milton, Massachusetts.

Charles Sedgwick Minot, biologist and educator, received his early education in Boston. At the age of sixteen, he entered the Massachusetts Institute of Technology and received the B.S. degree (1872). He obtained the D.Sc. degree in natural history from Harvard University (1878) after six years of independent study. Part of his time was spent in the physiological laboratory at Harvard Medical College with Henry P. Bowditch *(q.v.)*, and he also studied in Leipzig, Germany, and Paris, France, with Karl F. W. Ludwig and Louis-Antoine Ranvier. He returned home with fresh insights into the aims of the naturalist and methods of the science.

Minot was appointed to the Harvard faculty in 1880, first to the dental school and then to the medical school. He taught oral pathology and surgery and later became a professor of embryology and comparative anatomy (1892). He remained on the Harvard faculty to his death in 1914. He was credited with introducing new laboratory techniques in physiology and for establishing a collection of prepared sections of embryos that served as a model to other institutions. He invented the automatic rotary microtome to section embryos.

He was the author of *Human Embryology* (1892), *Bibliography of Vertebrate Embryology* (1893), *A Laboratory Textbook of Embryology* (1903), *The Problem of Age, Growth, and Death* (1908), and many articles and papers in scientific journals.

He was a founder of the American Society for Physical Research and a member of the American Academy of Arts and Sciences, the New York Academy of Sciences, the Philadelphia Academy of Arts and Sciences, the National Academy of Science, the British Association for the Advancement of Science, and other American and foreign associations. He was a fellow of the American Association for the Advancement of Science (secretary, 1885, vice-president of the biology section, 1890, president, 1901) and president of the American Society of Naturalists (1894), the Association of American Anatomists (1904–05), and the Boston Society of Natural History (1897–1914). He took part in the development of the Marine Biological Laboratory at Woods Hole (Massachusetts) and served as trustee (1888–1914). He received several honorary degrees.

REFERENCES: *AC; DAB; DSB; NCAB* (6:112); *TC; WWW* (I); *NYT,* November 21, 1914, p. 13.   *Richard M. Coger*

MITCHELL, Elmer Dayton. B. September 6, 1889, Negaunee, Michigan, to Samuel Sidney and Nellie (Morse) Mitchell. M. July 10, 1913, to Beulah Elizabeth Dillingham. Ch. two.

Elmer Dayton Mitchell, a leading figure in the development of the intramural sports movement in twentieth-century American education, received the A.B. (1912), A.M. (1919), and Ph.D. (1938) degrees from the University of Michigan.

He was a teacher and athletic director at Grand Rapids (Michigan) Union High School (1912–15) and athletic director and assistant professor of physical education at Michigan State Normal College (later, Eastern Michigan University) at Ypsilanti (1915–17). He returned to the University of Michigan as an athletic coach (1917–19), director of intramural athletics in 1919, and professor and chairman of the department of physical education, retiring in 1958. He invented the game of speedball in 1921.

A prolific writer, Mitchell authored, coauthored, and edited numerous books about play, sports, recreation, games, intramurals, and the history of physical education. Among them were *Intramural Athletics* (1925); *Theory of Organized Play* (1923) and *Practice of Organized Play* (1923), coauthored with Wilbur P. Bowen *(q.v.)*; and *Social Games for Recreation* (1935), *Active Games and Contests* (1939), and *Party Games for All* (1946), coauthored with Bernard S. Mason. He also coauthored *World History of Physical Education* (with Deobold B. Van Dalen and Bruce L. Bennett, 1953). Mitchell was editor of *Pentathalon* (1928–30) and *Journal of Health and Physical Education* (1930–43) and was founder and editor of the *Research Quarterly* (1930–43).

He was executive secretary of the American Association for Health, Physical Education and Recreation (1930–38) and president of the Michigan State Physical Education Association (1928) and the Intramural Directors Association (1924 and 1928). He received the honor award of the American Physical Education Association (1932), the Medal of Honor of the Ministry of Education and Health, Republic of Czechoslovakia (1939), and the Luther Halsey Gulick Award (1949), the highest honor given any member of the physical education profession.

REFERENCES: *LE* (III); *WW* (XXVIII); *WWAE* (XVIII); Norma Schwendener, *A History of Physical Education in the United States* (New York: A. S. Barnes and Co., 1942); Arthur Weston, *The Making of American Physical Education* (New York: Appleton-Century-Crofts, 1962). *Stratton F. Caldwell*

MITCHELL, Maria. B. August 1, 1818, Nantucket Island, Massachusetts, to William and Lydia (Coleman) Mitchell. M. no. D. June 28, 1889, Lynn, Massachusetts.

As a girl, Maria Mitchell assisted her father, a schoolmaster and astronomer, in rating chronometers for Nantucket's whaling fleet. She attended the local dame school, her father's school, and Cyrus Peirce's *(q.v.)* school.

In 1835, after working with Peirce, Mitchell opened a school for girls and in 1836 became librarian of the new Nantucket Atheneum, a position she held until 1856. Her father's observatory became a station for the United States Coast Survey, and in 1848 he was appointed to the visiting committee of the Harvard University observatory. Mitchell continued to work with her father and on October 1, 1847, using a two-inch telescope, she discovered a new comet. In 1852 Mitchell was given a five-inch telescope by Elizabeth Peabody *(q.v.)* as a gift from the women of America.

When Vassar College opened in Poughkeepsie, New York, Mitchell was appointed professor of astronomy (1865–88). At Vassar she was a pioneer in the photographic study of sunspots and the observation of Jupiter and Saturn and their moons. She used a twelve-inch telescope, at the time the third largest in the United States. Mitchell believed that women were natural observers and were well suited to study the natural sciences. She encouraged students to question and engage in independent research. She sought recognition of women's scientific abilities, application of scientific method to other fields, and an experimental approach to social problems.

Mitchell was one of the original computers of the *New American Ephemeris and Nautical Almanac* (1849). She was the first woman elected to the American Academy of Arts and Sciences (1848) and the American Philosophical Society (1869) and was vice-president of the American Social Science Association (1873). In 1850 she was elected to the American Association for the Advancement of Science. She founded the Association for the Advancement of Women (1873). She was awarded the Royal Danish medal for the discovery of a comet and received honorary degrees from

Hanover College and Columbia University.

REFERENCES: *AC; DAB; EB; NAW; NCAB* (5:236); *TC; WWW* (H); *NYT*, June 29, 1889, p. 5; Helen Wright, *Sweeper in the Sky* (Nantucket, Mass.: Nantucket Maria Mitchell Foundation, 1949).

Barbara Ruth Peltzman

MITCHELL, Samuel Augustus. B. March 20, 1792, Bristol, Connecticut, to William and Mary (Alton) Mitchell. M. August 1815 to Rhoda Ann Fuller. Ch. none. D. December 18, 1868, Philadelphia, Pennsylvania.

S. Augustus Mitchell, a major figure in the development of American geography, was a teacher who became dissatisfied with the presentations of geography textbooks of the day. He decided to write and publish geography materials and spent forty years in Philadelphia developing textbooks, maps, and manuals of geography. The demand for his works was great, and he employed a large staff to manufacture the books, which had many editions and revisions.

Mitchell employed J. H. Young as the engraver of his early maps, which were of a fine quality. Because people were interested in the newer parts of the country, there was a market for travel maps and guidebooks, which Mitchell produced along with school materials. He presented geography accurately to students and adapted the texts to the progressive capabilities of students.

He published *A New American Atlas* (1831) and maps of separate sections of the United States. A series of Tourists' Pocket Maps was begun in 1834 and was supplemented by *Reference and Distance Map of the United States* (1836). He also produced *Mitchell's Traveller's Guide through the United States* (1832), *An Accompaniment to Mitchell's Reference and Distance Map of the United States* (1834), *Mitchell's Compendium of the Internal Improvements of the United States* (1835), *An Accompaniment to Mitchell's Map of the World, on Mercator's Projection* (1837), *An Accurate Synopsis of the Sixth Census of the United States* (1843), *A General View of the United States* (1846), and *A New Universal Atlas* (1846). Materials were related to current events; maps of Mexico, Texas, Oregon, and California were issued as they became important. At the start of the Civil War he published *Map of the United States and Territories*, which indicated military fortifications.

Among his school materials were *Mitchell's Atlas of Outline Maps* (1839), *Mitchell's School Geography* (1839), *Mitchell's School Atlas* (1839), *Mitchell's Primary Geography* (1840), *Mitchell's Geographical Reader* (1840), *Mitchell's Ancient Atlas* (1844), *Mitchell's Ancient Geography* (1845), *Mitchell's Biblical and Sabbath School Geography* (1849), *Intermediate or Secondary Geography* (1849), *Easy Introduction to the Study of Geography* (1851), *Mitchell's Geographical Question Book*

(1852), *and First Lessons in Geography* (1860).
REFERENCES:*AC; DAB; WWW* (H). *Gorman L. Miller*

MITCHELL, Samuel Chiles. B. December 24, 1864, Coffeeville, Mississippi, to Morris Randolph and Grace (Chiles) Mitchell. M. June 30, 1891, to Alice Virginia Broadus. Ch. five. D. August 20, 1948, Atlanta, Georgia.

Samuel Chiles Mitchell attended school in Mississippi and was graduated from Georgetown (Kentucky) College with the M.A. degree (1888). He attended the University of Virginia (1891–92) and received the Ph.D. degree (1899) from the University of Chicago.

Mitchell was professor of history and Greek at Mississippi College in Clinton (1899–91), professor of Latin at Georgetown College (1891–95), and professor of history at the University of Richmond in Virginia (1895–1908 and 1920–45). He was president of the University of South Carolina (1908–13), the Medical College of Virginia (1913–14), and Delaware College (later, University of Delaware) from 1914 to 1920.

He was associate editor of the *Religious Herald* (1900–08) and editor of a volume *Social Life* in the series The South in the Building of a Nation. He was a member of the Southern Education Board, president of the Anti-Saloon League of Virginia (1901–03), and rector of the Virginia Normal and Industrial Institution (1904–06). He was a trustee of Hampton (Virginia) Institute, Union University, Richmond Woman's College, and the Jeanes Fund. He was a member of the Richmond, Virginia, school board (1904–06). He received eight honorary degrees from American colleges and universities.

REFERENCES:*LE* (II); *NCAB* (14:88); *WWW* (II); *NYT,* August 21, 1948, p. 15; *School and Society* 68 (August 28, 1948): 136. *S. S. Britt, Jr.*

MOEHLMAN, Arthur Bernard. B. August 10, 1889, Racine, Wisconsin, to John Henry and Helene (Coords) Moehlman. M. June 30, 1919, to Grace Fletcher. Ch. two. D. May 2, 1952, Naples, Florida.

Arthur Bernard Moehlman attended Racine (Wisconsin) public schools and the University of Michigan, where he received the A.B. (1912), M.A. (1921), and Ph.D. (1923) degrees. He studied at Cornell University in Ithaca, New York (1912–13).

Beginning as an elementary teacher in the Detroit (Michigan) public schools in 1912, Moehlman served as high school, evening high school, and summer high school principal to 1918. He was director of statistics, publications, and administrative research for the Detroit schools (1918–25) and professor of administration and supervision in the school of education at the University of Michigan (1925–51).

Moehlman was the author of *Child Accounting* (1924), *Public Education in Detroit* (1925), *Public School Relations* (1927), *Public School Finance*

(1927), *Public School Plant Program* (1929), *Public School Budget Procedure* (1929), *Public Elementary School Plant* (with others, 1930), *Social Interpretation* (1938), *School Administration* (1940), and *Improvement of Public Education in Michigan* (1945). He was the editor of *Nation's Schools* (1932–48).

A fellow of the American Association for the Advancement of Science, Moehlman was active in many professional associations and served as president of the American Educational Research Association (1929), the National Council on Schoolhouse Construction (1939–40), and the National Advisory Council on School Building Problems (1935–36). He conducted educational surveys in several states, was a consultant to public school systems in Michigan and Illinois, and was an adviser to the Michigan Department of Public Instruction (1932–50) and the United States Office of Education (1930–38). He served on the President's Advisory Committee (1936–38) and the Michigan Public Education Study Commission (1942–47).

REFERENCES: *LE* (III); *NCAB* (42:441); *WWAE* (VIII); *WWW* (III); *Michigan Education Journal* 30 (September 1, 1952):20; *Nation's Schools* 49 (June 1952): 124.   *John F. Ohles*

MOLLOY, Mary Aloysius. B. June 14, 1880, Sandusky, Ohio, to Patrick John and Mary (Lambe) Molloy. M. no. D. September 27, 1954, Rochester, Minnesota.

Mary Molloy received the Ph.B. (1903) and M.A. (1905) degrees from Ohio State University and the Ph.D. degree in English philology (1907) from Cornell University in Ithaca, New York.

She was a teaching fellow in English at Ohio State (1903–05) and a graduate fellow in English at Cornell (1905–07). She was assistant principal at Winona (Minnesota) Seminary (1907–11). The Franciscan order, which conducted the seminary, desired to establish a college for women. In 1911 Molloy was cofounder and dean of the new College of St. Teresa. In 1928 she became president, holding the office until her retirement in 1946. After the death of her father in 1922 she entered the Franciscan community and received the religious name of Sister Mary Aloysius.

During her thirty-nine years of active association with the college, Molloy worked to develop a standard liberal arts college that would prepare women to be apostolic Catholics and to excel in high school teaching, other professional fields, or advanced study. She won accreditation for the college from the North Central Association in 1917.

Her writing includes *Concordance to the Anglo-Saxon Translation of Bede's Ecclesiastical History* (1907), and *The Celtic Rite in Britain* (1910), and she collaborated on the *Wordsworth Concordance* (1911) and the *Horace Concordance* (1914). She authored various newspaper and journal articles on the Celtic revival and a series of pamphlets on topical religious and educational issues.

For twenty-five years Molloy was on the North Central Association's Commission on Institutions of Higher Learning (1918–43) and was the sole woman on the association's six-member ad hoc commission to draft new standards (1923). She was a member of many organizations, including the National Catholic Educational Association (first woman member of the Executive Committee of its College and University department and first woman vice-president, 1947). She was a cofounder of the Conference of Catholic Colleges for Women (secretary, 1918–33).

She received the papal medal, Pro Pontifice et Ecclesia (1918), the first time this distinction was conferred upon an educator. She was the first American woman decorated with the papal Cross of Merit of the Constantinian Order of St. George (1923).

REFERENCES: *LE* (III); *NCAB* (C:472); *WWAE* (VIII); *WWW* (III); *NYT,* September 30, 1964, p. 31, *New Catholic Encyclopedia* (New York: McGraw-Hill, 1967).   *Karen Kennelly*

MONROE, Paul. B. June 7, 1869, North Madison, Indiana, to William and Juliet (Williams) Monroe. M. August 26, 1891, to Mary Emma Ellis. Ch. three. D. December 6, 1947, Goshen, New York.

Paul Monroe was graduated with the B.S. degree (1890) from Franklin (Indiana) College and received the Ph.D. degree in sociology and political science from the University of Chicago (1897). He studied at the University of Heidelberg, Germany, in 1901.

Monroe was a high school teacher and principal for four years after graduating from Franklin College and then affiliated with Teachers College, Columbia University, as an instructor in 1897. He continued as director of the school of education (1915–23) and Barnard Professor of Education (1925–38). He was director of the International Institute of Education at Columbia (1923–38). He served as president of American College for Girls and Robert College in Istanbul, Turkey (1932–35).

In the first decades of the twentieth century, Monroe was a major educational historian and was instrumental in establishing the discipline of history of education. He was a leader in international education and conducted studies of educational systems in various countries and a survey of the Philippine schools for the United States government in 1913. He assisted the Chinese government in reorganizing China's schools in 1921.

Monroe compiled *Source Book in the History of Education for the Greek and Roman Period* (1901) and wrote *Thomas Platter and the Educational Renaissance of the Sixteenth Century* (1904), *Text-Book in the History of Education* (1905), *Brief Course in the History of Education* (1907), *Principles of Secondary Education* (1914), *China—A Nation in Evolution*

(1928), and *Founding of the American Public School System* (1940). He was editor-in-chief of the *Cyclopedia of Education* (five volumes, 1910–13), education editor for several encyclopedias, and editor of Brief Course of Educational Texts, Home and School Series (1914), and Technical Art Series (1914).

Vice-president of the China Foundation, Monroe was a cofounder and president of the China Institute of America and a founder and president of the World Federation of Education Associations (1931–33, 1935–43). He was a trustee for the International College of Smyrna, Syria (later, Beirut, Lebanon), American School of Sophia, Bulgaria, and Lingnan University in Canton, China. He received honors from the governments of Persia, Poland, China, and Japan and received honorary degrees from Columbia University, Franklin College, and the universities of Peking, China, Dublin, Ireland, and Brazil.

REFERENCES: *DAB* (supp. 4); *LE* (II); *NCAB* (36:336, B:206); *WWW* (II); William W. Brickman *(q.v.)* and Francesco Cordasco, "Paul Monroe's Cyclopedia of Education: With Notices of Educational Encyclopedias Past and Present," *History of Education Quarterly* 10 (Fall 1970): 324–37; *NYT,* December 7, 1947, p. 76; Edward H. Reisner, "Paul Monroe, 1869–1947," *Teachers College Record* 49 (January 1948): 290–93; Henry Suzzallo *(q.v.),* "Paul Monroe—An Appreciation," in I. L. Kandel *(q.v.),* ed., *Twenty-five Years of American Education* (New York: Macmillan Co., 1931).   *Natalie A. Naylor*

MONROE, Walter Scott. B. August 14, 1882, Chase, Kansas, to Jonathan S. and Mary Ruth (Albin) Monroe. M. May 1, 1907, to Lula V. Robnett. Ch. none. D. October 13, 1961, Palo Alto, California.

Walter Scott Monroe attended rural schools in Kansas and Missouri and Northwest Missouri College in Albany, Missouri, before receiving the A.B. (1905), B.S. (1907), and M.A. (1911) degrees from the University of Missouri at Columbia. He completed the Ph.D. degree (1915) at the University of Chicago while serving on the faculty of the Kansas State Normal School (later, Emporia Kansas State College) at Emporia (1912–18). His dissertation on the development of arithmetic as a school subject was published as a United States Bureau of Education bulletin in 1917.

Monroe was employed in Missouri as a teacher at a private academy in Columbia (1904–05), a high school principal in Vandalia (1905–07), and superintendent of schools in Norborne (1907–09). He was professor of education at Kansas State Normal School, where he organized a bureau of educational measurement.

He became director of the Bureau of Cooperative Research at Indiana University (1918–19) and at the newly formed Bureau of Educational Research at the University of Illinois in Urbana-Champaign (1919–50). He was acting dean of the college of education (1930–31 and 1945–47). He retired as Illinois' first Distinguished Professor of Education, Emeritus.

Monroe authored several widely used standardized tests in arithmetic, algebra, reading, and spelling (1915–20) and numerous reports, surveys, summaries, and compilations issued as bulletins of the Illinois Bureau of Educational Research (1920–36). He directed school surveys in Leavenworth, Kansas (1915), and Marion, Illinois (1924).

Monroe was an active compiler, interpreter, and disseminator of educational research results in the 1920s and 1930s. He founded and edited the first two editions of the *Encyclopedia of Educational Research* (1941, 1950), the first comprehensive work of its kind. His other major books and reports include *Educational Tests and Measurements* (1917), *Measuring the Results of Teaching* (1918), *An Introduction to the Theory of Educational Measurements* (1923), *Directing Learning in the High School* (1927), and the impressive historical and analytical *Teaching-Learning Theory and Teacher Education, 1890 to 1950* (1952). He coauthored *The High School* (with O. F. Weber, 1928), *Ten Years of Educational Research, 1918–1927* (with others, 1928), *Educational Psychology* (with J. C. De Voss and G. W. Reagan, 1930), *Directing Learning in the Elementary School* (with R. Streitz, 1932), *The Scientific Study of Educational Problems* (with M. D. Engelhart, 1936), and *Bibliographies and Summaries in Education to July 1935* (with L. Shores, *q.v.*, 1936). He edited a series of teacher-training books. He was associate editor of the *Journal of Educational Research* (1920–21).

He was president of the American Educational Research Association (1917) and the National Society of College Teachers of Education (1927). He was a member of several other professional organizations.

REFERENCES: *LE* (III); *NCAB* (53:442); *WW* (XXII); Henry C. Johnson and E. V. Johanningmeier, *Teachers for the Prairie: The University of Illinois and the Schools, 1868–1945* (Urbana: University of Illinois Press, 1972). *Ronald D. Szoke*
Norman J. Bauer

MONROE, Will Seymour. B. March 22, 1863, Hunlock, Pennsylvania, to Ransom and Emeline (Womelsdorf) Monroe. M. no. D. January 29, 1939, Burlington, Vermont.

After receiving the customary elementary and secondary education of the time, Will S. Monroe earned the A.B. degree (1894) from Stanford (California) University. He pursued graduate work at the universities of Paris, France, and Jena and Leipzig, Germany (1894–95), and at Grenoble, France, and Leipzig (1900–01).

Monroe was a teacher and principal in Luzerne County, Pennsylvania (1881–87), and superintendent of schools at Nanticoke, Pennsylvania

(1887–88), and Pasadena, California (1889–92). He was professor of psychology at Massachusetts State Normal School (later, Westfield State College) in Westfield (1896–1908) and at New Jersey State Normal School (later, Montclair State College) in Upper Montclair from 1908 to his retirement in 1925.

Monroe was a noted lecturer in the field of psychology, visiting at a number of universities in the United States and abroad. He proposed and expounded procedures and models that hastened the formal, systematic study of learning in children. His books include *Poets and Poetry of the Wyoming Valley* (1887), *Educational Labors of Henry Barnard* (1893), *Comenius' School of Infancy* (1896), *Bibliography of Education* (1897), *Child Study Outlines* (1898), *Comenius and the Beginnings of Educational Reform* (1900), *History of the Pestalozzian Movement in the U.S.* (1905), *Turkey and the Turks* (1907), *In Viking Land* (1908), *Sicily* (1909), *Bohemia and the Czechs* (1910), *Bulgaria and Its People* (1914), and *Edward Carpenter—An Appreciation* (1931). He was associate editor of *Monroe's Cyclopedia of Education* (1911–13).

He was active in numerous educational societies, including a fellow of the American Association for the Advancement of Science and the American Geographical Society. He was a delegate to many foreign and domestic congresses and expositions and chaired a subcommittee on the Balkans of the United States Commission of Inquiry for the Paris Peace Settlement. He built the Monroe Skyline, a forty-eight mile stretch of the Long Trail in Vermont. He was decorated by the city of Prague, Czechoslovakia, and the king of Bulgaria.

REFERENCES: *LE* (I); *NCAB* (42:139); *WWW* (I); *NYT,* January 30, 1939, p. 13.   *Kenneth L. Burrett*

MOORE, Ernest Carroll. B. July 20, 1871, Youngstown, Ohio, to John A. and Martha Jane (Forsythe) Moore. M. February 17, 1896, to Dorothea Lummis Roads. M. March 8, 1943, to Kate Gordon. Ch. one. D. January 23, 1955, Los Angeles, California.

Ernest Carroll Moore was graduated from Ohio Normal University (later, Ohio Northern University) with the A.B. (1892) and LL.B. (1894) degrees. He received the M.A. degree (1896) from Columbia University. During the academic year (1897–98) he was a fellow in education at the University of Chicago, from which he received the Ph.D. degree (1898).

In 1898 Moore went to the University of California at Berkeley as an instructor in philosophy and three years later became an instructor in education. From 1906 to 1910 he was superintendent of the Los Angeles public schools. He was a professor of education at Yale University (1910–13), and in 1913 he took a similar post at Harvard University.

Moore returned to California in 1917 to assume the presidency of the

MOORE, James   [913]

California State Normal School in Los Angeles. He led a movement to incorporate the school within the state university system, which led to the establishment of the Southern Branch, University of California (1919), with authority to grant college degrees. In 1927 it was called University of California, Los Angeles. Moore was professor of education and director of the university from 1919 to 1929, when he became director and vice-president. In 1931 he was made vice-president, provost, and professor of education. He resigned all but the professorship in 1936 and retired in 1941.

Moore was the author of *How New York City Administers Its Schools* (1913), *What Is Education* (1915), *Fifty Years of Education in America* (1917), *What the War Teaches about Education* (1919), *The Story of Instruction—The Beginnings* (1936), *The Story of Instruction—The Church, the Renaissances, the Reformations* (1938), and *I Helped Make a University* (1952). He also edited *Minimum Course of Study* (1922), *Thomas Starr King's Socrates* (1924), *Thomas Davidson's Education as World Building* (1925), *The Story of the United States by Those Who Made It* (1932), and *California Educators* (1950).

Moore was a member of the California Board of Charities and Corrections (1903–10 and president, 1903–06). He was a fellow of the American Association for the Advancement of Science, an honorary member of Phi Beta Kappa, and a member of the California Teachers Association, the New England Association of Colleges and Secondary Schools (president, 1914), and Western Association of Colleges and Secondary Schools (president, 1930), and many other organizations. He was the director of the Los Angeles Chamber of Commerce and a trustee of the Los Angeles Philharmonic Orchestra (1936). Moore was made an officer de l'académie, France (1919), and a chevalier of the French Legion of Honor (1932). He was awarded several honorary degrees.

REFERENCES: *LE* (III); *NCAB* (40:413); *WWW* (III); *NYT,* January 25, 1955, p. 25.   *Robert H. Truman*

MOORE, James. B. 1764, Virginia, to n.a. M. n.a. D. June 22, 1814, Lexington, Kentucky.

James Moore gained prominence during the early national period of America as a pioneer educator and clergyman of the Episcopal church in Kentucky. He went to Kentucky from Virginia some time before April 1792. He sought to affiliate with the Presbyterian church, but his trial sermon in 1793 was not approved by the presbytery. Moore declined reexamination and was dismissed. He turned to the Episcopal church in which he was ordained in 1794.

Moore became the director (principal) of Transylvania Seminary, a public educational institution located near the town of Danville, the first of its kind in that part of the country. The school experienced financial problems and was first conducted in his house. The trustees voted to relocate the seminary permanently at Lexington, Kentucky, in 1793. Moore continued as director until February 1794.

Doctrinal problems arose between religious groups with Moore's successor. The Presbyterian faction sought to establish a rival school, Kentucky Academy, at Pisgah. Although an Episcopalian, Moore was named second principal of the school in April 1796. He returned to Transylvania the next fall as president of the school. The two schools merged as Transylvania University in 1798. Moore was acting president and professor of logic, metaphysics, moral philosophy, and belles lettres (1799–1804).

Moore conducted services for a small group of Episcopalians in Lexington and organized a church in 1809, which he served as the first resident rector in Kentucky.

REFERENCES: *DAB; NCAB* (4:513); *WWW* (H).   *Joe L. Green*

MORGAN, Arthur Ernest. B. June 20, 1878, Cincinnati, Ohio, to John D. and Anna Frances (Wiley) Morgan. M. September 1904 to Urania T. Jones. M. July 6, 1911, to Lucy Middleton Griscom. Ch. five. D. November 16, 1975, Xenia, Ohio.

Arthur E. Morgan moved with his parents to St. Cloud, Minnesota, when he was two years old. He attended local public schools and enrolled in the University of Colorado at Boulder, but dropped out because of eyestrain.

Morgan had worked as a farmhand, miner, book seller, typesetter, and logger after graduating from high school and returned to St. Cloud, where he engaged in self-study and became qualified to practice civil engineering in 1902. He was a supervising engineer for the United States Drainage Investigations designing reclamation projects in the South (1907–09). He formed the Morgan Engineering Company in Memphis, Tennessee, in 1909 and reclaimed more than two million acres of land. He organized and was president of Dayton Morgan Engineering Company (1915). He was chief engineer of the Miami Conservatory District in Ohio (1913–21) and of the Pueblo, Colorado Conservatory District (1921).

In 1917 Morgan organized the progressive Moraine Park School with the support of Dayton (Ohio) businessmen. He was appointed president of Antioch College in Yellow Springs, Ohio, in 1920. He initiated the Antioch plan, which provided for alternating periods of study and work. In 1933 Morgan was appointed the first chairman of the Tennessee Valley Authority. His interest in cooperating with private utilities led to his dismissal by President Franklin D. Roosevelt in 1938. He became president of the Community Service, Inc.

Morgan was author of several books, including *Drainage of the St. Francis Valley in Arkansas* (1909), *Miami Valley and the 1913 Flood* (1915), *New Light on the Boyhood of Lincoln* (1918), *A Prospect* (1921), *My*

World (1927), *The Seedman* (1932), *The Long Road* (1936), *The Small Community* (1942), *Edward Bellamy* (1944), *A Business of My Own* (1946), *Industries for Small Communities* (1953), *Search for Purpose* (1955), *The Community of the Future* (1956), *It Can Be Done in Education* (1962), *Observations* (1968), and *The Making of the TVA* (1974).

A fellow of the American Association for the Advancement of Science, Morgan was president of the Progressive Education Association (1921). He served the government of India as a member of the University Commission (1948–49) and was the American director of a south India educational project. He was the recipient of several honorary degrees from American colleges and universities.

REFERENCES: *CA* (5–8); *CB* (July 1956 and January 1976); *LE* (II); *NCAB* (E:388); *NYT,* November 17, 1975; *WWAE* (VIII); *WWW* (VI).

Joan Duff Kise

MORGAN, John. B. June 10, 1735, Philadelphia, Pennsylvania, to Evan and Joanna (Biles) Morgan. M. September 4, 1765, to Mary Hopkinson. Ch. none. D. October 15, 1789, Philadelphia, Pennsylvania.

John Morgan, a pioneer in medical education, attended Nottingham School near Philadelphia and the College of Philadelphia (later, the University of Pennsylvania); he was in the first graduating class in 1757. In 1763 he was granted the M.D. degree from the University of Edinburgh, Scotland. He studied at the Académie royal de chirurgie in Paris and with Giovanni Morgagni in Italy (1764).

On his return to America in 1765, he suggested to the board of trustees of the College of Philadelphia the establishment of a school of medicine. On May 3, 1765, the first medical school in the colonies was opened at the College of Philadelphia with Morgan appointed to the first chair in the practice of medicine. He delivered *A Discourse upon the Institution of Medical Schools in America* at the 1765 commencement in which he noted a need for separating the functions of physician, apothecary, and surgeon and for establishing medical schools.

Morgan won a gold medal from John Sargent in 1766 for an essay published with others, *Four Dissertations on the Reciprocal Advantages of a Perpetual Union between Great Britain and Her American Colonies.* He received an appointment from the Continental Congress as director-general of hospitals and physican-in-chief of the Continental army. He came under criticism from subordinates and was dismissed from his position by the Congress in 1777. He published *A Vindication of His Public Character in the Station of Director-General of the Military Hospitals, and Physician-in-Chief of the American Army* (1777) in which he defended himself and demanded a court of inquiry; he was acquitted of all charges by President George Washington and Congress in 1779. He withdrew from public life and returned to private practice and his duties as professor and physician at the Pennsylvania Hospital.

Morgan was the author of *A Recommendation of Inoculation, According to Baron Dimsdale's Method* (1776). He was a member of the American Philosophical Society, the Royal Society of London, England, and the Belles Lettres Society of Rome, Italy, and he was a licentiate of the Royal College of Physicians of both London and Edinburgh. He made a suggestion that led to the establishment of the Philadelphia College of Surgeons in 1787.

REFERENCES: *AC; DAB; NCAB* (10:267); *TC; WWW* (H); Fielding H. Garrison, *An Introduction to the History of Medicine* (Philadelphia: W. B. Saunders Company, 1914), pp. 308–09.   *Richard M. Coger*

MORGAN, Lewis Henry. B. November 21, 1818, near Aurora, New York, to Jedediah and Harriet (Steele) Morgan. M. August 13, 1851, to Mary Elisabeth Steele. Ch. three. D. December 17, 1881, Rochester, New York.

Lewis Henry Morgan has been called the Father of American Anthropology. After graduating from Union College in Schenectady, New York, he read law for four years and was admitted to the bar in 1844. He practiced law in Rochester, New York (1844–61). Morgan became a member of a secret society, the Gordian Knot, which studied and perpetuated Indian lore and copied the Iroquois Confederacy; the society became known as the Grand Order of Iroquois.

Morgan became highly interested in Indians and made an extensive study of Iroquois and other tribes. He was adopted by the Hawk clan of the Seneca tribe of Iroquois, which provided him access to the tribal councils and gave him opportunities for further study. He published his researches on Indians in the *American Review* (1847) and the *Annual Reports of the Regents of New York* (1849–53). He received a grant to enlarge the Regents' Indian collection.

Morgan became the legal council for a railroad company operating in the Lake Superior iron region of Michigan in 1855. The job gave him an opportunity to study the Indian tribes of Michigan, Kansas, Nebraska, the upper Missouri, and as far north as the Hudson Bay Territory. He made notes on nearly seventy tribes.

With the support of the Smithsonian Institution, Morgan studied the primitive world in general. His studies partially validated the theory that Asiatic origins of American Indians could be shown through patterns of kinship relations. He concluded that there was a common origin and psychic unity of all races of men, all of whom passed from savagery through barbarism to civilization. Morgan also had an interest in the study of mind and instinct as manifested in lower animals.

He was the author of *The League of the Iroquois* (1851), *Laws of Consanguinity and Descent of the Iroquois* (1859), *The American Beaver*

(1868), *Systems of Consanguinity and Affinity of the Human Family* (1869), *Ancient Society* (1877), *On the Ruins of a Stone Pueblo* (1880), and *House and House Life of the American Aborigines* (1881).

Morgan was elected to the New York State Assembly (1861–68) and the New York State Senate (1868–69). In 1875 he helped to organize and was the first chairman of the section of anthropology of the American Association for the Advancement of Science and was president of the society in 1879. He was a member of the National Academy of Sciences and many other American and foreign scientific societies. He was awarded honorary degrees by the University of Rochester and Union College.

REFERENCES: *AC; DAB; EB; NCAB* (6:192); *TC; WWW* (H); *NYT,* December 19, 1881, p. 2; Carl Resek, *Lewis Henry Morgan: American Scholar* (Chicago: University of Chicago Press, 1960). *Robert R. Sherman*

MORGAN, Thomas Jefferson. B. August 17, 1839, Franklin, Indiana, to Lewis and Mary (Causey or Cansey) Morgan. M. 1870 to Caroline Starr. Ch. none. D. July 13, 1902, Ossining, New York.

Thomas Jefferson Morgan's father, a founder of Franklin (Indiana) College and an Indiana state legislator, died when Morgan was thirteen years old. Morgan received the A.B. degree (1861) from Franklin College, although he left in his senior year to enlist as a private in the Union army.

After serving three months in the army, he returned to civilian life and taught for a year in Atlanta, Illinois. Morgan reentered the army in 1862 and served with distinction for three years, rising to the rank of brigadier general. At the close of the Civil War, he resigned his commission and entered the Rochester (New York) Theological Seminary, graduating in 1868.

He was ordained a Baptist minister at Rochester, New York, in 1869 and held a pastorate at Brownville, Nebraska (1871–72). He served as president of the Nebraska Normal School (later, Peru State College) at Peru (1872–74) and taught homiletics and ecclesiastical history at Baptist Union Theological Seminary in Chicago (1874–81). Morgan went to Potsdam, New York, where he served as principal of the New York State Normal School (later, State University of New York College at Potsdam) (1881–83) and moved to Providence, Rhode Island, to become principal of the State Normal School (later, Rhode Island College) from 1884 to 1889.

In 1889 President Benjamin Harrison appointed Morgan United States commissioner of Indian affairs (1889–93). He outlined policies to promote the material welfare of the Indians, prepare them for American citizenship, and provide for their education. He became corresponding secretary of the American Baptist Home Mission Society (1893–1902) where he was able to provide leadership for the establishment of schools for thousands of blacks.

Morgan wrote several books, including *Reminiscences of Service with*

Colored Troops in the Army of the Cumberland, 1863–65 (1885), *Educational Mosaics* (1887), *Students' Hymnal* (1888), *Studies in Pedagogy* (1889), *Patriotic Citizenship* (1895), *The Praise Hymnary* (1898), and *The Negro in America and the Ideal American Republic* (1898). He also edited the *Baptist Home Mission Monthly* (1893–1902).

Morgan was an overseer of Columbian University (later, George Washington University) in 1889. He received honorary degrees from the University of Chicago (1874) and Franklin College (1894).

REFERENCES: *DAB; NCAB* (2:54); *TC; WWW* (I).   *Carol O'Meara*

MORGAN, William Henry. B. February 22, 1818, Logan County, Kentucky, to Joseph and Elizabeth (Adams) Morgan. M. November 30, 1852, to Sarah Anne Noel. Ch. five. D. May 16, 1901, Nashville, Tennessee.

William Henry Morgan, a pioneer dental educator, was twenty-seven years old before he was able to attend the Baltimore (Maryland) College of Dental Surgery, from which he was graduated in 1848.

Morgan practiced dentistry in Russellville, Kentucky (1848–49), and became a partner of T. B. Hamlin in Nashville, Tennessee. From 1876 to 1901 he practiced with his son, Henry W. Morgan. He was appointed professor of clinical dentistry and dental pathology at Vanderbilt University in Nashville, organized a department of dentistry, and served as dean (1879–1900). During his administration, the department became an outstanding dental education institution. He organized and directed the dental school of the Meharry Medical College, the first dental school for blacks in the country.

Active in professional associations, Morgan was organizer and president of the Southern Dental Association and the Tennessee State Dental Association (1867) and president of the American Dental Association (1870 and 1882) and the Central States Dental Association, the Mississippi Valley Dental Association, and the Nashville Dental Association. He was active in the Methodist church and served for thirty years on the book committee of the Southern Methodist Publishing House and was a trustee for twenty-three years and chairman of the board of trustees for ten years of the Central Tennessee College for Negroes (later, Walden University). He was appointed a member of the board of Indian commissioners by President Grover Cleveland.

REFERENCES: *NCAB* (8:228); *WWW* (H).   *John F. Ohles*

MORPHET, Edgar Leroy. B. January 25, 1895, Grass Creek, Indiana, to William Wesley and Rosalie (Backus) Morphet. M. December 19, 1932, to Camilla Matthews. Ch. two.

Edgar Leroy Morphet was graduated from Grass Creek (Indiana) high school in 1913, and after three months of study at Indiana State Normal

School (later, Indiana State University) in Terre Haute, taught in Washington County, Indiana (1913–14). Following the death of his father in 1914, he worked his way through the Indiana State Normal School, receiving the A.B. degree in 1918. He received the M.A. (1925) and Ph.D. (1927) degrees from Teachers College, Columbia University.

Morphet worked for two years with the Young Men's Christian Association in the rehabilitation and treatment of the mentally disturbed. He was an assistant high school principal at Stillwell, Indiana (1916–17), principal of Fairmount (Indiana) high school (1920–22), and a teacher and principal in the Philippine Islands (1922–24).

Morphet was a professor at Alabama Polytechnic Institute (later, Auburn University) from 1926 to 1928 and at the University of Alabama (1928–33). In 1933 Morphet became director of administration and finance in the Alabama State Department of Education, where he worked to modernize laws and financial provisions for schools. He served with the United States Office of Education as associate director for the first comprehensive study of local school units in the United States in 1935.

In 1936 Morphet accepted a position as director of administration and finance in the Florida State Department of Education. He participated in the codification of state school laws and directed a state educational policy study (1944).

In 1949 Morphet was appointed professor of education at the University of California at Berkeley, where he taught until he retired in 1966. He served as Fulbright Professor of Education at the University of Hong Kong (1955–56). He developed and supervised internship and field service programs for students and headed a University of California–sponsored project helping Brazilian professors and students in the social sciences (1962–64). Morphet was selected in 1966 to direct the Designing Education for the Future project in Denver, Colorado. When the project was completed in 1969, he directed the Improving State Leadership in Education project.

Morphet was coauthor of *Educational Administration* (with others, 1959) and *Financing the Public Schools* (with Roe L. Johns, 1960), and he edited *Comparative Educational Administration* (with Theodore L. Reller, 1962). He served as executive secretary and editor of publications for the Southern States Work Conference on Educational Problems and was an organizer of the National Conference of Professors of Educational Administration in 1947. He was consultant on finance to the White House Conference on Education (1955).

Morphet received the American Association of School Administrators Distinguished Service Award (1966), the Harry N. Rivlin Medal and Award from Fordham University, and the Council of Chief State School Officers Distinguished Service Award (1973).

REFERENCES: *LE* (V); *WW* (XXXIX); *WWAE* (XV).   *Marvin Gerber*

MORRISON, Henry Clinton. B. October 7, 1871, Oldtown, Maine, to John and Mary Louise (Ham) Morrison. M. July 29, 1902, to Marion Locke. Ch. three. D. March 19, 1945, Chicago, Illinois.

Henry Clinton Morrison was graduated from Dartmouth College in Hanover, New Hampshire, with the A.B. degree (1895) and received the M.S. degree (1906) from New Hampshire College (later, University of New Hampshire) at Durham.

He became principal of the Milford, New Hampshire, high school (1895–99) and then was superintendent of the Portsmouth, New Hampshire, schools (1899–1904). He was superintendent of public instruction for New Hampshire where he received national attention for the progressiveness of the state's schools, even in the face of ingrained Yankee skepticism and conservatism. After serving as assistant secretary to the Connecticut State Board of Education (1917–19) he went to the University of Chicago where he was professor of education (1919–37) and director of the laboratory schools.

He devised the Morrison unit plan as a substitute for lesson assignments in the high school and was a proponent of the junior high school and junior college. He advocated the abolition of report cards. He established himself as an expert in school finance and was the author of *The Financing of Public Schools in the State of Illinois* (1924), *School Revenue* (1930), and *The Management of the School Money* (1932). His most influential work was *The Practice of Teaching in the Secondary School* (1926), and he also wrote *Basic Principles of Education* (1934), *The Curriculum of the Common School* (1940), and *American Schools: A Critical Study of our School System* (1943). A collection of his addresses and essays was published as *School and Commonwealth* in 1937.

Morrison was a fellow of the American Association for the Advancement of Science and president of the American Institute of Instruction (1908–09). He received honorary degrees from the universities of Maine and New Hampshire.

REFERENCES: *CB* (May 1945); *LE* (II); *WWW* (II); Arthur B. Moehlman *(q.v.)*, "Henry Clinton Morrison: Master Teacher," *Nation's Schools* 35 (June 1945): 19; *NYT*, March 20, 1945, p. 19; Harry A. Brown, "Henry C. Morrison and His Contribution to American Education," *School and Society* 61 (June 9, 1945): 380–82.   *Ronald D. Szoke*

MORRISON, John Irwin. B. July 25, 1806, near Chambersburg, Pennsylvania, to Robert and Ann (Irwin) Morrison. M. 1832 to Catherine Morris. Ch. four. D. July 17, 1882, Knightstown, Indiana.

John Irwin Morrison was educated by local clergymen in Franklin County, Pennsylvania, and taught school briefly before moving to Washington County, Indiana (1824). He attended Miami University in Oxford, Ohio, obtaining the A.B. degree (1828).

He taught at Walnut Ridge, Indiana, shortly after arriving in the state and at Salem (Indiana) grammar school (1825–27). He returned to Salem in 1828 and opened the Washington County Seminary, where he remained until 1840. He also operated the Salem Female Institute (1835–39). In 1840 he was appointed professor of ancient languages at Indiana University in Bloomington, but after three years returned to the Washington County Seminary, remaining there until 1847.

Leaving teaching, he became a newspaper owner and editor of the *Washington Republican,* which he renamed the *Washington Democrat.* In 1850 he was a founder of the short-lived *Salem Locomotive* and was editor of the *Union Advocate* in 1861. Morrison was elected state representative from Washington County (1839–40), state senator (1847–50), and treasurer of the county (1856–60).

Morrison's most important service to education was as a member of the state constitutional convention in 1851. Chairman of the committee on education, he was responsible for the article on education establishing the office of state superintendent of public instruction. As a legislator, he helped enact laws providing teachers' institutes and creating the office of county superintendent of schools.

During the Civil War he was a commissioner on the board of enrollment for the draft. From 1865 to 1867 he was state treasurer. In 1872 he moved to Knightstown, where he was president of the school board from 1874 to 1877. He was a trustee of Indiana University (1847–55 and 1873–78).

REFERENCES: *DAB; TC; WWW* (H); Richard G. Boone, *A History of Education in Indiana* (New York: D. Appleton and Co., 1892); Annie Morrison Coffin, "John Irwin Morrison and the Washington County Seminary," *Indiana Magazine of History* 22 (June 1926): 183–93; Fassett A. Cotton *(q.v.), Education in Indiana (1793–1934)* (Bluffton, Ind.: Progress Publishing Co., 1934); Jacob P. Dunn, *Indiana and Indianans* (Chicago: American Historical Society, 1919), 1: 487–90.   *Ronald D. Cohen*

MORSE, Jedidiah. B. August 23, 1761, Woodstock, Connecticut, to Jedidiah and Sarah (Child) Morse. M. May 4, 1789, to Elizabeth A. Breese. Ch. three, including Samuel Finley Breese Morse, inventor of the telegraph. D. June 9, 1826, New Haven, Connecticut.

Jedidiah Morse was graduated from Yale College (1783) and opened a school for young ladies in New Haven, Connecticut. Dissatisfied with the treatment of geography in school textbooks from England, he wrote the first American geography text, *Geography Made Easy,* in 1784. He also authored *The American Universal Geography* (1789), *Elements of Geography* (1795), *The American Gazetteer* (1797), *A New Gazetteer of the Eastern Continent* (1802), *A Compendious History of New England* (with Elijah Parish, 1804), and *Annals of the American Revolution* (1814). He became identified as the Father of American Geography. During his lifetime his textbooks monopolized the field in the United States and were published extensively in Europe.

His teaching and the proceeds from his first geography text supported Morse while he pursued his ambition to enter the ministry. He was ordained in 1786 and served for thirty years at the First Congregational Church of Charlestown, Massachusetts. He exerted leadership in the church, particularly in support of orthodoxy and toward forcing Unitarian churches out of the Congregational fold. Dissension following the separation of Unitarian churches in 1816 led to friction within his own church and his retirement from the pulpit in 1819.

He founded and edited for five years the *Panoplist* (1815), a periodical espousing the orthodox point of view in the church, and he was one of the founders of Andover Theological Seminary (1808). He helped found the New England Tract Society (1814) and the American Bible Society (1816). He was secretary of the Society for Propagation of the Gospel, and his interest in American Indians led to his appointment by the secretary of war to study conditions of Indian tribes; his report was published in 1822. He was an outspoken partisan in politics and assisted in founding the Federalist periodical, *The Mercury and New England Palladium* (1801).

REFERENCES: *AC; DAB; NCAB* (13:353); *TC; WWW* (H). *John F. Ohles*

MORT, Paul R. B. February 21, 1894, Elsie, Michigan, to Emanuel L. and Barbara M. (Waltz) Mort. M. June 21, 1921, to Mildred Willey. Ch. two. D. May 12, 1962, Bronx, New York.

Paul R. Mort received the B.A. degree from Indiana University in 1916 and the A.M. (1922) and Ph.D. (1924) degrees from Columbia University.

In 1922 Mort began a long career at Teachers College, Columbia University, where he was director of the school of education (1929–35) and the advanced school of education (1935–40); he retired in 1959.

Mort advocated a more extensive education for the nation's children and increased financial support to education from the states and the federal government, but he was a strong advocate of local control of the schools. He served on numerous committees and government commissions to advise on educational programs. His conception of an equalization formula for financing education was utilized throughout the United States. As a founder and supporter of school study councils, he urged the improvement of education through cooperative research. His work with the Metropolitan School Study Council was the inspiration for many other study councils, including the Associated Public School Systems.

His books include *Individual Pupil* (1928), *Federal Support* (1935), *Adaptability of Public School Systems* (with Francis G. Cornell, 1938), *American Schools in Transition* (with Francis G. Cornell, 1941), *The Law and Public Education* (with Robert R. Hamilton, 1941), *A Look at Our*

Schools (with William S. Vincent, 1946), *Modern Educational Practice* (with William S. Vincent, 1951), *Introduction to American Education* (with William S. Vincent, 1954), *Principles of School Administration* (with Donald H. Ross, 1957), and *Public School Finance* (with Walter C. Reusser and John W. Polley, 1960).

Mort belonged to several professional associations and was president of the American Educational Research Association (1951). He received the Butler Medal (1933) and honorary degrees from Rutgers and Indiana universities.

REFERENCES: *LE* (III); *WW* (XXXII); *WWAE* (XX); *NYT,* May 13, 1962, p. 88. *Kenneth J. Frasure*

MORTIMER, Mary. B. December 2, 1816, Trowbridge, Wiltshire, England, to William and Mary (Pierce) Mortimer. M. no. D. July 14, 1877, Milwaukee, Wisconsin.

Mary Mortimer's family emigrated from England to New England, to New York City, and then to a farm in western New York. Orphaned at the age of twelve, she was raised by her oldest brother. At the age of twenty-one she attended Geneva (New York) Seminary, completing the four-year course in two years, while acting as a teaching assistant. She was principal of the Brockport (New York) Seminary (1841–46) and a teacher in the LeRoy (New York) Seminary (later, Ingham University) and in Milwaukee, Wisconsin. She opened a girls' school in Ottawa, Illinois, in 1849 but it was closed by a cholera outbreak.

Mortimer met Catharine Beecher *(q.v.)*, and they put Beecher's ideas for reforming the education of women into practice at the private seminary of Lucy A. Parsons in Milwaukee, Wisconsin. In 1857 the institution was chartered as a women's college with Mortimer as president, and in 1853 it was renamed the Milwaukee Female College.

Mortimer headed the college (1850–57 and 1866–74). She was principal of a seminary at Baraboo, Wisconsin, from 1857 to 1866. She retired in 1876 and was a founder of the Milwaukee Industrial School for Underprivileged Children and the Women's Club of Milwaukee. In 1852 Mortimer and Beecher organized the American Women's Educational Association.

Milwaukee Female College was merged to become Milwaukee-Downer College in 1895 and Lawrence University in 1964.

REFERENCES: *DAB; NAW; NCAB* (7:529); *WWW* (H).

Darlene E. Fisher

MOTEN, Lucy Ella. B. 1851, near White Sulphur Springs, Virginia, to Benjamin and Julia (Withers) Moten. M. no. D. August 24, 1933, New York, New York.

Born to a family of free blacks, Lucy Ella Moten moved with her family to Washington, D.C., so that she could receive an education at a tuition school and in one of the first public schools for blacks in 1862. She attended the preparatory and normal departments of Howard University in Washington (1868–70). She continued her education at the Salem (Massachusetts) Normal School (later, Salem State College) from which she was graduated in 1875. She also was graduated from the Spencerian Business College (1883) and earned the M.D. degree (1897) from Howard University.

After attending Howard University, Moten taught in Washington's O Street School (1870–73). Despite reservations about her age, Moten was appointed principal of the Miner Training School for Teachers on the personal recommendation of trustee Frederick Douglass in 1883. The Miner Normal School was the major source of teachers for Washington black schools. It was incorporated into the Washington public school system, and its program was upgraded and extended to a two-year course in 1896. Moten sought extension of the course to a four-year college program, but that was not accomplished until seven years after her retirement in 1920. In 1927 Miner Normal School became Miner College and, in 1955, merged with Wilson Teachers College to be the District of Columbia Teachers College.

At her death in New York City in 1933, Moten bequeathed over $50,000 to Howard University to be used for student aid. The District of Columbia named the Moten Elementary School in her honor in 1954.

REFERENCES: *NAW;* Thomasine Corrothers, "Lucy Ellen [*sic*] Moten," *Journal of Negro History* 19 (January 1934): 102–06.

Natalie A. Naylor

MOTON, Robert Russa. B. August 26, 1867, Amelia County, Virginia, to Booker and Emily (Brown) Moton. M. June 7, 1905, to Elizabeth Hunt Harris. M. July 1, 1908, to Jennie Dee Booth. Ch. five. D. May 31, 1940, Capahoosic, Virginia.

Born on a former Virginia slave plantation, Robert Russa Moton entered Hampton (Virginia) Institute at the age of nineteen, graduating in 1890.

Moton remained at Hampton as commandant of cadets (1890–1915). During his years at Hampton, he became associated with Booker T. Washington *(q.v.)*, accompanied him across the country on lecture tours, and became his protégé. When Washington died in 1915, the trustees of Tuskegee (Alabama) Institute chose Moton to head the school. He served at Tuskegee to his retirement in 1935.

Never the leader that Washington was, Moton had participated in the Niagara conference (1906) that had opposed Washington's leadership in black education. Moton believed that black militants and conservatives were working for the same goals in different ways. He introduced junior college programs in the 1920s that expanded into four-year programs. He restructured and restated the Tuskegee formula to meet the demands of a better-educated and race-conscious black middle class. Despite opposition from Howard and Fisk universities, he was able to have a Veterans Administration hospital located in Tuskegee, Alabama, following World War I.

Moton was the author of the Spingarn medal-winning *What the Negro Thinks* (1929) in which he attacked racial discrimination and advocated civil equality of the races. He also wrote *Racial Good Will* (1916) and the autobiographical *Finding a Way Out* (1920).

Moton helped found the Commission on Interracial Cooperation and was appointed by President Woodrow Wilson *(q.v.)* in 1918 to survey the opinion of black soldiers about the United States Army. He headed a commission of black leaders working with the presidential commission on the Mississippi River flood disaster in 1927 and was a member of the National Advisory Commission on Education and the Commission to Study Education in Liberia, chairman of the United States Commission on Education in Haiti (1930), and chairman of the National League on Urban Conditions among Negroes, a forerunner of the National Urban League. He was president of the National Negro Business League (1919–40), president of the Tuskegee Institute Savings Bank, director of the Dunbar National Bank in New York City, and a founder and president of the National Negro Finance Corporation of Durham, North Carolina. He was a trustee of the Phelps Stokes Fund and a member of boards of trustees of black schools, colleges, and universities. He was a director of Providence Hospital of Chicago and the National Health Circle. He was chairman of the committee on colored work and a member of the home division of the Young Men's Christian Association and the committee on church and race relations of the Federal Council of Churches of Christ in America. He was awarded the Harmon Award in Race Relations (1930) and received many honorary degrees from American colleges and universities.

REFERENCES: *DAB* (supp. 2); *LE* (III); *NCAB* (B: 75); *NYT,* June 1, 1940, p. 15; *WWW* (I); W. E. B. Du Bois *(q.v.),* "Moton of Hampton and Tuskegee," *Phylon* (Fourth quarter, 1940): 344–51; Mary White Ovington, *Portraits in Color* (New York: Viking Press, 1927); Mary White Ovington, *The Walls Came Tumbling Down* (New York: Harcourt, Brace, 1947).

Walter C. Daniel

MOWRY, William Augustus. B. August 13, 1829, Uxbridge, Massachusetts, to Jonathan and Hannah (Brayton) Mowry. M. November 15, 1849, to Rufina M. E. Weaver. M. April 29, 1858, to Caroline Aldrich. Ch. three. D. May 22, 1917, Hyde Park, Massachusetts.

When William Augustus Mowry was three years old, his father died, and he went to live on his grandfather's farm. Beginning at an early age, he supported himself by working on farms and in mills and by selling books. Mowry's formal education included attendance at Uxbridge (Massachusetts) Academy and Phillips Academy at Andover, Massachusetts. In 1854 he entered Brown University but discontinued after two years because of ill health.

Mowry taught at a district school in Rhode Island while attending Brown University and taught at the Providence (Rhode Island) High School. He served for two years as a captain in the Civil War. On his return to Providence in 1864, Mowry and a friend, Charles Goff, opened a private school for boys. Mowry was principal of the English and Classical School for twenty years. The school was recognized for its enlightened ideas about school hygiene, equipment, methods of teaching, and discipline. In 1884 he sold his interest in the school and moved to Boston. From 1891 to 1894 Mowry was superintendent of the public schools of Salem, Massachusetts. He was the executive head of the Martha's Vineyard Summer Institute (1887–1905), a pioneer program in pedagogy.

Mowry was the author of *Who Invented the American Steamboat?* (1874), *Nathaniel Mowry and His Descendants* (1878), *Studies in Civil Government* (1887), *Elements of Civil Government* (1890), *Talks with Boys* (1892), *A History of the United States* (1896), *The Uxbridge Academy* (1897), *First Steps in the History of Our Country* (1898), *American Inventions and Inventors* (1900), *Marcus Whitman and Early Oregon* (1901), *The Territorial Growth of the United States* (1902), *American Heroes* (1903), *American Pioneers* (with Blanche S. Mowry, 1905), *Essentials of United States History* (with Blanche S. Mowry, 1906), *Recollections of a New England Educator* (1908), and *Camp Life* (1909). He was editor of *Journal of Education* (1884–86) and *Education* (1886–91).

Active in educational associations, Mowry was president of the Rhode Island Institute of Instruction (1864–66), the American Institute of Instruction (1880–82), the Massachusetts Council of the American Institute of Civics (1885–87), and the department of higher education of the National Educational Association (1889). He was a member of the American Academy of Arts and Sciences, the New England Historic Genealogical Society, and the National Council of Education and was a founder of the American Historical Society. He served on school boards in Cranston (1864–66), and Providence (1869–74), Rhode Island, and Boston (1888–91), Massachusetts, and was a popular lecturer at teachers' institutes.

REFERENCES: *DAB; NCAB* (25:172); *NYT,* May 23, 1917, p. 13; *TC; WWW* (I); William Augustus Mowry, *Recollections of a New England Educator, 1838–1908* (New York: Silver Burdett and Co., 1908).

Harold D. Lehman

MULLANY, Patrick Francis (Brother Azarias). B. June 29, 1847, near Killenaule, County Tipperary, Ireland, to Thomas and Margaret (Ryan)

Mullany. M. no. D. August 20, 1893, Plattsburgh, New York.

Patrick Francis Mullany moved with his family from County Tipperary, Ireland, to Deerfield, New York, where they were among the first Irish Catholic immigrants. He was a student at Christian Brothers Academy in Utica, New York. On June 29, 1862, he joined the Brothers of the Christian Schools. He completed the classical course of study at Rock Hill College in Ellicott City, Maryland, in 1866. He was named Brother Azarias and became a noted teacher, administrator, author, and lecturer.

Mullany was a teacher in Albany, New York City, and Philadelphia and at the age of nineteen became a professor of mathematics and literature at Rock Hill College (1866–79) and served as president (1879–86). After a stay in Europe recuperating from the ill health that had forced his resignation from Rock Hill, he was professor of rhetoric and English literature at De La Salle Institute in New York City (1886–93). He was a founder of the Catholic Summer School in Plattsburgh, New York.

Among the books Mullany wrote were *An Essay Contributing to a Philosophy of Literature* (1874), *The Development of Old English Thought* (1879), *Aristotle and the Christian Church* (1888), *Books and Readings* (1890), *Phases of Thought and Criticism* (1892), *Essays Educational* (1896), *Essays Philosophical* (1896), and *Essays Miscellaneous* (1896).

REFERENCES: *AC; DAB; NCAB* (7: 525); *TC; Addresses and Letters Read at the Memorial Meeting in Honor of Brother Azarias* (Washington, D.C.: St. John's College, 1894); John Talbot Smith, *Brother Azarias* (New York: Benziger Brothers, 1897).   *David Delahanty*

MUMFORD, Frederick Blackman. B. May 28, 1868, Moscow, Michigan, to Elisha Charles Lindsley and Julia Ann (Camburn) Mumford. M. January 30, 1895, to Jessamine Kennedy. Ch. four. D. November 12, 1946, St. Charles, Missouri.

Frederick B. Mumford attended the local one-room school near his Moscow Township, Michigan, home and was graduated from Hanover (Michigan) High School. He attended Albion (Michigan) College (1885–88) and Michigan Agricultural College (later, State University) and was graduated with the B.S. (1891) and M.S. (1893) degrees. He studied at the University of Leipzig, Germany (1900), and the University of Zurich, Switzerland (1901).

He was an assistant at the Michigan Experiment Station (1891–93) and was an assistant professor at the Michigan Agricultural College (1893–95). In 1895 he was professor of agriculture and animal husbandry at the University of Missouri and served as acting dean of the college of agriculture and acting director of the agricultural experiment station (1903–05) and dean and director (1909–38).

A highly successful dean, Mumford directed the school to a leading position in the country. The faculty and student body increased in size, and five new departments were established between 1909 and 1919. Important improvements in agricultural methods and pioneering research in soil erosion and the development of new strains of seeds were realized during his administration.

Mumford was the author of *The Breeding of Animals* (1917), *Land Grant College Movement* (1940), *History of the Missouri College of Agriculture* (1944), and bulletins of the Agricultural Experiment Station. He served as a member of the Missouri State Board of Agriculture, chairman of the Missouri Council for Defense (1917–19), and federal food administrator for Missouri (1917–19). He was a member of the Missouri Commission for Relief and Reconstruction (1932), the Missouri State Planning Board, the Missouri Agricultural Debt Adjustment Commission, and professional organizations, including the Association of Land Grant Colleges and Universities (executive committee, 1920–41, and president, 1941). He was a fellow of the American Association for the Advancement of Science.

REFERENCES: *LE* (II); *WWAE* (XI); *WWW* (I); *Journal of Animal Science* 6 (February 1947): 102; John H. Longwell, *The Centennial Report, 1870–1970 of the College of Agriculture* (Columbia: University of Missouri, 1970); F. B. Mumford, *History of the Missouri College of Agriculture* (Columbia: College of Agriculture, University of Missouri, Bulletin 483, October 1944); *Missouri Historical Review* 41 (April 1947): 334–35.

John F. Ohles

MUNFORD, Mary Cooke Branch. B. September 16, 1865, Richmond, Virginia, to James Read and Martha Louise (Patterson) Branch. M. November 22, 1893, to Beverley Bland Munford. Ch. two. D. July 3, 1938, Richmond, Virginia.

A daughter of a prominent Virginia family, Mary Cooke Branch Munford was educated in private schools in Virginia and New York but was denied a college education by her family.

Sharing a sense of social responsibility through education, Mary Munford and her husband attended annual conferences of the Southern Education Board, an organization devoted to the improvement of public education in the South. She assisted Lila M. Valentine in organizing the Richmond Education Association, which sought to improve the education in the city schools, and served as president of the organization (1904–11). She was elected as the first woman member to the Richmond School Board in 1920 and served until 1931.

Munford was instrumental in bringing before the legislature bills designed to establish a college for women at the University of Virginia (1912–18). Women were finally admitted to the College of William and Mary beginning in 1918, the year it became a state-supported institution. Munford was a member of the board of visitors of the College of William and Mary and the University of Virginia.

The Munfords had a special interest in education for Negroes. While her husband served as a trustee of Hampton Institute, she assisted in the founding and served as trustee of the Virginia Industrial School for Colored Girls (1915). She was a trustee of Fisk University, the National League on Urban Conditions Among Negroes, and other racial organizations. She helped organize the first child study groups in Virginia. She was appointed by Theodore Roosevelt and William Howard Taft to presidential commissions on rural life.

REFERENCES: *LE* (I); *NAW; WWW* (I); *NYT,* July 4, 1938, p. 13.

Anne Raymond-Savage

MUNRO, William Bennett. B. January 5, 1875, Almonte, Ontario, Canada, to John McNab and Sarah (Bennett) Munro. M. February 19, 1913, to Caroline Sanford Gorton. Ch. one. D. September 4, 1957, Pasadena, California.

William Bennett Munro earned the A.B. (1895), M.A. (1896), and LL.B. (1898) degrees from Queens College, Kingston, Ontario. He engaged in postgraduate studies at the University of Edinburgh (Scotland). He received a second M.A. degree (1899) and the Ph.D. degree (1900) from Harvard University. He returned to Europe for a year of study at the University of Berlin, Germany.

Munro taught history and political science at Williams College in Williamstown, Massachusetts (1901–04). He served on the Harvard faculty as professor of government (1904–29) and for a time was chairman of the division of history, government, and economics. In 1929 Munro accepted appointment as Edward S. Harkness Professor of History and Government at the California Institute of Technology. He retired from active teaching in 1945 to become treasurer of the institute and a member of the board of trustees.

His published works include *Canada and British North America* (1904), *The Government of European Cities* (1909), *Initiative, Referendum and Recall* (1911), *Government of American Cities* (1912), *Selections from the Federalists* (1913), *Bibliography of Municipal Government* (1914), *Principles and Methods of Municipal Administration* (1916), *Leading Cases of the Constitution* (1917), *The Government of the United States* (1919), *Social Civics* (1922), *Municipal Government and Administration* (two volumes, 1923), *Current Problems in Citizenship* (1924), *The Governments of Europe* (1925), *The Invisible Government* (1927), *American Influences on Canadian Government* (1929), *Makers of the Unwritten Constitution* (1929), and *American Government of Today* (1930). He was an editorial writer for the *Boston Herald* (1907–21).

Munro was active in professional and civic organizations as a member of the Boston Budget Commission (1916), the American Political Science Association (president, 1927), and the American Association of University Professors (president, 1929–31) and a fellow of the American Academy of Arts and Sciences. He was a member of the board of overseers of Harvard University (1940–46). Munro received several honorary degrees.

REFERENCES: *LE* (II); *NCAB* (D:404); *WWW* (III); *NYT,* September 5, 1957, p. 29.   *Vincent Giardina*

MURCHISON, Carl Allanmore. B. December 3, 1887, Hickory, North Carolina, to Claudius Murat and Alice Penelope (Temple) Murchison. M. August 22, 1917, to Dorothea Powell. Ch. two. D. May 20, 1961, Provincetown, Massachusetts.

Carl Murchison received the A.B. degree (1909) from Wake Forest (North Carolina) College. He was a Rumrill Fellow at Harvard University (1909–10), studied at Rochester Theological Seminary (1910–13) and Yale University (1914–16), and was a Johnstone Scholar at Johns Hopkins University (1922–23), where he received the Ph.D. degree (1923).

Murchison taught psychology at Miami University in Oxford, Ohio (1916–17 and 1919–22). He served in World War I (1917–19). He joined the faculty at Clark University in Worcester, Massachusetts (1923–36), was department chairman (1924–36), and director of the Clark University Press (1926–36). He was editor of the Journal Press (1936–61). Murchison founded and edited many scholarly journals in the field of psychology.

Murchison was the author of *American White Criminal Intelligence* (1924), *Criminal Intelligence* (1926), and *Social Psychology* (1929). He was the editor of *Pedagogical Seminary and Journal of Genetic Psychology* (1924–61), Genetic Psychology Monographs (1925–61), *Journal of General Psychology* (1927–61), *Journal of Social Psychology* (1929–61), *The Psychological Register* (volume 2, 1929, volume 3, 1932), *The Foundations of Experimental Psychology* (1929), *Psychologies of 1925* (1926), *Psychologies of 1930* (1930), *A History of Psychology in Autobiography* (volume 1, 1930, volume 2, 1931; volume 3, 1936), *A Handbook of Child Psychology* (1931), *Handbook of General Experimental Psychology* (1934), *Handbook of Social Psychology* (1935), and *Journal of Psychology* (1935–61).

Murchison was a fellow of the American Association for the Advancement of Science and a member of professional associations. He was the recipient of two honorary degrees.

REFERENCES: *LE* (II); *WWW* (IV); *NYT,* May 22, 1961, p. 31.
                                                                John F. Ohles

MURLIN, Lemuel Herbert. B. November 16, 1861, Convoy, Ohio, to Orlando and Esther (Hankins) Murlin. M. October 12, 1893, to Ermina Fallass. Ch. none. D. June 20, 1935, Wayland, Michigan.

Lemuel Herbert Murlin's family settled in Mercer County, Ohio. At the age of sixteen he began teaching school in Convoy and Kalida, Ohio (1877–82). He left Ohio and went to Fort Wayne (Indiana) College where he taught from 1882 to 1886. He continued his education at DePauw University in Greencastle, Indiana, and received the B.A. (1891) and S.T.B. (1892) degrees.

Murlin was pastor of Methodist Episcopal churches in Fort Wayne, Indiana (1884–86), Knightsville, Indiana (1887–91), and Vincennes, Indiana (1891–94), before becoming president of Baker University in Baldwin, Kansas. During his administration at Baker (1894–1911) Murlin demonstrated administrative skills. He recruited students, extended campus facilities, balanced the university's budget, built its endowment fund, and was one of Kansas's most distinguished educational leaders.

Murlin became Boston University's third president in 1911. The student enrollment increased over seven times during his thirteen-year tenure. The university's endowment increased, new financial management was instituted, and the school of religious education and social services was established.

He returned to DePauw University and served as president during the last three years of his active professional life (1925–28). He introduced new administrative practices and reformed strict disciplinary codes. He retired from DePauw in 1928, and became pastor of the American Church in Berlin, Germany, but was forced to retire to his wife's family home in Michigan in 1929.

A prominent leader in the Methodist church, Murlin was president of the Educational Association of the Methodist Church (1905–15) and a delegate to general conferences of the church from 1900 to 1924 and to Methodist ecumenical conferences in London, England (1901), and Toronto, Canada (1911). He was a member of the Kansas state textbook commission and a special commission to reorganize the state educational administration. He was president of the Kansas Association of College Presidents, and Kansas director of the Religious Education Association and representative to the North Central Association of Colleges and Secondary Schools. He served as president of the American Association of Urban Universities (1920–25) and the New England Association of Colleges and Secondary Schools (1920–25). Murlin received honorary degrees from nine American colleges and universities.

REFERENCES: *LE* (I); *NCAB* (26:285); *TC; WWW* (I); Harold C. Case, *Harvest from the Seed: Boston University in Mid-Century* (New York: Newcomen Society in North America, 1957); George B. Manhart, *DePauw through the Years* (Greencastle, Ind.: DePauw University, 1962); "President Murlin of Boston University," *School and Society* 20 (November 22, 1924): 656; "Portrait of Lemuel Herbert Murlin," *Review of Reviews* 43 (June 1911): 6–11.   *Kim Sebaly*

MURPHREE, Albert Alexander. B. April 29, 1870, Murphree Valley, Blount County, Alabama, to Jesse Ellis and Emily Helen (Cornelius) Murphree. M. July 27, 1897, to Jennie Henderson. Ch. five. D. December 20, 1927, Gainesville, Florida.

Albert Alexander Murphree received his early education at Walnut Grove (Alabama) Academy and College (1880–87). In 1890 he enrolled in the Peabody Normal College (then part of the University of Nashville and, later, George Peabody College for Teachers). He received the A.B. (1894) and A.M. (1902) degrees from the University of Tennessee.

Murphree taught school at the age of seventeen in rural Tennessee schools. He became superintendent of schools in Cullman, Alabama, in 1892 and served as principal of the Summit (Alabama) Institute (1893). Upon completion of his work at Peabody in 1894, he accepted the principalship of a school in Cleburne, Texas; he suffered an almost fatal case of typhoid fever and decided to seek employment nearer his native state. He found a position as a Greek and mathematics teacher at the West Florida Seminary in Tallahassee (1895–97). At the age of twenty-seven, Murphree was president of the successor to the seminary, which had been renamed Florida State College (later, Florida State University). He served as president from 1897 to 1909.

He was selected president of the University of Florida in Gainesville in 1909, a position he held to his death in 1927. During his tenure as president, the university enrollment grew from under two hundred students to two thousand, and the physical plant was increased.

Murphree was president of the Florida Education Association (1906) and vice-president (1921) and president (1927) of the National Association of State Universities. He served as president of the Florida Baptist Conference (1922–24) and vice-president of the Southern Baptist Conference (1924–25). He was editor of the *Florida School Exponent* (1907–09). He was the recipient of two honorary degrees.

REFERENCES: *NCAB* (C:144); *WWW* (I); O. K. Armstrong, *The Life and Work of Dr. A. A. Murphree* (St. Augustine, Fla.: The Record Co., 1928).   *Phil Constans, Jr.*

MURPHY, John Benjamin. B. December 21, 1857, Appleton, Wisconsin, to Michael P. and Anna (Grimes) Murphy. M. November 25, 1885, to Jeanette C. Plamondon. Ch. five. D. August 11, 1916, Mackinac Island, Michigan.

John Benjamin Murphy received his education in the public schools and studied medicine under John R. Reilly of Appleton, Wisconsin. He was graduated from Rush Medical College in Chicago, Illinois, in 1879. He conducted a private practice (1879–82) and studied on the graduate level in Vienna, Austria, and in Germany at Heidelberg, Berlin, and Munich (1882–84).

Upon his return from Europe to Chicago, Murphy began to practice medicine with Edward W. Lee. Murphy was a specialist in abdominal surgery, a developing field as the result of bacteriological investigations and antispetic methods. He was an early investigator of the cause and treatment of peritonitis following appendicitis. In 1892 he produced the Murphy anastomosis button, a mechanical device for making rapid and accurate surgical connections within the intestinal and gastrointestinal tracts. Later he studied the surgery of the lungs and nervous system and was active in the surgery of bones and joints, particularly deformities resulting from infections.

Murphy was best known as a teacher of surgery. He began teaching in 1884 as a lecturer in surgery at Rush Medical College. He was professor of clinical surgery in the College of Physicians, Chicago (1892–1901), professor of surgery at Northwestern University Medical School (1901–05 and 1908–16), and professor of surgery at Rush Medical College (1905–08).

He was the author of many articles in professional journals and was editor of *General Surgery* (1911) and author of *The Surgical Clinics of John B. Murphy, M.D. at Mercy Hospital, Chicago* (five volumes, 1912–16). He was editor of *Yearbook of General Surgery* (1901).

Murphy was a member of many American and foreign associations. He was president of the Chicago Surgical Society and the Chicago Medical Society and vice-president of the National Association of Railway Surgeons. He was also a member of the Deutsche Gesellschaft für Chirurgie, Berlin, and the Surgical Society of Paris and was a fellow of the American Surgical Association and a member of the Twelfth International Medical Congress in Moscow, Russia.

Murphy received many honors at home and abroad. Notre Dame University awarded him the Laetare Medal (1902), and he was decorated knight-commander of the Order of St. Gregory the Great by the Vatican. He was awarded honorary degrees by the University of Illinois, Catholic University of America, and the University of Sheffield, England. The headquarters of the American College of Surgeons in Chicago was named the John B. Murphy Memorial, and Murphy Hospital in Chicago was also named in his honor.

REFERENCES: *DAB; NCAB* (13:602); *NYT,* August 12, 1916, p. 9; *WWW* (I).   *Darlene E. Fisher*

MURRAY, Lindley. B. June 7, 1745, Swetara, Pennsylvania, to Robert and Mary (Lindley) Murray. M. 1767 to Hannah Dobson. Ch. none. D. January 16, 1826, Holdgate, England.

The Murray family moved from Pennsylvania, first to North Carolina and then to New York City, where Robert Murray became a leading merchant. As the eldest of twelve children, Lindley Murray was expected to develop commercial interests; but he resisted these plans, and his father reluctantly consented to his studying law. Admitted to the New York bar, he engaged in a lucrative practice, which was interrupted for four years by the Revolutionary War. In 1783 ill health forced him to retire to a Hudson River estate, and in 1784, he sought a healthier climate in England, where he settled at Holdgate near York.

A devout Quaker, Murray published *The Power of Religion on the Mind* in 1787. At about the same time, he became interested in a Quaker school for girls that had been established by some friends in York. He assisted the teachers in preparing grammar lessons and with their encouragement wrote the *English Grammar* (1795), which has been credited as the first systematic study of grammar. The *Grammar* and subsequent works earned Murray the title Father of English Grammar. At the age of fifty, Murray embarked on a successful career writing schoolbooks despite a progressive deterioration of his health.

Over the next fifteen years Murray wrote *English Exercises* (1797), *Key to the Exercises* (1797), *An Abridgement of Murray's English Grammar* (1797), *English Reader* (1799), *Introduction to the English Reader* (1800), and *Sequel to the English Reader* (1801). A long interest in the study of French was reflected in *Lecteur français* (1802) and *Introduction au lecteur français* (1807). An *English Spelling-Book* (1804), a two-volume octavio edition of the *Grammar* and related books (1808) and a *First Book for Children* (n.d.) completed Murray's educational writings. Two religious works were published in 1812 and 1817.

By 1810, Lindley Murray was housebound. At the time of his death in 1826, he had gained recognition in England and the United States. His grammars and readers were used extensively in both English and American schools, and they were published as late as 1857 in the United States. His recognition also included honorary memberships in two New York literary societies, the Historical Society (1810) and the Literary and Philosophical Society (1816).

REFERENCES: *AC; DAB; NCAB* (7:178); *TC; WWW* (H); Elizabeth Frank, *Memoirs of the Life and Letters of Lindley Murray* (York, England: Longman, Rees, Orme, Brown, and Green, 1826).   *John F. Ohles*

MURSELL, James Lockhart. B. June 1, 1893, Derby, England, to James Cuthbert and Jean Murray (Lockhart) Mursell. M. December 30, 1919, to Alice Ethred May. Ch. one.

James Lockhart Mursell was educated at Edinburgh (Scotland) Academy, Taunton (England) School, and Kyre College in Adelaide, South Australia. He received the B.A. degree (1915) from the University of Queensland, Australia, and the Ph.D. degree (1918) from Harvard University. He also studied at the graduate level in New York City at Union Theological Seminary and Columbia University.

He was director of the research and library departments of the Inter-Church World Movement (1919–20). He was professor of psychology and education at Lake Erie College in Painesville, Ohio (1921–23), and professor of education at Lawrence College in Appleton, Wisconsin (1923–35), where he gained national prominence for his research and writing in education and music education. He advocated instruction in music by classroom teachers and the child-centered concept in music education. He joined the faculty at Teachers College, Columbia University, in 1935 where he served as chairman of the department of education and the department of music education until his retirement in 1959.

Mursell was the author of *Principles of Musical Education* (1927), *Psychology of School Music Teaching* (with Mabelle Glenn, 1931), *Psychology of Secondary School Teaching* (1932), *Principles of Education* (1934), *Human Values in Music Education* (1934), *Workbook in Principles of Education* (1934), *Streamline Your Mind* (1936), *Psychology of Music* (1937), *Educational Psychology* (1939), and *Psychology for Modern Education* (1952).

Mursell was a member of the research council of the Music Educators National Association (later, Music Educators National Conference).

REFERENCES: *LE* (III); *WW* (XXII); H. R. Wilson, "James L. Mursell," *Music Educators Journal* 49 (April 1963): 116–17; Leonard J. Simutis, "James Lockhart Mursell as Music Educator" (Master's thesis, University of Ottawa, 1961). *John F. Ohles*

MUZZEY, David Saville. B. October 9, 1870, Lexington, Massachusetts, to David W. and Annie W. (Saville) Muzzey. M. September 20, 1900, to Ina Jeannette Bullis. M. June 23, 1937, to J. Emilie Young. Ch. two. D. April 14, 1965, New York, New York.

David Saville Muzzey attended Harvard University and received the A.B. degree (1893), was graduated from the Union Theological Seminary in 1897, and received the B.D. degree (1907) from New York University. He studied at the University of Berlin, Germany (1897–98), and the Sorbonne in Paris, France (1898–99). He received the Ph.D. degree (1907) from Columbia University.

Muzzey taught mathematics at Robert College in Constantinople, Turkey (1893–94), and mathematics, classics, and history at the Ethical Culture School in New York City from 1899, and he was director of the history department from 1905. He began to teach at Barnard College of Columbia University in 1905 and continued there to 1940; he became Gouverneur Morris Professor of History at Columbia University in 1938, remaining there to his retirement.

Muzzey was particularly influential as a writer of textbooks and with Frank A. Magruder *(q.v.)* dominated the high school social studies market.

He attempted to depict realistically the American Revolution and other periods of American history and was attacked as unpatriotic and un-American. Among his books were *Rise of the New Testament* (1900), *Spiritual Heroes* (1902), *The Spiritual Franciscans* (1907), *Beginners Latin Book* (1907), *An American History* (1911), *State, Church, and School in France* (1911), *Readings in American History* (1915), *Life of Thomas Jefferson* (1918), *The United States of America* (1922–24), *History of the American People* (1927), *James G. Blaine* (1934), and *Ethics as a Religion* (1951). He was literary editor for the *Standard* of New York City.

Muzzey was assistant leader of the Society of Ethical Culture and received an honorable mention by the Pulitzer Prize jury for his book on James G. Blaine.

REFERENCES: *LE* (III); *WWW* (IV); *NYT,* April 15, 1965, p. 33.

John F. Ohles

MYERS, Garry Cleveland. B. July 15, 1884, Sylvan, Pennsylvania, to John Abner and Sara Alice (Besore) Myers. M. June 26, 1912, to Caroline Clark. Ch. three. D. July 19, 1971, Boyds Mills, Pennsylvania.

Educated in Pennsylvania public schools, Garry Cleveland Myers served as a country schoolteacher to support his education at Cumberland Valley State Normal School, from which he was graduated in 1905. He was appointed public school superintendent in Mercersburg, Pennsylvania. Continuing his formal education at Ursinus College in Collegeville, Pennsylvania, he received the A.B. degree (1909). He received the Ph.D. degree (1913) from Columbia University. He also studied at the University of Pennsylvania (1909–10).

Myers was professor of psychology and social science at Juniata College in Huntingdon, Pennsylvania (1912–14). In 1914 he became professor of psychology and education at the Maxwell Training School for Teachers in Brooklyn, New York, serving until 1918, when he joined the United States Army. He was the director of education at the First Recruit Educational Centre at Camp Upton, New York, where he developed textbooks and educational methods and trained teachers to staff other recruit educational centers (1918–19). He also served as director of Americanization programs.

In 1920 Myers was appointed head of the department of psychology at the Cleveland School of Education and was chairman of the division of psychology of the senior college of Western Reserve University (later, Case Western Reserve University), both in Cleveland, Ohio. A pioneer in methods of training children, Myers instituted a new course for parents under the auspices of the school of applied social sciences at Western Reserve. In 1927 he was appointed head of the division of parental education at the Cleveland College of Western Reserve University, serving in that capacity until 1940. He advocated enrichment of the school curriculum for the brighter pupil rather than accelerated promotions. Myers served as a leader in the public forums sponsored by the United States Office of Education (1937–39).

Myers was a productive researcher and writer throughout his long career. Among his publications were *New York City Penmanship Scale* (with Clyde C. Listen, 1914–18), *Army Lessons in English* (1918–20), *Language of America* (1921), *Myers' Mental Measure* (1921), *Measuring Minds* (1921), *Pantomime Group Intelligence Test* (1922), *Prevention and Correction of Errors in Arithmetic* (1924), *The Learner and His Attitude* (1925), *The Modern Parent* (1930), *Building Personality in the Child at Home* (1931), *Building Personality in the Child at School* (1931), *The Modern Family* (1934), *Homes Build Persons* (with C. C. Myers, 1951), *Creative Thinking Activities* (1965), *Headwork for Preschoolers* (1968), and *Headwork for Elementary Children* (with C. C. Myers, 1968).

He was founder and editor of *Highlights for Children* (1946–71), associate editor of *Education* and *Child Welfare Magazine* (1930–31), and editor-in-chief of *Children's Activities* (1934–46) and *Weedom's Modern Encyclopedia* (1931). He wrote a syndicated newspaper column, "The Parent Problem," for over thirty years.

A certified consulting psychologist, Myers was sought as a lecturer in child psychology. Active in many national, state, and local professional societies and civic groups, he was a fellow in the American Psychology Association, the American Educational Research Association, the Ohio Academy of Science (vice-president, 1936–37), and the American Association for the Advancement of Science. He was a member of the Society for Research in Child Development (president) and a member of the board of trustees of the National Association for Better Radio and Television (1959–60) and the Magazine Publishers Association (second vice-president, 1965). He was awarded the Citation of Merit by the National Association for Gifted Children (1967).

REFERENCES: *CA* (29–32); *LE* (III); *NCAB* (D:146); *WWAE* (XXII); *WWW* (V); *Who's Who in the East*, 12th ed. (Chicago: Marquis, 1969).

Charles M. Dye

MYERS, George William. B. April 30, 1864, Champaign County, Illinois, to Robert Henry and Mary Helen (Shawhan) Myers. M. June 27, 1889, to Mary Eva Sim. Ch. four. D. November 23, 1931, Chicago, Illinois.

George W. Myers received the B.L. (1888) and M.L. (1891) degrees from the University of Illinois and studied science at the University of Munich, Germany, where he received the Ph.D. degree (1896).

After teaching mathematics at the University of Illinois (1888–96),

Myers was associate professor (1896–97) and professor (1897–1900) of astronomy and applied mathematics and director of the observatory at Illinois; he planned the observatory and selected and installed the telescope. He was head of the mathematics department at Chicago (Illinois) Institute (1900–01) and was professor of the teaching of mathematics and astronomy at the University of Chicago from 1901 to his retirement in 1929. He was a pioneer in the field of correlated and unified mathematics.

Myers wrote many arithmetic textbooks, including *Rational Elementary Arithmetic* (with Sarah C. Brooks, 1905), *Myers-Brooks Elementary Arithmetic* (with Sarah C. Brooks, 1907), *First Year Mathematics for Secondary Schools* (with others, 1907), *Myers Arithmetic* (1908), *Geometric Exercises for Algebraic Solution* (with others, 1907), *Second-Year Mathematics for Secondary Schools* (with others, 1910), *Elementary Algebra* (with G. E. Atwood, 1916), *Elementary Algebraic Geometry* (1921), and *Elements of High School Mathematics* (1921). He translated *Experimental Physics* by Eugen Lommel (1899). He was a member of the editorial staff of *School Science and Mathematics* for thirty-one years and edited the Standard Service Arithmetics.

An internationally recognized scholar, Myers was a member of many mathematical and astronomical societies in the United States and foreign countries.

REFERENCES: *NYT,* November 24, 1931, p. 25; *WWW* (I); *Mathematics Teacher* 25 (January 1932): 44; *School Science and Mathematics* 32 (January 1932): 10–11.   *John F. Ohles*

MYERS, Phillip Van Ness. B. August 10, 1846, Tribes Hill, New York, to Jacob and Catherine L. (Morris) Myers. M. July 20, 1876, to Ida C. Miller. Ch. none. D. September 20, 1937, Cincinnati, Ohio.

Phillip Van Ness Myers studied at Gilmour Academy in Ballston Spa, New York, and received the B.A. (1871) and A.M. (1874) degrees from Williams College in Williamstown, Massachusetts. He studied law at the Yale University Law School (1873–74) and received the LL.B. degree (1890). While attending Williams, Myers traveled to South America as a member of the school's lyceum scientific expedition. With his brother Henry Myers, also a member of the expedition, he wrote a description of the trip, *Life and Nature under the Tropics* (1871). After his graduation from Williams, Myers traveled in Europe and Asia for two years and wrote *Remains of Lost Empires* (1875).

Following a brief experience in teaching, Myers moved to Columbus, Ohio, and practiced law and accepted the presidency of Farmer's College near Cincinnati, Ohio, in 1879. He was appointed to the University of Cincinnati in 1890 as a lecturer in history and political economy and instructor in rhetoric and served as dean of the academic faculty (1895–97).

In 1900 Myers resigned his position to protest the summary removal of several faculty members and his own reduction in status from professor to lecturer. The prestige Myers enjoyed forced a hearing on the matter before the university board of directors, but the action was sustained and Myers went into retirement. Sixteen years later, his contributions to the university were recognized by his appointment as honorary lecturer in history.

Many of Myers's books were used as texts in institutions of higher learning throughout the world. Among his writings were *Ancient History* (1872), *Mediaeval and Modern History* (1889), *General History* (1889), *Eastern Nations and Greece* (1890), *History of Rome* (1890), *History of Greece* (1897), *Rome, Its Rise and Fall* (1900), *The Middle Ages* (1902), *The Modern Age* (1903), and *History as Past Ethics* (1913).

Myers received honorary degrees from Belmont College, the University of Cincinnati, and Miami University.

REFERENCES: *NCAB* (12:149); *NYT,* September 21, 1937, p. 25; *WWW* (I); Reginald C. McGrane, *The University of Cincinnati: A Success Story in Urban Higher Education* (New York: Harper & Row, 1963).

Daniel D. Edgar

N

NASH, George Williston. B. December 22, 1868, Janesville, Wisconsin, to Newman Curtis and Elizabeth (Williston) Nash. M. November 17, 1903, to Adelaide M. Warburton. Ch. two. D. June 30, 1944, Bellingham, Washington.

George Williston Nash attended the public schools in Canton, South Dakota, and was graduated with the B.S. (1891) and M.S. (1895) degrees from Yankton (South Dakota) College. He studied at the University of Leipzig, Germany, and in Paris, France (1894–95), and pursued postgraduate studies in mathematics and astronomy at the University of Minnesota (1887–88).

Nash was publisher with his father of the *Sioux Valley News* in Canton, South Dakota (1891–92). He became an instructor in mathematics at Augustana College in Canton (1891). He was principal of Yankton College Academy (1893–97) and was professor of mathematics and astronomy at Yankton College (1897–1903).

Nash was state superintendent of public instruction in South Dakota (1903–05). He set up a system of uniform certification for teachers and worked for improved teaching standards. He served as president of the

Northern Normal and Industrial School (later, Northern State Teachers College) in Aberdeen, South Dakota (1905–14). During his administration there was a steady growth in enrollment and improved management of the school. He was president of the State Normal School (later, Western Washington College of Education) in Bellingham, Washington (1914–22). He resigned in 1922 to become the first president of the Congregational Foundation of Education in Chicago, Illinois. He returned to South Dakota as president of Yankton College in 1925 and served there until he retired in 1940. He returned to Bellingham, Washington, and continued to solicit financial assistance for Yankton College.

He was an elector for the New York University Hall of Fame (1925–44) and a director of the Chicago Theological Seminary. He was a member of the Washington State Board of Education and Joint Board of Higher Curricula (1920–21), a member of the youth service committee of Rotary International (1936–37), and a member of the advisory committee to the National Youth Administration for South Dakota. Nash was the recipient of several honorary degrees.

REFERENCES: *LE* (II); *NCAB* (39:527); *WWAE* (I); *WWW* (II).

Lawrence S. Master

NASH, Jay Bryan. B. October 17, 1886, New Baltimore, Ohio, to William L. and Harriet (Bryan) Nash. M. February 19, 1915, to Gladys Caldwell. M. 1935 to Emma R. Frazier. Ch. two. D. September 20, 1965, New York, New York.

Jay B. Nash, a leader in the new physical education movement, was graduated from Oberlin (Ohio) College with the A.B. degree (1911) and received the M.A. (1927) and Ph.D. (1929) degrees from New York University.

Nash moved to Oakland, California, where he taught in the public schools (1911–14) and was assistant director of recreation for the city (1915–18) under Clark Hetherington *(q.v.)*. He served for one year under Hetherington as assistant state supervisor of physical education in California (1918–19) before returning to Oakland to become superintendent of recreation and director of physical education (1919–26). Nash followed Hetherington to New York University where he was a member of the faculty (1926–53). Hetherington resigned in 1930 to return to Stanford University, and Nash became chairman of the department of health, physical education, and recreation and held that position in the school of education at New York University until his retirement in 1953. After he retired, Nash served as Fulbright lecturer to India (1953–54), dean of the college of health, physical education, and recreation at Brigham Young University in Provo, Utah (1954–55), and executive secretary of the New York State Association for Health, Physical Education and Recreation.

Nash made significant contributions in his interpretations of organic and emotional development, recreation, use of leisure, school and family camping, theory of play, skill learning, and health teaching. He added to the discipline the idea of the creative potential of play, suggesting that there is creativeness in every person.

Nash was the author of many books, including *Physical Education in Public Schools* (1921), *Organization and Administration of Playgrounds and Recreation* (1927), *Organization and Administration of Physical Education* (1931), *Standards of Play and Recreation Administration* (1931), *Spectatoritis* (1939), *Teachable Moments* (1939), and *Building Morale* (1942) and coauthor of *Paths to Better Schools* (1945), *Physical Education, Its Interpretation and Objectives* (1948), *Philosophy of Recreation and Leisure* (1953), *Opportunities in Health and Physical Education* (1953), and *Opportunities in Camping and Outdoor Recreation* (1963). He was editor of the five-volume *Interpretations of Physical Education* (1932).

Nash was active in professional associations and was president of the American Association of Health, Physical Education and Recreation (AAHPER) in 1942–43 and founder and president of the American Academy of Physical Education (1945–47). He received the Honor Award (1932) of the AAHPER, the Gulick Award (1940), and the Hetherington Award (1955). He received an honorary degree from Springfield College.

REFERENCES: *LE* (III); *NCAB* (A:187); *NYT,* October 11, 1965, p. 61; *WWAE* (XXII); *WWW* (IV); Ellen W. Gerber, *Innovators and Institutions in Physical Education* (Philadelphia: Lea and Febiger, 1971).

Richard B. Morland

NASH, Mell Achilles. B. July 20, 1890, Tryon, Texas, to Newton Achilles and Nancy Susan (Moody) Nash. M. August 6, 1916, to Mae Clarke. Ch. five.

Mell Achilles Nash was graduated from Central State Teachers College (later, Central State University) in Edmond, Oklahoma (1910), and received the A.B. (1919) and A.M. (1927) degrees from the University of Oklahoma. He also studied at the University of Michigan (1914).

Nash served in Oklahoma schools as a rural schoolteacher in Greer County (1908–10), principal of the high school in Granite (1910–12), superintendent of schools in Noble (1912–14), high school principal in Madill (1914–16), and superintendent of schools in Idabel (1916–19). He was chief high school inspector for the Oklahoma state department of education (1919–20). He was secretary of the Oklahoma Education Association and editor of the *Oklahoma Teacher* (1920–23). Nash was elected state superintendent in 1922 and was reelected in 1926, serving from 1923 to April 1927 when he resigned to accept the presidency of the Oklahoma College for Women (later, University of Science and Arts of Oklahoma) at Chickasha.

Nash served as president of the Oklahoma College for Women to 1943 and was credited as being a forceful leader who built the college into a quality institution. He served as chancellor of the Oklahoma State Regents for Higher Education (1943–61) and directed the development of state institutions during the period of rapid expansion following World War II.

Nash was a member of professional associations and was president of the State Board of Education of Oklahoma (1922–27). He established the Nash Award in 1943 to recognize outstanding students at the Oklahoma College for Women. He was awarded an honorary degree by the Oklahoma Baptist University in 1923. The Nash Library at the University of Science and Arts of Oklahoma is named in his honor.

REFERENCES: *LE* (III); *WWAE* (VIII); *WW* (XXXI); *Alumni News, Oklahoma College of Liberal Arts* (Spring 1974).   *John F. Ohles*

NEEF, Francis Joseph Nicholas. B. December 6, 1770, Soultz, Alsace, France, to Francis Joseph and Anastasia (Ackermann) Neef. M. July 5, 1803, to Eloisa Buss. Ch. five. D. April 6, 1854, New Harmony, Indiana.

Joseph Neef studied for the priesthood but discontinued his studies to join the French army under Napoleon Bonaparte when he was twenty-one years old. He was discharged from the army after being seriously injured at the battle of Arcola (Italy).

He was a teacher of languages and gymnastics at Johann Heinrich Pestalozzi's Burgdorf (Switzerland) School (1799–1803). He moved to Paris, France, where he founded a Pestalozzian school. In 1806 he moved to Philadelphia, Pennsylvania, under the sponsorship of William Maclure, learned the English language, and established the first Pestalozzian school in the United States in Falls of the Schuykill near Philadelphia (1808–12). He moved the school to Village Green, Philadelphia (1813–14). Neef moved to Louisville, Kentucky, where he conducted a school from 1814 to 1826.

Neef joined the New Harmony (Indiana) experimental Owenite community in 1826 as head of the community schools. When the community disintegrated in 1828, he moved to Ohio, first to Cincinnati and then to Steubenville in 1828 where he managed his last school. He retired to a farm in Jeffersonville, Indiana (1834), and then returned to New Harmony (1834–54).

A devoted Pestalozzian teacher, Neef's many schools were short-lived, in part because of his uncompromising position against established religion. He was the author of *Sketch of a Plan and Method of Education, Founded on an Analysis of the Human Faculties and Natural Reason, Suitable for the Offspring of a Free People and for All Rational Beings* (1808), which is considered the first pedagogical work published in English in the United States. His second book was a translation into English of *The*

Logic of Condillac as an Illustration of the Plan of Education Established at His School Near Philadelphia (1809). He also wrote *Method of Instructing Children Rationally in the Arts of Writing and Reading* (1813).

REFERENCES: *DAB; WWW* (H); Arthur E. Bestor, *Backwoods Utopias* (Philadelphia: University of Pennsylvania Press, 1950); George B. Lockwood, *The New Harmony Movement* (New York: D. Appleton and Co., 1905). *Thomas A. Barlow*

NEILL, Edward Duffield. B. August 9, 1823, Philadelphia, Pennsylvania, to Henry and Martha R. (Duffield) Neill. M. October 4, 1847, to Nancy Hall. Ch. five. D. September 26, 1893, St. Paul, Minnesota.

Edward Duffield Neill attended the University of Pennsylvania (1837–39) and transferred to Amherst (Massachusetts) College where he was graduated in 1842. He attended Andover (Massachusetts) Theological Seminary for one year, completed his theological studies in Philadelphia, was licensed to preach by the Presbyterian church in 1847, and was ordained in 1848.

He preached in Galena, Illinois, and established the First Presbyterian Church in St. Paul, Minnesota Territory, in 1849. He helped to establish the public schools in St. Paul and was the first superintendent of public instruction for Minnesota Territory (1851–53) and first state superintendent of public instruction when Minnesota became a state (1860–61). During the Civil War, he was chaplain for the First Minnesota Infantry (1861–62) and hospital chaplain in Philadelphia, Pennsylvania (1862–64). Neill was a private secretary to presidents Abraham Lincoln and Andrew Johnson (1864–69) and then was appointed consul to Dublin, Ireland (1869–71).

Neill founded the short-lived Baldwin School and College of St. Paul before the Civil War and, on his return to Minnesota in 1872, opened Jesus College, a religious but nonsectarian institution in Minneapolis, another unsuccessful venture. He persuaded Charles Macalester of Philadelphia to give a building for a college, raised an endowment, and renamed the college Macalester College in 1874. Neill was president of Macalester College to 1884, continuing from 1885 to 1893 as professor of history, English literature, and political economy and also as college librarian. He became pastor of the Calvary Reformed Episcopal Church in St. Paul in 1874 but later returned to the Presbyterian church.

Neill wrote many magazine articles and several books considered by historians to contain important documentary materials. Among his publications were *A History of Minnesota* (1858), *Terra Maria, or Threads of Maryland Colonial History* (1867), *History of the Virginia Company of London* (1869), *The English Colonization of America During the 17th Century* (1871), *Founders of Maryland* (1876), *Virginia Vetusta, The Colony under James I* (1885), *Virginia Carolorum* (1886), *Concise History of*

Minnesota (1887), and *Macalester College Contributions* (two volumes, 1890, 1892).

REFERENCES: *AC; DAB; NCAB* (9:411); *TC; WWW* (H); *Minneapolis Tribune,* September 27, 1893; *NYT,* September 28, 1893, p. 4.

Lawrence Byron Smelser

NEILSON, William Allan. B. March 26, 1869, Doune, Perthshire, Scotland, to David and Mary (Allan) Neilson. M. June 25, 1906, to Elisabeth Muser. Ch. three. D. February 13, 1946, Northampton, Massachusetts.

William Allan Neilson, educator and scholar, was educated in Scotland at Montrose Academy and Edinburgh University. He emigrated to Canada where he taught English at Upper Canada College in Toronto. He received the M.A. (1896) and Ph.D. (1898) degrees from Harvard University. He taught English at Bryn Mawr (Pennsylvania) College (1898–1900), Columbia University (1904–06), and Harvard (1900–04 and 1906–17).

In 1917 Neilson became president of Smith College in Northampton, Massachusetts, where he remained until his retirement in 1939. As president of Smith he beautified the campus and expanded the physical facilities. He raised admissions standards and initiated a junior year abroad program and a special honors program, which encouraged independent study and research.

Neilson was a prolific writer; his works include *Origins and Sources of the Court of Love* (1899), *The Essentials of Poetry* (1912), *The Facts about Shakespeare* (1913), *Burns: How to Know Him* (1917), *A History of English Literature* (1920), and *Intellectual Honesty* (1920). He was editor and coeditor of many works and associate editor of the Harvard Classics (1909) and the Harvard Classics Shelf of Fiction (1917). In 1934 he was editor-in-chief of *Webster's New International Dictionary* (second edition).

A strong supporter of humanitarian causes, he was cochairman of the Committee for the Protection of the Foreign Born, a director of the National Refugee Service, and a board member of the National Association for the Advancement of Colored People. At the time of his death in 1946 he was writing a history of Smith College. He received many awards and fifteen honorary degrees.

REFERENCES: *DAB* (supp. 4); *LE* (II); *NCAB* (33: 12); *WWAE* (VIII); *WWW* (II); *NYT,* February 14, 1946, p. 25.   *Thomas L. Bernard*

NEUMANN, John Nepomucene. B. March 28, 1811, Prachatitz, Bohemia, to Philip and Agnes (Lebisch) Neumann. M. no. D. January 5, 1860, Philadelphia, Pennsylvania.

John Nepomucene Neumann studied in Budweis, Bohemia, at the Pious Workers' Gymnasium (1823–31) and the Cistercian College theological seminary (1831–33). He completed his studies (1833–35) at the school of theology at Charles Ferdinand University in Prague, Bohemia (later, Czechoslovakia). He emigrated to the United States, where he was ordained in New York City in 1836.

Neumann was assigned to Williamsville, New York, as a missionary to the Niagara Falls area (1836–40). He entered the Congregation of the Most Holy Redeemer in 1840 and was the first to profess as a Redemptorist in the United States in 1842. He was assigned to St. James Church in Baltimore, Maryland (1842–44), and served as a missionary in Maryland, Virginia, and Pennsylvania. He moved to Pittsburgh, Pennsylvania, in 1844, where he built the St. Philomena Church and served as superior to the Redemptorist community. Returning to Baltimore, he was vice regent and vice provincial of American Redemptorist (1847–49) and consultant to the vice provincial and pastor of St. Alphonsus parish in Baltimore (1849–52). In Baltimore he assigned the Sisters of Notre Dame to parochial schools and was regarded as the founder of the order in the United States.

Neumann was appointed bishop of Philadelphia, Pennsylvania, in 1851 and was consecrated in 1852. During his eight-year tenure he erected over eighty churches, established the first diocesan school system, and built about a hundred parochial schools. He founded a preparatory seminary at Glen Riddle, Pennsylvania, and St. Joseph's College in Susquehanna County, Pennsylvania. He introduced into the diocese several orders of sisters and brothers and founded the Sister of the Third Order of St. Francis in Philadelphia.

Neumann wrote *Kleiner Katechismus* (1846), *Katholischer Katechismus* (1846), and *Biblische Geschichte des Alten und Neuen Testamentes zum Gebrauch der katolischen Schulen* (1849). Neumann was declared venerable in 1921, beatified in 1963, and canonized in 1977 as the first American male saint.

REFERENCES: *AC; DAB; EB; NCAB* (5:232); "Bishop Neumann Canonized; First Male Saint from U.S.," *NYT,* June 20, 1977, p. 1; *TC; WWW* (H).   *John F. Ohles*

NEVINS, Allan. B. May 20, 1890, Camp Point, Illinois, to Joseph Allan and Emma (Stahl) Nevins. M. December 30, 1916, to Mary Fleming Richardson. Ch. two. D. March 5, 1971, San Marino, California.

Allan Nevins, America's leading historian for over four decades, left his farm home at the age of eighteen and entered the University of Illinois where he received the A.B. (1912) and A.M. (1913) degrees.

Nevins was an instructor of English at Illinois (1912–13). He moved to New York City and began his work as a journalist as an editorial writer for the *Nation* (1913–18) and for several newspapers in New York, including the *New York Evening Post* (1913–23), the *New York Sun* (1924–25), and the *New York World* (1925–27).

Nevins joined the history department at Cornell University in Ithaca, New York, in 1928 but returned to New York City one year later to accept a similar position at Columbia University. He became De Witt Clinton Professor of American History in 1931 and held the position until his retirement in 1958. After his retirement, Nevins was a senior research associate at the Huntington Library in San Marino, California.

Nevins wrote over fifty books, edited at least seventy-five others, and wrote many articles and reviews. He compiled many biographical entries for the *Encyclopedia Britannica* and produced thirty-three entries for the *Dictionary of American Biography*. His first work to receive critical acclaim was *The American States During and After the Revolution* (1924). He received the Pulitzer Prize for biography in 1933 for *Grover Cleveland: A Study in Courage* (1932) and in 1937 for *Hamilton Fish: The Inner History of the Grant Administration,* and he received the Scribner Centenary Prize and the Bancroft Prize in 1947 for the first two volumes of his Civil War history, *The Ordeal of the Union* (1947). His studies of American industrialists forced historians to reappraise the dominance of economic self-interest as motivation in American social life.

Among his other books were *Life of Robert Rogers* (1914), *Illinois* (1917), *The Evening Post—A Century of Journalism* (1922), *American Social History Recorded by British Travellers* (1923), *The Emergence of Modern America* (1927), *Fremont, the World's Greatest Adventurer* (1927), *Henry White* (1930), *The Gateway to History* (1938), *John D. Rockefeller* (1940), *America in World Affairs* (1941), *A Brief History of Britain* (1943), *The Emergence of Lincoln* (two volumes, 1952), *The War for the Union* (two volumes, 1959, two volumes, 1961), *Herbert H. Lehman* (1963), and the last two of the eight volumes of *The Ordeal of the Union* (1971).

Nevins was the general editor of the American Political Leaders, the Yale Press Series, Chronicles of America Series, and the D. C. Heath Colleges and University History Series. Nevins initiated the popular *American Heritage* series. He encouraged the teaching of history in American high schools. He conceived and initiated the oral history project at Columbia University in 1948. Nevins was an interpreter of the American experience, especially the Civil War, and tried to produce historical narratives that enlivened the present through its clear analysis and exciting presentation of the past. He was credited with establishing the need to write history for the general public and attracting the general public to the need for historical understanding in daily affairs.

He served in the Office of War Information in Australia and New Zealand (1943–45) and as an information officer and cultural attaché in the United States embassy in London during World War II. Nevins spent an unprecedented two terms as Harmsworth Professor of History at Oxford

(England) University (1940–41 and 1964–65). He was president of the American Historical Association (1960), the American Academy of Arts and Letters (1966–68), and the Society of American Historians (1950–61), which he founded. He was a member of the Council on Foreign Relations and a trustee of the Woodrow Wilson International Center for Scholars from 1969 to his death. He was chairman of the Civil War Centennial Committee (1961–66). He anonymously donated money to establish a professorship in economic history at Columbia University in 1965, a chair that now carries his name. Nevins was awarded over twenty honorary degrees.

REFERENCES: *CA* (5–8); *CB* (October 1968 and April 1971); *LE* (II); *NCAB* (E:510); *NYT,* March 6, 1971, p. 1; *WWW* (V); Ray Allen Billington, *Allan Nevins on History* (New York: Charles Scribner's Sons, 1975); Henry Steele Commager *(q.v.),* "Obituary," *American Historical Review* 77 (June 1972): 869–72; *Journal of American History* 58 (September 1971): 535.   *Kim Sebaly*

NEWCOMB, John Lloyd. B. December 18, 1881, Sassafras, Virginia, to Benjamin Carey and Martha Jane (Coleman) Newcomb. M. October 24, 1924, to Grace Elliott (Shields) Russell. Ch. none. D. February 22, 1954, Charlottesville, Virginia.

John Lloyd Newcomb received the A.B. degree (1900) from the College of William and Mary and a degree in civil engineering from the University of Virginia (1903).

He worked for the Norfolk and Southern Railway (1903–05) and joined the faculty of the University of Virginia. He became dean of the school of engineering (1925), acting president (1931–33), and president of the university (1933–47). During the time he was president, the undergraduate program was reorganized, honors courses were instituted, enrollment increased, new buildings were constructed, including law and engineering buildings, and the Woodrow Wilson School of Foreign Service and International Affairs was established.

Newcomb was president of the National Association of State Universities (1943–44) and the American Association for the United Nations and was a member of the board of trustees of the Carnegie Foundation for the Advancement of Teaching. He was a member of the board of visitors of the United States Naval Academy and the board of trustees of the Virginia War Fund and the Special Committee on Aeronautical Research in Educational Institutions. He was a member of many organizations, including the Society for the Promotion of Engineering Education. He received four honorary degrees.

REFERENCES: *LE* (III); *NCAB* (F:98); *WWW* (III); *NYT,* February 24, 1954, p. 25.   *Robert Emans*

NEWELL, McFadden Alexander. B. September 7, 1824, Belfast, Ireland, to John and Agnes (Johnson) Newell. M. 1846 to Susanna Rippard. M. 1885 to Charlotte (Davies) Murrell. Ch. two. D. August 14, 1893, Havre de Grace, Maryland.

The son of an Irish educator, McFadden Alexander Newell studied with his father at a private school, at Queen's College in Belfast, Ireland, and Trinity College in Dublin, Ireland, from which he was graduated (1846).

Newell taught at the Mechanics Institute in Liverpool, England (1846–48). He went to the United States to visit relatives in 1848 and decided to stay. He was employed as an instructor of natural sciences in the Central High School (later, Baltimore City College) in Baltimore, Maryland (1850–54). He taught at Madison College in Uniontown, Pennsylvania, and then returned to Baltimore. He was an associate principal of a large business college he founded with his brother-in-law, James Rippard, and principal of a large grammar school for boys. He went to Pittsburgh, Pennsylvania, to teach with his cousins, John, James P., and Hugh Newell in the Newell Institute.

Returning to Baltimore in 1865, Newell was principal of the newly established Normal School (later, Towson State College) for teacher training, the first such institution in Maryland. In 1868 he also assumed the position of state superintendent of public instruction. A strong believer in formal teacher training, Newell continued in these positions for over two decades. At the normal school, he developed a model school, improved the curriculum, and established institutes for in-service training. He was president of the National Educational Association (1877–78), founded and edited the *Maryland School Journal* (1874–80), and coauthored with William R. Creery the Maryland Series of six readers for the Maryland schools, the first of which was published in 1868.

REFERENCES: *AC; NCAB* (12:512); Mary C. Cain, *The Historical Development of State Normal Schools for White Teachers in Maryland* (New York: Teachers College, Columbia University, 1941); Committee of the Alumni, *Seventy-five Years of Teacher Education* (Towson, Md.: The college, 1941); *NEA Proceedings* 33 (1894): 234–36.   *Richard J. Cox*

NEWLON, Jesse Homer. B. July 16, 1882, Salem, Indiana, to Richard Rosecrans and Arra Belle (Cauble) Newlon. M. December 29, 1909, to Letha Hiestand. Ch. none. D. September 1, 1941, New York, New York.

Jesse H. Newlon attended the University of Indiana, from which he was graduated with the A.B. degree (1907). He received the M.A. degree from Columbia University in 1914.

Newlon was high school principal in Charlestown, Indiana (1905–06), and taught history and mathematics in the New Albany (Indiana) high school (1907–08). He taught in Decatur, Illinois (1908–12), and was principal in the high school there (1912–16). He moved to Lincoln, Nebraska, as a high school principal (1916–17) and was superintendent of schools from 1917 to 1920. In 1920 Newlon became superintendent of the Denver (Colorado) public schools and stayed in that position for seven years. During his period of superintendency, fifteen schools were constructed in Denver.

Newlon resigned from his Denver position in 1927 to become director of education in the Lincoln School of Teachers College, Columbia University (1927–37). He was also chairman of the division of instruction (1934–38) and director of the division of foundations of education (1938–41).

Newlon served as an associate editor of *School Executive* from 1927 until his death in 1941. He authored *Administration of Junior and Senior High Schools* (with others, 1922), *The New Social Civics* (1926), *The Newlon-Hanna Speller* (with Paul R. Hanna, q.v., 1933), *Educational Administration as Social Policy* (1934), and *Education for Democracy in Our Time* (1939).

He was president of the National Education Association (1924–25) and a member of the executive boards of the Progressive Education Association and the American Association of Adult Education. He was a member of the Nebraska Children's Code Commission (1919–20), the American Historical Association Commission on Social Studies (1929–33), and the Commission on the Relations between Schools and College (1932). He received the Butler Medal from Columbia University (1925) and an honorary degree from the University of Denver (1922).

REFERENCES: *CB* (October 1941); *DAB* (supp. 3); *LE* (III); *NCAB* (32:358); *NYT,* September 2, 1941, p. 17; *WWW* (I).

Stanley A. Leftwich

NEWMAN, Samuel Phillips. B. June 6, 1797, Andover, Massachusetts, to Mark and Sarah (Phillips) Newman. M. May 31, 1821, to Caroline Kent. Ch. five. D. February 10, 1842, Andover, Massachusetts.

Samuel Phillips Newman, clergyman, educator, and author, was graduated from Harvard University with the A.B. (1816) and A.M. (1819) degrees, attended Andover (Massachusetts) Theological Seminary (1816–17), and was licensed as a Congregational preacher (1820).

He started to teach at Bowdoin College in Brunswick, Maine, in 1818 and served there to 1839. At Bowdoin, he was professor of ancient languages (1820), first professor of rhetoric and oratory (1824), and was acting president of the college (1830–33). He also served pulpits in Brunswick and in the vicinity. Newman was the first principal of the State Normal School at Barre, Massachusetts (1839), serving in this capacity to his death in 1842.

Newman wrote *Practical System of Rhetoric or the Principles and Practice of Style* (1827), which was published in sixty editions in the United

States. He also wrote *Elements of Political Economy* (1835).
REFERENCES: *AC; DAB; NCAB* (10:123); *TC; WWW* (H).

Joan Duff Kise

NICHOLS, Frederick George. B. March 18, 1878, Avon, New York, to George William and Ella (Fitzpatrick) Nichols. M. August 23, 1899, to Bessie Louise Winans. M. August 2, 1952, to Mabel A. Evarts. Ch. one. D. June 1, 1954, Rochester, New York.

Frederick G. Nichols was graduated from the Genesee Wesleyan Seminary in Lima, New York (1899), and Rochester (New York) Business Institute (1904). He studied law with the firm of Reed & Shutt in Rochester and at the University of Michigan.

Nichols was head of commercial departments at Montpelier (Vermont) Seminary (1899–1903), Martin School in Pittsburgh, Pennsylvania (1903–04), and the high schools at Schenectady, New York (1904–06). He was the first director of business for high and evening schools at Rochester, New York (1906–09 and 1911–18), and was associate principal of the Rochester Business Institute (1909–10). He was the first state supervisor of commercial education for the New York State Education Department (1910–11), the first assistant director of the Federal Board for Vocational Education in charge of the department of commercial education in Washington, D.C. (1918–20), and director of business education for Pennsylvania (1920–22). From 1922 to 1944, Nichols was an associate professor and taught courses in business education at the Graduate School of Education at Harvard University, where he was recognized as the leading pioneer in the field. He was an educational consultant after his retirement from Harvard in 1944.

The author of many articles and bulletins, Nichols wrote thirty-four books on business education, including *Elementary Bookkeeping* (1918), *Junior Business Training* (1923), *Commercial Education in the High School* (1933), *The Personal Secretary—Duties and Traits* (1935), and *Training for Economic Living* (1936), and he was coauthor of *Principles of Bookkeeping and Farm Accounts* (1913), *Brief Course in Commercial Law* (1913), *First Lesson in Business* (1920), and *Secretarial Efficiency* (1938). He was editor of a series of business education textbooks (from 1944) and was the first to sponsor the National Clerical Ability Tests (later, National Business Entrance Tests).

Active in professional associations, Nichols was president of the National Commercial Teacher-Training Association, the National Council of Business Education (1938–40), the Eastern Business Teachers Association (1921), the business education section of the National Education Association (1924), the Education Research Corporation (1938–44), and the Henry O. Peabody School Corporation (1944–46). He was the first recipient of the John Robert Gregg Award in Business Education (1953) and received an honorary degree from Harvard University (1924).

REFERENCES: *LE* (III); *NYT,* June 4, 1954, p. 23; *WWAE* (XIII); *WWW* (III); *American Business Education* 11 (October 1954): 55; *American Vocational Journal* 29 (September 1954): 46; "UBEA Salutes F. G. Nichols," *UBEA Forum* 8 (January 1954): 36. *John F. Ohles*

NORSWORTHY, Naomi. B. September 29, 1877, New York, New York, to Samuel B. and Eva A. (Modridge) Norsworthy. M. no. D. December 25, 1916, New York, New York.

Naomi Norsworthy attended the Trenton (New Jersey) State Normal School (later, Trenton State College), where she received a state diploma (1896). She attended Teachers College of Columbia University and was graduated with the B.S. (1901) and Ph.D. (1904) degrees.

A teacher in the Morristown (New Jersey) public schools (1896–99), Norsworthy spent most of her career at Teachers College, where she was an assistant in psychology (1901–02), tutor (1902–04), and instructor (1904–09). She was adjunct professor of psychology at Columbia (1909–16).

An outstanding public speaker, Norsworthy was the author of *The Psychology of Mentally Deficient Children* (1906). Two unfinished manuscripts were completed by colleagues and published as *How to Teach* (with George D. Strayer, *q.v.*, 1917) and *The Psychology of Childhood* (with Mary T. Whitley, 1918). Her brilliant career was ended with her death from cancer on Christmas Day, 1916.

REFERENCES: *DAB; NYT,* December 26, 1916, p. 11; *WWW* (I); Frances Caldwell Higgens, *The Life of Naomi Norsworthy* (Boston: Houghton Mifflin, 1918). *Gary C. Johnsen*

NORTH, Edward. B. March 9, 1820, Berlin, Connecticut, to Reuben and Hulda (Wilcox) North. M. July 31, 1844, to Mary Frances Dexter. Ch. one. D. September 13, 1903, Clinton, New York.

Edward North was the son of a prosperous farmer. He received his early education at Worthington Academy of Berlin, Connecticut, but at the age of fifteen went to Clinton, New York, to live in the family of his uncle, Simeon North, president of Hamilton College, and to prepare for college at the Clinton Grammar School. He was graduated from Hamilton College in 1841 as valedictorian.

After a year as a tutor he began to read law, but almost immediately was chosen principal of the Clinton Grammar School where he taught until 1843, when he was appointed professor of ancient languages at Hamilton College. At the age of twenty-three, he was the youngest full professor ever appointed at that institution. He was Edward Robinson Professor of Greek and held this position from 1862 until he resigned on November 16, 1901, after fifty-seven years of service.

During the 1871–72 school year North was secretary to the United States minister to Greece, John M. Francis, at Athens. After the death of President Henry Darling of Hamilton College, he served as acting president from April 1891 to November 1892. In addition to his classroom duties, North engaged in editorial work for the college, was a regular contributor to the college literary magazine, and served as college necrologist from 1855 to his retirement. He delivered many lectures and published innumerable papers on educational topics, had a wide acquaintance with the public and private schools of the state, and aided many of them in finding qualified teachers.

Among North's published works were *Uses of Music* (1858) and *Memorial of Henry Hastings Curran* (1867). In 1865 he served as president of the New York State Teachers' Association. From 1881 to his death, he was a trustee of Hamilton College. North was a member of many scientific and literary groups. Honorary degrees were conferred on him by the regents of the University of the State of New York (1869) and Madison (later, Colgate) University (1887).

REFERENCES:*AC; DAB; NCAB* (4:212); *NYT*, September 14, 1903, p. 7; *TC; WWW* (I); S. N. D. North, *Old Greek, A Memoir of Edward North* (New York: McClure, Phillips & Co., 1905).   *J. Franklin Hunt*

NORTHEND, Charles. B. April 2, 1814, Newbury (later, Newburyport), Massachusetts, to John and Anna (Titcomb) Northend. M. August 18, 1834, to Lucy Ann Moody. Ch. three. D. August 7, 1895, New Britain, Connecticut.

Charles Northend was a student in Massachusetts in the public schools at Newbury and Dummer Academy at South Byfield. He entered Amherst (Massachusetts) College in 1831 but was forced to withdraw at the end of his sophomore year for financial reasons.

In 1831. he became an instructor for several terms at the Dummer Academy. He was principal of the First Grammar School in Danvers, Massachusetts (1836–41), and at Epes Grammar School in Salem, Massachusetts (1841–52). He returned to Danvers as superintendent of schools (1852–55) where he instituted educational reforms and was active in professional associations. He moved to New Britain, Connecticut, as school visitor (assistant superintendent) from 1856 to 1879 and was superintendent of schools (1879–80).

Northend organized teachers' associations and conducted institutes for the discussion of teaching problems. In 1846 he was elected president of the Essex County Teachers' Association and served three terms. He was president of the American Institute of Instruction (1863–64) and a member of the New Britain school board in 1872.

After his retirement in 1880, Northend continued to participate in educational affairs by contributing articles to professional journals and updating new editions of his books. Among his many books were *The Common School Book-Keeping* (1845), *The American Speaker* (1848), *The Young Composer* (1848), *The Little Speaker and Juvenile Reader* (1849), *Dictation Exercises* (1851), *The Teacher and the Parent* (1853), *The Teacher's Assistant* (1859), *Exercises for Dictation and Pronunciation* (1862), *Selections for Analysis and Parsing* (1864), and *Entertaining Dialogues* (1876). He was editor of the *Connecticut School Journal* (1856–66) and associate editor of *New England Journal of Education* (later, *Journal of Education*).

REFERENCES: *AC; DAB; WWW* (H).   *Robert Emans*

NORTHROP, Birdsey Grant. B. July 18, 1817, Kent, Connecticut, to Thomas Grant and Aurelia (Curtiss) Northrop. M. February 18, 1846, to Harriette Eliza Chichester. Ch. five. D. April 27, 1898, Clinton, Connecticut.

Birdsey Grant Northrop attended school in Ellington, Connecticut. He was graduated from Yale College (1841) and the Yale Theological School (1845). His education was interrupted by periods of poor health and teaching at Elizabethtown, New Jersey. Northrop was pastor of the Congregational church at Saxonville, Massachusetts (1846–56). He was appointed agent of the state board of education in Massachusetts (1857).

Northrop was secretary of the Connecticut State Board of Education (1867–83). He organized a system of free and compulsory education and placed restrictions on employment of children in factories and mills of the state. He became active in efforts to beautify local communities and was a promoter of the observance of Arbor Day. He was active in securing restitution to Japan of an indemnity extracted by the United States after the Shimonoseki incident in 1863. He served as guardian for some of the first Japanese students to study in the United States, these students being financed by the funds returned to Japan by the federal government.

Among Northrop's writings were *Education Abroad* (1873), *Lessons from European Schools* (1877), *The Legal Prevention of Illiteracy* (1878), *Village Improvement* (1878), *Schools of Forestry and Industrial Schools of Europe* (1878), *Menticulture and Agriculture* (1881), *Rural Improvement* (1882), and *Arbor Day in Schools* (1892).

A participant in educational organizations, Northrop was president of the American Institute of Instruction, the National Superintendent's Association, and the National Educational Association (1873). He served as visitor to the United States Military Academy and trustee of Smith College and Hampton Institute.

REFERENCES: *AC; DAB; NCAB* (10:225); *NYT,* April 29, 1898, p. 7; *WWW* (H).   *Robert V. Shuff*

NORTHROP, Cyrus. B. September 30, 1834, Ridgefield, Connecticut, to Cyrus and Polly Bouton (Fancher) Northrop. M. September 30, 1862, to Anna Elizabeth Warren. Ch. three. D. April 3, 1922, Minneapolis, Minnesota.

Cyrus Northrop attended Williston Seminary in Easthampton, Massachusetts, and Yale College, where he was graduated with the A.B. degree (1857); he received the LL.B. degree (1869) from the Yale Law School.

Admitted to the bar in 1860, Northrop was unable to develop a paying practice. He became active in politics and spent two terms as a clerk in the Connecticut state legislature (1861–62) and was editor of the *New Haven Palladium* (1863). He taught rhetoric and English literature at Yale (1863–84). He also served as collector of duties for the port of New Haven (1869–81) and ran unsuccessfully for the United States Congress on the Republican ticket in 1867.

In 1884 Northrop reluctantly accepted the presidency of the University of Minnesota, a small institution with fewer than three hundred students, which subsisted on small appropriations from the legislature. He demonstrated rare powers as an administrator and was able to persuade the legislature to provide funds and the faculty to ensure quality educational programs. During his twenty-seven-year tenure as president (1884–1911), the University of Minnesota added twenty new buildings and schools of medicine, law, and agriculture. The size of the faculty and the number of students were increased.

Northrop was a member of the Minnesota State High School Board, a state examiner, and a member of the board of trustees of the Minneapolis public library. He was a popular public speaker and wrote many articles for periodicals. Some of his speeches and articles were published in *Addresses, Educational and Patriotic* (1910). He served as a delegate to the International Congregational Council in London in July 1891.

He was awarded five honorary degrees by American colleges and universities, and the Northrop Auditorium at the University of Minnesota was named in his honor.

REFERENCES: *AC; DAB; NCAB* (13:328); *NYT,* April 4, 1922, p. 17, and April 5, 1922, p. 16; *TC; WWW* (I); Oscar W. Firkins, *Cyrus Northrop, A Memoir* (Minneapolis: University of Minnesota Press, 1925); James Gray, *The University of Minnesota, 1851–1951* (Minneapolis: University of Minnesota Press, 1951); *Minneapolis Morning Tribune,* April 4, 5, 1922.

Lawrence Byron Smelser

NORTON, Charles Eliot. B. November 16, 1827, Cambridge, Massachusetts, to Andrews and Catharine (Eliot) Norton. M. May 21, 1862, to Susan Ridley Sedgwick. Ch. six. D. October 21, 1908, Cambridge, Massachusetts.

After graduation from Harvard University in 1846, Charles Eliot Norton was employed for three years by a Boston, Massachusetts, importing firm. He went to India in 1849 and traveled in India and Europe, returning to the United States in 1851. He engaged in business (1851–55) and was back in Europe under doctor's orders from 1855 to 1857.

Norton assisted in editing the writings of his father, Andrews Norton, a well-known clergyman and Harvard professor. He was editor of a paper of the Loyal Publication Society during the Civil War and was coeditor with James Russell Lowell of the *North American Review* (1864–68). He traveled again to Europe in 1868, where he studied Dante in Italy and laid the basis for his future reputation as a Dante scholar. He returned to Cambridge from Europe in 1873 and assisted Henry Wadsworth Longfellow in editing his translation of the *Divine Comedy*.

Norton began to teach art history at Harvard in 1873 and was professor of art history from 1875 to 1897. His activities in the field of literature were extensive and varied. One of his books, *Historical Studies of Church Building in the Middle Ages* (1880), had considerable influence on the architects of his day. He also wrote *Considerations on Some Social Theories* (1853), *The New Life of Dante* (1859), *Notes of Travel and Study in Italy* (1860), *A Gift of Dante* (1886), *Rudyard Kipling* (1889), *The Poet Gray as a Naturalist* (1903), and *Henry Wadsworth Longfellow* (1907), and he edited *A Book of Hymns for Young People* (1854), *Fairy Tales, Narratives and Poems* (1895), *The Complete Writings of James Russell Lowell* (1904), and *The Love Poems of John Donne* (1905). He was editor of *The Heart of Oak Books* (seven volumes, with Kate Stephens, 1893–94). He was a founder of *Nation* magazine.

Norton was a fellow of the American Academy of Arts and Sciences and the Imperial German Archaeological Society and founder and president of the Dante Society, as well as first president of the Archaeological Institute of America (1879–90). He was awarded the Order of the Crown of Italy and received honorary degrees from the English universities of Oxford and Cambridge and from Harvard, Columbia, and Yale universities.

REFERENCES: *AC; DAB; NCAB* (6:425); *NYT,* October 21, 1908, p. 1; *TC; WWW* (I).   *Roger H. Jones*

NORTON, John Pitkin. B. July 19, 1822, Albany, New York, to John Treadwell and Mary (Pitkin) Norton. M. December 15, 1847, to Elizabeth Marvin. Ch. two. D. September 5, 1852, Farmington, Connecticut.

When John Pitkin Norton's family moved to Farmington, Connecticut, the son attended Simeon Hart's school. Deciding to become a farmer, he was encouraged by his father to complete his education first. From 1838 to 1842 he worked on the family farm in the summer and studied in Albany, New York City, New Haven, Connecticut, and Boston. He was a student of Benjamin Silliman, Sr. *(q.v.),* Denison Olmsted *(q.v.),* and Benjamin

Silliman, Jr. *(q.v.)*. They encouraged Norton to study under James F. W. Johnston, an eminent Scottish agricultural chemist. He was in Scotland with Johnston from 1844 to 1846 and then analyzed plant proteins in the laboratory of Gerardus Johannes Mulder in Utrecht, Holland (1846–47).

Returning from Europe, he became professor of agricultural chemistry at Yale College (1846). With the two Sillimans, he started the department of scientific education at Yale, which later became the Sheffield Scientific School. Norton was named professor of agricultural chemistry, probably the first in the United States.

Norton's scientific reports were widely acclaimed and published by Scottish, English, and American agricultural societies. A prize essay submitted to the New York State Agricultural Society was published as the textbook *Elements of Scientific Agriculture* (1850). Norton edited Henry Stephen's *Farmer's Guide,* adding notes and an appendix, and contributed a series of articles to the *Cultivator* (Albany, New York, 1844–52). His only academic degree was an honorary M.A. awarded by Yale (1846).

REFERENCES: *DAB; DSB; NCAB* (8:255); *TC; WWW* (H).

M. Jane Dowd

NORTON, Mary Alice Peloubet. B. February 25, 1860, Lanesville, Massachusetts, to Frances Nathan and Mary Abby (Thaxter) Peloubet. M. June 6, 1883, to Lewis Mills Norton. Ch. five. D. February 23, 1928, Northampton, Massachusetts.

Alice Peloubet Norton attended Smith College in Northampton, Massachusetts, where she received the A.B. (1882) and A.M. (1897) degrees. She also was a student at the Boston Normal School of Household Arts (1896), Massachusetts Institute of Technology (1896–97), and the University of Chicago.

Norton was one of a group that organized the Sanitary Science Club, a study group under the leadership of Ellen H. Richards *(q.v.)*. Norton's husband died in 1893 after ten years of marriage and five children, and she entered the new field of home economics. She lectured at the Lasell Seminary in Newton, Massachusetts (later, Lasell Junior College in Auburndale), to 1899. She also lectured at the Hartford (Connecticut) School of Sociology (1894), Boston Young Women's Christian Association School of Domestic Science (1895–1900), Boston Cooking School (1896–1900), and at the Brookline (Massachusetts) High School, and she also supervised grammar school studies.

In 1900 Norton accepted a position at the Chicago Institute, which was under the leadership of Francis W. Parker *(q.v.)*. The institute became part of the school of education of the University of Chicago, where Norton was assistant professor of home economics (1901–04). She became assistant professor of household administration at the University of Chicago

(1904–13). She was dietitian of Cook County (Illinois) public institutions (1913–14). With Anna Barrows *(q.v.)*, she was a leader of the Chautauqua (New York) School of Domestic Science (1899–1905, 1915–19, and 1920).

One of the founders of the American Home Economics Association (1908), she was the first councilor-at-large (1909–13), secretary (1915–18), and editor of the *Journal of Home Economics* (1915–21). During World War I, she was home economics editor for the Home Conservation Division of the United States Food Administration (1917–18) and was editor of thrift leaflets of the War Savings Division of the United States Treasury Department (1919).

From 1921 to 1923, Norton was head of the home economics department at the Constantinople (Turkey) Women's College, which had been established with the assistance of the American Home Economics Association. She was acting chairman of the department of home economics at Indiana University (1924–25) and was associated with the Institute for the Coordination of Women's Interests at Smith College.

Norton was the author of *Food and Dietetics* (1904), *Food for Children (n.d.)*, and *The Cooked Food Supply Experiments* (1927). She was active in women's groups and professional associations.

REFERENCES: *DAB; NAW; WWW* (I); *Journal of Home Economics* 20 (September 1928); 651–58. *Darlene E. Fisher*

NOTESTEIN, Ada Louise Comstock. See COMSTOCK, Ada Louise.

NOTT, Eliphalet. B. June 25, 1773, Ashford, Connecticut, to Stephen and Deborah (Selden) Nott. M. July 4, 1796, to Sarah Maria Benedict. M. August 3, 1807, to Gertrude (Peebles) Tibbits. M. August 8, 1842, to Urania E. Sheldon. Ch. one. D. January 29, 1866, Schenectady, New York.

Eliphalet Nott was orphaned at an early age and reared and educated by his brother Samuel, a Congregational minister in Franklin, Connecticut. He enrolled at Brown University, bypassed the bachelor's degree, and received the M.A. degree (1795) after passing a special examination.

At the age of sixteen, Nott taught in the Franklin district school, was principal of Plainfield (Connecticut) Academy, and studied with a local pastor. He moved to rural New York as a Presbyterian minister in Cherry Valley where he founded an academy and served as a minister and teacher. He moved to Albany, New York, in 1798, where he was a successful clergyman. He campaigned for reform of the Albany public school system, and, at his urging, the Albany Academy was organized in 1813.

Nott was a trustee of Union College in Schenectady, New York, in 1800 and succeeded Jonathan Maxcy *(q.v.)* as president of the college in 1804. He was instrumental in securing a sound financial basis for the college through lotteries authorized by the New York state legislature. Disabled by a stroke in 1859, Nott continued as nominal president to his death in 1866. He had been head of Union College for an unprecedented sixty-two years.

During Nott's administration, engineering and medical schools and the Dudley Observatory were established. He introduced courses in agriculture and gardening, and military drills were instituted as physical training exercises. He provided courses in modern languages, modern history, and engineering as alternative subjects in the traditional liberal arts program.

Nott was the author of *Councils to Young Men* (1840) and *Lectures on Temperance* (1847). He invented and patented thirty scientific devices. He was active in the organization of the American Association for the Advancement of Education (president, 1850) and was a member of other educational associations. He was active in temperance, anti-slavery, religious, and civil liberty movements. He was awarded honorary degrees by Brown University and the College of New Jersey (later, Princeton University).

REFERENCES: *AC; DAB; NCAB* (7:170); *TC; WWW* (H); *NYT,* January 30, 1866, p. 4; Codman Hislop, *Eliphalet Nott* (Middletown, Conn.: Wesleyan University Press, 1971).

Roger Rasmussen

NOYES, William Albert. B. November 6, 1857, Independence, Iowa, to Spencer Williams and Mary (Packard) Noyes. M. December 24, 1884, to Flora Elizabeth Collier. M. June 18, 1902, to Mattie Laura Elwell. M. November 25, 1915, to Katherine Haworth Macy. Ch. six. D. October 24, 1941, Urbana, Illinois.

A research chemist and professor, William Albert Noyes attended country schools and was graduated with the A.B. and B.S. degrees (1879) from Iowa (later, Grinnell) College in Grinnell, Iowa. He received the Ph.D. degree (1882) from Johns Hopkins University in Baltimore, Maryland, where he studied with Ira Remsen *(q.v.).* He received a second Ph.D. degree (1889) from the University of Munich, Germany, studying under organic chemist Adolf von Baeyer.

He taught Greek and chemistry at Iowa College (1879–80). While in Baltimore, he was employed by the National Board of Health in a study of methods of water analysis. He held academic positions at the University of Minnesota (1882–83), the University of Tennessee (1883–86), and Rose Polytechnic Institute in Terre Haute, Indiana (1886–1903), where he was often the only member of the department.

In 1903 Noyes became the first chief chemist for the newly created United States Bureau of Standards, where he developed standard methods of analysis and standard specifications for chemicals. Noyes became chairman of the University of Illinois chemistry department where he built a strong graduate program (1907–26). The teaching staff more than doubled, and the number of graduate students increased more than six times. In 1926 Noyes became emeritus director of the chemistry laboratory where he continued to do research.

Noyes's specialty was organic chemistry. He introduced new analytic methods for detecting and estimating the amounts of benzene in illuminating gas, strychnine in the exhumed human body and phosphorus, sulfur, and manganese in steel and iron. In inorganic chemistry he sought to make more accurate determinations of the atomic weights of oxygen and chlorine.

He wrote textbooks on chemistry, including *Organic Chemistry for the Laboratory* (1897), *Elements of Qualitative Analysis* (1888), *Organic Chemistry* (1903), *Text-book of Chemistry* (1913), *Laboratory Exercises in Chemistry* (1917), *College Textbook of Chemistry* (1919), *Organic Chemistry* (1926), and *Modern Alchemy* (with W. Albert Noyes, Jr., 1932). He also wrote *Building for Peace* (1923) and *Building for Peace II* (1924). He was editor of *The Journal of the American Chemical Society* (1902–17) and first editor of *Chemical Abstracts* (1907–10), *Scientific Monographs* (1919–41), and *Chemical Reviews* (1924–26).

He was a fellow of the American Academy of Arts and Sciences and a member of many American and foreign associations, including the American Association for the Advancement of Science (chairman of the chemistry section, 1896 and 1918), the Indiana Academy of Science (president, 1912), and the American Chemical Society (secretary, 1903–07 and president, 1920). Noyes served on the Illinois State Board of Natural Resources (secretary, 1917–41). In 1922 he visited Europe to attend a meeting of Allied and Central Power chemists and was a delegate to a meeting of the International Union of Chemistry in Cambridge, England (1923). He received several honorary degrees and the Nichols Medal (1908), the William Gibbs Medal (1919) and the Priestley Medal (1935). The chemistry laboratory at Illinois was named for him.

REFERENCES: *DAB* (supp. 3); *DSB; LE* (II); *NCAB* (B: 314, 44:258); *WWAE* (VIII); *WWW* (II); *NYT,* October 25, 1941, p. 17.

Darlene E. Fisher

NUTTING, Mary Adelaide. B. November 1, 1858, Frost Village, Quebec, Canada, to Vespasian and Harriet Sophia (Peaselee or Peaseley) Nutting. M. no. D. October 3, 1948, White Plains, New York.

M. Adelaide Nutting, the first nurse appointed to a professorship in a university, was educated in the Waterloo, Quebec, village academy, at a nearby convent school, and at Bute House in Montreal. She studied art and music and performed in public on the piano. She taught music in the Cathedral School for Girls in St. Johns, Newfoundland (1882–83). She went to the United States from Canada in 1889. Interested in nursing and nursing education from the time she was a girl, she was a member of the first Johns Hopkins University nursing graduating class (1891).

Nutting stayed at Johns Hopkins Hospital in Baltimore, Maryland, as a head nurse (1891–93), assistant superintendent of nurses (1893–94), principal and superintendent of nurses (1894–1907), and successor to Isabel Hampton Robb *(q.v.)* as administrator of the Johns Hopkins Hospital School of Nursing in 1895.

In 1904 she helped draft the state of Maryland's first nurse-practice law. Through her leadership a department of nursing and health was established in 1910 at Teachers College, Columbia University, as an independently endowed unit with freedom to design its own curriculum. She encouraged creative teaching; the institution developed into an international center for nursing. She helped raise national standards and the quality of instruction.

The first comprehensive and critical survey of schools of nursing, published as *The Educational Status of Nursing* (1912), was directed by Nutting. She initiated a curriculum study of nursing schools, which was reported in *Standard Curriculum for Schools of Nursing* (1917), a guide to higher standards of nursing schools. She initiated the study of nursing and nursing education, which resulted in the Goldmark Report in 1923. In 1900 she helped to establish the *American Journal of Nursing* and, in collaboration with Lavinia Dock, wrote *A History of Nursing* (two volumes, 1907); she also wrote *A Sound Economic Basis for Schools of Nursing* (1926).

Nutting was a member of professional associations, and she was chairman of the committee on nursing of the Council for National Defense (1917–18) and honorary president of the Florence Nightingale International Foundation in London, England (1934). The Teachers College board of trustees established a professorship and the National League of Nursing Education established the Mary Adelaide Nutting Medal in her honor. She was awarded an honorary master's degree by Yale University.

REFERENCES: *DAB* (supp. 4); *NAW; WWW* (II); Ethel Johns and Blanche Pfefferkorn, *The Johns Hopkins Hospital School of Nursing, 1889–1949* (Baltimore, Md.: The Johns Hopkins Press, 1954); Isabel M. Stewart *(q.v.)* and Anne L. Austin, *A History of Nursing,* 5th ed. (New York: G. P. Putnam's Sons, 1962); Edna Yost, *American Women of Nursing* (Philadelphia: J. B. Lippincott, 1947).

Marie M. Seedor

O

OBERTEUFFER, Delbert. B. November 19, 1901, Portland, Oregon, to William Gaul and Roberta (Fox) Oberteuffer. M. June 10, 1935, to Katharine F. Hersey. Ch. one.

Delbert Oberteuffer, a leader in the development of twentieth-century physical education and health education, received the A.B. degree (1923) from the University of Oregon and the A.M. (1924) and Ph.D. (1929) degrees from Columbia University.

Oberteuffer taught at the University of Oregon (1924–28). He was Ohio state supervisor of physical education and health education (1929–32). Throughout the next four decades he was associated with Ohio State University as professor, chairman of the department of physical education for men, and chairman of the graduate division for health and physical education. Oberteuffer influenced the fields of health education and physical education through numerous publications, speeches, and leadership given to professional organizations, which helped develop a maturing, humane, and democratic physical education and health education.

His major publications include *Industrial Hygiene for Schools* (1930), *Personal Hygiene for College Students* (1930), *Health and Physical Education: A Course of Study for Junior and Senior High Schools* (volume 3, 1932), *Health in the World of Work* (1942), *School Health Education* (1954), and *Physical Education* (1956). He was editor of *The Journal of Health* (1959–73).

He was active in professional organizations as chairman of the Joint Committees on Health Problems in Education of the National Education Association and the American Medical Association (1956–58), president of the College Physical Education Association (1944–45) and the American Academy of Physical Education (1958–59), and a fellow of the American School Health Association (president, 1957–58). Many honors were accorded him, including the Luther Halsey Gulick Award (1959) for distinguished service in physical education and the Howe Award (1968) by the American School Health Association.

REFERENCES: *LE* (III); *WWAE* (XX); *WW* (XXXIV); Fred V. Hein, "In Appreciation: Delbert Oberteuffer, Ph.D.," *The Journal of School Health* 43 (November 1973): 555–56; "Highest Tribute," *Journal of Health-Physical Education-Recreation* 30 (October 1959): 28–29.

Stratton F. Caldwell

ODUM, Howard Washington. B. May 24, 1884, Bethlehem, Georgia, to William Pleasants and Mary Ann (Thomas) Odum. M. December 24, 1910, to Anna Louise Kranz. Ch. three. D. November 8, 1954, Chapel Hill, North Carolina.

Howard W. Odum attended Emory University in Oxford, Georgia, where he received the A.B. degree (1904). He received the A.M. degree (1906) from the University of Mississippi and the Ph.D. degree in psychology from Clark University in Worcester, Massachusetts (1909) and in sociology from Columbia University (1910).

Odum was coprincipal of Toccopolo (Mississippi) School (1904–05), an instructor at the University of Mississippi (1905–08), and a fellow at Clark University (1908–09). He was a researcher for the Philadelphia Bureau of Municipal Research (1910–12). He joined the University of Georgia in 1912 as an associate professor and professor of educational sociology (1912–19) and also was superintendent of the University Summer School for Teachers (1916–19). He was dean of liberal arts at Emory University (1919–20), which moved to Atlanta, Georgia, in 1919.

Odum joined the University of North Carolina, where he served as Kenan Professor of Sociology (1920–54). He established the school of public welfare (later, school of social work) in 1920 and served as its director to 1932; he initiated and was director of the Institute for Research in Social Science (1924–44). He owned a farm, where he bred prize cattle.

Odum was the author of many books, including *Social and Mental Traits of the Negro* (1910), *Systems of Public Welfare* (1925), *Southern Pioneers* (1925), *Sociology and Social Problems* (1925), *The Negro and His Songs* (1925), *Public Welfare and Social Work* (1926), *Negro Workaday Songs* (1926), *Man's Quest for Social Guidance* (1927), *American Masters of Social Science* (1927), *Rainbow Round My Shoulder* (1928), *Wings on My Feet* (1929), *Introduction to Social Research* (1929), *An American Epoch* (1930), *Cold Blue Moon* (1931), *Southern Regions of the United States* (1936), *American Regionalism* (1938), *American Social Problems* (1939), *American Democracy Anew* (1940), *Alabama Past and Future* (1941), *The States at Work* (1941), *Race and Rumors of Race* (1943), *Understanding Society* (1947), *The Way of the South* (1947), and *American Sociology* (1951). He founded and was editor of *Social Forces* (1922–54).

Odum was a member of civic and professional organizations, including the North Carolina Commission on Interracial Cooperation (1933–35) and the North Carolina State Planning Board (1935–54). He was president of the North Carolina Conference for Social Service (1936–37), the Southern Regional Council (1944–46), and the American Sociological Society (1930). He was a fellow of the American Association for the Advancement of Science (executive committee, 1939–43) and the Society of American Historians and assistant director of the President's Research Committee on

Social Trends (1929–33). During the Depression, he was chairman of the North Carolina Emergency Relief Administration (1933–35) and the North Carolina Civil Works Administration (1933–34).

He received awards, including the Catholic Conference of the South Award (1943), the Bernays Award (1945), the American Jersey Cattle Club Master Breeders Award, and the O. Max Gardner Award and was recipient of several honorary degrees.

REFERENCES: *LE* (II); *NCAB* (44:260); *NYT,* November 9, 1954, p. 27; *WWW* (III); *American Journal of Sociology* 60 (March 1955): 504–05; Lee M. Brooks, "Some Contributions of Howard W. Odum to Sociology," *Sociology and Social Research* 39 (March 1955): 224–29.

John F. Ohles

OGDEN, Robert Curtis. B. June 20, 1836, Philadelphia, Pennsylvania, to Jonathan and Abigail (Murphey) Ogden. M. March 1, 1860, to Ellen E. Lewis. Ch. two. D. August 6, 1913, Philadelphia, Pennsylvania.

Robert C. Ogden was educated in a Philadelphia city academy. At the age of fourteen he began to work in a dry goods store. In 1852 he moved to New York City with his father, who became a partner in the firm of Devlin and Company. Robert Ogden was a junior partner in the company.

Ogden served for a short time with Union forces in the Civil War. In 1879 he became associated with John Wanamaker, prominent Philadelphia retailer. In 1896 he opened a Wanamaker store in New York City and continued with Wanamaker to his retirement in 1907.

A friend of Samuel Chapman Armstrong *(q.v.),* the founder of Hampton (Virginia) Institute, Ogden became interested in the South during a business trip early in 1861. A trustee of Hampton Institute, he continued and expanded his interest in education in the South. In cooperation with southern educators and others of influence, he developed the Ogden movement, which promoted public education. Through conferences and as president of the Southern Education Board and the Conference for Education in the South and a member of the General Education Board, he distributed funds supporting school taxes and higher standards for southern schools.

Ogden was the author of a number of booklets, including *Samuel Chapman Armstrong* (1894) and *Sunday School Teaching* (1894). He was president of the directors of Union Theological Seminary and a director of Tuskegee (Alabama) Institute and Teachers College of Columbia University. He was a member of the Johnstown (Pennsylvania) Flood Relief Commission (1889). Ogden was the recipient of honorary degrees from Union College and Yale and Tulane universities.

REFERENCES: *DAB; NCAB* (14:415); *NYT,* August 7, 1913, p. 7; *WWW* (I).

Samuel A. Farmerie

O'GORMAN, Thomas. B. May 1, 1843, Boston, Massachusetts, to John and Margaret (O'Keefe) O'Gorman. M. no. D. September 18, 1921, Sioux Falls, South Dakota.

Thomas O'Gorman's family moved frequently when he was a child, living in Boston, Massachusetts, Chicago, Illinois, and St. Paul, Minnesota. The O'Gormans arrived in St. Paul with the family of Richard Ireland, whose son John Ireland *(q.v.)* was a lifelong friend of Thomas O'Gorman. O'Gorman attended Chicago and St. Paul schools (1850–53). At the age of nine he entered a seminary and a year later was sent to a minor seminary at Meximieux, France. He was graduated from the major seminary at Montbel, France (1863), and was ordained a priest at the age of twenty-two.

O'Gorman was a pastor in Rochester, Minnesota (1867–78), and then joined the Paulists in New York City (1878–82). He was called to Minnesota by Bishop John Ireland and was pastor in Faribault (1882–85) and rector of St. Paul Seminary and the College of St. Thomas in St. Paul (1885–90) where he also taught English, French, and dogmatic theology. In 1890 he became professor of church history at the newly organized Catholic University of America and in 1896 was named bishop of Sioux Falls, South Dakota, where he remained until his death in 1921. O'Gorman was noted as a builder of hospitals, churches, and schools.

O'Gorman was the author of *A History of the Roman Catholic Church in the United States* (1895). He served on the Taft Commission (1902) that dealt with the Vatican to resolve a problem over church lands in the Philippine Islands.

REFERENCES: *AC; DAB; NCAB* (12:417); *TC; WWW* (I); *New Catholic Encyclopedia* (New York: McGraw-Hill, 1967); *NYT,* September 19, 1921, p. 15.   *James M. Vosper*

O'HARRA, Cleophas Cisney. B. November 4, 1866, Bentley, Illinois, to Jefferson Wood and Paulina (Robertson) O'Harra. M. June 15, 1893, to Mary Phebe Marvel. Ch. four. D. February 21, 1935, Rapid City, South Dakota.

Cleophas Cisney O'Harra was educated in the public schools of Hancock County, Illinois. He received the A.B. degree (1891) from Carthage (Illinois) College (later, moved to Kenosha, Wisconsin) and the Ph.D. degree (1898) from Johns Hopkins University in Baltimore, Maryland.

O'Harra taught in the Hancock County schools and was an instructor in Latin and physics in the preparatory department (1891–92), professor of natural and physical sciences (1892–95), and vice-president (1894–95) at Carthage College. After receiving the doctorate, he was professor of mineralogy and geology of the South Dakota School of Mines (later, South Dakota School of Mines and Technology) from 1898 to 1911. O'Harra was president of the school (1911–35) and led the institution to recognition for the quality of its graduates.

O'Harra was the author of *Geology of Allegany County, Maryland* (1900), *A History and Bibliography of Geographical Exploration in the Black Hills Region* (1900), *The Mineral Wealth of the Black Hills* (1902), *The Badland Formations of the Black Hills Region* (1910), *O'Harra's Handbook of the Black Hills* (1913), *A Bibliography of the Geology and Mining Interests of the Black Hills Region* (1917), and *The White River Badlands* (1920). He was coauthor of several Black Hills geological folios published by the United States Geological Survey. He was editor of *The Black Hills Engineer.*

O'Harra was an assistant to the Maryland Geological Survey (1896 and 1897) and for several seasons was field assistant for the United States Geological Survey of the Black Hills (South Dakota) region. He was a member of the South Dakota Coal Commission (chairman, 1917–19), the state advisory board of the Federal Fuel Administration (1917–19), and the American Association for the Advancement of Science and a corresponding member of the Geological Society of Washington. He belonged to many scientific and engineering associations and was educational director of military training at the South Dakota School of Mines during World War I.

REFERENCES: *LE* (I); *WW* (XVIII); *WWW* (I); "Doctor Cleophas C. O'Harra," *The Black Hills Engineer* 22 (June 1935): 212–28.

John F. Ohles

OLDBERG, Oscar. B. January 22, 1846, Aefta, Sweden, to Anders and Frederika Katrina (Ohrstromer) Oldberg. M. May 19, 1873, to Emma Parritt. Ch. three. D. February 27, 1913, Pasadena, California.

Oscar Oldberg attended a Swedish elementary school and the Gefle (Sweden) Gymnasium (1857–60) and was apprenticed to an apothecary. He emigrated to the United States in 1865 and practiced pharmacy in New York City (1865–67).

Oldberg was professor of pharmacy at Georgetown (D.C.) University (1867–71). He served as chief clerk and acting medical purveyor at the United States Marine Hospital Service and also was a member of the faculty of the National College of Pharmacy (1874–81). He was a chemist for the Richardson Drug Company in St. Louis, Missouri, for two years and was professor of the College of Pharmacy in Chicago, Illinois.

In 1886 Oldberg was the first dean of the newly organized department of pharmacy at Northwestern University in Evanston, Illinois. He gained a national reputation as a pharmacy educator and played an important role in raising standards for pharmacy schools in the United States.

Oldberg was the author of important books in the field of pharmacy, including *The Metric System in Medicine* (1881), *Unofficial Pharma-*

copoeia (1881), *Companion to the United States Pharmacopoeia* (with Otto A. Wall, 1884), *Weights and Measures* (1885), *Home Study in Pharmacy* (1890), *Fifteen Hundred Examples of Prescriptions and Formulas* (1892), *Laboratory Manual of Chemistry* (with John H. Long, 1894), *Inorganic Chemistry, General, Medical and Pharmaceutical* (1900), *Pharmaceutical Problems and Exercises* (1902), *Lessons in Pharmacy* (1906), and *Pharmacy, Theoretical and Practical* (1913). He was editor of *The Apothecary* (1891–97).

A fellow of the American Association for the Advancement of Science, Oldberg was secretary of the Seventh International Pharmaceutical Congress (1893) and was a member of several state pharmaceutical associations. He was president of the American Pharmaceutical Association (1908). He received honorary degrees from the National College of Pharmacy and Northwestern University.

REFERENCES: *NCAB* (20:429); *WWW* (I).   *John F. Ohles*

OLIN, Stephen. B. March 2, 1797, Leicester, Vermont, to Henry and Lois (Richardson) Olin. M. April 10, 1827, to Mary Ann Eliza Bostick. M. October 18, 1843, to Julia Matilda Lynch. Ch. one. D. August 16, 1851, Middletown, Connecticut.

Stephen Olin was graduated from Middlebury (Vermont) College with the A.B. (1820) and A.M. (1823) degrees. He intended to study law, but suffered from ill health and went to South Carolina where he became a Methodist minister.

He taught school in Cokesbury, Abbeville District, in South Carolina (1820–23) and served as a junior preacher to Charleston, South Carolina, churches (1824–26). He was professor of ethics and metaphysics at the University of Georgia in Athens (1827–33). Olin became the first president of Randolph-Macon College in Mecklenburg County, Virginia (1834–37), and also served as professor of mental and moral science. He traveled in Europe and the Middle East (1837–40). He was elected president of Wesleyan University in Middletown, Connecticut, and served in the office from 1842 to 1851.

Olin was noted for his effective college leadership and his participation in debates of the Methodist Church General Conference in 1844, supporting an anti-slavery resolution but seeking later to resolve problems between the slavery and anti-slavery factions. He was credited with enlisting Methodist support for education. He was instrumental in founding the Evangelical Alliance in London, England, in 1846.

Olin was the author of *Travels in Europe, Arabia, Petraeea, and the Holy Land* (1843), and *Youthful Piety* (1853). After his death, his second wife, Julia Matilda, a well-known author, edited *The Works of Stephen Olin* (1853), *Greece and the Golden Horn* (1854), and *College Life, Its*

Theory and Practice (1867). He received honorary degrees from Yale and Middlebury colleges and Alabama and Wesleyan universities.

REFERENCES: *AC; DAB; NCAB* (9:429); *TC; WWW* (H). *John F. Ohles*

OLMSTED, Denison. B. June 18, 1791, East Hartford, Connecticut, to Nathaniel and Eunice (Kingsbury) Olmsted. M. 1818 to Eliza Allyn. M. 1831 to Julia Mason. Ch. seven. D. May 13, 1859, New Haven, Connecticut.

Denison Olmsted was educated in the local district school and was tutored in arithmetic by Governor John Treadwell, in whose home he was raised. He studied for college with James Morris and Noah Porter (*q.v.*) and was graduated from Yale College with the A.B. (1813) and A.M. (1816) degrees.

Olmsted served as a teacher in New London, Connecticut (1813–15), tutor at Yale (1815–17), and professor of chemistry, mineralogy, and geology at the University of North Carolina at Chapel Hill (1817–25). He returned to Yale as professor of mathematics and natural philosophy (1825–36) and natural philosophy and astronomy (1836–59).

Olmsted inaugurated the first geological survey of North Carolina in 1821 under the direction of the state board of agriculture. He reported on a complex theory explaining hailstones and published a report of observations of meteoric showers indicating their cosmic origin. He and Elias Loomis were the first Americans to observe the Halley comet in 1835. He held patents to the Olmsted stove and other inventions.

Olmsted wrote texts and other books, including *Thoughts on the Clerical Profession* (1817), *Students Commonplace Book* (1828), *Introduction to Natural Philosophy* (two volumes, 1831), *Compendium of Natural Philosophy* (1832), *Introduction to Astronomy* (1839), *Compendium of Astronomy* (1841), *Letters on Astronomy Addressed to a Lady* (1841), *Life and Writings of Ebenezer Porter Mason* (1842), and *Rudiments of Natural Philosophy and Astronomy* (1844). He also contributed many scientific papers, articles on religion, and biographical sketches. He was a member of many American and European scientific societies.

REFERENCES: *AC; DAB; NCAB* (8:121); *TC; WWW* (H).

John F. Ohles

OLNEY, Jesse. B. October 12, 1798, Union, Connecticut, to Ezekiel and Lydia (Brown) Olney. M. 1829 to Elizabeth Barnes. Ch. six. D. July 31, 1872, Stratford, Connecticut.

Jesse Olney was educated in Whitesborough, New York. He taught at Whitesborough and Binghamton, New York, and was principal of the Stone School in Hartford, Connecticut (1819–31). He left teaching in 1831 to engage in writing and politics. In 1833 he left Hartford, moving to

Southington (1833–54) and Stratford (1854–72), Connecticut.

Olney represented Southington for eight terms in the Connecticut legislature from 1835 and was state comptroller (1867–68). He was a strong supporter of the public-school movement and in the organization of the state board of education in 1838.

Olney was an important writer of schoolbooks. He was the author of *A Practical System of Geography* (1828), *A New and Improved School Atlas* (1829), *The Child's Manual* (1829), *The National Preceptor* (1830), *The Easy Reader* (1833), *A Practical System of Arithmetic* (1836), *The Family Book of History* (1839), *An Improved System of Arithmetic* (1839), *Olney's School Atlas* (1841), *The School Reader* (1842), *An Elementary Geography* (1847), *Olney's Quarto Geography* (1849), *A History of the United States* (1851), *Psalms of Life* (c. 1851), and *Olney's School Geography* (1853). Olney's schoolbooks were highly successful and served as important instructional tools in the 1800s.

REFERENCES: *AC; DAB; NYT,* August 17, 1872, p. 3; *WWW* (H).

Fredrick Chambers

OPPENHEIMER, J Robert. B. April 22, 1904, New York, New York, to Julius and Ella (Freedman or Friedman) Oppenheimer, M. November 1, 1940, to Katherine (Puening) Harrison. Ch. two. D. February 18, 1967, Princeton, New Jersey.

J Robert Oppenheimer attended the Ethical Culture School in New York City where he developed an early interest in mathematics and chemistry. He received the A.B. degree (1926) after three years of study at Harvard University. He studied at Cambridge (England) University (1925–26) and at the University of Göttingen, Germany (1926–27), where he received the Ph.D. degree. He studied on the postdoctoral level as a National Research Fellow at Harvard and the California Institute of Technology (1927–28) and was a fellow of the International Education Board at the University of Leiden, the Netherlands, and the Technische Hochshule in Zurich, Switzerland (1928–29).

Oppenheimer joined the faculties of both the University of California at Berkeley and California Institute of Technology in Pasadena (1929–47). At the University of California he built up the largest graduate and post-doctoral program in theoretical physics in the country. In 1941 he began to work with the atomic energy program at the Radiation Laboratory at the University of California. He was a full-time participant in the project in 1942 and became director of the Los Alamos (New Mexico) project in 1943. There he directed the development of the first atomic bomb, which was exploded on July 16, 1945. In 1947 Oppenheimer resigned his teaching posts to become director of the Institute for Advanced Study in Princeton, New Jersey, where he served to his retirement in 1966.

In 1954 Oppenheimer became involved in a celebrated controversy when the Atomic Energy Commission revoked his security clearance and excluded him from his consultative posts with the government. The charges against him centered on his associations with members of the Communist party in the late 1930s and early 1940s. Reversal of the government's negative position began with an invitation by President John F. Kennedy to Oppenheimer to a dinner at the White House for Nobel Prize winners in 1962. In 1963 he was awarded the Atomic Energy Commission's highest honor, the Enrico Fermi Award.

Oppenheimer was chairman of the general advisory committee to the Atomic Energy Commission (1947–52) and served in many advisory capacities on atomic energy matters to the secretary of war (from 1945), secretary of state, President of the United States, and United States representative on the United Nations Atomic Energy Committee. He was a fellow of the American Academy of Arts and Sciences, the American Physical Society (president, 1948), and the Royal Society and a member of other American and foreign scholarly associations. He was the recipient of several honorary degrees.

REFERENCES: *CB* (April 1964 and April 1967); *EB; NCAB* (G:365); *NYT,* February 18, 1967, p. 1; *WWW* (IV); Haakon Chevalier, *Oppenheimer, The Story of a Friendship* (New York: George Braziller, 1965); Philip M. Stern, *The Oppenheimer Case: Security on Trial* (New York: Harper & Row, 1969). *Leon W. Brownlee*

ORCUTT, Hiram. B. February 3, 1815, Acworth, New Hampshire, to John S. and Hannah (Currier) Orcutt. M. August 15, 1842, to Sarah Cummings. M. April 8, 1865, to Ellen Dana. Ch. five. D. April 17, 1899, Boston, Massachusetts.

Hiram Orcutt, the youngest of ten children of a poor farmer, struggled to receive an education. He was graduated from Dartmouth College in Hanover, New Hampshire (1842), supporting himself by teaching in academies and high schools during his first two years of study.

Orcutt was principal of Hebron (New Hampshire) Academy (1842–43). He was elected principal of Thetford (Vermont) Academy, a position he held from 1843 to 1855. He accepted an appointment in 1855 as principal of the Ladies Seminary at North Granville, New York, resigning in 1860 to establish the Glenwood Ladies' Seminary at West Brattleboro, Vermont. In 1864 he was appointed principal of the Tilden Ladies' Seminary at West Lebanon, New Hampshire, and served as principal of both the Glenwood and Tilden seminaries until 1868 when he sold his interests in the Glenwood Ladies' Seminary, continuing at the Tilden Seminary to 1880. He also served as superintendent of schools in Brattleboro, Vermont, and Lebanon, New Hampshire (1860–66).

A prolific writer of articles and books, Orcutt's major works include *Class Books of Prose and Poetry* (with Truman Rickard, 1847), *Gleanings from School-Life Experience* (1848), *Methods of School Discipline* (1871), *Teachers' Manual* (1871), *Parents' Manual* (1874), *Home and School Training* (1874), *School Keeping: How to Do It* (1885), and *Among the Theologies* (1888). He was editor of the *Vermont School Journal* (1861–65) and a member of the advisory board, associate editor, and subscription manager for the *New England Journal of Education*.

He was the representative of the town of Lebanon in the New Hampshire General Court (1870–72) and helped enact legislation to establish the Plymouth Normal School, provide for compulsory school attendance, and change the administration of schools from a district to a town system. He was secretary of the board of trustees of the Plymouth Normal School from its inception in 1870 to 1876. Orcutt was a frequent lecturer to teachers' institutes and active in the organization of educational associations.

In 1880 he moved to Boston as the proprietor of the New England Publishing Company. He served as manager of the New England Bureau of Education from 1875 to 1898. Orcutt received an honorary degree from Bates College.

REFERENCES: *DAB; NCAB* (7:129); *WWW* (H); Albert M. Hyamson, *A Dictionary of Universal Biography—Of all Ages and Of All Peoples* (New York: P. Dutton & Co., 1951), p. 460.   *Norman J. Bauer*

ORR, Gustavus John. B. August 9, 1819, Orrville, South Carolina, to James and Anne (Anderson) Orr. M. 1847 to Eliza Caroline Anderson. Ch. ten. D. December 11, 1887, Atlanta, Georgia.

Gustavus John Orr moved with his family from South Carolina to Georgia at the age of three. He attended school at Jefferson, Georgia, and attended Maryville (Tennessee) Seminary and the University of Georgia. He enrolled in Emory College in Oxford (later, moved to Atlanta), Georgia, graduating in 1844. He returned to his home county of Jackson, Georgia, to study law.

Financial problems led to his acceptance of the post of principal in Jefferson Academy (1847). He was principal of a school for girls in Covington (1848) and taught mathematics at Emory College from 1849 to 1866. He was president of the Southern Masonic Female College at Covington, Georgia (1867–70), and professor of mathematics at Oglethorpe University in Atlanta, Georgia (1870–72). Orr was appointed to represent Georgia in establishing the boundary between Georgia and Florida. Orr and B. F. Whitner, representing Florida, surveyed the line in 1859–60, providing an acceptable boundary and settling a long-standing dispute.

Orr was appointed state school commissioner in 1871 and was reappointed, serving to his death. He had been working in the Georgia Teacher Association from 1867 to 1870 to evolve a plan for organizing the Georgia schools. The first school law of 1870 accepted the plan of the association committee chaired by Orr and was the basis for the legislation that established the schools. He served as an agent for the Peabody Fund in Georgia and was active in the National Educational Association (vice-president, 1881, and president, 1882).

REFERENCES: *DAB; NCAB* (9:555); *WWW* (H); Dorothy Orr, *A History of Education in Georgia* (Chapel Hill: University of North Carolina Press, 1950). *John F. Ohles*

ORTON, Edward, Jr. B. October 8, 1863, Chester, New York, to Edward Francis Baxter (*q.v.*) and Mary Matilda (Jennings) Orton. M. October 30, 1888, to Mary Princess Anderson. M. October 6, 1928, to Mina Althea Orton. Ch. none. D. February 10, 1932, Columbus, Ohio.

Edward Orton, Jr., son of the first president of the Ohio State University, received the E.M. degree (1884) from Ohio State University and was employed by the Columbus Hocking Coal and Iron Company as a chemist and mine engineer (1885–87) and superintendent of the Bessie furnace at New Straitsville, Ohio (1887–88), where he produced the first commercial ferro-silicon iron. He was superintendent of the Victoria furnace at Goshen Bridge, Virginia (1889) and managed the Ohio Paving Brick Company of Columbus, Ohio, and the Acme Vitrified Brick Company of Cloverport, Kentucky.

Orton persuaded the Ohio legislature to provide for the establishment of a department of clayworking and ceramics at the Ohio State University in 1894. He was director of the department (1894–1915), the first of its kind in the world. He also was secretary (1895–1902) and dean (1902–06 and 1910–15) of the college of engineering. He served as Ohio state geologist (1899–1906). He established the Standard Pyrometric Cone Company (1900–32), which became the Orton Memorial Laboratory after his death. He served in the United States Army in World War I.

The author of *Clays of Ohio* (1884) and *The Clay-Working Industries of Ohio* (1893), Orton was active in professional associations. He founded the American Ceramic Society (1900) and served as secretary (1899–1919) and president (1930–31). He was a fellow of the Geological Society of America and the American Association for the Advancement of Science. He was awarded three honorary degrees. Mount Orton in Estes Park, Colorado, was named in his honor.

REFERENCES: *NCAB* (24:107); *WWW* (I). *John F. Ohles*

ORTON, Edward Francis Baxter. B. March 9, 1829, Deposit, New York, to Samuel Gibbs and Clara (Gregory) Orton. M. August 30, 1855, to Mary

Matilda Jennings. M. August 26, 1875, to Anna D. Torrey. Ch. six, including Edward Orton (q.v.), engineer and educator. D. October 16, 1899, Columbus, Ohio.

Edward Francis Baxter Orton was graduated from Hamilton College in Clinton, New York, in 1848. He studied with Asa Gray (q.v.) at the Lawrence Scientific School at Harvard University. He studied at the Lane Theological Seminary in Cincinnati, Ohio (1849–50). He spent a year at the Andover (Massachusetts) Theological Seminary (1854–55) and was ordained a Presbyterian minister.

Orton was an assistant in an academy at Erie, Pennsylvania (1848–49). He was a teacher in Franklin, New York, at the Delaware Literary Institute (1851 and 1853–54). He was appointed pastor of a church at Downsville, New York. He was later "silenced for heresy" for expounding the Darwinian theory of evolution.

Orton was professor of natural sciences at the New York State Normal School (later, State University of New York at Albany) in Albany from 1856 to 1859. He was principal of an academy at Chester, New York (1859–65), and was principal of the preparatory department and professor of natural history (1865–72), and president (1872–73) of Antioch College at Yellow Springs, Ohio. He also was assistant state geologist of Ohio (1869–75).

In 1873 Orton became the first president and professor of geology of the newly organized Ohio Agricultural and Mechanical College in Columbus. He was instrumental in renaming the Ohio institution the Ohio State University in 1878 and gaining popular acceptance of the university by the people of the state. He resigned as president in 1881, continuing to teach geology to his death in 1899. He also was chief of the Ohio geological survey (1882–99).

He was the author of *Economic Geology of Ohio* (two volumes, 1883, 1888) and *Petroleum and Inflammable Gas* (1887). Orton was a member of professional and scientific organizations in the United States and Europe and was president of the American Association for the Advancement of Science (1899), the Ohio State Sanitation Association (1884–85) and the Geological Society of America (1896). He received honorary degrees from Hamilton College (1875) and Ohio State University (1881).

REFERENCES: *AC; DAB; NCAB* (24:106); *TC; NYT,* October 17, 1899, p. 5; *WWW* (I); Simeon D. Fess *(q.v.), Ohio, A Four Volume Reference Library* (Chicago: Lewis Publishing Company, 1937), 4: 232–33.

Alfred J. Ciani

ORTON, James. B. April 21, 1830, Seneca Falls, New York, to Azariah Giles and Minerva (Squire) Orton. M. 1859 to Ellen Foote. Ch. one. D. September 25, 1877, Lake Titicaca, Peru.

The son of an outstanding theologian, James Orton planned to make theology his profession. Through associations with Henry A. Ward and others, he developed interests in the natural sciences. Orton accompanied two scientific expeditions to Nova Scotia and Newfoundland as an undergraduate at Williams College, from which he was graduated in 1855. He pursued his religious training at Andover (Massachusetts) Theological Seminary, graduating in 1858. He was ordained on July 11, 1860, and served in the ministry until 1866.

In 1866 the University of Rochester, New York, appointed Orton instructor in natural history to replace Henry Ward, who was on a leave of absence. He accepted a position teaching natural history at Vassar College in Poughkeepsie, New York, in 1869 and held that position until his death in 1877. He participated in three explorations in South America to the equatorial Andes and the region of the Amazon in 1867, 1873, and 1876. Orton collected many animal and plant specimens that were distributed to various museums, including the Smithsonian Institution at Washington, D.C., and the Museum of Natural History at Vassar, which Orton directed.

In 1876 a third expedition was organized with outside backing; the first two had been financed primarily by Orton. No narrative or collections resulted from this expedition; Orton died while crossing Lake Titicaca. His daughter Anna participated in international ceremonies dedicating a monument in honor of her father in 1921 that marks his grave on Esteves Island in Lake Titicaca.

Orton wrote several books, including a popular report of his first expedition, *The Andes and the Amazon* (1870). He also wrote *The Miner's Guide and Metallurgist's Directory* (1849), *The Proverbalist and the Poet: Proverbs Illustrated by Parallel or Relative Passages from the Poets* (1852), *Underground Treasures: How and Where to Find Them* (1872), *The Liberal Education of Women* (1873), and *Comparative Zoology: Structural and Systematic* (1876).

REFERENCES:*AC; DAB; DSB; NCAB* (11:280); *TC; WWW* (H); Edward Albes, "An Early American Explorer," *Bulletin of the Pan American Union* 39 (July 1914): 1–13; "An International Dedication Ceremony," *Bulletin of the Pan American Union* 45 (August 1922): 117–28; *NYT,* November 8, 1877, p. 8, Estuardo Nuñez, "Over the Andes and Along the Amazon," *Americas* 12 (March 1960); 27–31.   *Anita Bozardt*

OSBORN, Henry Fairfield. B. August 8, 1857, Fairfield, Connecticut, to William Henry and Virginia Reed (Sturges) Osborn. M. September 29, 1881, to Lucretia Perry. Ch. five. D. November 6, 1935, Garrison, New York.

The son of the founder and president of the Illinois Central Railroad, H. Fairfield Osborn attended the Lyons Collegiate Institute in New York City before he earned the A.B. (1877) and Sc.D. (1880) degrees from the College of New Jersey (later, Princeton University). He studied anatomy, histology, embryology, and comparative anatomy at various institutions in New York and London in the 1880s.

Osborn served at Princeton as assistant professor of biology and professor of comparative anatomy (1879–91). He went to New York City to serve as professor of zoology at Columbia University (1891–1910) and curator of the American Museum of Natural History. He served as the dean of the Columbia faculty of pure science (1892–95) and retired from teaching in 1910, but continued his research in zoology and association with the museum as president of the board of trustees (1908–33). Osborn was responsible for the collection and display of mammalian and dinosaur fossils. He made the museum a model learning center and assembled the largest collection of vertebrate fossils in the world. He made many expeditions to various parts of the world.

Osborn was the author of many articles and monographs; he also wrote *From the Greeks to Darwin* (1894), *The Age of Mammals* (1910), *Huxley and Education* (1910), *Men of the Old Stone Age* (1915), *Origin and Evolution of Life* (1917), *Impressions of Great Naturalists* (1924), *The Earth Speaks to Bryan* (1925), *Evolution and Religion in Education* (1926), *Creative Education* (1927), *Man Rises to Parnassus* (1927), *Fifty-two Years of Research* (1930), and *Cope, Master Naturalist* (1931).

Osborn was president of the American Society of Naturalists (1892), the American Morphology Society (1898), the New York Academy of Sciences (1898–1900), the Marine Biology Association (1896–1901), the New York Zoological Society (1909–23), the American Society of Paleontologists (1903), the Audubon Society of New York State (1910), the American Bison Society (1914–15), and the American Association for the Advancement of Science (1928). He was a trustee of the Brearley School for Girls (1894–1919), the Marine Biological Laboratory (1890–1901), the Hispanic Society of America (1909–24), and the New York Public Library (1911–19). He was a councillor of the National Academy of Sciences (1906–13), the American Philosophical Society (1907–19), and Institut de paléontologie humaine. He was a fellow of the New York Academy of Sciences, the American Geographical Society, and the American Academy of Arts and Sciences.

Osborn served with United States and Canadian geological surveys and was one of the founders of the New York Zoological Park. He was awarded twelve medals from American and foreign agencies and ten honorary degrees from American and foreign colleges and universities.

REFERENCES: *DAB* (supp. 1); *DSB;LE* (I); *NCAB* (C:26, 26:18); *TC; WWW* (I); *NYT*, November 7, 1935, p. 23; Florence Mulligan, ed., *Fifty-two Years of Research, Observation and Publication* by Henry Fairfield

Osborn (New York: Charles Scribner's Sons, 1930).

Vincent Giardina

OSBORNE, Estelle Massey Riddle. B. 1903, Palestine, Texas, to William H. and Betty Massey. M. April 15, 1932, to Riddle. M. June 27, 1947, to Herman P. Osborne. Ch. none.

As a girl, Estelle Massey Riddle Osborne wanted to be a dentist, but her family chose teaching for her. She studied at Prairie View State College in Texas, the only postsecondary educational institution in the state for blacks at the time. She taught elementary school in rural Texas and then decided against teaching any longer. While visiting her brother, a physician in St. Louis, Missouri, Osborne entered a diploma nursing class at City Hospital No. 2, graduating in 1923 and passing the registered nurse examination with the highest score in the state of Missouri for that year.

She was appointed head nurse of a ward in the hospital and quickly learned that the white supervisory staff would not favor her promotion, although the hospital served black patients. When white nurses with less experience were appointed to supervisory positions and served as her superiors, Osborne resigned her post and joined the staff of the municipal visiting nurses' organization. She decided to leave the nursing profession because of the prejudice she found in its administration but learned of a joint arrangement between the Lincoln High School, the Lincoln Junior College, and two hospitals in Kansas City, Missouri, where she could work as a nurse and teach night classes. This brought her into nursing education.

Osborne completed bachelor's and master's degrees in nursing education at Teachers College, Columbia University, New York City, earning the M.A. degree in 1931, the first ever awarded to a black nurse. She was appointed educational director at the Freedman's Hospital in Washington, D.C., and began her attack on the problems of Negro nurses on a national scale through volunteer services with the National Association of Colored Graduate Nurses.

After three years' work at Freedman's Hospital, she was one of fourteen investigators appointed by the Rosenwald Fund to conduct a two-year survey on making rural education more effectively serve the needs of poverty-stricken people in the South. The survey led to the establishment of health and other educational programs in many communities and to education of the public through published reports about poverty and health conditions among workers in the South. Federal programs for health improvement resulted from these studies. From 1945, she was the first black woman instructor in the department of nursing education at New York University.

In 1943 she was appointed consultant to the National Nursing Council for War Service, focusing upon the long-range plans for better nurses' training for Negroes. She published several articles on nursing education in the *Journal of Negro Education, Opportunity,* and *The American Journal of Nursing.* In 1946 the Estelle Massey Scholarship was established in her honor at Fisk University. She was presented the Mary Mahoney Award in recognition of her significant contributions to nursing education. She was vice-president of the National Council of Negro Women and on the executive committee of the Committee of Women in World Affairs.

REFERENCES: Herbert Morais, *History of the Negro in Medicine* (New York: Publishers Co., 1969), p. 255; "Estelle Massey Riddle Appointed to War Service Nursing Council," *Opportunity* (April 1943): 80; Harry A. Ploski and Ernest Kaiser, *AFRO USA* (New York: Bellwether Pub. Co., 1971), p. 884; *Who's Who in Colored America,* 7th ed. (New York: Burckel & Associates, 1950); Edna Yost, *American Women of Nursing* (Philadelphia: J. B. Lippincott, 1947).   *Walter C. Daniel*

O'SHEA, Michael Vincent. B. September 17, 1866, LeRoy, New York, to Michael and Margaret (Fitzgerald) O'Shea. M. June 1894 to Harriet Frisbie Eastabrooks. Ch. four. D. January 14, 1932, Madison, Wisconsin.

Michael Vincent O'Shea attended the LeRoy (New York) Academic Institute and received the B.L. degree (1892) from Cornell University at Ithaca, New York.

O'Shea was professor of psychology and education at the State Normal School (later, Mankato State University) at Mankato, Minnesota (1892–95). He was professor of pedagogy at New York State Teacher's College (later, State University of New York College at Buffalo) in Buffalo (1895–97). He was appointed professor of education at the University of Wisconsin in 1897, a position he held until his death in 1932.

During the first ten years of his career, O'Shea began a series of developmental studies, which he pursued for several decades. Lecturing throughout the United States on themes concerned with child welfare and education, O'Shea developed a reputation as a vigorous and dynamic popularizer of current educational theory. In 1905 he gave a series of lectures in Great Britain and began a study of education in England and Scotland. In the mid-1920s, O'Shea conducted studies of educational systems in Newark, New Jersey, and the states of Mississippi and Virginia.

Among O'Shea's many books were *Aspects of Mental Economy* (1900), *Six Nursery Classics* (1900), *Old World Wonder Stories* (1902), *Education as Adjustment* (1903), *Social Development and Education* (1904), *Dynamic Factors in Education* (1906), *Linguistic Development and Education* (1907), *Everyday Problems in Teaching* (1912), *Everyday Problems in Child Training* (1920), *Faults of Childhood and Youth* (1920), *First Steps in Child Training* (1920), *The Trend of the Teens* (1920), *Mental Development and Education* (1921), *Tobacco and Mental Efficiency*

(1923), *The Child, His Nature and His Needs* (1924), *Our Children* (1925), *The Reading of Modern Foreign Languages* (1927), *A State Educational System at Work* (1927), and *Newer Ways with Children* (1929). He edited the *World Book Encyclopedia* and served as chairman of the editorial board of the Children's Book Club and editor of *Junior Home Magazine, The Nation's Schools,* and *The Parent's Library.*

O'Shea served as chairman of American committees at the International Congress of Home Education at Liège, Belgium (1905), and Brussels, Belgium (1910). A member of many educational and scientific associations, he was a fellow of the American Association for the Advancement of Science and president of the Society of College Teachers of Education (1911–12).

REFERENCES: *DAB; WWW* (I); *NYT,* January 15, 1932, p. 21.

Harvey Feldstein

OSUNA, Juan Jóse. B. June 24, 1884, Caguas, Puerto Rico, to Juan Jóse and Cesárea (Rodriquez) Osuna. M. May 17, 1915, to Laura Mae Gates. M. August 22, 1923, to Margaret Logan Thompson. Ch. two. D. June 18, 1950, Arlington, Virginia.

Juan Jóse Osuna went to the United States in 1901. He attended the Indian Training School at Carlisle, Pennsylvania, and the State Normal School (later, Bloomsburg State College) at Bloomsburg, Pennsylvania, graduating in 1906. He received the A.B. degree (1912) from the Pennsylvania State College (later, University) and was graduated from Princeton (New Jersey) Theological Seminary in 1915. He was awarded the A.M. (1920) and Ph.D. (1923) degrees by Columbia University.

Osuna taught in the public schools in Mayaguez, Puerto Rico (1906–08), and was a missionary for the Presbyterian Board of Missions at Anasco, Puerto Rico (1915–17). He was professor of religious education at the Polytechnique Institute (later, Inter-American University) of Puerto Rico at San German. He traveled to Spain to study and conduct research in the development of education in Puerto Rico, gathering data for a doctoral dissertation (1920–21).

In 1922 Osuna joined the University of Puerto Rico at Rio Piedras as professor of education and was director of the summer school (1922–28) and dean of the college of education (1928–44), where he assumed the leadership in the education of teachers for the island schools.

While at the University of Puerto Rico, Osuna was acting chancellor (1935–36), traveled in Latin America on behalf of the World Federation of Educational Associations (1938–39), and was an exchange professor to Pennsylvania State College (1932–33). He was an educational consultant to the Bureau of Employment and Migration of the Puerto Rican Department of Labor (1948–49).

Osuna was the author of *Education in Puerto Rico* (1923), the publication of his research for his doctoral dissertation. He was assistant editor of *World Education* and a contributor to the symposium, Twenty-five Years of American Education, in 1924. He wrote many articles on education in Puerto Rico and was a member of many professional and scholarly associations and a fellow of the American Association for the Advancement of Science.

REFERENCES: *LE* (III); *WWAE* (I); *WWW* (III), *NYT,* June 20, 1950, p. 27.   *John F. Ohles*

OWEN, William Bishop. B. April 30, 1866, Union Station, Ohio, to Thomas Walter and Elizabeth (Bishop) Owen. M. October 3, 1890, to Lucy Caroline Anderson. Ch. three. D. February 17, 1928, Chicago, Illinois.

William Bishop Owen was graduated with the A.B. degree (1887) from Denison University in Granville, Ohio, and taught there for a year. He entered the Morgan Park Theological Seminary (later, the divinity school of the University of Chicago). After completing the seminary course, he remained as instructor of biblical Greek at the seminary. He studied in Germany at the University of Berlin (1897) and the University of Halle (1900–01). He was awarded the Ph.D. degree by the University of Chicago in 1901.

Owen taught at the Western Pennsylvania Classical and Scientific Institute (1887–88). In 1890 he opened a private preparatory school, South Side Academy, for the first freshman class of boys to be enrolled at the University of Chicago. This academy developed into University High School, one of the greatest experimental schools in the United States. Owen was a member of the University of Chicago faculty when it opened in 1892 and served to 1909 as examiner, associate professor of Greek, associate professor of education, and principal and dean of the University of Chicago secondary schools (1901–09).

He became president of the Chicago Normal School (later, Chicago State University) in 1909, where he led the school to college rank. He remained there to his death in 1928. Owen was the author of *Homeric Vocabularies* (1895) and was founder and editor of *The Chicago Schools Journal.* He introduced and developed the junior high school and proposed new methods of instruction for the Illinois normal schools as a member of the Illinois Normal School Board (1917–22). A member of professional associations, he was president of the Illinois State Teachers Association (1923) and the National Education Association (1922–23).

REFERENCES: *NCAB* (23:66); *NYT,* February 18, 1928, p. 17; *WWW* (I).   *Sara Throop*

OWRE, Alfred. B. December 16, 1870, Hammerfest, Norway, to Lewis and Laura Cecelie Owre. M. September 1, 1915, to Franc Charlotte Hockenberger. Ch. two. D. January 2, 1935, New York, New York.

Alfred Owre moved to the United States from Norway with his parents in 1884 and settled in Minneapolis, Minnesota. He attended public schools and the University of Minnesota, where he received the D.D.S. (1894) and B.A. (1910) degrees. He received the M.D. and C.M. degrees in 1895 from the College of Physicians and Surgeons at Hamline University in St. Paul, Minnesota.

Owre taught dentistry at the college of dentistry of the University of Minnesota (1893–1927) and was dean and professor of theory and practice of dentistry (1905–27). He served as dean of the school of dentistry at Columbia University (1927–34). A major figure in dental education, Owre established a separation of scientific dental schools from commercial training schools, promoted dentistry as a medical specialty, advocated dental care for all in need of it, and lengthened preparatory studies to provide for a broader general education. He engaged in an unsuccessful effort to merge the medical and dental professions.

Owre was the author of many articles and books, including *Prunes or Pancakes* (1926) and *Some Phases of Dental Education in the United States* (1931). A member of international dental congresses, he was president of the Minnesota State Dental Association (1902) and vice-president of the American Dental Association (1907). He received an honorary degree from Columbia University in 1929.

REFERENCES: *DAB* (supp. 1); *LE* (I); *NYT*, January 4, 1935, p. 21; *WWW* (I). *John F. Ohles*

P

PACE, Edward Aloysius. B. July 3, 1861, Starke, Florida, to George Edward and Margaret (Kelly) Pace. M. no. D. April 26, 1938, Washington, D.C.

Edward Pace attended public elementary school and Duval County High School in Jacksonville, Florida. He was a student at St. Charles College in Catonsville, Maryland (1876–80), and enrolled at the North American College in Rome, where he received the S.T.B. (1883) and S.T.D. (1886) degrees. He studied in Paris but soon transferred to the University of Leipzig, Germany, where he received the Ph.D. degree in 1891.

Pace was assigned to the diocese of St. Augustine (Florida) for a short time and joined the faculty of Catholic University in Washington, D.C. At

Catholic University he was professor of psychology (1891–94) and philosophy (1894–1935). He was dean of the school of philosophy on three separate occasions in his long career. He was vice-rector of the university (1925–36) and founded the department of education. The second psychological laboratory in the country was established on the campus in 1891.

Pace was editor of the *Catholic Encyclopedia* (1907–14), the first editor of *Studies in Psychology and Psychiatry,* and with Thomas Shields *(q.v.)* was cofounder and coeditor of the *Catholic Educational Review.* He and James H. Ryan were the first editors of *New Scholasticism* founded in 1926. He authored *A Mass for Every Day in the Year* (1916).

Founder and first president of the American Catholic Philosophical Association, Pace served as president of the American Council on Education (1925) and in 1929 was appointed to the National Advisory Committee on Education by President Herbert Hoover.

REFERENCES: *DAB* (supp. 2); *NCAB* (40:390); *WWW* (I); *New Catholic Encyclopedia* (New York: McGraw-Hill, 1967); *NYT,* April 27, 1938, p. 23.   *James M. Vosper*

PACKARD, Alpheus Spring, Jr. B. February 19, 1839, Brunswick, Maine, to Alpheus Spring and Frances Elizabeth (Appleton) Packard. M. October 1867 to Elizabeth Derby Walcott. Ch. none. D. February 14, 1905, Providence, Rhode Island.

Naturalist, entomologist, and physiologist, Alpheus S. Packard, Jr., showed an interest in natural science at an early age and was encouraged by his father to collect specimens and observe the wonders of nature. He was a student at Bowdoin College in Brunswick, Maine, where he studied natural history and specialized in entomology, graduating with the A.B. degree in 1861. He spent the summer with the Maine Geologic Survey and published his first scientific papers in entomology and geology. He was a student and assistant to Louis Agassiz *(q.v.)* at Harvard University. He received the A.M. degree from Bowdoin (1862) and the M.D. degree from Maine Medical School (1864).

He saw action as an assistant surgeon with the First Maine Veteran Volunteers during the Civil War. He became a librarian and custodian of the Boston Society of Natural History (1865–66), was appointed curator of the Essex Institute in 1866, and became curator and then director of the Peabody Academy of Science in Salem, Massachusetts (1866–78).

Packard founded the *American Naturalist* with Edward S. Morse, Frederick W. Putnam, and Alpheus Hyatt *(q.v.)* and served as editor-in-chief (1869–87). He was the state entomologist for Massachusetts (1871–73) and lectured at the Maine College of Agriculture and Mechanics (later, University of Maine), Massachusetts Agricultural College (later, University of Massachusetts), and Bowdoin College (1870–78).

His publications were numerous; among the most noteworthy were *The*

Guide to the Study of Insects (1869), *Cave Fauna of North America* (1888), and *Textbook of Entomology* (1898), which was considered the basic text for students of entomology. He also wrote several monographs on moths, of which his monumental three-volume account of the Bombycene moth is world renowned. His interest in J. B. Lamarck's philosophy led him to write *Lamarck, the Founder of Evolution; His Life and Work, with Translations of his Writings on Organic Evolution* (1901).

Active in professional and scientific groups, he was elected to the National Academy of Sciences (1872), was honorary president of the Zoological Congress in Paris (1889), and was appointed secretary to the United States Entomological Commission (1877). He founded the Neo-Lamarckian movement, which influenced the writings of early twentieth-century American taxonomists.

REFERENCES: *AC; DAB; DSB; NCAB* (3:102); *TC; WWW* (I); *NYT,* February 15, 1905, p. 1.   *Harold J. McKenna*

PACKARD, Silas Sadler. B. April 28, 1826, Cummington, Massachusetts, to Chester and Eunice (Sadler) Packard. M. March 6, 1850, to Marion Crocker. Ch. none. D. October 27, 1898, New York, New York.

Silas Sadler Packard, a pioneer in business education, moved with his family from Massachusetts to Fredonia, Ohio, in 1833. He attended district schools and spent a year attending the Granville (Ohio) Academy.

He began teaching penmanship (one of the first business education subjects) at the age of sixteen. In 1845 he was master of a school in Kentucky and moved to Cincinnati, where he taught penmanship in commercial schools and later added bookkeeping to the curriculum.

Packard was in Adrian, Michigan (1850–51), Lockport, New York (1851–53), and in Tonawanda, New York, where he started a weekly newspaper, the *Niagara River Pilot,* in 1853. In 1856 he became associated with Henry Bryant and Henry D. Stratton, who successfully promoted the chain of Bryant and Stratton business colleges. In 1858 Packard founded Packard's Business College in New York City.

Packard published a series of textbooks beginning in 1869, mainly in the business field. He published *Packard's Monthly* beginning in 1868 and continuing to 1870. He was a leader in opening office work to women through training programs and in persuading businessmen to hire women for clerical and secretarial positions. He was one of the first business school proprietors to sense the impact that the development of the typewriter (1867) would have on business in general and on office work in particular.

REFERENCES: *AC; DAB; NCAB* (3:72); *WWW* (H); Thomas L. Cahalan, "Silas Sadler Packard, Pioneer in American Business Education" (Ph.D. diss., New York University, 1955).

Richard D. Featheringham

PACKARD, Sophia B. B. January 3, 1824, New Salem, Massachusetts, to Winslow and Rachel (Freeman) Packard. M. no. D. June 21, 1891, Washington, D.C.

Sophia B. Packard's early education was received in the district school of New Salem, Massachusetts. She received a diploma from the Charlestown (Massachusetts) Female Seminary in 1850.

In 1838 at the age of fourteen she had begun to teach, alternating teaching with the pursuit of her education. She taught school at the Charlestown Seminary and in schools on Cape Cod until she returned to the New Salem Academy as preceptress and teacher in 1855. At New Salem Academy, Packard met her lifelong friend and colleague, Harriet E. Giles, a student at the academy. Giles taught with Packard at Orange, Massachusetts, for three years. They opened a school in Fitchburg, Massachusetts, for a short time and also taught together for five years (1859–64) at the Connecticut Literary Institute in Suffield.

In the fall of 1864 Packard became principal of Oriad Collegiate Institute in Worcester, Massachusetts. The school had been founded on two reform ideas: college education for women and abolition. Packard and Giles, who also taught at Oriad, left the institution in 1867. Packard was in business in Boston for several years and assisted the Reverend George C. Latimer, a Baptist minister, from 1870. She was a founder of the Woman's American Baptist Home Mission Society in 1877, served as first treasurer, and was corresponding secretary in 1878.

Parker and Giles went to Atlanta, Georgia, in 1881 and in the basement of the Friendship Church founded Spelman Seminary (later, Spelman College), a school for black women, with the support of the Baptist Home Mission Society. The school received financial support from John D. Rockefeller and was named for his wife's family. The school provided instruction in college preparatory studies, a normal course, and a higher scientific honor course. As the school grew, music and industrial departments and a course for training of nurses were added. It was chartered in 1888.

Packard went to Egypt and Palestine in 1890. She returned to the United States and died the following year. She was succeeded as president by Harriet Giles.

REFERENCES: *NAW; NCAB* (2:270); Dorothy Orr, *A History of Education in Georgia* (Chapel Hill: University of North Carolina Press, 1950); Florence Matilde Read, *The Story of Spelman College* (Princeton, N.J.: Princeton University Press, 1961).   *Rita S. Saslaw*

PAGE, David Perkins. B. July 4, 1810, Epping, New Hampshire, to n.a. M. December 16, 1832, to Susan Maria Lunt. Ch. none. D. January 1, 1848, Albany, New York.

David P. Page grew up on a modest farm in New Hampshire. He was interested in learning, but his father refused for years to let him attend a secondary school. He was finally allowed to attend Hampton (New Hampshire) Academy at the age of sixteen.

Page taught at a district school in Epping, New Hampshire, and at Newbury, Massachusetts, where he opened a private school at the age of nineteen. The school was a success, and he was appointed assistant principal and English school chairman at Newburyport High School, where he remained for twelve years (1831–43).

At Newburyport, Page gained respect as a speaker on education. He came to the attention of Horace Mann (*q.v.*) who had some of Page's speeches printed in pamphlet form. *The Mutual Duties of Parents and Teachers* (1838) was given to all public school teachers with instructions that it should be circulated to the parents of each teacher's pupils. Another speech printed in pamphlet form was *Advancement in the Means and Methods of Public Instruction* (1844).

Page was invited in 1844 to become head of New York's normal school at Albany under legislation passed in 1843; he was recommended for the position by Horace Mann. The Albany Normal School became the foundation for public higher education in New York, culminating in the establishment of the State University of New York.

In 1847 Page wrote *The Theory and Practice of Teaching,* which became one of the most widely used and influential pedagogical books in the United States. He wrote in detail how a teacher should learn the trade, practice it, and live his or her life.

REFERENCES: *AC; DAB; WWW* (H); Ezra Abel Huntington, *Funeral Discourse on David Perkins Page* (Albany, N.Y.: Albany Press, 1848); A. E. Winship (*q.v.*), *Great American Educators* (New York: American Book, 1900); Leonard Withington, "Funeral Remarks," *The Watchtower,* January 14, 1848.   *Charles E. Davis*

PAGE, Inman Edward. B. December 29, 1853, Warrenton, Virginia, to Horace and Elizabeth Page. M. 1878 to Zelia R. Ball. Ch. three. D. December 21, 1935, Oklahoma City, Oklahoma.

Inman Edward Page was born a slave and moved with his family to Washington, D.C., in 1862. He attended the private school of George F. T. Cook for three years and a night school run by George B. Vashon while he worked during the day. He entered Howard University of Washington soon after it opened in 1867 and worked his way through school landscaping the college grounds, as a janitor, and as a clerk at the Freedmen's Bureau. He left Howard in 1873 and attended Brown University in Providence, Rhode Island, as one of the first black students. He received the A.B. (1877) and A.M. (1880) degrees from Brown and was unanimously selected class orator by his white classmates.

Page taught at Natchez (Mississippi) Seminary (1877–78) and at Lincoln

Institute (later, University) in Jefferson City, Missouri (1878–80). He was appointed head of the institute in 1880 and served to 1898; he later returned as interim president (1922–23) on leave from the Oklahoma City (Oklahoma) schools. Under his leadership Lincoln Institute grew and was supported by state funds Page helped secure from the legislature.

In 1898 Page became the first president of the Colored Agricultural and Normal University (later, Langston University) in Langston, Oklahoma. By his resignation in 1915, the enrollment increased from forty-one students to a thousand. He served as president of Western Baptist College in Macon (later, Kansas City), Missouri (1916–18), and Roger Williams University in Nashville, Tennessee (1918–21). He was principal of Douglass High School and supervising principal of black elementary schools in Oklahoma City, Oklahoma (1921–35).

Oklahoma schools and buildings at Langston and Lincoln universities have been named in his memory. Page was the recipient of honorary degrees from Wilberforce and Howard universities.

REFERENCES: Elwyn E. Breaux and Thelma Perry, "Inman E. Page: Outstanding Educator," *Negro History Bulletin* 32 (May 1969): 8–12; William J. Simmons, *Men of Mark* (Cleveland, Ga.: M. Newell & Co., 1887); Kaye M. Teall, *Black History in Oklahoma* (Oklahoma City: Public Schools, 1971).

John F. Ohles

PAINE, John Knowles. B. January 9, 1839, Portland, Maine, to Jacob S. and Rebecca (Beebe) Downes Paine. M. September 7, 1869, to Mary Elizabeth Greeley. Ch. none. D. April 25, 1906, Cambridge, Massachusetts.

John Knowles Paine was the first professor of music in the United States. As a young child, he showed great musical talent and his parents, both of whom were talented musicians, encouraged his interest in music. He studied piano, organ, and composition with Hermann Kotschmar, an accomplished German musician who had settled in Portland, Maine. At nineteen years of age Paine went to Germany where he spent three years studying with the famous German organist, Karl August Haupt, and won acclaim on concert tours throughout Germany and in London as an accomplished organist (1858–61). He returned to the United States and performed brilliant organ concerts in Portland, Maine, and Boston, Massachusetts.

Paine was director of music at Harvard University and concurrently organist and choirmaster for the college (1862–73). Although music was not then offered for credit, he expanded the curriculum to include music theory and music history, as well as vocal and organ music. He was appointed assistant professor (1873) and two years later became the first person to occupy a university chair of professor of music in the United States, remaining in that position until his retirement thirty years later (1905). He taught some of America's greatest musicians, music critics, and music teachers. Paine did much to promote music as a component of general liberal education and was probably the first in this country to teach music as an art rather than as a trade.

He composed a number of musical works both for Harvard performances and for the general public, including *Mass in D,* which he conducted at a Berlin *Singakademie* concert in 1867, *St. Peter* (an oratorio, 1873), *In Frühling* (a symphony, 1880), vocal and orchestral music for *Oedipus Tyrannus* (1881), "Centennial Hymn" (1876) for the Centennial Exposition in Philadelphia, Pennsylvania (1876), and music for the World Columbian Exposition in Chicago, Illinois (1892), and for the St. Louis Exposition (1904).

Paine edited *Famous Composers and Their Music* (with Karl Klauser and Theodore Thomas, 1901) and wrote *History of Music to the Death of Schubert* (1907). He was awarded honorary degrees from Harvard and Yale universities.

REFERENCES: *AC; DAB; NCAB* (7:436); *TC; WWW* (I); George T. Edwards, *Music and Musicians of Maine* (New York: AMS Press, 1974), pp. 120–40; Louis C. Elson, *The History of American Music,* rev. ed. (New York: Macmillan, 1915), pp. 165–70; H. Wiley Hitchcock, *Music in the United States: A Historical Introduction* (Englewood Cliffs, N.J.: Prentice-Hall, 1969), pp. 130–32; *NYT,* April 26, 1906, p. 11.

Thomas A. Barlow

PAINTER, Franklin Verzelius Newton. B. April 12, 1852, Hampshire County, Virginia, to Israel and Juliana (Wilson) Painter. M. August 9, 1875, to Laura Trimble Shickel. Ch. six. D. January 18, 1931, Marion, Virginia.

Franklin Verzelius Newton Painter received the A.B. (1874) and A.M. (1877) degrees from Roanoke College (Virginia). He was graduated from the Theological Institute in Salem, Virginia, the following year and was ordained as a Lutheran minister. In 1882 he studied at the universities of Paris, France, and Bonn, Germany.

Painter taught modern languages (1882–1906) and education (1906–20) at Roanoke College. From 1906 he was president of a local cigarette machine company, teaching one course at Roanoke each semester. In the 1880s, Painter conducted summer normal institutes for teachers in Virginia and West Virginia before normal schools or departments of education were organized in many colleges in the area. He advocated changing teaching methods and supported more training for public-school teachers.

Painter wrote eighteen books, including *A History of Education* (1886), *History of Christian Worship* (with J. W. Richard, 1891), *Christian Wor-*

ship: Its Principles and Forms (1892), *Introduction to English Literature* (1894), *Introduction to American Literature* (1897), *History of English Literature* (1900), *The Reformation Dawn* (1901), *Poets of the South* (1903), *Elementary Guide to Literary Criticism* (1903), *Poets of Virginia* (1907), and *Introduction to Bible Study* (1911). He edited *Great Pedagogical Essays from Plato to Spencer* (1905).

He was the founder of the Virginia Teachers' Reading Association in 1885. He was awarded honorary degrees by Pennsylvania College and Susquehanna University.

REFERENCES: *LE* (I); *NCAB* (10:59); *TC; WWW* (I); William Edward Eisenberg, *The First Hundred Years, Roanoke College, 1842–1942* (Salem, Va.: Trustees of Roanoke College, 1942).   *Earl W. Thomas*

PALMER, Alice Elvira Freeman. B. February 21, 1855, Colesville, New York, to James Warren and Elizabeth Josephine (Higley) Freeman. M. December 23, 1887, to George Herbert Palmer *(q.v.)*. Ch. none. D. December 6, 1902, Paris, France.

Eager to acquire a college education, Alice Freeman Palmer persuaded her parents to permit her to enter the University of Michigan in 1872. While an undergraduate, she taught Sunday school and organized the Students' Christian Association, open to both men and women students. In 1876 she received the B.A. degree. She engaged in graduate study in history at Michigan but was not able to complete her doctoral dissertation.

Palmer found it necessary to take jobs to support herself and help her family. She taught at a girls' school in Lake Geneva, Wisconsin (1876–77), and served as a high school principal in Saginaw, Michigan (1877–79).

In 1879 she became head of the Wellesley (Massachusetts) College history department and became president of the college in 1882. During her administration she was instrumental in placing the college on a firm academic footing. She strengthened the faculty, made entrance examinations more rigorous, regularly sought the advice of department heads, and formed associations with selected preparatory schools. In 1887 she married George Herbert Palmer, a philosophy professor at Harvard University, and resigned her position at Wellesley.

Palmer continued to serve numerous educational and social causes. From 1892 to 1895, she was dean of women at the University of Chicago, where she was required to be in residence only twelve weeks annually. She wrote with George H. Palmer *The Teacher: Essays and Addresses on Education* (1908). She was a trustee of Wellesley College and a member of the Massachusetts Board of Education. She was awarded honorary degrees from the University of Michigan, Columbia University, and Union College.

REFERENCES: *DAB; NAW; NCAB* (7:328); *TC; WWW* (I); Alice M.

Fleming, *Great Women Teachers* (Philadelphia: J. B. Lippincott, 1965); George Herbert Palmer, *The Life of Alice Freeman Palmer* (Boston: Houghton Mifflin Co., 1908). *Nancy Baldrige Julian*

PALMER, George Herbert. B. March 19, 1842, Boston, Massachusetts, to Julius Auboyneau and Lucy Manning (Peabody) Palmer. M. June 15, 1871, to Ellen Margaret Wellman. M. December 23, 1887, to Alice Elvira Freeman *(q.v.)*. Ch. none. D. May 7, 1933, Cambridge, Massachusetts.

George Herbert Palmer entered Phillips Academy in Andover, Massachusetts, at the age of twelve, where he studied for two years. After an interval of travel and employment, he entered Harvard University, from which he received the A.B. (1864) and A.M. (1867) degrees. He taught for one year at Salem (Massachusetts) High School and then entered Andover (Massachusetts) Theological Seminary in 1865, studying philosophy. He spent two years abroad at the University of Tübingen, Germany, and then resumed his work at Andover, receiving the B.D. degree (1870).

Charles William Eliot *(q.v.)*, president of Harvard University, offered him a tutorship in Greek in 1870. Palmer accepted and began forty-three years of service to Harvard. He taught philosophy (1872–89) and also was curator of the Gray collection of engravings (1872–76). He was Alford Professor of Natural Religion, Moral Philosophy, and Civil Polity from 1889 to his retirement in 1913.

Palmer was a successful author and was known for his translations of the Greek classics, *The Odyssey of Homer* (1884) and *The Antigone of Sophocles* (1889). He was also the author of several volumes of philosophical and literary studies and biographies. His works include *Self Cultivation in English* (1897), *The Glory of the Imperfect* (1898), *The Field of Ethics* (1901), *The Nature of Goodness* (1904), *The Life and Works of George Herbert* (three volumes, 1905), *The Life of Alice Freeman Palmer* (1908), *The Teacher* (1909), *Intimations of Immortality in the Sonnets of Shakespeare* (1911), *The Problem of Freedom* (1911), *Trades and Professions* (1915), *Formative Types of English Poetry* (1918), *Altruism: Its Nature and Varieties* (1919), and *The Autobiography of a Philosopher* (1930).

Palmer was an overseer of Harvard University (1913–19) and a trustee of Wellesley College. He was a fellow of the American Academy of Arts and Sciences. He was the recipient of seven honorary degrees from American colleges and universities.

REFERENCES: *DAB; NCAB* (6:427); *NYT,* May 8, 1933, p. 15; *TC; WWW* (I). *Linda Cogar*

PALMER, Horatio Richmond. B. April 26, 1834, Sherburne, New York, to Anson B. and Abbey Marie (Knapp) Palmer. M. 1855 to Lucia A. Chapman. Ch. none. D. November 15, 1907, Yonkers, New York.

Horatio Richmond Palmer was educated at Rushford (New York) Academy and was instructed in music by his father and sister. He also studied music in New York City, Berlin, Germany, and Florence, Italy.

Palmer began to compose music at the age of eighteen and conducted a chorus at the age of twenty. He taught music at Rushford Academy (1855–57), became director of music in 1857, and directed a choir and cornet band. After the Civil War he moved to Chicago, Illinois, where he was a church choir director. In 1873 he moved to New York City and in 1881 took charge of the New York Choral Union. The group grew to a membership of over twenty thousand singers, and as many as four thousand sang in a single concert in Madison Square Garden under Palmer's direction. He organized similar groups in Brooklyn and Buffalo, New York, Philadelphia, Pennsylvania, and Washington, D.C. He was the first dean of the Summer School of Music at Chautauqua, New York (1877–91), conducted a music festival at Cortland, New York, for seventeen years, and was choir master of the Broome Street Tabernacle in New York City for eleven years.

Composer of some popular religious songs, Palmer was the author of *The Elements of Musical Composition* (1867), *Palmer's Theory of Music* (1876), *Palmer's Musical Catechism* (1881), *Palmer's Piano Primer* (1885), and *Palmer's Class Method* (1892). He compiled song books, including *The Song Queen* (1867), *Concert Choruses* (1898), and *The Song Herald* (1904). He was awarded honorary degrees by the University of Chicago and Alfred University.

REFERENCES: *AC; DAB; NCAB* (7:429); *WWW* (I). *Norman J. Bauer*

PANOFSKY, Erwin. B. March 30, 1892, Hanover, Germany, to Arnold and Caecilie (Solling) Panofsky. M. April 9, 1916, to Dora Mosse. M. to Gerda Sörgel. Ch. two. D. March 14, 1968, Princeton, New Jersey.

Erwin Panofsky received his early education at a gymnasium in Berlin, Germany (1901–10), and was a student at the universities of Freiburg, Berlin, and Munich; he received the Ph.D. degree (1914) from Freiburg.

Panofsky began his career as a teacher and professor of art history at the University of Hamburg, Germany (1921–33). He was visiting professor of fine arts at New York University and visiting lecturer at Princeton University (1934–35). He became a professor at the Institute for Advanced Study in Princeton, New Jersey, in 1935 and served there to his death in 1968. He also was Charles Eliot Norton Professor at Harvard University (1947–48) and Gottesman Lecturer at Uppsala (Sweden) University (1952). He was an authority on old movies, expert on Wolfgang Mozart, and was particularly knowledgeable about the history of the detective novel.

The author of a number of articles published in Germany, Austria, England, and America, Panofsky is best remembered for his books, including *Style and Medium in the Motion Picture* (1934), *Studies in Iconol-*

ogy (1939), *Albrecht Dürer* (1943), *Early Netherlandish Painting* (1953), *Meaning in the Visual Arts* (1955), and *Gothic Architecture and Scholasticism* (1957). With his first wife, Dora Mosse Panofsky, also an art historian, Panofsky was coauthor of *Pandora's Box* (1956).

Panofsky was a member of many American and European scholarly societies and received many awards, including the Junguis Medal from the University of Hamburg, the Haskins Medal of the Medieval Society of America (1962), and a gold medal from the republic of Italy. He received many honorary degrees from American and foreign colleges and universities.

REFERENCES: *NYT,* March 16, 1968, p. 32; *WWW* (IV); *Burlington Magazine* 110 (June 1968): 356–60.

Roger H. Jones

PARK, John Rocky. B. May 7, 1833, Tiffin, Ohio, to John and Elizabeth (Waggoner) Park. M. no. Ch. two, adopted. D. September 29, 1900, Salt Lake City, Utah.

John R. Park was graduated with the A.B. degree (1853) from Ohio Wesleyan University in Delaware, Ohio. He received the M.D. degree (1857) from New York University.

He practiced medicine for only a few months, when he accepted the superintendency of the Tiffin (Ohio) schools. By 1861 Park joined the Mormon (Latter-Day Saints) church, moved to Draper, Utah, and became principal of the local district school. Leaving Utah in 1862, he spent the next two years in Oregon teaching and in business. He returned to his position as principal of Draper Academy in 1864.

Park was elected president of the University of Deseret (later, University of Utah) in 1869 with specific instructions to reorganize the school and put it on a full-time operating basis. He is considered the first president of the University of Utah. In 1871 Brigham Young sent Park on a trip to the East and then to Europe to investigate institutions of higher education. Returning to Utah in 1872, Park began a twenty-three-year tenure as president. Under his administration, faculties of arts and science, education, law, and mines were established. The school of mines became a foremost institution of its kind and was one of the first doctoral degree-granting institutions in mining in the United States. Park hired a strong science faculty, which made the first geological, flora, and fauna surveys of Utah. By the time of his resignation in 1892, the school had a new campus and a new name, the University of Utah.

From 1896 until his death Park served as the first superintendent of public instruction for Utah. He was credited with a revision of the Utah school law and establishment of a vocational education program as part of the school curriculum. In tribute to his efforts in developing the University of Utah, the administration building was named after him in 1912. In 1922 a statue of Park by the renowned artist Mahonri Young was placed on the campus.

REFERENCES: *NCAB* (22:82); Ralph V. Chamberlin, *The University of Utah: A History of Its First Hundred Years, 1850 to 1950* (Salt Lake City: University of Utah Press, 1960); *Salt Lake Herald,* June 9, 1892.

Leo D. Leonard

PARKER, Francis Wayland. B. October 9, 1837, Piscatoquog, New Hampshire, to Robert and Millie (Rand) Parker. M. December 1, 1864, to Josephine E. Hall. M. November 23, 1882, to Frances Stuart. Ch. two. D. March 2, 1902, Pass Christian, Mississippi.

Francis Wayland Parker was referred to by John Dewey *(q.v.)* as the Father of Modern Education. He was born and reared in rural New Hampshire and attended an academy in Mount Vernon. He obtained his first teaching position in his home state in 1854 at the age of sixteen.

In 1858 Parker was called to teach at Carrollton, Illinois, where he remained until 1861, when he enlisted in the Union army. After being wounded at the battle of Deep Bottom, Virginia, he returned to action and in 1864 was brevetted colonel. After the war he served as principal of the grammar school in Manchester, New Hampshire (1865–68), and the district schools in Dayton, Ohio (1868–71). While in Dayton he put into practice some of his radical and experimental teaching methods: regimentation gave way to flexibility, strict curriculum requirements to the needs of individual learners, and rote memorization to exploration and discovery—methods reflective of the influence of Edward A. Sheldon *(q.v.),* whose *Object Lessons* pointed the way toward overcoming the formalism then prevalent in American schools.

In 1871 Parker went to Europe, where he studied at the University of Berlin. He studied the theories of John Amos Comenius, Johann Heinrich Pestalozzi, Johann Friedrich Herbart, and Friedrich Froebel, as well as new methods of teaching geography set forth by Carl Ritter and Arnold Guyot *(q.v.).* In 1875, after returning to the United States, Parker was appointed superintendent of schools at Quincy, Massachusetts, where he introduced science into the curriculum and permitted greater freedom and informality in classroom instruction and relaxed methods of discipline. He served as a supervisor of schools in Boston (1880–83) and principal of the Cook County (Illinois) Normal School (1883–96) and of its successor, the Chicago Normal School (later, Chicago State University), from 1896 to 1899. In 1899 he was president of the Chicago Institute, which had been established by a grant from Mrs. Emmons McCormick Blaine.

In 1901 the institute became affiliated with the University of Chicago with Parker as the first director of its school of education. Parker founded the progressive education movement. His educational ideas were expressed in *Talks on Pedagogics* (1894) and *Talks on Teaching* (1896). He also wrote *The Practical Teacher* (1883), *Course in Arithmetic* (1884), *How to Teach Geography* (1885), *Outlines in Geography* (1885), *How to Study Geography* (1889), and *Uncle Robert's Geography* (with Nellie L. Helm, four volumes, 1897–1904). He was editor of *The Elementary School Teacher and Course of Study*.

Parker was one of the founders and the first president of the Illinois Society for Child Study, the first organization of its kind in the United States. He received honorary degrees from Dartmouth College and Lawrence University.

REFERENCES: *AC; DAB; EB; TC; WWW* (I); Carroll Atkinson and Eugene T. Maleska, *The Story of Education* (Philadelphia: Chilton Company, Publishers, 1962), pp. 78–83; Jack K. Campbell, *Colonel Francis W. Parker: The Children's Crusader* (New York: Teachers College Press, 1967); Edward Dangler, "From Quincy to Chicago—The American Comenius," *The Harvard Educational Review* 13 (January 1943): 19–24; John Dewey, "In Memoriam—Colonel Francis Wayland Parker," *The Elementary School Teacher* 2 (June 1902): 704–08.   *Frederick C. Neff*
Joseph Engle

PARKER, Horatio William. B. September 5, 1863, Auburndale, Massachusetts, to Charles E. and Isabella (Jennings) Parker. M. August 9, 1888, to Anna Ploessl. Ch. three. D. December 18, 1919, Cedarhurst, New York.

Horatio Parker first studied music with his mother, a person of considerable artistic talent. He studied music in Boston with George W. Chadwick *(q.v.)* and others. He enrolled in the Royal Music School of Munich, Germany, at the age of nineteen, where he studied with J. G. Rheinberger. He was graduated in 1885 and returned to the United States, where he was professor of music at the Cathedral School of St. Paul in Garden City, Long Island, New York (1885–87), and at the National Conservatory of Music in New York City under Anton Dvorak, director (1887–93). He was organist at several churches, including the Holy Trinity Church in New York City (1888–93) and Trinity Church in Boston, Massachusetts (1893–1901).

Parker became professor of music theory at Yale University in 1894 and continued there to his death in 1919. He was Battell Professor of Music and became dean of the school of music from 1903. He was conductor of the New Haven (Connecticut) Symphony Orchestra, which was affiliated with Yale. He assumed responsibilities as organist of the Collegiate Church of St. Nicholas in New York and conductor of singing groups in Philadelphia, Pennsylvania, and Derby, Connecticut.

Parker was a major American composer, whose works include the oratorios *Hora Novissima* (1893) and *St. Christopher* (1902), the operas *Mona* (1912), which won a prize from the Metropolitan Opera Company, and *Fairyland* (1915), and many others. He was the author of *Music and Public Entertainment* (1911). He was a fellow of the American Academy of Arts and Letters and the American Guild of Organists and a member of many other organizations. He received honorary degrees from Yale and Cambridge (England) universities.

REFERENCES: *DAB; EB; NCAB* (35:91); *TC; WWW* (I); George W. Chadwick, *Horatio Parker* (New Haven: Yale University Press, 1921); John Tasker Howard and George Kent Bellows, *A Short History of Music in America* (New York: Thomas Y. Crowell Co., 1957); Wilfred Melloers, *Music in a New Found Land* (New York: Alfred A. Knopf, 1965); *NYT,* December 19, 1919, p. 15.   *Arved M. Larsen*

PARKER, Richard Green. B. December 25, 1798, Boston, Massachusetts, to Samuel and Anne (Cutler) Parker. M. April 20, 1820, to Mary Ann Moore Davis. M. c. 1848 to Catherine (Hall) Payson. Ch. five. D. September 25, 1869, Boston, Massachusetts.

Richard Green Parker received his education at the Boston Public Latin School and was graduated with the A.B. degree (1817) from Harvard University.

Parker began teaching on graduation from Harvard, and from 1825 he was associated with Boston public schools as grammar master of the East Roxbury Grammar School (1825–28), Mayhew School (1828–29), Franklin School (1830–36), and Johnson School (1836–53). On retiring, he established a private girls' school.

Parker was a major writer of schoolbooks, including *The Boston School Compendium of Natural and Experimental Philosophy* (1837), *Progressive Exercises in English Composition* (1832), and *Progressive Exercises in English Grammar* (with Charles Fox, 1834). He also wrote *Questions Adapted to Hedge's Logick* (1823), *A Sketch of the History of the Grammar School in East Parish, of Roxbury* (1826), and *A Tribute to the Life and Character of Jonas Chickering* (1854). He and James M. Watson (*q.v.*) prepared the National Reader Series (1858). His books were widely used but were also attacked in public as being subject to favoritism by the school committee. He contributed opera and concert reviews for Boston newspapers.

REFERENCES: *AC; DAB; WWW* (H); John A. Nietz, *The Evolution of American Secondary School Textbooks* (Rutland, Vt.: Charles E. Tuttle, 1966).   *Joan Duff Kise*

PARKHURST, Helen. B. March 7, 1887, Durand, Wisconsin, to James H. and Ida (Smallet) Parkhurst. M. no. D. June 1, 1973, New Milford, Connecticut.

Helen Parkhurst taught in a one-room school in Wisconsin at the age of sixteen. She attended the Wisconsin State Teachers College, graduating with the B.S. degree (1907). She studied summers at Columbia University (1908–10). She was a student in Germany at the University of Munich and in 1914 in Italy at the University of Rome, and with Maria Montessori, originator of the Montessori method of instruction. She was a fellow in education at Yale University (1942–43), where she received the M.A. degree (1943).

Parkhurst taught in rural elementary schools and at the Wisconsin State Teachers College (1909–10). She taught at the Edison School in Tacoma, Washington (1910–11), where she developed ideas that came to be called the Dalton laboratory plan. She returned to Wisconsin to teach at the Central State Teachers College (later, University of Wisconsin—Stevens Point) at Stevens Point (1912–14). Returning from Italy and her work with Maria Montessori, Parkhurst established a two-year Montessori College in New York City (1916–18).

She assisted the Upway Field School for Crippled Children of Pittsfield, Massachusetts, in establishing an experimental educational plan, the first application of Parkhurst's laboratory plan (1918–19). With financial assistance from Mrs. H. M. Crane, Dalton (Massachusetts) High School was reorganized on the plan. The school was considered to be a sociological laboratory. School work was divided into contract jobs with each student contracting for specific assignments, organizing his or her learning experiences, and reporting his or her progress to the teachers. Subject matter instruction was conducted in subject laboratories and special subjects, such as physical education, industrial arts, and art, could be conducted by group instruction.

Parkhurst returned to New York City in 1920, where she established the Dalton School, which she directed to her retirement in 1942. Invited by foreign governments to explain the Dalton plan, she established Dalton schools in England, Japan, and China; other countries also adopted the plan. She was president of Your Child, Inc., from 1942 and headed Research Associates, Inc., of New York City (1943–45). She was educational consultant to Hoffman School and Columbia Grammar School for Boys (1945–47).

Parkhurst produced radio and television programs, including "Child's World" (radio, 1947–49 and television, 1947–48) and the radio programs "Children Should Be Heard" (1950) and "Know Your Child" (1949–54). She was the author of *Education on the Dalton Plan* (1922), *Work Rhythms in Education* (1935), *They Found Johnny* (1947), *Exploring the Child's World* (1951), and *Undertow* (with Christine Hotchkiss, 1959).

A member of many educational organizations, Parkhurst was vice-president of the Children's Foundation (1939–41) and the International Education Association (1939–41). She was decorated by the government of the Netherlands and received many awards for educational, television and radio work.

REFERENCES: *NYT,* June 3, 1973, p. 66; *WW* (XXXI); *WWW* (VI); Evelyn Dewey, *The Dalton Laboratory Plan* (New York: E. P. Dutton, 1922); Helen Parkhurst, *Education on the Dalton Plan* (London: G. Bell & Sons Ltd., 1922).   *Robert D. MacCurdy*

PARKINS, Almon Ernest. B. January 10, 1879, Marysville, Michigan, to John H. and Mariah (Cooley) Parkins. M. June 29, 1905, to Eleanor Grace Stone. Ch. none. D. January 3, 1940, Nashville, Tennessee.

Almon Ernest Parkins received the B.Pd. (1906) and A.B. (1911) degrees from Michigan State Normal College (later, Eastern Michigan University) at Ypsilanti. In 1911 he entered the University of Chicago where he earned the B.S. (1914) and Ph.D. (1916) degrees.

Parkins taught agricultural geology and geography at the University of Missouri (1914–16). From 1916 until his death in 1940, he was professor of geography at George Peabody College for Teachers in Nashville, Tennessee. In 1936 he served as a field representative for the division of cotton of the Agricultural Adjustment Administration.

Parkins achieved national recognition through his writings, which include *The Development of Transportation in Pennsylvania* (1916), *Historical Geography of Detroit* (1918), and *The South, Its Economic-Geographic Development* (1937). He coauthored *Common School Geographies* (with Frank M. McMurry, *q.v.,* 1921), *Our Trees and How They Serve Us* (with Rufus S. Maddox, 1925), *The Geography of North America* (with George J. Miller, 1928), and *Our Natural Resources and Their Conservation* (editor with J. R. Whitaker, 1937). For many years he was editor of "Junior High School Geography" in the *Class Room Teacher.* He edited the *Annals of the Association of American Geographers* (1924–29) and prepared a series of maps for school and college use. He was chairman of the committee that compiled the 1933 *Yearbook of the National Society for the Study of Education.*

Parkins was a fellow of the American Association for the Advancement of Science and a member of many professional associations, including the Association of American Geographers (president, 1929), the National Council of Geography Teachers (president, 1925), and the Tennessee Academy of Sciences (president, 1922–23). In 1934 Parkins received the Distinguished Service Award of the National Council of Geography Teachers. He received an honorary degree from the Michigan State Normal College.

REFERENCES: *LE* (I); *NCAB* (38:469); *NYT,* January 4, 1940, p. 23; *WWW* (I).   *Harold D. Lehman*

PARRISH, Celestia Susannah. B. September 12, 1853, Swansonville, Virginia, to William Perkins and Lucinda Jane (Walker) Parrish. M. no. Ch. one, adopted. D. September 7, 1918, Clayton, Georgia.

Celestia Susannah Parrish attended a private school on her father's plantation near Swansonville, Pittsylvania County, Virginia. During the Civil War, both parents died, and she lived with an uncle and two aunts. She enrolled in a private school in Callands, Virginia. When her uncle died in 1867, Parrish became a teacher in a private school, in the Swansonville (Virginia) public school, and in other local schools (1869–74). She taught in the Danville (Virginia) schools (1874–83).

Parrish was a student in the Roanoke Female Institute in Danville (1874–76) and in Farmville, where she was graduated in 1886. She studied mathematics and astronomy at the University of Michigan (1891–92) and enrolled at Cornell University in Ithaca, New York, where she received the Ph.B. degree in 1896. She also studied summers at the University of Chicago (1897–99).

Parrish taught mathematics at the Roanoke Female Institute (1883–84) and State Normal School (1884–92). She joined the faculty of the new Randolph-Macon Woman's College in Lynchburg, Virginia, in 1893 as a teacher of mathematics, education, and psychology. In 1902 she became professor of education at the State Normal School at Athens, Georgia, where she established the first laboratory school in the South. From 1911 to 1918, she was supervisor of rural schools for the Georgia state education department.

Parrish was active in promoting the education of women in the South. She organized the first Young Women's Christian Association college in the South and was an organizer of the first southern branch in Virginia of the Association of Collegiate Alumnae (president, 1899–1902) and the Southern Association of College Women (first president, 1903). She was president of the Georgia Congress of Mothers.

REFERENCES: *DAB; NAW; TC; WWW* (I).   *Linda C. Gardner*

PARRISH, Edward. B. May 31, 1822, Philadelphia, Pennsylvania, to Joseph and Susanna (Cox) Parrish. M. 1848 to Margaret Hunt. Ch. five. D. September 9, 1872, Fort Sill, Indian Territory (Oklahoma).

Edward Parrish, pharmaceutical educator and founder and president of Swarthmore College, was educated at Friends' School in Philadelphia. He was apprenticed to his brother Dillwyn, a druggist. He attended the Philadelphia College of Pharmacy, graduating in 1842. He also attended the University of Pennsylvania.

Parrish opened a drugstore near the University of Pennsylvania where he instructed medical students in the back of his store, opening a school in

1849. He entered into a partnership with his brother and moved the school to the new store in 1850. He discontinued the school in 1864 when he became professor of materia medica at the Philadelphia College of Pharmacy and in 1867 taught the theory and practice of pharmacy, which he continued to his death in 1872.

In 1864 he was one of the founders of Swarthmore (Pennsylvania) College and served as secretary (1864–68) and president (1868–72). He was the author of *Introduction to Practical Pharmacy* (1855), *Summer Medical Teaching in Philadelphia* (1857), *The Phantom Bouquet* (1863), and *An Essay on Education* (1866) and many articles for the *Journal of Pharmacy*.

Parrish was a charter member of the American Pharmaceutical Society in 1852 (president, 1868–72) and belonged to other American and foreign societies. He was a delegate to the International Pharmaceutical Congress in London in 1858. In 1872 he served as a peace commissioner for the United States government in the Indian Territory.

REFERENCES: *AC; DAB; NCAB* (5:348); *TC; WWW* (H).

James M. Vosper

PARSONS, Frank. B. November 14, 1854, Mount Holly, New Jersey, to Edward and Alice (Rhees) Parsons. M. no. D. September 26, 1908, Boston, Massachusetts.

Frank Parsons received his early education at home and at Aaron Academy near Mount Holly, New Jersey. He entered Cornell University in Ithaca, New York, as a sophomore and was graduated in engineering and mathematics (1873). Following brief employment as engineer for a railroad (1873) and in a rolling mill (1874), he taught in a district school and taught French, mathematics, and drawing at the Southbridge, Massachusetts, high school (1874–81). He completed three years' study of law in one year and was admitted to the bar in 1881. His health suffered, and he went to New Mexico for three years of recuperation.

Parsons practiced law briefly, then accepted employment as a writer of legal textbooks for Little, Brown & Company (1885–97). Discovering interests and talents in writing and speaking, he devoted the last twenty years of his life to writing, teaching, and social reform. He lectured at the Boston University Law School (1892–1905). He took a leave of absence from Boston University to teach history and political science at the State College of Agriculture and Applied Science (later, Kansas State University) in Manhattan (1897–99). He spent a few months at Ruskin College for Social Service at Trenton, Missouri, in 1899 and returned to Boston.

He was a member of a commission sent to Europe by the National Civic Federation to study government, industry, and transportation (1901–02). In 1902 he lectured under the auspices of the Chicago University and after retirement from Boston University in 1905 was involved with founding the

Bread-winners College and the Vocational Bureau, where his work was recognized as pioneering in vocational guidance.

His writings include *The World's Best Books* (1889), *Philosophy of Mutualism* (1890), *Public Ownership of Monopolies* (1892), *Our Country's Need or a Scientific System of Industry* (1894), *The People's Lamps* (1895), *The Telegraph Monopoly* (1896), *Compulsory Arbitration* (1897), *The Drift of Our Century* (1897), *Rational Money* (1898), *The Drift of Our Time* (1898), *Legal Aspects of Monopoly* (1898), *New Political Economy* (1899), *Power of the Ideal* (1899), *Direct Legislation* (1900), *The Bondage of the Cities* (1900), *The City for the People* (1900), *Great Movements in the 19th Century* (1901), *The Story of New Zealand* (1904), *The Trusts, the Railroads, and the People* (1906), *The Heart of the Railroad Problem* (1906), and two books that were published posthumously, *Choosing a Vocation* (1909), and *Legal Doctrine and Social Progress* (1911). He also prepared pamphlets on economic subjects, edited economic publications, and contributed to numerous periodicals.

Parsons was a member of the American Academy of Political and Social Science, president of the National Public Ownership League and National Referendum League, director of the Co-Workers' fraternity, and vice-chairman of the National Non-Partisan League for Majority Rule. Parson's *Choosing a Vocation* and his efforts to aid youth in the Boston area in selecting vocations have led many writers in school guidance to call Parsons the Father of Vocational Guidance.

REFERENCES: *DAB; NCAB* (11:182); *TC; WWW* (I); Howard V. David, *Frank Parsons: Prophet, Innovator, Counselor* (Carbondale: Southern Illinois University Press, 1969); *NYT,* September 27, 1908, p. 11.

Paul L. Ward

PARTRIDGE, Alden. B. February 12, 1785, Norwich, Vermont, to Samuel and Elizabeth (Wright) Partridge. M. April 1837 to Ann Elizabeth Swasey. Ch. two. D. January 17, 1854, Norwich, Vermont.

Alden Partridge grew up in Norwich, Vermont, and attended Dartmouth College in Hanover, New Hampshire, from 1802 to 1805, when he entered the United States Military Academy at West Point, New York. He was graduated from the academy and was commissioned a first lieutenant in the Corps of Engineers in October 1806.

Partridge was assigned to West Point as an assistant professor of mathematics and remained at the academy for twelve years. He was West Point's first professor of the art of engineering in 1813. Appointed superintendent of the academy in 1815, his term ended with conflict between Partridge and his staff that led to a court-martial on charges of neglect of duty and insubord'nation. Sentenced to be discharged from the army in 1817, Partridge was allowed to resign his commission in 1818.

Partridge was an engineer on the project that established the northeastern boundary of the United States and Canada under the terms of the Treaty of Ghent. Believing a large standing army was dangerous, Partridge advocated a citizen soldiery as a necessity for a free society. Convinced that West Point would never be able to furnish all the officers needed, he established the American Literary, Scientific and Military Academy in Norwich, Vermont, in 1819. This was the first purely technical and military school for the training of citizen soldiery in the world. He moved the school to Middletown, Connecticut, in 1825, but four years later, he returned to Vermont, and his school was granted a charter by the state in 1834 as Norwich University.

Partridge introduced new ideas to higher education, including the laboratory method of instruction, the study of agriculture as part of the regular curriculum, courses in civil engineering, and courses in navigation. He established a summer school of engineering, where students spent several weeks in camps on practical engineering work, practice marches, and military tactics. Students of Norwich did not graduate at a specific time but received certificates as soon as they completed their course work.

Partridge resigned as president of Norwich in 1843 and developed other military schools throughout the East; seven such schools were established by 1853. He was active in the administration of these schools and lectured on military and historical subjects at them. He was a frequent contributor to journals and was the author of *An Excursion* (1822), *Lecture on Education* (1825), *The Art of Epistolary Composition* (1826), and *Journal of a Tour of Cadets* (1827).

Partridge served as surveyor-general of Vermont (1822–23) and was a member of the Vermont legislature in the 1830s. He was a lecturer on military and historical topics in many cities in the United States.

REFERENCES: *AC; DAB; NCAB* (18:322); *TC; WWW* (H); Ernest N. Harmon, *Norwich University, Its Founder and His Ideals* (New York: Newcomen Society in North America, 1951).   *Edward J. Durnall*

PASTORIUS, Francis Daniel. B. September 26, 1651, Sommerhausen, Franconia, Germany, to Melchoir Adam and Magdalana (Dietz) Pastorius. M. November 6, 1688, to Ennecke Klostermanns. Ch. two. D. September 27, 1719 (also given as c. January 1, 1720), Germantown, Pennsylvania.

Francis Daniel Pastorius grew up in Germany and was educated at Windsheim Gymnasium and attended universities at Altdorf, Strassburg, Basel, and Jena and received the J.D. degree (1676) from the University of Altdorf, Switzerland.

Pastorius practiced law in Windsheim and moved to Frankfort-am-Main. He traveled in Europe (1680–82) and became acquainted with William Penn. He became a land agent for a group of Frankfort Quakers (1683) and purchased land in Pennsylvania. He laid out the settlement of Germantown and served as a village official (1683-1707).

A professional public writer, Pastorius taught in a Friends' school in Philadelphia (1698-1700) and was master of a school in Germantown from 1702. He participated in the first protest against slavery in the colonies (1688). He was the author of several works, including a pamphlet describing the new settlement and providing advice to potential German emigrants, *Umständige Geographische Beschreibung der Allerletzt Erfundenen Provintz Pennsylvaniae* (1700). He also wrote *Four Boasting Disputers of This World Briefly Rebuked* (1697) and *A New Primmer or Methodical Directions to Attain the True Spelling, Reading and Writing of English* (n.d.).

REFERENCES: *AC; DAB; NCAB* (11:352); *WWW* (H); E. Gordon Alderfer, "Pastorius and the Origins of Pennsylvania German Culture," *The American-German Review* 17 (February 1951): 8-11; Arthur E. Englebert, "Francis Daniel Pastorius in His Literary Activities," (Doctoral diss., University of Pittsburgh, 1935); Charles F. Jenkins, "Francis Daniel Pastorius," *The American-German Review* 1 (December 1934): 22-25.

Samuel A. Farmerie

PATERSON, Donald Gildersleeve. B. January 18, 1892, Columbus, Ohio, to Robert and Rosa (Gildersleeve) Paterson. M. June 22, 1920, to Margaret Young. Ch. two. D. October 4, 1961, Minneapolis, Minnesota.

A student at Olivet (Michigan) College (1910-12), Donald G. Paterson received the B.A. (1914) and M.A. (1916) degrees from Ohio State University.

He was a graduate assistant at Ohio State University (1914-16), served as an instructor at the University of Kansas (1916-17), and was a consulting psychologist to the Scott Company in Philadelphia, Pennsylvania (1919-21). He was appointed to the faculty of the University of Minnesota in 1917 and served until he retired in 1960. He established the Counseling Bureau and the Industrial Relations Center at the University of Minnesota.

He was a prolific author with over two hundred publications to his credit, most of which were coauthored by colleagues and students; they include *Physique and Intellect* (1930), *Men, Women and Jobs* (1936), *Student Guidance Techniques* (1937), *How to Make Type Readable* (1940), *Local Labor Research* (1948), and *Studies in Individual Differences* (1961). He was an author of standardized tests, including the *Minnesota Mechanical Ability Tests* (1930) and *The Minnesota Occupational Rating Scales and Counseling Profile* (1941). He was associate editor of Mental Measurement Monographs series (1925-61), advisory editor to *Public Personnel Quarterly* (1939-41), and editor of *Journal of Applied Psychology* (1943-54).

Paterson was chairman of the technical committee of the National Occupational Research Program sponsored by the United States Employment Service (1934–40) and the committee on individual diagnosis and training of the Employment Stabilization Research Institute at the University of Minnesota (1931–45). He was a consultant to the training program for vocational counselors conducted by the Veterans Administration and was a member of the technical committee (1933–38) and committee on measurement and guidance (1936–41) of the National Research Council. He was a member of the Social Science Research Council and the White House Conference on Child Health and Protection (1927–30). He was a diplomate in Industrial Psychology in 1949 and a fellow in the American Association for the Advancement of Science and the American Psychological Association (secretary, 1931–37). He held memberships in the American Association of Applied Psychology (president, 1938–39) and the Minnesota Society of Applied Psychology (president, 1937) and was a member of many other organizations. He received an honorary degree from Ohio State University (1952).

REFERENCES: *NCAB* (53:158); *WWAE* (XVI); *WWW* (IV); *Journal of Applied Psychology* 45 (December 1961): 352; *Personnel and Guidance Journal* 40 (November 1961): 235.   *Bruce D. Mattson*

PATERSON, William Burns. B. February 9, 1849, Tullibody, Scotland, to John and Janet (Burns) Paterson. M. June 5, 1879, to Margaret Bingham Flock. Ch. five. D. March 14, 1915, Montgomery, Alabama.

William Burns Paterson attended school in Scotland but withdrew at the age of twelve because of health problems. He emigrated to the United States by working on a freighter.

Paterson worked his way from New York City to New Orleans, Louisiana, Columbus, Mississippi, and to Alabama at Mobile and Demopolis. Working with a dredging crew on the Black Warrior River, he taught black laborers to read and write during lunch breaks. He started the Hopewell day school outside Greensboro, Alabama, and moved it into the town in 1871.

In 1872 Paterson established Tullibody Academy for black students and maintained the academy to 1878 when he became principal of Lincoln Normal University in Marion, Alabama. Seeking better facilities, Paterson moved to a new site in Marion in 1879 and to Montgomery in 1887. Paterson directed the normal school to his death in 1915. The institution later became Alabama State University.

Paterson organized the Alabama State Teachers Association for black teachers in 1882 and served as its first president. Paterson Hall at Alabama State College and the W. B. Paterson Elementary School in Montgomery were named in his honor.

REFERENCES: *Alabama Historical Quarterly* (Summer 1974).

John F. Ohles

PATRI, Angelo. B. November, 1877, Italy, to Nicholas and Carmela Patri. M. 1910 to Dorothy Caterson. Ch. none. D. September 13, 1965, Danbury, Connecticut.

Angelo Patri was born in Italy and came to the United States with his parents. He attended New York City public schools and City College of New York, where he was graduated with the A.B. degree (1897). In 1898 he became a teacher in the New York City public schools. He studied pedagogical principles and methods at Columbia University where he received the M.A. degree (1904).

Patri was principal of Public School 4 (1908–13) and Public School 45 in the Bronx (1913–44), where he pioneered in providing liberal education for students. Besides studying reading, writing, and arithmetic, pupils were encouraged to develop their talents in the school's shops and courses where they could weave, draw, sew, write, work with clay, wood, and metal, play in an orchestra, or plant fruit and vegetables. Children were encouraged to develop creative skills while learning basic fundamentals.

Patri wrote a syndicated newspaper column, "Our Children." Among his books were *A School Master of the Great City* (1917), *The School That Everyone Wants* (1922), *Child Training, School and Home* (1925), *Problems of Childhood* (1926), *What Have You Got to Give* (1926), *The Questioning Child* (1930), *Parent's Daily Counselor* (1940), *Your Children in War Time* (1943), and *To Help Your Child Grow Up* (1948). He also wrote several books for children, including *Pinocchio in Africa* (1911) and *Pinocchio in America* (1928).

REFERENCES: *CB* (November 1940); *LE* (II); *WWW* (IV); *NYT*, September 14, 1965, p. 39.   *Anthony V. Patti*

PATTEE, Fred Lewis. B. March 22, 1853, Bristol, New Hampshire, to Lewis F. and Mary P. (Ingalls) Pattee. M. March 9, 1889, to Anna L. Plumer. M. November 25, 1928, to Grace (Gorrell) Garee. Ch. one. D. May 6, 1950, Winter Park, Florida.

Fred Lewis Pattee attended the New Hampton (New Hampshire) Institute and served a three-year apprenticeship as a journeyman printer. He received the A.B. (1888) and A.M. (1891) degrees from Dartmouth College in Hanover, New Hampshire. He studied in Germany at the universities of Göttingen (1902–03) and Marburg (1910).

Pattee was a school principal at Eatontown, New Jersey, Mendon, Massachusetts, and Coe's Northwood (New Hampshire) Academy (1890–94). He was professor of English and literature at Pennsylvania State College (later, University) from 1894 to 1928. He was one of the first to hold the position of professor of American literature (1918–28). After retirement he served at Rollins College in Winter Park, Florida (1928–41). He had been a visiting professor of American literature at the University of Illinois (1923–24) and professor of American literature at the Bread Loaf

Summer School of English at Middlebury, Vermont (1924–36).

Pattee was the author of many books, including *The Wine of May and Other Lyrics* (1893), *Pasquaney, a Study* (1894), *A History of American Literature* (1896), *Reading Courses in American Literature* (1897), *The Foundations of English Literature* (1900), *Mary Garvin* (1902), *The House of the Black Ring* (1905), *Elements of Religious Pedagogy* (1909), *The Breaking Point* (1911), *Compelled Men* (1913), *History of American Literature Since 1870* (1915), *Sidelights on American Literature* (1922), *The Development of the American Short Story* (1923), *Tradition and Jazz* (1924), and *The New American Literature* (1930). He edited the works of several authors and *Century Readings in the American Short Story* (1927), *Beyond the Sunset* (1934), *The First Century of American Literature* (1935), and *The Feminine Fifties* (1940).

Two honorary degrees were conferred on Pattee by Dartmouth College and one by Lebanon Valley College.

REFERENCES: *LE* (II); *NCAB* (A:228, 39:182); *NYT,* May 7, 1950, p. 108; *TC; WWW* (III); W. L. Werner and Arlin Turner, "In Memoriam: Fred Lewis Pattee, 1863–1950," *American Literature* 22 (January 1951): 573–74.   *John F. Ohles*

PATTERSON, Edwin Wilhite. B. January 1, 1889, Kansas City, Missouri, to Louis Lee and Roberta Ann (Wilhite) Patterson. M. December 28, 1915, to Dorothy Madison Thomson. Ch. three. D. December 23, 1965, Charlottesville, Virginia.

After attending the Kansas City, Missouri, public schools, Edwin Wilhite Patterson attended the University of Missouri from which he was graduated with the A.B. (1909) and LL.B. (1911) degrees. In 1920 he received the S.J.D. degree from Harvard University, where he was greatly influenced by Roscoe Pound *(q.v.).*

Admitted to the bar in 1911, Patterson practiced in Kansas City for four years before embarking on a career of teaching law. He taught successively at the universities of Texas (1915–17), Colorado (1917–19), and Iowa (1920–22) before joining the faculty of Columbia University in 1922.

Patterson conducted seminars with John Dewey *(q.v.)* on the influence of philosophy on law (1925–30). When the Cardozo Chair of Jurisprudence was created in 1945, Patterson was named to the post and served to his retirement in 1957. After his retirement from Columbia, he was a visiting professor at the University of Southern California (1958–59) and taught at the Judge Advocate General School in Charlottesville, Virginia (1961–65). Patterson was one of the most influential men in American legal education, particularly in establishing meaningful graduate law study at Columbia.

He was a prolific writer. His major contribution was *Men and Ideas of the Law* (1953). His other major works include *The Insurance Com-*

missioner in the United States (1927), *Cases and Other Materials on the Law of Insurance* (1932), *Essentials of Insurance Law* (1935), *Cases and Materials on Contracts* (1935), *Materials for Legal Method* (with others, 1946), and *Legal Protection of Private Pension Expectations* (1960).

Patterson served as an adviser on the Restatement of Restitution for the American Law Institute (1933–37) and was chairman of the American Bar Association committee on qualification and regulation of insurance companies (1935–50). He was in charge of the Revision of the New York State Insurance Law (1935–39); his work was a model for other states. He received an honorary degree from the University of Missouri.

REFERENCES: *CA* (1–4); *LE* (II); *NCAB* (51:426); *WWAE* (XVI); *WWW* (V); Harry W. Jones, "Edwin Wilhite Patterson: Man and Ideas," *Columbia Law Review* 57 (May 1957): 607–19; *NYT,* December 25, 1965, p. 13; Charlotte H. Sherr, comp., "The Writings of Edwin Wilhite Patterson," *Columbia Law Review* 57 (May 1957): 619–23.   *Robert H. Truman*

PATTERSON, James Kennedy. B. March 26, 1833, Glasgow, Scotland, to Andrew and Janet (Kennedy) Patterson. M. December 25, 1859, to Lucelia Wing. Ch. one. D. August 15, 1922, Lexington, Kentucky.

James Kennedy Patterson emigrated with his family from Scotland to America in 1842 and settled in Indiana. He began his studies at Hanover (Indiana) College in 1851 and was graduated as valedictorian with the A.B. degree (1856) and received the A.M. degree (1859) from Hanover.

He became principal of the Presbyterian Academy in Greenville, Kentucky (1856–59), and the preparatory department of Stewart College in Clarksville, Tennessee (1859–61). The academy closed with the start of the Civil War, and Patterson took a position as principal of Transylvania Academy in Lexington, Kentucky (1861–65). The University of Kentucky was organized in 1865, and Patterson was made professor of Latin, history, and metaphysics. In 1869 he became president of the Agricultural and Mechanical College of Kentucky, which had been established in 1865 as an adjunct to the university. Patterson visited Europe in 1875 and upon his return to Kentucky found dissension at the university that resulted in the separation of the Agricultural and Mechanical College from the University of Kentucky.

Patterson remained in control of the renamed State College, an institution without a campus and with a faculty of five and an inadequate budget. He established a campus in Lexington and led a fight for state aid from 1875 until 1882 when an appropriation bill was passed by the Kentucky legislature. The State College became the University of Kentucky. He retired as president in 1910.

Patterson wrote editorials for the *Louisville* (Kentucky) *Courier-Journal* from 1871 to 1874. He was a delegate to the International Geographical

Congress in Paris, France (1875), and the British Association in Bristol (1875) and Leeds (1890). He was a fellow of the Royal Historical Society of Great Britain and the Society of Antiquaries of Edinburgh, Scotland, and president of the Association of Land Grant Colleges (1903) and of other associations. He was a trustee of Hanover College and the University of Kentucky. He received honorary degrees from Lafayette and Hanover colleges and the universities of Vermont and Kentucky.

REFERENCES: *DAB; NCAB* (11:422); *TC; WWW* (I).

Donald C. Stephenson

PATTERSON, James Willis. B. July 2, 1823, Henniker, New Hampshire, to William and Frances Mary (Shepherd) Patterson. M. December 24, 1854, to Sarah Parker Wilder. Ch. two. D. May 4, 1893, Hanover, New Hampshire.

At the age of eighteen, after trying work as a farmer and bookkeeper, James Willis Patterson taught two years in the public schools in order to attend college. He studied at Henniker (New Hampshire) Academy (c. 1836–38) and received tutorial instruction in Greek. He entered Dartmouth College in 1844, where he gained recognition as a debater and scholar, graduating with honors in 1848.

Patterson served as principal of an academy in Woodstock, Connecticut (1848–51). First studying law, he was influenced by Henry Ward Beecher to study theology. He entered Yale Theological Seminary (1851), teaching at a ladies' boarding school to pay expenses.

In 1854 Patterson accepted a position at Dartmouth College as professor of mathematics and also taught political economy, intellectual philosophy, meteorology, and astronomy. In 1859 he was appointed professor of astronomy and meteorology. Patterson served as a school commissioner for Grafton County, New Hampshire, and secretary of the New Hampshire state board of education (1858–62). He became known as an advocate of common schools and a brilliant orator. He was elected to the New Hampshire Legislature (1862).

Patterson was elected to the United States House of Representatives and served two terms. He was the author of bills to provide free education to all children in the District of Columbia, regardless of race, and establish the first college for deaf mutes in Washington, D.C. (College for the Deaf, later Gallaudet College). He served a term in the United States Senate and became involved in the crédit mobilier scandal. Failing to win reelection to the Senate because of crédit mobilier, he took an extended trip through the British Isles.

Patterson again served in the New Hampshire legislature (1877–78). He was appointed state superintendent of instruction, a position he held from 1881 to 1893. As superintendent, he established county normal training schools and initiated a town rather than a district school system. He served for two years as president of the American Institute of Instruction. In 1893 he was appointed Willard Professor of Oratory at Dartmouth College but died shortly after. He received an honorary degree from Iowa (later, Grinnell) College in 1868.

REFERENCES: *AC; DAB; NCAB* (11:364); *TC; WWW* (H); J. K. Lord, *A History of Dartmouth College* (Concord, N.H.: Rumford, 1913); J. W. Patterson Papers, Dartmouth Library, Hanover, N.H.; George Willis Patterson, *James Patterson as Educator* (Concord, N.H.: Republican Press Association, 1893). *Fred L. Splittgerber*

PAYNE, Bruce Ryburn. B. February 18, 1874, near Morganton, North Carolina, to Jordan Nathaniel and Barbara Anne Eliza (Warlick) Payne. M. December 7, 1897, to Lula Carr. Ch. one. D. April 21, 1937, Nashville, Tennessee.

Bruce Ryburn Payne obtained his formal education at Trinity College (later, Duke University) in Durham, North Carolina, where he received the B.A. (1896) and M.A. (1902) degrees. He continued his education as a graduate student at Columbia University, where he received the M.A. (1903) and Ph.D. (1904) degrees.

Payne was principal of Morganton (North Carolina) Academy (1896–99), superintendent of county schools (1898–99), and instructor at Durham High School (1899–1902). He was professor of philosophy and education at William and Mary College in Williamsburg, Virginia (1904–05). In the fall of 1905 he became professor of secondary education at the University of Virginia and was professor of psychology (1906–10). He brought order to the university's system of student credits and courses of study. He established entrance requirements and reorganized the summer session, admitting women for the first time in the history of the university.

In 1911 he became president of George Peabody College for Teachers in Nashville, Tennessee, a position he held until his death. He started with a new campus with two buildings, industrial arts and home economics, that expanded to twelve buildings. He was a leader in directing the South's attention to the needs of its rural schools, and he strove for greater equality of educational opportunities for southern blacks. He was a leader in agricultural and conservation movements in the South.

Payne was the author of *Public Elementary Curricula* (1905) and co-editor of *Southern Prose and Poetry* (with Edwin Mims, 1910). He was active in many professional organizations, served as secretary to the Southern Association of Colleges and Preparatory Schools, and was the recipient of several honorary degrees.

REFERENCES: *DAB* (supp. 2); *LE* (I); *NCAB* (32:395); *WWAE* (I); *WWW* (I); *NYT,* April 22, 1937, p. 23. *Harold J. McKenna*

PAYNE, Daniel Alexander. B. February 24, 1811, Charleston, South Carolina, to London and Martha Payne. M. 1847 to Julia A. (Becroft) Ferris. M. 1853 to Eliza A. Clark. Ch. none. D. November 29, 1893, Wilberforce, Ohio.

Daniel Alexander Payne was the grandson of a freed slave who fought at Bunker Hill as a black soldier. Orphaned by the age of eight, he learned to read, write, and master mathematics with assistance from the Charleston, South Carolina, Brown's Fellowship Society and the Minor Moralist Society, a group of free Negroes organized to provide for the material needs of black orphans. Later tutored by Thomas Bonneau, he studied English grammar and Roman and Grecian history. By the age of thirteen, he had mastered Greek, Latin, and French.

At the age of eighteen Payne started a school for slaves in the house of Caesar Wright. The school was closed, and he was sentenced to prison after South Carolina passed laws outlawing schools for Negroes. After release from prison, he was ordained the first black African Methodist Episcopal (AME) minister (1844). He began a series of church reforms at the Bethel Church of Philadelphia, which triggered a great deal of criticism from his elders in the church, but he was elected a bishop in 1852 despite the opposition. Assigned to prepare a history of the AME church, his final work included a comprehensive review of over five hundred pages and thirty-seven chapters.

In 1856 Payne was appointed a member of the original board of trustees of Wilberforce (Ohio) University, a college established by the state of Ohio. By 1862 the trustees suspended operations because of insufficient funds. Payne, however, continued to express interest in the university and fought the effort of the state of Ohio to convert Wilberforce into an asylum for the mentally disturbed. Within a period of two years, he was able to purchase the institution and reopened it with about a dozen students. Payne was the first Negro president of a university in the Western world. United States Chief Justice Salmon Chase, General O. O. Howard, and Frederick Douglass sat on the board of trustees at Payne's invitation. By the end of Payne's tenure in 1867, the institution enjoyed freedom from debt, had a competent international faculty, and had graduated six classes. It had grown from twelve students in 1863 to over 150 from seventeen states in 1876. Richard Wright referred to Payne as the Negroes' First Apostle of Education.

REFERENCES: *AC; DAB; NCAB* (4:188); *TC; WWW* (H); Russell L. Adams, *Negroes Past and Present* (Chicago: Afro-American Publishing Co., 1969), p. 96; William H. Simmons, *Men of Mark* (Chicago: Johnson Publishing Co., 1970), p. 779; George Singleton, *The Romance of African Methodism* (New York: Exposition Press, 1952), pp. 68–69; Earl E. Thorpe, *Black Historians* (New York: William Morrow and Co., 1971), pp.

157–58; Edgar O. Toppin, *A Biographical History of Blacks Since 1528* (New York: David McKay Co., 1969–71), pp. 384–85; Charles Illian, "Wilberforce University: The Reality of Bishop Payne's Dream," *The Negro History Bulletin* 18 (March 1955): 141–42; Benjamin Brawley *(q.v.), Negro Builders and Heroes* (Chapel Hill: University of North Carolina Press, 1937).   *Lionel S. Duncan*

PAYNE, William Harold. B. May 12, 1836, Farmington, New York, to Gideon Riley and Mary Brown (Smith) Payne. M. October 2, 1856, to Sara Evaline Fort. M. July 6, 1901, to Elizabeth Rebecca Clark. Ch. five. D. June 18, 1907, Ann Arbor, Michigan.

William Harold Payne attended the Macedon (New York) Academy (1852–54) and the New York Conference Seminary at Charlottesville in 1854.

Payne taught in New York country schools (1854–56) and operated a school at Victor, New York, with his wife (1856–58). He was principal of the Union School at Three Rivers, Michigan (1858–64), superintendent of the Niles, Michigan, public schools (1864–66), principal of the Ypsilanti (Michigan) Seminary (1866–69), and superintendent of schools at Adrian, Michigan (1869–79).

In 1879 James B. Angell *(q.v.)*, president of the University of Michigan, recommended to the university regents that a chair of education be established at Michigan; Payne was appointed to the position, the first in the country (1879–88). He was chancellor of the University of Nashville, Tennessee, and president of the Peabody Normal College (later, George Peabody College for Teachers) from 1888 to 1901. He returned to the University of Michigan in 1901 on the death of Burke A. Hinsdale *(q.v.)* and remained there to his retirement in 1904. Payne sought increased pay for increased education and qualifications of teachers, in-service programs, and integration of liberal arts and methodology in teacher education programs. He was a proponent of compulsory education.

Payne was the author of *School Supervision* (1875), *Science and Art of Teaching* (1879), *Outlines of Educational Doctrine* (1882), and *The Education of Teachers* (1901), and he translated Gabriel Compayre's *History of Pedagogy* (1886), *Lectures on Teaching* (1888), *Elements of Psychology* (1890), and *Applied Psychology* (1893) and Jean-Jacques Rousseau's *Emile* (1892). He also edited David P. Page's *(q.v.) Theory and Practice of Teaching* (1885). He was editor and publisher of *The Michigan Teacher* (1864–69).

Payne received honorary degrees from the Western University of Pennsylvania (later, University of Pittsburgh) and the universities of Michigan and Nashville.

REFERENCES: *AC; DAB; NCAB* (8:134); *TC; WWW* (IV); Willis F.

Dunbar, *Michigan Through the Centuries* (New York: Lewis Historical Publishing Co., 1955); George C. Poret, *The Contributions of William Harold Payne to Public Education* (Nashville: George Peabody College for Teachers, 1931); Charles R. Starring and James O. Knauss, *The Michigan Search for Educational Standards* (Lansing: Michigan Historical Commission, 1969).   *H. J. Prince*

PEABODY, Elizabeth Palmer. B. May 16, 1804, Billerica, Massachusetts, to Nathaniel and Elizabeth (Palmer) Peabody. M. no. D. January 2, 1894, Jamaica Plain, Massachusetts.

Elizabeth Palmer Peabody's mother directed a private school where her children received their early education. Elizabeth Peabody studied Latin with her dentist father, who had taught at Phillips Academy in Andover, Massachusetts, and Greek with Ralph Waldo Emerson.

As a teenager, Peabody taught in her mother's school and opened her own school in Lancaster, Massachusetts, at the age of sixteen. She operated a school in Brookline near Boston (1822–23) and served as a governess in the home of Benjamin Vaughn in Hallowell, Maine (1823–25). With her sister Mary (later, the wife of Horace Mann, *q.v.*), she opened a school on Boston's Beacon Hill, which was first successful but eventually ran into financial problems (1825–34). While in Boston, Peabody became acquainted with William Ellery Channing and served for nine years as his secretary while continuing to teach.

In 1834, Peabody became associated with Amos Bronson Alcott *(q.v.)* in his Temple School in Boston. In 1836 she returned to Salem and later opened a school in a Boston boarding house. In 1840 she opened a bookstore in Boston with financial support from Channing; she maintained the store to 1850. She moved to her parents' farm in Newton, Massachusetts, where she engaged in writing. In 1859 she met Margarethe Schurz *(q.v.)* and became interested in the kindergarten movement of Friedrich Froebel.

In 1860 Peabody established the first American English-speaking kindergarten in Boston. She closed the kindergarten in 1867 and spent a year in Berlin and Hamburg, Germany, studying Froebelian methods. On her return to the United States, she engaged in lecturing and writing to promote the kindergarten movement. She retired to Concord, Massachusetts, where she was a member and lecturer at Alcott's Concord School of Philosophy (1879–84).

Peabody published the transcendental journal *The Dial* (1842–43) and *Kindergarten Messenger* (1873–75). She was the author of *Aesthetic Papers* (1849), *Crimes of the House of Austria* (1852), *The Polish American System of Chronology* (1852), *Moral Culture in Infancy and Kindergarten Guide* (with Mary Mann, 1864), *Kindergarten in Italy* (1872), *Reminiscences of Dr. Channing* (1880), *Genius and Character of Emerson*

(1885), *Letters to Kindergartners* (1886), and *Last Evening with Allston* (1887).

REFERENCES: *AC; DAB; NAW; NCAB* (12:350); *NYT,* January 5, 1894, p. 2; *TC; WC; WWW* (H); Alice Fleming, *Great Women Teachers* (Philadelphia: J. B. Lippincott, 1965); Agnes Snyder, *Dauntless Women in Childhood Education, 1856–1931* (Washington, D.C.: Association for Childhood Education International, 1972); Louise Hall Tharp, *The Peabody Sisters of Salem* (Boston: Little, Brown and Co., 1950).

Ann Stankiewicz

PEABODY, Endicott. B. May 30, 1857, Salem, Massachusetts, to Samuel Endicott and Marianne Cabot (Lee) Peabody. M. June 18, 1885, to Fannie Peabody. Ch. six. D. November 17, 1944, Groton, Massachusetts.

Endicott Peabody lived in Salem, Massachusetts, until he was thirteen and while there attended the Hacker School. In 1870 he moved with his family to London, England, and studied at Cheltenham School for five years and then Trinity College, Cambridge, graduating in 1878. During his stay in England, Peabody was influenced by Phillips Brooks and others and in 1881 enrolled in the Episcopal Theological Seminary in Cambridge, Massachusetts; he was ordained in 1884.

With a gift of land near Boston from the Lawrence family in Groton, Massachusetts, Peabody established Groton School on October 18, 1884, with twenty-seven boys and two masters besides himself. From the start, Groton School attracted an elite clientele; in addition to President Franklin D. Roosevelt, the alumni roll includes cabinet members, ambassadors and ministers, senators, congressmen, and many prominent figures in education, literature, publishing, the military, and philanthropy.

At Groton athletics, especially football, were stressed, and social responsibility was emphasized. Masters and students were urged to participate in the Groton School Camp operated in the summers at Squam Lake, New Hampshire, for underprivileged boys. Peabody maintained active membership in more than thirty committees and organizations, ranging from the Audubon Society to the Birth Control League of Massachusetts.

Peabody received an outpouring of affectionate tributes upon his retirement in 1940 after fifty-six years as active headmaster. Peabody lived in Groton until his death.

REFERENCES: *CB* (May 1940); *DAB* (supp. 3); *LE* (II); *NCAB* (A:308); *NYT,* November 18, 1944, p. 13; *WWW* (II); Frank D. Ashburn, *Peabody of Groton: A Portrait* (New York: Coward McCann, 1944).

Dennis G. Wiseman

PEABODY, Selim Hobart. B. August 20, 1829, Rockingham, Vermont, to Charles Hobart and Grace (Ide) Peabody. M. August 9, 1852, to Mary

Elizabeth Pangborn. Ch. none. D. May 26, 1903, St. Louis, Missouri.

Selim Hobart Peabody's clergyman father wanted his son to become a minister and supplemented his public-school education with lessons in Hebrew and Greek. When Selim was twelve years old, the father died, and his goal of obtaining a ministerial education was thwarted. At the age of fifteen, he became a carpenter's apprentice. After two years of work, he entered the University of Vermont, receiving the A.B. (1852) and A.M. (1855) degrees.

Peabody had a varied career as an educator, serving as principal of the Burlington (Vermont) High School (1852–53), professor of mathematics at the New Hampton Seminary in Fairfax, Vermont (1853–54), professor of mathematics and civil engineering at the Polytechnic College of Pennsylvania in Philadelphia (1854–59), principal of the high school at Fond du Lac, Wisconsin (1859–62), and superintendent of schools in Racine, Wisconsin (1862–65). He was professor of physics at the Chicago High School and conducted the first evening school for working men in Chicago (1865–71). He was professor of mathematics and civil engineering at Massachusetts Agricultural College (later, University of Massachusetts) from 1871 to 1874 and returned to the Chicago high school and evening school position in 1874.

Peabody joined the faculty of Illinois Industrial University (University of Illinois from 1885) as professor of mechanical engineering (1878–80) and was appointed president of the university (1880–91). During his term as president, the university received its first financial support from the state legislature. An agricultural experiment station was established in 1887. After his retirement in 1891, he was a participant in conducting international expositions: World's Columbian (Chicago, 1893), World's Fair (Paris, 1899), Pan-American (Buffalo, New York, 1901), Interstate and West Indies (Charleston, South Carolina, 1902), and Louisiana Purchase (St. Louis, 1904).

Peabody was the author of *Juvenile Natural History* (three volumes, 1869), *The Elements of Astronomy* (1869), *New Practical Arithmetic* (1872), *American Patriotism* (1880), and *Charts of Arithmetic* (1900). He also wrote the series Cecil's Books of Natural History. He was an editor of *International Cyclopedia* (1880).

Peabody was president of the Wisconsin State Teachers' Association and served as a spokesman for Wisconsin educators advocating state-supported normal schools and the initiation of teachers' institutes, a graded system of schools in the state, and establishment of high schools and state universities. He was also active in the Chicago Academy of Sciences (secretary, 1874–88 and president, 1892–95) and the National Council of Education (president, 1889–91). He received honorary degrees from the universities of Vermont and Iowa.

REFERENCES: *DAB; NCAB* (1:271); *NYT,* May 27, 1903, p. 9; *TC;*
WWW (I).   *Lew E. Wise*

PEARCE, Richard Mills, Jr. B. March 3, 1874, Montreal, Quebec, Canada,
to Richard Mills and Sarah (Smith) Pearce. M. November 6, 1902, to May
Harper Musser. Ch. two. D. February 16, 1930, New York, New York.

Richard Mills Pearce, Jr., a pathologist and medical educator, moved
from Montreal, Canada, to New England where he received his formal
education at Hillhouse High School in New Haven, Connecticut (1889–
90), and Boston Latin School (1890–91). He attended the Boston College of
Physicians and Surgeons (1891–93) and received the M.D. degree from
Tufts College Medical School (1894) and the Harvard Medical School
(1897). He studied at the University of Leipzig, Germany (1902).

Pearce was a resident pathologist at Boston City Hospital (1896–99),
served as an instructor in the department of pathology at Harvard, and was
pathologist to three Boston hospitals (1899–1900). He taught in the
department of pathology at the University of Pennsylvania (1900–03) and
became director of the Bender Hygienic Laboratory at Albany, New York,
and professor of pathology at Albany Medical College (1903–08). He was
chairman of the department of pathology at the Bellevue Hospital Medical
College in New York City from 1908 to 1910, when he accepted the first
chair of research medicine in America at the University of Pennsylvania.
He held this position until 1920, when he became director of the division of
medical education of the Rockefeller Foundation, a post he held until his
death in 1930.

In 1924 Pearce established the annual publication *Methods and Problems of Medical Education,* an international exchange of information and
opinion about medical education. A collection of his early contributions in
pathology and speeches on medical education was published in 1913 as
Medical Research and Education. He was chairman of the medical division of the National Research Council (1918) and a member of many
professional and scholarly associations, including serving as president of
the New York Pathological Society (1910), the Association of American
Pathologists and Bacteriologists (1912), the Rush Society (1913), the Philadelphia Pathological Society (1913), and the American Society of Experimental Pathology (1914–15). He was awarded an honorary degree by
Lafayette College (1915).

REFERENCES: *DAB; NCAB* (15:204); *NYT,* February 17, 1930, p. 21;
WWW (I).   *Richard M. Coger*

PEARSON, Eliphalet. B. June 11, 1752, Newbury, Massachusetts, to
David and Sarah (Danforth) Pearson. M. July 17, 1780, to Priscilla Holyoke. M. September 27, 1785, to Sarah Bromfield. Ch. five. D. September
12, 1826, Greenland, New Hampshire.

Eliphalet Pearson, the first principal of Phillips Academy in Andover, Massachusetts, was educated at Dummer Academy in Byfield, Massachusetts, and Harvard College (later, University) where he received the A.B. (1773) and A.M. (1776) degrees. During the Revolutionary War and while teaching grammar school in Andover, Massachusetts, he and Samuel Phillips manufactured gun powder and saltpeter for the Continental army (1775–78).

Pearson helped to write the constitution for the new Phillips Academy and was appointed principal (1778–86); he later served as president of the academy's board of trustees (1802–21). He was Hancock Professor of Hebrew and Oriental Languages at Harvard University (1786–1806). On the death of Harvard's president, Joseph Willard, in 1804, Pearson became acting president. He served for two years and returned to Andover in 1806 where he was ordained to the Congregational ministry. He helped found Andover Theological Seminary as a Congregational institution, was professor of sacred theology, and served as president of the seminary's board of trustees (1807–21).

A prominent intellectual and academic leader, Pearson engaged in professional activities, including being a founding member of the American Education Society and member of the American Academy of Arts and Sciences (secretary), the Society for the Promotion of Christian Knowledge (president), and the Massachusetts Historical Society. He was the author of a Hebrew grammar and a number of scholarly papers. He received honorary degrees from Yale College and the College of New Jersey (later, Princeton University).

REFERENCES: *AC; DAB; NCAB* (10:94); *TC; WWW* (H); *Massachusetts Encyclopedia of Biography* (Boston: American Historical Society, 1916).   *Thomas L. Bernard*

PECK, William Guy. B. October 16, 1820, Litchfield, Connecticut, to n.a. M. to n.a. M. to (n.a.) Davies. Ch. four. D. February 7, 1892, Greenwich, Connecticut.

William Guy Peck attended the United States Military Academy at West Point, New York, graduating in 1844 as head of his class. He took part in a survey of the defenses of the Portsmouth, New Hampshire, harbor and was with John Frémont's third expedition to the Rocky Mountains (1846). He served during the Mexican War with the Army of the West. He received the M.A. degree from Trinity College in Hartford, Connecticut, in 1853.

Peck was assistant professor of natural science at the military academy from 1846 until he resigned from the army in 1855. He was professor of physics and civil engineering at the University of Michigan (1855–57). He was professor of mathematics at Columbia College (1857–61) and professor of mathematics and astronomy at Columbia from 1861 until his death in

1892. When the school of mines was established in 1864, Peck was appointed head of the department of mechanics and also professor of mechanics.

He wrote *Elements of Mechanics* (1859), *Practical Treatise on Differential and Integral Calculus* (1870), *Elementary Treatise on Mechanics for the Use of Colleges and Schools of Science* (1870), *A Treatise on Analytical Geometry* (1873), *Manual of Practical Arithmetic* (1874), *Complete Arithmetic, Theoretical and Practical* (1874), *First Lessons in Numbers* (1875), *Manual of Algebra* (1875), *Manual of Geometry and Conic Sections* (1876), *Elementary Arithmetic* (1878), *Textbook on Popular Astronomy* (1883), *Elementary Treatise on Analytical Mechanics* (1887), and *Elementary Treatise on Determinants* (1887). He coedited with his father-in-law Charles Davies *(q.v.) Dictionary and Encyclopedia of Mathematical Science* (1855). He received honorary degrees from Trinity and Columbia colleges.

REFERENCES: *AC; NCAB* (5:520); *NYT,* February 9, 1892, p. 5; *WWW* (H); *New York Mail and Express,* February 9, 1892.

Robert McGinty

PEERS, Benjamin Orr. B. April 20, 1800, Loudoun County, Virginia, to Valentine and Eleanor (Orr) Peers. M. no. D. August 20, 1842, Louisville, Kentucky.

Benjamin Orr Peers was brought to Kentucky by his parents when he was three years old. He was educated at Bourbon Academy and entered Transylvania University in Lexington, Kentucky, in 1817. A teacher of Greek and Latin, Peers was graduated from Transylvania in 1820 and stayed to teach for the next two years. He studied at Princeton (New Jersey) Theological Seminary to become a Presbyterian minister but changed to the Episcopal church. He was graduated from the Theological Seminary of the Protestant Episcopal Church at Alexandria, Virginia (1826), and was ordained a deacon.

Peers was elected professor of moral philosophy at Transylvania in 1827 and served to 1830. He was sent east to examine the public education school systems by the governor of the state and, using the information, established a school system for the state. He has been called the Founder of the Public School System in Kentucky.

Peers opened a mechanics institute in Lexington (1829–30) and operated the Eclectic Institute in Lexington (1830–36). He was elected president of Transylvania University in 1833. Differences with the university trustees over the power of appointing members of the faculty led to his resignation in 1835. He opened a boys' school in Louisville and became first rector of St. Paul's Episcopal Church (1835–38).

Peers was editor of *The Journal of Christian Education* in New York

City from 1838 and was placed in charge of the Sunday school publications of the Episcopal church. He wrote an article on his idea of Christian education published in *The Journal of Christian Education* and two books, *Christian Education* (1836) and *American Education* (1838).

REFERENCES: *AC; DAB; NCAB* (4:514); *TC; WWW* (H); *The Biographical Encyclopedia of Kentucky of the Dead and Living Men of the 19th Century* (Cincinnati, Ohio: J. M. Armstrong & Co., 1878), p. 276; Walter Wilson Jennings, *Transylvania—Pioneer University of the West* (New York: Pageant Press, 1955), pp. 171–82.   *Thomas D. Meyers*

PEET, Harvey Prindle. B. November 19, 1794, Bethlehem, Connecticut, to Richard and Johannah (Prindle) Peet. M. November 27, 1823, to Margaret Maria Lewis. M. 1835 to Sarah Ann Smith. M. January 15, 1868, to Louisa P. Hotchkiss. Ch. three, including Isaac Lewis Peet *(q.v.)*, teacher of the deaf. D. January 1, 1873, New York, New York.

Harvey Prindle Peet grew up on a farm in northwestern Connecticut and was a promising student in the country school. He entered Phillips Academy in Andover, Massachusetts, in 1816 and Yale College in 1818, graduating in 1822.

Peet taught school at the age of sixteen and, on graduation from Yale, was employed by Thomas Hopkins Gallaudet *(q.v.)* as a teacher in the American School for the Deaf at Hartford, Connecticut. He remained there for eight years, teaching with Laurent Clerc *(q.v.)* and other experienced and skilled teachers of the deaf.

He moved to New York City as a teacher and principal of the New York Institution for the Instruction of the Deaf and Dumb (1831–67). He achieved great success at the school, building it from a small, poorly equipped institution to the largest and best-equipped establishment for deaf children in the United States. He retired in 1867 but continued to live at the school and served as an adviser to his son, Isaac Lewis Peet, who succeeded him.

Peet was the author of books for and about the deaf, including a series of elementary books for deaf mutes, *Course of Instruction for the Deaf and Dumb* (three volumes, 1844–49), which was used throughout the country. He also wrote *Scripture Lessons for the Deaf and Dumb* (1846), *Statistics of the Deaf and Dumb* (1852), *Report on Education of the Deaf and Dumb in Higher Branches* (1852), *Letters to Pupils on Leaving the New York Institution for the Deaf and Dumb* (1854), *Legal Rights of the Deaf and Dumb* (1856), and *History of the United States* (1869). He received honorary degrees from the regents of the University of the State of New York (1849) and Gallaudet College (1871).

REFERENCES: *AC; DAB; NCAB* (12:550); *TC; WWW* (H); *NYT,* January 2, 1873, p. 5.   *John W. Schifani*

PEET, Isaac Lewis. B. December 4, 1824, Hartford, Connecticut, to Harvey Prindle *(q.v.)* and Margaret Maria (Lewis) Peet. M. June 27, 1854, to Mary Toles, Ch. four. D. December 27, 1898, New York, New York.

After graduating from Yale College in 1845, Isaac Lewis Peet entered Union Theological Seminary in New York City; he was graduated in 1849 but was not ordained. He traveled to Europe and studied the latest methods of instructing the deaf (1851–54).

On his return to the United States from Europe in 1854, he became vice-principal of the New York Institution for the Deaf and Dumb, headed by his father. Peet became principal of the institution and served until his retirement (1867–92). He wrote *A Monograph on Decimal Fractions* (1866) and *Language Lessons Designed to Introduce Young Learners, Deaf Mutes and Foreigners to a Correct Understanding of the English Language on the Principle of Object Teaching* (1875). He contributed articles to professional journals, particularly the *American Annals of the Deaf.*

Peet was a member of many societies connected with his work, including the Medico-Legal Society of New York (president, 1886), the Conference of Superintendents and Principals of American Schools for the Deaf (president, 1896), and the Convention of American Instructors for the Deaf (executive committee, 1868–96). He helped secure legislation providing instruction for the deaf in New York State. He attended the international congress in Milan, Italy (1881), as a representative of American institutions for the deaf and dumb. Peet received an honorary degree from Columbia College in 1872.

REFERENCES: *AC; DAB; NCAB* (13:145); *NYT,* December 29, 1898, p. 7; *TC; WWW* (H). *John W. Schifani*

PEIRCE, Benjamin. B. April 4, 1809, Salem, Massachusetts, to Benjamin and Lydia (Nichols) Peirce. M. July 23, 1833, to Sarah Hunt Mills. Ch. five, including James Mills Peirce *(q.v.),* mathematician, and Charles Sanders Peirce *(q.v.),* American philosopher. D. October 6, 1880, Cambridge, Massachusetts.

Benjamin Peirce was graduated from Harvard University with the A.B. (1829) and A.M. (1833) degrees. He taught at Round Hill School in Northampton, Massachusetts (1829–31), and was a tutor in mathematics at Harvard (1831–33). Peirce served at Harvard as professor of mathematics and natural philosophy (1833–42) and Perkins Professor of Astronomy and Mathematics (1842–80).

In addition to recognition as an eminent American mathematician, Peirce gained distinction in many science fields, including physics, mechanics, astronomy, and navigation. About 1840 he worked nights in the Harvard observatory and was instrumental in the building of a new observatory. His lectures on astronomy at the time of the great comet of 1843 stimulated public interest in astronomy. With Joseph Henry, Alexander Dallas Bache *(q.v.)*, and others, Peirce organized the Dudley Observatory in Albany, New York, under Benjamin Apthorp Gould *(q.v.)* in 1855. He worked with the United States Coast Survey (1852–67) and succeeded Bache as superintendent of the survey (1867–74). He assisted in determining geographical locations for charting a general map of the United States. He was in charge of the American expedition to Sicily to observe an eclipse of the sun (1870) and organized two expeditions to observe the transit of Venus in 1874. He was consulting astronomer for the *American Nautical Almanac* (1849–67).

Peirce wrote mathematical texts, including *Elementary Treatise on Plane and Solid Geometry* (1835–36), *Elementary Treatise on Algebra* (1837), *Elementary Treatise on Plane and Solid Geometry* (1837), *Elementary Treatise on Plane and Spherical Trigonometry* (1840), *Elementary Treatise on Curves, Functions, and Forces* (volume 1, 1841 and volume 2, 1846), *Tables of the Moon* (1853), *A System of Analytic Mechanics* (1855), *Linear Associative Algebra* (1870), and *Ideality in the Physical Sciences,* published posthumously in 1881. He was associate editor of the *American Journal of Mathematics* (1878).

He was a fellow of the American Academy of Arts and Sciences and honorary fellow of the University of St. Vladimir in Kiev, Russia, and of the Royal Societies of Edinburgh, Scotland, London, England, and Göttingen, Germany. Peirce was a founder of the National Academy of Sciences (1863) and president of the American Association for the Advancement of Science (1853). He was an organizer of the Smithsonian Institution in 1847. Peirce was awarded honorary degrees by the University of North Carolina (1847) and Harvard University (1867).

REFERENCES:*AC; DAB; DSB; NCAB* (8:152); *NYT,* October 7, 1880, p. 2; *TC; WWW* (H); Victor F. Lienzen, *Benjamin Peirce and the U.S. Coast Survey* (San Francisco: San Francisco Press, 1968); F. B. Matz, "Benjamin Peirce," *American Mathematical Monthly* (1895): 173–79.

Daniel S. Yates

PEIRCE, Charles (Santiago) Sanders. B. September 10, 1839, Cambridge, Massachusetts, to Benjamin *(q.v.)* and Sarah Hunt (Mills) Peirce. M. October 16, 1862, to Harriet Melusina Fay. M. 1883 to Juliette Froissy. Ch. none. D. April 19, 1914, Milford, Pennsylvania.

The son of America's foremost mathematician of the era, Charles Sanders Peirce received a rigorous intellectual training in childhood. He received the A.B. (1859) and M.A. (1862) degrees and the Sc.B. degree (1863), the first of its kind, summa cum laude in chemistry, from Harvard University.

Appointed lecturer in the philosophy of science at Harvard (1864–65),

Peirce held lectureships in philosophy (1869–70) and logic (1870–71). From 1879 to 1884, Johns Hopkins University in Baltimore, Maryland, employed him as a lecturer in logic, and at various other times he lectured at Lowell (Massachusetts) Institute, Bryn Mawr (Pennsylvania) College, and Harvard.

Peirce worked for thirty years in the United States Geodetic Survey (1861–91) where he established a reputation in physics and philosophy. He was concerned with the relation of philosophy to scientific and empirical methods. His postulate that practical consequences are the sole test of ideas, a test that is ultimately social inasmuch as it depends upon the agreement of competent observers, exercised a critical effect directly upon the philosophical ideas and indirectly upon the educational theories of William James *(q.v.)* and John Dewey *(q.v.).* Peirce insisted upon the necessity of experimentation and project work in the teaching of science. He asserted that the aims of education are coterminous with the aims of life. He labeled his philosophy *pragmatism.*

Peirce was the author of *Photometric Researches* (1878), and he edited *Studies in Logic* (1883). He delivered lectures on his own work that were collected and published after his death as *Chance, Love and Logic* (edited by Morris R. Cohen, 1923), and *Collected Papers* (volumes 1–6 edited by Charles Hartshorne and Paul Weiss, 1931–35, and volumes 7–8 edited by Arthur W. Burks, 1958).

Peirce was a fellow of the American Academy of Arts and Sciences and a member of the National Academy of Sciences and other scientific societies. He was the brother of James Mills Peirce *(q.v.).*

REFERENCES: *AC; EB; DAB; DSB; NCAB* (8:409); *TC; WWW* (I); Justus Buchler, *Charles Peirce's Empiricism* (New York: Harcourt Brace and Co., 1939); Joseph Jastrow, "Charles S. Peirce as a Teacher," *Journal of Philosophy, Psychology and Scientific Method* 13 (December 21, 1916); G. S. Maccia, "The Educational Aims of Charles Peirce," *Educational Theory* 4 (July 1954): 206–12. *Joseph M. McCarthy*

PEIRCE, Cyrus. B. August 15, 1790, Waltham, Massachusetts, to Isaac and Hannah (Mason) Peirce. M. April 1, 1816, to Harriet Coffin. Ch. none. D. April 15, 1860, West Newton, Massachusetts.

Cyrus Peirce, Father of the First American State Normal School, showed unusual promise as a scholar in local schools and was sent to the Framingham (Massachusetts) Academy where he was tutored by the Reverend Dr. Charles Stearns of Lincoln, Massachusetts, to prepare for college. He was graduated from Harvard University in 1810 and from Harvard Divinity School in 1815.

Peirce began to teach school in West Newton, Massachusetts (1807–08), while he was a student at Harvard. He became principal of a private school at Nantucket, Massachusetts (1810–12 and 1815–18). He entered the ministry in 1818 as pastor of the North Reading (Massachusetts) Congregational Church and was ordained in 1819. In 1827 he returned to teaching, conducting a school with William Putnam in North Andover, Massachusetts (1827–31). He returned to Nantucket as a principal of a private school (1831–37) and with the local school committee developed a plan of organization for a public-school system; he served as the first principal of the Nantucket High School (1837–39).

Peirce was chosen president (1839–42 and 1844–49) of the first state normal school (later, Framingham State College) established in Lexington, Massachusetts. The school emphasized mastery of subject matter and included a model school where normal school students engaged in practice teaching with children from the community. He spent two years recovering his health in Nantucket (1842–44) and returned to the school, relocated in West Newton, Massachusetts.

Health problems again forced his retirement from the normal school, and he was asked to represent the American Peace Society at the World's Peace Congress in Paris, France, in 1849. On his return to the United States, Peirce served as an instructor in the West Newton English and Classical School in the building occupied by the normal school that had relocated in Framingham, Massachusetts. He taught there to his death.

REFERENCES: *DAB; WWW* (H); *Boston Transcript,* April 7, 1860; *The Massachusetts Teacher* (May 1860); Samuel J. May, "Memoir of Cyrus Peirce," *American Journal of Education* (December 1857): 275–308; Arthur O. Norton, ed., *The First State Normal School in America: The Journals of Cyrus Peirce and Mary Swift* (Cambridge: Harvard University Press, 1926).   *Stephen J. Clarke*

PEIRCE, James Mills. B. May 1, 1834, Cambridge, Massachusetts, to Benjamin *(q.v.)* and Sarah Hunt (Mills) Peirce. M. no. D. May 21, 1906, Cambridge, Massachusetts.

James Mills Peirce, son of Benjamin Peirce *(q.v.)* and brother of Charles S. Peirce *(q.v.),* received the A.B. (1853) and A.M. (1856) degrees from Harvard University and was graduated from the Harvard Divinity School (1859).

Peirce was a tutor in mathematics at Harvard (1854–58) and preached in Unitarian churches in New Bedford, Massachusetts, and Charleston, South Carolina (1859–60). He returned to Harvard as a tutor (1860–61), assistant professor and professor of mathematics (1861–85), and Perkins Professor of Astronomy from 1885. He served as secretary of the academic council (1872–90), dean of the graduate school (1890–95), and dean of the faculty of arts and sciences (1895–98). Peirce worked with President Charles Eliot *(q.v.)* in establishing elective courses at Harvard.

Peirce was the author of *A Text-Book of Analytic Geometry* (1857), *Three and Four Place Tables of Logarithmetic and Trigonometric Functions* (1871), *The Elements of Logarithms* (1873), and *Mathematical Tables Chiefly to Four Figures* (1879) and was editor of Benjamin Peirce's *Idealty in the Physical Sciences* (1881).

Peirce was a fellow of the American Academy of Arts and Sciences and the American Association for the Advancement of Science and a member of the American Mathematical Society and other groups.

REFERENCES,*A C; DAB; NCAB* (10:25); *TC; WWW* (I).   *John F. Ohles*

PENDLETON, Ellen Fitz. B. August 27, 1864, Westerly, Rhode Island, to Enoch Burrows and Mary Ette (Chapman) Pendleton. M. no. D. July 26, 1936, Newton, Massachusetts.

Ellen Fitz Pendleton was graduated as valedictorian of her class at Westerly (Rhode Island) High School (1882). She entered Wellesley College and was graduated with the A.B. (1886) and A.M. (1891) degrees. She was a student at Newnham College, Cambridge (England) University (1889–90).

Pendleton became a tutor in math at Wellesley in 1886 and, except for a year of study at Cambridge, England, and trips abroad, remained at Wellesley the rest of her life. She served as secretary of the college (1897–1901), dean (1901–11), and acting president. She became the sixth president (1911–36), succeeding Caroline Hazard *(q.v.)*; she was the first alumnae president.

In March 1914 fire destroyed the building that housed more than two hundred students, most of the classrooms, laboratories, and faculty offices. The next morning, Pendleton announced the beginning of an early spring vacation; three weeks later classes resumed in temporary facilities, and a major fund-raising campaign began. The physical recreation of Wellesley was accomplished through Pendleton's efforts. During her twenty-five-year administration, the size of the student body grew by fewer than one hundred, but fifteen impressive brick buildings were erected. The faculty was increased and salaries doubled. Endowment funds increased more than eightfold under a major fund-raising campaign she conducted.

Pendleton was noted as a builder and as an excellent business woman. She liberalized entrance requirements and introduced honors work, independent research, and a greater choice of electives. She sought to preserve high academic standards. Pendleton rejected efforts to introduce vocational training or narrow specialization into the Wellesley program.

She held many offices, serving as vice-president of Phi Beta Kappa, president of the College Entrance Examination Board, and vice-president of the Associate Board for Christian Colleges in China. When Edward Bok established the American Peace Prize in 1923, Pendleton was chosen the only woman on the committee to determine the recipient of the award. She was appointed by the State Department to represent women's colleges at the Inter-American Congress of Rectors, Deans, and Educators in Havana, Cuba (1930).

Pendleton retired in 1936 on the fiftieth anniversary of her graduation from Wellesley and the twenty-fifty anniversary of her presidency. Her estate was left to Wellesley to further the academic work of the college. She received many honorary degrees.

REFERENCES: *DAB* (supp. 2); *LE* (I); *NAW; NCAB* (A:190); *WWW* (I); *NYT,* July 27, 1936, p. 15.   *Ann Stankiewicz*

PENDLETON, William Kimbrough. B. September 8, 1817, Yanceyville, Virginia, to Edmund and Unity (Yancey) Pendleton. M. October 1840 to Lavinia M. Campbell. M. July 1848 to Clarinda Campbell. M. September 19, 1855, to Catherine Huntington King. Ch. seven. D. September 1, 1899, Bethany, West Virginia.

William Kimbrough Pendleton was born into a prominent Virginia family. He was graduated from the University of Virginia (1840), completing courses in classical, scientific, and philosophical studies and the law. Pendleton was admitted to the bar in 1840 and began to practice law.

As a young man Pendleton had become acquainted with the family of Bishop Alexander Campbell who was associated with a religious movement known as the Campbellites (the church later took the name Disciples of Christ). Pendleton's first two wives were daughters of Campbell, who was the founder and first president of Bethany (Virginia, later West Virginia) College. In 1841 Pendleton was appointed to the chair of philosophy and physics at Bethany and four years later was elected vice-president. Upon the death of Campbell in 1866, Pendleton was appointed president of the college and served until his resignation in 1886 after a forty-five year association with the school.

Following the Civil War, Pendleton was appointed a member of the constitutional convention for the new state of West Virginia. He worked for a free public school system, helped write the state school laws, and served as state superintendent of public schools (1873–80).

Pendleton was active in civic affairs and ran unsuccessfully for Congress as a Whig in 1854. Active in church affairs, he established a church of the Disciples of Christ in Eustis, Florida, where he had moved in 1886 on his retirement. He was a coeditor with Alexander Campbell and later editor of the *Millennial Quarterly,* a denominational publication (1846–70). He was associated with two other religious journals, *Christian Quarterly* and *Christian Standard.* He received an honorary degree from the University of Pennsylvania.

REFERENCES: *DAB; NCAB* (22:362); *TC; WWW* (H).

Harold D. Lehman

PENNIMAN, James Hosmer. B. November 8, 1860, Alexandria, Virginia, to James Lanman and Maria Davis (Hosmer) Penniman. M. no. D. April 6, 1931, Philadelphia, Pennsylvania.

James Hosmer Penniman attended the Free Academy of Norwich, Connecticut, and was graduated from Yale College with the A.B. degree (1884).

Following a year as a private tutor in Glyndon, Maryland, he taught at DeLancey School in Philadelphia, Pennsylvania, where he became head of the lower grades in 1900. He retired in 1913 and engaged in historical research and writing. He was a recognized authority on the life of George Washington and owned a comprehensive private library on Washington and his times.

Penniman founded the Maria Hosmer Penniman Memorial Library at the University of Pennsylvania (1916) in the memory of his mother, the Penniman Memorial Library of Education at Yale University (1920), and the Penniman Memorial Library of Brown University (1921).

Penniman wrote *A Graded List of Common Words Difficult to Spell,* (1891), *Prose Dictation Exercises from the English Classics* (1893), *The School Poetry Book* (1894), *Practical Suggestions in School Government* (1899), *Penniman's New Practical Speller* (1900), *Success* (1905), *Books and How to Make the Most of Them* (1910), *George Washington as Commander in Chief* (1917), *George Washington as Man of Letters* (1918), *The Alley Rabbit* (1920), *Children and Their Books* (1921), *George Washington at Mount Vernon* (1921), *Our Debt to France* (1921), *What Lafayette Did for America* (1921), and *Philadelphia in the Early Eighteen Hundreds* (1923). Penniman received honorary degrees from Marshall College and the University of Pennsylvania.

REFERENCES: *DAB; NCAB* (22:263); *WWW* (I); *NYT,* April 7, 1931, p. 27.   *Joan Williams*

PENNY, George Barlow. B. June 30, 1861, Haverstraw-on-Hudson, New York, to Joshua and Sarah J. (Barlow) Penny. M. August 25, 1887, to Jessie Smith. M. January 6, 1891, to Beulah Ray White. Ch. two. D. November 15, 1934, Rochester, New York.

George Barlow Penny studied music at Syracuse University and in New York City with Percy Goetschius *(q.v.)* and others. He received the B.S. degree (1885) from Cornell University in Ithaca, New York.

Penny taught at Girton College and Dalhousie College in Halifax, Nova Scotia, Canada (1885–87), and Metropolitan College of Music in New York City (1887–88). He established a school of music at the State Normal School (later, Emporia Kansas State College) in Emporia, Kansas (1888–90), and organized a school of fine arts at the University of Kansas in Lawrence (1890–1903). Penny organized a school of fine arts at Washburn

College of Topeka, Kansas (1903–07), and was organist at the Topeka municipal auditorium (1904–06).

In 1907 Penny moved to Rochester, New York, where he was dean of the Institute of Musical Art (1910–20). He established a four-year degree program, public-school teacher courses, and courses in the organ and musical appreciation. In 1920 George Eastman purchased the school and presented it to the University of Rochester as the Eastman School of Music. In 1922 Eastman presented the school with $12 million for equipment and an endowment fund. From 1920 Penny was professor of theory, history, and literature of music at the Eastman School.

Penny organized and conducted the Topeka (Kansas) Oratorio Society and the Rochester (New York) Oratorio Society, each with two hundred voices. He composed church music and lectured on music, architecture, and art for thirty years. He was dean of the Rochester chapter of the American Guild of Organists.

REFERENCES: *LE* (I); *NCAB* (C:369); *WWAE* (I); *WWW* (I).

John F. Ohles

PEPPER, William. B. August 21, 1843, Philadelphia, Pennsylvania, to William and Sarah (Platt) Pepper. M. June 25, 1873, to Frances Sergeant Perry. Ch. four. D. July 28, 1898, Pleasanton, California.

William Pepper, an American physician and medical education reformer, attended the University of Pennsylvania and received the A.B. (1862), M.D. (1864), and A.M. (1865) degrees. He traveled in Europe in 1871 studying methods of medical education and administration.

Pepper practiced medicine in Philadelphia and was a resident physician (1864–65) and pathologist and visiting physician (1865–68) at the Pennsylvania Hospital in Philadelphia. He started lecturing in anatomy in the medical school at the University of Pennsylvania in 1868; he continued as professor of clinical medicine (1876–84), provost (1880–94), and professor of theory and practice of medicine (1884–98).

In 1874 he established a teaching hospital at the University of Pennsylvania, the first hospital in the United States to be associated closely with a medical school. He founded the Nurses' Training School (1887). While provost, he established the Wharton School of Finance, the Binnett School for the graduate instruction of women, the veterinary school, the Wistar Institute of Anatomy and Biology, and the school of architecture. He instituted the university extension lectures that led to the establishment of the Society for the Extension of University Teaching. He was the first to record changes in the bone marrow in progressive pernicious anemia in 1875.

As medical director of the Centennial Exhibition held in Philadelphia in 1876, Pepper developed a model hospital. The medical services in this hospital were organized so efficiently that he was honored by the British and Norwegian governments.

Pepper was active in his private practice and in teaching, medical research, and writing. His writings include *Social Treatment of Pulmonary Disease* (1874), *Sanitary Relations in Hospitals* (1875), *High Medical Education* (1877), *Catarrhal Irritation* (1881), *Epilepsy* (1883), *Phthisis in Pennsylvania* (1886), and *Theory and Practice of Medicine* (1893). He edited *A System of Practical Medicine* (five volumes, 1885–86). He was a founder and editor of the Philadelphia *Medical Times* (1870–71).

He was founder in 1884 of the American Climatological Society (president, 1886) and president of the American Clinical Association (1886) and the Association of American Physicians (1891). He was a member of many other societies. In the name of his father, he founded and endowed the William Pepper Laboratory of Clinical Medicine at the University of Pennsylvania (1894), the first of its kind in the United States. He was a founder of the Pennsylvania Museum and School of Industrial Art. He presided at the Pan-American Medical Congress in Washington (1893). He was decorated by Sweden and received an honorary degree from Lafayette College.

REFERENCES: *AC; DAB; EB; NCAB* (1:345); *NYT,* July 30, 1898, p. 7; *TC; WWW* (H).   *Richard M. Coger*

PERRIN, Ethel. B. February 7, 1871, Needham (later, Wellesley), Massachusetts, to David C. and Ellen P. (Hooper) Perrin. M. no. D. May 15, 1962, Brewster, New York.

Ethel Perrin attended a private boarding school, was graduated from Howard Collegiate Institute in West Bridgewater, Massachusetts (1890), and matriculated at the Boston (Massachusetts) School of Gymnastics, where she was a student for two years and a faculty member for fourteen (1892–1906) under Amy Morris Homans *(q.v.).* She substituted for the directors of physical training at Smith College in Northampton, Massachusetts, for one year and at the University of Michigan the following year (1906–07).

In 1908 Perrin was selected to organize a physical training program for girls at Central High School (later part of Wayne State University) in Detroit, Michigan. She was appointed the first successful supervisor of physical culture for Detroit public schools in 1909 and served in this capacity until 1923. The program she developed served as a prototype of a modern and comprehensive program of physical education. The Detroit school course of study and the state course of study for Michigan physical education were nationally copied and widely used.

Perrin was the associate director of the Health Education Division of the American Child Health Association (1923–36), where she provided constructive promotional health consciousness on a national level. A founder and the chairman of the executive committee of the Women's Athletic Federation, she was instrumental in bringing about its merger with the women's athletic section of the American Physical Education Association (APEA), which provided principles for the conduct and leadership of girls' and women's sports.

The author of many professional articles, Perrin also wrote *One Hundred and Fifty Gymnastic Games* (with others, 1902), *A Handbook of Rhythmical Balance Exercises* (with Mary S. Sparks, 1906), *Play Day* (with Grace Turner, 1929), and two books for children, *Health in Play* (n.d.) and *My Health Book* (n.d.).

Actively engaged in professional leadership, Perrin was president of the Midwest Society of Physical Education (1917–18). In 1922 she was vice-president of the APEA, the highest position a woman could occupy. She was in its first group of honor awardees and was made a fellow in 1931. In 1946 she became the second woman to receive the profession's highest honor, the Gulick Award.

REFERENCES: *LE* (III); Ellen W. Gerber, *Innovators and Institutions in Physical Education* (Philadelphia: Lea and Febiger, 1971), "The Gulick Award, 1946," *Journal of Health and Physical Education* 17 (September 1946): 405; Elizabeth Halsey, *Women in Physical Education: Their Role in Work, Home, and History* (New York: G. P. Putnam's Sons, 1961); "In Memoriam," *Journal of Health, Physical Education, and Recreation* 33 (September 1962): 76; *NYT*, May 16, 1962, p. 41; Ethel Perrin, "Ethel Perrin—An Autobiography," *Research Quarterly* 12 (October 1941): 682–85.   *Adelaide M. Cole*

PERRIN, Porter Gale. B. September 17, 1896, Williamstown, Vermont, to Justus Newton and Laura (Gale) Perrin. M. September 20, 1926, to Dorothy Louise Merchant. Ch. three. D. September 9, 1962, Kirkland, Washington.

Porter Gale Perrin received the A.B. degree (1917) from Dartmouth College in Hanover, New Hampshire. He received the A.M. degree (1921) from the University of Maine and the Ph.D. degree (1936) from the University of Chicago.

Perrin taught history at a high school in Provincetown, Massachusetts (1917). He held a succession of teaching posts in English composition at the University of Maine (1919–21), Northwestern University in Evanston, Illinois (1921–22), Middlebury (Vermont) College (1922–25), and the University of Chicago (1925–29). He joined the faculty at Colgate University in Clinton, New York, as an assistant professor in 1929 and served as professor of English and department chairman from 1944 to 1947. From 1947 to his death in 1962, Perrin was professor of English at the University of Washington at Seattle.

Perrin wrote *The Life and Works of Thomas Green Fessenden* (1925),

Texts and Reference Books on Rhetoric before 1750 (1936), *An Index to English* (1939), *A Writer's Guide and Index to English* (1942), and *Guide to Modern English* (three volumes with R. Corbin, 1960, 1963). He also coedited two books of readings in literature.

Perrin was known nationally as an authority on modern American English style, usage, and grammar. He was active in several professional organizations, including the National Council of Teachers of English (chairman of the college section, vice-president, and president, 1947). He also served on many committees and was a trustee of the Research Foundation.

REFERENCES: *NCAB* (50:235); *WWAE* (XVI); *WWW* (IV); Robert C. Pooley, "Porter Gale Perrin," *College English* 24 (December 1962): 241-42; *NYT*, September 10, 1962, p. 29; *Seattle Times*, September 10, 1962, p. 33.   *Michael A. Balasa*

PERRY, William Flake. B. March 12, 1823, Jackson County, Georgia, to Hiram and Nancy (Flake) Perry. M. January 1, 1851, to Ellen Douglas Brown. Ch. seven. D. December 18, 1901, Bowling Green, Kentucky.

When he was ten years old, William Flake Perry and his family moved to Chambers County, Alabama, where only limited schooling was available. With what schooling he had, Flake taught school and studied law in Talladega County, Alabama (1848–53). In 1854 he was admitted to the bar, but never practiced because he was elected Alabama's first state superintendent of education that year. He was twice reelected and served until 1858. As state superintendent, he found few available funds, sparse population, indifferent and incompetent teachers and administrators, and inadequate public support. Despite the difficulties, he accomplished a great deal in the office.

In 1858 Perry resigned his position as superintendent and became president of the East Alabama Female College at Tuskegee, holding this position until 1862, when he enlisted in the Confederate army. Perry led his regiment in the assault at Gettysburg and later at Chickamauga, returned to Alabama after the war, and spent two years as a farmer.

In 1867 Perry went from Alabama to Kentucky where he was in charge of a military school at Glendale and then to Ogden College at Bowling Green where he was professor of English and philosophy. Perry wrote "The Genesis of Public Education in Alabama" for the *Transactions of the Alabama Historical Society for 1898*.

REFERENCES: *DAB; NCAB* (8:451); *TC; WWW* (I). *Walter J. Sanders*

PETRIE, George. B. April 10, 1866, Montgomery, Alabama, to George Laurens and Mary Jane (Cooper) Petrie. M. August 30, 1893, to Mary Barkwell Lane. Ch. one. D. September 6, 1947, Auburn, Alabama.

George Petrie was educated at the University of Virginia where he received the A.M. degree (1887) and at Johns Hopkins University in Baltimore, Maryland, where he received the Ph.D. degree (1891).

Petrie became professor of modern languages and history at Alabama Polytechnic Institute (later, Auburn University) in 1887 and remained there for his entire career. Petrie was dean of faculty (1908–22) and dean of the graduate school from 1922 to his retirement in 1942. In 1930 and 1931 he made weekly broadcasts "Topics of the Day," on a local radio station. Petrie was the author of *Church and State in Early Maryland* (1892), *Mace-Petrie American School History* (with William H. Mace, *q.v.*, 1919), and *Mace-Petrie Elementary History* (with William H. Mace, 1923). He was editor of three series of Alabama Polytechnic Institution Studies in Southern History.

He was president of the Alabama History Teachers' Association (1915), the Association of Graduate Deans of Southern Colleges (1932), and other organizations. He received an honorary degree from the University of Alabama.

REFERENCES: *LE* (II); *WWW* (II); *NYT*, September 7, 1947, p. 60.   *Jonathan C. McLendon*

PETTIT, Katherine Rhoda. B. February 23, 1868, near Lexington, Kentucky, to Benjamin F. and Clara Mason (Barbee) Pettit. M. no. D. September 3, 1936, Lexington, Kentucky.

Katherine Pettit was educated in Lexington and Louisville, Kentucky, and at the Sayre Female Institute of Lexington. Interested in the mountain people of Kentucky, she and May Stone agreed to conduct educational programs for rural mothers under the sponsorship of the Kentucky State Federation of Women's Clubs in 1899. They set up a tent in Hazard, Kentucky, and taught household skills to women in the camp and in private homes. During the summers of 1900 and 1901, they conducted day-long instructional sessions called "industrials" in Hindman and Sassafras.

Soliciting money for a permanent program, Pettit and Stone opened the Hindman Settlement School in 1902 under the sponsorship of the Women's Christian Temperance Union. Surviving fires, the school succeeded, and Pettit moved to Pine Mountain in Harlan County and opened the Pine Mountain Settlement School in 1914 with the assistance of Ethel de Long. From the school, they extended services to local schools and set up health centers in the communities of Big Laurel and Pine Fork.

Resigning from the Pine Mountain school in 1930, she spent five years working independently with unemployed miners, urging them to return to farming and teaching them improved farming methods. The University of Kentucky awarded Pettit the Algernon Sidney Sullivan Medal in recognition of her work (1932).

REFERENCES: *NAW; NYT*, September 5, 1936, p. 15; "Katherine

Pettit,'' *Register,* Kentucky State Historical Society (January 1937).

John F. Ohles

PHELPS, Almira Hart Lincoln. B. July 15, 1793, Berlin, Connecticut, to Samuel and Lydia (Hinsdale) Hart. M. October 4, 1817, to Simeon Lincoln. M. August 17, 1831, to John Phelps. Ch. five. D. July 15, 1884, Baltimore, Maryland.

Almira Hart Lincoln Phelps was educated by her parents and at the Berlin Academy in Middlebury, Vermont, run by her sister Emma Hart Willard *(q.v.).* She attended the Female Academy in Pittsfield, Massachusetts.

Phelps taught in a district school near Hartford, Connecticut, at the age of sixteen and also in Berlin and New Britain, Connecticut. She was principal of the Sandy Hill (New York) Female Academy (1815–17). After the death of her first husband, she became the head teacher in the science department (1823–27) of Emma Willard's Troy (New York) Seminary and vice-principal (1827–31).

Retired from teaching on her second marriage, Phelps returned as principal of the West Chester (Pennsylvania) Female Seminary (1838) and taught at Rahway, New Jersey. With her husband, she conducted the Patapsco Institute, a diocesan female school in Baltimore, Maryland (1841–49). After the death of her husband in 1849, she conducted the school until 1856.

She was not satisfied with the textbooks available and wrote her own. Her published works include *Familiar Lectures on Botany* (1829), *Dictionary of Chemistry* (1830), *Botany for Beginners* (1831), *Female Student or Fireside Friend* (1833), *Geology for Beginners* (1834), *Lectures on Natural Philosophy* (1835), *Lectures on Chemistry* (1837), *Natural Philosophy for Beginners* (1837), *Christian Households* (1858), *Hours with My Pupils* (1859), and several fictional titles. She edited *Our Country* (1868).

Phelps was the second woman elected to the American Association for the Advancement of Science and was a member of the Maryland Academy of Science, to which she donated her herbarium of about six hundred specimens.

REFERENCES: *AC; DAB; NAW; NCAB* (11:359); *TC; WWW* (H); *NYT,* July 16, 1884, p. 5; Emma Lydia Bolzau, *Almira Hart Lincoln Phelps: Her Life and Work* (Philadelphia: Science Press Printing Co., 1936).

Audrey N. Tomera

PHELPS, William Franklin. B. February 15, 1822, Auburn, New York, to Halsey and Lucinda (Hitchcock) Phelps. M. 1854 to Carolyn Chapman Livingston. Ch. one. D. August 15, 1907, St. Paul, Minnesota.

William Franklin Phelps received his education at Auburn (New York)

Academy (1834–38) and then alternately studied and taught in rural schools during the winters (1838–44). He was selected as the state student from Cayuga County to the New York State Normal School (later, State University of New York at Albany) in Albany in 1844 and was graduated in 1846. In 1845 he organized a model practice school at the normal school, which opened in 1846 as the first school of its kind with Phelps in charge.

From 1852 to 1855, he entered private business and traveled to regain his health. In 1855 Phelps organized the State Normal School (later, Trenton State College) at Trenton, New Jersey, and served as both principal and professor of the science of education until 1864. From 1856 he was also principal of the Farnum Preparatory School in Beverly, New Jersey. In 1864, Phelps moved to Minnesota where he reorganized and headed the State Normal School (later, Winona State College) at Winona until 1876. Phelps was president of the normal school (later, University of Wisconsin—Whitewater) at Whitewater, Wisconsin (1876–78). He was superintendent of the Winona, Minnesota, public schools (1878–79 and 1882–83). He served as secretary of chambers of commerce in Minnesota at Winona (1881–86), St. Paul (1886–87), and Duluth (1887–90). He was director of Minnesota normal schools (1896–1903). He lived in St. Paul, Minnesota, from 1890 to his death.

Phelps was the author of *Teachers' Handbook* (1875, translated into Spanish for use in the Argentine Republic), and volumes of reports on New Jersey and Minnesota normal schools. He revised and edited H. W. Pearson's *A Nebulo-Meteoric Hypothesis of Creation* (1902). He also wrote several monographs for the Chautauqua textbook series. He was editor of *Chicago Educational Weekly* (1867–68).

Phelps was active in professional organizations as an organizer and first president of the National Normal School Association (1858–63) and president of the National Educational Association (1875–76). He presided at the first international conference of educators at the Centennial Exhibition in Philadelphia, Pennsylvania, in 1876 and received an award at the French Exposition in Paris in 1878.

REFERENCES: *AC; DAB; NCAB* (12:480); *WWW* (IV).

James R. Layton
Mary Paula Phillips

PHELPS, William Lyon. B. January 2, 1865, New Haven, Connecticut, to Sylvanus Dryden and Sophia Emilia (Linsley) Phelps. M. December 21, 1892, to Annabel Hubbard. Ch. none. D. August 21, 1943, New Haven, Connecticut.

William Lyon Phelps assisted his clergyman father in publishing a Baptist weekly in Hartford, Connecticut, as typesetter, copyreader, book reviewer and writer. As a student at the Hartford (Connecticut) Public High School he was asked to leave because of his poor academic record but later was graduated as an honor student. He was graduated with the A.B. degree (1887) from Yale College and in 1891 received both the A.B. degree from Harvard University and the Ph.D. degree from Yale.

He taught for a year at Harvard (1891-92) before joining the Yale faculty where he taught English literature (1892-1933) and was Lamson Professor of English Literature (1901-33).

Upon his retirement from Yale in 1933 at the age of sixty-eight, he continued to write magazine and newspaper articles and give public lectures and radio broadcasts that spread his views on life and letters.

Phelps admired modern authors and introduced a course on the modern novel at the beginning of the century. He taught Stephen Vincent Benet, Thornton Wilder, Phillip Barry, and Sinclair Lewis, all of whom became famous in American literature. He was a pioneer in the teaching of contemporary drama. His course on Tennyson and Browning was one of the most popular with generations of students. He has been credited with playing a major role in popularizing the teaching of contemporary literature.

Phelps wrote twenty-six books, mainly on literature, but some of philosophy and religion, including *The Beginnings of the English Romantic Movement* (1893), *Essays on Modern Novelists* (1910), *Essays on Russian Novelists* (1911), *Teaching in School and College* (1912), *The Advance of English Poetry* (1918), *Human Nature in the Bible* (1922), *Happiness* (1926), *Essays on Things* (1930), *What I Like in Prose* (1934), *Autobiography with Letters* (1939), and *The Children's Anthology* (1941).

Phelps was a fellow of the American Academy of Arts and Sciences and the American Geographical Society and was a member of many other scholarly and literary societies. He received gold medals from the Holland Society, the National Society of New England Women, and the Connecticut Foot Guard. He was the recipient of many honorary degrees from American colleges and universities.

REFERENCES: *CB* (January 1943 and October 1943); *DAB* (supp. 3); *EB; LE* (II); *NCAB* (A: 375, 32:444); *WWW* (II); *Hartford Daily Courant,* August 22, 1943, p. 5; *NYT,* August 22, 1943, p. 37.

Arthur E. Soderlind

PHILBRICK, John Dudley. B. May 27, 1818, Deerfield, New Hampshire, to Peter Philbrick and his wife (n.a.). M. 1843 to Julia A. Putnam. Ch. none. D. February 2, 1886, Danvers, Massachusetts.

John Dudley Philbrick attended Pembroke Academy for a term or two each year for four years. He was graduated from Dartmouth College in Hanover, New Hampshire, in 1842.

Philbrick taught in a school in Roxbury, Massachusetts (1842-44), and became an assistant in the English High School in Boston (1844-47). In 1847 he was appointed principal of the Quincy School in Boston, where he made many changes in the school, including utilization of single desks instead of the two-pupil ones. He drastically reduced punishment by whipping and added drawing and music to the curriculum.

Disappointed when passed over when the superintendent's office was vacated in 1852, Philbrick accepted a position as principal of the Connecticut State Normal School (later, Central Connecticut State College) at New Britain. He was appointed Connecticut state superintendent of schools (1853–57). The Boston superintendency was again vacated, and Philbrick was appointed to the post at the age of thirty-eight and remained in that post to 1874 and then served again from 1876 to 1878. Philbrick gained a national reputation while in Boston for his administration of the Boston schools and his participation in the discussion of education at the national level.

He was an author of textbooks and works on education, including *Primary School Tablets* (1860), *American Union Speaker* (1865), *Primary School Speaker* (1866), and *City School Systems in the United States* (1885). He was editor of the *Massachusetts Teacher* and *Connecticut Common School Journal* (1854–56).

Philbrick was an organizer and president of the Massachusetts Teachers' Association and president of the National Teachers' Association (later, National Education Association, 1863), the Connecticut Teachers' Association, and the American Institute of Instruction (1857–59). He served ten years on the Massachusetts State Board of Education and represented the United States commissioner of education at the Paris Exposition of 1878. He was awarded the French Legion of Honor and honorary degrees from the University of Edinburgh, Scotland, and Dartmouth and Bates colleges.

REFERENCES: *AC; NCAB* (12:242); *NYT,* February 3, 1886, p. 5; A. E. Winship. *(q.v.), Great American Educators* (New York: American Book Co., 1900).   *John F. Ohles*

PHILLEO, Prudence Crandall. See **Crandall, Prudence.**

PHILLIPS, John. B. December 27, 1719, Andover, Massachusetts, to Samuel and Hannah (White) Phillips. M. August 4, 1743, to Sarah (Emery) Gilman. M. November 3, 1767, to Elizabeth Hale. Ch. none. D. April 21, 1795, Exeter, New Hampshire.

John Phillips entered Harvard College before he was twelve years old and received the M.A. degree in 1735, delivering the Latin salutatory oration at graduation. For some months Phillips taught school and settled in Exeter, New Hampshire. He engaged in preaching but turned to business and operated a country store. Phillips accumulated property, chiefly through speculation in real estate and lending money at high rates of interest. He was interested in public affairs and held several offices, including moderator of town meetings (1778 and 1779) and member of the General Court (1771–73) and was colonel of the Exeter Cadets.

Phillips was recognized as a philanthropist and made liberal gifts to Dartmouth College, including a professorship of biblical history and literature. Shortly after the founding of Phillips Academy in Andover, Massachusetts (1781) he corresponded with his nephew, Samuel Phillips, regarding the establishment of a similar school in Exeter. The act of incorporation for the new institution, to be called the Phillips Exeter Academy, was dated April 3, 1781, but the school was not opened until 1783.

Phillips contributed thirty thousand dollars to the establishment and development of Phillips Academy in Andover and gave much of his remaining fortune to Phillips Academy in Exeter. He was the first president of the Exeter board of trustees, a member of the Andover board (president, 1791–94), and a trustee of Dartmouth College (1773).

REFERENCES: *AC; DAB; NCAB* (10:103); *TC; WWW* (H).

Robert C. Morris

PHYSICK, Philip Syng. B. July 7, 1768, Philadelphia, Pennsylvania, to Edmund and Abigail (Syng) Physick. M. September 18, 1800, to Elizabeth Emlen. Ch. seven. D. December 15, 1837, Philadelphia, Pennsylvania.

Philip Syng Physick, the Father of American Surgery, attended a local school in Philadelphia and received the B.A. degree (1785) from the University of Pennsylvania. After studying with the distinguished Philadelphia physician, Adam Kuhn, he went to London, England, in 1788 and studied at the Great Windmill Street School under John Hunter. In 1790 Physick was appointed a house surgeon to St. George's Hospital in London. One year later, Hunter offered him a position as his personal assistant, but Physick declined and went to Edinburgh, Scotland, where he received the M.D. degree (1792).

Physick returned to Philadelphia but had difficulty in establishing a medical practice; several years passed before he earned a sufficient income. During the yellow fever epidemics of 1793 and 1798 he conducted many postmortem studies of the victims. He twice contracted the disease himself. His fame as a surgeon spread, and he was elected a surgeon at the Philadelphia Hospital (1794–1816). In 1800 Physick began giving lectures on surgery at the University of Pennsylvania. In 1805 he became professor of surgery, holding this position until his health forced him to resign in 1831. He published little, but his surgical views and experiences were preserved largely by the writings of his nephew, John Syng Dorsey.

Physick promoted the use of manipulation instead of mechanical methods of traction in the reduction of dislocations, the introduction of new methods in the treatment of hip-joint diseases by immobilization, and the development of a modified splint for fractures of the femur and ankle.

He was the first to use the stomach tube and invented needle forceps, used to tie deeply placed vessels, and the guillotine tonsillotomy. He introduced animal ligatures in surgery and established the practice of leaving them in the tissues to become absorbed. He performed the first successful operation of an arteriovenous aneurysm, which had followed venesection, in 1804.

Physick was president of the Phrenological Society of Philadelphia (1822) and the Philadelphia Medical Society (1824), an honorary fellow of the Royal Medical and Chirurgical Society in London, England, and a member of the Academy of Medicine of France.

REFERENCES, *AC; DAB; NCAB* (6:391); *TC; WWW* (H); John H. Talbott, *A Biographical History of Medicine* (New York: Grune and Stratton, 1954), pp. 731–32.   *Richard M. Coger*

PICKARD, Josiah Little. B. March 17, 1824, Rowley, Massachusetts, to Samuel and Sarah (Coffin) Pickard. M. August 24, 1847, to Cornelia Van Cleve Woodhull. Ch. three. D. March 27, 1914, Cupertino, California.

Josiah Little Pickard received his early education in the Lewiston, Maine, public schools and in the academy of the Reverend David B. Sewall. He was graduated from Bowdoin College in Brunswick, Maine, with the A.B. (1844) and A.M. (1847) degrees. He was principal of the academy of North Conway, New Hampshire, for one year.

Pickard established an academy at Platteville, Wisconsin, in 1846 and remained there to 1860. The school gained a reputation as a secondary school and later became a state normal school. He served as superintendent of public instruction for Wisconsin (1860–64) and became superintendent of the public schools of Chicago, Illinois; he was reelected annually until he resigned in September 1877.

In June 1878 Pickard was chosen president of the State University of Iowa. During his nine-year presidency, the university's endowment grew, and dental and pharmaceutical colleges were established. He resigned in 1887 but stayed in Iowa City doing literary and historical work until 1900. He lectured on topics in education.

Pickard was the author of *School Supervision* (1890) in the International Education Series of William T. Harris *(q.v.)*. He also wrote *Brief Political History of the United States* (1892) and *History of State University of Iowa* (1900). He was president of the National Educational Association (1871), the Iowa Historical Society (1871–1900), and the National Council of Education (1877–78). He received honorary degrees from the University of Chicago and Beloit and Bowdoin colleges.

REFERENCES: *AC; NCAB* (12:512); *NYT,* March 29, 1914, sec. IV, p. 6; *WWW* (I); *Platteville* (Wisconsin) *Journal,* April 1, 1914; James Alua

Wilgus, *The History of the Platteville Academy* (Platteville, Wis.: State Teachers College, 1942). *Arnold Lien*

PICKERING, Edward Charles. B. July 19, 1846, Boston, Massachusetts, to Edward and Charlotte (Hammond) Pickering. M. March 9, 1874, to Elizabeth Wadsworth Sparks. Ch. none. D. February 3, 1919, Cambridge, Massachusetts.

Edward Charles Pickering studied at the Boston Latin School and received the B.S. degree (1865) from the Lawrence Scientific School at Harvard University.

An instructor at the Lawrence Scientific School (1865–67), Pickering was Thayer Professor of Physics at the Massachusetts Institute of Technology (MIT) in Cambridge (1867–76). At MIT he introduced the laboratory method of instruction and established the first physical laboratory in the United States, where the students conducted their own experiments. In 1876 he became professor of astronomy and director of the Harvard College Observatory. In 1874 he married the daughter of Jared Sparks *(q.v.)*.

Representing a departure from the traditional astronomy, Pickering utilized photometric techniques to study the light and spectra of the stars. He invented a meridian photometer, compiled a photographic library of three hundred thousand glass plates, and established a foundation for spectral classification. He established an observatory in Arequipa, Peru, to observe the southern stars.

The author of *Elements of Physical Manipulation* (two volumes, 1873–76), Pickering edited seventy volumes of annals and other publications of the Harvard College Observatory. A fellow of the American Academy of Arts and Sciences, he was a member of many other American and foreign associations and an honorary member of foreign societies. He was president of the American Astronomical Society (1906) and the founder and first president of the Appalachian Mountain Club. He was decorated by the German government and received the Henry Draper Medal and the Rumford (1901) and Bruce (1908) gold medals and the Royal Astronomical Society Gold Medal twice (1886 and 1901). He was awarded several honorary degrees from American and foreign colleges and universities.

REFERENCES: *AC; DAB; DSB; EB; NCAB* (6:424); *NYT,* February 4, 1919, p. 11; *TC; WWW* (I). *Harold J. McKenna*

PICKET, Albert. B. April 15, 1771, Connecticut, to n.a. M. May 8, 1791, to Esther Rockwell Hull. Ch. five. D. August 3, 1850, Cincinnati, Ohio.

Albert Picket was a student of Noah Webster *(q.v.)* for a short time in 1782 and was largely self-educated. He moved from Connecticut to New York City in 1794 where he opened the Manhattan School, a school for women, which was considered to be one of the first schools to provide advanced education for women.

Picket conducted the school for many years and moved to Cincinnati, Ohio, in 1826, where he was principal of the Cincinnati Female Seminary, served on the board of education, and was a trustee of Cincinnati College. He sought to establish a normal school but was not successful.

Picket is primarily known as the founder and editor in January 1811 of *Juvenile Monitor, or Educational Magazine,* commonly believed to have been the first educational periodical in the United States. The venture was short-lived as was *The Academician,* a periodical he published with his son John W. Picket. Albert Picket was also the author of schoolbooks, including *Union Spelling Book* (1804), *The Juvenile Expositor* (1806), *The Juvenile Mentor* (1813), *The Juvenile Instructor* (1818), and *Analytical School Grammar* (1823). With his son he also wrote *Geographical Grammar* (1816), *Essentials of English Grammar* (1829), *Principles of English Grammar* (1837), *Picket's Primer* (1836), and *The Normal Teacher* (1845).

With Alexander Kinmont, Picket established the Western Academic Institute and Board of Education, from which was founded the Western Literary Institute and College of Professional Teachers, an association engaged in the promotion of public education in Ohio and seventeen other states along the Ohio and Mississippi rivers. Picket delivered the opening address to the institute in 1834 and frequently spoke before it and other groups. He prepared "Teaching Reading," which was read for him to the July 1850 Ohio State Teachers' Association in Springfield, Ohio.

REFERENCES: *DAB; WWW* (H); James J. Burns, *Educational History of Ohio* (Columbus: Historical Publishing Co., 1905).   *Wendy M. Losey*

PIERCE, John Davis. B. February 18, 1797, Chesterfield, New Hampshire, to Gad and Sarah (Davis) Pierce. M. February 1, 1825, to Millicent Estabrook. M. October 28, 1829, to Mary Ann Cleveland. M. 1833 to Harriet Reed. Ch. four. D. April 5, 1882, Medford, Massachusetts.

John Davis Pierce was graduated from Brown University (1822) and continued his study for the ministry at Princeton (New Jersey) Theological Seminary.

Pierce joined the American Home Missionary Society in 1831 after leaving pastorates in Sangerfield, New York, and Goshen, Connecticut, in a wave of anti-Masonic demonstrations. Pierce settled in Marshall, Michigan, where he met Isaac Crary *(q.v.),* Michigan's first congressman and chairman of the constitutional convention's education committee. Through Crary, Pierce influenced the articles on education in the state's constitution.

During his five-year tenure as the first Michigan superintendent of public instruction (1836–41), Pierce drew up plans for the organization and support of a system of primary schools, provided for the establishment of the

University of Michigan, and set up procedures for the sale of lands granted to the territory for the support of public education. Pierce organized the state into school districts and helped formulate state school laws that required appointment of school inspectors, provided for a library in each district, governed the length of schooling, and established qualifications for teachers. He drew ground plans for a model schoolhouse that were used throughout the state. His plan for the state university provided for a board of regents, establishment of the first three academic departments, and the initiation of a building program. Pierce initiated and edited *The Journal of Education* (1838–40), the first common school journal in that region of the country.

Pierce returned to Marshall in 1841 where he served the Congregational church (1842–47) and was elected to the state house of representatives (1847). He was chairman of the committee on federal relations that passed resolutions opposing slavery in the state. He supported legislation that established the state's first normal school. Pierce retired from state service after serving as a member of the constitutional convention in 1850.

Pierce gave the dedicatory address at the state's first normal school (later, Eastern Michigan University) in Ypsilanti, Michigan (1852), and retired there in 1853. During the remaining years of his life he frequently spoke at teachers' institutes and the normal school. He was elected to his last official position when he became the county superintendent of schools for Washtenaw County (1867–68).

REFERENCES: *AC; DAB; WWW* (H); Claude Eggertsen, ed., *Studies in the History of American Education* (Ann Arbor: University of Michigan, 1947); Charles O. Hoyt and R. Clyde Forst, *John D. Pierce: Founder of the Michigan School System, A Study of Education in the Northwest* (Ypsilanti, Mich.: The Scharf Tag, Label and Box Co., 1905); *NYT*, April 6, 1882, p. 2; Avis L. Sebaly, "Michigan State Normal Schools—Teacher Colleges in Transition" (Ph.D. diss., University of Michigan, 1950); Kent Sagendorph, *Michigan: The Story of the University* (New York: E. P. Dutton & Co., Publishers, 1948).   *Kim Sebaly*

PIERCE, Sarah. B. June 26, 1767, Litchfield, Connecticut, to John and Mary (Peterson) Pierce. M. no. D. January 19, 1852, Litchfield, Connecticut.

Orphaned at the age of fourteen, Sarah Pierce was left in the care of her brother, Colonel John Pierce, paymaster general of the Continental army. She and her sister Nancy were sent to New York City to be educated.

Pierce started teaching groups of two or three students in her Litchfield, Connecticut, dining room. Her school gained a reputation and enrolled increasing numbers of students. The citizens of Litchfield provided a building for the school in 1798. As enrollment continued to grow, the building was enlarged, and the school became known as the Litchfield Female Academy.

The academy was well known for its academic instruction and training in manners. It was nationally respected for almost forty years. The curriculum included reading, writing, spelling, grammar, composition, arithmetic, geography, history, painting, dancing, and needlework. When the textbooks that were available seemed dull, Pierce wrote her own. Religious instruction was given by the Reverend Lyman Beecher in return for tuition for his three children, including Catharine Beecher *(q.v.)*.

Pierce conducted the school by herself until 1814 when her nephew, John Pierce Brace, who had been educated at Williams College, came to assist her. He took over the principalship of the school in 1825 and remained until 1832 when he left to become principal of the Hartford (Connecticut) Female Seminary. Pierce returned to the academy in 1833 and continued for another decade. She was the author of *Sketches of Universal History* (four volumes 1811–18), written in a question and answer form.

REFERENCES: *NAW;* Emily N. Vanderpoel, *Chronicles of a Pioneer School* (Cambridge, Mass.: University Press, 1903).

Marie V. Stephenson

PIERPONT, John. B. April 6, 1785, Litchfield, Connecticut, to James and Elizabeth (Collins) Pierpont. M. September 23, 1810, to Mary Sheldon Lord. M. December 8, 1857, to Harriet Louise (Campbell) Fowler. Ch. six. D. August 27, 1866, Medford, Massachusetts.

John Pierpont, an 1804 graduate of Yale College, taught in an academy at Bethlehem, Connecticut, and served five years as a tutor to a South Carolina family (1805–09). He began legal studies in 1810 and was graduated from the Litchfield (Connecticut) Law School in 1812. Unsuccessful in law practice and in conducting a dry-goods business (1814–15), he entered Harvard Divinity School and was graduated in 1818. He was ordained a minister of the Hollis Street Church in Boston, Massachusetts, in 1819 and served the church to 1845. His ministry was characterized by support for temperance and the abolition of slavery, the state militia, and imprisonment for debt.

While secretary of the Boston School Committee, Pierpont suggested that a new school be called English High School, a designation subsequently used throughout the United States. He compiled textbooks that departed from tradition by excluding roles for elocution and that included selections from Shakespeare. Among his books were *The American First Class Book* (1823) and *The National Reader* (1827). He also wrote *Airs of Palestine and Other Poems* (1843) and *The Anti-Slavery Poems of John Pierpont* (1843).

Concerned that he did not confine himself to religious activities, Pierpont's congregation accused him of wasting time "in the making of books." Vindicated by an ecclesiastical council, Pierpont resigned in 1845. Later he served pastorates in Troy, New York (1845–48), and West Medford, Massachusetts (1849–58), was gubernatorial candidate for the Abolition party, congressional candidate for the Free Soil party, a Union army regimental chaplain, and a United States Treasury Department clerk.

REFERENCES: *A C; DAB; NCAB* (6:155); John A. Nietz, *Old Textbooks* (Pittsburgh: University of Pittsburgh Press, 1961); *NYT,* August 30, 1866, p. 3.   *Mary Harshbarger*

PIERSON, Abraham. B. c. 1645, Southampton, Long Island, New York, to Abraham and n.a. (Wheelwright) Pierson. M. 1673 to Abigail Clark. Ch. none. D. March 5, 1707, Killingworth (later, Clinton), Connecticut.

Abraham Pierson received his elementary and secondary schooling from his father and the Reverend John Davenport and in common schools in New Haven, Connecticut. He studied theology and the classics at Harvard College and was graduated in 1668. He and a college classmate studied theology to prepare for the Congregational ministry under the Reverend Roger Newton of Milford, Connecticut, until May 1669.

After declining a call to Woodbridge, New Jersey, Pierson was ordained in 1669 as copastor with his father of the Congregational church in Newark, New Jersey. Pierson was pastor from his father's death in 1678 until 1692 when an ecclesiastical policy dispute with parishioners caused him to leave Newark. He moved to Greenwich, Connecticut, and in 1694 accepted a call as pastor in Killingworth (later, Clinton), Connecticut, in a congregation that was split by dissension. Pierson brought peace and unity to the church and served to his death.

Pierson was recognized in his time as an excellent scholar. With James Pierpont he laid the foundations for what later became Yale College. A charter establishing a Collegiate School of Connecticut was granted by the General Court of Connecticut in October 1701; Pierson was named one of ten trustees. When the trustees met for the first time on November 11, 1701, he was elected rector of the school that was first located in Saybrook, Connecticut. The institution was renamed Yale College in 1745 and Yale University in 1879.

Because Saybrook was nine miles from Pierson's parish and the parishioners opposed his moving from Killingworth, the first students were instructed in the Killingworth parsonage, with commencements held in Saybrook. An unpublished textbook Pierson wrote on physics was used in manuscript form at Yale with considerable success.

REFERENCES: *A C; DAB; NCAB* (1:164); *TC; WWW* (H); Edwin Oviatt, *The Beginnings of Yale* (New Haven, Conn.: Yale University Press, 1916).   *Walter F. C. Ade*

PIKE, Nicholas. B. October 6, 1743, Somersworth, New Hampshire, to James and Sarah (Gilman) Pike. M. to Hannah Smith. M. January 9, 1779, to Eunice Smith. Ch. six. D. December 9, 1819, Newburyport, Massachusetts.

Nicholas Pike received the A.B. (1766) and M.A. (1770) degrees from Harvard College.

He was master of the first public grammar school in Newburyport, Massachusetts, a position he held from 1773 to around 1800. He opened a private evening school in the Newburyport town hall in 1774 and a private school for young ladies in 1775. He conducted these schools until 1783. In addition to educational activities, he served as town clerk of Newburyport, one of five selectmen of the town, justice of the peace, and town surveyor.

Pike was the author of the first textbook on arithmetic published in America, an eight-volume treatise entitled *A New and Complete System of Arithmetick, Composed for the Use of the Citizens of the United States* (1788) and an abridged edition of his textbook, *Abridgement of the New and Complete System of Arithmetick, Composed for the Use and Adapted to the Commerce of the Citizens of the United States . . . for the Use of Schools and Will Be Found to Be an Easy and Sure Guide to the Scholar.* Pike was said to have completed his book for publication in 1785 but withheld it until he was able to file copies with several states to have the copyright registered in his name.

In addition to his textbooks, Pike edited Daniel Ferning's *The Ready Reckoner, or the Trader's Useful Assistant* (1794). He was a fellow in the American Academy of Arts and Sciences.

REFERENCES: *DAB; NCAB* (20:362); *WWW* (H).

Katharine W. Hodgin

PILLSBURY, Walter Bowers. B. July 21, 1872, Burlington, Iowa, to Harrison and Eliza Crabtree (Bowers) Pillsbury. M. June 16, 1905, to Margaret M. Milbank. Ch. two. D. June 3, 1960, Ann Arbor, Michigan.

Walter Pillsbury received the A.B. degree (1892) from the University of Nebraska and the Ph.D. degree (1896) from Cornell University in Ithaca, New York. He joined the faculty of the University of Michigan in 1897 as an instructor, and by 1910 he had obtained the rank of professor of psychology. From 1929 until his retirement (1942) he was chairman of the department of psychology.

Beginning with his first book, *Attention* (1906), Pillsbury presented an analysis of attention theories. In addition to his concern for interesting or holding the attention of students, his other works investigated such important areas as reading processes, mental fatigue, and the sources of the sensation of movement. Among his earlier works are *Psychology of Reasoning* (1910), *Essentials of Psychology* (1911), *Fundamentals of Psychology* (1916), *Psychology of Nationality and Internationalism* (1919), and *Education as the Psychologist Sees It* (1925). In 1928 Pillsbury co-authored with Clarence L. Meader *The Psychology of Language,* which combined the expertise of a linguist and a psychologist to provide some new points of approach. His later works include *History of Psychology* (1929), *An Elementary Psychology of the Abnormal* (1932), *Psychology of Memory* (1938), and *Handbook of Psychology* (with Leon A. Pennington, 1942).

Pillsbury was active in professional associations, including the American Psychological Association (president, 1910–11) and the American Association for the Advancement of Science (vice-president and chairman of section H, 1913). He was chairman of the editorial committee of *Studies in Psychology,* honoring Edward Bradford Titchener *(q.v.).* He received an honorary degree from the University of Nebraska (1934).

REFERENCES: *LE* (III); *NCAB* (44:450); *WWAE* (XIV); *WWW* (IV).

Jean L. Easterly

PINNEY, Norman. B. October 21, 1804, Simsbury, Connecticut, to Butler and Eunice (Griswold) Holcomb Pinney. M. no. D. October 1, 1862, New Orleans, Louisiana.

Norman Pinney was graduated from Yale College in 1823, studied for the Protestant Episcopal ministry, and was ordained by Bishop Thomas C. Brownell *(q.v.)* in 1831.

He was a teacher of classical language at Washington (later, Trinity) College in Hartford, Connecticut (1826–31), until his ordination, when he became rector of Christ Church in Mobile, Alabama. He resigned after a few years because of doctrinal differences and later became a Unitarian.

In 1836 Pinney founded Mobile (Alabama) Institute as a school for boys. The school was successful, and many of its students became prominent citizens of Mobile. He set forth his educational philosophy in a short booklet, *The Principles of Education as Applied in the Mobile Institute* (1836). Believing that education was too theoretical and did not meet the needs of a democracy, he emphasized Latin, English, composition, mathematics, and sports and placed little emphasis on history, science, and modern languages.

He went to New Orleans in 1862 to establish a school for youth but became ill and died.

Pinney authored several schoolbooks, including *Practical French Teacher* (1847), *First Book in French* (1848), *The Progressive French Reader* (1850), *The Practical Spanish Teacher* (with Juan Barcel, 1855), *Easy Lessons in Pronouncing and Speaking French* (1860), and *French Grammar* (with Emile Arnoult, 1861), as well as keys to the texts. His French textbooks were adopted by a number of colleges, among them Harvard and the University of Pennsylvania.

REFERENCES: *AC; DAB; NCAB* (5:159); *WWW* (H); *Daily Picayune* (New Orleans, Louisiana), October 2, 1862.   *S. S. Britt, Jr.*

PIRSSON, Louis Valentine. B. November 3, 1860, Fordham, New York, to Francis Morris and Louisa (Butt) Pirsson. M. May 17, 1902, to Eliza Trumbull Brush. Ch. none. D. December 8, 1919, New Haven, Connecticut.

Louis Pirsson had almost no family life as a youth. His father was in South America, his mother died when he was four years old, and he was left without relatives in New York City after the death of his maternal grandparents. At the age of nine, he was placed with the family of the Reverend William J. Blain, a Presbyterian pastor who lived on a small farm near Amsterdam, New York. Blain was a strict disciplinarian and a good teacher for Pirsson, who acquired a taste for literature and natural history in the pastor's library.

Pirsson entered Amenia (New York) Academy at the age of sixteen. He moved with that school when it became the South Berkshire Institute in New Marlboro, Massachusetts, in 1878. He attended the Sheffield Scientific School of Yale University, where he was awarded the Ph.B. degree with honors (1882).

Pirsson remained at the Sheffield Scientific School as a laboratory assistant and instructor in analytical chemistry (1882–88). He taught chemistry for one year at the Brooklyn Polytechnic Institute (1888–89) but resigned that position to become a voluntary assistant geologist with the United States Geological Survey. He spent the summer of 1889 at Yellowstone National Park, where he found his vocation as a geologist. He returned to Yale for an academic year to study crystallography, mineralogy, and petrology. He studied in Europe at the world's leading schools of petrology at Heidelberg, Germany, and Paris, France (1891–92).

Professor George J. Brush, Pirsson's Yale adviser, asked him to return to Yale to become an instructor in mineralogy and lithology. He was subsequently professor of physical geology from 1897 to 1919. Pirsson was given positions of importance in the Sheffield Scientific School as a member of the governing board (1892), assistant director (1897), trustee (1912), and member of the university council. He was associate editor of the *American Journal of Science* (1897–1919) and was an assistant consultant (1893–1904) and geologist for the Geological Survey (1904–19).

Pirsson was one of four American petrologists to formulate an entirely new system for classifying igneous rocks. He was the author of the widely used *Rock and Rock Minerals* (1908) and author of part 1 of the most widely used textbook in physical geology, *Textbook of Geology* (1915).

REFERENCES: *DAB; NCAB* (28:199); *WWW* (I); J. P. Iddings, "Louis Valentine Pirsson," *Science* 51 (May 28, 1920): 530–32; *NYT,* December 9, 1919, p. 17.   *Isadore L. Sonnier*

PITMAN, Benn. B. July 24, 1822, Trowbridge, Wiltshire, England, to Samuel and Mariah (Davis) Pitman. M. 1849 to Jane Bragg. M. 1881 to Adelaide Nourse. Ch. four. D. December 28, 1910, Cincinnati, Ohio.

Benn Pitman began his career as a teacher, author, and court reporter at the age of fifteen when, after mastering his brother Isaac's new system of phonetic shorthand, he taught the subject in Isaac's private academy in England. Pitman perfected the outlines in his brother's first edition of shorthand and helped Isaac compile numerous textbooks on the subject. Pitman and another brother, Joseph, were enthusiastic about the phonetic principle and lectured extensively on the system throughout England. He briefly turned his attention to architecture, but his interest in phonography was so great that he returned to the lecture circuit and, for a while, managed a publishing house in England.

In 1852 at Isaac's suggestion, Pitman sailed with his wife and two children to the United States where he introduced Pitman shorthand in Philadelphia, Pennsylvania, and Canton, Dayton, and Cincinnati, Ohio. In Cincinnati he founded and presided over the Phonographic Institute, a combination school and publishing house.

After active service in the Civil War, Pitman became the official shorthand reporter for the United States government. He recorded and compiled the proceedings of a number of trials, including those of the assassins of President Lincoln, the Buell investigation, the New Orleans, Memphis, and Indiana riots investigation, and the Ku Klux Klan.

Later Pitman directed his attention to professional recording of conventions, political rallies, and lawsuits. His wife sold his shorthand textbooks, which he had elaborately decorated. His artistic talent earned him a position at the Cincinnati Art Academy, where he taught art and wood carving for many years. He invented the electrochemical process of relief engraving.

Pitman wrote *The Reporter's Companion* (1854), *Manual of Phonography* (1854), *Phonographic Teacher* (1857), *History of Shorthand* (1858), *The Phonographic Dictionary* (with Jerome B. Howard, 1883), *A Plea for American Decorative Art* (1895), *Sir Isaac Pitman, His Life and Labors, Told and Illustrated by Benn Pitman* (1902), and *A Plea for Alphabetic Reform* (1905). He compiled and edited *The Assassination of President Lincoln and the Trial of the Conspirators* (1865) and *Trials for Treason at Indianapolis* (1865).

REFERENCES: *AC; DAB; NCAB* (4:87); *TC; WWW* (I); *N Y T,* December 29, 1910, p. 9.   *Louise H. Wheeler*

PITTMAN, Marvin Summers. B. April 12, 1882, Eupora, Mississippi, to John Wesley and Ellen (Bradford) Pittman. M. February 13, 1915, to Anna Terrell. Ch. two. D. February 27, 1954, Statesboro, Georgia.

Marvin Summers Pittman received the A.B. degree (1905) from Millsaps

College in Jackson, Mississippi. He received the M.A. degree (1917) from the University of Oregon and the Ph.D. degree (1921) from Columbia University.

Pittman was a teacher of science and mathematics in a Monroe, Louisiana, high school (1905–07), superintendent of the Madison Parish (Louisiana) schools (1907–09), and professor of history at the State Normal College (later, Northwestern State University of Louisiana) in Natchitoches, Louisiana, from 1909 to 1912. He was director of rural education at the State Normal School (later, Oregon College of Education) in Monmouth, Oregon, from 1912 to 1918. From 1921 to 1934 Pittman was on the staff at Michigan State Normal College (later, Eastern Michigan University) at Ypsilanti, first as director of rural education and then as director of teacher training. He observed rural schooling in several European countries (1928), Mexico (1929), and Cuba (1932).

Pittman became president of Georgia State Teachers College in Statesboro. He served in that capacity from 1934 to 1941 and from 1943 to 1947. He was director of instruction at the Louisiana State Normal College (1942–43).

After his retirement from the Georgia State Teachers College, Pittman served as a member of a special commission on rural education that was sent to West Germany by the War Department (1947). He worked in South Korea under assignment of the United States Army to help organize South Korean teachers' colleges and departments of education (1948). He served as an educational consultant to the Institute of International Education (1951) and headed a special mission for technical assistance to Costa Rica (1951–53). Pittman was recognized as a rural education expert and was an adviser on the administrative aspects of teacher education.

Pittman wrote *Value of School Supervision* (1921), *A Guide to the Teaching of Spelling* (with Hugh Clark Pryor, 1921), *Successful Teaching in Rural Schools* (1922), *Problems of the Rural Teacher* (1924), *The Value of School Supervision Demonstrated with Zone Planning in Rural Schools* (1925), *The Practical Plan Book* (1931), and *Profitable Farming* (1932).

Pittman was a member of many professional associations, including the Louisiana State Teachers Association (president, 1911–12) and the Georgia Association of Colleges (president, 1938).

REFERENCES: *LE* (III); *NYT,* February 28, 1954, p. 92; *WWW* (III). *Robert D. Heslep*

POLAND, William Carey. B. January 25, 1846, Goffstown Center (later, Grasmere), New Hampshire, to James Willey and Sarah Jane (Ayer) Poland. M. March 25, 1882, to Clara Frances Harkness. Ch. three. D. March 19, 1929, Providence, Rhode Island.

William Carey Poland received the A.B. (1868) and M.A. (1871) degrees from Brown University in Providence, Rhode Island. He also studied in Germany at the universities of Berlin and Leipzig (1875–76) and the Berlin Museum (1878) and in France and Italy (1878–79).

Poland served as principal of Worcester (Massachusetts) Academy from 1868 until 1870 when he began his long association with Brown University as an instructor in Greek and Latin. In 1892 he became professor of the history of art at Brown and remained until he retired as professor emeritus in 1915. Poland served the university as curator of the Museum of Classical Archaeology (1889–93) and director of the Museum of Fine Arts (1893–1915).

Poland was the author of numerous books, including *Syllabus of Ten Lectures on Archaeology* (1893), *Notes on Art in the 19th Century* (1900), *Notes and Questions on the History of Art During the Period of Renaissance* (1901), *Lecture Outlines on the History of Roman and Medieval Art* (1906), *Robert Feke, the Early Newport Portrait Painter* (1907), and many articles in newspapers, educational journals, and in the *American Journal of Archaeology*.

He was secretary of the Commission of Colleges in New England on Admission Examinations (1886–1905), director of the American School of Classical Studies at Athens, Greece (1891–92), and president of the Rhode Island School of Design (1896–1907). He was a member of many other associations.

REFERENCES: *NCAB* (22:356); *NYT*, March 20, 1929, p. 29; *WWW* (I).   *Roger H. Jones*

POLLOCK, Louise Plessner. B. November 29, 1832, Erfurt, Germany, to Frederick Wilhelm Plessner and his wife (n.a.). M. to George H. Pollock. Ch. five. D. July 24, 1901, Stony Man Camp, Virginia.

Frederick Wilhelm Plessner, father of Louise Plessner Pollock, was a retired Prussian army officer and writer of textbooks. He took charge of the education of his youngest daughter, who was sent to Paris at the age of sixteen to study French. There she met George H. Pollock of Boston, whom she married two years later.

Pollock became interested in the kindergarten movement in 1859 when German relatives sent her books on child training, hygiene, and physiology. When her husband suffered from illness and financial difficulties, she became employed as a translator and author of stories for periodicals. In 1862 she translated Lena Morgenstern's *Paradise of Childhood* and adopted Morgenstern's system of child training with her own family.

Responding to a request of Nathaniel T. Allen (*q.v.*), principal of the West Newton (Massachusetts) English and Classical School, she established a kindergarten, said to be the first "pure" kindergarten in the United States. In 1874 she studied the kindergarten movement in Berlin,

Germany, and returned to open the Le Droit Kindergarten in Washington, D.C. She actively and unsuccessfully campaigned for national legislation to establish a free national kindergarten normal school. With the Le Droit Kindergarten, she conducted a class to train nursery maids in child care, a procedure copied in a number of cities across the country. In 1883 she opened the Pensoara Free Kindergarten and later was principal of the National Kindergarten and Kindergarten Normal Institute.

Pollock wrote four lengthy articles on the kindergarten for the *Friend of Progress* magazine in 1863, among the first contributions to literature in the field in the United States. She was the author of *National Kindergarten Manual* (1889), *National Kindergarten Songs and Plays* (1880), and *Cheerful Echoes* (1888).

REFERENCES: *WC; Washington* (D.C.)*Post,* July 27, 1901; *Kindergarten Review* 12 (September 1901): 35.   *John F. Ohles*

POOR, John. B. July 8, 1752, Plaistow, New Hampshire, to Daniel and Anna (Merrill) Poor. M. November 2, 1777, to Sarah Folsom. M. January 7, 1789, to Jane Neely. Ch. ten. D. December 5, 1829, York Haven, Pennsylvania.

John Poor completed his studies at Harvard University and turned to education as a profession. Not much is known of his early career, but he became head of the Young Ladies Academy in Philadelphia on June 4, 1778. The academy grew in importance and attracted students from Canada, Nova Scotia, and the West Indies, as well as from other states. On February 1, 1792, Poor and several prominent Philadelphians obtained a state charter, the first granted to an institution established for the education of girls in the United States. The academy failed to receive state financial aid on a par with that of boys' academies, but provided a broad curriculum for young women. The academy was unique in educating girls as homemakers, as well as providing instruction in the sciences, history, literature, and moral philosophy.

Poor remained principal of the academy until 1809 when he moved to Solebury, Pennsylvania. He conducted a school for girls in New Hope, Pennsylvania (1815–27), and retired in 1827.

REFERENCES: *DAB; WWW* (H); Mabel Newcomer, *A Century of Higher Education for American Women* (New York: Harper, 1959).

Patricia L. Earls

PORTER, Arthur Kingsley. B. February 6, 1883, Stamford, Connecticut, to Timothy Hopkins and Maria Louisa (Hoyt) Porter. M. June 1, 1912, to Lucy Bryant Wallace. Ch. none. D. July 8, 1933, Bay of Donegal, Ireland.

A. Kingsley Porter received his early education at the Browning School in New York City. He entered Yale University in 1900 and received the

B.A. (1904) and B.F.A. (1917) degrees. He attended the Columbia University School of Architecture in New York City (1904–06). While a student at Columbia he wrote the two-volume *Medieval Architecture: Its Origins and Development,* which was published in 1909 when he was twenty-six years old. At the time of its publication, it was the most important addition made by an American scholar to the history of medieval architecture.

Porter taught the history of art at Yale University. He served as a lecturer (1915–17) and as an assistant professor (1917–19). Yale granted Porter a leave of absence so that he might accept an invitation from the French Ministry of Instruction, Department of Fine Arts, to be liaison adjutant with the Commission d'histoire monument; he was assigned to the Service des oeuvres d'art dans la zone des armées (1918–19). Returning to the United States in 1920, he accepted a position as professor of fine arts at Harvard University where he inaugurated classes in which he prepared many young American art historians. He was the first William Dorr Boardman Professor of Fine Arts (1924). He was exchange professor at the Sorbonne, Paris, and held the Hyde lectureship at French provincial universities during the 1923–24 academic year.

Porter was the author of an impressive number of works in his field. Among them were *The Construction of Lombard and Gothic Vaults* (1911), *Lombard Architecture* (four volumes, 1915), which was awarded the Grande medaille de vermeil of the société française d'archeologie, *Romanesque Sculpture of the Pilgrimage Roads* (1923), *Spanish Romanesque Sculpture* (two volumes, 1928), *The Crosses and Cultures of Ireland* (1931), and two plays, *The Seven Who Slept* (1919) and *The Virgin and the Clerk* (1929). He also wrote more than eighty articles for periodicals and anthologies and served as editor of *Art Studies* (1925–33).

Porter was a member of many American and European professional associations. Among the honors he received were honorary degrees from the University of Marburg, Germany (1927), and Williams College (1932). He traveled to Ireland in 1933 to engage in the study of the prehistoric culture of that country. He disappeared during a storm off the island of Inishbifin and was presumed to have drowned in the Bay of Donegal, Ireland.

REFERENCES: *DAB* (supp. 1); *LE* (I); *NCAB* (40:572); *NYT,* July 10, 1933, p. 1; *WWW* (I). *Roger H. Jones*

PORTER, Noah. B. December 14, 1811, Farmington, Connecticut, to Noah and Mehetabel (Meigs) Porter. M. April 13, 1836, to Mary Taylor. Ch. none. D. March 4, 1892, Farmington, Connecticut.

Noah Porter received the A.B. (1831) and A.M. (1834) degrees from Yale College. After serving as head of the Hopkins Grammar School in New

Haven, Connecticut (1831–33), he returned to Yale as a tutor (1833–35) and student of theology. Ordained in 1836, he was pastor of Congregational churches in New Milford, Connecticut (1836–43), and Springfield, Massachusetts (1843–46).

In 1846 Porter was appointed to the new chair in moral philosophy and metaphysics at Yale, a position he held to his death in 1892. Porter was president of Yale for fifteen years (1871–86). During his tenure he directed the reorganizing of the schools of law and medicine and changes in the departmental structure. Many new buildings were added to the campus. Although students were allowed to take some elective courses, Porter resisted changes in the required curriculum. He favored an emphasis on the classical languages and mathematics, the textbook and the recitation method of instruction, compulsory institutional religion, and strict segregation of the sexes.

Porter defended the traditional course system of American colleges in *American Colleges and the American Public* (1871). He was also the author of *The Human Intellect* (1868), *Books and Reading* (1870), *Elements of Intellectual Science* (1871), *Science of Nature vs. the Science of Man* (1871), *Science and Sentiment* (1882), *Evangeline, the Place, the Story and the Poem* (1882), *Life of Bishop George Berkeley* (1885), *Elements of Moral Science* (1885), and *Critical Exposition of Kant's Ethics* (1886), and he was chief editor of *Noah Webster's Dictionary* (1864 and 1890).

Porter was awarded honorary degrees by several American colleges and the University of Edinburgh in Scotland. He was the brother of Sarah Porter *(q.v.)*, founder of Miss Porter's School.

REFERENCES: *AC; DAB; NCAB* (1:171); *TC; WWW* (H); George S. Merriam, ed., *Noah Porter: A Memorial By Friends* (New York: Charles Scribner's Sons, 1893); *NYT,* March 5, 1892, p. 4.   *Walter F. C. Ade*

PORTER, Sarah. B. August 16, 1813, Farmington, Connecticut, to Noah and Mehetabel (Meigs) Porter. M. no. D. February 17, 1900, Farmington, Connecticut.

Sarah Porter was educated with her brothers at the Farmington (Connecticut) Academy, which was exclusively male until she was admitted. At the age of sixteen she became an assistant teacher there. At the age of nineteen, she joined her brother Noah *(q.v.)* at New Haven, Connecticut, to study with Ethan Allen Andrews *(q.v.)* who founded an institute for young ladies.

From 1832 to 1841, Porter taught in schools in Springfield, Massachusetts, Philadelphia, Pennsylvania, and Buffalo, New York. She returned to Farmington in 1841 and taught a class of fifteen day pupils, but the financial burden on her family was too great. In 1843 she opened a day school in an upper room of the "Old Stone Store" and later rented rooms at a private home. This school became one of the best-known boarding schools for girls in the United States, Miss Porter's School.

Porter taught most of the subjects offered by the school. Scholarly achievements were secondary to culture, character development, religious training, and physical activities. Frequent excursions into the woods and countryside were made for nature study and concerts and lectures were scheduled at the school. Students were allowed to pursue studies at their own pace without examinations, grades, and rules, which Porter felt would interfere with the desire to learn. Porter's pedagogical principles were compared with those of the later progressive educators. She saw the future role of her students as homemakers rather than as career women; the school was not college-preparation oriented.

In 1885 former students presented Porter with an art building. In 1902, after her death, the Sarah Porter Memorial Building, a parish house in Farmington, was dedicated to her memory. Her brother Noah was president of Yale University.

REFERENCES: *AC; DAB; NAW; NCAB* (10:292).

Barbara Ruth Peltzman

POSSE, Nils. B. 1862, Stockholm, Sweden, to Knut H. Posse and his wife (n.a.). M. to Rose Moore Smith. Ch. none. D. December 18, 1895, Boston, Massachusetts.

Nils Posse was graduated from a Swedish secondary school and completed gymnastics and fencing courses at the Swedish Royal Military School and the Royal Central Institute of Gymnastics. He became interested in medical gymnastics when he arrived in Boston, Massachusetts, in 1885 and was employed by Mary Hemenway to teach twenty-five women instructors the Swedish system of educational gymnastics.

He became the first teacher at the Boston Normal School of Gymnastics, endowed by Hemenway (1889–90), and started his own school, the Posse Normal School, in 1891. Posse made extensive use of the Chautauqua lecture circuit to present the Swedish system of gymnastics and taught short courses at Martha's Vineyard Summer Institute and summer courses at the Boston Normal School. He was in charge of an exhibit at the Chicago World's Fair (1893) sponsored by Swedish gymnastic societies and athletic clubs.

During his brief professional life, he translated an article on massage by Dr. Douglas Graham into Swedish and the Swedish physician Björnström's work *Hypnotism—Its History and Present Development* into English (n.d.), and he was the author of *The Swedish System of Educational Gymnastics* (1890), *Handbook of School Gymnastics of the Swedish System* (1891), *The Special Kinesiology of Educational Gymnastics* (1894), and articles in professional journals on Swedish gymnastics. The first number of each *Posse Gymnastics Journal* for 1892 to 1895 had an article by him.

Posse is credited with introducing gymnastics into schools in fifty-two cities and assisting in the establishment of clinics for medical gymnastics in most of the larger hospitals in Boston. After his death in 1895, his wife continued his work.

REFERENCES: Ellen W. Gerber, *Innovators and Institutions in Physical Education* (Philadelphia: Lea & Febiger, 1971); C. W. Hackensmith, *History of Physical Education* (New York: Harper & Row, 1966); *Herringshaw's Encyclopedia of American Biography of the Nineteenth Century* (Chicago: American Publishers Association, 1898); Emmett Rice, John Hutchinson, and Mabel Lee *(q.v.)*, *A Brief History of Physical Education* (New York: Ronald Press, 1926); *Boston Globe,* December 19, 1895, p. 1.

E. A. Scholer

POTEAT, William Louis. B. October 20, 1856, Caswell County, North Carolina, to James and Julia A. (McNeill) Poteat. M. June 24, 1881, to Emma Purefoy. Ch. three. D. March 12, 1938, Wake Forest, North Carolina.

William Louis Poteat spent his early childhood on Forest Home, a North Carolina plantation. He entered Wake Forest College (later, University) in Winston-Salem, North Carolina, in 1872 and received the A.B. (1877) and A.M. (1889) degrees. He studied law for a short time and later studied at the Marine Biological Laboratory at Woods Hole, Massachusetts, and at the Zoological Institute in Berlin, Germany.

Poteat taught biology at Wake Forest (1889–1905) and was a pioneer in the use of laboratory instruction. He served as president of Wake Forest (1905–27). As a biologist, he was able to reconcile the teaching of evolution and strong religious beliefs, but the question was repeatedly raised and occupied much of his time when the controversy raged nationally in the 1920s. He took an active role as a social reformer and was a leader in movements to improve prison conditions, revise child labor laws, seek better treatment of the insane, and make changes in the setting of railroad rates.

Poteat was the author of *Laboratory and Pulpit* (1901), *The New Peace* (1915), *Can a Man Be a Christian Today?* (1925), *The Way of Victory* (1929), and *Stop-Light* (1935).

He was active in many organizations, including serving as president of the North Carolina Academy of Science (1902), the North Carolina Convention of the Anti-Saloon League (1918–23), the North Carolina Conference for Social Service (1918–19), the Southern Baptist Education Association (1921–23), and the Council of Church Schools of the South (1923). He was a member of the board of managers of the American Baptist

POTTER, Alonzo [1049]

Missionary Union (1888–1903) and the Baptist Publications Society (1898–1903) and a trustee of the Baptist Theological Seminary. He received honorary degrees from five universities.

REFERENCES: *LE* (I); *NCAB* (28:132); *WWW* (I); Suzanne Cameron Linder, *William Louis Poteat, Prophet of Progress* (Chapel Hill: University of North Carolina Press, 1966); *NYT,* March 13, 1938, sec. 2, p. 8.   *Linda C. Gardner*

POTTER, Alonzo. B. July 6, 1800, Beekman, New York, to Joseph and Anne (Knight) Potter. M. 1824 to Sarah Maria Nott. M. 1841 to Sarah Benedict. M. 1865 to Frances Seaton. Ch. seven. D. July 4, 1865, aboard ship in San Francisco Bay, California.

Alonzo Potter attended district schools and an academy in Poughkeepsie, New York. He was graduated from Union College in Schenectady, New York, in 1818. He studied for the ministry with the Reverend Dr. Samuel H. Turner and was ordained a deacon (1822) and priest (1824) in the Episcopal church.

Potter was employed as a bookseller in Philadelphia. In 1819 he was a tutor at Union College and in 1822 was named professor of mathematics and philosophy; he remained at Union as professor of mathematics and natural philosophy until 1826. He was rector of St. Paul's Church in Boston (1826–31). He returned to Union as professor of moral philosophy and political economy, a position he held (1831–45) until his election to the episcopate. He was vice-president of Union College (1838–45).

On May 23, 1845, he was chosen bishop of the diocese of Pennsylvania, remaining in this office until his death in 1865. As bishop he reestablished and reorganized the Protestant Episcopal Academy, established vocational institutes, founded the Divinity School of the Episcopal Church in Philadelphia (1863), helped establish thirty-five new churches in Philadelphia, and established the Episcopal Hospital in Philadelphia.

Potter was the author of *Political Economy, Its Objects, Uses and Principles* (1840), *The Principles of Science* (1841), and *The School and the Schoolmaster* (with George B. Emerson, *q.v.,* 1842), a copy of which was placed in every school in New York and Massachusetts. He also wrote *Handbook for Readers and Students* (1843) and *Discourses, Charges, Addresses, and Pastoral Letters* (1858). He edited Harpers Family Library (seven volumes). He delivered Lowell Lectures in Boston between 1845 and 1849, which were published after his death as *Religious Philosophy: or Man and the Bible Witnessing to God and to Religious Truth* (1870). He received honorary degrees from Harvard University and Union and Kenyon colleges.

REFERENCES: *AC; DAB; EB; NCAB* (3:470); *NYT,* July 21, 1865, p. 5; *TC; WWW* (H).   *Norman J. Bauer*

POTTER, Elisha Reynolds, Jr. B. June 20, 1811, South Kingston, Rhode Island, to Elisha R. and Mary (Mawney) Potter. M. no. D. April 10, 1882, South Kingston, Rhode Island.

Elisha Potter, Jr., prepared to attend Harvard University at Kingston (Rhode Island) Academy. He entered Harvard in 1826 and was graduated in 1830. He studied law in the office of Nathaniel Searle of Providence, Rhode Island, and was admitted to the bar on October 9, 1832.

Potter was adjutant general of Rhode Island (1835–37). In 1839 he became a representative in the state general assembly, served one year, sat in the state constitutional convention (1841–42), and was elected as a Whig candidate to the United States House of Representatives (1843–45). He was on a commission of three that met with President John Tyler during an uprising in 1842 known as the Dorr war.

He returned to Rhode Island from Washington and became interested in reorganizing the state educational system. He was appointed commissioner of public schools (1849–54). He promoted efficient school administration and sought to keep sectarian interests out of public education. Potter served in the upper house of the state legislature from 1861 to 1863 and became an associate justice of the supreme court of Rhode Island in 1868; he held that office until he died in 1882.

Potter was founder and editor (1852–53) of *Rhode Island Educational Magazine.* He wrote many books, including *The Early History of Narragansett* (1835), *A Brief Account of Emissions of Paper Money, Made by the Colony of Rhode Island* (1837), *Considerations on the Questions of the Adoption of a Constitution and Extension of Suffrage in Rhode Island* (1842), and *Memoir Concerning the French Settlements and French Settlers in the Colony of Rhode Island* (1879).

REFERENCES: *AC; DAB; TC; WWW* (H); *NYT,* April 11, 1882, p. 5.

Walter J. Sanders

POUND, Louise. B. June 30, 1872, Lincoln, Nebraska, to Stephen Bosworth and Laura (Biddlecombe) Pound. M. no D. June 28, 1958, Lincoln, Nebraska.

Louise Pound was educated privately before her matriculation at the University of Nebraska, where she received the B.A. degree (1892) with a diploma in music and the M.A. degree (1895). After summer courses at the universities of Chicago (1897 and 1898) and Heidelberg, Germany, she received the Ph.D. degree (1900) from the University of Heidelberg.

Starting as a teaching fellow in English at the University of Nebraska, she rose to full professor by 1912 and served for many years as department head; she remained there until her retirement in 1945.

Pound wrote many articles on education, linguistics, literature, and folklore and prepared editions of Tennyson's *Lancelot and Elaine* (1905), the major poems of Gray and Goldsmith (1907), Shakespeare's *Henry VI, Part One* (Tudor Shakespeare Series, 1912), *The Ancient Mariner and Other Poems* (1920), and *American Ballads and Songs* (1922). *Selected Writings of Louise Pound* was published in 1949. She was editor of the University of Nebraska Studies in Language, Literature and Criticism (1917–40) and senior editor (1925–33) and associate and department editor (1933–38) of *American Speech.* An adviser to *Southern Folklore Quarterly* and the *Bulletin of the American Association of University Professors,* she served on advisory boards of *New England Quarterly* (1928–30), *American Literature* (1929–45), *Folk-Say* (1929), and *College English* (1939–46).

Pound was active in many civic and professional associations; she was acting state head and chairman of the overseas relief committee of the National League for Woman's Service during World War I and a member of the woman's committee of the Nebraska State Council of Defense (1918).

A sports enthusiast from childhood, she was an excellent ice skater and bicyclist and held tennis championships, including Nebraska state (1891 and 1892), women's western (1897), and central western and western women's doubles (1915). Her golf championships included local women's (1906–23, 1925–27), city (1926), and state and women's (1916). She was the first woman elected to the Nebraska Sports Hall of Fame in 1955 three years before her death. She was a sister of Roscoe Pound *(q.v.),* law educator.

REFERENCES: *LE* (II); *NCAB* (E:379, 46:538); *WWAE* (XIII); *WWW* (III); *NYT,* June 29, 1958, p. 69; *Who's Who of American Women,* 1st ed. (Chicago: Marquis, 1958). M. Jane Dowd

POUND, Roscoe. B. October 27, 1870, Lincoln, Nebraska, to Stephen Bosworth and Laura (Biddlecombe) Pound. M. June 17, 1899, to Grace Gerrard. M. June 30, 1931, to Lucy (Berry) Miller. Ch. none. D. July 1, 1964, Cambridge, Massachusetts.

Roscoe Pound was one of the world's first scholars in modern jurisprudence and has been called the Schoolmaster of American Law. He displayed an early enthusiasm for botany and earned the B.A. degree (1888) in the study of botany and the M.A. (1889) and Ph.D. (1897) degrees in plant geography, ecology, and parasitic fungi at the University of Nebraska.

Pound was admitted to the Nebraska bar in 1890 after one year of study at Harvard Law School. He practiced law privately until 1901 when he became commissioner of appeals in the Supreme Court of Nebraska. He was associate professor of law at the University of Nebraska (1901–03) and served as dean (1903–07). Pound taught at Northwestern University (1907–09) and the University of Chicago (1909–10). He joined the faculty at the Harvard Law School in 1910 and taught there to his retirement in 1947, serving as Story Professor of Law (1910–13) and Carter Professor of Jurisprudence (1913–37). Although he never received a degree in law, he was dean of Harvard Law School from 1916 through 1936. During his tenure he presided over the school's "golden age." Under his leadership the curriculum was enlarged from a study of private and corporate law to include government law.

Pound was a prolific author. His books include *The Phytogeography of Nebraska* (with Frederic E. Clements, 1898), *Readings on the History and System of the Common Law* (1904), *Readings in Common Law* (1906), *The Spirit of the Common Law* (1921), *Interpretations of Legal History* (1923), *Introduction to the Philosophy of Law* (1925), *Criminal Justice in America* (1930), *Appellate Procedure in Civil Cases* (1941), *Administrative Law* (1942), *Social Control Through Law* (1942), *The Ideal Element in Law* (1958), *Jurisprudence* (five volumes, 1959), and books on Freemasonry. He wrote many essays and delivered lectures in universities around the world.

Pound was one of the founders and first director of the Botanical Survey of Nebraska from 1892 to 1903. A fungus parasite that he discovered was classified and named *Roscoepoundia*. He mastered many languages, including French, German, Italian, Spanish, Sanskrit, Greek, Latin, and Hebrew. His sister was Louise Pound *(q.v.)*.

Pound served on a number of judicial commissions during his career. He was Nebraska commissioner of uniform state laws (1904–07) and served on the justice section of the Institut international de cooperation intellectuelle established by the League of Nations, the American-British Claims Arbitration Group (1925–26), the Wickersham Commission on Law Observation and Enforcement (appointed by President Herbert Hoover, 1929–31), and the National Conference of Judicial Councils (director from 1938). He served the Republic of (Nationalist) China in the reorganization of the judicial system (1946–49). He was a fellow of the American Association for the Advancement of Science and was president of the American Academy of Arts and Sciences (1935–37) and the International Academy of Comparative Law in London (1950). He received many honorary degrees from American and foreign colleges and universities and was awarded the American Bar Association Medal (1940). The University of Nebraska established the Roscoe Pound Lectureship (1950) and the Harvard Law School established the Roscoe Pound Chair of Law (1950).

REFERENCES: *CB* (May 1947); *EB; LE* (II); *NCAB* (E:378); *NYT,* July 2, 1964, p. 1; *WWW* (IV); *Time* 84 (July 10, 1964): 46.

Vincent Giardina

POWELL, Lawrence Clark. B. September 3, 1906, Washington, D.C., to G. Harold and Gertrude Eliza (Clark) Powell. M. March 26, 1934, to Fay Ellen Shoemaker. Ch. two.

Lawrence Clark Powell moved with his parents to southern California in 1911 where he was graduated from high school in 1924. He received the B.A. degree (1929) from Occidental College in Los Angeles. He taught English for a short time at Occidental and then worked in a bookstore for a year. In 1931 he entered the University of Dijon in France, where he earned the Ph.D. degree in English and American literature (1932).

On his return to the United States, he entered an apprenticeship in the antiquarian book trade in Los Angeles. He received a certificate of librarianship in 1937 from the University of California at Berkeley and joined the staff of the Los Angeles Public Library. He worked in the acquisitions department of the library of the University of California at Los Angeles (UCLA) from 1938 to 1943. He became university librarian and director of the William Andrews Clark Memorial Library (1964). Under his directorship, the libraries at UCLA tripled in size.

In 1960, Powell became first dean at the new school of library service at UCLA. Relinquishing his role as university librarian in 1961, he remained as dean of the library school and director of the Clark Memorial Library until his retirement in 1966.

Powell was a book collector and a writer of articles and books, with over five hundred titles to his credit. His books include *An Introduction to Robinson Jeffers* (1932), *Robinson Jeffers, the Man and His Work* (1934), *Manuscripts of D. H. Lawrence* (1937), *Philosopher Pickett* (1942), *Islands of Books* (1951), *Land of Fiction* (1952), *The Alchemy of Books, Sky, Sun and Water* (1954), *Books West Southwest* (1957), *The Malibu* (with W. W. Robinson, 1958), *A Passion for Books* (1959), *Books in My Baggage* (1960), *Act of Enchantment* (1961), *The Sea* (1962), *The Little Package* (1963), *Fortune and Friendship* (1968), and *Bookmans Progress* (1968).

Powell was a Guggenheim Fellow in Great Britain (1950–51). He was a member of library associations and served as president of the California Library Association (1950) and the Bibliographical Society of America (1954–55).

REFERENCES: *CA* (21–22); *CB* (June 1960); *LE* (III); *WW* (XXXVIII); Betty Rosenberg, *Check-list of the Published Writings of Lawrence Clark Powell* (Los Angeles: University of California, 1966).   *Gary D. Barber*

POWELL, William Bramwell. B. December 22, 1836, Castile, New York, to Joseph and Mary (Dean) Powell. M. May 1865 to Minnie Paul. Ch. one, Maud Powell, violinist. D. February 6, 1904, Mount Vernon, New York.

William Bramwell Powell was the son of a Methodist circuit preacher-farmer. In his youth he went to school when he could arrange to and helped his father carry out household chores and farm duties. The family moved to Illinois, where he received the major portion of his public education. He was enrolled in the preparatory department of Oberlin (Ohio) College and completed his education at Wheaton (Illinois) College.

For the next twenty-five years, Powell held a variety of administrative positions in the school systems of Illinois as principal of a school in Hennepin (1860–62) and superintendent of schools at Peru (1862–70) and Aurora (1870–85). At Aurora, he established a training school for teachers, which used high school graduates who showed teaching promise as assistants in the various departments.

Powell went to Washington, D.C., where he was superintendent of schools (1885–1900). His administration was marked by disagreements over the methods employed in his schools, which were considered progressive by their supporters and loose and unstructured by their detractors. He instituted the use of trained supervisors to assist classroom teachers, increased the number and variety of courses taught in the teacher-training school, and established the first commercial high school in the country. He was forced to resign from the superintendency during a congressional investigation of his school administration.

After leaving Washington, Powell was employed briefly by the D. Appleton Publishing Company for whom he made an extensive tour and study of the educational needs in the Philippines, including the need for textbooks. He was active in a number of professional societies and organizations. Powell was one of the founders of the National Geographic Society.

Powell wrote a number of books, including *How to Talk* (1882), *How to Write* (1882), *How to See* (1886), *Normal Course in Reading* (1889), *How to Teach Reading* (with Emma J. Todd, 1889), *A Rational Grammar of the English Language* (with Louise Connolly, 1899), and *A History of the United States for Beginners* (1900).

REFERENCES: *DAB; NCAB* (13:120); *WWW* (I).   *J. K. Ward*

POWERS, James Knox. B. August 15, 1851, Lauderdale County, Alabama, to William and Rosanna (Reeder) Powers. M. January 31, 1879, to Louise A. Reynolds. Ch. two. D. August 15, 1913, Florence, Alabama.

James Knox Powers attended the preparatory and collegiate departments at Wesleyan University in Florence, Alabama. He was a tutor there from 1870 to 1871. He was graduated from the University of Alabama with the A.M. degree (1873) after two years of study; he earned the highest grades in the history of the university.

He was professor of mathematics at the State Normal College in Florence, Alabama (later, University of North Alabama) from 1873 to 1897, and president (1888–97). He served as president of the University of Alabama from 1897 to 1901 when he was associated with a publishing company until 1911. Powers returned to educational administration as president of State Normal College in 1911. He was a progressive educator.

He was the author of numerous addresses and educational reports. He coauthored with John M. Colaw and Frank W. Duke *School Arithmetic*

(1908) and was editor of *Southern Education* (1892). He was an organizer of the Southern Educational Association and president of the Alabama Educational Association. Powers was grand dictator of the Knights of Honor of Alabama (1886–88) and president of the Southern Association of Colleges and Preparatory Schools (1900–01). He received an honorary degree from the University of Alabama (1897).

REFERENCES:*NCAB* (15:362); *TC; WWW* (I).   *Teri Bland*

PRANG, Mary Amelia Dana Hicks. B. October 7, 1836, Syracuse, New York, to Major and Agnes Livingston (Johnson) Dana. M. October 7, 1856, to Charles Spencer Hicks. M. April 15, 1900, to Louis Prang. Ch. one, D. November 7, 1927, Melrose, Massachusetts.

Mary Amelia Dana Hicks Prang was educated at Mary B. Allen's Female Seminary in Syracuse, New York, and, when the school moved, in Rochester, New York. She was graduated in 1852 at the age of sixteen. She married Charles Spencer Hicks, a young Syracuse lawyer, who was drowned in 1858, leaving her with a daughter.

To support herself and her child, Prang became supervisor of drawing in the Syracuse public schools (1868–78). Moving to Boston in 1879, she accepted the position of author-editor of the Prang Educational Company Publications founded by Louis Prang. She studied at Massachusetts Normal Art School and at the school of the Boston Museum of Fine Arts. On April 15, 1900, Mary Dana Hicks married Prang, a German lithographer who had emigrated to Boston around 1848. After her marriage, she retired from the publishing company.

Mary Prang wrote many articles and books, including, *The Use of Models* (with John S. Clark, 1887), *Form Study Without Clay* (1887), *Prang Complete Courses in Form Study and Drawings* (1889–94), *The Prang Elementary Courses in Art Instruction* (with others, 1897–1900), *Notes on Egyptian Architecture and Ornament* (1899), *Art Instruction for Children in Primary Schools* (1900), *Suggestions for Color Instruction* (with others, 1893), and *The Prang Drawing Books and Manuals* (four sets).

Prang was active in the National Education Association, the Eastern Drawing Teachers' Association, and the Public School Art League. She earned the A.A. degree from Radcliffe College in 1916 and the Ed.M. degree from Harvard University in 1920 at the age of eighty-four. She was active in the arts until her death in 1927.

REFERENCES: *DAB; NAW; NCAB* (27:414); *NYT,* November 10, 1927, p. 25; *TC; WWW* (I).   *Kathryn D. Lizzul*

PRATT, Caroline. B. May 13, 1867, Fayetteville, New York, to Henry S. and Lydia C. (Rowley) Pratt. M. no. D. June 6, 1954, New York, New York.

Caroline (Carrie) Pratt grew up on her parents' farm. When she was sixteen years old, she taught one summer in the local one-room school and in the fall became a full-time teacher at the local primary school. In 1892 she received a scholarship to study at Teachers College, Columbia University. She labeled the Froebelian doctrines taught there "mythical fol-de-rol" and changed her major to manual training.

In 1894 after graduation from Teachers College, Pratt became a teacher in the Normal School for Girls in Philadelphia. She attended a summer course at the sloyd manual training school in Sweden, which influenced her thinking. Pratt became a friend of Helen Marot, organizer of the Women's Trade Union League, who showed her the conditions slum children lived under. Pratt said the function of the school was to develop in children the kind of thinking and working attitudes that would enable them to take over their own future growth.

Pratt went to New York City in 1913 and founded her first school exclusively for five-year-olds in 1914. Most of the pupils were the children of Greenwich Village artists and writers. The school expanded and moved to new quarters in 1921. The name was changed from Play School to the City and Country School and admitted children from five to thirteen years of age.

Pratt believed that a school should fit the children, not the children the school. This theory and its application made her a well-known and controversial figure in the early days of progressive education. She believed children have a natural curiosity and desire to learn; curiosity should be stimulated and satisfied. New York City became her textbook, geography was studied on field trips in the city, and games of cowboys and Indians were used to teach history. She designed wooden blocks with which her pupils reproduced what they had seen on trips; her blocks came to be used in schools throughout the world. She believed that the child needs to be free to learn for himself.

Pratt retired in 1945 and wrote her autobiography, *I Learn from Children* in 1948. She also wrote *Before Books* (with Jessie Stanton, 1926) and *Experimental Practice in the City and Country School* (with Lula E. Wright, 1924).

REFERENCES: Robert H. Beck, "Progressive Education and American Progressivism: Caroline Pratt," *Teachers College Record* (December 1958): 129–37; *NYT,* June 7, 1954, p. 23; and June 12, 1954, p. 14; Caroline Pratt, *I Learn from Children* (New York: Simon & Schuster, 1948); Evelyn Weber, *The Kindergarten* (New York: Teachers College Press, 1969).   *Barbara Ruth Peltzman*

PRATT, Orson. B. September 19, 1811, Hartford, New York, to Jared and Charity (Dickinson) Pratt. M. July 4, 1836, to Sarah M. Bates (and nine other wives). Ch. forty-five. D. October 3, 1881, Salt Lake City, Utah.

In the early days of Mormonism in Utah, Orson Pratt was a pioneer advocate of higher education. His early formal education consisted of nine short rural school terms; the rest was self-acquired.

When the Mormons established the short-lived University of Nauvoo at Nauvoo, Illinois, Pratt became the first professor of mathematics. He went to the Salt Lake Valley in Utah in 1847. He went to England where he presided over European Mormon churches (1848–50) and edited *The Millenial Star*. From 1851 to 1869 he served in the Utah provincial legislature, presided over the church in the United States, and edited *The Seer* in Washington, D.C. He was a missionary in Austria and eight times in England.

Pratt served as professor of mathematics and astronomy (1869–74) at the University of Deseret (later, University of Utah). He wrote *New and Easy Method of Solution of the Cubic and Biquadratic Equations* (1866).

Pratt spent many years in the service of the Mormon church. He was one of the Twelve Apostles in 1835 and served in that office until his death in 1881. His most important contribution was formulating Mormon theological doctrine.

His other writings include *The Kingdom of God* (1849), *Absurdities of Immaterialism* (1849), *New Jerusalem and the Fulfillment of Modern Prophecy* (1849), *Divine Authenticity of the Book of Mormon* (1850–51), *Great First Cause* (1851), *Necessity for Miracles* (1857), *Universal Apostacy* (1857), *Does the Bible Sanction Polygamy* (1876), and *Key to the Universe* (1879).

REFERENCES:*AC; DAB* (supp. 1); *NCAB* (16:17); *TC; WWW* (H); Ralph C. Chamberlain, *The University of Utah—A History of Its First Hundred Years, 1850–1950* (Salt Lake City: University of Utah, 1960); Edward R. Hogan, "Orson Pratt as a Mathematician," *Utah Historical Quarterly* 41 (Winter 1973); T. Edgar Lyon, "Orson Pratt: Early Mormon Leader" (Master's thesis, University of Chicago, 1932); *NYT*, October 8, 1881, p. 5.

Steven H. Heath

PRATT, Richard Henry. B. December 6, 1840, Rushford, New York, to Richard S. and Mary (Herrick) Pratt. M. April 12, 1864, to Anna Laura Mason. Ch. four. D. March 15, 1924, San Francisco, California.

Richard Henry Pratt, advocate of American Indian rights and educational opportunity, was educated in the Logansport, Indiana, public school. He was apprenticed to a tinsmith in 1846. Pratt enlisted in the Union army eight days after the bombardment of Fort Sumter in April 1861 and fought in Kentucky, Tennessee, and Georgia.

For a short time he was in the hardware business. At the age of thirty-seven, Pratt received a commission in the regular army. Serving as a captain at Fort Arbuckle, Indian Territory, in 1875, he began his association with native Americans. His later contact with various Indian tribes as a jailer of Indian prisoners at Fort Marion, Florida, was influential in the development of Pratt's interest and beliefs about Indian education. He conducted a school for those in the prison and came to believe in the need for the education of the Indians. Pratt served with the Bureau of Indian Affairs until his retirement from the army in 1903.

In 1879, with Secretary of the Interior Carl Schurz, Pratt founded the Carlisle Indian School in old cavalry barracks at Carlisle, Pennsylvania. The school educated over four thousand Indian children from seventy-seven tribes during his twenty-four-year tenure as superintendent.

The elementary and secondary curriculum included academic and industrial education. The school was only partially successful in preparing graduates for college; most of the graduates chose or were forced to return to the reservation. Pratt's strong attacks on the reservation school system led to his retirement from the Carlisle School. After his retirement in 1904, Pratt continued his crusade for Indian rights.

Pratt's writings and addresses were edited by Robert M. Utley in 1964 as *Battlefield and Classroom: Four Decades with the American Indian, 1867–1904*. He received an honorary degree from Dickinson College (1898).

REFERENCES: *DAB; NCAB* (13: 89); *WWW* (I); *NYT*, March 16, 1924, p. 23; Paul Prucha, ed., *Americanizing the American Indian* (Cambridge: Harvard University Press, 1973).   *Peter Moses*

PRESSEY, Sidney Leavitt. B. December 28, 1888, Brooklyn, New York, to Edwin Sidney and Orie Belle (Little) Pressey. M. 1918 to Luella Cole. M. 1934 to Alice Margaret Donnelly. Ch. none.

Sidney Leavitt Pressey was a student at the University of Minnesota (1908–09) and was graduated from Williams College in Williamstown, Massachusetts, with the A.B. degree (1912); he received the A.M. (1915) and Ph.D. (1917) degrees from Harvard University and began a long and versatile career as a research psychologist. In 1921 he accepted a position at Ohio State University; he became emeritus professor of educational psychology on his retirement in 1959.

In the early 1920s Pressey became concerned with the lack of student activity in the learning process. He developed a machine that administered tests and provided students with immediate knowledge of the correctness of their responses, considered the first teaching machine. The instructional methodology Pressey developed, called *adjunct autoinstruction,* was a forerunner of some of the principles utilized in programmed instruction. He was active in educational, developmental, and abnormal psychology, and his research efforts made a substantial contribution to the field of reading and gerontology.

Among Pressey's publications were *Introduction to the Use of Standard Tests* (1922), *How to Handle Test Scores* (1924), *Mental Abnormality and Deficiency* (with L. C. Pressey, 1926), *Research Adventures in University Teaching* (1927), *Introduction to the Use of Standardized Tests* (1931), *Psychology and the New Education* (1933), *Casebook of Research in Educational Psychology* (with J. E. Jenney, 1937), *Life: A Psychological Survey* (with others, 1939), *Educational Acceleration* (1949), and *Psychological Development through the Life Span* (1957).

Pressey was a fellow of the American Association for the Advancement of Science (vice-president of section I, 1946), the Ohio Academy of Science (vice-president and chairman of the section on psychology, 1949), and the American Psychological Association (president, division on aging, 1946 and on teaching 1948) and a member of the Ohio Psychological Association (president, 1951), the American Association of Applied Psychology (council member), the Midwestern Psychological Association (president, 1943), and many other groups. He received an honorary degree from the Ohio State University (1960), and the learning resources center at Ohio State was named the Sidney L. Pressey Hall.

REFERENCES: *LE* (III); *WW* (XXVIII); *WWAE* (XV); Robert J. Havighurst *(q.v.)*, ed., *Leaders in American Education* (Chicago: University of Chicago Press, 1971); Lisa Holstein, "A Lifetime of Saying 'Let's Get Going,' " *On Campus* (Ohio State University), May 27, 1977, p. 7.   *David Alan Gilman*

PRESTON, Josephine Corliss. B. May 23, 1873, Fergus Falls, Minnesota, to John Wesley and Josephine (Kinney) Corliss. M. to n.a. Preston. Ch. none. D. December 10, 1958, Renton, Washington.

Josephine Corliss Preston attended Carleton College in Northfield, Minnesota, and was a teacher in rural Minnesota elementary and high schools (1887–1903).

Preston served as superintendent of the Walla Walla (Washington) County schools (1903–12) and was state superintendent of public instruction from 1912 to 1929, when she lost in the 1928 Republican primary to Noah D. Showalter *(q.v.)*. Preston was credited with reorganizing the Washington schools, providing housing for rural teachers, consolidating small school districts, increasing state aid to schools, promoting vocational education, and significantly raising standards for certification of teachers.

A member of the state board of education (1911–13), Preston was chief executive of the state board for vocational education, president of the state library commission (1921–28), and trustee of the Ellison White Lyceum Bureau in Portland, Oregon (1920–26). She was president of the National

Education Association (1919–20) and the Council of State Superintendents and Commissioners of Education (1925–26). She was a member of the executive committee of the Washington Education Association (1918–28) and was chairman of the rural section of the World Federation of Education Associations (1923).

Preston contributed series of articles to *The Instructor* (1931–32) and *School Board Journal* (1934–36). She served on the War Emergency Education Commission during World War I and received honorary degrees from Whitman and Carleton colleges.

REFERENCES: *LE* (I); *WWW* (III); *Seattle Times,* September 12, 1958, p. 45.   *John F. Ohles*

PRIESTLEY, James. B. n.a., Virginia or Pennsylvania, to n.a. M. n.a. D. February 6, 1821, Nashville, Tennessee.

James Priestley was brought into the home of William Graham, the first rector of Liberty Hall Academy (later, Washington and Lee University) in Lexington, Virginia. He studied at the academy and taught mathematics there (1782–84).

Priestley was a tutor in the classics at Annapolis and Georgetown, Maryland. He was the principal of several schools, including Salem Academy at Bardstown, Kentucky (1788–92), a classical school in Georgetown, D.C. (1792–96), and the Baltimore (Maryland) Academy (1796–98). The Baltimore Academy building was destroyed by fire in 1798, and Priestley conducted another academy in Baltimore from 1798 to 1803. He became the first principal of Baltimore (Maryland) College in 1803.

In 1809 Priestley became the second president of Cumberland College (later, George Peabody College for Teachers) in Nashville, Tennessee. The college became an important institution of higher education but was closed in 1816 for financial reasons. Priestley opened a girls' academy near Nashville but returned as president of Cumberland College when it was reopened in 1820; he died shortly after.

Priestley was an organizer with John Carroll of the Maryland Society for the Promotion of Useful Knowledge in 1800.

REFERENCES: *DAB; NCAB* (8:130); *TC; WWW* (H).   *John F. Ohles*

PRITCHETT, Henry Smith. B. April 16, 1857, Fayette, Missouri, to Carr Waller and Betty (Smith) Pritchett. M. January 19, 1881, to Ida Pritchett Williams. M. June 9, 1900, to Eva McAllister. Ch. five. D. August 28, 1939, Santa Barbara, California.

Henry Smith Pritchett was the son of Carr W. Pritchett, who founded and was president (1866–73) of Pritchett School Institute (later College) at Glasgow, Missouri. He received the A.B. (1875) and A.M. (1879) degrees from Pritchett College. He received the Ph.D. degree (1894) from the University of Munich, Germany. He studied at the United States Naval Observatory (1876–78).

Pritchett was assistant astronomer at the United States Naval Observatory (1878–80). He served as professor of astronomy and mathematics and director of the observatory at Washington University in St. Louis, Missouri (1883–97), superintendent of the United States Coast and Geodetic Survey (1897–1900), and president of the Massachusetts Institute of Technology (1900–06).

Selected by Andrew Carnegie in 1906 to be president of the newly created Carnegie Foundation for the Advancement of Teaching, Pritchett worked for Carnegie's goal of a free pension system for college teachers. He discovered a confused state of higher education and found it necessary to define a college. He evolved the concept of high school programs being identified through a specific number of course units, which became known as Carnegie units. He had to abandon the free pension idea and established the principle of joint contributions by institution and teacher. From his pension work developed the Teachers' Insurance and Annuity Association in 1918, which Pritchett served as president (1918–30).

Under Pritchett's leadership, the Carnegie Foundation sponsored a number of famous studies on educational problems of the day, including Abraham Flexner's *(q.v.)* study of medical education and others on the education of lawyers, dentists, teachers, and engineers and with educational systems of various states and Canada, testing programs, and collegiate athletics.

Pritchett was a member of astronomical expeditions in the 1890s and established the Federal Bureau of Standards during his superintendency of the Coast and Geodetic Survey. He was the author of many scientific papers, *What Is Religion?* (1904), and *The Social Philosophy of Pensions* (1930). He was a fellow of the American Academy of Arts and Sciences and the American Association for the Advancement of Science and a member of many other associations. He received many honorary degrees from colleges and universities in the United States and Canada, as well as honors from the governments of France and Greece.

REFERENCES: *DAB* (supp. 2); *LE* (I); *NCAB* (C: 498, 29:124); *NYT*, August 29, 1939, p. 21; *TC; WWW* (I); Abraham Flexner, *Henry S. Pritchett, A Biography* (New York: Columbia University Press, 1943).

Carey W. Brush

PROCTOR, William Martin. B. January 26, 1875, Denver, Colorado, to Alexander and Tirzah (Smith) Proctor. M. June 15, 1901, to Agnes Elida Adams. Ch. three. D. October 28, 1937, Palo Alto, California.

William Martin Proctor worked for four years as a stenographer and court reporter at Snohomish, Washington, before entering Whitman College in Walla Walla, Washington, from which he was graduated with the A.B. degree (1901). He studied for three years at the Chicago (Illinois) Theological Seminary and received the B.D. degree (1904). He received the M.A. (1916) and Ph.D. (1919) degrees from Stanford (California) University.

Proctor served as a pastor in the Congregational churches at Spokane and Ritzville, Washington, for five years. He taught at the State Normal School (later Eastern Washington State College) in Cheney, Washington (1909–10), and was professor of education and dean of the faculty at Pacific University in Forest Grove, Oregon (1910–1915). From 1916 until 1937, he was a member of the faculty at Stanford University and served as chief of the division of teacher training (1917–33) and faculty secretary in the school of education (1933–37). Proctor also served as a lecturer on education at San Francisco College for Women (later, Lone Mountain College) (1922–37).

Proctor authored *Psychological Tests in the Guidance of High School Pupils* (1923), *Educational and Vocational Guidance* (1925), *Vocations* (1929), *The Junior High School* (1930), and *Workbook in Vocations* (with C. G. Wrenn, *q.v.*, and G. R. Benefield, 1931). He edited *The Junior College* (with Nicholas Ricciardi, 1927), *The Six-Four Plan at Pasadena* (1933), and the 1936 edition of the *California Journal of Secondary Education,* and he contributed articles to a number of journals.

Proctor was a member of the school board of Los Altos, California (1917–19), a member of the board of the Stanford campus school (1920–24), and director of curriculum revision for San Francisco (1925–30) and Sacramento (1928–32). He was a member of a California committee to survey secondary education (1928–32), a national committee on standards in secondary education representing the Western Association of Secondary Schools and Colleges (1934–37), director and chairman of the executive committee of Menlo (California) Junior College (1929–37), director of education at Camp Fremont, California, during World War I, and coordinator of the United States Veteran's Bureau for Stanford (1919–24). He was a member of the National Vocational Guidance Association (president, 1933–34) and other professional associations. He received an honorary degree from Whitman College.

REFERENCES: *LE* (I); *NCAB* (28:341); *WWAE* (VIII); *WWW* (I); *NYT,* October 29, 1937, p. 21.   *Paul L. Ward*

PROSSER, Charles Allen. B. November 20, 1871, New Albany, Indiana, to Rees William and Sarah Emma (Leach) Prosser. M. December 30, 1896, to Zerelda Ann Huckeby. Ch. one. D. November 26, 1952, Minneapolis, Minnesota.

Charles Allen Prosser attended public schools and a business college at New Albany, Indiana, and received the B.A. (1897) and M.A. (1906) degrees from DePauw University in Greencastle, Indiana, and the LL.B. degree (1898) from the University of Louisville, Kentucky. He was a graduate student at Columbia University (1908–10), where he received the Ph.D. degree (1915). He was admitted to the bar in 1898.

Prosser was a principal of elementary schools for two years, a teacher for five years, and a superintendent of schools from 1900 until 1908. He was superintendent of the Children's Aid Society, New York (1909–10), assistant commissioner of education for the state of Massachusetts (1910–12), and secretary of the National Society for Promotion of Industrial Education (1912–15). He was director of the William Hood Dunwoody Institute in Minneapolis, Minnesota (1915–45). During World War I he served two years as director of the Federal Board for Vocational Education in Washington, D.C., where he wrote legislation providing for federal aid for vocational training and the Vocational Rehabilitation Act. Prosser was frequently asked to write laws concerning vocational education.

For several year Prosser was an editor for the Century Company and a member of the consulting editorial board of the *Nation's Schools*. He contributed to *The New Harmony Movement* (by George B. Lockwood, 1913) and wrote *The Teacher and Old Age* (1913), *Vocational Education in Democracy* (1925), *Have We Kept the Faith?* (1929), *Evening Industrial Schools* (1929), *Vocational Education and Changing Conditions* (1934), *Secondary Education and Life* (1939), and *Development of Vocational Education* (1951). He edited *Shop Training Manual* (1941), *Machine Shop Training* (1942), *Welding Training Units* (1942), and the Vocational Education Series (1944).

In Minnesota he served as a member of the governor's Interim Commission on the Blind, was president of the State Council for the Blind, a member of the State Crime Commission (1929), and chairman of the Minneapolis Employer and Employee Board (1935). He was a director of the Federal Board for Vocational Education (1917–19) and a member of the President's Commission on Agriculture and Industrial Education (1914), a consultant to the National Youth Administration (1940) and the Office of Co-ordinator of Inter-American Affairs, a member of the War Production Board (1944), and an arbitrator for the American Arbitration Association.

REFERENCES: *LE* (I); *NCAB* (42:44); *WW* (XXII); *WWAE* (VIII); *NYT*, November 28, 1952, p. 26. *Lee H. Smalley*

PROUD, Robert. B. May 10, 1728, Yorkshire, England, to Robert and Ann Proud. M. no. D. July 5, 1813, Philadelphia, Pennsylvania.

Robert Proud was the son of an English farmer with sufficient means to send him to village school and later to a boarding school. In London in 1750, he became tutor for the sons of the scientist Timothy Bevans. Proud emigrated to Philadelphia where he ran a boys' school (1759–70) and became master of Friends Public School (1761–70). In 1770 he joined his brother John in a mercantile venture, which failed by 1776. During the

Revolutionary War, he assembled a collection of source materials for the early history of Pennsylvania and wrote the first history of the state. He returned to Friends School to teach mathematics and ancient languages from 1780 to 1790.

Abandoning the classroom in 1791, Proud started to prepare his history for printing. A dozen public-spirited citizens, including several former pupils, contributed toward the publication in 1797–98 of the two-volume *History of Pennsylvania in North America, from the Original Institution and Settlement of That Province . . . in 1681, until after the Year 1742.*

REFERENCES: *DAB; WWW* (H); Charles West Thomson, "Notices of the Life and Character of Robert Proud" in Edward Armstrong, ed., *Memoirs of the Historical Society of Pennsylvania* (Philadelphia: McCarty and Davis, 1826).

M. Jane Dowd

PUGH, Evan. B. February 29, 1828, Oxford, Pennsylvania, to Lewis and Mary (Hutton) Pugh. M. February 4, 1864, to Rebecca Valentine. Ch. none. D. April 29, 1864, Bellefonte, Pennsylvania.

The first president of Pennsylvania State University, Evan Pugh became a blacksmith's apprentice at the age of sixteen. He bought his apprenticeship contract in 1847 and attended the Manual Labor Seminary at Whitestown, New York, where he studied the classics and learned shorthand to take notes in his classes. In 1849 Pugh returned to Chester County, Pennsylvania, where he taught in the local East Nottingham school district. He inherited property, including the Jordan Bank Seminary, and opened an academy there (1850–53).

He went to Europe from 1853 to 1857, where he studied in Germany at the universities of Leipzig, Göttingen, and Heidelberg and at the University of Paris, France. He received the Ph.D. degree (1856) from Göttingen and studied agricultural chemistry with J. B. Lawes at Rothamstead, near London, England (1857–59). He demonstrated that plants do not absorb free nitrogen.

On his return to the United States, he became president of the Agricultural College of Pennsylvania, which had just received a charter. He helped write the Morrill Act, which provided land grants to the states to establish agricultural and mechanical colleges. He lobbied for passage of the act and, on its passage in 1862, persuaded the Pennsylvania legislature to provide those funds to his institution. He organized the college, engaged a faculty, and enrolled a student body. Before his death, he had established a program of graduate studies, and eleven students were enrolled in the graduate program in 1864.

REFERENCES: *AC; DAB; NCAB* (11:320); *TC; WWW* (H); *Penn State Alumni News* 46 (January 1960).   *Peter J. Bachmann*

PUTNAM, Alice Harvey Whiting. B. January 18, 1841, Chicago, Illinois, to William Loring and Mary (Starr) Whiting. M. May 20, 1868, to Joseph Robie Putnam. Ch. four. D. January 19, 1919, Chicago, Illinois.

Alice Harvey Whiting Putnam, the youngest daughter of a wealthy Chicago merchant, was educated privately at home and at the Dearborn Seminary.

Concerned about the education of her children, she attended a lecture by Elizabeth Peabody *(q.v.)* on the kindergarten. She organized a class of parents in 1874 to discuss Friedrich Froebel's *Mother Play;* the group later organized the Chicago Kindergarten Club (1883). After attending Anna J. Ogden's training school in Columbus, Ohio, Putnam opened the first kindergarten in Chicago in her home and within two years added a training class for young women, which has been called the pioneer training school of the West. In 1880 Putnam and Elizabeth Harrison *(q.v.)* founded the Chicago Froebel Association, which sponsored a kindergarten training school Putnam supervised from 1880 to 1910.

Concern for the study of kindergarten philosophy resulted in Putnam's acquaintance with Francis W. Parker *(q.v.),* who became principal of Cook County Normal School in 1882. The Froebel Kindergarten Association moved its headquarters to the normal school, and Putnam joined Parker's staff as a part-time lecturer in kindergarten theory and director of the demonstration kindergarten. She was a nonresident reader in kindergarten education in the correspondence department of the University of Chicago (1906–17).

In 1886 the Froebel Association was given permission by the Chicago Board of Education to conduct a kindergarten in Brennan School, and others were allowed to open as rooms became available. In 1899 the Chicago public school system adopted kindergartens in the school, and credit was given to Putnam for her enthusiasm, tireless work with parents and teachers, and influential connections in Chicago society.

Putnam served as president of the Chicago Kindergarten Club (1890) and the International Kindergarten Union (1901), which she founded. A mothers' conference called by Putnam and Elizabeth Harrison in Chicago in 1894 and the subsequent Congress of Mothers in Washington in 1897 later became the National Congress of Parents and Teachers.

REFERENCES: *NAW;* "Evolution of the Kindergarten Idea in Chicago," *Kindergarten Magazine* 5 (June 1893): 729-33; *Pioneers of the Kindergarten in America* (New York: The Century Co., 1924), pp. 204-22; Agnes Snyder, *Dauntless Women In Childhood Education, 1856–1931* (Washington, D.C.; Association for Childhood Education International, 1972); Evelyn Weber, *The Kindergarten* (New York: Teachers College Press, 1969).

Elizabeth S. Oelrich

PUTNAM, Rex. B. June 7, 1890, Buffalo Gap, South Dakota, to Jay and Rebecca (Sutton) Putnam. M. June 20, 1919, to Elinor Gertrude Snow. Ch. two. D. May 19, 1967, Milwaukie, Oregon.

Rex Putnam was graduated from the State Normal School (later, Black Hills State College) in Spearfish, South Dakota, and received the B.A. (1915) and M.A. (1929) degrees from the University of Oregon in Eugene.

Putnam taught in Oregon high schools at Springfield (1915–16) and Salem (1916–18) and taught science in a Tacoma (Washington) high school (1918–23). He returned to Oregon as superintendent of schools at Redmond (1923–32) and Albany (1932–37). He was state superintendent of public instruction (1937–60). During his superintendency, he reduced the number of school districts from about three thousand to about four hundred units. He was instrumental in obtaining passage of the School District Consolidation Act of 1957. He promoted preservice and in-service programs for teachers and early instruction in social hygiene (including sex education) and vocational studies. He laid the groundwork for the establishment of community and technical colleges in the state.

Putnam was active in professional associations, serving as president of the Oregon High School Principals Association (1932), the Oregon Superintendents of the First Class Association (1935), and the National Council of Chief State School Officers (1946). He was a member of the State Apprenticeship Commission, the Oregon State Textbook and Curriculum Commission, the advisory committee for vocational education of the United States Office of Education (1947–49), and a trustee of the state library board.

REFERENCES: *LE* (III); *WW* (XXXI); *WWAE* (XVI); *American School Board Journal* 95 (July 1937): 37; *School Executive* 57 (November 1937): 125.   *Howard C. Zimmerman*

Q

QUACKENBOS, George Payn. B. September 4, 1826, New York, New York, to George Clinton and Catharine J. (Payn) Quackenbos. M. 1846 to Louise B. Duncan. Ch. one, John Duncan Quackenbos *(q.v.)*. D. July 24, 1881, New London, New Hampshire.

George Payn Quackenbos was graduated from Columbia College (later, University) in 1843. After spending a year in North Carolina, he returned to New York City to study law. In 1847 he founded the Henry Street Grammar School and was associated with the Collegiate School from 1855 to 1868, serving as principal (1858–68).

Quackenbos was a prolific textbook writer. His textbooks were usually divided into lessons, had many illustrations, and were subject to numerous revisions to achieve the intention printed in the preface to most of the books: the pupil "should find his textbook interesting, and be won to study by the pleasant trains of thought it suggests and clearness of style and story." Quackenbos's *First Lessons in Compositions* (1851) represented his belief that "parsing is secondary to composing." Among his other books were *Advanced Course of Rhetoric and Composition* (1854), *Illustrated School History of the United States* (1857), *Natural Philosophy* (1859), *Elementary History of the United States* (1860), *Primary History of the United States* (1860), *An English Grammar* (1862), *First Book in Grammar* (1864), *Primary Arithmetic* (1867), *Illustrated Lessons in Our Language* (1876), which advocated "language before grammar" and had many engravings by A. R. Waud at a time when such illustrations were rare in language study books, *An American History* (1877), and *A Higher Arithmetic* (1879).

Quackenbos revised and translated textbooks written by others and prepared dictionaries, including an edition of Spiers and Surenne's *French and English Pronouncing Dictionary* (1872). He also contributed articles to many journals and newspapers. Wesleyan University conferred an honorary degree on him in 1863.

REFERENCES: *AC; NCAB* (13:301); *NYT,* July 26, 1881, p. 5; *TC;* John A. Nietz, *Old Textbooks* (Pittsburgh: University of Pittsburgh Press, 1961).   *David Delahanty*

QUACKENBOS, John Duncan. B. April 22, 1848, New York, New York, to George Payn *(q.v.)* and Louise B. (Duncan) Quackenbos. M. June 28, 1871, to Laura A. Pinckney. M. June 1916 to Louise D. White. Ch. none. D. August 1, 1926, Lake Sunapee, New Hampshire.

John Duncan Quackenbos grew up in New York City and attended the Collegiate School, where his father was rector and the author of several of the textbooks used by the pupils. He was graduated with the A.B. (1868) and A.M. (1871) degrees with first honors from Columbia College (later, University) and received the M.D. degree (1871) from the College of Physicians and Surgeons at Columbia.

He practiced medicine in New York City in 1871 but maintained close ties with Columbia for the next twenty-four years as tutor in rhetoric and history (1870–84), adjunct professor of English language and literature (1884–91), and professor of rhetoric and secretary of the faculty (1891–94). From 1891 to 1893 he was professor of rhetoric at Barnard College for Women.

Upon retiring from Columbia, he devoted himself to the practice of medicine, specializing in nervous and mental diseases and in psychotherapy. He was engaged in experiments to prove that psychic measures would be useful in controlling physical disease, breaking drink and drug habits, and in the transformation of character.

A prolific writer, Quackenbos was the author of twenty-five educational works and medical monographs, including *Appletons' School History of the World* (1876), *History of Ancient Literature* (1878), *A History of the English Language* (1884), *Advanced Course in Composition and Rhetoric* (1885), *Appletons' Physical Geography* (1887), *Appletons' Geography for Little Learners* (1889), *Appletons' School Physics* (1891), *Practical Rhetoric* (1896), *Hypnotism in Mental Moral Culture* (1900), *Hypnotic Therapeutics* (1908), *Enemies and Evidences of Christianity* (1909), *Standing Forests* (1909), *Body and Spirit* (1916), a psychic novel *Magnhild* (1919), and *Rational Mind Cure* (1925).

He was a member of many medical and scholarly associations.

REFERENCES: *AC; NCAB* (6:171); *TC; WWW* (I); *NYT,* August 2, 1926, p. 17.   *Robert W. Blake*

QUILLEN, Isaac James. B. February 9, 1909, Bishop, Maryland, to Isaac Edward and Ida Cecelia (Collins) Quillen. M. November 5, 1932, to Viola Harte Lewis. Ch. none. D. August 4, 1967, Stanford, California.

I. James Quillen received the A.B. degree (1929) from the University of Delaware and the M.A. (1932) and Ph.D. (1942) degrees from Yale University.

Quillen was a store manager for the Atlantic and Pacific Tea Company (1929–30) and teacher and head of the social studies department of the Shelbyville (Delaware) public schools (1932–34). He was assistant professor of social science and director of social studies at the laboratory school at the Colorado State College of Education (later, University of Northern Colorado) at Greeley (1934–36). He was director of social studies at Menlo (California) School and Junior College (1936–42) and a member of the faculty of Stanford (California) University from 1936 and acting dean (1952–53) and dean (1953–67) of the school of education.

Quillen was the author of *Colorado, The People and Their Government* (1936), *Making a Resource Unit* (1942), and *Textbook Improvement and International Understanding* (1948). He was coauthor of *The Challenge of Education* (1937), *Social Education* (1939), *The Future of the Social Studies* (1939), *The Social Studies in General Education* (1940), *Ten Communities* (1940), *This Useful World* (1941), *Our World and How We Use It* (1942), *Making the Goods We Need* (1943), *Charting Intercultural Education* (1946), *Living in Our Communities* (1946), *Education for Social Competence* (1948), *Living in Our America* (1951), *Citizens Now* (1952), and *American Values and Problems Today* (1956). He was general editor of a series of social studies textbooks for Scott, Foresman & Company from 1946.

Quillen served with the United Nations Educational, Scientific, and Cultural Organization secretariat in Paris, France, in charge of the improvement of textbooks and teaching materials (1948–49), was codirector of the Stanford Social Education Investigation (1938–44), and was cochairman of the Stanford Workshop on Education for War and Peace (1942). He was a member of the international relations committee (chairman, 1958–59) and the National Commission for the Project on Instruction (1960–63) of the National Education Association. He was president of the National Council for the Social Studies (1944). He received the George Washington Egleston Historical Prize from Yale University (1942) and an honorary degree from the University of Delaware (1958).

REFERENCES: *LE* (III); *WWAE* (XXII); *WWW* (IV); "I. James Quillen," *Social Education* 31 (November 1967): 629.   *John F. Ohles*

QUINCY, Josiah. B. February 4, 1772, Boston, Massachusetts, to Josiah, Jr., and Abigail (Phillips) Quincy. M. June 6, 1797, to Eliza Susan Morton. Ch. seven. D. July 1, 1864, Quincy, Massachusetts.

Josiah Quincy was graduated from Phillips Academy in Andover, Massachusetts, and Harvard University with honors in 1790. He studied law and became interested in politics. A Federalist, he served in the state senate and the United States Congress (1804–12), where he opposed the embargo, the War of 1812, and the annexation of the Louisiana Territory. The purchase of Louisiana and the issue of slavery led him to advocate the secession of Massachusetts from the Union.

Declining reelection to Congress, he was a state legislator and judge. He was Boston's second mayor (1823–28) and built Faneuil Hall market, reorganized the fire department, advocated water and sewer systems, controlled vice, and opened correctional and work houses. Because of debts from the institution of civic reforms, he opposed high schools for girls in Boston's school system.

Quincy was elected Harvard's fifteenth president in 1829. The college had reached a low ebb in financial condition, student enrollment, faculty morale, curriculum, and reputation, when he took control of the institution. Changes in grading systems, improved discipline, and increasing course offerings restored the university to a stable condition. He solicited funds from alumni for scholarships and established the Harvard Astronomical Observatory in 1844. After resigning in 1845, he conducted agricultural experiments, and wrote and spoke on public affairs.

He wrote *The History of Harvard University* (1840), *The History of the Boston Athenaeum* (1851), *A Municipal History of Boston* (1852), *Memoir of John Quincy Adams* (1858), and various other memoirs and pamphlets. He was an overseer of Harvard University (1810–29). Active in scholarly associations, he was vice-president of the American Academy of Arts and Sciences, the Massachusetts Historical Society, and the American Philosophical Society. He received honorary degrees from Yale College, the College of New Jersey, and Harvard University. Statues of Quincy were erected in front of the Boston city hall and in Saunders Theater in Cambridge.

REFERENCES: *AC; DAB; NCAB* (6:417); *TC; WWW* (H); Robert A. McCaughey, *Josiah Quincy 1772–1864, The Last Federalist* (Cambridge: Harvard University Press, 1974).   *David Delahanty*